Comparing Economic Systems
A Political-Economic Approach

Andrew Zimbalist
Smith College

Howard J. Sherman
University of California, Riverside

COMPARING ECONOMIC SYSTEMS

A Political-Economic Approach

Academic Press, Inc.
(Harcourt Brace Jovanovich, Publishers)

ORLANDO ■ SAN DIEGO ■ SAN FRANCISCO ■ NEW YORK ■ LONDON
TORONTO ■ MONTREAL ■ SYDNEY ■ TOKYO ■ SÃO PAULO

To my mother, Dorothy H. Zimbalist,
with love from Andy

To Barbara
with love from Howard

Academic Press, Inc.
Orlando, Florida 32887

United Kingdom Edition Published by
Academic Press, Inc. (London) Ltd.
24/28 Oval Road, London NW1 7DX

ISBN: 0-12-781050-1
Library of Congress Catalog Card Number: 84-070233
Printed in the United States of America

CONTENTS

Preface xiii

Part One. Introduction 1

1. Political and Economic Systems 3
    Plan of the Book 3
    The Political-Economic Approach 5
    Socialism and Capitalism 6
      Arguments for Capitalism 9
      Arguments against Socialism 9
      Arguments against Capitalism 10
      Arguments for Socialism 11
    Democracy and Dictatorship 13
    Developed and Underdeveloped Economies 14
    Hypotheses Concerning Politics and Economics 15
      No Necessary Relation 16
      Politics Determined by Economics 16
      Closely Related, But Not the Same 18
    Comparing Economic Systems 23
      The Standard of Living 23
      Static Efficiency 24
      Economic Growth and Dynamic Efficiency 25
      Equality of Income Distribution 25
      Full Employment and Macroeconomic Stability 26
      Economic Freedoms and Noneconomic Factors 26
    Controversies among Comparative Economists 28
    Recommended Readings 29

Part Two.   Market Economies and the Government   31

2. Japan.   Business and Government Coordination   33
   Background   34
   Corporate Structure and Finance   36
   Household Savings   41
   Labor Market Institutions   43
     Lifetime Employment   45
     Seniority-based Wages   47
     Company Unionism   48
     Worker Participation   48
     Wages   50
     Other Employee Compensation   52
   Role of the State   52
   Summary and Conclusion   59
   Recommended Readings   61

3. Sweden.   The Middle Way   62
   Background   63
   Social Services and Benefits   66
   The Cooperative Sector   69
   Industrial Democracy   70
   Labor Market Characteristics and Policies   74
   Fiscal Policy   81
     Taxation   83
   Monetary Policy   86
   Supply Management   88
   Capital Formation   90
   Conclusion   91
   Recommended Readings   92

4. France.   Indicative Planning   93
   The Monnet Plan   96
   Performance of the First Plan   98
   Later Plans   99
   Performance of Planned Goals   103
   The Socialist Government of Mitterrand (1981–)   106
   Different Views of Planning and Management   108
   Managing the Nationalized Firms   109
   Macro Performance under the Mitterrand Government   111
   Recommended Readings   114

Part Three.   Central Planning: The Soviet Case   115

   Soviet Economic Institutions: Differences from the
     United States   116
   Government Ownership of Industry   116

Government Ownership of Agriculture   117
Central Planning   118
Central Planning and the University   118
Public Health, Education, and Housing   120
Soviet Economic Institutions: Similarities to the
        United States   121
Privately Owned Consumer Goods   121
Work for Money Wages   122
Worker Mobility   123
Plan of Part Three   123

5. USSR. Development from 1917 to 1928   125
Russia before 1917   125
The Immobilization of the Peasant   126
The Extremely Low Level of Agricultural Productivity   127
Political Evolution, 1905–1917   128
War Communism   129
Political Evolution, 1917–1921   133
Socioeconomic Causes of Soviet Dictatorship   135
Czarist Russia   135
The Underground Viewpoint   136
Civil War   136
The Peasant Majority   136
Foreign Intervention   136
Economic Backwardness   138
The New Economic Policy   138
Beginnings of NEP (1921–1923)   139
Agriculture   139
Industry   139
Trade   139
Labor   140
Finance   140
Planning   140
The Scissors Crisis (1923–1924)   141
The End of NEP (1924–1928)   142
Agriculture   142
Industry   145
Trade   146
Finance   146
Planning   147
The Great Debate   149
The Stalinist Solution   153
Recommended Readings   157

6. USSR. Development from 1928 to the Present   158
Political History, 1928 to 1956   158
Economic Backwardness and Rapid Industrialization   159
Political Development, 1956 to the Present   161

Soviet Ideology: Democracy and Dictatorship   162
The First Five-Year Plan (1928–1932)   165
The Second Five-Year Plan (1933–1937)   169
The Third Five-Year Plan (1938–1941)   170
Growth in the 1930s   171
The Second World War (1941–1945)   174
Reconstruction (1945–1950)   174
Soviet Economic Growth, 1950 to the Present   176
   Growth in a Centrally Planned Economy   176
   Production Is Determined by Capital, Labor, Natural
     Resources, and Technology   176
   Population and Growth   177
   Full Capacity Growth   178
The Political-Ethical Issues: Consumption vs. Investment   180
A Statistical Overview of Soviet and U.S. Growth since
     1950   182
   Industrial Performance   182
   Agricultural Performance   182
   Consumption Performance   183
   Performance of Total Output (GNP)   184
Why the Soviet Economy Has Grown Faster Than the U.S.
     Economy   184
The Decline of Soviet Growth Rates   185
   Soviet Labor Productivity   186
   Capital Productivity   187
   Combined Factor Productivity   188
The Slowdown in Soviet Growth   190
   Consequences of a Maturing Economy   190
   Strategic Planning Decisions   191
   Systemic Elements   192
   Exogenous Factors   193
Appendix 6A.   Problems with Soviet Statistics   194
Appendix 6B.   Soviet vs. U.S. "Defense Spending"   198
   Tentative Conclusions   201
   Recommended Readings   202
   Recommended Readings for Appendix 6A   203
   Recommended Readings for Appendix 6B   203

7. USSR. The Operation of Central Planning   204
   Forms of Enterprise   207
   The Ministry System   208
   The Organization of the Planning Mechanism   210
   The Price System   214
     Retail Prices of Consumer Goods   215
     Prices of Labor Services (Wage Rates)   216
     Industrial Wholesale Prices   217
     Agricultural Prices   217

The Second Economy   218
Appendix 7A.   Soviet Planning for International Trade   220
Method of Planning International Trade   220
The Volume of Trade   221
Recommended Readings   224
Recommended Readings for Appendix 7A   225

8. USSR.   Planning for Balance   226
Aggregate Balance   226
No General Unemployment   226
Causes of Inflation   227
The Lack of Balance and Its Cure   229
Problems of Coordination   232
Input-Output Method   234
Problems of the Soviet Balance Method   235
Limitations of Input-Output Method   238
Appendix 8A.   The Input-Output Technique   240
Recommended Readings   246

9. USSR.   Planning for Efficiency   248
Need for Rational Prices   248
Optimal Conditions and Planning   249
Information and Computation Problems   251
Central and Decentralized Solutions   252
A Tentative Summary of Conclusions   253
The "Law of Value" in the Soviet Union   255
History of the Debate   255
Marxist Economic Laws and Planning Models   260
Prices and Efficiency   262
The Importance of Prices in Soviet Planning   263
Price Policies   264
Summary of the Planning Debate   266
Choice of Technology   267
Decision Making, Democracy, and Efficiency   271
Appendix 9A.   Linear Programming in the Soviet
          Context   273
An Example   276
Recommended Readings   278

10. USSR.   Class Structure: Rulers, Managers, Workers, and
          Farmers   280
The Soviet Ruling Class   280
Mobility   284
Soviet Income Distribution and Inequality   285
Stratification of the Soviet Working Class   286
Soviet Managers   289
Soviet Industrial Workers   292

Soviet Agricultural Workers   295
Appendix 10A.   Trade Unions   300
Soviet Trade Unions   300
Polish Trade Unions   303
U.S. Trade Unions   310
Recommended Readings   311

11. USSR.   Reform and Regression, after 1965   313
Political Background of Reform   313
Marx on Socialism   313
Socialist Economic Theories   313
Yugoslav Experience   314
Economic Problems Leading to Reform   314
Problems of the Soviet Enterprise   315
(1) False Reports   316
(2) Easier Plans   316
(3) Poorer Quality   317
(4) Fewer Styles   317
(5) Easiest Mixture   317
(6) Extra Supplies   318
(7) Hidden Reserves   318
(8) Extra Labor   318
(9) Storming   318
(10) Resistance to Innovations   319
The Liberman Debate   319
Official Reforms   322
What Happened to the Reforms?   323
Fewer Incentive Indicators, Mainly Profitability   324
Use of Rent and Interest on Capital   325
Decentralized Investment   325
Long-term Contracts without Changes   326
Continuing Contradictions   327
Recommended Readings   329

Part Four.   Central Planning: The Developing Countries   331

12. China.   A Changing Model   333
Background   333
Economic Development and the Transformation of the
Chinese Economy   337
Great Leap Forward (1958–1960)   339
The Cultural Revolution   345
The Post-Mao Reforms   352
Industrial Reform   353
Agricultural Reform   357
Reform Problems   361

Conclusion   362
Recommended Readings   364

13. Cuba. Socialism Next Door   365
     Background   367
     Early Development Strategy   370
     Planning in the 1960s   371
     Economic Change, 1970–1975   374
        Material Incentives   375
        Worker Participation   377
        Income Distribution   378
     Economic Change since 1975   380
     Achievements of the Cuban Revolution   382
     Soviet Economic Aid   385
     Prospects   389
     Conclusion   389
     Recommended Readings   391

Part Five.   Market Socialism   393

14. The Theory of Market Socialism   395
     The Economics of Market Socialism   396
     Alternative Market Socialist Models   401
     Recommended Readings   402

15. Hungary. Plan and Market   403
     Background   403
     Early Economic Reform   406
     The New Economic Mechanism   407
        Agriculture   412
        Foreign Trade   415
     NEM: The Second Phase   417
        Prices   417
        Industrial Structure   418
        Labor   419
     Evaluation   421
     Recommended Readings   423

16. Yugoslavia. Self-Management and the Market   424
     Early Economic Policy: The Emergence of the Yugoslav
          Model   426
     Economic Reforms of 1965   428
     Income Distribution   432
     The Economic Theory of Worker Management   434
     Yugoslav Worker Management in Practice   438
     The Reforms of the 1970s   440

Conclusion   443
Recommended Readings   444

Part Six.   Conclusion   447

17. **Comparing Economic Systems**   449
General Remarks   449
Market Decentralization of "Socialist" Economies   450
Administrative Decentralization of "Socialist"
Economies   451
Evaluating Performance   454
Methodology   454
Criteria and Performance   456
Economic Growth   456
Efficiency   458
Distribution of Income   460
Economic Stability   461
Economic Freedoms   465
Consumer Choice   465
Worker Participation   466
Occupational Choice   467
Final Remarks   468
Appendix 17A.   A Controlled Comparison: East and West
Germany   469
Per Capita Income and Growth   470
Efficiency   471
Stability   472
Income Distribution   472
Other Criteria   472
Recommended Readings   473

Index   475

PREFACE

The adjective *political-economic* in the title of this book indicates that we employ in the book a somewhat broader analysis than is usual in the comparative analysis of economic systems. Rather than restricting our approach to the narrowly economic, we encompass in it the political system, because we believe that politics and economics cannot be neatly separated. For this reason, we do not organize the book as is often done, by providing chapters on different subjects—labor, for example, or money and credit—and then offering just a few pages on the economy in each country. Instead, we provide full, integrated political-economic case studies of several representative countries. Our unique approach is explained in detail in Chapter 1.

Authors' Division of Labor

The chapter on China was written initially by an expert in that field, Victor Lippit. In order to conform to the style and approach of the book, it was partly rewritten and edited by the authors. The rest of the book was written jointly by Howard J. Sherman and Andrew Zimbalist, with each doing approximately half of the work.

Acknowledgments

We wish to thank the many people who reviewed all or part of the manuscript and gave us constructive criticisms: K. C. Kogiku, Victor Lippit, Allan Miller, Lynn Turgeon, Gyorgy Varga, Gyorgy Adam, Janos Kornai, Michael Simai, Ed Hewett, Laszlo Drechsler, Andrea

Deak, Zsuzsa Ferge, Marton Tardos, Istvan Martos, Allan Larsson, Andy Martin, Anna Hedborg, Kjell-Olof Feldt, Sten Wikander, Karl-Olof Faxen, Clas-Erik Odhner, Lars Hansson, Andrew Wechsler, Debbie Milenkovitch, Laura Tyson, Lajos Hethy, Takeo Iguchi, Chalmers Johnson, Joe Berliner, Charles Staelin, Nola Reinhardt, Arthur MacEwan, Susan Eckstein, Claes Brundenius, Bob Kuttner, Sam Bowles, Eric Einhorn, John Logue, Carl Riskin, Lydia Nettler, Howard Wachtel, William Mandel, E. K. Hunt, Paul Adler, Irwin Wall, Ellen Comisso, Murray Yanowitch, Harry Shaffer, Steve Goldstein, Sinan Koont, Jens Christiansen, and Mike Chinoy.

Howard Sherman is grateful to the University of California, Riverside, Research Committee for its funds in support of some of the research that went into this book. He also wishes to thank Shirley Pigeon and Kaylyn Gary for excellent typing and editing, as well as Paul Sherman for research help.

Andrew Zimbalist gratefully acknowledges the support of the Smith College Picker Fellowship. He also wishes to thank Darcy Naumowicz, Cindy Kruhm, and Lisa Morris for excellent research and editorial work, and Beki Mahieu for proficient and punctual typing.

One

INTRODUCTION

1

POLITICAL AND ECONOMIC SYSTEMS

In this chapter we begin by giving the reader the plan of the whole book. Then we discuss our particular political-economic approach. After this discussion we present some definitions of the main kinds of political and economic systems, and we follow them with theoretical arguments from various points of view about how political and economic systems relate to each other. Finally, we discuss the criteria for evaluating different political-economic systems.

Plan of the Book

The major portion of this book analyzes and compares different types of economic systems. Part 2 of the book discusses Japan, Sweden, and France, all three of which are basically *market capitalist* systems. A *capitalist* system is, roughly, an economic system in which the means of production are mainly privately owned by individuals who invest capital (that is, money put into productive facilities) and who are called capitalists. Capitalists buy plant, equipment, and raw materials. They hire workers, who are paid at a specified wage per week, per hour, or per piece produced. Everything produced by workers is owned by the capitalist and is sold, generally, at a profit. Goods are sold in a *market*, which is defined as an arena where goods and services exchange for each other or for money and where firms compete against one another for the consumer's dollar by means of price differentials and advertising. The result is some set of prices and outputs, according to the conditions of demand and supply. The United States, Sweden, France, and Japan are not pure capitalist systems because all four make a fairly large use of government intervention in production and/or in distribution of income. The United States is much closer to a pure capitalist model than the others, but even it differs from the pure model. It has a large amount of government demand for goods and services. The U.S. economy also has control through giant corporations, which often collude or coordinate rather than compete. The other three countries differ even more from the pure model, and their economic performance is also different from that of the United States.

Part 3 of this book examines in great detail one centrally planned, allegedly socialist economy, the Union of Soviet Socialist Republics (the USSR or Soviet Union for short). We examine both the theory of a perfect centrally planned economy and the actual operation of the Soviet Union, which is quite different. Almost all industry in the Soviet Union is government owned and all production is directed, in theory, by a central plan (though in practice much is left for local discretion and much happens that is unplanned or not under government control). We concentrate as heavily as we do on the Soviet Union because it has the largest production of any planned economy, has been in existence much longer than the others, and has generally served as a model for the other planned economies.

We ask and attempt to answer many questions about the Soviet Union: What are the basic institutions of the Soviet economy? How well does it perform? Who decides how much is invested every year? Are there interest rates, savings accounts, insurance policies? How did the Soviet Union grow so fast and develop from a backward, agricultural economy in the 1920s to the second largest industrial producer today? Why has Soviet growth been slowing down? What is the relation of the Soviet political system to its economic system? And so on.

Part 4 investigates the evolution of the economies of China and Cuba. These countries are like the USSR in having central planning and are considered to be socialist. Their economies are distinct, however, in that they are still at an earlier stage of development. Because of their different histories, these countries each have societies and cultures that are very different from each other as well as from the Soviet Union. Although it is commonly believed that all centrally planned economies have similar structures and performance, we shall see that, just as is true among the market economies, there is significant variability among them. This economic variability reflects their distinct social and political histories.

Part 5 outlines the theory of market socialism, a system built on collective ownership but making more use of the market than of planning. After examining its theoretical strengths and weaknesses according to various writers, we turn to the practical experience of Hungary and Yugoslavia. Hungary has a large degree of decentralization and uses market mechanisms extensively. Hungary is still mainly in a framework of central planning, however, and has enterprises run by state-appointed managers, with most profit going to the state. In Yugoslavia, each enterprise is run by a workers' council; all profits after taxes are used as the council decides (within certain constraints), and enterprises compete in a modified market, setting their outputs—and sometimes their prices—accordingly.

Finally, Part 6 attempts to summarize the lessons learned from the study of these systems—according to various experts who differ among themselves. It then attempts to compare the performance of the various economic systems studied in this book by applying the evaluative criteria developed later in this chapter.

The Political-Economic Approach

Most of the writing that has been done on comparison of economic systems concentrates on such narrow "economic" issues as efficiency and growth. For example, a high quality comparison of East and West Germany has been done in these terms by Gregory and Leptin.[1] While recognizing the usefulness of such studies, we believe that each country must be seen as an organic whole, with an economic-political-social system that evolves in a distinct way over time.

To begin with, the economic structure is not purely technically determined. It consists of two interacting parts. First, there are the material forces of production—plant and equipment (or *capital*), natural resources (called *land* by the classical economists), human beings with given skills (or *labor*), and technology. Technology states the *technical* relations of production, that is, the necessary proportion of raw materials, machines, and human labor to produce at minimum cost. Secondly, however, there are the *human* relations of production, such as the relation between slaves and slave owners or between workers and managers. Thus, the economic structure is composed of both technical-material elements and human relations.

How this economic structure interacts with the political structure (such as a democratic election mechanism or dictatorial decision making by a small group) is a vital controversy of great importance to comparative economics. Do U.S. capitalists control U.S. politics? Do U.S. fiscal and monetary policies help or hinder U.S. growth? Did Soviet economic backwardness and underdevelopment contribute to political control by a very small, self-selected group? Does the repressive Soviet political system help account for slowing economic growth?

---

1. Paul Gregory and Gert Leptin, "Similar Societies Under Differing Economic Systems: The Case of the Two Germanies," *Soviet Studies* 29 (Oct. 1977): 519–42.

There are many points of view on these questions among economists. Some tend to think of politics and economics as being very separate, with the choice of political leaders having very little to do with economic relationships, and with political leaders free to choose whatever course they wish to influence the economy (though everyone agrees that political decisions can influence the economy). Other economists see political systems as being completely determined by economic relations; some argue that capitalism always produces democracy and socialism always produces dictatorship, while others argue that capitalism always produces dictatorship and socialism always produces democracy. An intermediate position (held by the authors and by many other economists) is that political and economic structures interact in complex ways, and there is no simple correlation between them. So political democracy may be observed in some degree with either capitalism or socialism under given circumstances. Yet political structures are heavily influenced by economic relations. For example, economic wealth influences U.S. elections, and the low level of economic development sets the context for Soviet dictatorship. Also, however, economic relations are heavily influenced by political relations; U.S. government policies have great effects on U.S. growth, while Soviet political leaders plan their whole economy.

These are not issues to be settled in a few sentences, so the above must be considered as opening, rather than resolving, questions for the reader. All of the arguments involve words like *capitalism, socialism, planning, market socialism, central* or *workers' control*, and *developed* or *underdeveloped countries*. How these words are defined determines how the conclusions are stated. Since the conclusions vitally affect our lives, how these words are defined is not a dull matter of semantics but involves a set of burning controversies in comparative economics. We therefore turn to a consideration of these definitions and the controversies surrounding them. The reader should note that such complex definitions cannot be determined merely by turning to the dictionary or to any other authority. Every social scientist must use those definitions and concepts that seem to be most useful in the understanding of a problem. Any reasonable definition may be used so long as it is consistent and unchanging, but it helps to keep definitions close to popular notions, so that communication is easier.

Socialism and Capitalism

Pure *capitalism* is defined as a system wherein all of the means of production (physical capital) are privately owned and run by the capitalist class for a profit, while most other people are workers who work for a salary or wage (and do not own the capital or the product). We emphasize that none of our four chosen examples of capitalism—the United States, Japan, Sweden, or France—are pure capitalist systems and that they differ greatly among themselves. Thus, it is incorrect to infer anything directly from a theoretical analysis of pure capitalism and apply the inference to any of these four actual economies, and it is also incorrect to infer that what we find for one of them must be true of the others.

Pure *socialism* is defined as a system wherein all of the means of production are owned and run by the government and/or cooperative, nonprofit groups. Again, we reiterate that our chosen examples of socialism in this book—the USSR, Cuba, China, Hungary, and Yugoslavia—are each very different from a pure system and differ among themselves. So no consideration of pure socialism can necessarily tell you how the USSR operates, and a fact about Soviet operation does not necessarily tell you how China operates.

Our very narrow, bloodless, and apolitical definition in purely economic terms of *socialism* will not please anyone. Most Americans define socialism as a society (like the USSR) run by government bureaucrats who tell everyone what to do, a society that lacks any democratic decision making. Most socialists, on the contrary, define socialism as the extension of democratic decision making into the economic sphere: a cooperative society where everyone is equal in power and decision making, and there is democratic rule over the economy by the vast majority (those who do the work).

Socialism is sometimes defined as "public ownership," so the question arises as to what is meant by "public." Suppose there is a dictator in a centrally planned economy. In this case, does public ownership and control simply mean government ownership and control, with the government controlled by the dictator? Many socialists argue that "public" implies a democratic process of discussion and election by the entire public in both the political and economic spheres. Therefore, only a government derived democratically could possibly be called socialist. A dictatorial, undemocratic socialism would be a contradiction in terms according to this argument. In this view, the Soviet Union, which has government ownership and a dictatorship, could not be called socialist—neither could any of the other countries with dictatorships and government ownership.

The problem with accepting this argument is that most people—including most economists—do commonly refer to the USSR, Eastern Europe, China, and Cuba as socialist. So it would be confusing to call them something else. Moreover, they are certainly not capitalist because (1) the means of production are not privately owned; and (2) they lack many of the usual features of capitalism, such as periodic heavy unemployment (on the contrary, we shall see that these countries usually have labor shortages). So one would need another name for this type of system. Plenty of names are available. The Soviet Union has been called state capitalist, state socialist, bureaucratic collectivist, and etatist or statist, to mention only a few.

We cannot settle this controversy here, which is really not about words but about the relation of democracy and socialism. There is a huge literature on this topic, some of which is listed in the Recommended Readings at the end of this chapter. To avoid confusing readers, we will use the term *socialism* in the popular sense to describe the Soviet Union and similar systems. Yet it should be kept firmly in mind that socialism may mean control by central planners or control by local workers and consumers, and socialism may be run by democratic decision making or dictatorial decision making.

Analytically, however, our definition of socialism in terms of ownership and control by government and/or collective groups has the merit that it is possible to apply it without enormous controversy. Of course, pure capitalism and pure socialism exist nowhere, even on our narrow definitions. The U.S. economy has some cooperative and government ownership, while the Soviet economy has some private ownership. One should really speak of degrees of capitalism and socialism. For practical purposes, however, we note that the U.S. economy is over 90 percent privately owned, so it is predominantly capitalist and we do call it capitalist. Similarly, the Soviet economy is over 90 percent government and collectively owned and run, so it is predominantly socialist and we do call it socialist.

Cuba, China, Hungary, and Yugoslavia have much wider areas of private ownership among farmers and small business, but they are predominantly government or collectively owned and run, so we call them socialist. Japan is run by a close partnership of government and business; France has about 30 percent government ownership; and Sweden has very extensive welfare programs (unemployment compensation, health care, social security, etc.) as well as employee retraining and other programs to influence the economy. Yet the Japanese, Swedish, and French economies are all largely owned and run by private capitalists and rely primarily upon the market mechanism to allocate resources, so we call them capitalist. Of course, the more mixed an economy is, the less it will operate in the way that our theory may predict for a pure system. In addition to observing these domestic characteristics, it is important to note that Japan, Sweden, and France are very tightly tied into the international capitalist market through exports and imports of goods, services, and capital. These international ties strongly constrain the range of feasible domestic policies. To some extent, as we shall see, even the socialist countries are part of the international marketplace and are much affected by that relationship.

Arguments for Capitalism

What are the major arguments that economists have used in favor of a capitalist or a socialist system? Economists who advocate capitalism, mainly the so-called classical and neoclassical economists, stress the following arguments for capitalism:

1. Capitalism is a very efficient system. Resources follow relative prices, which follow demand. When demand for a good goes up, the price of the good rises and more resources (land, labor, and capital) are devoted to producing the good. Hence, consumers get what they want because capitalists compete for the consumer dollar by producing those things which the consumers desire. Prices are as low as possible because any capitalist who charges higher prices than necessary will be undercut by the competition. Price signals and resource allocation happen automatically and require no government intervention.

2. Capitalism is also dynamically efficient, so it produces rapid growth. It is dynamically efficient because competition among capitalists forces them to put money into research and to apply new inventions as soon as they are available. Thus, as each capitalist competes to lower his or her costs, to sell more goods, and to get a large share of consumer demand, growth will be stimulated.

3. As we shall see later in detail, it is argued that capitalism is the best foundation for political democracy because anyone can go into business for himself or herself. The millions of small businesses ensure that there is no control over what is produced; there is no control over what can be said and who says it in independently owned newspapers, radio, and TV stations; and workers are free to change jobs if they don't agree with the managers.

Arguments against Socialism

Most classical and neoclassical economists argue that socialism is not a good system for the following reasons:

1. A system where everything must be centrally planned by government bureaucrats must be so complex and lacking in information that it will be terribly inefficient. Lacking market prices, planners would need millions of bits of data on consumer preferences, resource availability, and technology. Information will always be deficient and, even with information, it will be impossible to solve the millions of necessary equations in reasonable time. Consumers will not get what they want, prices will be set arbitrarily, and enterprises will not produce at the lowest possible cost.

2. With no private entrepreneurs, there will be no incentive for new research, invention, or innovation in industry, so growth will be retarded.

3. Since the government will control all of the means of propaganda and all of the jobs, the party in power will be able to stay in power forever and will gradually become a dictatorship.

Arguments against Capitalism

Many economists who criticize capitalism are called Marxists, since they are inspired by the work of Karl Marx (1818–1883). Others who are critical of the present capitalist system include many environmentalists, post-Keynesians, many institutionalists (such as the followers of Thorstein Veblen), and other radicals with assorted suggestions for change.

The arguments against capitalism include the following:

1. Capitalists exploit workers, that is, the entire product is made directly or indirectly by the workers, but the workers are paid a wage that is far below the total product produced by the workers. Therefore, the source of all profits is the labor of workers. This is an unfair system. It leads to vast wealth for a few capitalists, but it leads to only adequate wages for most workers and to poverty for some workers in low-paid jobs or for the unemployed. For example, in the United States, about 85 percent of the economically active population are wage-earning and salaried workers, while fewer than one-half of 1 percent are capitalists who live primarily off property income (rent, interest, and profit). Yet the top one-half of 1 percent control over two-thirds of all stocks and bonds and all have incomes well over $100,000 a year. On the other side, the bottom 20 percent of income earners receive only 5 percent of total income, and 35 million people live below the official poverty level.

2. Capitalism leads to wide fluctuations of output, with a few years of boom times followed by a few years of recession or depression. The unplanned nature of capitalism—and the lopsided distribution of income—leads inevitably to imbalances in supply and demand. These imbalances bring on the periods of recession or depression, which create significant human hardship. Thus, capitalism leads to some unemployment most of the time and heavy unemployment periodically.

3. The prices generated by the forces of supply and demand on the market reflect only private costs. So a company that pollutes a river in carrying on its production does not have to pay the people who use the river for drinking water, fishing, or swimming. Such prices do not constitute a socially efficient basis for allocating resources, so government intervention is required. The govern-

ment is also needed to provide so-called public goods, such as public parks, lighthouses, street lights, and defense, which will not be produced if left to the market.

4. Capitalist competition must lead to elimination of the weakest firms, causing concentration into giant corporations. The giant firms have monopoly power to charge higher prices, pay less attention to consumers and less attention to lower costs, and do less research and innovation.

5. Finally, capitalist economic power means that the capitalists control the political structure through money spent to buy the media (controlling radio, TV, and newspapers), to buy the voters through advertising, to buy the politicians and political parties, and to lobby. Even if these methods fail to convince governments to promote capitalist interests, it would still be the case that the economic structure would cause politicians to bow to capitalist desires in order to induce the capitalists to invest in the economy, promote prosperity, and promote full employment. None of these things can be accomplished in capitalism unless capitalists see a good outlook for profits. Hence, either directly or through the economic structure, capitalists always have a strong control over the political structure (although workers' pressure may force reforms at times).

Arguments for Socialism

Economists favoring socialism note that there are at least two possible types of economic mechanisms under socialism. There is *centrally planned socialism*, which is defined as a system in which the central government plans all major prices, outputs, and technologies; the plan is a law which must be obeyed by managers. There is also *market socialism*, which is defined as a system in which each socialist firm decides within limits its own prices, outputs, and technologies through the competitive market system. A market socialist system may use government-appointed managers with the profit going to the government, or the firm may be run by a workers' collective with profits going back to all the worker-owners. In reality, all socialist economies use a mixture of plan and market; but the USSR, China, and Cuba have leaned more toward planning, while Hungary and Yugoslavia have leaned toward greater use of the market.

Some arguments hold for both types of socialism; others, for only one type. Arguments for socialism are as follows:

1. Any type of socialism gets rid of private profit, so workers are no longer exploited and the distribution of income is a just one. (Existing socialist economies do allow some small business and some small-scale private farming.)

2. Socialism allows economic planning; central planning can assure that there is no unemployment, because planners can always start enough projects to use all available labor. Central planning can also assure that there is no inflation, because planners, in theory, can always keep buying power at or below the level of full employment output, since all incomes are planned. (Of course, unplanned events may cause inflationary pressure.)

3. Under centrally planned socialism, all resources can be fully employed at all times, so there can be a faster rate of growth.

4. Market socialism has a fair distribution of income but eliminates all bureaucracy, so it can be as efficient as or more efficient than capitalism. Market socialism with control by a workers' collective puts all decision making in the workers' hands, so it is true economic democracy.

5. Since there are no large concentrations of economic wealth, the political process can be truly democratic for the first time. It is true that in a planned economy, all jobs would be controlled by the government. But jobs in a centrally planned socialist economy can and should be covered by a civil service system, as government jobs are now covered in the United States. Under the civil service system, many jobs are filled by an objective testing mechanism, and no one may be fired without just cause. Thus, workers' jobs are protected more fully from political bias and racial or sexual bias than under private enterprise; in fact, the percentage of women and minorities is higher in U.S. government jobs protected by civil service than in private U.S. firms. It is also true that, by definition, if everything is government owned and planned, then the media would also be run by the government. Even in that case, the examples of the Public Broadcasting System in the United States and the British Broadcasting System show that the opposition can be guaranteed free speech and equal time (in both systems, it has been more commonly the administration in power that has complained about the publicly owned media being too independent).

6. Market socialism may make use of decentralized enterprises controlled cooperatively by the workers who work in them. Then jobs cannot be threatened by government bureaucrats or by capitalists, and the media can be run by various cooperative, nonprofit groups (such as the Pacifica radio network in the United States).

The arguments presented here in theory about pure capitalist or socialist systems cannot be easily resolved. In this book, we will present in-depth discussions of particular economies, from which readers may draw their own conclusions. Our concluding chapter will sum up some of the known data and the differing points of view about it.

Democracy and Dictatorship

The basic point of any democracy is to accomplish decision making by the majority of all the people. There are two necessary features to this process. First, there must be a mechanism for election of representatives in which every adult has the right to vote and in which every group has the right to present competing candidates. The only other way for people to participate in decision making is a town meeting or a referendum, but a town meeting is impossible for a large nation and referenda can be used only for a few main issues. Second, there must be ways for every competing group to have access to the media to state freely the opposing views. There is no democracy if only one view can be stated or heard.

It is important to recognize that according to our definition democracy is not a goal or an end; it is rather a process or procedure for arriving at decisions. One may like or dislike the decisions and still be in favor of the political process on the grounds that there is no better alternative. As Joseph Schumpeter, an economist who wrote one of the most famous studies of this problem, stated, "Democracy is a political *method*, that is to say, a certain type of institutional arrangement for arriving at political—legislative and administrative—decisions and hence incapable of being an end in itself, irrespective of what decisions it will produce under given historical conditions."[2] For simplicity, any country fulfilling these two procedural conditions will be considered by us to be a democracy, but we emphasize that many perspectives consider this definition too narrow. It should also be noted that many observers would define industrial democracy as the right of workers to control their enterprises (or perhaps the whole economy) as a necessary part of democracy. On this definition, Yugoslavia might be called a democracy, even though it has only one party and no competing opposition party in national elections. The Soviet Union claims to be democratic in the sense that the Communist party—which is the only party allowed—represents the working class, so the working class (which is a majority) rules.

The fact that we call the United States a democracy indicates only that the formal democratic procedures are followed; it does not rule out the possibility that the economic institutions load the game so that the interests of the capitalist class may dominate the political process. The fact that the Soviet Union is called a dictatorship does not mean that its policies are always contrary to the interests of the majority, though they may be.

It should be emphasized, moreover, that many political scientists as

---

2. Joseph Schumpeter, *Capitalism, Socialism, and Democracy* (New York: Harper and Row, 1950), 242.

well as economists would disagree with our narrow procedural definition of democracy, even on the national scale (and we have already
mentioned that many would consider industrial democracy in the
firm very important). The procedural definition is mainly negative,
specifying that constraints should not be put on political parties or
individuals seeking election or on anyone who wishes to speak or
write. Many writers emphasize a positive view of liberty, the freedom
to develop and become what one wants, the right to a job so that one
can earn the basic necessities, and the actual means to speak or write.
Negative liberty to do something, in the sense that one is not prevented from acting by the interference of others or coercion of others,
still does not guarantee the positive freedom to act, because one may
not have the necessary means or opportunities. Thus, U.S. capitalism
and its democratic procedures guarantee that no obstacles will be
placed in the way of a worker who wishes to move from Maine to
California, but a family may be utterly unable to move for economic
reasons. Anyone has the freedom to open a business in the United
States without the government stopping him or her, but only a small
percentage have the money to do so. Anyone may own a newspaper
company or a radio broadcasting company or a television station
without prohibition by the U.S. government, but very few people have
the money to do so. No one in the United States is prohibited from
going to the best universities, but most people lack the $15,000 or
more a year necessary for tuition and expenses. Thus, our narrow
procedural definition based on negative liberties is lacking according
to theories that consider class differences. For simplicity and communication we make use of the most popular definitions, but we are
aware that popular speech on political-economic systems suffers
from a deficiency of categories and therefore may be misleading if its
limitations are not made clear.

On our very narrow definitions of democracy and dictatorship, it is
a fact that the more developed capitalist countries are all democracies. It is also a fact, however, that *most* capitalist countries are not
democracies; these are all the less developed economies of Asia,
Africa, and Latin America. The Communist countries allow only one
party, so they are all dictatorships by our procedural definition—
though they would all claim to be economic democracies.

Developed and Underdeveloped Economies

The *developed* economies are defined to be those that are mainly
urban and industrialized and have a much higher standard of living
than the less developed. (Obviously, the countries defined as highly
developed today will look terribly backward and underdeveloped by
the standards of a hundred years in the future, but that is irrelevant.)
The *less developed* (or "underdeveloped," a less precise but more

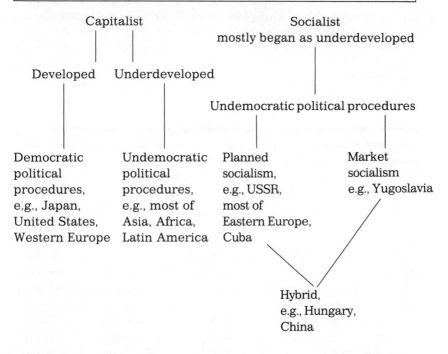

Figure 1.1
Typology of Political-Economic Systems

commonly used term) economies are defined to be those that are mainly rural and agricultural and have much lower standards of living than the more developed. It follows that the more developed economies have better education, better health care, higher use of human energy, and so forth. A few of the less developed or underdeveloped economies are developing rapidly, but most are not. Most of Africa, Asia, and Latin America contain less developed or underdeveloped economies. The USSR, Cuba, China, and most of the economies of Eastern Europe were underdeveloped when they became socialist. China remains a less developed economy.

From the preceding definitions, we can construct a typology (shown in Figure 1.1) of all current systems (leaving aside some remnants of earlier historical systems).

Hypotheses Concerning Politics and Economics

How capitalism or socialism, market or plan, is related to democracy depends on how we understand the broader issue of how economic systems are related to political systems. We can distinguish three types of hypotheses: (1) there is no necessary relation between economic and political systems, (2) economic and political systems are really one and the same thing (or one is fully determined by the other), and (3) economic and political systems are different but do have certain necessary relationships and reciprocal influences on each other.

No Necessary Relation

Most neoclassical economists (but not all) assume in the application of their theory that there is no necessary relation between economic and political systems. Thus, a country may have capitalism and democracy or capitalism and military dictatorship; similarly, a country may have socialism and democracy or socialism and dictatorship. Of course, they agree that government *policy* may affect the economy. For example, under capitalism a subsidy for building ships may encourage shipbuilders to invest more than they otherwise would. They also agree that economic conditions affect governments. For example, an inflation might induce a government to reduce its spending.

In this view, choices of policy are made on rational grounds and are not determined by conflicting interests of socioeconomic classes. Thus, if an economist determines the optimal way to solve problems of unemployment and inflation, the government will adopt that policy. A few exceptions are often mentioned. Politicians may be stupid or corrupt or influenced by a few greedy union leaders. In this case, the optimal policy may not be followed or may be postponed. Politicians are frequently lectured by neoclassical economists on the virtues of administering unpleasant medicine for the long-run good of all, even though the medicine may hurt most voters in the short run.

A great many U.S. political scientists agree with this outlook on government, although they express it in a more sophisticated way in their discipline. In the *pluralist* view, which was dominant for some decades but is now under heavy attack (but has not been replaced by any other consensus), all interest groups in the economy compete in any election, they win representation according to their strength among voters, and the representatives then reach the best possible compromises. The pluralists recognize that some groups are more powerful than others; for example, there are more dog owners than stamp collectors, and millionaires make more political contributions than the unemployed. Overall, however, they believe that political leaders may affect the economy (within limits) but that economic interests do not determine political decisions.

Politics Determined by Economics

Several economists have an opposite view. Milton Friedman and Frederick Hayek present a very conservative view, in which the nature of the economic system fully determines the political system. Capitalism automatically tends to produce democracy, while socialism automatically tends to produce dictatorship.[3]

Capitalism leads to democracy for several reasons. Everyone is free to set up a business (if they have the money), free to move where they wish (if they have a job and money), and free to publish any book or newspaper or produce any television program they wish (if they have the money). There is economic democracy because everyone with a dollar can spend it as he or she wishes (according to the number of dollars). No government bureaucrat can tell anyone what job to take, what business to open, where to move, or what to buy. People are free to work where they will (or to be unemployed).

Socialism leads to dictatorship for the same reasons in reverse. Socialism—as defined by Friedman and Hayek—means that you cannot open a business. A government bureaucrat tells you where to work, what to do, and what to produce, and the government determines what is available to buy. Government bureaucrats control the newspapers, book publishing, television, and so forth. Since everyone is dependent on the government, the ruling party can establish a dictatorship.

Strangely enough, some dogmatic Marxists (but not Marx) agree with Friedman and Hayek that the economic system fully determines the political system—this view is commonly called *economic determinism*. These economic determinists on the left, however, conclude that capitalism always produces dictatorship, while socialism is always democratic. The Marxist economic determinists argue that throughout history economic power always results in political power. Roman slaveholders controlled the Roman Empire. Feudal landowners controlled feudal states (the king was always a feudal landowner). Southern U.S. slaveholders before the Civil War controlled political power in the South.

Under capitalism (as in the United States), the Marxist determinists claim that democratic forms are a disguise for a dictatorship of big business or the capitalist class. Money talks in capitalism. The capitalist corporations control the government by using money for (1) control of the media, such as newspapers and television, which are owned and run by big business; (2) control of candidates through campaign contributions; (3) control of parties through the candidates and through further legal and illegal contributions; and (4) lobbying and bribery. By these means they normally control the House of Representatives, the Senate (22 of whom at present are millionaires); the Cabinet (most of whom at present are millionaires); and the President. They find confirmation of this thesis in the actions of the politicians, such as President Ronald Reagan, in favor of the wealthy.

---

3. See, e.g., Milton Friedman, *Capitalism and Freedom* (Chicago: University of Chicago Press, 1962).

They argue that workers, with no extra time and no extra money to spend, have no political power in any capitalist economy. Furthermore, they argue that the very structure of capitalism is such that, no matter who gets elected, the elected representatives must follow policies favorable to capitalists (such as reducing taxes on capitalist corporations, while cutting school lunches for poor children). If the elected representatives do not follow such policies, then capitalists will not invest and will not provide employment—and capitalists may even take their capital outside the country to invest in low-wage, high-profit countries, such as Taiwan. Control of jobs by corporations is a powerful tool, not only for control of the individual voter but also for setting limits on government policies.

On the contrary, according to those Marxists who are strict determinists, under socialism the power of the capitalist class is ended; no one has any large economic fortune, so no one can control the political process through the use of economic power. Therefore, socialism must be politically democratic.

Closely Related, But Not the Same

One extreme view finds no necessary relation between politics and economics, while the other extreme claims that the two are always identical in content (because economics determines politics). An intermediate view says that economics and politics have close and necessary relations but do not fully determine each other.

The well-known economist Joseph Schumpeter stresses that on his definitions (which are similar to our definitions), political democracy and socialist economies are two quite different things that may or may not go together. "Between socialism as we defined it and democracy as we defined it there is no necessary relation: the one can exist without the other. At the same time, there is no incompatibility: . . . the socialist engine can be run on democratic principles."[4] Yet this says only that there are no necessary relations *by definition*. Schumpeter, however, does believe that there are necessary relationships between political and economic systems; it is simply much clearer if one establishes these relations from the facts rather than from definitions. Furthermore, the relations are not simple but are rather complex; for one thing, causation runs both ways, not just from economics to politics.

Schumpeter agrees with Friedman that early capitalism comes into being in close relationship to political democracy; he believes that they are produced by the same forces. Yet Schumpeter also recognizes that under capitalism "in some cases political life all but resolves itself into a struggle of pressure groups,"[5] which greatly dis-

---

4. Schumpeter, *Capitalism, Socialism, and Democracy*, 284.
5. Ibid, 298.

torts the democratic process. He will not join socialists in saying that genuine democracy is impossible under capitalism, but he does say that with respect to democracy "capitalism is rapidly losing the advantages it used to possess."[6]

Schumpeter does argue that under a planned socialist economy there is the problem that politicians in the government would have some control over jobs in industry. He seems to believe, however, that mechanisms such as civil service protections could be quite sufficient to prevent such potential control from having serious negative effects. In fact, he says there is no reason to believe that a Minister of Production would "interfere more with the internal working of individual industries than English Ministers of Health or War interfere with the internal working of their respective departments."[7]

Finally, Schumpeter does warn that a country needs to be economically developed to a sufficient level when it adopts a socialist structure or it will not be able to maintain a democratic structure. "It goes without saying that operating socialist democracy in the way indicated would be a perfectly hopeless task except in the case of a society that fulfills all the requirements of 'maturity'"[8] as he has explained them. These requirements of maturity include many of the attributes that come only with economic development, such as a fully literate population. This condition is considered a very important one by many writers, as noted later.

For those who see politics and economics as different but reciprocally related to each other, one can begin with the point that the capitalist economy does influence the political structure. Because of its economic power, the capitalist class tends to dominate the political structure (through the political parties, use of the media, and so forth). Some qualifications include the facts that there are divisions within the capitalist class itself, and the workers do have some political influence.

Under capitalism, economic power does tend to dominate the political sphere, but it is also true that politics and ideology strongly influence the economic sphere. Day-to-day political actions may modify or intensify depressions or inflations and may speed or hold back research and innovation (by means of tax policies, subsidies, credit policies, public spending, and so forth). Moreover, political revolutions have led to change in economic relations: the French Revolution ended feudalism in France, while the Russian Revolution ended feudalism and capitalism in Russia. Of course, these political revolutions did not come out of nowhere; they were prepared (or "determined," if you wish) by long economic evolution of conflicting class interests and changing economic and political forces. In short,

---

6. Ibid.
7. Ibid., 301.
8. Ibid.

there is a two-way interaction between economic and political structures.

In this view, the economic growth of Russia created an alliance of class forces, which led the Revolution to end czarist autocracy in Russia in March 1917 and began to move toward establishment of a capitalist economy with democratic procedures. But economic growth also created a working class, which led a socialist revolution in November 1917 (aided by Russian economic and military weakness in World War I). The tragedy of this socialist revolution lay in the fact that it took place in a backward, underdeveloped country and was not followed (as the Communists expected it to be followed) by socialist revolution in Western Europe. On the contrary, the Russian Revolution was opposed by military intervention and economic blockade by the United States, Japan, and Western Europe. This backward, struggling, isolated country felt under immense pressure to modernize, industrialize, and develop a whole new economy overnight.

The weak, old Russian Empire was transformed into the modern, strong Soviet Union. But that success was at the expense of democratic and working-class control of the government. To develop with extreme rapidity—with no outside help—meant extreme sacrifices by the agricultural and industrial working class. It meant a very unpopular government—one that required declines in consumption to near starvation levels for much of the population for several years. Such an unpopular government could hold power only by repression and undemocratic means. This led to a Soviet government controlled by a small number of men (and very few women), consisting of the top Party leaders, government leaders, planners, and top military men. This small, self-selected crew continue to cling to power, with the top leaders getting older and older—and, in some instances, even decrepit.

The dictatorship and "socialism" of the Soviet Union were spread to all of Eastern Europe by the Red Army as it liberated the area from fascism. Therefore, these countries—except for Yugoslavia and Albania, which led their own armed liberation—cannot be considered as entirely separate cases. Of course, with the passage of decades many of the East European countries have expressed some of their historical identity in attempting to alter the Soviet-imposed model. Hungary has been very obvious in its recent successful deviations (and is considering contested parliamentary elections for 1985). Independent socialist revolutions took place in Yugoslavia, Albania, China, Cuba, and Vietnam (as well as ones too recent to analyze in Mozambique, Angola, and Nicaragua). *But all of these were also backward, underdeveloped countries at the time of their socialist revolutions.* Therefore, full-scale socialism has come to countries only (1) when they were underdeveloped economically (or not "mature" in Schumpeter's terminology); or (2) by diffusion through military power from an underdeveloped, socialist country. In the Soviet case the underdevelopment and drive to develop seems to have been a major factor behind its dictatorship (given many other historical circumstances, discussed in detail in Part 3).

Central economic planning in the Soviet Union began only *after* Stalin was dictator, so planning cannot be considered the initial cause of Soviet dictatorship. In the Yugoslav case, a dictatorship was established by a popular leader, Tito, right after the revolution. The Yugoslavs began with planning after the revolution, but a break with the Soviet Union led to the introduction of: (1) workers' councils controlling the enterprises, (2) extensive use of the market, and (3) some loosening of political controls, but a continuation of the basic one-party dictatorship. So, in Yugoslavia, workers' councils, use of the market, and dictatorship coexist under "socialism." It should be noted that market and dictatorship, along with private ownership, also coexist in most capitalist countries, that is, in most underdeveloped countries, which constitute the largest number of capitalist countries. It thus appears that there is a strong tendency for economic underdevelopment (not capitalism or socialism, nor planning or markets) to lead to one-party or military dictatorships.

Why has underdevelopment generally been accompanied by dictatorship in both capitalist underdeveloped countries and socialist underdeveloped countries? First, underdevelopment means illiteracy and lack of mass communications, both of which make democracy difficult. Underdevelopment means rural isolation of most people, which makes democracy difficult. Underdevelopment means grinding poverty, so people have no time for politics, and they worry about the next meal, not democracy. One cause of underdevelopment has been the rigid political control of a small, landowning aristocracy, whose wealth comes from exploitation of the peasantry. This rule by aristocrats over a poverty-stricken population is commonly expressed through a dictatorship, which sustains the rule by repression. Thus, none of the countries with socialist revolutions—USSR, China, Cuba, Yugoslavia, Mozambique, and so forth—had democracy before the revolution. This means that there was no democratic tradition, but an armed struggle in a civil war to achieve socialism—hardly a good beginning for peaceful democratic procedures.

Second, when an underdeveloped country has a socialist revolution, the leaders are under enormous pressure to institute very rapid development. They want to do this to give economic development to their people, to prove their success to the rest of the world, and to establish prestige and military defense. Unfortunately, an ultra-rapid industrialization drive is very unpopular in the short run because the resources must be generated mostly by holding down the living standards of their own people, for example, by selling grain abroad rather than consuming it. Since this course of action means constant or lower consumption for some years for a people already on the edge of starvation, it can be carried out only through repression and dictatorship. Thus, underdevelopment breeds dictatorship, and a rapid development drive may strengthen the tendencies toward dictatorship.

We have noted in some detail the influence of economic conditions and structures on political procedures, but it is also clear that the political sphere is a major influence on the economic sphere. In the United States, for example, private property is upheld by the law and the police. The policies of the Reagan administration have shifted income distribution to favor the rich. Decisions on the federal budget directly influence the degree of unemployment or inflation. Labor laws have sometimes added to the strength of labor and have sometimes decreased the strength of labor.

Finally, as we shall see in detail in Parts 3 and 4, in any centrally planned economy, political decisions directly determine the allocation of resources, rate of growth, and distribution of income. Most political controversies in the United States at this time are over the federal budget. Most political controversies in the Soviet Union are over the central Plan, which includes not only the federal and regional budgets but also the budget and directives affecting every Soviet enterprise. More generally, Alec Nove points out that "If the state owns the means of production, then the nature of the state, its political processes, its power relations, are crucial determinants of production relations."[9]

The absence of the market mechanism (what Adam Smith called the invisible hand) in planned economies requires information to be disseminated and decision making to be conducted on some basis other than individual self-interest. This, in turn, assures that economic decisions and actions assume a more social-political character in planned than in market economies. Accordingly, the performance and evolution of planned economies over time depend heavily on the nature of social and political relations in each country. For instance, much of the excessive centralization of the Soviet economy can be traced to the cultural and historical conditions at the time of the Russian Revolution rather than to central planning itself.

Another illustration of Nove's point that the political process of the Soviet Union is a determinant of the production relations comes from the fact that the Soviet political system seems to be a major drag on its economic growth in the present era. The Soviet leaders want a highly developed technology and an advanced scientific intelligentsia, but at the same time they want to limit freedom of expression. The Soviet historian and dissident, Roy Medvedev, writes that:

---

9. Alec Nove, "Is There a Ruling Class in the USSR?" *Soviet Studies* 27 (Oct. 1975): 631.

The scientific and technical revolution, which is inevitable in the USSR, just as it is elsewhere in the world, will bring about changes in the social structure and its economic base that will prove incompatible with the system of unlimited rule by a single individual (or by a small group). Extreme centralization and lack of democracy in politics, economics, and culture; . . . the absence of free exchange of ideas and information—all of this becomes an enormous impediment to the development of the productive forces.[10]

Comparing Economic Systems

This book examines the performance of different types of economic systems in various countries. What are the criteria for judging their comparative performance? We shall state the usual criteria, but the reader must understand clearly that there is significant controversy among economists on these issues. We will state our view of the proper criteria and then note the disagreements.

The Standard of Living

The most obvious criterion on which to compare economies is the standard of living achieved by the people in a country, usually measured by the income per capita. One might think it is sufficient to say that country X has a higher standard of living than country Y to prove that one country has a better economic system than another, at least in this one respect. Yet it is not so simple. Each country has a different history and different resources. How do we compare a country rich in oil with one that is not? Is it fair to compare the standard of living in two countries when one has just been devastated by war and the other has not? Moreover, if a country has just adopted a new economic system, the fact of its present standard of living does not prove anything about the new economic system.

Moreover, the income per capita reflects only a narrow materialistic criterion; what about the effect of the economic system on the quality of life and the subjective attitudes of the people in it? What, for instance, does capitalism do to the way that people think? One writer comments that "Max Weber has called it 'the spirit of capitalism' and described it as a value system which elevates the acquisition of riches pursued systematically through hard work, frugality, and thrift to the dignity of a way of life and of an ultimate goal."[11] He goes on to say, "In

10. Roy Medvedev, cited in William G. Rosenberg, "Democratic Dissent in the U.S.S.R.," *Democracy* 3 (Summer 1983): 123.

11. Walter Weisskopf, "Economic Growth Versus Psychological Balance," in *The Capitalist System*, 1st ed., ed. Richard Edwards, Michael Reich, and Thomas Weisskopf (New York: Prentice-Hall, 1972), 380.

distinction from previous societies where the pursuit of wealth and hard work were considered as inferior activities and as a curse, left to slaves, women, and inferior social groups, industrial society made the acquisition of wealth morally acceptable and considered it as a moral obligation."[12] Are these acquisitive attitudes historically generated by capitalism a plus or a minus; and how do we measure their effect compared to attitudes in other societies? There are no easy answers to such questions.

There are other problems in the use of the standard of living or the per capita income as a comparative criterion. What if the average income per person is very high, but a very small group of people have all the income, and the rest have very little? This is the case in some small Arab oil kingdoms. So one cannot really consider the *average* per person without looking at the distribution of income. Furthermore, there is disagreement whether more television sets or more doctors per thousand population spells a high standard of living. Is a high standard of living defined by more cigarettes or more hospitals, more real estate salesmen and stockbrokers or more teachers and entertainers, and more flashy cars but at the same time more smog and crime in the streets?

Because of the difficulties of making such comparisons as well as the unfairness of comparison on the basis of a given income per capita, we do not make use of this criterion but instead look at five other criteria that are more precisely defined and that make legitimate comparisons of the performance of different systems. These criteria are: (1) static efficiency, (2) economic growth and dynamic efficiency, (3) equality of income distribution, (4) full employment and macroeconomic stability, and (5) economic freedoms and noneconomic factors.

Static Efficiency

The term *static efficiency* refers to the amount of output from a given amount of inputs (land, labor, and capital) and level of technology. Roughly speaking, we are thinking of productivity: how efficiently are the given resources organized and used? The object is to maximize social welfare by efficiently using existing resources and attaining the highest level of production technically possible. The output, of course, consists of millions of different products, so it is also necessary that the assortment of different outputs should reflect the demand of consumers.

In other words, efficiency refers both to the highest output from given resources and to the best mixture of outputs according to social needs and preferences. Of course, in a capitalist economy, the demand for products depends not just on need or desire but also on

---

12. Ibid.

money income (the fact that a poor person desires a fur coat will not affect the demand). Therefore, the most "efficient" mix of outputs in a capitalist economy depends partly on income distribution.

Because of data limitations, measurement problems, and adjustments for quality, it is extremely difficult to estimate reliably levels of static efficiency across countries. More will be said on these points in later chapters.

Economic Growth and Dynamic Efficiency

Another criterion of performance is economic growth. In part, this depends on dynamic efficiency, that is, the growth rate of output relative to the weighted growth rate of inputs. Different systems are better or worse at generating new technology or selecting new investment projects.

Economic growth depends on, among other things, the amount of income saved and invested each year. Other things being equal, the higher the investment ratio (investment divided by national income), the higher the growth rate will be. In a centrally planned socialist system, the government gathers savings through taxes and from the profit of government-owned firms; it then invests in planned projects—and is always short of resources relative to the possible projects generated by planners, political leaders, and consumer pressure.

In a capitalist system new investment depends in the first place on making profits, which are the main source of new capital. If wages are held down and profits are very high, then there is a plentiful supply of capital. Notice the implication that more unequal income distribution causes more savings (by the wealthy) and so more potential capital. Yet this potential will not be actually invested unless capitalists expect a profit from future sales. But future sales depend on consumer demand, which will be greater generally if income is more equally distributed. For countries relying heavily on foreign trade, exports are also a vitally necessary part of demand. Without sufficient demand, output and employment must fall. Thus, growth is also crucially related to the distribution of income.

Equality of Income Distribution

To have justice and fairness in the world, it might be argued that the distribution of income and wealth should not be such that one person has insufficient food from a low wage at a dirty job while someone else can be a glutton with a very high income from inherited wealth. One philosophical school, the Utilitarians, argues that a poor person gains more utility from an extra dollar of income than a rich person. Hence, every time the government transfers a dollar from a rich to a poor person, it is increasing aggregate social utility.

At any rate, the degree of equality of income distribution is considered one criterion of good performance by most comparative economists. If more equality of income distribution is accepted as a goal, then some other economic achievements may appear less favorable. For example, from the early sixties until the late seventies Brazil had a very high rate of growth and many observers referred to the Brazilian "economic miracle." Brazil's income distribution, however, became more and more unequal, and by most assessments the poor majority did not benefit from the growth.

Full Employment and Macroeconomic Stability

At the moment of this writing, U.S. unemployment is at a level of twelve million human beings who want jobs but cannot get them. Numerous studies indicate a high correlation of unemployment with mental illness, divorce, malnutrition, and crime—so the human suffering is very great. Suppose that those U.S. workers who are employed have greater productivity than employed workers in country X. But suppose country X has full employment. Is the U.S. economy or the X economy performing better? In addition to full employment, other criteria for macroeconomic stability include price and output stability as well as international payments equilibrium.

Economic Freedoms and Noneconomic Factors

One criterion—discussed in detail already—is whether a particular economic system tends to produce more democracy or tends to create dictatorship. Some people view political democracy (general decisions made by the voters or their representatives in an atmosphere of free discussion) and economic democracy (running the economy and/or the firm by democratic decisions of all the participants at each level) to be important ends in themselves. They are also means of achieving the ends of efficiency or equality. If we start with a capitalist system, economic democracy by all the workers in a firm or by all of the public would probably reduce the concentration of wealth and increase the equality of income distribution. If we start with a planned economy, political democracy would enable economic plans to better reflect the desires of the majority of the public. Since the mix of outputs would more closely approach the desires of most people (rather than the will of a small group of dictatorial leaders), one might argue that the efficiency of the system would be improved. In fact, if everyone could participate in decision making for the economy—or the firm—it might also improve the incentive to work.

Economic freedom is often interpreted by neoclassical economists to mean the freedom of consumers to choose what products they wish and the freedom of workers to change jobs when they wish. The neoclassicals stress the fact that these two aspects of economic freedom exist under capitalism. The critics of capitalism note that the right of consumers to choose products is limited by their income under capitalism. A rich person may choose a diamond ring and a fur coat, but a poor person cannot choose them, even though he or she may desire them. A poor person may not even be able to choose to buy sufficient food for a decent diet. Furthermore, the right to choose one's job under capitalism is limited by extensive unemployment and unequal levels of educational attainment. Therefore, many writers have defined economic freedom as the right of every consumer to a minimum adequate standard of living and the right of every worker to be employed. In brief, one would ideally like to have both the negative freedoms not to be prohibited from changing jobs or from buying what one wants *and* the positive freedoms to have enough money and enough job security to actually buy the necessities of life and to actually be able to move to a new location when one wants. To be sure, economists of all or most ideological persuasions consider "economic security" a desirable goal; that is, a guarantee of a minimum income even if one is sick, handicapped, old, or unemployed through no fault of the individual.

An economic system may also have particular effects on things beyond the political-economic sphere. For example, a system built on private profit with no regulation is alleged by some critics to be more destructive of the environment than other economic systems—because of the intense drive to maximize private profit and because the private balance sheet of a corporation does not record environmental destruction as a cost. Socialist planners would allegedly consider the environment when planning for the nation, but a socialist enterprise manager or even a planner under political pressure for maximum production may neglect the environmental impact. A system built on slavery, such as the U.S. South before the Civil War, may employ racism as a rationale for keeping slaves (who are said to be inferior and suited to heavy labor, while the masters are superior and suited to supervision, leisure, and consumption of huge amounts of products of good taste).

We mentioned above that Marx criticized capitalism for creating alienated workers. To the extent that capitalism causes alienation (for the reasons given by Marx), the system tends to create unhappiness, loneliness, anxiety, mental illness, and so forth. Communist dictatorships, according to their critics, also create alienation among most of the population (because of the feeling of political helplessness, as well as the actual costs, humiliations, and irrationalities of a nondemocratic system).

Clearly, these social criteria defy rigorous quantification. Indeed, many of the economic performance criteria are also difficult to measure, and for many countries relevant data are not available. In this book we will forgo any attempt to assess directly the comparative performance of economic systems until the concluding chapter, where a full discussion is provided. Nonetheless, the reader is urged to keep the above criteria in mind as he or she learns about the different economies discussed in this book.

Controversies among Comparative Economists

Economists differ over the evaluation of different political-economic systems for three main reasons.

First, even if economists could agree on the list of comparative criteria (and most would include the same things), a list of criteria does one no good at all unless we know how to weight the different criteria. Should we give greater weight to efficiency or to democratic participation, to growth or to equality? Economists, like everyone else, differ greatly over the importance of the different criteria.

Second, it is not easy to get clear on the facts in comparing economies. We shall find, for example, that even comparisons of U.S. and Soviet national product levels or rates of growth are extremely difficult or impossible to obtain—at least, with any consensus on the details among observers. Comparison of static or dynamic efficiency among countries is even more difficult. There is no agreement among defenders of capitalism, market socialism, and central planning on the definition or meaning of democratic decision making, so how can one measure it?

Third, economists often describe the system they advocate in terms of how pure theory says that it presumably could be, rather than how it actually is. They then compare their perfect system with some actually existing system that they dislike; the perfect system described by pure theory always wins the comparison. For example, conservative U.S. economists may describe—in theory—what the U.S. performance would be if (1) government played no economic role, and (2) there was only pure and perfect competition (with no giant monopoly firms and no labor unions). Or, for example, socialists may describe a system of planning with (1) ability to calculate perfectly and immediately and (2) completely democratic processes of control of the planning process by the public. In examining the performance of these purely hypothetical systems, there is plenty of room for economists to make entirely different assumptions and different analyses and to reach completely different conclusions.

Thus, in comparative economics there are differences over (1) the weight to be assigned to different criteria, (2) the facts of performance of real societies, and (3) theories about the performance of a perfect model. We shall not try to settle these controversies in this book; rather, we shall try to present the different points of view in some depth. Although we shall present the different points of view, the reader should also be aware that authors always present their own views more persuasively than other views. (Though some authors claim to be absolutely fair, they never are.) The reader, then, is well-advised to stay alert for bias in any comparative analysis (and we will appreciate comments and feedback whenever you believe we are distorting some view or omitting some important fact).

Recommended Readings

1. E. J. Mishan, *What Political Economy Is All About* (Cambridge, England: Cambridge University Press, 1982).

2. Alec Nove, *The Economics of Feasible Socialism* (Boston: George Allen and Unwin, 1983).

3. Harry Shaffer, *Women in the Two Germanies* (New York: Pergamon Press, 1981).

4. Howard J. Sherman and James L. Wood, *Sociology: Radical and Traditional Perspectives* (New York: Harper and Row, 1980).

5. Morris Bornstein, ed., *Comparative Economic Systems*, 4th ed. (Homewood, Ill.: Irwin-Dorsey, 1979).

6. Charles E. Lindblom, *Politics and Markets: The World's Political Economic Systems* (New York: Basic Books, 1977).

7. Martin Carnoy and Derek Shearer, *Economic Democracy: The Challenge of the 1980s* (White Plains, N.Y.: M. E. Sharpe, 1980).

8. Andrew Zimbalist, ed., *Comparative Economic Systems: An Assessment of Knowledge, Method, and Theory* (Boston: Kluwer-Nijhoff, 1983).

9. Detailed description of U.S. economic institutions and performance may be found in E. K. Hunt and Howard J. Sherman, *Economics: Introduction to Traditional and Radical Views* (New York: Harper and Row, 1981). Also includes extensive bibliography for further study.

10. For a dissident East European viewpoint, see Rudolph Bahro, *The Alternative in Eastern Europe* (London: New Left Books, 1981).

11. For a radical debate on the nature of existing "socialist" systems, see Paul Sweezy and Charles Bettelheim, *On the Transition to Socialism* (New York: Monthly Review Press, 1980).

12. Theda Skocpol, *States and Social Revolutions: A Comparative Analysis of France, Russia, and China* (New York: Cambridge University Press, 1980).

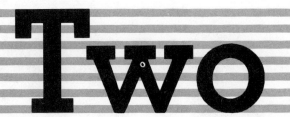

MARKET ECONOMIES AND THE GOVERNMENT

This part of the book discusses three economies that are still basically capitalist in nature but where the government plays an important role. They are predominantly capitalist in the sense that most ownership of the means of production is private. In that private sector, the capitalist class owns both the means of production and the product; capitalists decide what to produce, how to produce it, and who to hire; and workers must sell their labor power in the marketplace. These three economies resemble the United States in having a *tendency* toward inequality between a wealthy capitalist and professional class and a less affluent working class, and a *tendency* toward substantial periodic unemployment. What is fascinating is that their different historical developments, their different cultural and political traditions, and their different use of government in the economy produce very different results from the United States. Thus, the patterns of growth, unemployment, income distribution, and labor relations are all quite different from the U.S. pattern (and different from each other).

In Japan there has been a so-called economic miracle of rapid growth. One factor in achieving this growth has been the very close coordination of business and government in a voluntary sort of planning mechanism. How well it has worked, including its benefits and costs to Japanese workers, is discussed in detail.

In Sweden the government assists in providing for an individual's welfare from birth to death. Women are given a paid leave for pregnancy and birth—and fathers may also get time off for child care. The elderly are covered by social insurance. Health care is virtually free. Unemployment has been kept below 4 percent. So the harshness of the private enterprise system, which mostly is still intact in Sweden, is mitigated. It is a thorough welfare state.

Finally, the chapter on France discloses that this country has also had a close association of government and business in a process called *indicative planning*. In 1981, the French voters put a socialist party into office, which is committed to more welfare programs, nationalization of several more industries, and more democracy in planning—but the economy remains about two-thirds in private control.

Together, these three country case studies illustrate the considerable diversity among industrial capitalist economies, especially when compared to the United States. Yet they also illustrate that, despite the heterogeneity of institutions and performance, the advanced market economies experience common underlying tendencies and policy choices. By providing a discussion of the relevant political and historical contexts of these economies, we hope to elucidate some of the sources of these similarities and differences.

2

JAPAN

BUSINESS AND GOVERNMENT COORDINATION

At the turn of the century Rudyard Kipling unprophetically wrote, "The Jap has no business savvy." Today, American and European business executives are busily trying to emulate Japanese management practices.

By practically any standards of economic performance, Japan has far surpassed the rest of the world's economies in its rapid and balanced post–World War II development. Between 1949 and 1970 the Japanese economy grew at the unprecedented real annual rate of 10.5 percent per year; that is, its Gross National Product (GNP) doubled in less than every seven years. During the 1970s Japan's GNP grew at a rate of 5.2 percent per year despite conditions of international recession. Between 1980 and 1983 the Japanese GNP increased at a real average annual rate of 3.8 percent notwithstanding the deteriorating world economy.[1] In 1981, Japan, a country the size of Montana with 117 million inhabitants, had the second largest market economy in the world and a per capita income some 80 percent of the U.S. level. (This figure varies with the yen-dollar exchange rate.)

Japan is almost totally lacking in many important raw materials. The country imports over 90 percent of all of its energy resources, virtually all of its oil, iron ore, and nonferrous ores, and a substantial portion of its foodstuffs. Despite this import dependence and the manifold multiplication of petroleum prices during the seventies, Japan managed to run balance-of-trade surpluses throughout the

---

1. Unless otherwise indicated, figures on the Japanese economy are from the *Monthly Finance Review* published by the Research and Planning Division of Japan's Ministry of Finance.

decade. Its international reserves grew from $4.8 billion in 1970 to $31.9 billion in 1979. Japan's trade balance has remained strong in the early eighties.

Since 1970 Japan has combined economic growth with a concerted and effective campaign against environmental pollution. In 1975, for instance, Japan devoted some 3 percent of its GNP to anti-pollution efforts. In addition, these accomplishments have been accompanied by very low rates of unemployment since the late fifties (between 1.1 and 2.7 percent!), relatively high labor force participation rates (62 to 68 percent), and a comparatively equal distribution of income. Together these features and achievements have been dubbed the "Japanese economic miracle."

In recent years there has been a proliferation of publications purporting to explain the basis of Japan's economic success and to draw lessons for the United States. Although a consensus among scholars has not been reached, most agree that certain factors stand out as having had a strong bearing on Japanese economic performance. In what follows, we shall provide a brief, stylized overview of the Japanese economy, concentrating on those institutions and policies unique to Japan.

Background

The historical heritage, both structural and cultural, of the postwar Japanese economy is still subject to broad debate. Many authorities trace certain current-day practices and institutions back to earlier historical periods; others find roots in the new policies of the World War II era or the Allied occupation, and still others argue that modern Japanese institutions are strictly post–World War II phenomena. It is not our intention to shed new light on these questions. We believe that many historical legacies are difficult to identify and often assert themselves in subtle, even inscrutable, ways. Nonetheless, certain historical patterns and relationships have been more continuous and pronounced and have had a clear impact on the Japanese development model.

During the Tokugawa period (1603–1868) of hereditary military dictatorships the historical basis for state involvement in the economy was laid. Confucianism was restored as the official philosophy, extolling the virtues of obedience, propriety, benevolence, and knowledge. These values promoted the early growth of an educational system and a skilled labor force beyond the economy's absorptive capacity of human capital.

The government established rigid and extensive controls over economic activity in its effort to preserve the status quo in an essentially feudal society. Foreign trade remained closed until 1854 when it was forced open by colonialist aggression. Growing external commercial and military pressure forced a modernization on Japan, which came in 1868 with the overthrow of Tokugawa rule, known as the Meiji Restoration. The fear of foreign domination led the new rulers to actively promote industrialization.

In addition to loosening the feudal knots of the social structure, the new government took several important economic measures. The government set up trading companies to aid importers and exporters in dealing with foreign language, customs, regulations, and institutions. It sent representatives abroad to learn about modern production technologies, management methods, culture, and recreational activities; it also imported foreign technical specialists to train the Japanese in various areas.

According to Rosovsky, from 30 to 40 percent of capital formation (excluding the military sector) between 1887 and 1936 was undertaken by the government.[2] These figures, however, understate the qualitative contribution of the state to early economic development. The government directly invested in basic industry and infrastructure, including railroads, communications, shipbuilding, military production, mining, textiles, and other manufacturing activities. Under the prevailing conditions, most of these investments were regarded as quite risky. After these ventures were well established, the state began (starting around 1880) to sell these companies at well below market prices to select members of elite groups.

As a result of unequal trade treaties, Japan did not have control over its own tariff policy until 1911. The state was thus compelled to aid infant industry through subsidies, marketing and training support, control of foreign investment, and other measures. These Japanese government efforts to establish control over its trading patterns as an inferior member of the late-nineteenth-century world economy might well be the basis for many post–World War II trade policies, such as Japan's notorious nontariff commercial barriers.

The specific economic policies of the government were decided upon and implemented by a powerful state bureaucracy. Historically, the bureaucracy was created by and responsible to the emperor. It was legitimized by the examination system, which certified incoming bureaucrats to be well-educated (perhaps the highest virtue in the prevailing value system). By the 1890s, the Meiji oligarchs also sought legitimation for their own political power and introduced an ineffectual, token parliament. The existence of a strong, professional government bureaucracy that was unconstrained by a weak parliament established for the state sector a modus operandi that is little changed today, even under conditions of formal political democracy. We will deal further with this subject later.

---

2. Henry Rosovsky, *Capital Formation in Japan, 1868–1940* (Glencoe: Free Press, 1961), 24.

Largely as a result of increasing military aggression, the state grew more involved in the Japanese economy during the early decades of the twentieth century. Japan's military excursions were, of course, to culminate in its alliance with the Axis powers and then in its ultimate defeat in the Second World War. The costs of World War II to Japan were high: 40 percent of Japan's capital stock was destroyed and 2.8 million citizens were killed. (It should be pointed out, however, that wartime destruction probably had the effect of spurring the introduction of new technology and, paradoxically, of giving Japan a competitive cost edge for certain products.) The terms of surrender brought U.S. occupation of Japan until April 1952 as well as a constitutional requirement that Japan not maintain military forces. In practice, this provision has been partly circumvented by the so-called self-defense forces, but spending on defense has been consistently less than 1.5 percent of Japan's GNP. The Allied occupation also played a key role in reshaping Japan's economic and political institutions, although the details of this process do not directly concern us. (Apart from the brief U.S. occupation, throughout its history Japan was never penetrated by an occupying foreign power, which helps to account for the country's ethnic homogeneity.)

We may, then, decipher certain unambiguous historical legacies that became part of Japan's postwar strategy of economic development: a strong, interventionist state, fully accepted by the business community; policy making and implementation through a powerful, skilled government bureaucracy; a highly educated population; and a low burden of defense expenditures.

Corporate Structure and Finance

In this section, we discuss in detail several salient features of Japan's industrial organization: (1) the dominant role played by industrial groups (coalitions of enterprises) and their trading companies, (2) sharp industrial dualism, (3) excessive leveraging or unusually high debt/equity ratios, and (4) a very high rate of investment (and saving). One final characteristic, and probably the most important, the coordination and guidance of enterprises by the state bureaucracy, will be discussed in a subsequent section of this chapter.

There are three basic patterns of industrial groups. The first we shall call *zaibatsu-type bank groups*, roughly corresponding to the family-owned zaibatsu dating to the nineteenth century. The zaibatsu groups are coalitions of usually dozens of large enterprises, all connected to a major city bank and a trading company. They were broken up during the Allied occupation but were quickly reassembled in the early and mid fifties. The member companies own stock in one another, have interlocking directorates, and borrow heavily from the associated bank and trading company. One well-known example of a zaibatsu bank group is Mitsubishi, which contains twenty-eight core companies all tightly associated, or some sixty large companies with a looser affiliation, as well as the Mitsubishi bank and trading company.

These large enterprises are also linked to constellations of subordinate enterprises and small subcontractors through stock ownership, shared directors, and (often exclusive) trade ties. The top one hundred nonfinancial enterprises have around forty-three hundred enterprises under them.

A second category of industrial group is what we shall call the *German-type bank group*. In these groups, a somewhat smaller number of enterprises are all closely associated with a common bank, but the enterprises lack formal ownership bonds with one another.

Finally, there are *large industrial groups*, such as Toyota, Sony, Hitachi, and others, which are tied to no specific bank but are associated with scores of subordinate companies. Together the ten largest industrial groups account for approximately 50 percent of Japan's GNP. This high level of vertical integration and conglomeration represents a significant degree of nonmarket coordination of decision making; it also facilitates the formal and informal government coordination among companies and sectors that will be described below. (The close, and often exclusive, association of large companies with their subcontractors is also held to explain Japan's efficient system of "just-in-time" inventory management. Slower economic growth during the early eighties, however, has strained these relations.)

Japan's trading companies, as we saw, date back to the nineteenth century. Today, there are some sixty-seven hundred trading companies. The largest nine are called general trading companies (GTCs) and play a truly dominant role in the Japanese economy. In 1978 the nine GTCs had combined sales of $228 billion and accounted for 48 percent of Japan's exports and 51 percent of her imports.

The GTCs continue to perform their traditional role of assisting in the penetration of foreign markets and securing the purchase of necessary inputs and raw materials. Because of their size and the fact that they operate on both the import and export sides of the market, the GTCs can also reduce the risks (for their 750-odd affiliated companies) associated with exchange rate fluctuations and seasonal variations in demand and price. GTCs also provide import and export credits and account for over one-third of Japanese direct foreign investment, helping them gain control over the supply of essential imports. Finally, the GTCs are widely used as financial intermediaries by city banks, which prefer to loan to the financially robust GTCs and have the GTCs loan to the small and medium-sized companies to which they are tied.

The role of the large commercial banks in the industrial groups is naturally to provide capital. What is different about Japanese commercial banks is that the capital is provided in prodigious amounts

Table 2.1
Debt/Equity Trend in Japanese Industry

	1968	1971	1974	1977
Debt (as a share of total capitalization)	83.1%	84.2%	85.7%	85.9%
Equity (as a share of total capitalization)	16.9%	15.8%	14.3%	14.1%
Debt/equity ratio	4.9	5.3	6.0	6.1

Source: Naoto Sasaki, *Management and Industrial Structure in Japan* (Oxford: Pergamon Press, 1981), 26.

and that the direction and size of the loan as well as the interest rate are often controlled or influenced by a government organ. Most bank loans are also essentially guaranteed by the Bank of Japan. This takes us into the realm of corporate finance.

Although the pattern is slowly changing since the late seventies, most Japanese corporations have an extremely low ratio of stockholders' equity to total capital. The great bulk of company capital comes from debt rather than from the issuance of stock. Most debt, in turn, takes the form of bank loans rather than corporate bonds.

In contrast to the situation in U.S. corporations, where the average share of equity (stock) in total capitalization is around 50 percent, the typical Japanese company relies on borrowing for over 80 percent of its capital. Through the seventies, the average debt/equity ratio of Japanese corporations was still rising (see Table 2.1). (This average masks the fact that certain high-growth sectors such as electronics and computers have "matured." Thanks to strong profits, very favorable depreciation allowances, access to foreign capital markets, and liberalized regulations on the Tokyo Stock Exchange, such sectors are no longer dependent on bank loans for the majority of their investment financing.)

The equity that is held in Japanese companies is concentrated in a few hands. In 1972, 69 percent of the shares held in the Tokyo Stock Exchange were held by one-half of 1 percent of the stockholders.[3] Institutions, as opposed to individuals, held two-thirds of all shares. In the U.S. the largest institutional stockholders are pension funds, insurance companies, and other financial institutions. "In Japan, by contrast, the institutional shareholders are usually the banks and trading partners of a company whose shares they own. They have

---

3. Henry Wallich and M. Wallich, "Banking and Finance," in *Asia's New Giant: How the Japanese Economy Works*, ed. H. Patrick and H. Rosovsky (Washington, D.C.: Brookings Institution, 1976), 307.

bought their shares not so much for dividends as to ensure the cooperation of the company as a borrower or customer or supplier."[4] Many
maintain that this circumstance gives Japanese companies a more
long-run perspective in making business decisions. Japanese companies are thus more likely to be patient and engage in projects with
lengthy gestation periods. Japanese success with semiconductors is
often attributed to this characteristic; and the early dropping of semi-
conductor projects by G.E., Westinghouse, and RCA is seen as a
reflection of their irrational emphasis on short-run profits, a compulsion forced upon them by stockholders looking for quick returns.

Generally, corporate loans come either from their affiliated banks
or from a government financial agency such as the Japan Development Bank. In both cases, the direction, size, and terms of the loan are
influenced by government policy.

Commercial banks are said to engage in "overloan"; at times, they
loan out in excess of 100 percent of their deposits. Banks are dependent on the Central Bank (Bank of Japan (BOJ)) for funds to expand
their lending capacity. The BOJ, in turn, will generally extend funds
only to banks that are connected with a company in a state-targeted
growth sector. This practice provides an incentive for the banks to
affiliate with firms in designated sectors. In some cases, this affiliation
is accomplished by setting up a new enterprise, which could generate
overcapacity in the sector. This system helps to account for frequent
industrial production growth above planned levels as well as the
Japanese drive to find foreign markets.

An important public channel for loans to industry is provided by the
so-called postal savings system operated by the government. Individuals can deposit funds in post office branches and receive the
same rate of interest available at a commercial bank. The incentive to
save through the postal system is that the annual interest on the first
three million yen[5] deposited is tax-exempt. Moreover, this limit applies to the account, not to the individual. A person can open separate
accounts at as many different post office branches as he or she desires
and receive the limit exemption on each account. The postal savings
system provides an important tax shelter, especially for the wealthy
since Japan has a nominally progressive rate structure.

By 1980, the total amount of postal savings was estimated at fifty-five
trillion yen, representing four times the assets of the world's largest
commercial bank, the Bank of America, or almost twice the total sum
deposited in Japan's city commercial banks. Here again, according to
the priorities worked out by the Ministry of Finance (MOF) and the
Ministry of International Trade and Industry (MITI), the funds are

---

4. Rodney Clark, *The Japanese Company* (New Haven: Yale University
Press, 1979), 102.

5. As of July 1984 there were approximately 240 yen to the dollar.

channeled in the form of subsidies and low-interest loans to stipu-
lated areas of the economy through the Fiscal Investment and Loan
Plan (FILP) under the MOF and the Japanese Development Bank
(JDB).

The Japanese corporate income tax creates a preference among
Japanese firms for debt financing. As in the United States, interest
payments on debt are deductible from taxable income, while stock
dividends must be paid after the income tax is fully levied. The preference for debt and the resulting capital structure make the firm particularly sensitive to changes in the interest rate. In normal periods the
rate has been kept low and many rates have been set below a market
level, complementing the system of government rationing or guidance of funds.

Beyond pointing out the elaborate mechanisms for channeling
funds and the substantial government control over their allocation, it
is necessary to note that the absolute availability of capital funds in
Japan has been very high. This is a direct consequence of Japan's
having the highest savings rate in the capitalist world (at the expense
of present consumption). In 1980, for instance, Japan's savings ratio
(gross savings as a percentage of GNP) was 30.7 percent, versus 23.1
percent in West Germany, 17.3 percent in Sweden, 21.7 percent in
France, 19.2 percent in Great Britain, and 18.3 percent in the United
States. With sufficient aggregate demand, high savings and high investment, of course, go together and generally promote fast growth.

Until the mid seventies the Japanese government was a net saver,
contributing to national savings along with the corporate and household sectors (see Table 2.2). Between 1955 and 1972 government saving amounted to between 21 and 41 percent of government revenues.
The lion's share of this saving took the form of government investment in infrastructure, but government saving also exceeded govern-

Table 2.2
Japanese Savings by Sector as a Percentage of GNP

	Households		Government		Business		Total	
	1970–75	1976–80	1970–75	1976–80	1970–75	1976–80	1970–75	1976–80
Gross savings	17.2	19.3	6.6	2.4	14.1	10.2	37.9	31.9
Gross investment	6.6	11.3	5.9	6.8	23.9	15.7	36.4	33.8
Net lending	10.5	8.0	0.7	−4.4	−9.8	−5.5	—	—

Source: *The Economist* (Oct. 23, 1982): 69.
Note: Gross saving by government is defined as budgetary revenues minus
current expenditures.

ment investment by 1 to 18 percent between 1955 and 1972, providing net capital funds to the private sector.[6]

Low defense spending and low debt-service payments were key factors keeping down public expenditures and allowing for budgetary surpluses. With yearly budgetary surpluses, monetary as opposed to fiscal policy was the principal short-term instrument for dealing with business cycles. Since the late seventies, however, Japan has had significant government deficits.

The corporate sector has tended to make modest net contributions to national savings. Whereas the share of retained earnings in corporate profits has been high, lower profit rates and high debt-service burdens have restricted corporate savings.

Household Savings

The main ingredient behind Japan's high savings ratio is high household savings as a share of disposable income. For example, whereas this ratio has fluctuated around 5 percent in recent years in the United States, in Japan it has been around 21 percent. What we attribute the Japanese households' prodigious frugality to is therefore a very central question. Below we shall enumerate some possible explanations.

1. Savings may promote growth, but growth may also promote savings. As incomes rise it takes a while for households to adjust their consumption patterns upward. The faster the rise in incomes, in general, the greater will be the proportional lag in consumption, i.e., the greater will be the saving. So growth in this sense is self-generating. Japan, of course, fits this pattern well, and this factor is likely an important one behind Japan's high household savings.

2. Consumer and mortgage credit markets have been rather underdeveloped. Home buyers, for instance, are required to make a minimum down payment of 40 percent of the purchase price. Moreover, since land is scarce, home prices are relatively high. Nevertheless, some 60 percent of Japanese households own their homes. These factors require households aspiring to home ownership (or major durable goods purchases) to save a high share of their income.

3. Social security benefits are low (in 1976 they averaged around a thousand dollars per beneficiary per year) and retirement age is young (55 to 60). Workers are thus well-advised to save for old age. Companies normally provide a lump sum payment upon retirement rather than an annuity. This payment can be as high as four

---

6. Wallich and Wallich, "Banking and Finance," 15.

years of wages and varies by company and length of employment. Such large lump sum payments in contrast to annuities also induce savings.

4. It is standard practice for Japanese companies to set a relatively low basic wage and then offer large bonuses (based loosely on profits) twice a year. These bonuses have been rising as a share of the basic wage over time and in 1978 averaged 35.8 percent of the basic wage for all employees in manufacturing. Again, as lump sum payments they encourage saving.

5. Japan today has a comparatively young population. In June 1982 there were 7.5 working people for each retiree (this ratio in the U.S. and Western Europe is close to 3 to 1). Since retired persons tend to use up savings and workers tend to save, Japan's demographic balance has also promoted saving. The Japanese birthrate, however, declined sharply in the early fifties and has stayed low. Life expectancy, meanwhile, rose to 73.3 years for males and 78.8 years for females by 1980, second only to Iceland in longevity rates in the world. These trends will alter the demographic pattern considerably in the near future. By the year 2000 it is projected that the Japanese will have only three workers per retiree. This shift will lower the aggregate propensity to save as well as impact upon Japan's employment system, as we shall see below.

6. There is no capital gains tax on assets (except land), and there are substantial exemptions on interest and dividend income. These provisions stimulate saving, but also tend to redistribute income regressively.

7. Some believe that frugality is an intrinsic part of the Japanese character or value system. For instance, Ezra Vogel writes, "Japanese students also learn the value of saving, as every pupil in every elementary school saves a few yen each week over several years to finance the sixth grade school trip."[7] It is difficult to know what importance to ascribe to this educational custom or how to identify its origins. Similar things are known to happen in the U.S. schools. Other experts, such as Nathan Glazer,[8] argue that it is hard to perceive a clear link between Japanese culture and savings. We will remain agnostic on this dispute.

These, then, are the major explanations for Japanese thriftiness. It should be self-evident that many of these savings-promoting features are either nontransferable or not desirable to other economies.

---

7. Ezra Vogel, *Japan as Number One* (Cambridge: Harvard University Press, 1979), 177.

8. Nathan Glazer, "Social and Cultural Factors in Japanese Economic Growth," in Patrick and Rosovsky, *Asia's New Giant.*

Labor Market Institutions

By most conventional standards, Japan's labor market has performed very well. The economy has had virtually full employment since the late fifties (with inflation levels comparable to those in the United States). Lengthy strikes are virtually nonexistent. Industrial accident rates are among the lowest in the world. Absenteeism, averaging 1.9 percent during 1981, is the lowest among the industrialized capitalist countries. Workers are well educated, disciplined, and hardworking; and, according to many, decision making in enterprises is more open and democratic than elsewhere in the advanced capitalist world. From the Japanese employers' point of view there is one additional advantage: Japanese wages plus benefits are considerably below the levels prevailing in other industrialized nations. There are few U.S. managers who do not look enviously at the Japanese system of labor relations.

The official unemployment rate in Japan averaged 1.2 percent between 1967 and 1973 and 1.9 percent between 1973 and 1980. The unemployment rate averaged 2.2 percent in 1981 and fluctuated between 2.2 and 2.8 percent during the period January 1982 through May 1984.[9] The fact that these rates are three or four times below what is currently considered the "natural" rate of unemployment in the United States might lead the reader to question whether the Japanese define and measure unemployment as we do in the United States. The answer is no, but most methodological differences are minor. A recent study by the U.S. Bureau of Labor Statistics concluded that if Japan were to use the U.S. concepts in defining unemployment, its unemployment rate would nevertheless be unchanged; that is, the upward and downward biases would cancel each other.[10]

While this judgment might be generous to Japan, it is noteworthy that the Japanese labor force participation rate has been consistently above that of the United States, primarily because of higher labor force participation rates among men. The most important bias appears to be cultural and is not taken into account by the Bureau of Labor Statistics study. There appears to be a much stronger presumption in Japan than in the United States that a woman's natural place is in the home. Consequently, a larger share of discharged women in Japan do not seek new employment and are not counted as unemployed. In 1982, the labor force participation of Japanese women was

---

9. These and other figures are taken from the *Monthly Finance Review*, No. 133 (July 1984), published by Japan's Ministry of Finance.

10. U.S. Bureau of Labor Statistics, *International Comparisons of Unemployment*, Bulletin 1979 (Washington, D.C.: U.S. Government Printing Office, Aug. 1978), 3, 12. A September 1983 study released by the Japanese embassy in Washington concluded that methodological differences lower the measured rate in Japan by a mere two-tenths of one percentage point.

48.0 percent, compared to 52.7 percent for U.S. women. Although participation rates are similar, Japanese women's wages are 53 percent of the wages of their male counterparts, in contrast to the U.S. female-to-male median wage ratio of 60 percent. Moreover, Japanese women are to an overwhelming extent part-time workers.

What accounts, we might ask, for the Japanese success in maintaining unemployment below 3 percent of the labor force with rates of inflation comparable to other OECD (Organization for Economic Cooperation and Development) countries? First, rapid economic growth with only mild and brief recessions has generated strong and steady demand for labor. Second, as we shall see below, the combination of weak labor unions, the prevalence of large semiannual bonuses, and economic dualism[11] have all served to keep the basic wage level low relative to worker productivity. This circumstance has reinforced the demand for labor.

Tight labor markets are often associated with rising worker militancy, particularly if unit labor costs are falling. But full employment in Japan has been compatible with a high degree of industrial peace. Relative to other advanced market economies, Japan had a low level of industrial conflict in 1971; by the end of the decade this advantage had multiplied severalfold (see Table 2.3). With the figures adjusted for the size of the labor force (using Japan as the base), for the years covered the U.S. economy lost on average 8.6 times as many work days from industrial disputes (primarily strikes) as did the Japanese economy.

This combination of labor market successes is usually ascribed to what the Japanese call their *three sacred treasures*: lifetime employment, seniority-based wages, and company unionism. We shall discuss these in turn.

Lifetime Employment

The origins of the lifetime employment system in Japan are sometimes traced back to pre-Meiji times and sometimes to the 1920s, but the system in its present form did not begin to emerge until the 1950s as a response to the then incipient labor shortage. The name of the system is misleading and it has been widely misunderstood. It refers to an employment pattern whereby a person, upon completing school, begins work at a specific company and is more or less guaranteed a job at the company until retirement. Moreover, the incentive structure is such that the overwhelming majority of workers do stay with the same company.

In its pure form this system is applied only in large companies and

---

11. Economic dualism refers basically to the coexistence within the Japanese economy of a sector with large, capital intensive, unionized firms and another sector with small, labor intensive, nonunionized firms.

Table 2.3
Work Days Lost from Industrial Disputes

Work days lost (in millions)

	1971	1973	1975	1977	1979
Japan	6.03	4.60	8.06	1.52	0.93
United States	47.6	27.9	31.2	35.8	34.8
France	4.4	3.9	3.9	3.7	3.7
Sweden	0.84	0.01	0.36	0.87	0.28

Index of work days lost relative to size of labor force

	1971	1973	1975	1977	1979	Avg.
Japan	100	100	100	100	100	100
United States	431	328	211	1,263	2,069	860
France	181	207	119	593	1,000	420
Sweden	188	28	60	756	413	290

Source: Calculated from the International Labor Organization, *Yearbook of Labor Statistics*, 1981.

only to the designated permanent employees in these enterprises. *Women are almost completely excluded from this system, which covers only 25 to 30 percent of the labor force.* It must also be noted that retirement age is young; until recently, it was 55 years and now varies between 55 and 60 for most workers.

Even though the system is adopted only by a subset of companies, it is still appropriate to ask how large Japanese enterprises can guarantee jobs for their workers for "lifetime" while large U.S. enterprises cannot do so. Doesn't this commitment hurt enterprise adjustment to the business cycle and serve to lower profits, and doesn't it create inefficiency and inflexibility in the allocation of labor?

So-called lifetime employment does have certain negative effects, but it has generally been perceived to have on balance a positive impact. On the negative side, it can result in overstaffing during economic downturns. Furthermore, since the system requires the retention of less competent workers, it can lead to a less qualified staffing of certain positions relative to what would exist without the system.

The positive consequences are many. Lifetime employment (1) results in lower worker turnover and, hence, reduced recruitment and job training expenses; (2) achieves less worker resistance to technological change and job reassignment; and (3) in general, fits into the strategy of developing a personal, familylike atmosphere in the enterprise; an atmosphere which, it is usually held, engenders greater worker loyalty and effort.

The lifetime employment system is also more flexible than is often recognized. For instance, a large company facing reduced demand for its output has several options to cut costs and lower output short of outright layoff or dismissal. One option involves the circumstance that, as we indicated above, not all employees of large companies are covered by permanent employment rights. A large and growing number of workers are temporary and do not belong to the company union. It has been estimated that as many as 15 percent of all manufacturing employees are in this status. In certain companies the proportion runs much higher. Temporary employees can be laid off.

Another option is based on the sharp economic dualism of Japan's industrial structure. Over 50 percent of Japan's manufacturing labor force works in enterprises employing fewer than one hundred workers, compared to around 25 percent in the United States. A very large share of these small Japanese firms are subcontractors for larger companies and often do business solely with the parent company. Japanese automobile companies, for instance, purchase 65 to 70 percent of their parts and materials from their subcontractors. That is, rather than doing a substantial portion of, say, parts machining in the parent company itself, where workers (1) are unionized, (2) are largely under lifetime employment, and (3) receive higher wages by a factor of 30 to 40 percent as well as greater nonwage benefits, the parent company farms out this work to its subcontractors. It thereby obtains lower manufacturing costs and also enhanced flexibility. When demand for the company's final output falls, the parent company can cut its orders to the subcontractors. It is then the subcontractors that lay off workers, and the lifetime employment privileges for parent company workers are protected.

A third choice—another possibility owing to Japan's industrial structure—is to send workers from one company to another within the same industrial group. During the last recession, for example, Nissan (producers of Datsun) sent several hundred steelworkers to work in a fish hatchery. Production workers are also used for carrying out social works projects (e.g., landscaping, construction and maintenance of recreational facilities, etc.) during periods of slack demand.

Other production or cost-cutting options include: reducing bonuses, lowering benefits, eliminating overtime work, encouraging employees to take their holidays early, inducing older workers into early retirement, or using the slack period for worker training and education. Government agencies have also been generous in granting subsidies to enterprises to hold on to excess workers during recessions.

Finally, if push comes to shove, so-called permanent employees can be furloughed at partial pay (usually 60 to 90 percent of the basic wage) or they can even be discharged. Although this option is legally permissible, companies try hard to avoid it since it undermines the family attitude on which Japanese labor relations are founded. Notwithstanding, on occasion it is unavoidable. In the fall of 1981, for example, the Maruzen Oil Co. (Japan's fourth largest oil refinery) announced it would discharge twelve hundred of its forty-six hundred workers. Before making this move, however, the company took several economizing steps, including cutting the pay of corporate officers by one-half. Moreover, the discharges were to occur over a three-year period.

Seniority-based Wages

The second so-called sacred treasure is the seniority-based wage system. In its pure form this system provides guaranteed wage increases and/or promotions for length of service. If decision-making authority corresponded rigidly to the hierarchy of the company's organizational chart, this system would produce a gerontocracy. One clear intent of the system is to provide a strong incentive for workers to stay with the same firm and, of course, to develop a loyalty to that firm.

The strict implementation of this system creates too many problems to be workable in a competitive economic environment. Several adaptations have proved necessary. If the senior, as distinct from the most competent, people move to the top of the organization, then it is necessary to move decision making down the organization to where the best qualified are found. This consideration, presumably, has been a major force behind the practices in Japanese firms of decentralizing information and decision making, having new ideas circulate widely and seeking consensus. To be sure, these practices may be efficient in companies outside Japan as well.

Another adaptation has been to modify the rules of the game. In some cases, one can observe a trend toward the separation of the wage system and the promotion system so that a subordinate might be earning more than his superior. In other cases, the wage system has developed to consider both seniority and merit or merit alone. Indeed, a September 1977 Ministry of Labor survey found that 43 percent of enterprises were basing wage increases on merit alone.

Part of the pressure to reward merit or skill has come from marked demographical shifts. The fact that the birth rate fell off after 1950 has a twofold consequence for the seniority wage: first, it has produced a current swelling in the 35 to 50 age group; and second, it has meant a dearth of skilled labor available out of high schools and universities. The former circumstance means that the pool of mid-career employees far exceeds the room at the top levels of the organizational charts. Thus, not all can expect promotion, and a non-seniority-based competition ensues for the top positions.

The shortage of skilled labor at the entry level has forced up the wages of younger workers and has narrowed the differential for seniority. Wage competition at the entry level also has induced younger workers to test the market more often, raising considerably the rate of turnover. If these tendencies proceed too far, they will begin to erode the basis for enterprise familism.

Other systemic adaptations to the demographical shift are also possible. Enterprises might improve the employment conditions for female workers or they might push back the retirement age. It remains to be seen which adaptations will predominate.

Company Unionism

The third sacred treasure is company unionism. Approximately one-third of the Japanese labor force is unionized. The collective bargaining unit and the locus of union power is at the enterprise level. This has been the case since the reconstruction of the union movement after World War II. There is only one union per company, as a rule, so the union cuts across all craft boundaries and includes all regular blue- and white-collar employees up to the management level. Among other things, this arrangement gives management greater flexibility in shifting job assignments to cover for absenteeism, to adjust to new technology, or to respond to demand shifts among products.

There is a tendency for union presidents to be key workers, such as crew chiefs, about to be promoted into management. Union presidents enjoy higher salaries and perquisites than rank-and-file workers. Japanese unions generally perceive a unity between the interests of management and workers, and union leaders commonly adopt a management perspective. Galenson and Odaka quote a personnel manager of a large Japanese corporation on his view of the proper role of unions: "Unions improve morale, develop mutual respect and confidence and prevent sabotage."[12] The founding slogan of the Nissan Company labor union was "Those who truly love their union, love their company."[13] Rank-and-filers who question union policy often find themselves not getting promoted or not receiving standard wage increases.

Worker Participation

Despite the tight discipline and emphasis on conformity, there are aspects of Japanese management practices that are relatively open and democratic. The most well-known and successful example of shop floor worker participation is the so-called quality control (Q.C.) circle, which dates back to the early 1950s. A principal idea behind the circles is that workers are closer to actual production than managers and they, therefore, can frequently perceive and offer constructive solutions to problems more readily than can management.

---

12. Walter Galenson and K. Odaka, "The Japanese Labor Market," in Patrick and Rosovsky, *Asia's New Giant*, 640.

13. John Junkerman, "We Are Driven," *Mother Jones* (Aug. 1982): 22.

A typical enterprise has dozens of Q.C. circles, and each circle has an average of ten workers. Circles meet once every one or two weeks for about an hour, usually during breaks or after work hours. The workers' participation is voluntary, and normally the workers do not receive direct remuneration for productivity increases based on the suggestions or activities of the circles. Nonetheless, promotion and basic-wage increases are often contingent on worker attitudes, so belonging to a successful Q.C. circle may be rather helpful. Participants are trained in problem-solving techniques, including statistical methods. The groups discuss a wide range of subjects: product quality improvements, cost reductions, worker safety, tooling, inventory policy, maintenance, etc. The process is aided by the practice of having company engineers regularly go to the shop floor to discuss production with the workers—yielding better-informed workers as well as better-informed engineers.

The circles are widespread throughout Japanese industry, although their scope and significance varies from sector to sector. Steel and autos are two sectors where they play a particularly important role. For instance, Toyota Motors in 1980 reported that on average there were 17.8 suggestions per employee, of which management adopted close to 90 percent.[14] One recent survey of 276 plants found that the nationwide mean benefit/cost ratio from Q.C. circle suggestions was 80 to 1.[15]

Some companies, it appears, get carried away in calling for expressions of worker loyalty. Quality circles enter into strong competition (or emulation) to "out-loyalty" one another—staying after hours, giving up breaks or even vacation time, etc. Japanese workers put in many more hours than European or U.S. workers. For instance, in 1979 the estimated annual average of hours worked in manufacturing was 2,150 in Japan versus 1,700 in West Germany, 1,550 in Italy, 1,800 in France, 1,500 in Sweden, and 1,900 in the U.S.[16]

The inevitable result is work intensification. Perhaps this, in addition to the many positive features mentioned above, helps to explain why Ezra Vogel was able to report, "In 1976 none of the major European car producers (Fiat, Renault, or Volkswagen) was able to produce as many as twenty cars per man year of labor, but Nissan employees produced 42 cars per man year and Toyota turned out 49."[17]

14. Robert Cole, "The Japanese Lesson in Quality," *Technology Review* (July 1981): 38.

15. Christopher Gray, "Total Quality Control in Japan: Less Inspection, Lower Cost," in "Japan: Quality Control and Innovation," *Business Week*, special section, July 20, 1981, 24.

16. W. L. Chilton, "The Unit-Labor-Cost Race: Who's Gaining: Who's Losing," *Citibank's World Outlook* (Oct. 1982): 5.

17. Vogel, *Japan as Number One*, 12.

Wages

Job security and relative equality in company pay scales undoubtedly aid the success of Japanese worker participation. With job security, the Japanese worker does not have to fear that productivity-increasing suggestions will put workers out of their jobs. More equal pay scales (Toyota chief executives are paid *$200 less an hour* than GM executives!) give workers the sense that rewards from productivity increases are more fairly distributed. Both factors contribute to the atmosphere of enterprise familism and loyalty. (To the extent that inequality and discrimination prevail, these conditions tend to be more readily accepted in Japan than elsewhere because of the persistent vestiges of Japan's feudal heritage.)

Compressed intraenterprise wage scales are complemented by other practices that help to generate the sense of an egalitarian community within companies. For instance, there is one Japanese word, translated "earnings," used to refer to both wages and salaries. Earnings are paid on a monthly, rather than an hourly, basis for all permanent employees, and the use of piece rates is rare. All employees share the same cafeteria and other facilities. It is likely, however, that wage disparities will grow in the future as remuneration becomes more a function of skill and interenterprise wage bidding becomes more prevalent. It should also be added that despite salaries that are low relative to their American counterparts, Japanese executives enjoy very generous fringe benefits. (In 1979, so-called corporate social expenses came to $13.8 billion.)

In spite of generous executive fringe benefits, the combination of a relatively compressed earnings distribution, full employment, favorable demographical balance, and explicit government intervention to increase the incomes of farmers (as well as small wholesalers and retailers) has produced in Japanese society a comparatively equal overall distribution of income (see Table 2.4).

The difference between public and private sector earnings for workers with similar educational backgrounds is less in Japan than in the United States. The effect of this fact is twofold: (1) it brings highly qualified individuals into the public sphere, helping to account for the economic influence and effectiveness of government policy; and (2) it is more likely that sufficient numbers of competent, technically trained individuals will be attracted to teaching positions. This circumstance is surely one of the reasons that Japan is able to consistently turn out more engineers than we do in the United States (twice as many are graduated per year on a per capita basis).

Finally, a word about the absolute level of wages in Japan: While overall real compensation (including bonuses and benefits) has risen very rapidly in Japan, it has not kept up with the growth in worker productivity. Between 1970 and 1981 real hourly compensation in Japanese manufacturing rose by 54 percent, while productivity (per

Table 2.4
After-tax Distribution of Household Income
(Including Transfers) in Selected Countries

		Percentage of total income		
	For year	Household Income— Lowest 10%	Household Income— Highest 10%	Ratio (highest to lowest)
France	1970	1.4	30.5	21.8
West Germany	1973	2.8	30.6	10.9
Sweden	1972	2.6	18.6	7.2
United States	1972	1.7	26.1	15.4
Japan	1969	2.7[a]	27.8	10.3
Great Britain	1973	2.4	23.9	10.0

Source: Malcom Sawyer, "Income Distribution in OECD Countries," *OECD Economic Outlook* (Paris: July 1976): 19.

Note: Data adjusted for household size.

a. This figure means that the poorest 10% of Japanese households in terms of income received 2.7% of all household income.

man-hour) rose by 110 percent. When converted at the average exchange rate for each year, hourly compensation in Japan rose from 21.8 percent of the U.S. level in 1970 to 52.6 percent in 1981 (see Table 2.5). Although these dollar-equivalent wage calculations are highly sensitive to fluctuations in the exchange rate, it is clear that, with a wide margin for error, Japanese exporters still enjoy a considerable labor cost advantage over many of their foreign competitors.

Table 2.5
International Rates of Hourly Compensation
in Manufacturing in Current Dollars
(Including Bonuses and Benefits)

Country	1970	1980	1981	1981[a]
France	2.05	10.55	9.59	7.57
West Germany	2.26	12.68	11.00	10.06
Japan	1.07	6.02	6.63	5.72
Sweden	3.50	14.85	13.57	11.17
United States	4.90	11.44	12.61	12.61

Source: W. L. Chilton, "The Unit-Labor-Cost Race: Who's Gaining: Who's Losing," *Citibank's World Outlook* (Oct. 1982): 2.

Note: Most of the increase in money wages between 1970 and 1980 is due to inflation and does not denote increases in the standard of living.

a. At July 1982 exchange rates.

Other Employee Compensation

In addition to bonuses, enterprise-provided social benefits are an important component of employee compensation as well as an integral part of the campaign to promote enterprise familism and loyalty. Such benefits are far-ranging and can include: housing credit; company housing; medical insurance with company clinics or hospitals (supplementing or superseding the national health insurance system); retail and service shops; mutual aid credit provisions for marriages, births, accidents, etc.; cultural, sport, and recreational facilities and clubs; and more. In 1978, all manufacturing enterprises had an average expenditure of 12.2 percent of payroll on legally required social benefits plus an average of 13.0 percent on non-mandatory benefits.[18] Large enterprises spend considerably above these average levels.

Social benefits also come in the form of special attention and service for personal problems. Factory department chiefs, for example, often get involved in personal problems of their workers, such as mediating a marriage squabble or setting the terms of a divorce settlement. This emphasis on personal rather than contractual relations is rooted in Japanese culture and has helped Japan avoid the burdensome expenses of a litigious society. (There are some 13,000 lawyers in Japan, 1.1 per thousand inhabitants, versus 600,000 in the U.S., 26.6 per thousand inhabitants.) Surveys asking workers whether they would prefer a department chief who demanded hard work but did something for them personally in nonwork matters or the opposite type of supervisor have consistently shown that 80 percent or more want the paternalistic-type supervisor.[19]

The personalism and paternalism of company culture, in turn, have reduced the role of the state in providing social welfare benefits to its citizens. Lower government transfer payments along with restricted military spending in Japan have yielded a smaller share of government expenditures in Gross Domestic Product (GDP) than elsewhere in the OECD bloc. Despite this, the state has played and continues to play a leading role in Japanese economic affairs. In the next section, we turn to an analysis of this phenomenon.

Role of the State

Until recently, casual empiricism might well have led one to conclude that low taxes and a small government role lay behind Japan's economic success. It should be clear from Table 2.6, however, that Japanese government expenditures as a share of Gross Domestic

18. Chilton, "The Unit-Labor-Cost Race," 3.
19. Glazer, "Social and Cultural Factors," 854.

Table 2.6
Government Expenditure Share of
Gross Domestic Product

	1967	1973	1980	Percentage of Increase in Govt. Share, 1967–80	Average Annual Rate of Real GDP Growth, 1967–80 (%)
Japan	18.3	25.4	31.6	72.7	6.7
West Germany	38.2	40.5	46.1	20.7	3.7
France	39.0	38.5	46.3	18.7	4.1
United States	31.8	32.0	33.1	4.1	2.9

Sources: Bank of International Settlements, *Fifty-First Annual Report* (June 1981): 24; OECD, *Main Economic Indicators*, various issues.

Product are now nearly on a par with the government share in the United States. (If the shares were adjusted for the disparity in military expenditures, the share of the Japanese government would be approximately five percentage points above the U.S. government share in 1980.) Moreover, Japan's rapid growth has been accompanied by a rapidly rising government share since the mid sixties. The government share in Japan has risen three and a half times faster than in West Germany, almost four times faster than in France, and over seventeen times faster than in the United States since 1967. Yet the Japanese rate of economic growth was at least 50 percent higher than the rate in these countries and more than double the rate in the United States. Nonetheless, the true story behind the government role in the Japanese economy is not told by these numbers.

Earlier in the chapter we discussed the crucial role played by the state during the industrialization drive of the nineteenth century. After establishing much of the industrial sector with public funds, the state sold off enterprises at bargain prices to private ownership and subsequently nurtured these enterprises with favorable economic policies. Among other things, this course of action established a strong symbiotic relationship between the Japanese government and the business community. Rather than resenting government interference, Japanese businessmen generally have welcomed it. Through heavy campaign financing and ties through their national federation, the business community has enjoyed an intimate relationship with the Liberal Democratic Party, which has governed Japan since 1955.

Public economic policy making is basically in the hands of the professional government bureaucrats rather than the elected legislature. The independent decision-making power and prestige of the bureaucracy is historically rooted as explained above. The leading economic bodies in the government bureaucracy (MITI, MOF, Ministry of Agriculture and Forestry, Ministry of Construction, Ministry of Transport, and the Economic Planning Agency) set economic policy with very few constraints. Committees of experts make recommendations to the leading organs of the bureaucracy which are invariably passed through the Diet (parliament) with little or no modification or are simply implemented directly. It is the accepted wisdom, for instance, that in the Japanese budgetary process appropriations precede authorizations (the opposite of the U.S.). Chalmers Johnson asserts that this order has been broken only once when in 1972 the coupling of rare opposition unity and government mishandling provoked a small cut in proposed defense spending.[20]

The Japanese bureaucracy is professional rather than political. Only twenty-four ministers are politically appointed (at least one thousand posts in the U.S. government bureaucracy are politically selected); the rest of the Japanese bureaucracy is chosen on professional merit. In 1977, fifty-three thousand Japanese citizens took the higher level public official exam and only thirteen hundred passed, a fact that suggests that entrance into the bureaucracy is highly competitive. The bureaucracy's strong, independent decision-making role and its prestige lead it to attract Japan's most capable individuals.

Whereas the economic bureaucracy often takes its own initiative in formulating policy, it maintains very close relations with the business community. Economic bureaucrats from MITI and other state agencies regularly meet with representatives from the business community. It is not uncommon for bureaucrats working on a particular industrial sector to have dinner with the top executives and managers of the sector's enterprises several nights a week and, on occasion, in the company of the Prime Minister. The tab is picked up by the company. This Judge Gary–type dinner is not viewed as corrupt or improper but as the best way to coordinate information and set rational industrial policy. Further solidifying the links between the bureaucracy and industry is the widespread practice of *amakudari* (literally "descending from heaven"), whereby the top bureaucrats in a given economic sphere retire from the public sector at an early age and assume a top managerial post in a private company of the same sector.

Some analysts have used the term *Japan Inc.* to describe this hand-in-glove relationship between industry and government. However, the term is misleading. It does not capture the fact that there are occasional disagreements among sectors of the government bureaucracy and between the bureaucracy and industry. MITI cannot

20. Chalmers Johnson, *MITI and the Japanese Miracle* (Stanford: Stanford University Press, 1982), 10.

coerce industry to implement its proposals, and there have been several instances where its powers of persuasion have failed.[21]

The Japanese economic policy-making apparatus concerns itself primarily with supply management as opposed to the emphasis on demand management in the U.S. economy. Supply management also goes by the names *indicative planning* or *active industrial policy*. The basic premise is that the private sector alone has insufficient vision, coordination, resources, and risk-bearing ability to conduct its affairs in an optimal manner. To alleviate bottlenecks, to avert overproduction, to anticipate market shifts, to develop and deploy unchartered technology, the government is needed to assist in the sharing of information, pooling of resources, and overall collaboration of efforts. As a result of the successful implementation of this approach, MITI has referred to the Japanese system as a *plan-oriented market economy.*

When MITI was formed out of the old Ministry of Commerce and Industry in 1949, it quickly turned its attention to developing a dynamic, export-promoting/import-retarding industrialization strategy. The plan MITI evolved actually defied the conventional comparative advantage approach to international trade. Rather than emphasizing labor-intensive, low-technology industries, MITI chose to promote the heavy and chemical industries in the early fifties. The rationale was that this approach was consistent with a dynamic comparative advantage analysis. If Japan concentrated on nongrowth, traditional export sectors instead of modern, growth industries, it would confine its whole economy to slow growth and backwardness in the long run. Through an aggressive use of the policy levers at its disposal, MITI first instigated the rapid development of the electric power, shipbuilding, coal, and steel industries from 1953 to 1955; then the petrochemical, heavy machinery, and auto industries in 1955; the electronics and synthetic rubber industries in 1957; and the airplane industry in 1958.

During the first half of the 1950s textiles and fibers represented 30 percent and machinery represented 14 percent of Japan's exports. By the first half of the 1960s textiles and fibers had fallen to 8 percent and machinery had risen to 39 percent of Japanese exports. Attributing this overhaul of Japan's export composition to the policies of MITI, Chalmers Johnson writes: "This shift of industrial structure was the operative mechanism of the economic miracle."[22]

This view, which assigns a central role to government supply management in Japanese economic development, is widely held. It is therefore useful to inquire in greater detail into the mechanisms and

---

21. Toshimasa Tsuruta, "Japan's Industrial Policy" (paper presented at MIT Conference on Lessons from Japan, November 1982). Forthcoming in conference volume edited by Lester Thurow.

22. Johnson, *MITI and the Japanese Miracle*, 31.

levers employed for implementing the policies of Japan's economic bureaucracy. It is important to realize that while only some measures deal directly with foreign trade most policies affect Japanese exports and imports either directly or indirectly. Because Japan is a country very poor in natural resources, balance of payments difficulties were the effective constraint on Japanese development through the mid sixties. Thus, government policy was explicitly designed to advance exports and restrict imports. In 1964 the Japanese balance of payments turned positive and has stayed positive ever since. Beginning in the 1960s there has been a gradual liberalization of foreign trade and exchange controls.

We have already discussed one of the economic bureaucracy's key levers—the control over and supply of low- or no-interest funds to targeted industries. Such funds have constituted an important share of raised capital for prioritized sectors. These funds have also been used by the government to influence, if not determine, the number of enterprises in an industry. A leading expert on Japanese economic development, Henry Rosovsky, has remarked on the uniqueness of this practice: "Japan must be the only capitalistic country in the world in which the government decides how many firms there should be in a given industry and then sets about to arrange the desired number."[23]

Prioritized sectors have also benefited from special depreciation and tax benefits. For instance, in 1951 companies were given a tax exemption for up to 50 percent of their export earnings and this exemption was raised to 80 percent in 1955. As a result of pressure from GATT (General Agreement on Tariffs and Trade), these exemptions were replaced in 1964 by less obvious deductions and new accelerated depreciation prerogatives. Export industries have also benefited from import duty exclusion and sizable direct government subsidies. A subsidiary of MITI, the Japanese External Trade Organization (JETRO), operates eighty offices around the world to assist Japanese exporters in gathering marketing information and penetrating foreign markets. In this regard, JETRO's activities complement those of the major trading companies.

On the import protection side the economic bureaucracy has used discriminatory tariffs, import quotas, subsidies for domestic producers, import restrictions based on foreign currency allocations, foreign currency cartels, and other nontariff barriers to trade. Nontariff barriers to trade have been most effective in protecting domestic producers and, until recently, were compatible with the enforcement of international tariff treaties. Since all earned foreign currency had to be deposited with the government within ten days and MITI issued

___

23. Henry Rosovsky, "What Are the Lessons of Japanese Economic History," in *Economic Development in the Long Run*, ed. A. J. Youngson (London: George Allen and Unwin, 1972), 244.

licenses for the right to deal in foreign exchange and, hence, imports, the government had effective control over imports. "MITI made every effort to suppress imports of finished goods, particularly those which competed with domestic products, but it urgently sought imports of modern technology and machinery."[24] MITI had this power to grant licenses for foreign exchange until 1980. Here again, the large Japanese trading companies assisted this effort in refusing to import finished goods which would compete with the output of their domestic clients. (Since 1980 Japan's low interest rates have led to an undervalued yen, which in turn has provided for continued export promotion and import retardation.)

Japan is notorious for the use of standards and testing procedures as nontariff barriers to trade. To protect domestic car producers from foreign competition technical requirements were set, for example, regarding the precise placement of mirrors and other accessories or the so-called kimono guard (no space between back bumper and chassis to avoid strangulation of kimono wearers by passing cars). Testing procedures often involved several stages, each with long delays. Taken together these hurdles were frustrating and costly (often prohibitively so) to the foreign producer.

(Since late 1982 there has been some relaxation in standards testing and other nontariff import barriers. Further relaxation has been promised by the new Japanese Prime Minister Nakasone. To avoid excessive cynicism on this point, it is perhaps useful to note that Japan imported 6,758 cars from the United States in 1980. On a per capita basis this amount is double the number of U.S. cars imported by France and just below the number imported by West Germany in 1980.[25] Nonetheless, it is a far cry from the 1.8 million-odd Japanese cars per year imported by the United States, and it should be noted that U.S. car companies own production facilities and produce cars in Western Europe but not in Japan. Of course, the economic meaning of such comparisons is dubious.)

Although many tariff and nontariff impediments have been eased or removed, several are still in place. Some of the most troublesome currently to the United States concern agriculture. Because of severe gerrymandering, rural districts and small towns elect over 300 of 491 representatives in the Japanese Diet. The ruling Liberal Democratic Party (LDP) gets most of its support from these areas and less than 30 percent of the urban vote. This being the case, the LDP must carefully cultivate the continued support of Japan's farmers. "[Consequently,] agriculture has been the most heavily protected of industries. Even the most modest liberalization of agricultural imports has been the subject of prolonged and anguished debate and even now 20 farm

---

24. Johnson, *MITI and the Japanese Miracle*, 217.

25. Calculated from Japan–U.S. Study Group, *Japan's Economy and Japan–U.S. Trade* (Tokyo: The Japan Times), 219.

products, including rice, wheat, meat and dairy products, remain under quantitative import controls."[26] Domestic price supports for major crops have been among the highest in the world. In 1974, for example, the government spent $2.3 billion on farm price supports compared to $3.5 billion for national defense. In January 1983 Japan reduced tariffs on tobacco and other food items. Yet, despite intense pressure from U.S. trade negotiators, the Japanese government thus far has been unwilling to further liberalize their import quotas on beef and citrus products. To do so, they fear, would threaten the twenty-seven-year tenure of the LDP at the head of Japan's government.

Three additional policy areas of the economic bureaucracy merit discussion. First, although there is almost no government ownership of manufacturing operations, the government has been active in providing, owning, and operating infrastructural facilities (communications, transportation, utilities, industrial parks, etc.). Second, MITI has been very much involved in the procurement of and negotiation of the terms for foreign technology. MITI has successfully bargained for Japanese control over the use of imported technology as well as for lower fees and royalties.

Third, and the most important policy lever according to many, the economic bureaucracy has engaged in various kinds of "administrative guidance." The most prominent form of administrative guidance is the so-called *recession cartel*. During periods of slower growth or stagnating demand, MITI calls together the companies in an industry to discuss the restriction of output and prevent "excessive competition." Typically, these cartels lay plans for limiting production capacity, delaying or dividing up investment projects, and, sometimes, arranging for mergers. During the 1960s there were over nine thousand mergers, mostly involving small enterprise.

Another type of cartel is the *rationalization cartel*, again usually orchestrated by MITI. These are industry groups which exchange technology, share research and development, standardize goods production, arrange specialization by enterprises along product lines, establish queuing for investment projects, make common use of transportation, storage, or marketing facilities, etc. Between 1961 and 1973 there were an average of close to one thousand cartels per year that were exempt from antitrust law.[27]

A variety of the rationalization cartel was established by MITI in 1982. This involved the creation of a government Institute for New Generation Computer Technology—itself an extension of MITI's strategy dating back to 1971 to develop knowledge-intensive indus-

---

26. Philip Trezise, "Politics, Government, and Economic Growth in Japan," in Patrick and Rosovsky, *Asia's New Giant*, 773.

27. Richard Caves, "Industrial Organization," in Patrick and Rosovsky, *Asia's New Giant*, 487.

tries. The Institute has a ten-billion-yen budget for ten years and will bring together the leading research scientists of Japan's electronics companies. The goal is to develop a fifth-generation computer capable of receiving input and instructions in ordinary language and of reasoning and making judgments like a human brain. MITI has also recently organized large-scale, long-term, joint-research projects in ceramic engines, "synthetic metals," and biotechnologies.[28]

The role of the economic bureaucracy and especially MITI has changed over time. Much of the early policy was focused on overcoming the balance of payments constraints to growth and making arrangements for importing technology. In the early eighties, economic circumstances no longer necessitate export stimulation or import retardation, and political circumstances militate for the opposite approach. Accordingly, the economic bureaucracy has given up most of its foreign exchange controls. Furthermore, Japan has essentially caught up technologically. It is no longer as important for MITI to bargain for importing foreign technology as it is for MITI to assist in the pushing out of technological frontiers. Thus, the levers and priorities of the economic bureaucracy have shifted, but the preponderant state function of guiding and facilitating Japanese development is still in place.

Summary and Conclusion

The chief ingredients of the so-called Japanese economic miracle might be summarized as being threefold: high savings; effective and peaceful labor relations; and efficient, forward-looking, and extensive government intervention. The environment that gave rise to these characteristics is complex, to say the least. It emerged out of a historical process of constant interaction among the cultural, political, and economic spheres of society. Japan has successfully evolved a set of internally consistent institutions, also consistent with rapid economic growth. Borrowing from the Japanese model piecemeal may be either problematic or impossible.

This is not to say that other governments cannot develop their own policies for, say, increasing saving, generating greater worker involvement in industry, or initiating an active industrial policy that are consistent with their own political economic institutions. Indeed, in most cases it seems they must do these things and more for their country's economic well-being. The option of having no industrial

---

28. For a discussion of current MITI activities, see Yasunobu Otori, "Ceramic Engine: Technological Frontier," *The Oriental Economist* (Apr. 1982): 48–51; and the *Testimony of Douglas Fraser before U.S. House of Representatives, Committee on Energy and Commerce on H.R. 1234, The Fair Practices in Automotive Products Act* (Apr. 12, 1983).

policy, for instance, appears to be a nonoption. The question is whether the government takes *ex ante* measures to guide industry in positive directions or engages in *ex post* or inadvertent industrial policy, lacking vision and coordination.

There is also the question of how fully Japan of the future will be able to copy Japan of the past. The prolonged world economic recession is bringing new pressures to bear on the Japanese economy, which depends on foreign trade for some 17 percent of her GNP. The Japanese economy has successfully averted demand-side difficulties, in large measure as a result of consistently and rapidly expanding exports. However, in 1982 exports fell for the first time in thirty years. With world demand stagnating or falling, the Japanese government in recent years has had to undertake unprecedented expansionary fiscal policy and to run ever-growing budgetary deficits. Japanese financial markets are not well-suited to large government borrowing and are under considerable strain. Undoubtedly, financial regulations and institutions will have to be liberalized in coming years.

Demographic shifts are challenging Japanese labor market institutions. Promotion by seniority is no longer taken for granted, and signs of attenuating company loyalty are increasingly rife. The recent growth of venture capital operations has resulted in the emergence of thousands of new enterprises and the exodus of top technical and managerial personnel from large companies. The trend toward more competitive labor markets will likely widen earnings inequality, which will play back upon social relations in the enterprise. Additionally, demographic realignments will put downward pressure on the savings ratio.

Repression and economic growth helped to elicit union cooperation with management in the fifties. As growth slows in the eighties, some unions may return to their earlier conflict orientation. Many public sector unions are already controlled by socialist groups and represent another threat to Japan's longstanding labor peace.

There is also evidence of attitudinal shifts among young people. "In a recent national survey, the majority of teenagers viewed their parents' lives as uninteresting and unfulfilling."[29] The teenagers seemed to be reacting to the unquestioning company loyalty syndrome, lack of personal initiative or of different life experiences, and the perceived unidimensional focus on material possessions of their parents. To the extent that such attitudes withstand the pressures to conform that come with age and responsibility, there will have to be further accommodations in Japan's political economic institutions. To be sure, sustained affluence has affected social attitudes in other countries. It is, after all, understandable to opt for more leisure and less

---

29. Susan Chira, "Against the Japanese Grain," *New York Times Sunday Magazine* (June 20, 1982): 28.

work as incomes rise. If the Japanese hunger for growth erodes, they will have lost a major contributory asset to their economic miracle.

Recommended Readings

1. H. Patrick and H. Rosovsky, eds., *Asia's New Giant: How the Japanese Economy Works* (Washington, D.C.: Brookings Institution, 1976).

2. Two interesting and balanced treatments of Japanese labor/management relations can be found in Rodney Clark, *The Japanese Company* (New Haven: Yale University Press, 1979), and Robert Cole, *Work, Mobility and Participation: A Comparative Study of American and Japanese Industry* (Berkeley: University of California Press, 1979). A good, accessible discussion of Japanese agriculture and its transformation is provided in Ronald Dore, *Shinohata: A Portrait of a Japanese Village* (New York: Pantheon, 1978).

3. Chalmers Johnson, *MITI and the Japanese Miracle* (Stanford: Stanford University Press, 1982).

4. Edwin Reischauer, *The Japanese* (Cambridge, Mass.: Harvard University Press, 1981).

5. Chalmers Johnson (ed.), *The Industrial Policy Debate* (San Francisco: Institute for Contemporary Studies Press, 1984).

6. Current information on and analysis of the Japanese economy are available in several journals. Among the best are *Japan Economic Journal, The Oriental Economist,* and the *Far Eastern Economic Review.*

3

SWEDEN

THE MIDDLE WAY

Sweden's 8.3 million people enjoyed a per capita Gross National Product of $13,520 in 1980, behind only West Germany and Switzerland among the advanced market economies. Its long-term growth record from 1870 to 1976 of 2.5 percent average per year is the best in Western Europe. Yet most people think neither of rapid growth nor of high living standards when they think of Sweden. They think, rather, of what Marquis Childs has called Sweden's "Middle Way."[1]

In 1976, after forty-four years of government headed by the left-wing Social Democratic Party, Sweden had one of the smallest public sectors in Western Europe with only 5 percent of industrial production originating in state-owned enterprises. Yet, at the same time, Sweden had developed the most extensive system of social services with greater income, race, and sex equality and the fullest eradication of poverty among the world's market-oriented economies. Perhaps most notably from a macroeconomic point of view, Sweden has since World War II consistently maintained very low unemployment rates (between 1.5 and 4 percent), along with very high labor force participation rates (over 70 percent in recent years) and rates of inflation in line with other developed market economies.

These accomplishments have implied both high taxes and a large role for the government in economic regulation and redistribution. Yet, contrary to the arguments of Milton Friedman and other libertar-

---

1. Marquis Childs, *Sweden: The Middle Way* (New Haven: Yale University Press, 1961). See also Marquis Childs, *Sweden: The Middle Way on Trial* (New Haven: Yale University Press, 1980).

ians, big government in Sweden has not meant restricted democracy and freedom. On the contrary, Sweden has maintained one of the most participatory and thoroughgoing democracies in the world. For instance, in contrast to voter turnouts in recent U.S. presidential elections of around 50 percent of eligible voters, national elections in Sweden (once every three years) inspire upwards of 90 percent of the electorate to go to the polls. In order to preserve diversity of opinion in the media, the government subsidizes newspapers that are in financial difficulty. Since the social democratic papers receive less business advertising, they receive some 60 percent of such subsidies.

National referenda have been held on vital political questions. Most recently, in March 1980, following extensive public debate, nation-wide study groups, and mock votes in schools, 75 percent of eligible Swedes chose among three alternatives regarding the future use of commercial nuclear power. Sweden's numerous foreign-resident workers have the right to vote in local elections, thus including them in part of the political life of the nation. Additionally, political democracy has been carried over to the economic sphere to a greater extent than elsewhere in the capitalist world.

Until the 1970s the Swedish "Middle Way" prospered in both economic and political terms. In that decade, however, a combination of domestic and international forces weakened the economy and challenged the country's longstanding political equilibrium. In what follows we shall present a brief historical overview of Sweden's development, a discussion of its unique socioeconomic characteristics and institutions, and an analysis of Sweden's economic model and its performance.

Background

The historical absence of feudalism and serfdom, the existence of early electoral and parliamentary practices, and the high degree of ethnic homogeneity all helped set the basis for Sweden's emerging democratic and egalitarian institutions in the twentieth century. Furthermore, the traditional open field system in agriculture with small, rotating plots encouraged the development of tightly knit, highly collective rural communities.

When Sweden's first major industrialization drive was launched in the 1870s, some 75 percent of the labor force worked the land. The rapid formation of an urban working class out of self-employed, collectively oriented, ethnically uniform ex-farmers led to vigorous union organizing by the 1880s. In 1889, the Social Democratic Party (or SAP, its commonly used Swedish acronym) was founded, with fifty of the seventy founding organizations being trade unions. The national trade union federation, the LO, was formed in 1898. The close and strong historical ties between the SAP and LO remain today; approximately 60 percent of the Party's membership comes from the LO.[2]

In direct response to the forming of a centralized national trade union, an employers' federation, SAF, was established in 1902. Following a period of industrial unrest, the LO and SAF reached an accord in 1906 wherein the SAF recognized the right of workers to unionize and collectively bargain, and the LO recognized the right of employers to hire, fire, and organize production. Industrial relations, however, remained unsettled until the LO/SAF Basic Agreement at Saltsjobaden in 1938. In this agreement the LO and SAF accepted each other as equals. The agreement set procedures for grievance bargaining, outlawed industrial actions directed at third parties, and restricted the right to declare a strike or lockout to the national bodies of the LO or SAF, respectively. In establishing centralized control over industrial actions the agreement set the basis for the system of national wage bargaining. It also, in effect, removed the strike weapon as a power resource for labor. With its political party, the SAP, in office from 1932 to 1976, the LO was willing to encourage industrial peace and cooperation between labor and capital. The focus of the LO's demands for economic justice would be the political rather than the industrial sphere. The SAF, in return, would cooperate with the government.

The government at the time of the Saltsjobaden Agreement was headed by the SAP, which, in order to gain a majority in the Parliament, had entered a coalition with the Farmers' Party. Representing landowning farmers, the Farmers' Party naturally favored private property. Thus, despite the proclaimed socialist aims of the SAP, the SAP agreed to forgo the nationalization of productive property in exchange for support from the Farmers' Party for their program to redistribute income through progressive taxation, income transfers, and the provision of social services.

Until the mid thirties Sweden's rate of labor strife was among the highest in the industrialized countries. Following the 1938 agreement a downward trend in strike activity began, and by the 1950s and 1960s Sweden had the lowest incidence of strikes among the advanced capitalist economies.

The emergence of labor peace contributed to Sweden's steady growth during the first half of this century. Sweden's neutrality kept her essentially out of World Wars I and II; and, as the first market economy to consciously engage in pump priming during the early thirties, Sweden was able to bypass the depths of the international

---

2. Unless otherwise indicated, data on the Swedish economy come from the following two sources: OECD, *Sweden: Economic Survey*, various years; or, *Fact Sheets on Sweden*, published by the Swedish Institute in Sweden. This latter source is virtually comprehensive, is regularly updated, and is available through the Swedish Information Service of the U. N. Mission in New York.

depression. With Sweden's production facilities unscathed from the Second World War and with the aid of a 1949 devaluation of the krona, the Swedish economy set off on an export-led boom which continued to the late sixties.

After 1965, the traditional leading exports of Sweden began to encounter increasingly tough competition. Sweden was the world's leading iron ore exporter in the early sixties, but the development of large open-pit iron ore mines in Australia and Brazil, together with cheaper labor and new bulk carriers lowering shipping costs, rapidly reduced Sweden's share in the export market. By the mid seventies Brazil and Australia were each exporting four times as much ore as Sweden. Increasing competition in pulp and paper supplies from the U.S., Canada, and elsewhere, where tree maturation time was considerably shorter, undermined previous Swedish dominance in European timber product sales. The striking advance of technology in Japanese industry and its cheaper labor gradually challenged Swedish export markets in shipbuilding, steel, and cars. The shipbuilding market was also challenged by Spain, South Korea, and Brazil. These sectoral problems were, of course, compounded by the international recession and skyrocketing oil prices of the seventies. For Sweden, a country that exports half of its industrial production and imports all of its oil, these developments contributed to a falling rate of profit, diminished capital formation, and slower economic growth.

The government responded to this situation by expanding its labor market programs in order to meet its commitment to full employment. Public employment grew rapidly as employment in private industry fell after 1965. The private sector responded in large measure by accelerating the growth of subsidiaries abroad through foreign investment. Whereas Swedish industry invested on average some 500 million krona per year abroad during the mid sixties, by the late seventies this figure had multiplied seven times to 3.5 billion krona per year of foreign investment. In 1960, Swedish manufacturing subsidiaries abroad employed some 100,000 workers; by 1970 this number was up to 183,000, and by 1980 it stood at 400,000 (or almost one-half of total industrial employment within Sweden).

Despite higher rates of return abroad and gradually lowered profits taxes in Sweden, business savings in the seventies as a share of GNP was less than one-half of what it was in the fifties and sixties. Thus, to reduce the growing deficit in its international payments and restore health to its economy in general, Swedish policy makers had to grapple with the question of how to raise industrial productivity and increase capital formation.

The LO and SAP were concerned that increased capital formation not come at the expense of greater income and wealth inequality. Meanwhile, the coalition between the private property oriented Center (formerly Farmers') Party and the SAP had ended in 1957, so the Social Democrats were less reserved about supporting public capital formation and ownership. The SAF and nonsocialist political parties called for greater stimulus to private capital formation.

With the aid of growing popular reaction against SAP-supported nuclear power, the nonsocialist party coalition was able to oust the SAP by a narrow margin in the 1976 elections. Ironically, the economic recession led this new coalition government to nationalize more industry in a space of two years than the SAP had nationalized in over forty-four years. With large parts of the iron ore, steel, shipbuilding, and textile industries added to the public sector, government-owned enterprise grew to account for some 10 percent of industrial production. Campaigning for lower taxes, the nonsocialist parties retained a one-seat parliamentary edge in the 1979 elections.

In the midst of the severe international recession, the economic situation within Sweden continued to deteriorate. The most significant economic problem in political terms was Sweden's growing level of unemployment. In fact, the unemployment rate doubled between the 1979 and 1982 national elections. Although the unemployment rate was only 4 percent at the time of the September 1982 elections, this rate represented a postwar record high and became the decisive issue in the political campaign. With over 90 percent of the electorate voting, on September 19, 1982, Olof Palme and the Social Democrats were returned to office with a solid majority in the Parliament.

Social Services and Benefits

Social insurance and welfare expenditures come to around 25 percent of GNP in Sweden, compared to approximately 10 percent in the U.S. The benefits are extensive and very generous by U.S. standards and would require a separate book to be discussed fully.[3] In the following paragraphs we shall only scratch the surface of Sweden's "cradle to grave" provision of social assistance.

Suppose you are married, you live in Stockholm, and you have just become a parent. Suppose, further, for purposes of grammatical convenience, you are the male of the couple. You are entitled to the parental benefit, which gives you or your wife a six-month leave (at 90 percent pay) from your work. You or your wife is also entitled to an additional three months that you may take any time up to your child's eighth birthday and yet another three months at a fixed daily allowance of 37 krona (approximately $5). You or your wife may also take

---

3. A good discussion of Sweden's welfare benefits can be found in Childs, *The Middle Way on Trial*, 1980. An excellent article on the availability of benefits and services to men and women as well as the overall position of women in Swedish society is Letty Cottin Pogrebin's "A Feminist in Sweden: I Have Seen the Future and It (Almost) Works," *Ms.* magazine, Apr. 1982, 66–88.

up to sixty days' leave per year per child (again at 90 percent pay) when your child is sick. Alternatively, you may elect to take eighteen months' leave from the time of your child's birth and be guaranteed your job. Both parents also have the right to shorten working hours to three-fourths of normal until the child's eighth birthday (pay is proportionately reduced).

You, as parents, receive a child allowance for each child under the age of sixteen. At the end of 1981, this equaled 3,000 krona (around $430) per year. Primary, secondary, and university education is free. Students over sixteen also receive a study allowance of over 2,000 krona per year.

Furthermore, your family will have virtually all of its medical expenses covered by national health insurance. You may choose to visit either a public clinic or hospital as an outpatient or to visit a private practitioner. If you select the former, you pay a set fee of 20 krona (around $3) per visit; and if you choose the latter, you usually pay 30 krona per visit. (Approximately 15 percent of physicians in Sweden are private.) Your child is entitled to free dental care until the age of sixteen; thereafter at least 50 percent of dental fees are covered. Wholesale and retail pharmaceutical companies have been run by the state since 1971, and drugs are either free or heavily subsidized. Patients cover no more than 3 percent of total medical cost through their out-of-pocket expenditures. The rest is paid by Sweden's twenty-six county governments. The sources of funding are a 10.6 percent payroll tax on the employer levied by the county government as well as federal government subsidies. Despite some shortcomings, the overall quality of health care in Sweden is reputed to be excellent.

As a worker you enjoy, as do all Swedish workers, a guaranteed five weeks' paid leave per year on top of twelve paid holidays. If you are sick, you receive 90 percent of your wage beginning the second day of your illness.

Your chances of being laid off during a recession are low as a result of government subsidies and stockpiling grants; nevertheless, if your employer should decide to lay you off, he or she must give you from one to six months' prior notice, depending on your age and length of service. If you then join the small ranks of Sweden's unemployed, you receive compensation averaging around two-thirds of your normal pay from your union *(90 percent of Sweden's blue-collar workers and 70 percent of Sweden's white-collar workers are unionized)* or from public funds. (These benefits are taxable, so the net pay is above two-thirds of normal net because of Sweden's progressive income tax structure.) The benefits are payable for up to 300 days for workers under fifty-five and up to 450 days for workers over fifty-five.

Beginning at age sixty you can enter phased retirement up to age sixty-five. If you elect this option, you must cut back at least five hours per week but you must continue to work at least seventeen hours. The state pays you 65 percent of your basic wage for the hours you do not work (50 percent for those electing the option after January 1, 1981). This benefit is financed by a 0.5 percent payroll tax.

When you retire (eligibility begins at age sixty-five), you benefit from Sweden's two-tiered pension system. (Low-income individuals also usually receive a municipal housing subsidy.) The first tier is the basic pension, which provides a fixed income, indexed to the rate of inflation, to all pensioners. Since 1960, a supplementary pension has been added which varies according to income. Together the pensions total about two-thirds of average income during a person's fifteen best-paid years.

The basic pension is financed out of an 8.3 percent payroll tax, and the supplementary pension, out of an 11.75 percent payroll tax. Despite the fact that 16.2 percent of Sweden's citizens are over sixty-five, compared to 10.7 percent in the U.S., the Swedish pension system has consistently run a surplus. This surplus, which currently plays a large role in Sweden's capital markets (to be discussed below), was formed deliberately in anticipation of predicted demographic shifts. The percentage of Swedes over sixty-five is projected to peak at 21 percent in the year 2020.

These welfare benefits, albeit only partially enumerated above, constitute an impressive level of social assistance. They carry an equally impressive price tag. Large payroll taxes place a heavy burden on Swedish industry, which compounds the difficulties of remaining internationally competitive. In 1965, payroll taxes amounted to 7 percent of payroll; by 1979, because of new social legislation, they had grown to approximately 33 percent of payroll. On top of this 33 percent, an additional 5 percent of payroll on average is paid by the employer into privately negotiated pensions. In Table 3.1 we see that all nonwage labor costs (including public and private pension contributions, insurance payments, payroll taxes, costs of occupational training, and pay for times not worked) came to 61.5 percent of wages

Table 3.1 Ratio of Nonwage Labor Costs to Wages and Salaries in Manufacturing		
	1975 (%)	1978 (%)
West Germany	64.4	69.0
Sweden	47.4	61.5
United States	31.6	35.2
Japan	16.1	19.2

Source: Organization for Economic Cooperation and Development (OECD), *Sweden: Economic Survey* (June 1981): 44.

and salaries in Swedish manufacturing in 1978. As seen in Table 3.1, by 1978, fringe benefits for Swedish workers were considerably higher (relative to income) than those in the United States and Japan.

The Cooperative Sector

The special significance of the cooperative sector of the Swedish economy is twofold. First, its broad scope and longevity are unique for a market economy. Movements of industrial, financial, and retail cooperatives have emerged in many capitalist economies, but they have generally succumbed to competitive economic and hostile ideological forces over time. Small pockets of cooperatives, such as Mondragon in Spain or, to a lesser degree, the plywood cooperatives in Puget Sound, Washington, sometimes persist, but they have not spread and endured elsewhere as they have in Sweden. Second, and as a partial explanation of the above, Swedish cooperatives are a reflection of the strong collectivist spirit in Swedish culture, this spirit having its origin in the egalitarian organization of agricultural production by cooperatives prior to the nineteenth-century enclosure movement. Swedish cooperatives receive a further boost from the federal government, paying only a 32 percent tax on net income versus the 40 percent rate levied on corporations.

The first nonagricultural cooperatives in Sweden were founded by idealistic liberals in the mid nineteenth century. Most were short-lived. The cooperative movement was not put on a secure foundation until some forty societies came together in 1889 to form the *Kooperativa Forbundet* (KF). KF began with wholesaling. Then, when private retailers boycotted their wholesale distribution, they went into retailing. They soon turned to certain production activities to offset the market power of monopolies. Today, KF runs two thousand retail stores, from small shops to large department stores, and has 18 percent of the total retail market. KF's industrial subsidiaries produce a variety of consumer goods, paper and pulp products, plastics, tires, machinery, building materials, etc. Together with Sweden's two largest trade unions, KF owns one of the country's largest insurance companies. Through another subsidiary, KF refines oil and operates four hundred gasoline stations with 16 percent of that market. In 1979, KF had total sales of 23 billion krona and was Sweden's second largest company. Half of Sweden's households belong to KF. Like all Swedish cooperatives, KF has a democratic organization; it is owned and operated by its members, each with one vote.

Construction cooperatives account for close to one-fourth of new housing. Three other cooperatives, involved in food production, processing, and marketing, are among the twenty-five largest companies in Sweden. Together all Swedish industrial cooperatives account for around 4 percent of industrial production and 7 percent of industrial employment.[4]

Agricultural producer cooperatives dominate Swedish food production, accounting for 80 percent of food sales. For a northern country, with less than 10 percent of its land arable and less than 4 percent of its labor force in agriculture, Sweden's agricultural cooperatives are remarkably successful. Sweden is nearly 85 percent self-sufficient in food. (This high proportion is accounted for in part by government subsidies to and protection for domestic agriculture.) Although most observers agree that there is little idealism or sense of mission left in Sweden's cooperative movement, the cooperatives' long-term success and their extension certainly make them a notable and interesting feature of the Swedish economy.

Industrial Democracy

The practice of centralized collective bargaining—and the requirement that the national trade union must give its sanction before a local union can strike—had resulted in the neglect of many factory or shop floor specific demands of workers. Prior to the 1970s little had been done by the Social Democratic government to ameliorate the oppressive conditions of piecework and organizational hierarchy in much of Swedish industry.[5] Meanwhile, progressive social change was moving forward in other spheres of society, including ever higher levels of educational attainment for the work force, effective implementation of full employment policy, and generous provisions for sick leave. These factors combined to produce frustrated expectations for rewarding work, as well as high absenteeism and high turnover in the 1960s. Indeed, by December 1969 it also appeared that Sweden's longstanding industrial peace was being threatened. In that month a wave of sizable and long wildcat strikes erupted in the state-owned iron mines. The central union's hold on members' loyalty seemed to be eroding.

These circumstances brought a response both from industry and from government. From the mid sixties there was a proliferation of

---

4. Figures have been calculated from the 1981 annual report of the Kooperativa Forbundet and a 1981 report commissioned by the Swedish government on the cooperative sector. For background on the Swedish cooperative movement see Frederic Fleisher, *The New Sweden* (New York: McKay Co., 1967), Ch. 3; and Roland Huntford, *The New Totalitarians* (New York: Stein and Day, 1972), Chs. 1 and 2.

5. An interesting first-hand account of working life in one large Swedish factory is available in English: G. Palm, *The Flight from Work* (Cambridge: Cambridge University Press, 1977).

management-initiated work reorganization schemes with the apparent intention of increasing worker participation and satisfaction. However, many of the more dynamic and successful experiments were cut back or terminated. A 1973 study by a member of the Government Commission on Industrial Democracy concluded:

> Both Norwegian and Swedish experience point to the fact that despite the proven superiority of workers' management on the shop floor (both in productivity and work satisfaction) this form of organization seriously threatens the established organizational structure and managerial ethics. . . . The goals of preserving the existing differences in power, status and income by far are more important values than the overall efficiency of the firms.[6]

One of the earlier and most far-reaching of these management-sponsored work-reorganization experiences occurred at the new Volvo plant in Kalmar, where the traditional assembly line is replaced with a system of subassembly stations. Computer-controlled dollies move the car from one work station to another. At each station a team of ten to twenty workers assembles a "natural unit" (e.g., electrical system, steering mechanism) onto a stationary car body. Each station has a two-car buffer (or waiting station for two cars ready for assembly) entering and another leaving the work area. These buffers provide some flexibility in work speed and some additional worker control over the length of their breaks. The system functions with considerable job enlargement and job rotation. Further, the workers' training program is four weeks long instead of the four hours that is usual at conventional assembly plants.

There are bay windows at each work station which provide an ample view of the Swedish countryside. The two-story, hexagonal plant is uncommonly quiet for an auto assembly operation, and one hears soft-rock music at several work stations. Each work team has its own restrooms, equipped with lockers, showers, and sauna.

Beginning in 1971, rank-and-file workers were called upon to participate in generating ideas for the physical design and work flow process of the planned factory at Kalmar. The plant opened in early 1974. Today, Volvo Kalmar is touted to be a pioneering testimony to the malleability of modern technology and the possibility of building humane work places.

Among other things, the improved working conditions and more open communications system between workers and managers at Volvo Kalmar have improved morale and work quality, lowered absenteeism and turnover, and elicited worker innovations and greater effort. The buffer and job rotation systems greatly reduce the

6. Lars Karlsson, "Experiences in Employee Participation in Sweden: 1969–1972," Program in Participation and Labor-Managed Systems (Ithaca: Cornell University, 1973), 51.

probability and impact of production bottlenecks. Together these attributes have contributed to significant cost reductions. The Kalmar concept has been copied and extended at other Volvo and Saab plants throughout Sweden.[7]

The LO and SAP, however, were not content to leave the initiative to management. Prime Minister Olof Palme declared that, Sweden having already achieved political and social democracy, the seventies would be the decade of economic democracy. Beginning in 1972, a series of important legislative acts were passed that statutorily expanded worker rights and decision-making powers in Swedish industry. The first law, in 1972, required that two worker representatives be on the board of directors of all firms with a hundred or more employees. This law was superseded by a 1976 law that extended this provision to all firms with twenty-five or more employees.

Several different laws were enacted in 1974. One revises the worker participation act of 1949 and gives the worker-elected safety steward the right to call a stop to work he or she considers to be unsafe. The safety steward may take off as much time as necessary from production work to perform his or her duties as steward with no loss in pay. The steward is also trained in a course on worker health and safety during regular working hours. This act was extended by the Work Environment Act of 1978. Any worker can stop his or her own work to consult with the safety steward. Furthermore, a labor-management safety committee is established which is provided with full information on planned work-place changes and can hold up implementation of such changes until the changes conform to safety requirements. Another 1974 law established that a worker is presumed innocent until proved guilty in labor court and thus retains his or her job while a dispute is being adjudicated.

The greatest legislative step in terms of industrial democracy was taken with the 1976 "Act on Employee Participation in Decision-Making" (or MBL, by the Swedish acronym). First, the MBL strikes down the provision dating back to the 1906 LO/SAF agreement giving ownership the sole prerogative to "direct and allocate work." Hereafter, the functions of management could no longer be excluded from the realm of collective bargaining. Second, the MBL requires employers to inform their workers of all matters of importance concerning the firm, with no allowances made for managerial secrecy. Third, the MBL obligates employers to initiate negotiations with workers over all major company decisions, such as new investment, relocations, etc. Fourth, the law gives legal standing to the union interpretation of a broad range of contract provisions pending the decision of the labor court.

---

7. For more examples and a good discussion of technological design and worker participation in Sweden see Eric Einhorn and John Logue, *Democracy on the Shop Floor?* (Kent, Ohio: Kent Popular Press, 1982). Much of the discussion of Kalmar is based on an October 1982 visit to the plant by A. Zimbalist.

This law opened broad possibilities for greater worker participation in decision making. However, the employers, emboldened by the 1976 and 1979 elections of a nonsocial democratic parliamentary majority, resisted many of the provisions of the MBL. Thus, the act probably raised worker expectations more than it raised actual worker participation. A 1982 survey of the Swedish Center for Working Life found that 82 percent of the respondents felt that they had some additional influence since the MBL, yet only 25 percent said they had enough influence.

It has been this desire for greater influence, in part, that has propelled the current campaign for wage earner funds. The original wage earner fund proposal came from a 1975 report to the LO of a committee headed by Rudolf Meidner. The Meidner report argued that meaningful employee influence in enterprise decision making could come only with employee ownership. Moreover, growing worker ownership would counteract the extreme concentration of corporate wealth ownership that had resulted from corporate self-financing, wage solidarity policy, and the tax laws (discussed in the section on fiscal policy later in this chapter). In 1979, 0.3 percent of households owned 50 percent of all stock shares held by individuals, just over 1 percent of households held 75 percent of such shares, and an additional 10 percent held the remaining 25 percent of shares.[8] Any further stimulus to corporate capital formation through subsidies or lower taxes would exacerbate this inequality and, therefore, be politically impracticable. According to the Meidner report, then, to promote the needed capital formation, it was necessary to disperse the ownership of corporate wealth. The original Meidner plan recommended that 20 percent of profits each year go into collective funds (for purchasing corporate stock) administered by employee representatives. Depending on profit rates and other assumptions, this plan would have given employees controlling interest in most companies after twenty years.

The Meidner plan was amended several times. During the 1982 campaign the SAP and LO were calling for wage earner funds to be established during the next administration. These funds were to be fed by a 1 percent extra levy on payroll and a 20 percent tax on excess profits. Thereby, an estimated five to six billion krona would accumulate in the fund per year and would be used to buy stock in the name of the workers. Many details of the fund's management were left to be worked out.

Naturally, the SAF (employers' federation) and opposing political parties propagandized vigorously against the funds. Reminiscent of their opposition to the Supplementary Pension Fund of 1960, they

---

8. LO, *The Labor Movement and Employee Investment Funds* (Stockholm: LO, 1982), 32–33. Also see: Rudolf Meidner, *Employee Investment Funds* (London: George Allen and Unwin, 1978), 34–37; Roland Spånt, *Wealth Distribution and Its Development in Sweden* (Stockholm: Arbetslivcentrum, 1980).

argued that the funds would (1) threaten private ownership, (2) misallocate capital away from the most profitable investments, (3) lower aggregate investment, and (4) lower employment.

The wage earner funds idea, in fact, received only lukewarm support from Sweden's workers. This together with the virulent opposition from private capital led the Social Democrats, once in office, to postpone the introduction of the funds. Instead, in November 1982 the Social Democratic government suggested a temporary 1983 plan that required companies to pay a sum equal to 20 percent of dividends into the Fourth Supplementary Pension Fund (a management body well respected by Swedish business). Since the October 1982 devaluation was expected to lead to higher corporate profits in 1983, the SAP maintained that the only way of obtaining the necessary wage restraint from labor was by allowing this indirect form of profit sharing. The Palme government submitted a final wage earner fund bill to Parliament in November 1983. It is expected to be passed and implemented in 1984. The bill contains many of the features outlined above, with some greater restrictions on the yearly and total fund accumulations. The funds are to be governed by five regional boards with government-appointed administrators. The opposition has pledged to abolish the funds if it is returned to office in the September 1985 elections.

Labor Market Characteristics and Policies

Since World War II Sweden has pursued what some have called an ultra-Keynesian full employment policy. Unemployment rates between 1½ and 4 percent have prevailed even during recessions since 1945. In September 1982 a record postwar high unemployment rate was reached at 4 percent. The rate has since dropped. Making this excellent employment performance yet more remarkable is Sweden's high labor force participation (see Table 3.2), which has hovered at 69.5 percent to 72 percent (percentage of noninstitutionalized persons between the ages of sixteen and seventy-four in the labor force), some ten percentage points above the corresponding rate in the U.S. in recent years. (Adjusting for the methodological differences in obtaining participation rates between the two countries would close the gap by a few points.)

One important factor behind the high labor force participation rate in Sweden is the high rate of female participation. In 1981, 65.7 percent of all noninstitutionalized women between the ages of sixteen and seventy-four were gainfully employed. This female participation climbed swiftly during the seventies: in 1970, 30 percent of the labor force was female; in 1979, 45 percent of the labor force was female. It is also significant to note that the female rate of pay averaged 89 percent of the male rate in 1977 (up from 80 percent in 1969) in contrast to the U.S. ratio of approximately 60 percent.

Table 3.2
Labor Market Indicators

	1975 (%)	1976 (%)	1977 (%)	1978 (%)	1979 (%)	1980 (%)
Unemployment rate (% of labor force)	1.6	1.6	1.8	2.2	2.1	2.0
Persons affected by labor market measures (% of labor force)	2.3	2.7	4.0	3.9	3.4	2.8
Labor force participation rate	69.6	69.8	69.9	70.2	71.0	71.5
Consumer Price Index (% change from previous year)	9.8	10.1	11.5	10.1	7.2	12.1

Source: OECD, *Sweden: Economic Survey*, various years.
Note: The meaning of labor market measures is explained later in this chapter.

Finally, it is to Sweden's further credit that, unlike the situation in other Western European nations, immigrant workers are granted the same rights as Swedish workers. Among other things, this means that their work visas are not terminated when slack develops in the labor market during recessions. Approximately 5 percent of the Swedish labor force is made up of foreign guest workers.

An inquisitive reader may by this time be asking herself or himself two questions: how is economic policy able to achieve these results and what are the costs involved?

The theoretical origin of Sweden's full employment/active labor market strategy is a 1951 report by Gosta Rehn and Rudolf Meidner to the LO Congress, entitled *Trade Unions and Full Employment*.[9] By the mid fifties this report had been accepted by the government and incorporated into fiscal policy; it remains today. Rehn and Meidner were charged by the LO with the mandate to design a noninflationary fiscal policy that would maintain full employment without calling for wage restraint. Naturally, from the union's point of view this latter point was indispensable.

To comprehend the Rehn–Meidner proposal, it is first necessary to understand the LO's policy of *wage solidarity*. In order to preserve the

---

9. Actually, the notion that the government could maintain full employment by increasing its spending (and aggregate demand) was developed in Sweden during the 1930s at the Stockholm School of Economics. The Stockholm School's theoretical contributions came more or less simultaneously with those of John Maynard Keynes, although many aspects of their models differed.

long-term basis for union solidarity and to pursue equity, the LO has bargained with the SAF on the basis of the principle "equal pay for equal work." This means, for instance, that a skilled machinist should receive the same wage whether he is working for a large, very profitable firm or a small, less profitable firm. However, since the LO did not have access to a detailed, nationwide job classification system and could not bargain centrally for every individual's job, the LO followed the strategy of bargaining for higher percentage increases for low-wage jobs than for high-wage jobs. The resulting narrowing of wage differentials would, it was hoped, approximate the goal of "equal pay for equal work."

It does appear that the solidarity policy succeeded in narrowing wage differentials. Whereas in 1959 those with above mean earnings earned on average 17 percent above the mean for industrial workers and those below the mean earned 13 percent below, in 1974 those above the mean earned on average only 7 percent above the mean and those below the mean earned only 7 percent under the mean. That is, the spread fell from 30 percentage points to 14 percentage points over the period.[10] Wage equality, together with Sweden's progressive tax system, has produced a more egalitarian overall income distribution than in other advanced capitalist nations (see Table 2.4).

In addition to furthering equality, the wage solidarity policy had a somewhat perverse impact on industrial structure. If wages were equalized between capital intensive or strong enterprises, on the one hand, and labor intensive or weak enterprises, on the other, then profits in the former would be higher and in the latter lower than they would otherwise be. The latter would be less able to compete, would have their profit margins squeezed, and might go under or be bought out by a stronger firm. Less developed regions offering lower initial returns on investment could have their growth jeopardized for the same reason. Thus, the policy of wage solidarity would tend to foster industrial concentration and unequal regional development.

The Rehn–Meidner plan, in part, was to have the state subsidize employment in weaker sectors or regions with the notion that such selective action would not put pressure on already tight labor markets and, thus, would not generate inflationary wage increases. Similarly, the state could sponsor certain public service employment, such as sheltered workshops for the handicapped, without aggravating the tautness of normal labor markets. Finally, to promote labor and capital mobility and lower frictional and structural unemployment Rehn and Meidner argued for an extensive program of government and in-plant worker retraining. In contrast to a demand-oriented, expansionary fiscal policy which might generate full employment but only with significant inflationary pressures, this policy would reduce wage pressure in firms hurt by wage solidarity,

---

10. Meidner, *Employee Investment Funds*, 30–31.

selectively create employment in slack labor markets, and enhance mobility, thereby improving the unemployment/inflation trade-off. In large measure, the Rehn-Meidner model has been successful.

Today, the Rehn-Meidner model is usually referred to as Sweden's active labor market policies. These policies are primarily implemented by the central Labor Market Board (LMB) and its county subsidiaries. This Board has broad powers and a large budget to influence the level and distribution of employment opportunities in the economy. In addition to granting subsidies to firms in weaker sectors or regions and creating public service employment, the LMB has also: subsidized firms for hiring women in traditionally male jobs; given grants to firms for abstaining from laying off workers; offered special allowances for retaining older employees; subsidized stockpiling to maintain employment; administered a massive national program for retraining workers; and, along with the Ministry of Finance, managed the investment funds system (more on this later).

The labor market training system has capacity for little more than 1 percent of the labor force at any given time. The courses have an average length of four to five months so the program can accommodate 3 percent or more of the labor force each year. Courses are free and trainees receive above-subsistence allowances which exceed unemployment benefits.

In Table 3.2 it is seen that between 2 and 4 percent of Sweden's labor force owes its jobs to labor market measures in recent years. In fiscal year 1977/78 expenditures on labor market policy reached a record 9 percent of the national budget, falling to 6.5 percent the next year. One manifest cost, then, of these programs is the extra taxes or borrowing needed to finance them.

Other costs, however, are less apparent. For instance, does the pursuit of full employment engender inflationary wage pressure? Or, to what extent do these policies distort market signals and thereby promote inefficiency?

The impact of full employment on wage settlements and price developments is quite complex. Although Sweden's rate of inflation has been slightly above the OECD average during the seventies, Sweden has also had a substantially lower rate of unemployment and has had to import all of its oil, or over 70 percent of its energy supply.

As mentioned above, every year or two the LO and SAF bargain centrally to set an average wage increase for Swedish industry, generally with low wage sectors receiving greater percentage gains. In theory, the average gain reflects the competitive position in the industrial export sector, which accounts for some 50 percent of total industrial output. Thus, Sweden would be able to protect its international market share in the face of incremental changes in market conditions.

As defined in the so-called EFO model (developed by Swedish economists Edgren, Faxen, and Odhner) the contracted wage increase could equal productivity growth in the sector exposed to foreign competition plus international price increases without suffering a deterioration in Sweden's competitive position internationally. However, heightened price instability and variable exchange rates after 1973 made it increasingly difficult to predict price changes. The application of the formula, then, became more ambiguous and problematic during the seventies.

In practice, massive discrete changes occurred, such as the opening of low wage, rich iron ore mines in Australia and Brazil and the rapid emergence of modern shipbuilding in Brazil and South Korea, where the average wage level is one-eighth that in Swedish shipbuilding. In 1976, productivity in Swedish shipbuilding was less than double that in South Korea and Brazil, so Swedish unit labor costs were approximately four times those of Sweden's new competitors. It was not possible to strike an LO/SAF bargain that would adjust for this sharp disparity. The fast decline in Sweden's world market shares and the shrinking world market in steel, shipbuilding, textiles, and timber products cut deeply into Swedish industry's profits.

Another complicating factor is "wage drift," that is, locally negotiated wage increases above the rate set in national agreements. In order to preserve adherence to the wage solidarity policy on the part of unions in growth sectors of the economy, the LO must allow these unions to squeeze additional wage increases out of highly profitable companies. Yet, in order to maintain the unity and solidarity represented by a single nationally negotiated wage bargain, the LO must achieve the highest increase consistent with the prevailing economic conditions. If wage drift accounts for too much of overall wage increases, the low-paid sectors object. Conversely, if wage drift is too small, the high-paid sectors object. Thus, LO must walk a fine line in its bargaining strategy.

The 1974 agreement, for instance, did not anticipate the coming banner year for corporate profits. The nationally contracted wage increase for that year was 5.1 percent; and wage drift, caused by the unexpectedly large profits, was an additional 8.1 percent for a total average nominal wage increase of 13.2 percent. This was too much drift to maintain organizational cohesion within the LO, so the LO was aggressive in bargaining over the 1975/76 settlement. This agreement provided for a huge 39 percent increase in hourly labor costs over a two-year period. This increase coincided with the appreciation of the krona, low productivity increases, an expansionary fiscal policy, and weak world markets, thus contributing to a sharp erosion in Sweden's international competitiveness. Since the 1975/76 agreements, however, negotiated wage increases have been moderate and wage drift has been reduced from an annual rate of near 7 percent in 1974–76 to close to 3 percent in 1978–80, in part reflecting lower profit margins. Indeed, other than the 1974–77 period, the aggregate record does not suggest strong inflationary pressure from wages.

The bottom row of Table 3.3 approximates the change in unit labor cost, which fell in all periods since 1965, save 1974–77. If payroll taxes

Table 3.3
Wages, Productivity, and Inflation:
Annual Rates of Growth over Period

	1965–70 (%)	1970–74 (%)	1974–77 (%)	1974–79 (%)	1978 (%)	1979 (%)
(a) Productivity (mfg. + mining)	7.0	5.8	0	2.5	5.9	7.0
(b) Hourly wages (mfg. + mining)	9.0	9.8	13.3	10.9	6.6	8.1
(c) Consumer Price Index	4.4	7.6	10.5	9.7	10.2	7.0
(d) Unit labor costs = b − a − c	−2.4	−3.6	2.8	−1.3	−9.5	−5.9

Source: OECD, Sweden: *Economic Survey*, various years.

Note: The approximate calculation of the percentage change in unit labor costs is made on the assumption that the numbers in lines (a) through (c) represent instantaneous rates of change.

were added to hourly wages, the same conclusion would hold, albeit with lesser magnitude. The aggregate statistics, however, do not tell the whole story. Since less efficient and less profitable operations come under additional pressure in Sweden because of the wage solidarity policy as well as the depreciation allowances of the investment funds system (see the section on fiscal policy later in this chapter), there is a higher rate of restructuring and shutdown among stagnating firms in Sweden than elsewhere. Thus, a good part of the continuing productivity growth is explainable by the ongoing dissolution of low productivity enterprises as opposed to new entries or expansion of existing productive capacity. This dissolution has taken place without an increase in unemployment as a result of the rapid expansion of public service employment. Total employment in the private industrial sector has, in fact, been declining since 1965.

It is therefore quite possible that a sizable share of industrial enterprises have been paying out real wage increments in excess of productivity growth. This, of course, would generate some upward cost pressure in these enterprises. It is likely that during the seventies some of this pressure was absorbed by lower profits as well as by higher prices.[11]

---

11. The EFO model provides a complementary explanation. If productivity increases in the export sector exceed those elsewhere in the economy and the export sector position determines wage increases, then the domestic sector will experience cost pressure. This problem can be resolved either by price increases or lower profits. The presence of managed devaluations of the krona and wage drift contract clauses in the seventies and early eighties, however, weakens the explanatory power of the EFO model.

Overall, Sweden's system of centralized wage bargaining seems to have helped contain inflationary pressure. Sweden's large unions recognize that responsibility goes along with their political leverage. This compromise posture has been an important ingredient behind Sweden's economic success. However, with the Social Democrats out of office and workers' political leverage consequently diminished, there was an unprecedented strike and lockout for ten days during May 1980 that affected one-fourth of the labor force. A year later, in May 1981, twenty thousand white-collar employees went on strike for one week in Sweden's five largest private companies. Since October 1982 the Social Democrats have once again been in power, and general industrial peace is anticipated by most observers (even in the face of a decreasing standard of living and experimentation with more decentralized wage bargaining).

The practice of central wage bargaining existed through 1982. In 1983 a few sectors negotiated on a decentralized basis, and all sectors are scheduled to reach a decentralized bargain in 1984. It is too early to predict how, if at all, this change will affect Sweden's wage structure and labor relations.

The question of whether Sweden's active labor market policy has jeopardized or enhanced the economy's dynamic efficiency is not easily answered. We shall raise some relevant considerations in the sections that follow. For now, it is important to clarify a related theoretical point.

In a market economy, according to marginal productivity theory, the profit maximizing firm will hire labor to the point where the laborer's marginal revenue product equals the laborer's wage. This is an efficient solution to the firm since to hire fewer workers or to hire more workers would result in lower profits. Yet, what is privately efficient and what is socially efficient may not coincide. The firm considers only private costs. If the government does not force the firm to internalize social costs, then private and social costs diverge.

Let us illustrate this proposition. Assume that for ethical reasons a society decides that each individual, whether employed or not, should have at least a $6,000 annual income to cover basic necessities. Suppose a Mr. Haig is employed at Company X producing hats and is paid $8,000 a year. Mr. Haig produces four thousand hats a year, and each hat sells for $2.00 (assume the marginal revenue is also $2.00). Now, because of a drop in demand, the price of hats falls to $1.50. Company X will now lay Mr. Haig off.

When demand fell for hats, it rose for some other product(s). Assume the growth industry is home computers, that Mr. Haig does not have the skills to work producing microcomputers, and that wages are downwardly rigid. Hence, Mr. Haig cannot find alternative employment. Society's welfare loss or the net social cost incurred from this layoff can be reckoned on the product side as follows. The society loses the production of four thousand hats valued somewhat below $1.50, say $1.25. (In order for the additional output to be sold, the price would have to be lowered unless demand were perfectly elastic at $1.50.) That is, it loses $5,000 worth of hats. Moreover, were the extra hats to be produced, there would be a welfare gain of $500 in consumer surplus. (Mr. Haig will receive a $6,000 income maintenance payment; but, while this payment is a cost to the taxpayers, from society's point of view it is a transfer and represents no net change in welfare assuming a distributionally neutral social welfare function[12] apart from the minimum allowance and assuming an efficient tax system.) Thus, there is an annual net welfare loss (social costs exceed social benefits) of $5,500 resulting from the layoff.

Consider three possible policies by the government. One: the government can choose to do nothing and simply endure the welfare loss of $5,500 a year while Mr. Haig remains unemployed. Two: the government can choose to subsidize the hat employer to the tune of $3,000 (assuming a marginal revenue of $1.25) in order to induce the retention of Mr. Haig. From a microeconomic or political point of view, policy two is clearly preferable to policy one. The layoff and $5,500 social loss are averted, and the cost to the taxpayers is reduced from $6,000 (the income maintenance transfer) to $3,000 (the employment subsidy). Three: the government can pay a home computer company to train and employ Mr. Haig. Policy three is also obviously preferable to policy one and probably also to policy two. (Whether it is preferable to policy two would depend on, among other things, the permanence of the demand shift from hats to computers.)

Clearly, the government could pursue other policies as well; e.g., it could run the labor retraining program itself or it could nationalize the hat industry and employ Mr. Haig directly. The essential point here is that the divergence of social and private costs provides a theoretical justification for the government to intervene in the labor market and help preserve full employment. From this perspective, then, much of Sweden's active labor market policies may promote efficiency rather than impede it.

We have reached these conclusions utilizing traditional marginal productivity theory. Similar conclusions, justifying Sweden's active labor market policies, could be obtained through various alternative theoretical perspectives.

Fiscal Policy

Sweden is notorious for having the most burdensome taxes and largest government expenditures as a share of GNP in the capitalist world. In 1979, for instance, Sweden led all OECD countries, with total

---

12. The social welfare function is basically society's preference map or ordering for all goods and services (including distributional and other outcomes).

government spending equaling 57.1 percent of Gross Domestic Product. In the same year, the federal government budget deficit amounted to 9.6 percent of GNP. These numbers often leave the impression that the Swedish government chokes off private initiative and crowds out private corporations from the capital markets. In fact, neither of these impressions is generally correct. The Swedish government actually is a net saver rather than dissaver and, thus, is a net supplier of funds to the capital market.

The figure of 57.1 percent is itself misleading. The numerator, total government spending, includes transfer payments, but the denominator, GDP, does not. If we net out the transfer payments and consider only government purchases of goods and services, then the amount of government spending comes to 28.7 percent of GDP in 1979. Table 3.4 compares the share of government in consumption and investment for various advanced capitalist economies.

Another way of looking at this matter is to compare the share of collective consumption (including social services such as health care, unemployment insurance, child care programs, government administration, education, defense, etc.) with that of private consumption in GNP. Sweden's share of collective consumption in GNP is actually in line with that in other West European nations (though higher than the U.S.), but Sweden finances a larger share of its collective consumption through the government. Some people, of course, believe that collective consumption through the public sector is more efficient than private consumption since it allows services to be better planned

---

Table 3.4
Shares of GNP by Expenditure in Selected Countries
(1979, current prices)

	U.S. (%)	Japan (%)	W. Germany (%)	France (%)	Sweden (%)
Consumption	83.8	68.1	74.4	77.2	81.5
Private	63.7	58.4	54.6	62.1	52.4
Public	20.1	9.7	19.8	15.1	29.1
Gross investment	15.6	31.7	22.6	21.3	19.5
Private	10.8	15.0	12.4	8.9	7.8
Housing	4.8	6.8	6.5	7.0	5.0
Public	. . .	9.9	3.7	5.4	6.7
Changes in inventories and foreign balance	0.6	0.2	3.0	1.5	−1.0

Source: M. Hallvarson, *Swedish Industry Faces the 80s.* (Stockholm: The Federation of Swedish Industries, 1981): 30.

Note: The proportions given here are as a share of GNP, not GDP, and therefore differ slightly from other cited figures.

and more equally distributed. Further, they argue, collective consumption merely replaces goods and services that would be consumed privately and, hence, does not crowd out investment spending. On the other hand, most conservative economists believe that collective consumption reduces free choice and is less efficient than private consumption. It could also reduce saving or investment by taxing the rich in order to provide low-income groups with consumption goods or services they would otherwise be unable to afford.

Taxation

Let us now turn to consider the principal source of government spending, the Swedish system of taxation. Payroll taxes have already been discussed. The other prominent form of business taxation is the profit tax. Corporations pay a proportional tax of 40 percent of net income to the national government and a proportional tax averaging 29 percent (but varying from 25 to 34 percent depending on the county) to the local government. The local tax for corporations, however, is deductible from net income for national tax purposes. Thus, the total nominal rate of income taxation averages 57 percent for corporations. There are, however, a number of very favorable provisions and allowances which lower the effective rate of the corporate profit tax considerably, especially for the faster growing and more capital intensive companies.

From the 1930s to 1955, Swedish companies were allowed "free depreciation"; that is, they could write off the value of their machinery and equipment as quickly or as slowly as they pleased. Since 1955 depreciation rules have been in effect. The current rules are quite liberal. A corporation may choose either a 30 percent declining balance method, writing off 30 percent of the undepreciated amount each year, or a 20 percent rule, writing off 20 percent of the initial value each year. At any point a company can switch from the 30 percent to the 20 percent rule. At most, then, all machinery and equipment can be depreciated within five years, considerably faster than the physical deterioration of the assets. This process is known as accelerated depreciation. It allows the company to pay lower taxes now in exchange for higher taxes later and, hence, amounts to an interest-free loan from the government (the value of this loan being equal to the imputed interest on the tax amount postponed).

Since the onset of depreciation rules in 1955, the investment funds system, a Swedish fiscal policy innovation, has become important. The investment funds system permits a company, at its discretion, to set aside up to 40 percent of its pretax income. Of the amount set aside 46 percent must go into a noninterest-bearing blocked account in the Central Bank. The remaining 54 percent becomes part of the enterprise's working capital. The blocked amount is released when the Ministry of Finance and the Labor Market Board decide the economy is in a downturn and would benefit from more investment spending. The first general release came in 1958; since then, the releases have become increasingly frequent. Releases can also be industry or region specific, if the LMB is trying to promote employment or growth in a particular area. To encourage use of funds during releases, an additional 10 percent of investment spending is allowed as a deduction.

The investment funds system has the advantage of being a highly flexible counter-cyclical policy instrument. The system can be invoked by a release of funds without first being cleared through the legislative process, thus avoiding the normal enactment lag of fiscal policy. Company allocations to the investment reserve grew from 0.4 percent of GNP in the mid fifties to 2.3 percent in 1975. Most observers agree that the system has been effective in evening out the Swedish business cycle.

From the company's point of view, the system permits a substantial reduction in its tax burden. Highly profitable and rapidly expanding companies are able to take fullest advantage of the investment reserve. It is significant to note that the available tax reduction is contingent on new investment. This feature of the investment funds system helps to account for its political acceptability.

Together with the liberal inventory valuation provision, intermittent investment tax incentives, and favorable depreciation allowances, the investment funds system has helped to lower the effective rate of profit taxation. Over time, the effective rate has continued to drop as the statutory rate has gone up. The falling tax has helped to offset the declining pretax profit margins of Swedish corporations. Whereas business profits taxes were 12 percent of all taxes in 1950, in 1975 they were only 3 percent. The national profit tax as a share of value added in industry dropped from 10.4 percent during 1953 to 1957 to 2.4 percent during 1973 to 1975. The legal, statutory rate is compared with the actual, effective rate in Table 3.5. The rate is an average for all corporations; the rate is lower for high profit companies and higher for low profit companies. The regressive system of

Table 3.5
Tax Rate on Profits (Sum of National and Local)

	1958 (%)	1960 (%)	1965 (%)	1970 (%)	1974 (%)	1975 (%)
Statutory	52	49	50	54	55	55
Effective (average)	51	32	30	28	10	26

Source: Villy Bergstrom, *The Political Economy of Swedish Capital Formation*, Department of Economics, University of Uppsala, Working Paper Series, no. 3 (Uppsala, 1979): 5, 12.

enterprise taxation joins the wage solidarity policy in furthering industrial concentration.

In contrast, the personal income tax in Sweden is highly progressive. At the national level, rates run from a minimum of 2 percent up to 58 percent. The municipal tax is the same for individuals as for corporations, but for individuals it is not deductible from income for the national tax. The combined income tax rate thus goes from roughly 28 percent to 85 percent.

Capital gains on assets held under two years are taxable as ordinary income. For certain assets (e.g., houses) the acquisition cost is adjusted upward with the CPI (Consumer Price Index) for tax computation purposes. Assets held over two years are subject to reduced taxation, depending on the type of asset and length of ownership. For corporate stock, after two years 40 percent of gains are taxable; for bonds, after five years gains are not taxed. The system of personal deduction and special provisions is substantially different from that in the U.S. For instance, in Sweden interest payments on all debts are deductible. This provision (modified in 1982) along with the sharply progressive tax structure has rendered many income groups insensitive to the interest rate.

On top of the income tax, individuals with assets over 200,000 krona pay a progressive wealth tax levied at between 1 and 2.5 percent. Thus, wealthy individuals with high incomes and low deductions may pay taxes in excess of their incomes. Other taxes include: a nationwide value-added tax of 20 percent, intermittent investment taxes, and special excise taxes on unhealthy or sumptuous items.

By the late seventies it became clear that the Swedes were growing intolerant of their increasingly heavy tax obligations. Individuals in medium tax brackets (between one and two times the income of an average production worker) faced a marginal tax rate of 68 percent in 1978. (This is true if the first breadwinner in a family increased his or her earnings. If a second breadwinner in a family entered the labor force, however, the rate would be 37 percent. Earned incomes of husbands and wives are taxed separately in Sweden.)[13] Black market activities were generally recognized to be growing, and the Social Democrats as well as the nonsocialist parties accepted the need for a change. Several changes were made.

First, in 1977 tax brackets were indexed to the rate of inflation. (In 1981 increased energy prices were removed from this indexing.) Second, in November 1979 the government presented legislation setting a tax limit of 85 percent of income for all personal taxation including wealth. Third, in December 1980 the tax on dividend income was reduced by 30 percentage points. Finally, in April 1982, a coalition of the Liberal, Center, and Social Democratic Parties passed

13. OECD, *Sweden: Economic Survey* (1981): 29.

a tax reform that lowers the top marginal rate of combined local and national taxation to 50 percent for all but the top 10 percent of income earners. Those in the top 10 percent are to have their rate reduced by 5 percentage points. This tax reduction will be phased in over three years. The reform also reduces the deduction on interest payments for high income earners and adds a 2 percent employers' payroll fee for 1983 to help finance the income tax reduction.

Monetary Policy

As is the case with other small economies so heavily exposed to international trade and finance, monetary policy in Sweden is largely derivative and money supply changes are poorly correlated with changes in the price level. Policy targets for the money supply would be feasible only with a freely floating exchange rate, which would bring greater price instability. (The krona was fixed in relation to the dollar until March 1973 when Sweden joined the European "snake," linking the krona to other European currencies but having these combined currencies fluctuate relative to the dollar. Sweden withdrew from the snake in August 1977 and has managed several devaluations of its currency since then—the latest being a 16 percent devaluation in October 1982.)

The Central Bank (Riksbank) is governed by political appointees with three-year terms. Large government deficits in recent years have been financed partly out of increases in the domestic money supply as well as through large government borrowing domestically and abroad.

Although interest rates in Sweden have paralleled those in the U.S. in recent years, they have not had the same contractionary effect because spending in Sweden is less sensitive to the interest rate. The inelasticity of spending with respect to the interest rate has enabled the monetary authorities since 1979 to maintain high interest rates with an eye to external equilibrium. One reason for interest inelasticity is the fact that the level of housing construction is planned each year by government agencies. The financing is then arranged in separate agreements with the banks and the insurance companies (the public pension system playing the largest role). The creditors are now given the market interest rate, but the rate charged borrowers is subsidized out of the government budget. Construction expenditures are thus relatively autonomous of monetary policy and interest rates. Apart from the small state-owned sector in industry, housing is the only sectoral investment which is planned by the government.

The other sectors manifesting insensitivity to the interest rate are households and agriculture. Households tend to be rate insensitive since the combination of high inflation, high marginal tax rates, and full income tax deductibility lower the real interest rate to zero or below for households in the upper income brackets. For example,

Table 3.6 Percentage of Private Consumption Covered by Price Controls, February 1979

	Percentage
Sweden	60
Denmark	81
United States	0[a]
West Germany	40
Great Britain	61
Italy	27

Source: M. Hallvarson, *Swedish Industry Faces the 80s* (Stockholm: The Federation of Swedish Industries, 1981), 133.

a. Hallvarson appears to have underestimated the extent of price controls in the U.S. economy, where price controls have existed on public utilities, natural gas, air fares, and other items.

suppose the rate of inflation is 10 percent, the tax bracket is 50 percent, and the interest rate is 16 percent. Half of the 16 percent is a tax deduction, making the effective nominal rate 8 percent; and the real rate is 8 percent minus 10 percent, or −2 percent. Lars Wohlin, the governor of the Central Bank under Fälldin, estimated "that, for average income levels, the nominal interest rate would have to rise to 35 percent before the real rate exceeds zero while, for high income levels, the nominal rate would have to rise over 50 percent."[14]

Agricultural producer prices are heavily subsidized by the government. They are set in annual negotiations between the government and agricultural organizations on the basis of the goal to keep farmers' net incomes in line with other groups. Thus, a rise in interest costs to farmers would likely be passed on in the form of higher negotiated price increases, rendering the agricultural sector interest-rate insensitive. The sole sector likely to be highly sensitive to higher interest rates is the export sector. It receives no interest subsidies and it must price competitively. The phasing in of the April 1982 tax reform should improve interest rate sensitivity in the economy and help to normalize credit markets.

Like other West European governments, the Swedish government resorts periodically to sectoral or general price controls (see Table 3.6). The General Price Control Act of 1956 (extended yearly) empowered the Swedish government to introduce various forms of price

14. Cited in Andrew Martin, "Economic Stagnation and Social Stalemate in Sweden," in Joint Economic Committee's *Monetary Policy, Selective Credit Policy, and Industrial Policy in France, Britain, West Germany and Sweden* (Washington, D.C.: U.S. Government Printing Office, 1981), 214.

control (e.g., freezes, ceilings) and to require companies to give prior notice of planned price hikes. There is a National Price and Cartel Office which administers these controls. In recent years this office has been rather active. A temporary general price freeze was imposed in 1977 but was replaced in March 1978 by a requirement of advance notice of price increase. Another general freeze was imposed in March 1980 and lifted on May 16, 1980. Then, together with a 9 percent devaluation of the krona and other stabilization measures, on September 14, 1981, a new general price freeze was imposed for the remainder of 1981.

Supply Management

The Swedish government issues long-term planning reports. These reports are based on extensive conversations and meetings with industrial, union, and government leaders. They facilitate a wide-ranging exchange of information; however, next to nothing is done by the Swedish government to implement the planning reports' projections. In fact, the Swedish government does considerably less than other West European and Japanese governments to consciously direct the pattern of investments among various industries. Swedish government support for research and development tends also to be smaller as a share of all R & D expenditure than elsewhere. Apart from subsidies for housing and agriculture, the major government sectoral interventions until recently came through procurements and R & D support in defense, utilities, and space and nuclear research, as well as investment fund releases to promote regional development.

Since 1976 the state-owned sector of industry has grown from employing just over 5 percent of the industrial labor force to over 10 percent. After the state expanded its ownership to the steel, shipbuilding, and forestry sectors, it affected sectoral capital allocation by reducing or restructuring capacity in these areas. Whereas less than 5 percent of industrial production received state subsidies of some form in 1975, between 10 and 15 percent has been subsidized in recent years.[15]

One hallmark of Swedish government selective intervention to date has been that it has favored the declining rather than the growth sectors of the economy. This practice follows largely from the policy of subsidizing weak firms to retain workers or from taking over failing industries to maintain full employment. This tendency to support declining areas is in distinct contrast to the pattern of government

---

15. Mats Hallvarson, *Swedish Industry Faces the 80s*. (Stockholm: The Federation of Swedish Industries, 1981): 139.

intervention in other West European nations (see Table 3.7). Table 3.7 also shows that the other West European governments, to a lesser extent, do intervene to bolster declining sectors.

This pattern is a further indication that, despite having a larger role in the economy since 1976, the Swedish government has not played an active role in planning for and orienting economic growth. Supply management in the private sector with government collaboration as practiced in Japan, West Germany, France, and elsewhere does not appear to be an important feature of the Swedish economy. Although Sweden has extremely concentrated industrial and financial sectors,

Table 3.7
Allocation of Government Funds to Industry, 1970–1977
(R & D Grants, Sectoral Grants, and
Regional Grants)

	Sweden[a] (%)	W. Germany (%)	France (%)	United Kingdom (%)
Declining sectors				
Coal mining	—	12	17	10
Shipbuilding	51	5	7	9
Steel	9	—	7	14
Textiles and clothing	2	3	1	1
Forest products	6	5	—	1
Other	5	2	—	2
Subtotal	73	27	32	37
Growth sectors				
Nuclear power equipment	2	14	14	5
Aerospace	10	10	27	27
Electronics & computers	3	16	15	16
Mechanical engineering	—	17	2	5
Automobiles	8	3	4	4
Chemicals	2	8	4	4
Subtotal	25	68	66	61
Other	2	5	2	2
Total	100	100	100	100

Source: Boston Consulting Group, *A Framework for Swedish Industrial Policy*, vol. 1 (Boston: Boston Consulting Group, 1978), 83.
  a. Includes small business programs.

their broad exposure to international competition makes cartel-type practices more problematic. Whether the government plays such a role in harnessing and directing capital in the future is a central subject in current political debates in Sweden.

Capital Formation

Sweden is still in the process of attempting to rejuvenate its shattered traditional export sector. Engineering products have filled some of the gap left by sharp declines in shipbuilding, iron ore, and forestry products, but ongoing export strength will require a vigorous program of retooling, expansion of old facilities, and investment in new areas. Such a program depends on saving and effective channeling of funds into profitable projects. As a share of net national saving, business saving has steadily fallen from 38.3 percent during 1950 to 1954 to 4.2 percent during 1972 to 1976. Over this interval public saving has increased from 24.2 percent to 60.8 percent of net national saving, the share of household saving remaining fairly constant at around 35 percent.

The main source of this public saving has been the previously described supplementary pension system. When the system was begun in 1960, Sweden's social insurance funds accounted for less than 1 percent of net national saving. By 1972 to 1976, they accounted for over 37 percent. Until 1974, supplementary pension funds were used exclusively on the credit markets, providing direct loans to business or indirect loans through banks or government intermediaries as well as loans to the housing sector. Largely as a result of fears of excessive leveraging (high debt/equity ratios) in industry, the supplementary pension funds (through the newly established Fourth Fund) were allowed to purchase stock in private companies beginning in 1973; the purchase of equity was and is statutorily limited to a small share of the pension's accumulated funds.

By 1981, equity had been purchased in forty-two different companies and totaled 1.4 billion krona in share value. The Fourth Fund is limited to holding 10 percent of outstanding shares in any given company. At the end of 1981 it held over 5 percent of equity in LM Erickson and Volvo, two of Sweden's largest companies.[16] Although publicly owned and managed, the Fourth Pension Fund has acted to maximize its return on investment rather than to implement social or political goals. As such, it has gained the confidence of the business community; and once-serious concern in the private sector regarding public ownership of industry through the Fourth Fund is now dissipated.

---

16. The Fourth Fund Board, *Annual Report* (1981): 6–7.

Because of shifting demographical patterns, the supplementary pension system will come to play a smaller and smaller share in Sweden's capital markets. The question thus remains how to stimulate additional capital formation.

It comes as no surprise that the SAF calls for lower taxes and fewer regulations in order to stimulate more private capital formation. It is the contention of the SAF that the market will provide signals to enterprising corporate leaders about what and how to produce if they are left unencumbered by government action. Furthermore, since the economic environment is less certain and more risky today than during the steady growth of the fifties and sixties, higher rates of profitability must be tolerated. The SAF has also argued that the new regulations of the 1970s giving workers more control over decision making at the work place will impede the necessary process of rationalization and innovation.

The LO and SAP have argued for public capital formation via the creation of wage earner funds discussed above. It is their contention that the market does not provide adequate signals about the future and that the choice of what investments will be most beneficial in the long run can be made effectively only through planning. Moreover, they believe that stimulating additional private capital formation will lead to unacceptable increases in inequality in the distribution of wealth and income. The LO and SAP also feel that workers will not stand in the way of rationalization and innovation, even if it means more capital intensive processes. On the contrary, they believe that the choice, deployment, and use of new technologies will be greatly facilitated by worker involvement.

Finally, as pointed out above, the size of company earnings is a major factor in worker demands for wage drift. To combat inflation and regain international competitiveness, wage restraint is judged to be crucial. Yet, if workers are not allowed to share in the fruits of corporate investment, they will be unlikely to engage in wage restraint.

Conclusion

The Swedish political economy is unique. It has struck a delicate balance between growth and equity and has given both capital and labor very considerable influence in political and economic decision making. The Swedish mixture of regulated markets, private and public ownership, extensive social benefits, and full employment constitutes a "middle way" that, according to many, has combined some of the best features of capitalist and socialist societies (and avoided many of their worst features).

For decades many believed the Swedish model was stable. With hindsight we see that Sweden's equilibrium was easier to preserve during an era of strong economic growth. As growth has slowed since the late sixties, social conflict over limited resources has intensified. Some observers feel that Sweden is at a turning point. In this view, the time has come for an unavoidable choice between pushing forward with the reforms of the seventies from worker participation to worker ownership *or* accepting an economy based on private ownership of the means of production and restructuring incentives accordingly.

Yet capital and labor in Sweden have struggled and reached accommodations in the past. An air of compromise characterized the early measures of the new Palme government and the Swedish stock market responded quickly with a robust rally.

In 1983, the Swedish economy began to grow again. Wage restraint has been exercised. The large October 1982 devaluation of the krona succeeded in stimulating exports and retarding imports. Industrial profits have picked up. Yet, at this writing, the prospect of some form of increased worker ownership remains a strong bone of contention as well as a possible destabilizing element. Nevertheless, the Swedish model has surprised observers with its resiliency in the past, and it is not unlikely that it will do so again.

Recommended Readings

1. Rudolf Meidner, *Employee Investment Funds* (London: George Allen and Unwin, 1978).

2. Assar Lindbeck, *Swedish Economic Policy* (Berkeley: University of California Press, 1974).

3. B. Ryden and V. Bergstrom, eds., *Sweden: Choices for Economic and Social Policy in the 1980s* (London: George Allen and Unwin, 1982).

FRANCE

INDICATIVE PLANNING

France has had a long tradition of state intervention in the economy (*dirigiste*) as well as protectionism against foreign industries. There were some voices raised in favor of a laissez faire economy and free trade in the nineteenth century, but government intervention tended to grow in the last half of the century. The government became involved in the transportation sector in the 1850s. By the 1890s, the government controlled a considerable percentage of the railways. The Bank of France was a semipublic institution, but it had little power over most financial activities and was largely controlled by financiers for a long, long time. The government also worked hard to maintain the status quo in agriculture. It did that by using protective tariffs to make it more expensive to import competing products.

The French governments of this period were in no hurry to industrialize, preferring to keep the country largely agricultural, as it was, in order to maintain the existing cultural and sociological conditions. In the period from 1890 to 1914, moreover, the socialist parties gained strength, and the ideology of socialism spread among the French population.[1,2]

During the First World War in 1914–1918 the Germans occupied much of French industry in the northeast of France. The economic crisis and the long war forced the government into a large degree of state control of industry, despite a contrary ideology among some of the government coalition parties. The government activities were

---

1. See Richard F. Kuisel, *Capitalism and the State in Modern France* (New York: Cambridge University Press, 1981).

2. Considerable material and ideas for this chapter came from discussions with a historian working on modern France, Professor Irwin Wall, of the University of California at Riverside.

paid for mostly by means of borrowing and partly by a new income tax.

In the 1920s there was a move to return to "normalcy," in other words, a move back toward less governmental intervention. At the same time, however, the CGT (General Confederation of Labor) suggested a program of syndicalism. In their scheme syndicalism meant control of each enterprise by an autonomous board of (1) workers, (2) consumers, and (3) public representatives from the government. Syndicalism meant a high degree of decentralization, though the CGT moved toward a scheme for some central planning in the 1920s.

France escaped the Great Depression until 1931; then the depression hit hard, and there was a continuous decline in production until 1938 (except for a brief rise in 1936 under Blum). In this period many cartels were formed and competition declined. The government encouraged the cartels because it felt they would be better able to resist the depression than would small business. In 1936 a popular front government of Socialists and Radicals came to power; it nationalized part of the armaments industry and more of the railroads and increased the national power over the banking industry (especially the Bank of France). It also legislated the 40-hour week, paid vacations, collective bargaining, and other prolabor measures.

During the Second World War, Germany occupied most of France, while a collaborationist government existed in the unoccupied part at Vichy. The Vichy government instituted some "war planning," some technocratic modernization drives, and widespread controls. During the war the whole Resistance movement agreed that the economy should be freed from fascism and from "capitalist oligarchy" (because many capitalists had collaborated with the Fascists). Most of the Resistance leaders agreed that there should be a national economic council, some degree of planning, and some amount of nationalization—but all of the proposals were very vague and hid many conflicts among different groups.

In 1945 production was only a third of the prewar level. Much of big business had collaborated with the Fascists, and the Communist party was very popular because of its role in the Resistance. All of this created a climate in favor of major economic changes. A Socialist government in 1946 (supported by the Communists and the labor unions) nationalized about 20 percent of all industry and began to move toward some kind of central planning. Nationalization included (1) several big deposit-taking banks; (2) almost all public utilities, including electric power and gas; (3) more railroads; (4) about half of the aircraft industry; (5) the insurance industry; (6) the coal industry; and (7) the Renault automobile company. The expressed motives for nationalization included (1) to punish collaborators among big business, (2) to put key public services under public control, (3) to direct a rapid recovery, (4) to modernize the relatively backward French economy, and (5) to foster patriotism.

Since the trade unions were supporting the government, workers' committees were formed not only to improve work conditions but also to stimulate production among workers. Former owners (except collaborators) were compensated when industry was nationalized. In most cases, the public enterprises were supposed to be run by tripartite boards of workers, consumers, and the government. These boards were supposed to set policy and appoint managers, subject to approval by the ministers. Actually, each industry has been run somewhat differently. Usually, the minister appointed the manager, with the approval of the whole Cabinet. The tripartite boards soon came to have little power, as we shall see.[3] Although there was supposed to be some planning by the government, there has never been any direct (nonmarket) coordination among the various nationalized industries. The only partial exception was that the government (in an informal and confidential manner) instructed the government-controlled banks to give easier credit to favored industries.

The far Left in France has always advocated more control and planning by a Socialist government, as well as more plant-level workers' control. The Communists wanted workers' control, provided the Communist-dominated CGT represented the workers. In 1947, however, the U.S. offered the Marshall Plan to France, which included a large amount of help in the form of grants and low-interest loans. But the Marshall Plan had three strings attached to it. First, the Communist party had to be removed from the government. Second, there had to be much less spending on social welfare programs. Third, there had to be more spending in the private sector and less spending in the public sector, as well as less spending in basic industries and more in light industry.

Because the Communist party (which favored central planning) was ousted in 1947, the strong pressure for more government control through a central economic plan was ended. Ironically, the one exception to this circumstance was the peculiar relation that first existed between the Marshall Plan administrators and the French government planners. The Marshall Plan was providing one-third of French investment capital, so the American administrators had enormous influence over the French planners. So, as long as the Marshall Plan lasted, the Americans pushed for a powerful government plan, since it was basically under their control. The French government had no alternative but to go along. When the Marshall Plan ended, the importance of the French planning agency was progressively downgraded while other agencies of government (such as the Ministry of Finance) became more important in economic policy making.

At the same time, in order to keep out Communist influence, the nationalized industries became more centrally controlled. At this

---

3. Staff of *Dollars and Sense*, "Vive Le Nationalization," *Dollars and Sense* 73 (Jan. 1982): 8.

point the labor movement (largely Communist led) withdrew from the planning process because its voice was being ignored. Communist directors were purged from the nationalized enterprises, and this situation contributed to the "insurrectionary" strikes of November–December 1947 and October–November 1948. Labor claimed that if it had stayed in the planning process, it would only have been used as a mask for the real control. Control of the nationalized industries was mostly shifted out of the hands of the enterprise planning boards. Power shifted downward into the hands of the appointed managers, as well as upward to the ministers, who both appointed the managers and judged their performance.

The Monnet Plan

Jean Monnet, the minister in charge of planning in 1946, consulted only with businessmen in drawing up his plan. With the departure of the Communists in 1947, French planning changed from its beginning in actual central planning to what is called *indicative planning*. Indicative planning means that the plan merely indicates which areas might be the best ones in which the economy should grow, and business is requested to invest in those sectors. The government provides indirect incentives or sanctions but exerts no direct or compulsory control over them. Only the nationalized industries are expected to follow the plan in detail—and even they might not do so if the minister in charge or the director of the enterprise decides not to follow the plan (as is frequently the case).[4]

The main impact of the Monnet Plan (1947–1951) was a process of education. It brought much information as well as new management techniques to business. It ran many seminars to educate business in the latest technology and strategies for sales of French goods abroad. One important result of indicative planning was the provision of extensive market research to business. Indicative planning is built on the assumption that more information will smooth out sectoral bottlenecks and the business cycle. It also assumes that known national goals will enhance the aura of certainty in the economy, and such an atmosphere will inspire more investment—and the investment will be better for the country because it will be made with more knowledge of future trends.

More specifically, it has been argued that most capitalist economies overinvest in boom periods. Good indicative planning, however, because it provides more correct information, might reduce investment at such times and increase it in times of contraction. This view seems,

4. The most helpful single reference for this period, and for most of this chapter, is Stephen S. Cohen, *Modern Capitalist Planning: The French Model* (Berkeley: University of California Press, 1977).

at least for France, overly optimistic because it overstates the possibilities of correct information gathering and dissemination as well as their effects. The problems of information gathering include the following: (1) much information is kept secret; (2) there is intentional deception of the government by business; and (3) it is difficult to aggregate the individual corporate views of the future since each corporation has a different view of profitable investment opportunities and of its share of the market.[5] Even with the correct information on paper before them, business people usually are caught up in the frenzy of speculative expansion near the cycle peak. Then, during the recession, business people are affected by the atmosphere of pessimism.

What has actually been done in French indicative planning—from 1947 to the present—is to have the top planners or the ministers take the previous year's production and then project what the increase in demand will be for the next five years. Next, on this basis, the technicians compute a one-year plan. To this estimate of demand is added the technical information (coefficients) regarding the amount of inputs necessary for the estimated output. The planners prepare and publish this information in the indicative plan. In order to accomplish its planned goals, the government uses various kinds of incentives or sanctions.

The switch from actual planning to indicative planning in 1947—after the Communists were pushed out of the government—meant that the process consisted mostly of consultations with business. The planners and the business people together decide (1) what goals business wants and (2) what favors must be given to business to encourage economic growth. This has been the essence of French indicative planning. (We shall examine its structure in detail in different periods, since the precise mechanisms have evolved somewhat over time.) Note the similarity of French planning to the Japanese symbiosis of business and government; it appears that the deficiencies of the competitive market process have impelled many capitalist countries to turn to an increased role for government in collaboration with business.

The means used to induce business to cooperate include: (1) low-interest loans to provide cheap capital in areas considered vital; (2) accelerated depreciation of capital so as to give a larger tax break to those who invest; (3) various other tax reductions for business; and (4) outright grants to some businesses in favored sectors. It should be noted that this type of planning shifts income away from working class taxpayers to owners of corporations. (We shall examine below—in the section on "Later Plans"—the very limited participation of

---

5. A very clear discussion of the advantages and disadvantages of indicative planning is in Melaku Lakew, *History, Theory, and Practice of Indicative Planning* (Ph.D. diss., University of California, Riverside, 1981).

labor and Parliament in the planning process.) The lack of labor participation in the governmental and planning process, the regressive taxation policies, and the subsidies to business have all helped France to become the country with the most unequal income distribution among the major industrialized countries (see Table 2.4). The table shows quite clearly that the ratio of income of the top 10 percent of income receivers to income of the bottom 10 percent is much higher in France (21.8 to 1) than it is in the other highly developed capitalist countries.

Performance of the First Plan

Numerous writers do attribute to French planning some successes in eliminating production bottlenecks and scarcity of key raw materials in the period from 1944 to 1950 and in inducing business to make more investments for economic growth in the period from 1950 to 1960. Since that time, until the election of Mitterrand in 1981, planning was much looser and it accomplished less. In the view of its critics, while indicative planning may give some small boost to stability and growth under many circumstances, it is too weak to solve the fundamental problems of inflation, unemployment, or business cycles because these problems involve much more than a flow of more information to business.

During its early years, indicative planning undoubtedly did have a strong impact. This impact was due partly to the influence of labor in its first years, partly to the Marshall Plan administrators, and partly to the fact that about two-thirds of all capital investment came from the government, mostly in the form of long-term, low-interest loans to approved projects. Even as late as the period from 1952 to 1959, 80 percent of all business borrowing was based on low-interest loans from the government or on low-interest loans made by financial institutions and guaranteed by the government.

The Monnet Plan of 1946 concentrated on the long-term development of just a few industries—and did a good job of ensuring that those industries recovered from the war. There was no overall plan for the whole economy. There was no consideration of industry interrelations. The planners had very little data. French statistics were poor because companies refused to give information to the government. There were actual plans only for coal, electricity, cement, agricultural machinery, steel, and transport, these being considered the most vital industries for French recovery. These industries received government financing; most of the others were left out in the cold, with no financing available.

In the period from 1948 to 1950, prices and profits rose much faster than wages. Therefore, workers' share of national income declined in this period. There were also heavy military expenditures (mostly for the Vietnam War), which led to a large government deficit. The deficit amounted to half of the budget and was financed by a rapid increase in the money supply, which led to inflation. Because of these and other problems, the goals of the Plan for 1950 were not met until 1952.

Later Plans

In the 1950s and 1960s, however, the planners progressively lost authority (even though the Plan became more and more sophisticated). The government made fewer and fewer loans. The Plan had less and less impact. The Plan came to be treated merely as a policy statement of one department of the government. The planners in this period for the most part recommended use of the usual Keynesian tools of monetary and fiscal policy.

Business recognized this environment and its constraints; but within those constraints, business did as it wished in order to maximize its profits. The nationalized firms also tended to act exactly like profit-maximizing commercial firms with independent managers in a market environment. Indeed, many nationalized firms, such as Renault, have long been recognized as among the most efficient firms in France; but they do not act in a concerted way under a unified plan.

The fact that France had very good rates of growth in the 1950s and 1960s—higher than U.S. growth rates—led many writers to assert that French planning was very effective, mostly because it reduced uncertainty for business. It is worth remembering, however, that this period was generally one of good growth in most of the advanced capitalist countries. So the French growth may have been helped by indicative planning, but it is hard to disentangle planning from other favorable factors. France, with indicative planning, did better than the United States, which had no planning; but it did not do as well as West Germany and Japan, which used other forms of business–government cooperation, and it did not do as well as many of the centrally planned economies. A very extensive comparative analysis of the facts and performance of different systems in different countries would be necessary for any generalizations to be made about the performance effects of indicative planning. Instead, we shall discuss here some of the details of what actually happened, so as to give the reader a feel for the nature of French planning.

More French plans followed the first. They were each about four years long, with some gaps between; and some were a little unclear as to the exact dates for starting and stopping. Roughly, the dates of each plan are as follows: Second Plan, 1954–1958; Third Plan, 1958–1961; Fourth Plan, 1962–1965; Fifth Plan, 1966–1970; Sixth Plan, 1971–1975; and Seventh Plan, 1976–1980.

In the 1960s, direct government investment in state-owned industries was still 35 percent of all French industrial investment; but it does not appear that all of this investment was done according to one unified plan. In fact, most of the investment was done quite independently under separate managers. So even public investment did not follow the Plan, and private investment followed it even less. The fact is that the Planning Commission has no direct control over the public sector. The Finance Ministry has some direct control, but for the most part the state-owned industries go their own way and do as they wish.

As of 1977, the Planning Commission had only forty planners and only ninety other staff people and secretaries. These data emphasize that the planners are not expected or required to plan the whole economy in detail; rather, they set out some general directions for the leading economic sectors. After a four-year Plan is adopted, it is not implemented by the planning agency but by the Finance Ministry, to the extent that it is implemented at all. Yet the Finance Ministry was composed in large part for many years of conservatives who did not believe in planning. The conclusion of most experts is that French planning has had some effect on macroeconomic performance, but it has been a very small effect at most times.

In theory, the Parliament gives the final approval to any Plan before the Plan is carried out. In practice, Parliament has had little power. Either the Plan is not even mentioned in Parliament, or it is discussed rather briefly and approved in a perfunctory way.

As noted earlier, in the drawing up of the Plan labor has had little or no influence. Labor did not participate in the drawing up of the Second and Third Plans at all; because this was the height of the Cold War, Communist-led unions had no communication with the establishment. In later Plans the non-Communist unions (*Force Ouvrier* and the CFTC) had a small amount of participation. Some unions began to urge an attempt at greater participation in order to have a little bit of influence. This circumstance may change in the Mitterrand administration, but the situation is still unclear.

Most of the planning preparation is done in conferences between the planners and big business. The planners have had a strong preference for consulting with the giant firms, because having consultations with thousands of small firms is not practical, while consulting with a few large firms is relatively easy. One result of this situation has been that the indicative plan has encouraged the formation of larger firms by mergers and cartels. Besides ease of planning, the more important reason for encouraging larger firm size is so that firms have the ability to compete successfully in the European Common Market area and in world markets. As a result, one expert, Stephen Cohen, concludes: "In France . . . cartels and monopolies are traditional, omnipresent, and encouraged."[6]

Even though the French practiced a more institutionally formal

---

6. Cohen, *Modern Capitalist Planning*, 73.

method of indicative planning than the Japanese, the Japanese efforts at supply management and market coordination through MITI (Ministry of International Trade and Industry) and other government agencies (see Chapter 2) have been notably more successful. One apparent reason for this disparity of results is that in France there was a historical distrust and lack of cooperation among labor, business, and government, while in Japan there was a historical basis for close cooperation between business and government. Moreover, in Japan there has not been active opposition by the unions to government–business planning. Finally, changing of governments in France has generated less deliberate and more inconsistent policy goals.

In France, in the earliest period after World War II, indicative planning was supported by the unions but actively opposed by almost all of business. Over time, after the Communists left the government, the unions did not participate in the planning process and usually opposed the plans. Big business very slowly came to enter and participate in French planning, but small and medium business continued to oppose—or at least suspect—it.

The planners and the managers of big business tend to have the same social background and to come from the same schools. They also interchange positions frequently. For example, from 1960 to 1970, 25 percent of the Finance Ministry staff later became business executives. Not only do the unions complain about the apparent coziness of the planners and big business, so does much of small business. Claude Seibel, an expert on the French economy, writes: "One can conclude, therefore, that planning is done by big business for big business."[7]

The planners aim to help big business to be more efficient. The Plan is constructed by industry branch. In the highly concentrated industries, the planners work mostly with the big firms. In these branches all of the information comes from the big firms. Most of the targets are set in consultation with the big firms. In the less concentrated industries, the planners work with the trade associations. "The essence of French planning . . . is the planning of each industry by its own members, acting as a great cartel, with the civil service sitting in on the game and sweetening the pot."[8] In other words, planning does have an effect in aiding collusion in the direction chosen by big business, but it has had little effect in meeting national goals (except when government goals happened to coincide with business goals). After the Plan is constructed, each firm agrees to do its share by collusion with the others. "Good" or legal collusion is, according to the usual

---

7. Claude Seibel, "Planning in France," in Morris Bornstein, ed., *Comparative Economic Systems*, 4th ed. (Homewood, Ill.: Irwin-Dorsey, 1979), 66.

8. David Granick, *The European Executive* (New York: Doubleday, 1962), 155.

view of the French planners, that which follows the Plan and "the general interests of production."

It is important to understand that the main instruments of planning are subsidies and tax breaks to firms in the favored industries. So they are not only consulted, but they are then given the favors they desire in order to be cajoled to do what they probably proposed in the first place. Thus, the Plan permits big business "to obtain, in the name of the national interest, public funds at low interest rates and tax exonerations. . . ."[9]

One can see the influence of business in some detail in a study made of the composition of the planning commissions. In the Third Plan, there were nineteen "Modernization Commissions," which formulated the details of the plan.[10] These commissions consisted of 612 people, including 206 businessmen, and 136 civil servants (mostly with the same social background as the businessmen). There were also 13 bankers, 34 technical experts, and 57 trade union representatives. Finally, there were 66 miscellaneous others, including farmers, chamber of commerce representatives, doctors, architects, and innkeeper representatives. In the Fourth Plan, the planning commissions included 437 businessmen, 202 civil servants, 237 miscellaneous representatives, and 114 trade unionists.[11]

The French Left argues that the planning process should be more democratic, and that its end result should be binding on the economy, not merely indicative. By "democratization" the Left means the proportional participation of all sectors and social classes, including more representatives of the workers and consumers, in the drawing up of the plan. The French center also talks about "democratization," but to them it means more participation of labor in carrying out the plan, but not in formulating it.

The attitudes of the French trade unions (before the present Socialist government) as reflected in their debates over tactics and strategy with regard to planning were quite interesting. Some trade unionists took the position of *fundamental opposition*, which meant no participation. These unions included the ones led by the Communist party, that is, most locals of the CGT. At the other extreme were conservative unions that followed a policy of *unconditional participation*, mostly those unions concerned only with wages and working conditions narrowly defined. Those unions that participated unconditionally in the planning process appeared to endorse the very pro-business results of the planning process, and even sometimes declared that "union members should not strike against their own plan." Their members generally have been dissatisfied with these results and have applied pressure to pull out of the planning process.

9. Gilbert Mathieu, *Le Monde*, Mar. 2, 1962, p. 17.

10. This study is reported in Pierre Bauchet, *Economic Planning: The French Experience* (New York: Praeger, 1964), 36.

11. Cohen, *Modern Capitalist Planning*, 194.

Of course, the unions that stayed out of the planning process could have no effect upon the results. There was much pressure, therefore, from the rank and file inside the Communist-led unions for some form of participation; so the Communist-dominated CGT has slowly moved toward greater involvement in the planning process.

In the late 1970s, still before the Socialist government, a third position, called *critical participation*, emerged. The trade unionists espousing this position, mostly left Socialists, argued that it is better to offer some constructive suggestions to change the Plan in the direction of workers' interests rather than just sitting on the sideline while business shapes the Plan as it wishes. This is a new and complex position, because it means being involved in the process while frequently criticizing the result. A fine line must be walked between being merely obstructionist and becoming placid collaborators in a probusiness plan.

Performance of Planned Goals

As mentioned earlier, the First Plan failed to achieve its 1950 goals until 1952. After that, there was a confused hiatus of a year, with the Second Plan actually beginning in 1954. As a result of much-improved national income accounting and statistical data, the Second Plan (1954–1958) endeavored to be a comprehensive plan for the whole economy, not just a few industries. Unfortunately, however, from the planner's point of view, the Second Plan had even less authority and control than did the First Plan. The main reason was that there was much less investment funding by the central government (as the Marshall Plan ended). Much more investment was self-financed by business, so the government had considerably less leverage to use on business to control the direction of the investment. The result was a Plan that looked more comprehensive and more sophisticated but had less impact on actual economic events.

The Second Plan emphasized productivity, automation, and cost cutting, all of which resulted in additional pressure on labor to do more and be paid less. Production did grow rapidly, but it grew in ways very different from what had been planned.[12] The distortion was due mainly to the impact of the Algerian War, which meant a huge increase in military spending as well as an increase in inflation.

The Third Plan (1958–1961) was similar to the Second Plan in that its scope was comprehensive. It was technically even more sophisticated than the Second Plan. It was, however, even less effective in achieving its goals because no major interests—other than some of the companies that helped to formulate it—were strongly committed

---

12. Ibid., 151.

to its major goals (at least by the time it went into effect). The major problem was seen to be the fact that imports were much greater than exports, creating a balance of trade deficit. The Plan called for a considerable increase in exports, while imports were to increase only by 10 percent. In reality, imports increased by 58 percent, so it failed in its main goal.

Like the Second and Third Plans, the Fourth Plan (1962–1965) failed to meet some of its principal goals. The Plan still lacked effective economic controls; some actual outputs fell far short of the targets, while others went way beyond them. For example, coal production reached only 39 percent of its target and all productive investment only 80 percent of its target; yet the armaments and aerospace industries achieved 914 percent of their targets.

Three major reasons were alleged to be the cause of these failures. It was said, first, that the planners made mistakes; second, that any projections are impossible in a complex economy; and third, that planners cannot possibly foresee all the exogenous shocks that may hit an economy. But none of these reasons seem sufficient. More careful planning with the use of the latest techniques could achieve the planned goals with a fair degree of accuracy (according to other historical experiences to be discussed in later chapters). A more fundamental reason for the failure of these three Plans was that French indicative planning had insufficient force. It could not control the private sector because it could not issue any direct commands. In France it did not even control the so-called public corporations because they were semiautonomous, directed to maximize profit as their sole goal and supervised by other government ministries. Short-term government monetary and fiscal actions responded to unforeseen emergencies day by day, with little or no attention being paid to the Plan.

The Fifth Plan (1966–1970) deemphasized physical targets. It concentrated on only short-run Keynesian monetary and fiscal controls and it did not really attempt to push for long-run goals concerning growth or allocation. French planning for its domestic goals also became more uncertain when France was fully integrated into the European Economic Community in the early 1960s. Having a common market meant an economy "open" to all the influences of its neighboring economies, so France by itself would have less control of its output totals in any industry.

In spite of some attempts to get them involved, the trade unions did not, for the most part, participate in producing or implementing the Fifth and Sixth Plans. Moreover, the government's short-term measures were no more coordinated with the Plan in the Sixth Plan than they had been in the Fifth Plan. In the Fifth Plan, many industries did achieve their targets, but overall public investment reached only 83 percent of its target. At the same time, private investment was 140 percent of its planned target. In this period of conservative governments, the economy was shifted away from the public sector toward the private sector, even more than the goals of the Plans anticipated.

The Sixth Plan (1971–1975) was more detailed and had 1,600 equations. The planners had large numbers of advisers in devising the Sixth Plan; the advisers included some 2,926 people, mostly notables from various areas. Yet the two major trade union federations (the CGT and the CFDT) pulled out of the planning process because they opposed its basic probusiness orientation. In spite of all the eminent advisers and the high degree of mathematical sophistication, this Plan failed to a greater degree than any of its predecessors, largely because of the recession of 1974–75. Instead of rapid growth, there was slow growth or stagnation accompanied by increasing unemployment in 1975. Prices rose 60 percent. France entered a period of stagflation, that is, both stagnation and inflation.

When Giscard d'Estaing was elected in 1974, he was anti-Plan. He argued that (1) the Plan had failed to predict events, and (2) the planners were not trustworthy. According to Giscard, the planners were macroeconomic model builders who were harmless, but they were also as useless as their very abstract and complex models. Further, Giscard asserted that the planners were left-leaning "social technocrats" who worried about making the Plan relevant to social problems rather than merely concentrating on economic growth. A reduced role for planning fit Giscard's pro–laissez faire views. Instead, the government pursued a restrictive macroeconomic policy, including higher sales taxes, higher income taxes on wages and salaries, higher interest rates, and stricter control of the money supply, all designed to reduce inflation but increase saving among capitalist investors. It also ended price controls and removed some fees from corporations to encourage capitalist enterprise. Industrial policy, however, continued to be pursued outside the framework of the plan. Despite the free market rhetoric of Giscard, many observers have argued that government intervention in and control over financial markets increased during his time in office.

Since the government had little interest in it, the Seventh Plan (1976–1980) was almost forgotten. When it was finally allowed to go forward, its formulation involved minimal public participation and it established few targets. It set only a small number of modest goals in particular industries, with the agreement of big business in those industries. Even these limited goals were not met because of the stagnant economy of the seventies.

In many ways, all of this planning activity has not changed the French economy very much. For example, in 1973, all government expenditures in France were 32 percent of GNP, while central government expenditures were 19.6 percent of GNP. This was remarkably similar to the U.S. levels of government expenditure (though the level has now risen much higher under Mitterrand). Over a long period, the French economy under indicative planning did better than some capitalist countries in growth and worse than others. France achieved an average annual GNP growth rate of 4.0 percent from 1960 through 1978. In the same period, the mostly unplanned U.S. economy grew at a rate of 2.4 percent a year, while the partially planned Japanese economy grew at 7.6 percent a year. Since so many other factors affect growth, it is difficult to say how much indicative planning had to do with any of these differences in growth rates. In terms of stability over the business cycle, the French economy has also behaved very similarly to other (unplanned) European capitalist economies.

The Socialist Government of Mitterrand (1981–)

How did the Socialists come to win a majority in France?[13] The Socialist party was often part of a governing coalition in the 1950s and did not strongly advocate any extension of socialism. In the 1960s, the Gaullists achieved an absolute majority and drove the Socialists to the opposition. In this situation, the Socialists became more radical under the leadership of Mitterrand. He committed the party to an alliance with the Communist party (which had also been in the opposition since 1947) and reoriented it to a more socialist type of program. The left and right Socialists, however, have continued to disagree with each other over the scope of socialism and the extent of nationalization that the Socialist party should advocate.

The alliance of the Communist and Socialist parties helped to strengthen the Socialists electorally and to give them a more militant image. The left was also aided by various socioeconomic tendencies. For one thing, the number of farmers was declining. In 1954, 27 percent of the whole economically active population was in agriculture, but by 1976 the number dropped to only 11 percent. This hurt the Gaullists because farmers had been one of their main social bases. At the same time the number of students was growing, with most of them on the left. Finally, growing unemployment was hitting many manual workers and even some intellectual and professional workers. The increasing complexity of the society and the harshness of individual competition for limited jobs gave many people a sense of alienation. All of these trends led to a desire to change society. These changes, together with the unemployment and inflation of the early eighties, finally resulted in the election of Mitterrand in 1981.

The flavor of the new Socialist government is best characterized by some of its immediate measures. First, there was an amnesty for 6,235 nonviolent prisoners, which represents about one-seventh of all pris-

---

13. See, for an interesting analysis, Tony Daley and Jonas Pontusson, "The Left Victory in France," *Socialist Review* 11 (Nov.–Dec. 1981): 9–56.

oners in France. Second, the minimum wage was raised by 10 percent. Third, the family housing allowance was raised by 25 percent. Fourth, minimum old-age pensions and handicapped pensions were raised by 20 percent. Fifth, all cases of extradition against illegal immigrants were suspended until the cases could be reconsidered. Sixth, the government pledged to support and enforce the new, much more liberal abortion and birth control laws that had just been passed.

The Mitterrand government has nationalized two very different sectors of industry. On the one hand, it has nationalized some declining industries that were in need of help. These industries include steel, chemicals, and synthetic textiles. From these industries, the government will inherit only losses—a similarity to other nationalizations carried out in Western Europe. On the other hand, several high-technology, growth industries—thought to be profitable—have been nationalized as well. They include telecommunications, major parts of consumer and industrial electronics, and computers. Other specific firms nationalized include a large aircraft firm (Dassault, mostly military planes) and a large munitions firm, as well as firms in glass, paper, and chemicals. After delicate negotiations, the government also took control of three companies that have big foreign interests: ITT–France (telephone equipment), Honeywell–Bull (computers), and Roussel–Uclaf (chemicals). It turns out, however, that all but one of the newly nationalized firms lost money in 1982; and it has been alleged that stockholders knew that most of them were headed for losses (which is why there was little opposition).

All French banks have been nationalized except small, local, regional, cooperative, or independent banks. Foreign-owned banks were not nationalized. The nationalized banks now hold 90 to 95 percent of all domestic deposits. Since the state traditionally controlled the allocation of most credit in the economy, it remains to be seen what is gained by this extension of public ownership in the financial sector.

The total industries now nationalized include eleven groups, constituting about 33 percent of French industry. Since about 18 percent had been nationalized prior to Mitterrand, the Socialists have raised the share of nationalization by 15 percentage points, depending on which estimates and definitions are used. In all, the nationalized firms plus all other government agencies now employ about 50 percent of all French workers. The other 50 percent are employed in some two million private businesses. The government has pledged not to nationalize any of these businesses but rather to aid and encourage them in any way possible.

It is worth emphasizing that the new nationalizations have significant popular support partly because many of the previously nationalized firms have performed so well. Renault and Air France, for instance, are very efficient, profitable, and successful companies. Three French banks that have been nationalized for a long time rank among the top ten banks in the world. The nationalized railroad system has a train that travels 230 miles an hour on the Paris–Lyon route and has been praised for its efficiency.

Another reason why the government has met less business opposition than might be expected is the fact that the previous stockholders are receiving very generous compensation for their stock. In fact, the prices of most of these stocks actually rose after it was known that the firms were to be nationalized![14] No foreign assets have been touched.

Furthermore, in addition to its early social measures, the government has ordered four additional, more significant measures, most of which are very popular. First, to undo the historical overcentralization of French government, the Socialist administration has decentralized a great deal of power to the municipal and regional governments, even though their opponents are in power in many of these local units. Second, capital punishment has been abolished, ending the use of the guillotine. Third, the workweek has been reduced from 40 to 39 hours, and a decision has been made to lower it eventually to 35 hours (although it is unclear at this time just when that will happen). Fourth, the retirement age for receiving social security pensions has been lowered to 60.

Different Views of Planning and Management

Within the French Socialist party, not to mention the rest of French society, there are many conflicting views of how planning should be run, what its goals should be, how the nationalized firms should be managed, and how much worker self-management there should be.

The French Socialist party is for *autogestion*, or self-management, but what does it mean? The right and center Socialists, including Mitterrand, see it as a political affirmation of freedom of association, participation in the political process, and other liberties to express individual views and to control the state through democratic processes. The left Socialists see it as workers' control of the work place and of the means of production.

The two groups also have totally different notions of "planning." To the right-wing Socialists, planning means encouraging voluntary actions by business to follow an indicative plan, the function of which is to correct some misallocations and imbalances. The left-wing Socialists see the Plan as a substitute for the market system, a way by which the French people can direct their own economic destiny rather than have business direct it.

---

14. For this fact and other facts later in this chapter, we are grateful for the use of unpublished work by Professor Irwin Wall, University of California at Riverside.

There are also different notions of the management of nationalized firms, already mentioned above. The right-wing Socialists (and Premier Mauroy) favor the independence of each unit, with the units of a large size so that they can better compete in the international market, have more sales, and bring France more prestige. Their position implies that the aim of each firm, run by its manager, should be to maximize profits and not to provide extra jobs. The left-wing Socialists see nationalization as a means to socioeconomic liberation, with a more equitable income distribution, provision of more jobs to the full employment level, and more control for workers over their work life.

Managing the Nationalized Firms

One of the big criticisms of previous French planning was its undemocratic nature. How has the Mitterrand government been moving in this respect? First of all, we must examine who it has appointed as managers; then we will look at their powers vis-à-vis the government, consumers, and workers.

The Mitterrand government has mainly appointed "experienced administrators and technocrats" as managers of the nationalized firms.[15] Two former managers were retained in their jobs after nationalization. Bank manager jobs were mostly filled "by highly qualified bankers whose Socialist credentials are equally impeccable." Most of those appointed were already lower executives in various firms or banks, but with Socialist leanings. Thus, unlike the Chinese during the Great Leap Forward and Cultural Revolution, when they were more concerned to appoint reds than experts (on the grounds that one could learn the job, but loyalty was more important), the French have appointed experts who are a little pink.

Many American analysts believe that the control of the banking and credit system is even more important for the Socialist government than the direct control of industry, since control of the purse is decisive. It is therefore worth noting that two "veteran Rothschild bank [officers]" were named to head two of the newly nationalized banks.[16] But all newly appointed managers of banks and other firms were formally members of the Socialist party, except one Communist who was named head of the state coal authority. An example of one person named who is both expert and deeply pink is Alain Gomez. He is 43 years old, is a left Socialist according to his own statements, and was trained at France's elite Graduate School of Administration and at the Harvard Business School. He was division president of another

---

15. See Felix Kessler, "France Selects Officers for Firms It Nationalized," *Wall Street Journal*, Feb. 18, 1982, p. 32.

16. Ibid.

company before being named to head the new nationalized company in electric equipment.

One executive of a newly nationalized firm, who had been simply reappointed to his old job, has already quit. The Communist party had opposed his appointment in the first place because he had fired thousands of workers before nationalization. He asserts that he quit because he was given "impossible" targets while not being given enough capital for investment to buy new equipment.[17] He also wanted to allow more foreign investment, but the government did not agree. He expressed dislike of the shorter workweek and was opposed to higher social benefits. Finally, he argued that the company needed an austerity program of job and wage cutbacks rather than any kind of expansion. It is hard to understand why he accepted the appointment in the first place.

There are many tensions within the government and between the government and the managers over whether the government goal should be more jobs, especially in the nationalized firms, or whether it should simply be maximizing profits in the firms. In this context, it is important to know how much power will go to the manager versus the government or consumers or workers. To democratize planning and management, one way to proceed is to give large amounts of power to decentralized boards of consumers and workers. Another way to go is to keep power centralized in the hands of the government but to have plenty of detailed discussion and control in Parliament. In the latter method, the whole population participates indirectly through its elected representatives; if nationalized firms make mistakes, the party in power can be blamed and will suffer in the next election.

The present French government has so far chosen neither of these two roads of democratization. The tendency has been to decentralize power to the firms, but not to allow increased participation in the firms' decision making by the workers and consumers. Thus, Premier Pierre Mauroy has said, "Nationalization will not be statization. We shall protect the identity and autonomy of the national companies thus created. They will enjoy full responsibility as companies, being called on to act on their own initiative at the national level as well as on the international level."[18] Mauroy makes it clear that neither the planners, nor the ministers, nor the Parliament will have much direct control over the nationalized firms.

At the firm level, who will have control? For many years, all French firms with over fifty workers have had works committees (*Comités d'Entreprise*) representing the workers in disputes. The nationalized firms have also had administrative councils (consisting of workers, consumers, and government representatives), but they too have far

---

17. Felix Kessler, "Resignation Rocks Socialist France," *Wall Street Journal*, July 22, 1982, p. 25.

18. Pierre Mauroy, quoted by Dan Cook, "France Nationalizing 4 Big Concerns," *Los Angeles Times*, July 9, 1981, Part I, p. 5.

less power than the manager or the minister and can only give advice. "In some firms the councils can influence management and production decisions, but in many others they have been relegated to planning summer camps for employees' children."[19]

During the elections, and for some years before, the Socialist party emphasized *autogestion*, that is, self-management for workers. Now that the Socialists are in power, however, less has been heard about this idea. One reason is that the Communists dominate the unions in many of the nationalized firms. The Mitterrand government, therefore, fears that this would mean Communist dominance of enterprise policies through the administrative councils or the works committees or any new forms of workers' control.

Rather than develop workers' participation or control, the government has so far expanded the rights of union organizing, increased the information flow from companies to unions, increased individual rights of workers, and improved grievance procedures. They have not, however, allowed any workers' participation or infringement on managers' decisions—and certainly no workers' control over firms. The tendency has been to substitute improved collective bargaining for self-management. The bargaining has been mostly tripartite in form: by labor, by business, and by government representatives until a consensus has been formed. Even this mildly reformist type of bargaining should be universal and centralized if it is to be effective. In France, however, centralized bargaining is difficult because most workers (70 percent) are not represented by unions, there are three different union federations, and each local union has a large measure of autonomy.

Rather than workers' or Parliamentary control, the Minister of Industry says that undemocratic (and inefficient) state bureaucracy will be prevented because "a sufficient entrepreneurial autonomy will be respected. Each corporation will naturally act in concert with the Ministry of Industry and in the framework of the Plan, but the strategies and development of each will be left to the initiative of the enterprise itself."[20] In summary, it appears that at present: (1) most decisions are being left at the firm level, with no new significant planning power at the national level; and (2) decisions at the firm level are being made by old-style expert managers on conventional criteria of profit maximizing, with no control by workers or consumers.

Macro Performance under the Mitterrand Government

The Socialist government of Mitterrand came into power in 1981 with high hopes and expectations by the populace. It was faced with rising unemployment and stagnation in a worldwide recession. Therefore,

---

19. Staff of *Dollars and Sense*, "Vive Le Nationalization," 8.
20. Ibid.

in addition to the social measures, labor legislation, and nationalization mentioned above, it launched an emergency plan to stimulate the economy and move toward full employment. The combination of all of these measures was very popular. At the end of its first year, the Mitterrand government had an unprecedented popularity index of 60 percent. The continued worldwide recession, however, and lack of great success in combating it in France have now led to considerable disillusionment and attacks by both Left and Right.

What were the specific full-employment measures of the Mitterrand government? An emergency two-year interim plan for 1982 and 1983 was launched (there was no mass participation in the planning; it was claimed that time was too short). The government has made major new investments in the nationalized industries (planned at 75 billion francs for 1983). But nationalized firms have long been under orders to hire workers only to maximize profits, not to help solve the unemployment problem. Since there is a worldwide glut of many of the goods produced by the French nationalized industries, they are unable to expand production. For example, Renault must sell its cars in the United States and other foreign countries, but this market has declined drastically during the recession. Under the circumstances, it comes as no surprise that the nationalized industries have expanded but very slowly and cautiously.

Two-thirds of French production remains in private hands. To stimulate this area, the Mitterrand government began with a very expansionary Keynesian-type policy of increased government spending on social programs (as noted above) and public works—the opposite of the policy of cutting government spending as practiced by the Thatcher government in the United Kingdom and the Reagan government in the United States. Mitterrand also gave direct incentives to private investment, such as tax credits and low-interest loans.

In the context of the international recession and financial instability, however, the measures were not very successful. In early 1983 the unemployment rate rose back up to the 1981 level of 8 percent. That was still several percentage points below the Reagan or Thatcher unemployment levels, but for a socialist government this level is unacceptable to its supporters. The Mitterrand government claims to be at the mercy of international capitalism. France is said to have suffered from high U.S. interest rates, which make borrowing for investment more difficult for French firms (as well as U.S. firms). France also suffers from insufficient demand for its exports, a demand that decreases as income drops in other capitalist countries.

One reaction to these domestic problems—allegedly caused by international capitalism—has been increased protectionism. *Protectionism* is defined as putting up barriers (by tariffs or quotas or other means) to the products of other countries.

A second reaction to falling exports has been a drive to cut costs, in order to make French products more price attractive. Cost cutting has been achieved, in part, by reducing real wages, that is, by not allowing nominal wages to rise as rapidly as prices. But this action necessitated a complete turnaround from the earlier Keynesian measures, aimed at stimulating employment and raising wages, to a new set of austerity measures, designed to lower employment, cut costs, and fight inflation. The new austerity program was announced in March of 1983.

Still another reason in the international arena was given for this sudden change in domestic policy. It was said that the expansionary policies—more social spending and higher wages—had failed. The reason stated was that the increased income of French workers was not being spent for French goods but for imports, especially from West Germany and Japan. So expansionary policies in France led to more jobs in West Germany and Japan; but their effect in France was only higher costs, inflation, and greater trade deficits. These problems, in turn, provoked a two-pronged policy: (1) protection against foreign goods and (2) austerity at home to lower French costs and increase French exports. The austerity measures include higher rates for gas, electricity, telephone, and train fares, as well as a compulsory loan to the government by all wage earners (except the very lowest).

The Socialist austerity policy began with a four-month wage and price freeze. It continued with the usual cuts in social programs and tax increases. But austerity, as such, does not sound socialist and smells very bad to the government's main supporters, since it appears anti–working class. So Mitterand does not call it *austerity*, but *rigor*. The policy of rigor means holding down wages, cutting social programs, and raising taxes. Thus, the Socialists have been impelled by circumstances largely beyond their control to follow a more traditional course—one that in many respects contradicts their initial policies.

The concrete economic aims of the Socialist government were announced as: (1) more welfare and redistribution, (2) nationalization of some industries, (3) more rights for labor, (4) self-management by workers, and (5) full employment. The government has progressed with respect to its first three goals but has not yet introduced a program for increasing worker participation in management and has made no gains with respect to full employment. To be sure, in late 1983 employment prospects are bleak, and Mitterrand is facing increasing pressure from labor as well as from his coalition partners, the Communist party. At the same time, other macroeconomic problems, such as inflation, international payments deficits, and low investment, remain to be solved.

The Socialist project in France is to build a socialist economy through a peaceful and gradual parliamentary transition. This project has been undertaken before, notably in Chile under Allende, and is fraught with difficulties. Whereas Mitterrand's policy of nationalization is consistent with French political culture, it is perceived as a threat by the capitalist economic world. Since the French are and wish to continue to be part of the capitalist international trading sphere, their potential for future structural modifications is constrained. Ironically, perhaps, the potential in France for further successful change along socialist lines seems to be directly proportional to the strength of the international capitalist economies.

Recommended Readings

1. Stephen S. Cohen, "Recent Developments in French Planning: Some Lessons for the United States," U.S. Congress, Joint Economic Committee, *Hearings* (Washington, D.C.: U.S. Government Printing Office, Dec. 26, 1977), pp. 1–26.

2. John Hackett and Anne-Marie Hackett, *Economic Planning in France* (Cambridge, Mass.: Harvard University Press, 1963).

3. David Liggins, *National Economic Planning in France* (Lexington, Mass.: Lexington Publishers, 1975).

4. Vera Lutz, *Central Planning for the Market Economy* (Washington, D.C.: American Enterprise Institute, 1965).

5. Claude Seibel, "Planning in France," in Morris Bornstein, ed., *Comparative Economic Systems*, 4th ed. (Homewood, Ill.: Irwin-Dorsey, 1979).

6. John Sheahan, *Promotion and Control of Industry in Postwar France* (Cambridge, Mass.: Harvard University Press, 1963).

7. J. Zysman, *Political Strategies for Industrial Order, State, Market, and Industry in France* (Berkeley: University of California Press, 1977).

8. Saul Estrin and Peter Holmes, *French Planning in Theory and Practice* (New York: George Allen and Unwin, 1983).

9. Stephen Cohen and Peter Gourevitch (eds.), *France in the Troubled World Economy* (London: Butterworth, 1982).

10. Stephen Cohen, James Galbraith, and John Zysman, "Credit Policy and Industrial Policy in France," U.S. Congress, Joint Economic Committee, *Monetary Policy, Selective Credit Policy, and Industrial Policy in France, Britain, West Germany and Sweden* (Washington, D.C.: U.S. Government Printing Office, 1981).

11. Jacques Delors, "The Decline of French Planning," in Stuart Holland, ed., *Beyond Capitalist Planning* (New York: St. Martin's Press, 1978).

Three

CENTRAL PLANNING: THE SOVIET CASE

We have examined France, where a new government is pledged to a socialist economy and a democratic political structure. In the rest of this book we shall examine several other countries claiming to be socialist already. The vision of socialism has clearly moved millions of people in the last two hundred years to fight for it—and sometimes to die for it. It is still a moving slogan in most of the world, from the socialism proclaimed in India to African socialism to East European, Russian, Chinese, and Cuban socialism.

What is this vision of socialism that has moved so many people and countries? It is a vision of putting a stop to poverty, exploitation, and unemployment forever. It is a vision of the end of all repression by governments, of an end to race and sex discrimination, and of an end to imperialism and war. This vision is to be realized by ending the capitalist system of private profit making, by ending competition of one against another, by ending a system where average working people feel that they have no control of the economy, and by establishing a new type of society based on more egalitarian and democratic principles. It would be a society in which people learned and practiced cooperation, not competition. The economy would be democratically controlled and carefully planned for the benefit of everyone, not for the few. This vision of socialism was advocated by Karl Marx in the nineteenth century. While many countries that claim to be socialist have had considerable economic success, they still have a long way to go in cultural, economic, and political terms if they are ever to achieve the beautiful vision of Marx.

In this part of the book we examine the Soviet Union, which proclaimed the first "socialist" country (and which officially endorses "Marxism") but which has achieved very little of the old socialist or

Marxist vision. We shall see that, on the one hand, the Soviet Union has had some magnificent economic achievements. First, it survived against the intervention of fourteen foreign countries in 1918–1919, against the forces of the old regime in a civil war, and against an enormous fascist war machine from Germany in the Second World War. Second, it did create an economy with no capitalists and with central planning and public ownership of all industry. Third, it developed in the 1930s from a backward, less-developed, agricultural, rural economy to the second largest economy in the world, highly developed in many sectors, mostly industrial, and mostly urban. It has had no unemployment since 1928, a very high level of growth from 1928 to the mid 1960s, universal health care, and an end to illiteracy with rapid growth of college education.

On the other hand, the Soviet Union is plagued with inefficiency, bottlenecks, stagnant productivity, low quality goods, and long lines of consumers who are often unable to find what they want. Moreover, if socialism means democratic control of the economy, then the Soviet Union is not socialist. The Soviet Union is controlled by a small group of men. This small group controls the government, using repressive means to discourage or stop all opposition, allowing very little freedom of speech, no real elections, and no democratic control. The government runs the economy.

Soviet Economic Institutions: Differences from the United States

Government Ownership of Industry

One of the basic differences between the Soviet Union and the United States lies in the ownership of productive facilities. In the United States, most land and factories are privately owned. In the Soviet Union, most land and factories are publicly owned. The public ownership tends, of course, to mean public direction and therefore usually means planning. The principal type of household income in the Soviet Union is wage income for labor. On the other side, in the United States income consists not only of wages but also of profit, rent, dividends, and interest. These latter incomes are derived basically from private property; thus, most U.S. planning is necessarily limited in scope to the confines of single enterprises, in which decisions reflect the search for private profit.

Even in the Soviet Union, there are some exceptions to socialist production. One *can* work for oneself in the Soviet Union. Thus, there are some people, a large absolute number but a small percentage of the whole, who do not work for the government. They produce goods or services privately by themselves, and they can sell these goods or services; this category includes some doctors, lawyers, farmers, and handicraftsmen. No one, however, can employ someone else for a wage for private profit—this is viewed as exploitation (though some East European countries and China do allow a certain amount of small business).

Most Soviet industrial enterprises are owned and operated by the "public," represented by the Soviet government. The only exceptions are a very small percentage of enterprises that are cooperatives, mainly composed of handicraft workers. In the public enterprises, the government, or some agency of the government, appoints a manager. This manager is solely responsible for the performance of the factory, and his bonus is based on how well the factory performs. His performance and his conduct are checked by numerous agencies, and he may be promoted, transferred, or fired at any time. In turn, he hires and fires all the other workers at the enterprise.

The government grants the enterprise its plant and equipment and initial working capital, though the government has begun to charge interest on capital. After the initial grant of capital, however, the enterprise is then made financially independent. In theory, it must meet all costs of wages and materials out of current revenue. It must also replace or repair depreciated and broken plant and equipment out of its revenues from sales. And it is normally expected to show a profit above all of its costs. In practice, Soviet firms often have losses and are given subsidies.

Government Ownership of Agriculture

Most farming constitutes an exception to pure socialist production. Most Soviet farms are theoretically cooperative. The government owns the land; however, it leases the land to the farm for 99 years. The profits are supposed to be split among the farmers. These units are the so-called collective farms. Collective farming means that the farmers pool their resources, work the land together, and divide the profits among themselves. It is required, of course, that a great deal of income be set aside for communal consumption and reinvested for further expansion. Further, there are obligatory deliveries of crops to the government at low prices, in effect a tax in kind, which cut sharply into collective farm profits.

There are also "state farms" in the Soviet Union. These farms are run essentially like factories. They are publicly owned and are controlled and operated by the government, which simply hires farmers to work on them. This is easiest to do with a mass-production type crop like wheat. The amount of land under state farms has been increasing absolutely and relatively, partly because huge new areas in Western Siberia were brought under cultivation and partly because of discontent with the collective farm as a form of economic organization. There is also a substantial sector of tiny private plots, held by individual collective and state farmers, producing a very large percentage of Soviet meat and vegetables.

Central Planning

Most important orders originate from the Politburo of the Communist party and the Council of Ministers, but additional orders to the enterprise may come from regional or local government bodies. Further orders may originate in or be transmitted through the agency directly supervising the enterprise, whether that agency is associated with a regional governing body or with the central ministry directing some industrial area. Finally, all of these orders from governmental or supervisory bodies are supposed to be in accord with the Plan, which emanates from the Central Planning Board (*Gosplan*) or its subordinate agencies. The enterprise manager is solely responsible for the performance of the factory, then, only in the sense that he must execute all of the orders he has received within the constraint of the resources allocated to him.

Gosplan (as will be seen in detail in a later chapter) first collects information up the ladder of agencies from the enterprise in order to evaluate the last year's performance and the present conditions and possibilities. Then Gosplan is told by the Council of Ministers what goals it must strive to meet. On these bases, it draws up a general plan for the whole economy, though details of production and allocation are provided only for a couple of thousand commodities. The draft plan is then shown to all agencies on down the ladder to the enterprise. After all of these units have added their detailed modifications and suggestions, Gosplan draws up the final draft.

The Plan is supposed to provide sufficient investment for the desired rate of growth, guarantee balance among all the industrial needs and outputs, and choose the "best" assortment of goods. Later chapters examine just how the planners must calculate so as to achieve balanced growth and optimal choices of assortments of goods and technologies. At any rate, the Central Planning Board (Gosplan) hands the Plan over to appropriate government bodies to enact it into law, and it is then passed on with detailed elaborations at each intermediate level until the enterprise receives a formidable document. This document is supposed to tell the enterprise for a year—or some other period—exactly what to produce, how to produce it, what prices to charge, and what funds it may use.

Central Planning and the University

Central planning is totally unlike the unplanned U.S. system. To help the reader get a feel for it, we may compare it to some U.S. institutions. Apart from nations, the largest planned economic unit in the world is the U.S. Defense Department. Like the Soviet economy, it has a plan for every year, in which it attempts to list everything from nuclear bombs to tanks to bullets. Plans are given as commands from the Joint Chiefs of Staff to armies to divisions to regiments to companies and, finally, to each platoon. Each level of command adds its own detail to the plan until the individual soldier is told exactly what to do. The plan for material goods to be bought must be approved by Congress and then the goods are bought from industry (private, in the U.S. case).

A university is another large type of planning unit. In the University of California, for example, the Board of Regents gives commands to each of the nine campuses. Then the administration of each (headed by one of the nine chancellors) makes those commands more detailed and binding on faculty, staff, and students. Yet most universities also have a certain amount of democratic participation by those who are affected. Faculty usually have a major role in deciding (1) what courses are to be offered, (2) what degrees are to be given, (3) who is to be hired and fired, and (4) what the content of their courses is to be. Faculty then act as a level of command over students.

In general, the market principle with dollar votes is not applied in decisions regarding the allocation of resources within a university. Rather, decisions are made through an administrative structure which, to a greater or lesser extent, gives some voice to faculty and to students, depending on the issue and the school. In the absence of a market-type mechanism, some administrative instrument for consultation is usually desirable. In some cases, students may feel consultation alone is tokenistic; they want votes or decision-making powers. Yet it is clear to faculty, and (one hopes) to most students, that it is better to locate most decisions at the level where information and experience are maximized.

How are resources allocated at a university? Consider the curriculum. Were each department governed by a market mechanism, the popular courses would offer additional sections and the unpopular courses would be eliminated. Popularity would be determined not simply by the number of students enrolling, but also by the price each student would be willing to pay to enter the course. The allocation of students to courses, then, would be affected by the income at each student's disposal; that is, a student from a rich family would be able to buy his or her way into courses. Further, popular professors would see their incomes rise while unpopular teachers would see their incomes fall and would possibly become impoverished or unemployed.

What problems do you see in applying market principles to the university? Why, if at all, is it desirable to have a market govern the allocation of resources outside but not inside the university?

In place of the market, curriculum is generally set by each department and by interdepartmental committees. It is presumed that the student as a consumer lacks complete information. The faculty has more information and experience and, hence, sets the curriculum not by a popularity poll but through the application of educational principles and collegial discussion. In short, the selection of courses to be offered (and/or required) is made administratively, not by the market. That is, it is made interpersonally without necessary reference to the price mechanism. Administrative decision making also characterizes the allocation of resources in a planned economy.

The fact that decision making is administrative, however, does not necessarily mean that the consumer, producer, or student is ignored. Many universities and departments, for instance, have student course critiques. Student evaluations, albeit not usually decisive, often influence the choices made about retaining professors or offering courses. Effective student input is likely not only to make the student feel involved and more motivated but also to improve the quality of decisions regarding faculty and curriculum.

Alternatively, were students to dominate rather than merely influence the decision-making process, it is probable that most faculty would find themselves in short order reducing assignments and giving all A's—a circumstance most would regard as a dilution of the educational process. There is, then, an argument for attempting to balance input from below, or student participation, with expertise in reaching administrative decisions in the university. As we shall see, many economists believe that the same holds true for centrally planned economies.

Other sets of issues that could be decided by the market or by plan are, for example, (1) which dormitory does a student live in? and (2) what kind of food shall be served at the dormitory? Dormitory domicile could be decided in a number of ways: by how much a student is willing to pay to live in a particular dorm; by the autocratic plan of an administrator; by the first-come, first-served principle; by lottery; and so forth. What kind of food is to be served could be decided by a nutritionist, by the cook according to what is cheapest, by student demand in terms of money, or by a democratic vote of the students.

What, then, is the optimal degree of participation or "popular control" in the university? This question is sufficiently complex when applied to a society of ten thousand individuals. It is formidable when applied to an entire economy involving millions of people and goods. Yet it is precisely this set of administrative questions and decisions that must be handled in a centrally planned economy. If nothing else, the market, by relying on self-interested individual decision making, in response to impersonal signals, provides an easy way out.

Public Health, Education, and Housing

One of the basic areas of difference between the Soviet Union and the United States lies in the Soviet practice of providing virtually free health service, largely subsidized education, and heavily subsidized housing. There is no tuition, so education is free to the average student. In addition, some 80 percent of students receive stipends. The student with high grades is given a larger fellowship, adequate to buy textbooks, pay for room and board, and have some left over. Students work under great competitive pressure for grades, not only for higher fellowships but because educational achievement determines future jobs.

A great deal of money is spent on the free health service of the Soviet Union. That U.S. citizens still have to *pay* money for medical services is considered extremely barbaric by Soviet citizens, who often question U.S. tourists quite incredulously on this point. Of course, the Soviet taxpayer is paying for health services indirectly. The Soviet citizen can also purchase health services directly through doctors in officially sanctioned private practices or through the black market.

Housing is an area of striking difference between the United States and the USSR—it is a sphere of consumption in which Soviet inferiority is greatest (some of this inferior housing is due to the massive destruction of World War II). True, rent charges are almost negligible in the Soviet Union, but this low rent is paid for inadequate housing. By law not more than a very small percentage of a citizen's income may go for rent. Whereas the average U.S. citizen spends 25 to 30 percent of his or her income for rent, the average Soviet citizen spends less than 5 percent. All rental units are, of course, rationed and subject to price control. It is necessary to ration them because people would be willing to pay a great deal more than 5 percent of their income for better and more adequate living quarters.

Soviet Economic Institutions: Similarities to the United States

In everyday activities there are many obvious similarities between Soviet and U.S. economic life.

Privately Owned Consumer Goods

While the Soviets do not allow private ownership of the means of production, this prohibition does not apply to consumer goods. The consumer goods market in the USSR operates very similarly to its American counterpart. In every town and city, stores line the streets, and individuals can buy everything from tomatoes to television sets, provided they have the money—more expensive durable goods can even be bought on the installment plan. Consumer goods become the private possessions of those who buy them. Consumer goods as well as cash can even be passed on by their owners, when they die, to relatives or friends. Land is not considered a consumer good; it is possible, however, to own one's own house. As we noted earlier, government enterprises often produce low quality goods, there is a poor assortment of goods, rationing is used occasionally for some scarce goods, and customers are forced to stand waiting in long lines.

Since the government dominates production and distribution, consumers' only recourse is often the black market.

Work for Money Wages

A second important point of similarity between the everyday economic life in the Soviet Union and in the United States is that in both countries the majority of people work for money wages. In the industrial sector of the Soviet Union, wage income is the only form of income, with some minor exceptions. The term *wages* is used broadly here to include monthly salaries, bonuses and commissions, time wages (paid by the hour, day, or week), and also piecework wages (according to the number of pieces one produces). In the past, the Soviet Union relied very heavily on piecework for incentive reasons. More recently, piecework has been deemphasized. The basic notion according to which wages are supposed to be paid is the "socialist" principle, namely, "from each according to his ability, and to each according to the work that he produces."

The distribution of wages and salaries within and among industries is also strikingly similar in the Soviet and U.S. economies. The greater the skill or effort required to do a particular job, the higher the pay (one difference is that the Soviet Union has a very small income tax and is talking of abolishing it altogether). And the higher the pay, the more commodities one is able to buy in the retail markets. This is the "carrot" which motivates capitalist and socialist workers alike. It is the overriding principle of labor allocation and income distribution under both systems. Distribution according to "need" has proceeded a long way in the Soviet Union in the areas of medical care and education, while heavy subsidies for food staples, housing, transportation, and other basic goods has assured their supply to low-income earners.

While the distribution of wage and salary payments is similar in the two countries, the overall income distribution is more unequal in the United States. This unequal income distribution is due primarily to the high incomes received in the United States in the form of profits and dividends, interest, and rent—incomes from ownership of property. Incomes from these sources have been abolished, of course, in the USSR. The highest paid individuals in the USSR are the dancers, artists, writers, composers, and others in the fine arts. Not only are they paid high wages, but they receive a high income from royalties. Also near the top of the pay pyramid are the scientists and leading university professors. As already noted, a very high premium is placed on education in the USSR. It is probably as difficult to get into the average Soviet college as it is to get into one of our top universities. The Soviet system is very much a merit system in which education is one of the major stairways to the top. This is not to deny the unofficial value for the job seeker of having political pull, of being the right nationality, and so forth. Finally, at the very top of the heap are the political leaders, who have high incomes (how high is secret), access to special stores, and unlimited terms in office.

Worker Mobility

Another major area of similarity is the ease with which workers can change jobs. Soviet workers are now completely free to move from job to job, though they are discouraged from doing so. In fact, a major problem has always been excessive labor turnover, far greater than that which characterizes the U.S. labor market. In the 1930s, labor turnover in industry reached a peak of over 150 percent—on the average each worker changed jobs one and one-half times a year. This implies almost a whole new work force in each factory each year. People are simply looking for better situations and moving to higher paying jobs. Before 1956, many administrative devices were used to try to reduce the turnover, and severe penalties could, in theory, be imposed for transgressions. However, because of the extreme labor shortage which has always existed in the Soviet industrial sector (the reasons for which are discussed in a later chapter), managers of enterprises trying to hire workers have been willing to collude with those seeking new jobs, and penalties have rarely been applied. In 1956, most of these penalties were abolished. At present, a worker is free to move as long as he or she gives two weeks' notice.

Plan of Part Three

We have presented in this introduction a brief sketch of some features of the present Soviet economy. In the chapters that follow we will explore how the Soviet economy arrived where it is today. We examine political and economic development from before the Revolution in 1917 to the reforms of 1965. Then we look at the operation of central planning in that period. After that, we examine some theoretical issues of planning. Within this framework we investigate the class structure of the Soviet Union and the economic behavior of managers and workers. Finally, we look at the reforms of 1965 and their failure.

5

USSR
DEVELOPMENT FROM
1917 TO 1928

To understand the changes in the economic structure and development of the Soviet Union since the Revolution in 1917, it is useful to
begin by reviewing conditions prior to that date. What were the per-
sistent trends that acted in such a way as to cause those revolutionary
changes?

Russia before 1917

Although the serfs were emancipated in 1861, the Russian class structure some forty years later was still basically feudal. That is, the
majority of the population was tied to the land and consisted of either
lowly peasants or aristocratic landlords. The middle class as a group
was still negligible. The ruling elite continued to be the coalition of the
Czar, the military officers, and the landlords. The emancipation reform, despite its liberal appearance, was essentially a victory for the
aristocracy. Every serf was given his freedom as well as the right to an
allotment of land. The terms which fixed the conditions for the transfer of land to the peasants, however, were very harsh.

The landlord was to lose both land and services, but he was to be
compensated by annual money payments for forty-nine years. The
terms of the compensation were, in effect, determined by the landlord himself within limits set by the state. The landlord could choose
between granting a larger allotment of land in exchange for a larger
redemption payment, or a smaller amount of land with a smaller
redemption payment. After the terms were decided upon, the responsibility for collection was assigned to the village commune
(known as the *mir*), which was to distribute the burden equally among

its members. Thus, each peasant came under the jurisdiction of the village commune, and as a member of the commune he was obliged to contribute his share of the redemption payments. The redemption payments were calculated in a manner so as to set an unrepayable burden on the "liberated" serfs. As a consequence, as each year passed, the village commune fell deeper and deeper into debt, and by the end of the century total peasant debts had expanded severalfold in most areas.

A major principle of life in the village commune was economic equality. To assure equality, the village practiced periodic repartitioning of the land, so that no one family would be any more, or less, favored by the different qualities of land than any other—though the family was awarded more land according to the number of able-bodied workers. This system of repartition was almost universal in the poorer northern regions, where the amount given by the emancipation to the peasants was greater; but it was almost nonexistent in the richer black-earth region of the Ukraine, where the landlord gave only the minimal amount.

The drive for equality was implemented in still another unique, and perhaps even more dramatic, way. Since the land occupied by each commune was not always uniform with regard to fertility, availability of water, hills, rockiness, or location, equality was achieved by dividing up each qualitatively different piece of land among all the families in the village. In areas in which the land was of very uneven quality, each farmer sometimes found himself cultivating not one solid lot but as many as thirty or forty narrow strips, sometimes only a few feet in width. There were several economic consequences of this agricultural system, discussed below.

The Immobilization of the Peasant

Since the village allocated tax charges on the basis of the number of workers per household (regardless of whether they stayed there or moved elsewhere), the peasant could not leave the commune without increasing the burden on the rest of the family. Thus, in those areas where the land was held in common and the taxes paid in common, the peasant was effectively immobilized. This system prevented the peasant from moving to the cities to try other occupations. Therefore, it reduced the extent of the division of labor in Russia and also reduced the possibility of the formation of an urban working or middle class. Only after the Stolypin Reforms of 1907 (and some further reforms through 1911) were the peasants encouraged to get private plots and withdraw from the commune. These reforms, which were promulgated as a result of the uprising of the peasants in 1905, abolished the redemption payments and ended the commune's collective responsibility for tax payments.

The Extremely Low Level of Agricultural Productivity

In the areas where the commune periodically repartitioned land, there was little incentive to raise the productivity of the land, since the gains would only be reaped by the next user of the land after the subsequent partitioning. The parceling of land into narrow strips also had a disastrous impact on efficiency for obvious reasons: it was impossible to use any but the most primitive implements on the strips; each farmer had an enormous amount of walking to do to get from strip to strip; and it has been estimated that in some regions about one-seventh of the land went into "boundaries."

About 80 percent of the people worked in agriculture, but they lived at a very low standard of living because of the low productivity. Czarist Russia's yield per worker in wheat was on a level with Asiatic countries, such as India, and was considerably below even the poorest European countries, such as Serbia and Italy. Primitive wooden ploughs were still used by a majority of all peasants.

It was basically because of the low agricultural productivity that the Russian national income per person in 1914 was less than 25 percent of England's and less than 15 percent of that of the United States. Moreover, we should keep in mind the extreme variations in living standards resulting from variations in ownership among the peasantry. In 1914, the richest 10 percent of the landowners owned 35 percent of the land. At the other end, the poorest 17 percent of the landowners owned only about 2.5 percent of the land. This means that, on the average, the richest 10 percent owned fourteen times as much land as the poorest 17 percent.

Another feature of Czarist Russia was the predominance of foreign investors in industry. The lack of entrepreneurship and the lack of a middle class left the direction of industry to the ruling elite, who invited foreign investors to establish heavy industry (since it was needed for military purposes). As a result, the most important Russian industry was to a considerable extent in the hands of British, French, and German investors.

Foreigners owned nearly half the capital in the coal industry and more than 80 percent in the oil and steel industries. In a typical colonial pattern, Russia exported raw materials and agricultural products and imported mostly finished manufactured goods. Since most Russian industry was established either by the government or by large foreign investors, enterprises were usually built on a very large scale. One finds the paradoxical situation that although Russia had comparatively little industry (because of the extra-long survival of serfdom), the industry which did exist was quite modern and consisted of very concentrated units. In fact, a majority of workers worked in factories that employed more than 500 workers. This high degree of concentration went together with a small middle class, thereby limiting political support for the existing economic system and making the subsequent change to socialism easier.

In the 1890s and 1900s Russian industrial output grew rapidly, especially as a result of the great investment in railway construction. Between 1890 and 1914, industrial output almost quadrupled. Nevertheless, intensive industrialization occurred primarily in the limited regions around Moscow and St. Petersburg. More than 85 percent of the population still lived in the countryside. Of the 10 percent of the labor force who actually worked in "industry," a very large number were employed in handicraft work rather than in mechanically powered factories. At the same time, the living conditions of the Russian urban worker were described as a hundred years behind those of western Europe. Although the Russian working class was numerically very small, the fact that it had a miserable standard of living and was concentrated in large factories in a few areas made it a potentially strong base for revolutionary movements.

Political Evolution, 1905–1917

In addition to these economic trends, certain political trends may be noted. Radical political movements and ideas came clearly to the surface in 1905 and then culminated in the Bolshevik Revolution of 1917. The most important revolutionary factor was the growing aspiration of the peasants, goaded by their hunger for land, to expropriate the large landed estates.

There was also an increasing bitterness against the militaristic policies of the Czarist regime. This strong antiwar sentiment was the natural consequence of Russia's humiliating defeats in several wars. The sentiment was reinforced by the fact that the peasantry had to carry the main burden of any war effort, both through the payment of taxes and the bearing of arms.

Furthermore, there was an increasing political consciousness among the workers, who felt that they were being exploited by the government and by foreign entrepreneurs. The fact that workers were highly concentrated in the centers of industry helped to crystallize this consciousness and made their organization much easier. Trade unions and socialist parties spread among the industrial workers in the early 1900s. The lost war against the supposedly "inferior" Japanese in 1905 brought the situation to a boiling point.

The 1905 rebellion was a nationwide attempt by the peasants as well as the workers to redress their grievances against the Czarist regime. It failed because it lacked enough organization to unite the country against the Czar. An organization was created, however, by the striking workers of St. Petersburg in 1905; it was called a council, or *soviet*, of all the workers. The soviets were at first merely propaganda bodies, but even in 1905 they began to exercise some governing functions. The 1905 revolution failed, but the greatly worsened conditions in Russia that resulted from Russia's participation in World War I led to another attempt at revolution in March 1917. The so-called March Revolution succeeded in overthrowing the Czarist regime.

The revolutionary movement and the soviets, which immediately assumed some government powers, both were controlled at first by liberals and moderate socialists. By April of 1917 the peasants as well as the soldiers had joined the workers in creating soviets to express their wishes. The war, however, was continued by the new government, and this created a further worsening of the conditions that had brought the revolt against the Czar. The inefficient agricultural sector, controlled in part by absentee landlords, produced very little after the best part of its labor force had been drafted into the army. During 1917, the remaining peasant producers withheld much of their food from the market because they were paid in rubles whose value was rapidly declining as a result of severe inflation. The effects of these agricultural deficiencies were terrible food shortages both in the cities and at the front.

In the towns, the relatively small Russian industry (acting under directives of a highly inefficient bureaucracy) could not produce even sufficient ammunition, let alone maintain rapid communications or transport of supplies. As the economy further deteriorated and the power of authority declined, the peasants began illegally to confiscate the landlords' estates. For example, in September 1917, the landowners in just one small province (Tambov) complained that twenty-four estates were burned by the peasants in just three days while the local government did nothing about it. The burnings and confiscations accelerated in October and November. At the same time, grass-roots factory committees formed by workers began to take over control of industrial enterprises.

Gradually, in these circumstances, the soviets began to swing to the Left. The Bolsheviks first took a majority in the workers' soviets in the cities. Then the peasants' soviets swung from the Right to the left Socialist Revolutionaries. Finally, the Bolsheviks came to control most of the soldiers' soviets at the front. The soviets everywhere took on more and more of the functions of government. When the Bolsheviks (later called Communists) achieved a majority in the soviets, they were able to launch a successful revolution; they took power on November 7, 1917.

War Communism

The conditions faced by the Bolsheviks were far from ideal. The Bolsheviks took over in the gravest of economic crises and soon were to face the gravest of political crises: civil war. The Bolshevik program called for peace for the soldiers, land to the peasants, and bread for the workers. They did achieve a peace with the Germans, though at an enormous cost in land and population. Landlord estates were confiscated and divided into twenty-five million individual farms. Similarly, in industry the local factory committees tried to take over the management of the factories, but the Bolshevik government took away this authority, centralized decisions, and appointed managers.[1]

The Bolshevik program originally called only for a strict regulation or "control" of capitalism by a worker-directed government and not for immediate confiscation or nationalization of capitalist enterprises. The Bolsheviks envisioned on the economic side (after the seizure of power) a long and slow transition toward a socialist economy. In 1918, however, further considerations of long-run peacetime economic policy were halted by the eruption of the civil war. From an already faltering economy, destroyed and exhausted by war and revolution, the Bolsheviks had to mobilize resources for their own defense. To understand the economic measures that followed, we must look at the entire situation.

In addition to civil war, there was foreign intervention against the Communists by the armies of Britain, France, Japan, and the United States. As a result of the war with the Germans, the civil war, and the foreign invasions, by 1920 Soviet industrial production had fallen to between 10 and 20 percent of the prewar level of 1913. The major coal and iron-ore producing area, the Donets Basin, which supplied the industrial centers of the North, was in the hands of anti-Bolshevik Russians and foreigners for most of the civil war. Furthermore, the stoppage of oil supplies from Baku drastically reduced industrial fuel supplies, and the lack of coal from the Donets necessitated an almost complete transfer to wood fuel on the railways. Moreover, many factories ceased operating because of desertions and lack of food in the cities. The managers deserted to the West, and workers went back to the countryside (where there was at least some food). Leningrad (known as St. Petersburg before the Revolution), previously a city of some two and a half million persons, became a ghost town of only eight hundred thousand. In fact, there were only half as many workers in industry in 1920 as in 1914, and the productivity per worker in 1920 was only about a third of what it had been in 1914. Consequently, industrial production was estimated at only 14.5 percent of the 1914 level.

All the usual sources of finance were blocked. The government lacked the machinery for tax collection. External loans and financing became politically impossible as the Western nations enforced an embargo on the new Communist nation. The only recourse to cover

---

1. The political events (and much economic background) from 1917 to the mid 1920s is detailed most thoroughly in the monumental, multivolume work of E. H. Carr, *History of Soviet Russia* (London: Macmillan and Co., 1950).

government expenses was to continue the inflationary policy of printing more money (in the face of restricted supplies of products). In fact,
after 1918, inflation proceeded at a disastrously accelerated pace. By
October 1920 the purchasing power of the ruble was no more than 1
percent of what it had been in 1917.

The production of agricultural products for the market began to
contract. The farmer (former peasant, now the owner of land) found
little incentive to produce for the market when the industrial goods
for which he wished to exchange his own products were either not
available or else were sold for fantastically inflated prices. He preferred to hoard his surplus food or simply reduce production and
exchange it for leisure. The Russian farmer, for the first time in
history, possessed the product of his own land; and he would consume
it himself if he could not sell it at a reasonable price in real terms.

In such a situation the Soviet government could not obtain the
resources it needed through the market. Yet military needs somehow
had to be filled. Soldiers needed, at a minimum, food and rifles and
ammunition. Squads of men were sent into the countryside to "req-
uisition" by force supplies of food from the rich and middle farmers,
who might have a surplus over and above the needs of their own
families.

In the early months of Communist rule obtaining military supplies
from industry was just as difficult as obtaining food from farmers. No
sweeping nationalization proposals were made by the new Communist government. In November 1917, the government authorized only
local workers' "control" or supervision over factory owners. Yet
many private owners and managers closed their factories and fled
the country. Workers temporarily ran production in those factories.
Managers who stayed were at first responsible only to the workers'
councils. But this brief experiment in workers' control was ended
almost immediately. The Bolsheviks decided that local workers' control would result in inefficiency and chaos. Industrial management
was taken over, in essence, by government functionaries. There was a
vigorous opposition to this measure within the Communist party and
among many rank-and-file workers who maintained that the goal of
democracy within the enterprise could not be postponed and that
workers' control would actually help efficiency and incentives.

The civil war became acute in the summer of 1918. Thus, as a
necessary military measure, the Bolsheviks nationalized and put
under central control all large-scale factories by the end of 1918. By
1920 all middle-sized and even many small factories had been
nationalized as well—and were also controlled from the center.

Since inflation had essentially wiped out the exchange value of
money, all supplies from farm and factory were requisitioned by the
government and then reallocated primarily in terms of military requirements. And so there came into existence *War Communism*—in
effect, a centralized substitute for the market in the determination of

income distribution and resource allocation. Although in theory the society or the workers as a whole (represented by government) not only owned but also directed every single industrial enterprise, there was in reality no comprehensive planning or coordination of economic activity. It was true that government attempted to run nearly every detail of the economy, but it was mostly *local government*. There was no overall central output plan, and most of the vast number of ad hoc central directives were ignored by local authorities. Central interference was expressed only from time to time in emergencies, and then only in brief campaigns or through "shock" tactics (further discussed below).

A central feature of War Communism, and key to the whole system, was the requisitioning of food supplies from the farmers. The food surplus extracted from the countryside was allocated to two users. First, it went to the industrial enterprise in the form of primary raw materials. In return, industry was expected to produce the goods needed by a wartime nation. The very scarcity of resources required the strictest control over them.

Second, the food went to the soldiers and to the industrial workers. The workers were paid their wages in kind (in goods rather than money), which generally meant no more than bare subsistence food portions. This situation had serious consequences. For one thing, the reduction of "income" to the barest levels did not leave any incentive for labor to work in the factory. Furthermore, wage differentials are the usual means of allocating labor to its most productive employment. Since wage differentials were very much reduced by the food-ration wages, which varied little from job to job and industry to industry, labor itself had to come under the administrative control of the government. Labor was "militarized" or conscripted for peaceful work into so-called labor armies and allocated by the central government to the best of its ability.

Some loyal ideologues tried to create a virtue out of necessity and applauded the features of this system of War Communism as bearing the hallmarks of Full Communism. The use of money and market relations had been eliminated by the physical allocation of goods and services. There was public ownership of the means of production and relative equality in income distribution. Obviously, this was a communism based on equality in poverty and was very far from the abundance that could free men and women from toil envisioned by Marx.

The extreme centralization of decision making led to a great deal of administrative delay. To break the ensuing shortages and bottlenecks, use was made of the "shock" system of planning. This system simply meant (in lieu of a comprehensive plan, which did not exist) that all-out effort was centered on the success of a few enterprises, which happened to be militarily important at that moment. Unfortunately, this approach tended to persist, in modified form, throughout much of subsequent Soviet history. Furthermore, in these early years few loyal workers knew much about administration, while few good administrators felt any loyalty to the Soviet government.

By the end of the civil war in 1921, the recklessness of continuing such a course became clear to almost everyone. The peasant, estranged from the system by the policy of requisitioning, simply cut production to just that amount necessary for subsistence consumption for his family. Why should he produce for a government that appeared hostile to his desires and was unable to pay for his goods? As a result, the political alliance with the peasantry was falling apart. For the nation, this situation threatened starvation and the eventual downfall of the party in power.

In addition to peasant dissatisfaction, the urban working class itself was frustrated and angry with the system, partly for its inefficiency and partly for alleged injustices in distribution. Workers were suspicious of government-sponsored trade unions as well as all higher economic agencies. There was no economic democracy in the enterprises, since worker control had been replaced by state-appointed managers. There was no political democracy, since other parties were mostly prohibited and the Communist party dictated every move (including actions in the soviets). By the end of 1920, there were strikes, protest demonstrations, and protest resolutions by whole factories. Then Kronshtadt, the naval base where the Communist revolution had received its strongest support, rebelled in favor of *soviets without Communists*. This was the final blow to War Communism. The Communist leadership, and especially Lenin, decided that the time was ripe for a complete economic reform, as well as political changes.

Political Evolution, 1917–1921

The decline of freedom and the rise of a new repressive dictatorship in the Soviet Union proceeded in four stages in its political forms: (1) prohibition of monarchist and capitalist parties, (2) prohibition of other socialist parties, (3) prohibition of factions in the Communist party, and (4) prohibition of freedom of speech in the Party (and outside it) and, under Stalin, the use of death penalties. In the months after the Revolution in 1917, there was immediately some small opposition to the Soviet government. This circumstance was used as an excuse for the banning of all monarchist and capitalist parties and for the prohibition of monarchist and capitalist newspapers. It was said at first that this was only a temporary prohibition until things returned to normal.

The other socialist parties were for the most part allowed to continue. Their status from day to day depended on how threatening the war situation was and also on whether or not they were supporting the war effort. When the civil war and foreign intervention ceased in 1921, one would have expected that the other socialist parties would have been afforded more freedom. That did not happen.

When the Communist party congress met in 1921, the civil war had been won, but the Communists now felt even more threatened by their previous allies and supporters. The poor peasants of Russia mostly had supported the Bolsheviks as long as there was a threat that the reactionary armies would win and restore the land to the landlords. Without that threat, all of the peasants strongly resented the continued requisitioning of food from the countryside without payment. They became openly rebellious. Also, as noted above, the sailors of the Baltic fleet and the industrial workers at Kronshtadt felt that the Communists were doing a poor job and were heading toward dictatorship. They still strongly supported the Revolution; they wanted socialism and workers' control, but they no longer wanted the Communists. This position horrified the Communists, because these sailors and workers had been among their most committed political and military supporters. So the Communist party felt threatened and surrounded like a small fort under siege.

In this situation, the Communist party took three momentous steps within a short period. First, they prohibited all other socialist parties and their newspapers—and prosecuted those that continued to function. This measure was said to be a temporary one. Second, they prohibited all factions within the Communist party. This move was said to be a measure to gain discipline and strength against any attempts to split the Party. But it was said very loudly that it would not restrict free speech in the Party; it would restrict only conspiratorial and organized movements. This was also said to be a temporary measure.

Neither of these "temporary" measures was ever revoked. They became permanent features of the Soviet system. During the 1920s, as we shall see, free speech did continue within the Communist party. There were far-ranging and very interesting debates, which we shall follow in part. Opponents might be demoted by vote of a Congress or any other leading body, but they were never put in prison. By 1928, however, all dissenting viewpoints were stilled, unrepentant opponents were either jailed or exiled, and Stalin's faction won complete control. To look even further ahead, we shall find that in the 1930s, all freedom of speech was ended even within Stalin's own faction. All of Stalin's enemies—and all of his supposed enemies—were jailed. Then, for the first time, executions began in the mid 1930s.

Thus, 1921 marked the beginning of the use of the big stick and repression in Soviet politics. At the very same time, the third important event was the New Economic Policy, a carrot held out to the peasants in the form of economic policies that allowed them to trade freely in the marketplace. Before turning to the New Economic Policy, however, we must deal directly with this question: Why did the Soviet Union become a dictatorship, even though the Revolution was fought in the name of extending democracy?

Socioeconomic Causes of Soviet Dictatorship

Conservative theorists have long argued that central planning and bureaucracy under socialism must inevitably lead to a dictatorship of a few people at the top. Socialist theorists, however, reply that Soviet dictatorship was established in spite of collective ownership and planning, not because of them. Other factors that socialist writers claim must bear the primary responsibility are: (1) the anti-democratic tradition of Czarist Russia; (2) the underground training of the Bolshevik leaders, which resulted in anti-democratic Leninist ideology and practice; (3) the effect of the Russian civil war, including a rapid decline in the urban working class (and the death of many worker-activists); (4) the effect of foreign intervention; and (5) the overwhelming realities of economic backwardness and illiteracy, combined with the industrialization drive to end backwardness.

Czarist Russia

Prerevolutionary Russia, headed by the Czar, was an absolute autocracy for most of its history; it was strongly militaristic and imperialistic in nature and was supported by a landowning nobility. Most of the population consisted of illiterate and poor peasants. Ideas of political democracy came very late in Russia, and for some time after the French Revolution they influenced only the small number of the intelligentsia. The great Russian writers of the nineteenth century did write many perceptive fictional attacks on tyranny and bureaucracy, but these writings influenced only some of the few who could read. They praised the local, collective democracy in the Russian village (called the *mir*). After the abortive revolution of 1905, there was only a token degree of parliamentary political democracy practiced from 1906 to 1917. The Russian Duma (parliament) was neither popular nor effective. There was thus very little consciousness of democracy and very little practical experience with democracy among the Russian people. Not only was there limited political suffrage and very limited power in parliament, there was also very little liberal tradition of freedom of speech and other individual rights. It is true that the Russian intellectuals praised the liberal tradition, but most of the Russian people had very little practice with democracy until 1917, so the tradition was not deeply rooted.

The Underground Viewpoint

The repressive laws of the Czarist government forced Russian Marxists to pursue an illegal conspiracy. Therefore, they instituted a very strict discipline within the Party, did not always hold elections for top officers, and enforced orders from the top down. To be sure, for most of the period between the 1905 and 1917 revolutions, the leaders of the Bolshevik party were in exile and, hence, had minimal contact with Party cadre in Russia or with the working masses they purported to represent.

In theory, Lenin argued for "democratic centralism," which meant democratic election of central officers plus strict obedience to orders from the elected officers. A democratic internal debate would lead to a decision, followed by centralized, disciplined action. Czarist repression made elections impossible in the Party and made democratic internal debates very fragmentary and limited, yet the Communist leaders still demanded obedience to orders. The tradition by which the Party led the masses, and the top leaders directed the Party, was probably necessary for political and military action and was not too detrimental before the 1917 Revolution. Since anyone could leave the Party without harm, the Party could ask only for voluntary self-discipline.

Few revolutionaries thought about what might happen if the Party became the all-powerful ruler of the nation. When the Party came to power, persuasion gave way to censorship and coercion. Under Stalin, voluntary discipline in the Party would be replaced by external compulsion. At that point, the old tradition of a centralized and disciplined Party was a pretext through which its leader would be able to control all discussion in the Party, forbid any opposition, and tell every member what to do. Since no other parties would be allowed, that would mean that the leader of the Communist party controlled the whole political sphere.

The Russian Revolution of November 1917 resulted in a government of "soviets," that is, councils of workers, peasants, and soldiers, led by the Communist party (Bolsheviks). Within a month after the Revolution, the first step against political democracy was taken when all the parties (and all the newspapers) advocating capitalism or monarchism were banned. This was partly explained as a temporary measure during the violence of the Revolution and attempts at counterrevolution. But it was also given a more ominous meaning as a "natural act of proletarian dictatorship," according to some Party spokesmen.

Nevertheless, there were free elections to a Constituent Assembly (which was to write a constitution), in which the biggest winner was the Socialist Revolutionary party—and the Bolsheviks ran a poor second. Then two months later the Constituent Assembly was dispersed because, it was said, the attitude of the people had greatly changed and the Socialist Revolutionary party had split. Thus, elections to the Assembly were now outdated. This was a reasonably democratic argument, except that new elections to the Assembly were not called, then or ever.

Civil War

Many democratic forms tend to fall by the wayside during any violent and rapidly changing civil war. After the bitterness of civil war, it is not easy to let the opposition immediately reenter politics. The long and bloody civil war, worsened by foreign intervention, made immediate initiation of widespread political democracy very unlikely. The civil war killed off some of the old working class and dispersed much of the old working class to the countryside. In fact, the number of urban workers shrank from a small 2.6 million in 1917 to an even smaller 1.2 million in 1920. Furthermore, the unpopular measures necessary for warfare alienated many former supporters. As a result, the few surviving old Bolsheviks felt as if they were a tiny remnant defending a besieged fortress, with the necessity to act dictatorially.

The Peasant Majority

Socialism was designed by Marx, as interpreted by Lenin, to meet the needs and desires of an urban working class. Urban workers, however, were a small minority in a country with a huge peasant majority. If the Communists—who held the allegiance of most of the urban workers (and that began only around September 1917), but who held the allegiance of only a tiny number of peasants—were to rule this backward, agrarian country, it had to be by a minority dictatorship. Even within the urban working class, the Communist party was only a small minority until just before the Revolution. But later the Communist leaders merely dictated to the urban workers as they dictated to everyone else (it became a dictatorship over the proletariat).

Foreign Intervention

A large number of foreign capitalist countries (including the United States, England, France, and Japan) intervened militarily against the Soviet Communists in the years 1918–1921. Furthermore, the economic blockade of the Soviet Union was continued for many years. Foreign threats never ceased until they culminated in the devastating Nazi invasion in 1941. This was followed by the Cold War in the 1950s.

The foreign threats, wars, and blockades made economic progress more difficult, necessitated a militaristic atmosphere, and, therefore, made political democracy objectively more difficult. They are also used, however, as a rationale for repression by some of the ruling elements in the Soviet Union.

Economic Backwardness

The Soviet economy of the 1920s was much less developed than the advanced capitalist economies. The harshness of the drive to industrialize—with its unpopular demands for sacrifices—was an important reason for the increasingly repressive dictatorship of the late 1920s and the 1930s.

The New Economic Policy

As we have seen, the farmer's reaction to government requisitioning was simply to hoard more and produce less. Unless the government could provide the farmer with an incentive to produce more, the towns would starve. To remedy this situation, Lenin introduced the New Economic Policy (NEP). First, the government abolished requisitioning and reintroduced a free market in agricultural goods. Second, as a substitute for requisitions, a single tax consisting of a set percentage of his output was levied on the farmer. This would be his only responsibility to the government, and it was payable in goods rather than money. Any other surpluses could be sold on the open market for money or exchanged for industrial goods. Third, most of the large nationalized industrial units were allowed to respond to the demand registered on the market by deciding independently of the central government what and how much to produce. Fourth, most small businesses and handicraft enterprises were denationalized. Fifth, middlemen or private traders (called NEPmen) were allowed to bring the wholesale goods to retail markets and collect any windfall gains. In this way, the period of requisitioning, central allocation of material supplies, and instructions to producers was over for the time being with the exception of a few of the most important industries.

Some have seen the period of the NEP as a successful experiment in market socialism.[2] This view does not recognize the failure of heavy industry to expand beyond previous capacity during this period. It was precisely this problem—that is, how to spark the development of heavy industry—which later became the subject of bitter controversy culminating in the introduction of full-scale central planning in 1928. At the other extreme were those foreign commentators who declared that NEP was the beginning of the end of the socialist experiment and presaged an eventual return to capitalism. This theory ignored the fact that NEP fitted perfectly Lenin's view of a long, smooth transition period into socialism (whereas War Communism had been an unexpected and forced interruption of the process). To really understand

---

2. See V. N. Bandera, "The NEP as an Economic System," *Journal of Political Economy* 71, 3 (June 1963).

the workings of the NEP, one must take a closer look at the economy of the time.

Beginnings of NEP (1921–1923)

Agriculture

In the early days of NEP, agricultural goods were scarce relative to industrial goods and sold at first at high prices on the market (because 1921 was a year of crop failure and famine in some regions). These favorable prices for agriculture provided an additional incentive for the farmer to produce as much as he could for the market. In fact, the government retreated even further and allowed the richer farmers to lease land and even to hire the poorer farmers for wages. In succeeding years, agricultural production did increase in response to the new measures of the NEP. Indeed, the recovery was rapid and resulted in real gains to the farmer, and especially to the larger-scale farmers.

Industry

The New Economic Policy toward industry was to make enterprises independent both financially and operationally. Small government-owned businesses were leased out for private independent management (though government-managed enterprises still produced 92 percent of the output in 1923). Furthermore, each large government-run enterprise was expected to make its own production decisions, to be financially responsible, and to be economically efficient. Financing of enterprise activities from the government budget was abolished by 1922 (with the major exception of the railroads). A firm could now obtain funds only from its own revenues or through bank credit. The immediate result of the introduction of competition among the different industrial producers was a relative decline in industrial prices. This situation only reinforced the favorable terms of trade for agriculture versus industry (that is, one unit of agricultural good A could "buy" more and more of industrial good B). But industrial cartels, or trusts, were soon formed to collaborate on fixing prices at artificially high rates. Each trust could plan the output and prices of its own factories, merely submitting the plan to the government for final sanction.

Trade

Private trading organizations expanded rapidly and soon controlled 90 percent of the retail trade. Many of the gains from the NEP were reaped by the notorious NEPmen, who cashed in on the difference between a low price paid to the farmer and a high price received from the city dweller for food. Also, small businesses and retail traders were allowed to hire up to ten or twenty workers and to sell the products of their labor at a profit. It was in this area of small business and trade that capitalism flourished under NEP.

Labor

Under the NEP, restrictions on labor mobility were abolished. The laborer was free to change his or her job. Wages were no longer centrally set on an egalitarian basis but were differentiated by the "market" according to productivity. Trade unions were formed, partly to negotiate wage contracts for the worker, but also to increase the general culture and welfare of the working class. Actually, however, the Communist party kept firm control of the unions as well as the enterprises with whom they were supposed to negotiate. The right to strike existed in theory but was not often exercised in practice. The later history of Soviet trade unions is discussed in the appendix to Chapter 10.

Finance

Government financial policy during the first part of the NEP was conservative in outlook. An attempt was made to return monetary and fiscal policy to what was considered "safe, healthy" orthodoxy—though in practice money was still being printed at a fast rate. Bank deposits were supposed to be secured against governmental requisitions. For the ideal future, a balanced budget was envisioned with government expenditures eventually to be covered by tax revenues from industry and agriculture. Actually, by the end of 1923 only two-thirds of state expenditures were covered by tax revenues. This situation was still highly inflationary—prices were rising at more than 50 percent per month in 1923, and the price index stood at, roughly, one billion times the 1913 level. It was nevertheless a great improvement over the situation at the end of 1921 when 90 percent of all government expenditures were financed by the printing press. Inflation was not finally brought under control until the Monetary Reform of the spring of 1924.

Planning

Central planning went into eclipse. It came to be thought of as strictly contradictory to the spirit of NEP. The mood of the central government leadership was to give every encouragement to NEP, to stress its ability, and to strengthen the farmer's and merchant's confidence in it. The theoretical rationale behind this approach was the economists' notion that private demand and market forces would encourage economic development. The demand for durable consumer and light industrial goods generated by a prospering agricultural sector would spur growth in those industries. They, in turn, by demanding more inputs (machines and raw materials), would spur a response in the heavy industry which furnished supplies to them.

Investment policy was clearly in line with this approach as credits were more readily given to high-profit, quick-turnover industries. Only Leon Trotsky, a leading Bolshevik, and a few of his followers called for central planning to "control" the market, though even he did not call for planning to replace the market. Trotsky warned the Party of the consequences of neglecting heavy industry and called for planning to redress the growing imbalance between light and heavy, private and socialized, sectors of industry. But he stood alone and was ignored at this time. Most of the other Party leaders justified the lack of planning under NEP as part of the necessarily long transition period from capitalism to communism.

The Scissors Crisis (1923–1924)

During 1923 and 1924 a crisis arose which can be seen as a turning point in the NEP period. As we have said, in the first days of NEP, in 1921 and in 1922, the terms of trade favored agriculture relative to industry. Yet agriculture soon made a complete recovery and, as industrial supply lagged behind, the terms of trade began to change against agriculture. Food prices dropped drastically relative to prices of industrial goods, which remained in short supply despite the increased demand, in part due to a slower recovery and in part due to the fact that the industrial cartels were consciously acting to restrict competition. Thus, at the beginning of 1923 industrial production had risen only to about a third of the 1914 level, but agriculture had almost reached the 1914 level. Furthermore, by the end of 1923 about 190 of the 360 industrial trusts had joined syndicates for the explicit purpose of preventing competition.

Whereas agricultural prices had previously risen relative to industrial prices, they now fell further and further behind. These price movements resembled a scissors when drawn graphically, and this experience has been aptly called the *scissors crisis*. During 1923 the price ratio moved three to one in favor of industry and against agriculture. This situation was of grave portent. The farmer was able to buy less and less with the meager returns he received from the sale of his products. What incentive would he have to produce for the market if the goods he desired were priced far out of his reach? The economy was again threatened with a contraction in agricultural output. The NEP was thus plagued by the same disease that had helped bring War Communism to an end. The problem was far from solved.

The various leaders of the Soviet Union saw the problem in different ways. There were those on the Right (Bukharin and others) who viewed it essentially as a problem internal to the agricultural sector. They prescribed "remedies" that would increase the motivation of the private farmer by offering him additional incentives, that is, the freedom to accumulate wealth or "enrich themselves." Others, those on the Left (Trotsky, for example), claimed that the problem lay in the industrial sector, in its inability to recover, to expand supply at lower costs, and thus to reduce prices.

At this time Bukharin, the spokesman for the Right, was able to win support for his view from a majority of the Party. Bukharin attacked the monopoly position of industry and its artificially high prices. He also maintained that the well-being of the town depended not upon the twenty-six million small farms that barely produced enough for themselves but upon the relatively small number of richer farmers (kulaks) who produced primarily for commercial sale. The larger farmer was willing to sell his goods since he was eager to grow wealthy. Hampered by restrictions on the sale and renting of land and on the employment of labor, as well as low prices for his output, he began to sell less. It was this trend that had to be reversed. Therefore, the government decided to support the well-to-do farmer and enacted new laws that permitted him to hire labor and to lease land.

In the fall of 1923 the Soviet government took action against the high industrial prices. The government reduced the flow of bank credit to the trusts, forcing them to unload excessive inventories of finished products in order to obtain the funds to continue operating. In addition, maximum price ceilings were set on some goods, and cheaper foreign goods were imported in a few cases. Finally, less efficient plants were closed, so production costs could be decreased. Industrial prices were indeed lowered almost 20 percent by the end of 1924. Also, efforts were made to raise farm prices. The government paid more for its own grain and encouraged the export of grain.

The "scissors" did begin to close to some degree in 1924, and for the rest of the NEP the price spread was never again quite so acute. Nevertheless, the scissors never fully closed and the peasants never again had the same relative incentive to sell their surpluses that they had in 1921–22. Farm production increased very slowly, and the share brought to market continued to decline because of the relatively high prices of industrial goods and heavy taxes. The discontent among farmers once again threatened the emerging political alliance of workers and farmers.

The End of NEP (1924–1928)

Agriculture

The richer farmers took advantage of their powers under NEP to expand, at the expense of the poorer farmers. Many of the poorer farmers lost their land and became hired workers. The increasing differentiation of the farming population that resulted was so antithetical to socialist ideology that repercussions were soon felt in a growing resentment by the Communists toward this "capitalist" farmer class. While the right wing of the Party wanted to placate the richer farmers as a necessary evil in agricultural development, the left wing wanted to capitalize on the growing resentment in order to restrict and heavily tax richer farmers.

In spite of the surface agitation, however, it was a fact that most of Soviet agriculture resembled too closely for comfort the situation under the Czars. The Russian villager remained an extreme individualist, very conservative technically as well as politically, still using the primitive methods of his ancestors. Since agricultural productivity was so low and had such poor prospects for improvement, Soviet industry would certainly not make significant progress if it were constrained to an advance no more rapid than that of agriculture. In the late 1920s, a considerable flow of tractors and other machinery did begin to reach the villagers. Yet most of the peasant holdings were much too small to utilize efficiently such heavy equipment.

As early as 1925–26 (the harvest year runs from October 1 to September 30) the total agricultural area reached 95 percent of the prewar average while the gross harvest was even higher than prewar. Since industry was not to reach the prewar level until the end of 1927, agriculture seemed to be in a good condition, but it still had some major problems. One critical agricultural problem remained which had to be confronted at once: although agricultural output had reached the prewar level, the agricultural surplus available to be marketed outside of the village was still far from the prewar level. It had, in fact, reached only 70 percent of the prewar level in 1925–26. Yet this agricultural surplus was needed (1) to feed the growing urban working population, (2) to provide the exports to be exchanged for machinery, and (3) to be used as inputs in industrial processing and production. Clearly, it was an essential ingredient in any rapid industrialization program. In effect, the agricultural surplus had to be the "savings" upon which investment for rapid industrialization depended.

Why was the marketable surplus of agriculture much smaller in the 1920s than it had been in prerevolutionary Russia? Even the Communist party found it hard to put all the blame on the rich peasant, or kulak, since the kulaks produced only 15 percent of the total output (though they had produced about 50 percent before the war). The kulak did exert an additional restraining influence over the market through his role as a middleman, trader, and speculator in the grain market; but just how much harm this speculation did is hard to document.

On the contrary, it is quite clear that the problem lay with the behavior of the great mass of poor and middle peasants, who now produced some 85 percent of the total grain. Generally speaking, the problem was simply that the relatively equal distribution of land achieved by the peasants was itself the main reason for the decline of the marketable surplus. The agrarian revolution of 1917 and the modest monetary tax on the peasants that was introduced during NEP had resulted not only in peasant control but in the ability of the peasants to keep much of the harvest for their own consumption (which had previously been at or sometimes below subsistence level).

In order to show the problem more concretely, we present in Table 5.1 a comparison of the grain market situation of the prerevolutionary period with that of the Soviet period of the mid 1920s. The table shows that in both periods the largest production units (landowners' estates and, later, collective farms and state farms) produced a small part of the total grain. But each large unit marketed almost half of its total production. One problem was simply that state and collective farms

Table 5.1
The Grain Market Problem, 1914 and 1927

Type of farm	Grain production (% of total)	Ratio of marketed grain to grain production (%)
Prerevolution (1913–14)		
Landowners	12	47
Kulaks (or rich peasants)	38	34
Poor and middle peasants	50	15
Total (in %)	100	26 (average percentage marketed)
Total (in poods)[a]	5,000,000,000	1,300,000,000
Soviet (1926–27)		
State and collective farms	2	47
Kulaks (or rich peasants)	13	20
Poor and middle peasants	85	11
Total (in %)	100	13 (average percentage marketed)
Total (in poods)[a]	4,749,000,000	630,000,000

Source: The Central Statistical Department of the USSR, cited in Stalin, in International Press Correspondence (June 14, 1928).
a. 1 pood equals 36 pounds.

owned only one-sixth as much land and produced only one-sixth as much total grain as had the large landowners before the Revolution. The next largest production units (those held by the kulaks or rich peasants) declined in land area and production by more than half since the Revolution, and they also declined considerably in the percentage of grain marketed. Nevertheless, it is clear that the major source of the problem lay with the smallest landholdings (those of the poor and middle peasants), whose share of land and production rose, in the two time periods, from 50 to 85 percent, but who marketed only 15 percent of their grain before the Revolution and only 11 percent at the later time.

The great egalitarian advance in land ownership—an unfortunate advance from the viewpoint of development planning—proved to be the greatest barrier to rapid industrialization in that it reduced the marketable agricultural surplus. This land reform had the further disadvantage of reducing the size of the average landholding to such an extent that it was unprofitable to buy and use efficiently more modern agricultural machinery. In addition, the marketable surplus was reduced even further because of the continued high industrial prices and the successful attempts to hold down agricultural prices— thus inducing farmers to use more of their output themselves rather than to offer it for sale on the market. As a result of these continued and ever-worsening terms of trade, grain collections by the government in 1927–28 were about 14 percent lower than the previous year, although the total grain production had fallen only a little more than 7 percent. The downward trend in collections continued into the harvest year 1928–29.

Industry

During the period 1924 to 1927 industrial production rose rapidly (see Table 5.2). Official data for the period are probably biased upward, but they do indicate well enough the general trends in production.

Table 5.2 Volume of Industrial Output in the USSR, 1913–1927	
Year	**Output**
	(as % of 1913)
1913	100
1917	71
1921	31
1925	73
1926	98
1927	111

Source: Central Statistical Board of the USSR, *National Economy of the USSR* (Moscow: Foreign Languages Publishing House, 1957), p. 41.

Most of the increase in industrial production, however, consisted of output from reconstructed facilities rather than from newly built plant and equipment. By 1927, reconstruction was complete and the more demanding job of capital expansion loomed ahead. Moreover, the emphasis during this period had been on light industry rather than on the heavy industry that required so much larger and longer-term commitment of resources. The Party came to agree on the need for rapid industrialization and began to devote more and more resources to it. The main issue under discussion was how and where to get the resources for further industrial investment. Trotsky was still being attacked for overestimating the importance of rapid industrialization, and the tempo and methods of industrialization remained vague. We shall return in detail to the issues of the great debate over industrialization in a later section.

Trade

During the latter years of NEP, the government and cooperatives became dominant in wholesale trade. In retail trade, however, private traders were still quite important. Finally, in foreign trade in the early 1920s, in addition to the government trading agency, there had been some trade by industrial "trusts" and even by individuals. Now, a complete monopoly of foreign trade was given to one government agency, a condition which has persisted ever since. Yet foreign trade was not as useful to industry as expected, partly because of barriers set up by foreign countries and partly because of a lack of grain collected for export. In the earliest years of the Soviet regime many anti-Communist countries joined in the *cordon sanitaire*, an attempt to cut off all trade with the Soviet Union—even in medical supplies. By the late 1920s, however, a gradual increase in the number of countries willing to trade with the so-called Bolshevik menace had resulted in a substantial recovery in foreign trade—though a few nations have maintained special political barriers against Soviet trade to this day (as we shall see in a later chapter).

Finance

The hyperinflation was finally ended by a monetary reform in the spring of 1924. All outstanding cash currency, 800 quadrillion of so-called sovnaks, were called out of circulation and redeemed for 15 million new rubles, that is, at a rate of roughly 50 billion sovnaks per ruble. The treasury was no longer allowed to finance budget deficits by printing notes; deficits had to be covered by bank credit.

Since the bank was a creature of the government, however, this restriction may have been more word than deed. Direct income taxes, collected mostly from the farm population, had been the most important source of government revenue in the first few years of NEP. Sales and excise taxes, however, were becoming more important all the time, especially after the "right wing" managed to have the income tax on farmers reduced in 1925. The importance of sales taxes meant that the increased expenditure on heavy industry fell as a burden, no longer on the rich farmers alone, but on all groups of the population (and sales taxes fall more heavily in percentage terms on the poorest workers). Meanwhile, inflationary deficit spending was much reduced, and price control held prices fairly stationary.

Planning

Serious attempts at central planning did begin by 1924 or 1925, but they were limited to the segments of heavy industry most closely controlled by central authorities. Actually, the most ambitious earlier planning was the plan for electrification of the whole country, begun in 1920 by the State Commission for Electrification, known as GOELRO. Electrification was given priority at Lenin's insistence, and we are reminded of his aphorism: "Soviets plus Electrification equals Communism." In 1921, the GOELRO was merged into the State Planning Commission (or Gosplan).

More general planning first developed out of attempts at control of the soaring industrial prices. Some general planning was also necessary to eliminate the heavy unemployment that had resulted from the flood of the rural population into the more attractive towns. The combination of rising urban population and a lack of capital for plant and equipment presented the early Soviet government with a type of unemployment problem common to many other underdeveloped countries.

The first thing that might be called an attempt at overall planning of the whole economy was the document issued by the State Planning Commission, which was known as the *Control Figures for 1925-26* (though there were a few control figures issued as early as 1923-24).[3] This little hundred-page booklet was epoch-making as the first pioneering effort to formulate a rational and unified plan, rather than compile a mere collection of the proposed projects of different government departments. It was very sketchy, however, and had little practical effect, though it greatly stimulated further efforts. It was more in the nature of a trial run and was not really meant to be operational.

From 1926 to 1928 the government attempted to formulate the First Five-Year Plan. Besides the argument over the practical content of

---

3. The earliest recorded effort was by P. I. Popov and others, *Balance of the National Economy of the USSR in the year 1923-24*, published in Russian in 1926; its introductory chapter was translated in Nicolas Spulber, ed., *Foundations of Soviet Strategy for Economic Growth: Selected Soviet Essays, 1924-1930* (Bloomington: Indiana University Press, 1964).

the Plan (to be discussed in the next section), Soviet leadership was held back by more theoretical uncertainties. The most eminent Communist theoreticians (Bukharin, Trotsky, and others) all agreed that a socialist economy needs no value theory nor theory of political economy because these relate only to "capitalism." Under socialism the economy would do whatever the planners wanted it to do without regard for economic laws, since "economic laws" apply only to the unregulated operation of a market economy and do not restrict the freedom of planners. This view leaves little room for a scientific approach to planning, except for engineering details. Those who held this view, that planners are completely free to set any goals, were called the *teleologists*.

On the other side were the *geneticists*, who insisted that planning was rigidly bound by the present state of things and had only limited room for maneuvering within existing trends. An example of the genetic approach was Kondratiev's argument that "planning work must avoid a fetishism of oversize calculations, which must bow before an understanding of those processes which are in actual motion in the economy; we must grasp these basic processes which confront us."[4]

Thus, he believed that planning must passively subordinate industrial growth to whatever development rate agriculture is likely to show. Another example of this line of thought was the argument by Bazarov and many others that the rates of growth in economic development would unavoidably follow descending curves according to the laws of diminishing marginal productivity. These writers were mostly older technical economists, who believed that the planners could only observe the "empirical regularities" of the past and then predict the "objective tendencies" of the future on that basis. Once again, this left little room for understanding how to construct a plan for the way economic development should take place. Even more defeatist were those (such as Rykov) who were just plain skeptical of man's ability to really construct a workable plan of any kind.

Obviously, in practice the planner must first know the existing conditions and past trends, but he then does have some freedom to choose among alternative roads of future development. The planner can use only existing resources, but he may use them in a large number of possible ways, some perhaps very different from the ways that have been used in the past. Eventually, the Soviet debaters came to realize that the practical questions were which methods of development to use, how fast to grow, and in what possible directions the economy might evolve.

---

4. Cited in M. Dobb, *Soviet Economic Development since 1917* (London: Routledge and Kegan Paul, rev. ed. 1966), 353.

The Great Debate

It is now time to turn to the political and economic debates of the period concerning the best road to a further growth of the economy. There are two different aspects to the problem of growth in a socialist economy. First, there is the question of the *initial* construction of socialist industry, especially in a country with only an underdeveloped agricultural economy. The second question concerns the rate of growth of an *established* socialist industry (considered in the next chapter of this book).

The whole period of the 1920s in the Soviet Union was witness to a vigorous debate on methods of rapid initial development.[5] The left wing of the Communist party, led by Trotsky in the 1920s, took the view that NEP must be quickly ended and a transition made to the rapid growth of socialist industry. They considered it necessary to build large-scale industry on the basis of modern technology but also considered it necessary for such modern technology to be extended into the countryside by the fullest encouragement of agricultural cooperatives to replace the tiny peasant farms. Yet Trotsky considered that the international political situation would prevent such a development until the revolution could spread to more advanced economies, capable of furnishing political support and economic aid to Soviet Russia. In this context, he denied "the possibility of socialism in a single country." Trotsky argued instead that:

> ... the contradiction inherent in the position of a workers' government functioning in a backward country where the large majority of the population is composed of peasants, can only be liquidated on an international scale in the arena of a worldwide proletarian revolution, [and that] the real growth of the socialist economy in Russia can take place only after the victory of the proletariat in the more important countries of Europe.[6]

Although Trotsky was the main proponent of the notion that socialist industry could not really expand rapidly in the Soviet Union until after the revolution triumphed in Europe, he nevertheless was also the main proponent of the attempt to industrialize as rapidly as possible, while recognizing the difficulty of doing so under the existing conditions. (In fact, it seems that Trotsky later came to believe that economic growth was possible under these conditions but that such forced industrialization would lead to harsh political dictatorship over the proletariat.) The argument in favor of the all-out expansion of industry at the expense of agriculture came to be the

---

5. For a comprehensive discussion, see Alexander Erlich, *The Soviet Industrialization Debate, 1924–28* (Cambridge: Harvard University Press, 1960).

6. Cited in Dobb, *Soviet Economic Development*, 178.

principal plank of Trotsky's opposition faction in the Party. He contended that it was unfortunate but true that rapid industrialization
under the existing circumstances could come only at the expense of
the peasantry. Furthermore, Trotsky argued strongly that such industrial expansion could be achieved only by detailed and comprehensive economic planning under the direction of the State Planning
Commission.

The more systematic economic analysis of the left-wing position
was clearly stated by the very original Soviet economist, Preobrazhensky.[7] Preobrazhensky spoke of the need for "primitive socialist accumulation." Marx had described "primitive capitalist
accumulation"[8] as the period in which "capitalist" countries first
acquire the initial capital for rapid industrialization; they acquire
most of it by piracy or colonial plunder or the slave trade, or some
other means of extraction from other countries.

Primitive socialist accumulation means the accumulation of capital
for socialist industry from "the surplus product of all pre-socialist
economic forms." Of course, when socialism comes to an advanced
private enterprise economy, the primitive accumulation will be completed by the revolutionary acquisition of all large firms. In a relatively underdeveloped economy, however, there is little to take over,
so the problem is one of constructing industry from scratch.

Where could capital be obtained? The Soviet Union in the 1920s had
neither the desire nor the strength to engage in the imperialist
plundering of other countries. It was also impossible to obtain large
foreign loans or investments. Most foreign governments still backed
the return of the pre-Soviet government or even the Czars. Moreover,
they feared that the Soviets might confiscate any new loans and
investments just as they had done the old. At any rate, they were more
willing to hinder Soviet development than help it.

Thus, the Soviet Union would have to develop solely from its own
meager resources. Preobrazhensky argued that up to a half of all the
profits of Soviet trade and industry were going into private hands
under the NEP. He advocated nationalizing these enterprises so as to
increase the profits available for government investment in industry.
Yet Preobrazhensky pointed out that Soviet industry was still so small
that, even including private profits, the internal reinvestments of its
surplus product (above workers' wages and replacement costs)
would mean only minute amounts of new capital each year. A big
push in investment was necessary to create new factories in the many
related industries all at once. Without this initial surge of capital
creation, development could never get off the ground, let alone gain
momentum.

---

7. See E. A. Preobrazhensky, "On Primitive Socialist Accumulation" (written 1926), translated in Spulber, *Foundations of Soviet Strategy.*

8. See Marx, *Capital*, Vol. I, Part VIII.

Since sufficient capital could not be obtained from foreign countries nor from the infant Soviet industry, the only remaining possibility was to extract it from agriculture. In agriculture, presocialist private ownership prevailed. In fact, in 1928 there were still twenty-six million private farms in the Soviet Union. The left wing, led by Preobrazhensky, urged that the agricultural surplus be extracted by high taxes and by setting high monopoly prices on the industrial goods that farmers must buy (which amounts to the same thing as taxation of the product of the private farmers).

The right wing of the Communist party, led by Bukharin, criticized this policy on several grounds.[9] First, they argued that it would not succeed because the farmer would either cut back production or use his ingenuity to hide his products and then either consume them himself or sell them on the black market. Second, Bukharin argued that such a harsh policy would break the vital political alliance between the workers and the farmers.

Third, Bukharin presented his own policy, which he believed would reach the same goal more easily. He had been impressed by the results of the NEP, which had allowed freedom for private trade and private agriculture. Under the NEP, large-scale industrial output had tripled from 1920 to 1924, though this was reconstruction and not new expansion. So Bukharin recommended more of the same, which would allow the farmer to prosper and grow rich. Eventually he would use moderate taxes on the farmer to build industry, while very gradually forming voluntary farmer cooperatives to end the rule of rich farmers. Bukharin wrote:

> ... the ideologists of Trotskyism believe that a maximum annual transfer from the peasant agriculture into industry secures the maximum rate of development of industry in general. But this is clearly incorrect. The maximum continued rate of growth will be experienced... when industry will advance on the basis of rapidly growing agriculture.[10]

Another right-wing writer, Rykov, expressed the idea that industry would eventually acquire the capital for expansion simply out of the continually increasing turnover of goods traded between agriculture and industry.[11]

Preobrazhensky and Trotsky countered with two arguments. First was the political argument that the right-wing policy would strengthen the rich farmers and thereby weaken the Communist political base. Second, the Left argued that their own policy of rapid industrialization would eventually result in an increased flow of manufactured consumer goods to the villages, which would finally

---

9. See, e.g., N. I. Bukharin, "Notes of an Economist" (first published in 1927), in Spulber, *Foundations*, 258–265.

10. Bukharin, "Notes of an Economist," 260.

11. Cited in Dobb, *Soviet Economic Development*, 187.

solve the so-called scissors problem and peasant dissatisfaction once and for all. Third, they claimed that small amounts of resources drawn very gradually from agriculture would never get industry moving on a basis of self-sustaining expansion (because of the necessity for an initial "big push" to development).

Stalin, leading the Center faction, first joined with the Right to defeat the Left and to exile Trotsky. Then he swung over to an ultra-left position to help defeat the right wing. Finally, when Stalin became sole ruler, he "solved" the problem.

This political evolution may be traced most clearly through the record of the Congresses of the Communist Party of the Soviet Union during the 1920s. At the Tenth Party Congress in 1921 Lenin introduced the New Economic Policy, based on a temporary retreat to more private capitalism and more use of the market. The Eleventh Party Congress in 1922, still under Lenin, endorsed the NEP but called for no further retreats from socialism. At the Twelfth Party Congress in 1923, with Lenin sick and unable to attend, the right-wing policy became evident in the enthusiastic arguments for the continuation of NEP and for further strong alliances with all of the peasantry. The Thirteenth Party Congress, in 1924 after the death of Lenin, attacked Trotsky's policies, alleging that they meant rapid industrialization only with impossible sacrifices by the peasantry. Instead, Stalin— supported by the other main leaders, Kamenev, Zinoviev, and Bukharin—supported the right-wing policy of relying on the rich peasants to build up agriculture as a base for eventual industrial expansion. Some important concessions were made to the rich peasants at this time, as noted earlier.

In 1925 at the Fourteenth Party Congress, Stalin and the Center faction fully supported the right-wing policies, of which Bukharin had become the major spokesman. They continued to call for conciliation with the rich peasant and a policy of "balanced growth," which meant (according to the Left) that industrial development would continue to be limited by the snail's pace of agricultural development. Now, however, Kamenev and Zinoviev had joined Trotsky in the Left opposition. They emphasized that industry must be rapidly developed, even if it meant taking resources from agriculture. Bukharin replied that NEP was not so much a retreat as "a regrouping of forces and an advance upon a reorganized front line." On the contrary, he called for an end to the last remnants of War Communism, that is, an end to any hostility toward the rich peasant. The Left feared the policy of letting the rich peasants lease land and hire workers; even more, they feared that the whole peasantry was gaining economically at the expense of industry and the urban worker. Stalin replied that the rich peasant and the private trader were really not doing so well as the Left opposition thought they were. He stated that in internal trade the share of the private trader had declined to 25 percent, while the share of the government had risen to 50 percent and the share of the cooperatives had risen to 25 percent. He generally avoided, however, specific figures on agriculture, where concentration in favor of the rich peasant was continuing at a fair pace.

In 1926 and 1927 the right wing (led by Bukharin, Rykov, and the trade union leader, Tomsky) continued to argue loudly for the encouragement of peasant agriculture, even at the risk of restoring petty capitalism in the countryside. Bukharin argued that agriculture must be given top priority for a long time, during which government-owned industry would develop parallel to peasant agriculture, each helping the other. The rate of growth of industry would, presumably, have to be held back to the slow rate of agricultural growth. Bukharin even made a political faux pas once by saying to the peasants (in a speech in April 1925), "enrich yourselves." As late as 1928, Bukharin was still arguing that the lack of food and consumer goods was mostly caused by the fact that industry was expanding too rapidly, and its rate of growth should be lowered accordingly. A follower of his (Frumkin) wrote in November 1928 that "we should not hinder the kulak undertakings in their production," state farms should not be expanded too rapidly, and less should be invested in industry than had been planned.[12]

Against this continued right-wing outpouring, the Left argued that as a result of lenient government policies the rich peasants were growing in power. In various regions, the rich peasant farms numbered from 15 to 25 percent of the total, had 25 to 45 percent of the total cultivated land, and owned 40 to 60 percent of the agricultural machinery. Stalin's answer to the left opposition was to expel all of them from the Party in October 1927, two months before the Fifteenth Party Congress. Trotsky was exiled to Siberia and then out of the country.

The Stalinist Solution

The interesting and thoroughly unexpected development (certainly unexpected by Bukharin and the Right) was that at the Fifteenth Party Congress Stalin adopted the left policies and attacked the Right. Stalin claimed that industry had recovered the prewar level by 1926 and had surpassed it by 18 percent in 1927. While industry was doing well, in agriculture the total harvest was barely above prewar. Thus, the critical grain production was only 91 percent of prewar, and the marketed surplus of grain was only 37 percent of prewar. Stalin concluded that collectivization was necessary: "The way out is to unite the small and dwarf peasant farms gradually and surely, not by pressure but by example and persuasion, into large farms based on

---

12. Ibid., 205.

common, cooperative cultivation of the soil, with the use of agricultural machines and tractors and scientific methods of intensive agriculture."[13] He defended this sudden policy shift by arguing that conditions had changed considerably since the last Party Congress, that now the peasants were in a mood favorable to collective farming, that the Party was now strong and capable enough to lead the change, and that industry was now enough developed to supply the new collective farms with sufficient machinery and tractors. Whether this argument was true or merely politically convenient, the Fifteenth Party Congress (packed with Stalin's supporters) agreed "to build the industrialization program upon the introduction of large-scale farming on cooperative lines as its cornerstone."

Stalin's solution to economic development was bloody and costly, but it did accomplish his objectives. He "persuaded" the unwilling farmers (and not only the small farmers, but especially the richer farmers) to give up their private farms and livestock and to join collective farms. These collectives were supposed to be cooperative ventures but were actually under strict central control. It should be noted that the earlier proposals by Bukharin had only casually mentioned peasant cooperation and collectives, and even Trotsky had thought of the process as a very long and gradual one, not an overnight collectivization. Thus, until Stalin acted in favor of collectivization in 1928, no one else had seriously considered it as more than a minor component in raising the marketed agricultural surplus.

At the end of 1928, the pace of collectivization was suddenly accelerated. Then the state increased its forced collections from the collective farms. Peasant resistance grew, and the brutal process of forced collectivization soon led to violence.

Stalin's "persuasion" to collectivize, which began in earnest in the fall of 1929, was marked by a civil war in which large numbers of peasants were killed or exiled to Siberia for resisting collectivization. Livestock were slaughtered by the farmers, and crop production fell. Yet Stalin succeeded in two objectives. First, the large size of collectives eventually allowed the introduction of machinery and more efficient farming (though they were anything but efficient in the first few years). Second, and this was most important, in spite of the lower total production, he greatly increased the amount of grain actually marketed and available for government use as "capital." That Stalin succeeded in increasing grain collections is clear (see Table 5.3).

Production of grain rose only a little, but government procurements—collected from the farms—doubled from 1928 to 1930. Even with a famine in 1931, the government still increased its collections a little more. This would have been impossible to achieve had the

---

13. Ibid., 222.

Table 5.3
Output, Government Collections, and Exports of Grain—
1928 to 1932

	Output	Government collections	Exports
	(in millions of tons)		
1928	73	11	0.1
1929	72	16	0.3
1930	77	22	4.8
1931	70	23	5.1
1932	70	19	1.7

Source: Michael Ellman, "Did the Agricultural Surplus Provide the Resources for the Increase in Investment in the USSR During the First Five Year Plan?" *Economic Journal* (Dec. 1975): 847.

peasants not been collectivized. In collective farms and under strict government control, farmers were no longer in a position to withhold grain either for speculation or for their own use. The government levied upon the farms so-called obligatory deliveries—in effect, a tax in kind—which had first claim on whatever output was produced. The amount of deliveries was based on the number of acres owned by the farm or in cultivation. Thus, it did not matter how much the farm produced, or whether or not there was a famine; the state's share remained stable since it was based on acreage, not output. The state did pay the farms for these deliveries—but at a fraction of their true cost of production, not to mention the high prices at which grain products were eventually sold in state stores. In effect, then, the mass collectivization combined with the obligatory deliveries was Stalin's technique for forcing the peasant to provide the bulk of the "capital" for the industrialization drive of the first two Five-Year Plans.

When we say that agriculture provided the "capital" for Soviet industrialization, we must be clear exactly what did and did not happen. Investment in 1932 in Soviet industry rose to four times its 1928 level. Some of this, in the form of raw materials and machinery and factories, came mainly from industry and construction themselves. Some of the investment came from imports, paid for mostly by' exports of Soviet grain (which rose, as shown in Table 5.3, from one hundred thousand tons in 1928 to over five million tons in 1931).

Agricultural output did *not* increase, nor did the agricultural surplus increase according to some analysts (in fact, there has been an extensive debate—led by J. Millar—in which the actual amount and importance of the agricultural surplus in this period has been strongly questioned).[14] Collectivization, however, did increase government collections of grain, potatoes, and vegetables.[15] These foods were used (1) for exports and (2) to feed millions of new workers in the cities. Since collectivization depressed rural living conditions—by its forced collections of food at low prices—it helped motivate millions of farmers to move to the cities to provide an industrial labor force. Of course, farmers were also attracted by the greater conveniences in the cities. At any rate, agriculture did (1) provide the industrial labor force, (2) feed it, and (3) pay for industrial imports by agricultural exports.

Farmers then constituted the majority of the Soviet population, as in most underdeveloped countries. Stalin's solution, therefore, amounted to keeping most of the population at a very low level of consumption, while using their "surplus" product for investment purposes. Since investment reached 25 to 35 percent of national income, this circumstance naturally resulted in a very rapid economic growth. Once industry got under way, the problem became a little easier since more of industry's own resources could be reinvested for further expansion. This solution meant high profits and restriction of wages, again postponing the increase of current consumption, this time, however, at the joint expense of the urban and rural worker.

Obviously, this model of economic development not only presumes heroic sacrifices in present consumption initially and for many years to come, but it also continues to reinforce the arguments for one-party dictatorship. No people will freely vote for such unpopular and drastic development measures in normal circumstances. Only a one-party dictatorship allowing no opposition could possible enforce these "temporary" measures for the development of an "infant" economy. This situation was surely a basic ingredient prolonging the Stalinist dictatorship in its protection of the "infant" USSR against the temptations of its own populace (who were in favor of more present consumption). But, one wonders, who decides when the infant is grown up enough to introduce democracy?

---

14. The literature is all cited in three articles by Millar: James Millar, "Soviet Rapid Development and the Agricultural Surplus Hypothesis," *Soviet Studies* 22 (July 1970): 77–93. James Millar, "Mass Collectivization and the Contribution of Soviet Agriculture to the First Five-Year Plan," *Slavic Review* 33 (Dec. 1974): 750–66. James Millar, "A Note on Primitive Accumulation in Marx and Preobrazhensky," *Soviet Studies* 30 (July 1978): 384–93. Also see Ellman, cited in Footnote 15.

15. See Michael Ellman, "Did the Agricultural Surplus Provide the Resources for the Increase in Investment in the First Five Year Plan?" *Economic Journal* (Dec. 1975): 859. Also see Michael Ellman, "On a Mistake of Preobrazhensky and Stalin," *Journal of Development Studies* 14 (Apr. 1978): 353–56.

Recommended Readings

1. For detailed discussion of 1861 to 1917 development see Alexander Gerschenkron, "Problems and Patterns of Russian Economic Development," in Cyril E. Black, ed., *Transformation of Russian Society* (Cambridge: Harvard University Press, 1960).

2. Leonard Shapiro, *The Communist Party of the Soviet Union* (New York: Vintage, 1960).

3. A critical account of Soviet economic policies is in Alexander Baykov, *The Development of the Soviet Economic System* (Cambridge: The University Press, 1947).

4. A sympathetic account of the whole Soviet period is in Maurice Dobb, *Soviet Economic Development since 1917* (London: Routledge and Kegan Paul, Ltd., rev. ed., 1966).

5. A critical analysis of the Soviet debates appears in Alexander Erlich, *Soviet Industrialization Debate* (Cambridge: Harvard University Press, 1960).

6. The Soviet leaders and economists speak for themselves in the translations in Nicolas Spulber, ed., *Foundations of Soviet Strategy for Economic Growth: Selected Soviet Essays, 1924–1930* (Bloomington: Indiana University Press, 1964).

7. The definitive history of the Soviet economic and political developments of the early 1920s is E. H. Carr, *History of Soviet Russia* (London: Macmillan and Co., Ltd., 1950). This has appeared in several volumes with different subtitles.

8. Maurice Brinton, *The Bolsheviks and Workers' Control, 1917–1921* (Detroit: Black and Reed, 1972).

9. R. W. Davies, *The Industrialization of Soviet Russia*, Vols. I and II (New York: Macmillan, 1980).

10. Isaac Deutscher, *The Unfinished Revolution* (London: Oxford, 1967).

11. Editors of the Current Digest of the Soviet Press, *The USSR Today* (Columbus, Ohio: Current Digest of the Soviet Press, 1981), fifth ed.

12. David V. Smith, ed., *Bibliographic Guide to Soviet and East European Studies* (Boston: G. K. Hall and Co., 1981 ed.).

6

USSR

DEVELOPMENT FROM 1928 TO THE PRESENT

In this chapter we begin with a sketch of Soviet political development from 1928 through 1956. We then examine the major reason why dictatorship continued and intensified in much of this period. We look at the ideology that sustained Stalinism and then examine political-economic development from 1928 through 1950. These investigations are followed by a general theoretical discussion of economic growth in centrally planned economies. Finally, we present and analyze the Soviet growth record from 1950 to the present.

Political History, 1928 to 1956

We saw how, after the Revolution, democracy and freedom were limited step by step: (1) banning monarchist and capitalist parties, (2) banning other socialist parties, and (3) banning factions within the Communist party. Freedom of discussion continued in the Party until 1928, when Joseph Stalin won undivided power. His main opponent, Leon Trotsky, was exiled in 1928 and was finally murdered in Mexico in 1940. The other old Bolshevik leaders, such as Bukharin, mostly confessed their "errors" and continued to work under Stalin's direction until the mid 1930s. In the purge trials from 1936 to 1938 most of the old Bolshevik leaders were executed. Tens of thousands of possible—or even rumored—opponents were killed. Not only were Communists in other factions executed, but most of the potential leaders from Stalin's own faction were executed. For example, three-fourths of his own handpicked delegates to the Communist Congress of 1934 were eventually executed, according to Nikita Khrushchev, Stalin's successor.

With a small group of loyal supporters, Stalin ruled alone from 1928 until his death in 1953. Stalin ruled not only the Soviet Union but also all the other Communist parties of the world through an organization known as the Communist International. In the Soviet Union, in this fourth political stage, no freedom of speech was allowed, and violators were punished with prison or death. After Stalin's death, the Soviet leaders continued most of Stalin's policies of repression until 1956. Even in that period (1953–1956), however, no one was actually executed for political crimes except the old chief of the secret police, named Beria. In 1956 came major changes that will be explored later. The question here is why dictatorship increased throughout the 1930s and continued at only slightly lower levels until 1956.

Economic Backwardness and Rapid Industrialization

In 1917 the Soviet Union was a poor and economically underdeveloped country. Many of its resources and industries were foreign-owned. A great many of the underdeveloped countries, from the Soviet Union to Somalia, have tended toward both "socialist" state ownership of the means of production and a dictatorial one-party control of political life. Why should economic backwardness generate both state ownership and dictatorship? These are countries that have a burning desire for rapid economic growth. Yet, they are also largely poor, agrarian countries with little modern industry in buildings, equipment, skilled workers, or experienced managers.

Government ownership (which they call socialism) is viewed as a useful instrument of industrialization in the underdeveloped countries. For one thing, there are few educated and experienced planners; thus, the central government can best make use of the ones that exist, whereas many decades might be required for the voluntary emergence of bold, private entrepreneurs. Furthermore, the extreme lack of capital in the underdeveloped countries can most easily be remedied by governmental control of resources. The government can tax the rich, gather the small savings of the poor, and expropriate foreign profits, in order to invest by itself in new factories and equipment.

It is thus clear why "socialist" government ownership may be chosen as an instrument to overcome backwardness; but why does backwardness also generate one-party dictatorship? The reason lies within exactly the same set of circumstances.

There is a conflict between rapid long-run growth and immediate consumption. Concretely, the Soviet leadership discovered that to gather the resources required to build industry, it was necessary to take some food and raw materials away from the farm population. Without foreign investment, agriculture had to be the main source of the resources to build industry quickly (though real wages were also reduced).

As shown in Chapter 5, Stalin "solved" the resource problem by forcefully putting the peasantry into collective farms from which the entire surplus could be taken (though there is controversy over its importance). This course of action was at the cost of a long stagnation or drop in living standards and was accompanied by violent resistance by much of the farm population. Such a sudden and unpopular transformation (unpopular to the peasant majority) could not have been accomplished without a dictatorship. The main historical issue is whether the Soviet industrial transformation could have been made somewhat more slowly and with more democratic consent.

A democratic socialism could *not* have industrialized as rapidly as the Soviet Union did, since the necessary sacrifices by the peasantry did not meet the approval of the peasants—who were the majority of the voters. It certainly may be argued that a slower industrialization would not have allowed the Soviet Union to survive the attack of Hitler's Germany; this was Stalin's strongest and most defensible argument for super-rapid industrialization. (On the contrary, some writers have argued that a more democratic regime would have strengthened the political loyalty of the Soviet people on the eve of World War II.) At any rate, it is clear that this all-out industrialization drive was a key factor in the intensification and perpetuation of Stalin's dictatorship in the 1930s.

In the early 1940s there was extensive mobilization for the Second World War, which continued the atmosphere of emergency, discipline, and repression of dissenting views. The Second World War devastated the Soviet economy, leaving twenty million people dead and a third of all factories and housing destroyed. The late 1940s witnessed an effort to recover and reindustrialize within a few years, entailing enormous sacrifices and requiring repression for the same reasons as the initial industrialization drive. This was followed by the Cold War in the 1950s, which artificially continued the same atmosphere.

Briefly, according to most of the expert studies, there are three groups of reasons for the continuing Soviet dictatorship. First, there was the prerevolutionary situation: (1) the system of production was still part feudal; (2) there was autocratic rule by the Czar, with very little experience with democratic process; (3) the opposition parties were driven underground, so they did not develop a democratic process or tradition among their members but had, rather, an elitist or vanguard view of their role; (4) poverty and illiteracy prevented knowledgeable political participation; and (5) the rural, backward economy made ultra-rapid industrialization a Socialist goal. Second, there was the rough process of transition, including (1) the First World War, (2) the Revolution and bloody civil war, (3) foreign intervention by fourteen armies, (4) chaos, economic devastation, and very low production, and (5) an already tiny urban working class, much of which was killed or dispersed. Third, later developments included (1) a harsh industrialization drive, taking surplus from agriculture, (2) collectivization of unwilling peasants, which resulted in extensive violence, (3) the enormous destruction of the Second World War, and (4) the Cold War, which isolated the Russians and led to a continuing heavy military burden. (Note that most dictatorships in the capitalist countries are also in developing countries.)

Political Development, 1956 to the Present

In 1956, at the Twentieth Party Congress of the Soviet Communist Party, Khrushchev pointed out that the situation since 1917 had greatly changed with respect to "counterrevolutionary" violence. Because of the power of the Soviet Union and China, Khrushchev held that in those countries with a long democratic tradition there may occur in the future a peaceful transition to socialism through a parliamentary majority. The power of the Soviet Union and China makes a difference (according to Khrushchev) because most of the violence of civil war in modern times can be attributed to foreign intervention. The 1917 Revolution in Russia was brief and largely peaceful before the intervention of foreign powers. The mildly socialist Spanish government of 1936 might have quickly overcome Franco but for his powerful Italian and German backing. Therefore, Khrushchev said, if foreign intervention is prevented, in many countries socialism may come into power and remain in power in a peaceful and full democratic manner. This proposition of Khrushchev remains controversial among Communists, with many rejecting it. The Eurocommunists—especially in Italy—do believe in a peaceful and democratic transition to socialism in the countries of advanced capitalism where high incomes, literacy, and democratic traditions prevail; but few accept it for the Third World countries where poverty, illiteracy, and dictatorship prevail.

Although their steps were slow and hesitant, the post-Stalin Soviet leadership—dealing with an educated population in an urban industrialized country—did liberalize Soviet politics to an extent. First, there is some evidence that, in addition to the General Secretary and the tiny Politburo, the more numerous Central Committee members are now more fully involved in the decision-making process. Second, there has been some increased tolerance of criticism in the press. Third, Stalin's police terror has been denounced, the number of political prisoners has been reduced, due process has increased, and there have been only two political executions since the execution of the secret-police chief, Beria, in 1953 (both victims were convicted of foreign espionage).

Nevertheless, the Soviet elite wishes to defend its privileged position, so progress is not smooth, and there has been some regression to Stalinist-type methods. The most important manifestations of this regression have been, in foreign policy, the tragic invasions of Hungary and Czechoslovakia, the support of repression in Poland, and the military intervention in Afghanistan and, in domestic policy, the continued censorship and harassment of any Soviet opposition.

Soviet Ideology: Democracy and Dictatorship

The reality of the Soviet Union (or Union of Soviet Socialist Republics, to give it its full title) is that it has government ownership plus a one-party political dictatorship. Stalinist ideology claimed that this was "socialism" plus a "dictatorship of the proletariat." It is socialism only if that is defined in the narrowest possible legalistic way to mean government ownership of the means of production. If *socialism* means ownership and control by the people, the public, or even the working class, then the Soviet socioeconomic system is something else. Neither is it capitalism: there is virtually no private ownership; no private dividends or profits; no inheritance of private capital; no private exploitation; and no general unemployment because of over-production. It might be called "governmentism" or "statism."

On the political side, the term "dictatorship of the proletariat" was used as a smokescreen by Stalin. Marx spoke in a general sociological manner of the "dictatorship of the bourgeoisie" to mean bourgeois rule, *whether democratic or dictatorial in political form*. Similarly, Marx used the term "dictatorship of the proletariat" to mean rule by the working class. Since the working class is the vast majority, it could rule *only* through democratic political forms. Hence, "dictatorship of the proletariat" meant democratic working class rule for Marx. Since it has been used so differently, as a fig leaf in Communist countries to cover political dictatorship by a small group, the term "dictatorship of the proletariat" has become ambiguous and misleading, according to those Marxists who believe that socialism without democracy is not true to Marx's vision of socialism.

To see how Marx used the term "dictatorship of the proletariat," one need only read his one case study of it. Marx's example of a dictatorship of the proletariat (or socialist democracy) was the short-lived Paris Commune of 1871, under which the city of Paris had multiple conflicting parties, elections, freedom of speech, workers' councils managing the factories, and other democratic practices. Marx wrote that "the Commune was formed of the municipal council-lors, chosen by universal suffrage in various wards of the town, re-sponsible and revokable at short terms."[1] Marx assumed that so-cialism meant democratic, public control of the economy and local workers' control of production; he certainly never condoned dictato-rial rule by a small elite over the government and the economy.

---

1. Karl Marx, *The Civil War in France* (New York: International Publishers, 1948), 12.

Conversely, Lenin in *State and Revolution*, written in the midst of the Russian Revolution and never completed, did lay a theoretical basis (though confused and nebulous) for the later Stalinist attack on democratic processes. Lenin presents a two-stage view of socialism and the socialist state. The first form of the socialist state is a "dictatorship of the proletariat." It implies more than the class rule of the working class, which was all that Marx meant by it. For Lenin, it means an unrestricted attack on the bourgeoisie by the workers' state to ensure the transition to socialism. It means no voting rights and no civil liberties for the capitalists or their political parties.

The second stage comes, according to Lenin, when the capitalist class has been completely eliminated and socialism begins to evolve into a classless, coercion-less communism (in which all goods and services are free, so there is *no* income inequality). In this second stage, Lenin followed Marx and Engels in speaking of the "withering away of the state" as coercion becomes unnecessary. Lenin wrote:

> It is constantly forgotten that the . . . withering away of the State means the withering away of democracy. . . . Democracy is a *state* which recognizes the subordination of the minority to the majority, i.e., an organization for the systematic use of *force* by one class against another, by one section of the population against another.[2]

When Leninists speak of the state, they speak mainly of the coercive apparatus of repression against the majority (or against the minority), including armies, police, and prisons. Any Marxist would agree that such repressive instruments should "wither away." In fact, the Soviet state built up an enormously strong secret police, army, and concentration camps—while explaining that these were "temporary" measures on the road to "withering away of the state." That argument might be useful to the Soviet party and government leadership; most West European and U.S. Marxists do not accept it as a satisfactory explanation.

To be sure, it seems perfectly clear that a socialist society must *increase* the government administration of economic activity (even if many decisions are decentralized to the local level). When the people, or the working class, take over the economy, they must have a mechanism for running it. So the purely administrative (nonrepressive) functions of local, regional, national, and world government will not wither away but must grow. The point is not to deny the need for administration, but to see that it is democratic in form and content. Unlike the anarchists (and Lenin in *State and Revolution*), Marx and Engels were clear that a democratic process is necessary even in a classless society so that the masses of people can participate in the

---

2. V. I. Lenin, *State and Revolution* (New York: International Publishers, 1932), 52.

decision-making process over the administrative functions of government. The alternative, as in the Soviet Union, is for the vastly expanded range of government economic decisions to be made undemocratically by a small group.

The first line of the Stalinist defense of dictatorship—still sometimes heard today—is that the class struggle becomes more violent under socialism, partly because remaining capitalist elements panic and partly because of foreign spies. So all the Communists executed by Stalin were really agents of foreign capitalists! The second line of Stalinist defense—also still heard today—contradicts the first line of defense: There is not increasing class conflict, but absolute harmony, only one class, so there is no need for democracy. Here is a utopian vision, used to defend repression, execution of opponents, and one-party (Soviet-party) dictatorship![3]

In truth, were there to be an open democratic socialist society, there would still be inequalities and conflict, even if all the "capitalists" should disappear. There is still a range of income distribution, differences in training, differences between city and rural areas, and differences between the few in political leadership and the millions not in leadership positions. Mao Zedong himself emphasized that even in socialism there are conflicts or "contradictions" between farm workers and industrial workers, between manual workers and intellectuals, and between ordinary individuals and government leaders or bureaucrats.[4]

Thus, even in a perfect socialism, there may be conflicts over educational reforms, which may pit the short-run interests of teachers against students. There may be conflicts over locating hospitals in city or rural areas, which may lead to short-run differences of interest between farm workers and industrial workers and, possibly, hospital workers. Each of these segments of the working class would have the right in a democratic socialist society to elect its own representatives and voice its own views. This requires factions within one party or entirely different parties. But each individual or group would have some vehicle to exercise free speech in an organized way with or against the majority of other voters.

The ongoing repression of the opposition and the disruption brought by leadership succession struggles in the Soviet Union and China underscores the desperate need in socialism (as in capitalism) for an orderly, democratic process of choosing leadership. Once leadership is chosen, it is forever necessary to criticize its errors and inefficiency. Both China and the Soviet Union allow and encourage criticism of the previous leaders, but never of the man in power. Thus,

---

3. See the astonishing defense of Stalinism in William Z. Foster, *History of the Three Internationals* (New York: International Publishers, 1953), 271.

4. Mao Tse-tung, *On the Correct Handling of Contradictions among the People* (New York: New Century Publishers, 1957).

Nikita Khrushchev was a near deity while in power but was reviled for all his mistakes *after* he was dethroned. The brilliant Marxist Rosa Luxemburg criticizes Soviet theory and points out the need for a nonviolent process of criticizing the *present* top leadership:

> Freedom only for the supporters of the government, only for the members of one party—however numerous they may be—is no freedom at all. Freedom is always and exclusively freedom for the one who thinks differently. Not because of any fanatical concept of "justice" but because all that is instructive, wholesome, and purifying in political freedom depends on this essential characteristic.[5]

In other words, in the viewpoint of democratic socialists, it is only by the exercise of freedom of speech and free elections that errors can be corrected, a minority can become a majority, a new leadership can be elected, and a leader can be prevented from becoming a dictator.

Socialism has the potential, according to democratic socialist arguments, to be more democratic than capitalism because there will be no private concentration of economic power which could control newspapers, television, and donations to political parties. Yet, dictatorship and lack of freedom, *if* they exist under government ownership, can be even more dangerous because there is concentration of economic power in the government. To protect citizens against arbitrary government control of jobs or of the media, it is necessary (as discussed in Chapter 1) to establish civil service guarantees against firing without cause, the right of the opposition to present its views in government-owned media, the right to use other nonprofit media, and the right of any party to compete in free elections.

We have now dealt with Soviet political development (briefly mentioning its economic context), as well as its defending ideology and its critics. It will be made clear in the following discussion that Soviet political development has profoundly affected Soviet economic development. The autocratic and repressive political culture in the USSR has led to excessive centralization and rigidity in its economic planning apparatus and has thereby hindered the quest for greater economic efficiency. We must now examine the economic development in the Soviet political context—remembering that politics and economics are never separate in reality.

The First Five-Year Plan (1928-1932)

The production targets which were finally accepted in 1929 for the period 1928–1933 were based on the following three optimistic assumptions: (1) no serious failure in harvests would occur during the

---

5. Rosa Luxemburg, *The Russian Revolution* (Ann Arbor: University of Michigan Press, 1961, written 1918), 69.

five-year period, (2) an expansion of exports and imports would occur, and (3) there would be increases in productivity and rising grain yield per acre. *Consumption was planned to increase by a "slight" 75 percent over the five-year period, but net investment in heavy industry was to increase by more than 200 percent.* The Five-Year Plan called for a fourth to a third of national income to be put into net investment (whereas net investment in Czarist Russia had averaged only about a tenth of national income). The *share* of consumption in national income was to fall from 77 percent to 66 percent, though we have noted that its absolute value was planned to increase about 75 percent in real terms as a result of the projected growth in output.

Collectivization of agriculture was to proceed at an extremely conservative pace. If this initially planned pace of collectivization (shown in Table 6.1) had been followed, there probably would have been no large-scale disruption of agriculture.

In the second year, 1929–30, of the Five-Year Plan, Stalin decided to revise upward the plan targets and thus effect an increase in the tempo of development. To accomplish this, he began an intensive collectivization drive. Stalin deemed it necessary to force the pace in agriculture if the main drive in industry was to be successful. The point was that a much greater surplus of food was needed to feed the rapidly growing urban working class, and only collectivization could ensure this flow from country to town. In other words, the Communist government was unable to extract more grain from the peasants without collectivization.

To some extent, the acute difficulties of the next three years—the slaughtering of livestock, the accentuated shortages of supply on the retail markets, the unanticipated enlargement of the labor force—can all be attributed to this forcing of the pace of collectivization in agriculture. In addition, all of the three conditions postulated above as prerequisite for plan fulfillment turned out to be less than favorable: (1) there *were* harvest failures, (2) the terms of international

---

Table 6.1
The Planned Collectivization

	Rural population (calculated in millions of farmers)		
	1927–28 (actual)	1932–33 (plan)	1933–34 (plan)
Collectivized	1.1	12.9	18.6
Private	122.0	121.0	116.9

Source: Naum Jasny in Franklyn Holzman, *Readings on the Soviet Economy* (Chicago: Rand McNally & Co., 1960).

trade moved drastically against the Soviet Union, and (3) productivity did not rise very much, mostly because of the disorganization caused by the vast transition from rural to urban life. All of the shortfalls in output below planned levels came out of consumption rather than investment. The result was that production of investment goods (according to somewhat biased official Soviet figures) increased by four times, but at the expense of consumption and current output.

The First Five-Year Plan was officially described as successfully completed in December 1932, just four and a quarter years after it began. According to official claims, planned investment targets were exceeded, though consumption fell far below the targets (and actually declined significantly according to Western estimates). In fact, investment in heavy industry was 50 percent higher, and investment in all industry 33 percent higher, than the planned targets for the whole five years! The production capacity of the iron and steel industry was increased by nearly two-thirds, and the beginnings of two entirely new metallurgical complexes were established at Kuznetsk in Western Siberia and at Magnitogorsk in the Urals. The machine-tool stock in the engineering industry was increased by nearly 100 percent, and electric power generating was also doubled.

There was also an important long-run gain registered in the improvement in the quality of labor. Thus, there was a 250-percent increase in the number of "specialists" in the economy, meaning persons with some kind of technological education at the university or secondary school level. It is true that the inexperience and lack of familiarity of most workers with machinery prevented any significant increase in productivity in this period. In later years, however, an important economic gain was reaped from the investment in human beings, both in schools and in on-the-job training.

In agriculture, meanwhile, only the poorest peasants were happy to join the collectives; the middle and rich peasants (kulaks) resisted bitterly. Yet the rich peasants held almost all the capital equipment and livestock, so the collectives could not be successful without their participation. Thus, the period of tolerance of the kulak suddenly ended—many were killed or exiled. The right-wing policy of letting them lease land and hire other peasants for wages was forbidden forever. On the contrary, the village soviets were allowed to take by force kulak livestock and capital equipment and all property above a certain minimum and to give it to the collective farms.

Conservatively estimated, the human toll reached hundreds of thousands. In 1929, only 4 percent of peasant households had been collectivized. By 1930, accelerated drive had forced the collectivization of 58 percent of the peasant households.

This first collectivization drive touched off violent peasant resistance. The slaughtering of privately held livestock drastically reduced the number of draft animals and cattle. By 1931, the number of cattle had fallen by one third, sheep and goats by one half, and horses by one fourth.

To prevent further disasters, Stalin reduced the pressure for collectivization in March 1930. People were allowed to leave the collective farms, and by May 1930, the percentage of collectivized households fell to 28 percent; by September, to 21 percent. Strong economic preferences given to the collective farmer and more gradual and judicious use of force, however, soon "persuaded" many to return. Thus, by a year later, in 1931, there were again 52 percent of the peasants on collective farms. In fact, by 1936, 90.5 percent of the peasantry was collectivized; this amount included virtually all the peasants located in heavily populated rural areas.[6]

The slaughter of draft animals left a gap in animal power used for cultivation, a gap which the small though rapidly growing number of machines was unable to fill (one reason for the small harvests of the early years of collectivization). Low grain yields and bad harvests contributed to a decline in product per acre. Yet government collections were maintained by the increase in sown area under collective farms. By the end of 1932, sown area under state and collective farms had increased eightfold over the 1928 level. Even more important, collectivization gave the government control of whatever output was produced, so the grain supply available to the state markedly increased.

In addition to the collective farms, the years 1929–30 and 1930–31 saw some effort to create gigantic state farms, to be run as government-owned factories. The collectives, we may recall, were supposed to be run as cooperatives with all profits and losses accruing to the members (though, in fact, their management was closely controlled by the central government until the reforms of the mid 1960s). The state farm was thus more "socialist" in character, and the Soviet government sank a very large investment into the state farms. They were mechanized as far as possible and run on a large scale. They did increase their production in these years, but *not* to a degree commensurate with the investment in them.

In summary, we can say that in spite of all the unforeseen calamities and in spite of some gross inefficiency and wastefulness, the First Five-Year Plan was successful in building the basis of future industrial production—the primary objective of the planners. Because of unforeseen difficulties, however, consumption did not rise by the planned 50 to 75 percent, but actually fell. This consumption decline resulted in vast human misery. In effect, an industrial base was built at the expense of the current consumption of the peasants and, to a lesser extent, industrial workers.

---

6. Naum Jasny, "Early Kolkhozy and the Big Drive," in Franklyn Holzman, *Readings on the Soviet Economy* (Chicago: Rand McNally & Co., 1960).

The Second Five-Year Plan (1933–1937)

The Second Five-Year Plan (covering the five years from 1933 through 1937) was devoted to the "completion of the reconstruction of the whole economy on a higher technical basis." The official idea was to advance not quite so rapidly but to really learn the new technologies and to solidify the industrial structure already erected. There was a strong effort to improve labor productivity both on the farm and in the new factories. A small decrease in the investment ratio was envisioned, and the emphasis was placed on consolidation and qualitative improvement. There was to be a relative increase in investment in consumer goods, and consumer goods output was *planned* to grow more rapidly (18 percent a year) than capital goods (14 percent a year). In fact, three-fourths of total investment was still in heavy industry, particularly in iron and steel, machine tool production, and nonferrous metal industries. Financially, the lessened pressures for investment and the fact of greater consumer goods production (partly the fortuitous result of bumper crops in 1935 and 1937) were reflected in the achievement of stable retail prices in 1936 and 1937.

The link between agriculture and industry improved during the Second Five-Year Plan. Supply deliveries became obligatory, were regularized as much as possible, and were paid for in advance at official purchase prices. These prices were so low as to constitute another form of taxation. The deliveries guaranteed a certain minimum supply to the towns, on the basis of which industrial plans and forecasts could be made. After more dislocations and disproportions in the first year of the Second Five-Year Plan, supplies of food to the cities did indeed improve markedly. By 1938, the agricultural surplus procured by the state was actually 250 percent higher than it had been in 1928.[7] By 1935, the improved supply had made it possible to abolish rationing.

The productivity of labor rose *faster* in the Second Plan than the planners had assumed. This was due in part to the greater incentives and in part to the fact that workers (who had formerly been farm workers) were finally learning how to use machinery. The former farm workers had come to accept some of the discipline and life style appropriate to factory work. At the same time, productivity was improved by the fact that many of the new, modern plants built in the First Plan period were just now being put into use and were reaching full capacity; they were staffed by workers who had eventually learned their jobs after several years of what amounted to on-the-job training. Although the labor force doubled in the First Plan, it rose

---

7. See Abram Bergson and Simon Kuznets, *Economic Trends in the Soviet Union* (Cambridge: Harvard University Press, 1963).

only gradually in the Second Plan, so industry had time to absorb further arrivals in an orderly manner.

The period of the Second Plan was generally a period in which the sacrifices of the First Plan were belatedly reflected in significant economic gains. By the end of the Second Plan, the Soviet Union surpassed all Western European countries in absolute production, though not in per capita production. By 1937, some 80 percent of all industrial output came from brand new or completely renovated factories built during the Five-Year Plans since 1928. Specifically, the capacity to produce iron and steel increased 400 percent between 1928 and 1938. The production of tractors and railway locomotives grew until the Soviet Union was the world's largest producer. Furthermore, during the Second Plan period alone—according to somewhat biased Soviet official figures—the output of machinery rose by 300 percent, though its target had been only 200 percent (but Western observers estimate that it actually only doubled).[8] On the other side, some consumer goods—especially textiles—fell far, far behind their planned goals, though they did rise somewhat in this period.

One indicator of the epochal changes in Soviet economic and social structure is the population figures for those years. According to the censuses, the urban population doubled from 1926 to 1939, while the rural population actually fell by 5 percent in those years, thus reflecting a vast internal migration from country to city, and from agriculture to industry—as well as the extensive loss of life from the harsh collectivization drive. From 1928 to 1938, the number of wage and salary earners had grown from 10 percent to more than a third of the labor force (most of these being urban workers), while cooperative producers (mostly collective farmers) grew to a full 55 percent of the whole. In the same period, the self-employed peasants, handicraft workers, landowners, and "capitalists" had shrunk from about 90 percent to little over 10 percent of the occupied population.

The Third Five-Year Plan (1938–1941)

The Third Five-Year Plan was formulated under the threat of war and was terminated after three and one-half years by the outbreak of war. Industrial growth targets were set at only 14 percent a year, much below the goals of the First and Second Plans. The reason for the lower-planned pace of economic development lay in the diversion of increasing amounts of resources to armaments. Not only were new plants built for military production, but existing plants—especially agricultural machinery factories—were converted to military uses.

---

8. See Norman Kaplan and Richard Moorsteen, "An Index of Soviet Industrial Output," *American Economic Review* (June 1960): 235.

Thus, not only consumption but even investment in productive facilities were curtailed by the defense effort. By 1940, investment plus defense spending together took at least half the Soviet national income. By 1941, defense spending had risen to three times the 1938 level and was far higher than productive investment. As a result, living standards declined again after 1937–38.

Growth in the 1930s

Table 6.2 shows the rates of growth of Soviet industry (leaving aside other sectors for the moment) in the 1930s, as calculated by the Soviet government and by various British and American observers.

Some interesting observations can be made about the data shown in Table 6.2. First, the very high Soviet figures are not so incredible when we note that, for each of the Plan periods, the highest non-Soviet estimates are much closer to the Soviet estimates than to the lowest estimates of their Anglo-American colleagues (though the Soviets' data are certainly higher than *any* foreign estimates). Second, *all* observers estimate very high growth rates for the first two

---

Table 6.2
Rates of Growth of Soviet Industrial Production, 1928–1940

Period	Source of data[a]					
	Official Soviet	Seton	Hodg-man	Jasny	Nutter	Kaplan-Moor-steen
First Five-Year Plan, 1928–1932:	19.2	16.0	14.5	13.3	8.8	11.4
Second Five-Year Plan, 1933–1937:	17.1	16.0	16.6	11.7	14.8	10.1
Third Five-Year Plan, 1938–1940:	9.4	6.7	5.0	6.8	3.8	1.8

Sources: Official Soviet figures from Central Statistical Board of the USSR, *National Economy of the USSR* (Moscow: Foreign Languages Publishing House, 1957), 41. Seton data from Francis Seton, "The Tempo of Soviet Industrial Expansion," *Manchester Statistical Society* (Jan. 1957), 30. Hodgman data from Donald Hodgman, *Soviet Industrial Production, 1928–51* (Cambridge: Harvard University Press, 1954), 89. Jasny data from Naum Jasny, *The Soviet Economy during the Plan Era* (Palo Alto, Calif.: Stanford University Press, 1951). Nutter data from G. Warren Nutter, *Growth of Industrial Production in the Soviet Union* (Princeton, N.J.: Princeton University Press, 1962), 158. Kaplan-Moorsteen data from Norman Kaplan and Richard Moorsteen, "An Index of Soviet Industrial Output," *American Economic Review* (June 1960): 235.

a. Figures given are for percentage of growth per year.

Five-Year Plans, averaging among them well over 12 percent per year for the 1928–1937 period. At that time, correctly or incorrectly, the rest of the world was impressed by the contrast with the United States, which was in a great depression and had a zero rate of industrial growth from 1929 to 1939. Third, all estimates show a severe decline in the growth rate in the Third Plan, reflecting the dislocation caused by war preparation (and also, perhaps, the purges of managerial personnel). Finally, one observer finds the same rate of growth in the First and Second Plans, and two find a *higher* growth rate in the Second Plan than in the First Plan! This makes sense since many factories that were constructed in the First Plan only came into operation in the Second Plan.

The question still remains as to why there is such a great range among these estimates of growth. Certainly, political bias plays some role, but we must look more carefully to understand how the same data can be used to reach such different estimates. To begin with, the USSR did not publish much data between the mid thirties and the mid fifties. The lack of availability of reliable information also meant that each investigator had to provide a (different) method to fill in the gaps.

These statistical difficulties were magnified in the 1930s because the Soviet economy did not merely grow quantitatively but was completely transformed from a rural, agricultural economy to an urban, industrial economy. How can such a transformation be adequately measured? One unique problem was that village handicrafts were being replaced by urban factory production. In the official figures, the rural handicraft production had not been recorded, whereas all factory production was recorded (one reason for the high official estimates). Second, in this period of political repression and dictatorship (especially after the purges of 1936 and 1937), Stalin used his control to keep some figures hidden and to issue some exaggerated claims by the use of peculiar definitions. Really abundant and reasonably defined Soviet economic statistics became available only after Stalin's death (though quite a bit of data were available until the mid 1930s). The third problem created by the rapid transformation was rapid changes in the quality of old products and the introduction of many new products, each of which involves arbitrary decisions on weighting in the construction of output indexes.

Last, the simple fact of a drastic change in the composition of the national product caused a difficult statistical problem. For example, let us say that the whole national product consisted in 1928 of shoes and steel. Suppose that far more shoes than steel were produced in 1928, so that shoes were *relatively* abundant and cheap while steel was scarce and expensive (that is, the price of steel was relatively high compared to the price of shoes). Finally, let us assume that from 1928 to 1937 the production of shoes increased by 10 percent, whereas the production of steel increased by 1,000 percent. As a result, in 1937 steel was relatively more abundant and its price was much lower relative to the price of shoes than it had been in 1928.

Changes of almost this magnitude did occur in the First and Second Five-Year Plans. But then what can we say about the growth of the total shoes-plus-steel national product? Was it 10 percent or 1,000 percent or some number in between? The estimate will depend on the weight, or "importance," of steel versus shoes, which in turn depends on the relative prices we attach to the two goods. Valued in 1928 prices (when steel was very high priced), the growth would be very high, weighing more strongly the 1,000-percent growth of steel. Valued in 1937 prices, however, when steel was less high priced and carried less weight, the growth of the total product would be much lower, reflecting more strongly the 10-percent growth of the shoe production. This qualitative change in the composition of Soviet output is one fundamental reason for the vast range of statistical estimates of growth for the period; each observer used a different set of price-weights, and each system was equally valid on its own assumptions (a numerical example of this problem and a more detailed discussion of Soviet accounting procedures are presented in Appendix A to this chapter). It should perhaps be noted here that after the 1930s, the broad industrial composition of Soviet output changed somewhat less rapidly, so estimates for the period after the Second World War fall within a much narrower range.

So far we have been speaking only of industrial production, but the economy includes several other sectors, which may move at very different rates. In fact, we have seen that in the 1930s agriculture had a poor growth record, and other sectors of low priority, such as services, also grew slowly. Therefore, the national income grew more slowly than industrial production.

The official Soviet data claim that Soviet National Income grew 14.6 percent a year from 1928 through 1940. A study by Abram Bergson claims that, if 1928 price-weights are used, the Soviet National Income grew 11.9 percent per year between 1928 and 1937.[9] On the other hand, if 1937 price-weights are used, the Soviet National Income grew only 5.5 percent per year between 1928 and 1937. Of course, even 5.5 percent is a high annual rate of growth, achieved by very few countries for a period as long as ten years. But the 11.9 percent rate—calculated by Bergson—is truly an exceptional rate of growth. The political impact of the rapid Soviet growth rate on the rest of the world was especially magnified by the fact that the rest of the world was in depression with mass unemployment in most of the 1930s. In fact, at the time, the important political point about the Soviet system was not its growth rate but the mere fact that it could prevent depression.

---

9. Abram Bergson, *The Real National Income of Soviet Russia since 1928* (Cambridge: Harvard University Press, 1961).

The Second World War (1941–1945)

At the beginning of the invasion of the USSR in 1941, German output alone was greater than Soviet output; Germany plus its allies and occupied countries produced twice the Soviet output. Moreover, in the very important coal, iron, and steel industries Germany alone produced more than the USSR. The Soviet Union, however, was able to convert its production very rapidly, so a huge percentage of all its resources was soon devoted entirely to the war effort.

Nevertheless, Soviet production declined very sharply because Hitler swiftly took over an area which had contained one-half of Soviet prewar production capacity. The invaded area included up to 70 percent of Soviet coal mining, 60 percent of iron ore production, and over 50 percent of steel capacity. It included an important breadbasket of the USSR, containing a third to a half of the area sown in grain. In addition, the German army ultimately killed at least twenty million Soviet citizens.

The main economic salvation of the Soviet Union was achieved by an amazing mass evacuation of skilled workers and whole factories to the eastern regions of the USSR. Over half the populations of Kiev and Kharkov were evacuated. And whole factories were evacuated from many other areas. In addition, there was much new construction in the eastern areas during the war. Civilian consumption was, of course, cut to the bone. External assistance during the war, largely from the United States via lend-lease, totaled some $12 billion.

When the Soviet Army retreated, it pursued a scorched-earth policy, attempting to destroy all productive facilities that could not be moved. Subsequently, when the Germans retreated, they destroyed virtually all that remained, especially Soviet factories and housing. The result was a great decline in Soviet production by the end of the war. This wartime destruction is also one explanation for the fact that Soviet housing is still very poor. Thus, official Soviet figures claim that the war destroyed the homes of 25 million people and leveled about 2,000 towns and about 70,000 villages. In sum, the Soviet government calculated that "the war retarded our industrial development for eight or nine years, that is approximately two five-year plans."[10]

Reconstruction (1945–1950)

Immediately following the war, a large number of plants that had produced war goods were converted to civilian use. Then the process of reconversion to peacetime uses and reconstruction of devastated factories was formalized in the Fourth Five-Year Plan, running from

---

10. Malenkov, cited in Maurice Dobb, *Soviet Economic Development since 1917* (London: Routledge and Kegan Paul), 313.

March 1946 through 1950. The main task of the plan was to rebuild and reequip the destroyed enterprises. The emphasis, therefore, was on investment in the western regions that had been laid waste by the war.

The emphasis was also inevitably on producer goods and investment in heavy industry so as to restore and surpass the prewar level. Thus, there was still little room for consumer goods or housing. Although consumer goods production did increase, living standards still had a long way to go to reach a comfortable level.

In the period from 1946 to 1950 the Soviet economy succeeded in reconstructing the productive capacity destroyed by the war. It was officially claimed that the prewar production level was reached by 1948 (partly by the addition of the new facilities built in the East), but prewar factories and equipment were not all restored until 1950. Housing was restored at a still slower pace, in part because housing uses up a great deal of capital per unit of output (about fifteen rubles of capital to one ruble of housing).

During the war large numbers of workers had been shifted from agriculture and consumer goods production to military production or to the army. This shift meant that goods available to consumers were decreasing, while the money wage bill was actually increasing, as a result of high wage rates and overtime in military production. This imbalance led to inflationary pressures, higher prices of consumer goods, and the necessity for rationing of food and other items. At the same time, through sales of food in the collective farm markets at soaring prices (where rationing and price control did not apply), many farmers amassed huge hoards of rubles.

By the end of 1947, agricultural production had improved enough so that wartime food rationing could finally be ended. At the same time a monetary reform was put into operation. The object was to replace the old ruble whose value had fallen during the war (when rubles in circulation had probably increased by at least 250 percent), and to do so primarily by soaking up the excess buying power and money hoards of those who had made profits from wartime speculation. To that end, the reform was designed so that it would hit disproportionately those with large hoards of cash, especially those held by the farmers.

The 1947 reform, therefore, allowed the exchange of cash at the rate of only one new ruble for ten old ones. *Bank* deposits, on the other hand, were exchanged at the rate of one new ruble for one old one up to three thousand rubles. Bank deposits over three thousand rubles were exchanged at progressively lower ratios. This reform (coupled with increasing production of consumer goods) was successful in ending the inflationary spiral. Thus, the following years saw the successful implementation of a policy of money wages rising slower than labor productivity and the accomplishment of price reductions once a year. By 1954, state retail prices, which had tripled during the war, were back down to only 20 percent above the 1940 level, implying that real wages had risen very significantly from the wartime low.

Soviet Economic Growth, 1950 to the Present

We shall begin with a general theoretical discussion of economic growth in centrally planned economies. We shall then turn to consider the Soviet growth record, both by itself and in relation to U.S. growth. After presenting the statistical picture, we shall consider the following analytical questions: (1) what have been the sources of Soviet growth? and (2) what factors lie behind the secular decline in Soviet growth rates since 1950?

Growth in a Centrally Planned Economy

Suppose that a centrally planned economy, such as the Soviet Union, can always make its *aggregate* effective demand rise as rapidly as aggregate supply, though *particular* goods may be unsalable for various reasons. Thus, there are no retardations nor depressions caused by lack of demand. If the problems of demand are thus eliminated, then growth will depend simply on how fast output can be expanded.

Since all problems of demand are assumed away, the remaining supply problem may be resolved into two questions. First, how much of each input (such as land, labor, and capital) can be procured under existing circumstances for use in production? Second, how much output can be obtained from these inputs in the production process?

Production Is Determined by Capital, Labor, Natural Resources, and Technology

Many different physical inputs constitute the production base of an economy. For convenience, these may be grouped into the three categories of capital, labor, and natural resources. *Capital* includes inventories of raw materials and goods in process as well as all plant and equipment. *Labor* means the number of woman- and man-hours available as well as the degree of skill of the available labor force. The term *natural resources* is defined as all useful materials, including land, known to be in the territory of the economy. Resources may be depleted by use or by natural erosion, but may be increased, for example, by new geological discoveries or improved recovery methods. *Technology* is the knowledge that determines how much output can be produced by various combinations of inputs. Therefore, the level of potential output is a function of the presently available (1) capital, (2) labor, (3) natural resources, and (4) technology. A thorough analysis of the growth potential of any existing economy should consider each of these inputs in turn as well as the interrelations among them.

The real gross national product of the United States grew by 3 percent a year from 1919 to 1956.[11] Part of that growth was due to the growth of the labor force and part to the growth of the capital stock; but more than half the growth was accounted for by technical improvements.[12] No one would deny the importance of improvements in technology or the quality of labor or capital; and, therefore, no one denies the urgent need for such things as research, education, and public health measures.

In order that the analysis may consider only the quantitative growth of a factor, changes in its quality—such as improvements in labor skills by education—will be lumped together with technological change. First, economic growth theorems will be solely related to growth of labor, and then solely related to the growth of capital. The other factors, however, and especially technology, will always be brought into the picture through their effects on the amount produced per unit of labor or of capital.

Population and Growth

After allowing for frictional movements from job to job, we may assume that the labor force in a centrally planned economy is always fully employed (this assumption is discussed in a later section). Potential growth of output is then determined by the growth of the labor force and by the amount produced per unit of labor.

The "law" of diminishing returns states that the successive increases in total output, as additional workers are hired beyond a certain level, will be less and less. It holds true only if capital, natural resources, and technique remain unchanged, and after some minimum level of employment is reached (where there are enough workers for the necessary division of labor). Given these assumptions, the law of diminishing returns cannot be other than true. All other things remaining the same, it is obvious that if enough workers are crowded onto a single plot of land or even the entire world, the crowding alone will eventually cause the product of an additional worker to decline. But, of course, "other things"—especially technology—do not remain the same over time. Furthermore, many of the classical economists, Malthus for example, went much further than the truism embodied in

11. U.S. Congress, Joint Economic Committee, Staff Report, *Employment, Growth, and Price Levels* (Washington, D.C.: U.S. Government Printing Office, 1959), xxiii.

12. See, e.g., E. D. Domar, "On the Measurement of Technological Change," *Economic Journal* 71 (Dec. 1961): 709–29; also R. M. Solow, "Technical Progress, Capital Formation, and Economic Growth," *American Economic Review* 52 (May 1962): 76–86. For more recent estimates, see John Kendrick, "Survey of the Factors Contributing to the Decline in U.S. Productivity Growth," Federal Reserve Bank of Boston, *The Decline in Productivity Growth*, Conference Series #22 (Boston: Federal Reserve Bank, June 1982).

the law of diminishing returns. They predicted that diminishing returns per worker in the economy as a whole *would* come about in actual fact. The Reverend Malthus reached this dismal conclusion on the grounds that population increase would be very rapid and would far outweigh the slow increase of capital, technology, and resources.

The Malthusian population controversy has great importance in the Soviet Union, China, and other centrally planned economies, both in theory and in practice. Marx called the Malthusian theory of people breeding like rabbits a slander on the human race.[13] Marx wanted to emphasize that the evils of poverty—both in the advanced capitalist countries and in the colonial and semicolonial countries—are *not* primarily caused by too much population but are social diseases caused by too much exploitation and profit making.

Even if we accept the idea that the Soviet brand of socialism can ensure a high rate of growth of output, this does not imply that the rate of growth per person could not be higher if there were less population growth. In other words, additional workers may add to the total product, but surely a point could be reached where the number of workers grows faster than the amount of capital. In that case, each additional worker has less capital with which to work, so—other things remaining constant—he or she will produce less than the previous worker. Thus, more population may mean greater absolute growth of product (good, perhaps, for military and prestige purposes) *but* a slower growth of output per worker (and therefore a heavy drag on the improvement of individual welfare). China seems to have recognized this in practice with a belated birth control drive, albeit with very hesitant theoretical recognition of the problem.

Full Capacity Growth

So far, we have concentrated on the increase of the labor force and its product per worker. It is more interesting and useful for our purposes, however, to estimate the potential growth of output in relation to the increase of capital and the product per unit of capital. Of course, the output per unit of capital will reflect changes in technology, natural resources, and the labor supply.[14]

In discussing growth, it is useful to state a simple relationship between output and capital at any given moment. *The national prod-*

---

13. For a full presentation of Marx's views on Malthus, see R. L. Meek, ed., *Malthus: Selections from Marx and Engels* (New York: International Publishers, 1958).

14. This approach is detailed in E. D. Domar, "Expansion and Employment," *American Economic Review* 37 (Mar. 1947): 34–35. For empirical data on the ratios and the average growth rate, see, e.g., Simon S. Kuznets, *National Product since 1869* (New York: National Bureau of Economic Research, Inc., 1946).

uct or output (Q) must equal the output per unit of capital (K) times the amount of capital in use. Thus, we may write the simple formula: output = (output/capital) × capital, or $Q = (Q/K) \times K$. This formula, obviously, is true by definition; but it is fruitful to think in these terms.

In the United States there are about three dollars of capital goods in use for every dollar of our annual national product. So our ratio of output to capital is about one-third. Therefore, when the value of our capital stock, including all machines and factories, was about $3 trillion, we produced annually about $1 trillion output.

Now this analysis may be extended to a growing economy. The "rate of growth of output" ($\dot{Q}$) is defined to be the increase in output (ΔQ) as a ratio to present output. Expressed as a formula, it is: rate of growth = (increase in output)/output, or $\dot{Q} = \Delta Q/Q$. For example, if the economy produced $100 last year, and it now produced $103, then the rate of growth is 3/100, or 3 percent a year.

If we begin with the expression

$$\dot{Q} = \frac{\Delta Q}{Q} , \tag{1}$$

and multiply the right-hand side by $\Delta K/\Delta K$ (which equals one and, hence, does not change the equality), we obtain

$$\dot{Q} = \frac{\Delta Q}{Q} \times \frac{\Delta K}{\Delta K} , \tag{2}$$

where ΔK equals the change in the capital stock. If we now rearrange the variables, we arrive at an interesting and useful growth equation:

$$\dot{Q} = \frac{\Delta Q}{\Delta K} \times \frac{\Delta K}{Q} . \tag{3}$$

Notice that an increase in the capital stock (ΔK) is the economist's definition of "net investment" (and, for simplicity, we shall assume no depreciation). Let us also assume (because it is generally true in a centrally planned economy) that the amount of investment is just equal to the amount of saving (S). Therefore, the increase in the capital stock (ΔK) is equal to investment as well as to saving. Thus, the growth identity of equation (3) can be stated in these terms: the rate of growth is equal to the incremental output/capital ratio ($\Delta Q/\Delta K$) times the share of output going to saving or investment. That is, the rate of economy growth is proportional to the productivity of the new investments and the rate of investment (or saving, S/Q).

Let us take an example of the use of this equation of growth. If the ratio of saving to output is 12 percent, and if the ratio of increased output per year to investment is one-fourth, then we find:

Rate of growth: ¼ × 0.12 = 0.03, or 3 percent a year.

Alternatively, if the saving ratio were to rise to 30 percent of output (it has been around this level in the USSR since 1928) and the incremental output to capital ratio remained at one-fourth, then we find:

Rate of growth = ¼ × .30 = .075, or 7.5 percent a year.

Both the saving ratio and the growth rate increased two and a half times. So, other things being equal, the greater the sacrifice of consumption out of current output, the higher will be the rate of growth of output. Clearly, the lower the initial standard of living, the greater is the human sacrifice which accompanies a given saving ratio.

The Political-Ethical Issues: Consumption vs. Investment

Up to this point, the issue of economic growth has been examined in the cold economic terms of the basic so-called Harrod-Domar growth equation.[15] Now it is necessary to investigate why the question of investment versus present consumption is a vital political issue around which Soviet politics must turn and by which Soviet lives are determined. (The same is true for all other centrally planned economies.)

On the ideological side, it may be noted that the Soviet economists follow a similar growth model derived from Marx. Actually, in the 1920s several Soviet economists, notably G. A. Feldman,[16] devised some quite sophisticated dynamic growth models as tools of long-term planning. Unfortunately, the Stalinist dictatorship distrusted any innovation in the social sciences and attacked these models as "bourgeois formalism" and "mathematical formalism." As a result, Feldman's pioneering work was ignored for several decades, while Soviet growth planning was left to political whim.

At any rate, the Soviet economists now use models derived from the reproduction schemes in Volume 2 of Marx's *Capital*, which anticipated the Harrod-Domar model by many decades. Although it was cruder mathematically, Marx's model showed all the essentials. It states implicitly: (1) what the conditions are for a steady growth at full capacity, and (2) that the growth rate of output will be higher if there is a higher ratio of producer goods to consumer goods (or of investment to consumption).

---

15. See Domar, "On the Measurement of Technological Change."

16. See the discussion in Evsey D. Domar, "A Soviet Model of Growth," *Essays in the Theory of Economic Growth* (New York: Oxford University Press, 1957). The original Feldman article, "On the Theory of Growth Rates of National Income," is translated in Nicolas Spulber, *Foundations of Soviet Strategy for Economic Growth: Selected Soviet Essays, 1924–1930* (Bloomington: Indiana University Press, 1964).

Of course, these Marxist models also show that the economy with the higher ratio of investment will *eventually* also have a larger amount of consumption—but the interesting question is how many years the populace must wait for increased consumption. The issue of how much sacrifice will lead to how much growth *is* an economic question. A decision to sacrifice current consumption, however, is a political and ethical one, not an economic one (so it would be made by all the voters in a democratic socialist society). It should also be noted that it is possible to go too far in reducing consumption, even from the cold and calculating viewpoint of economic growth. To reduce consumption opportunities below some point will lower labor productivity and, after some time, may even cause strikes or revolutions. A certain minimum percentage of consumption remains necessary if the gains made by more saving and investing of capital are not to be canceled out by negative side effects. To put it another way, there are definitely both political and economic maximum limits to the possible percentage of saving and investment.

Finally, on the ideological front, one must note a strange and false notion, which Stalin raised to the level of an unassailable dogma. This notion is that steady growth cannot be achieved unless the investment sector always grows faster than the consumption sector.[17] Actually, Marx merely showed that this is sometimes the case in a "capitalist" economy and that in its extreme form it is a disproportion that usually leads to a depression. Since the Soviets do not claim to have a capitalist economy, it is hard to see the relevance of this notion to the USSR. The real reason for Stalin's doctrine that investment goods *must* grow faster was merely to reinforce the arguments for even more investment. In reality, steady growth may be achieved with any constant positive rate of net investment; the investment sector must grow more rapidly than the consumption sector only if one wishes not steady, but constantly accelerating, growth.[18] In the Soviet Union in the 1930s it was, of course, vitally necessary to raise the level and percentage of investment by a drastic amount if industrialization was to be seriously begun.

There are still heated political disputes over the ratio of investment to national income, but the debate is over a small percentage either way. These disputes are decided by power struggles within the ruling group, though desire for popular support may influence the leaders' decision.

---

17. An extended critique of this doctrine may be found in P. J. D. Wiles, *The Political Economy of Communism* (Cambridge: Harvard University Press, 1964), 272–300.

18. See the similar view by a Soviet economist in V. Volkonskii, "Methods of Mathematical Economics and the Theory of Planning and Administering the Economy," translated in *Problems of Economics* 10 (1967), 1–14.

A Statistical Overview of Soviet and U.S. Growth since 1950

Industrial Performance

In Table 6.3 we present various estimates of U.S. and Soviet industrial growth since 1950. Two things can be seen from this table. First, United States industrial production has grown more slowly than Soviet industrial production over the period. From 1951 to 1978, according to official Soviet data, the Soviet growth rate was 9.1 percent per year, though the CIA estimates Soviet growth at 7.4 percent per year. Either estimate of Soviet growth is higher than the official U.S. growth rate of 3.4 percent per year. The reasons *why* Soviet industrial growth has been higher than U.S. growth are discussed below.

Second, Soviet industrial production has grown over the whole period, 1951–1978, very rapidly by any historical or comparative standards. *But* Soviet industrial *growth rates* have declined continuously in this period (by either CIA or official Soviet estimates). The reasons *why* Soviet growth rates have declined are also discussed below.

Agricultural Performance

Virtually every study of Soviet agriculture has shown it to be in trouble. A study by the Wharton Associates shows that over the eighteen years of rule by Leonid Brezhnev (1964–1982) agricultural output grew by only 1.7 percent a year.[19] Productivity per farm worker rose very little in this period. In 1965 a Soviet farm worker supplied agricultural produce to six persons; the same worker supplied eight persons in 1981. U.S. agricultural productivity grew much faster, from one farm worker supplying forty-three persons in 1965 to one farm worker supplying sixty-five persons in 1981. Thus, Soviet labor productivity did rise a bit in agriculture, but it fell comparatively from 14 percent to 12 percent of the U.S. level.

Consumption Performance

The Wharton study finds that Soviet living standards rose considerably in this period (in spite of the mediocre agricultural performance). For all goods and services (including public or collective ones) consumption *per person* rose in the Soviet Union at 2.7 percent per year in the period from 1964 to 1982.[20] Yet, reflecting the decline in

---

19. Wharton Econometric Forecasting Associates, "The Soviet Economy under Brezhnev and Its Outlook under Andropov," in *Centrally Planned Economies, Current Analysis* 2, 91 (Nov. 16, 1982): 2.
    20. *Ibid.*, 1.

Table 6.3
Real Growth Rates of U.S. and Soviet Industrial Production (Annual Average)

	1951–55	1955–60	1961–65	1966–70	1971–75	1976–78	1951–78
U.S. (official)	6.2	2.4	7.2	4.0	1.8	4.6	3.4
Soviet (by CIA)	10.6	9.8	6.6	6.3	5.9	3.8	7.4
Soviet (official)	13.1	10.4	8.6	8.5	7.5	5.1	9.1

Sources: F. Douglas Whitehouse and Ray Converse (both from the CIA), "Soviet Industry, Recent Performance and Future Prospects," U.S. Congress, Joint Economic Committee, *Soviet Economy in a Time of Change* (Washington, D.C.: U.S. Government Printing Office, 1981), 806. Also CIA, *Handbook of Economic Statistics, 1981* (Washington, D.C.: U.S. Government Printing Office, 1981).

industrial growth rates, the *rate of growth* of consumption per person declined from 3.0 percent in 1971–1975 to 1.7 percent in 1976–1980 (and an estimated 1.2 percent in 1981–1982).

In relative terms, the CIA finds that Soviet food consumption per person was only 43 percent of U.S. food consumption per person in 1965 but had risen to 53 percent of U.S. food consumption per person in 1980.[21] (Of course, part of this increase was based on imported grain.) More specifically, the CIA finds that Soviet ". . . per capita consumption of meat and dairy products [rose] from 27 percent of U.S. consumption in 1955 to 48 percent in 1977. Even larger gains were made in the provision of consumer durables and household services."[22] On the other hand, in the service sector (such as restaurants and barber shops) the CIA finds the Soviet Union falling further behind. The service sector, however, is notoriously difficult to calculate; for example, how does one compare the inflated prices of U.S. medical services to Soviet medical services? The index number problem, to be discussed in Appendix A to this chapter, will also affect these conclusions. Last, the CIA calculates the Soviet consumption *per person* of all goods and services (including public or collective ones) rose from 29 percent of the U.S. level in 1955 to 36 percent in 1977.[23]

In terms of investment in expansion of the economy, the CIA estimates that Soviet investment was only 46 percent of U.S. investment

21. *Ibid.*, 20.

22. Imogene Edwards, Margaret Hughes, and James Norem (all from the CIA), "U.S. and USSR: Comparisons of GNP," in U.S. Congress, Joint Economic Committee, *Soviet Economy in a Time of Change* (Washington, D.C.: U.S. Government Printing Office, 1979), 371.

23. *Ibid.*, 371.

in 1955 but had risen to 116 percent of U.S. investment by 1977.[24] Whether one believes these fairly conservative estimates, or wishes to consider higher Soviet estimates, it is clear that Soviet investment is rising faster than U.S. investment and is now higher in absolute terms in an average year. This is an important clue to Soviet growth performance. On the one hand, a higher absolute amount of investment is one reason why the Soviet economy has been growing faster than the U.S. economy. On the other hand, since the Soviet economy is still smaller than the U.S. economy, a higher amount of investment means that a much larger part of Soviet resources goes into expanding the economy. The effect is higher growth but a greater relative burden at present for Soviet citizens. It should also be noted that the Soviet incremental output/capital ratio has fallen significantly over the last thirty years, so more and more investment is needed to yield the same increment to output.

Performance of Total Output (GNP)

Finally, when all sectors are combined, the total is the gross national product (GNP). Comparisons of the GNP of two countries are not easy to make (see Appendix 6A), so the CIA estimates must be taken with a grain of salt. They use the geometric mean of ruble and dollar estimates, which is far from perfect, as Appendix 6A suggests. Still, the direction of their estimates is certainly correct, even though the exact percentages may not be reliable. They find that Soviet GNP was only 40 percent of the U.S. level in 1955; Soviet GNP rose to 50 percent in 1965; and Soviet GNP rose further to 60 percent of the U.S. level in 1977.[25] From 1951 to 1979, the CIA finds that the growth rate of Soviet GNP was 4.9 percent compared to a U.S. growth rate of GNP of only 3.4 percent[26] (Soviet official data claim their rate was closer to 7 percent). Thus, even on the conservative CIA estimates, the Soviet production of all goods and services is gaining on the U.S. level.

Why the Soviet Economy Has Grown Faster Than the U.S. Economy

How can we explain the fact that the Soviet economy has grown faster than the U.S. economy, both in the 1930s and from 1950 to the present? First, a planned economy can be directed to gather the resources for a high investment rate if there is a political decision to do so. The Soviet

---

24. *Ibid.*

25. *Ibid.*, 370.

26. See U.S. Congress, Joint Economic Committee, *USSR: Measures of Economic Development, 1950–1980* (Washington, D.C.: U.S. Government Printing Office, Dec. 8, 1982), 20.

leaders have made this decision (without consulting the Soviet people), so they have had a much higher rate of investment than the U.S. economy. Investment is not determined by individuals but by the government plan. The government obtains the resources both from taxes and directly from the profits of government-owned enterprises. The Soviet investment ratio is approximately 30 percent of national income compared to approximately 15 percent in the United States.

Second, the centrally planned economy of the USSR does not suffer from general unemployment. The reasons for this circumstance are discussed in Chapter 8 concerning balance in a planned economy. Of course, to say that workers are fully employed does not mean that they are working most efficiently—that issue is discussed below and in Chapter 9 on efficiency. Similarly, no factory is ever underutilized in the Soviet economy for lack of demand, though it may be underutilized at times because of a shortage of inputs. Since the U.S. economy frequently has high unemployment (10.8 percent in December 1982) and low utilization of capacity (68 percent in December 1982), avoiding such conditions is a major advantage of Soviet planning.

Third, Soviet planners have made a major effort in research and development. A U.S. Department of Commerce study found that in 1950 the U.S. economy had 159,000 scientists and engineers employed in research and development, whereas the USSR had only 125,000.[27] By 1979, however, while the U.S. employment in research and development had increased to 610,000, Soviet employment in research and development had increased to 957,000. In institutions of higher education alone, in 1950 there were 18,000 full-time equivalents in U.S. research and development, and the same number in the USSR. In 1976, however, full-time equivalents in research and development in U.S. higher education institutions had grown to 69,000, while the comparable Soviet number had grown to 134,000. In spite of the heavier Soviet investment in research, the Soviets have had problems in industrial innovation (for reasons to be discussed later).

The Decline of Soviet Growth Rates

According to both Soviet and CIA estimates, the growth rate of Soviet GNP has a long-run declining trend. Moreover, according to CIA estimates, the Soviet growth rate has fallen even faster than the U.S. rate has fallen in the 1951–1979 period. By CIA estimates (which are controversial) U.S. growth was actually faster than Soviet growth in the four years 1976–1979. Soviet growth, however, was again faster (by

---

27. Louvan Nolting and Murray Feshbach, *Statistics on Research and Development Employment in the USSR*, U.S. Department of Commerce, Census Series P-95, No. 76 (Washington, D.C.: U.S. Government Printing Office, 1981), 44–47.

Table 6.4
Real Growth Rates of U.S. and Soviet GNP (Annual Average)

	1951–55	1956–60	1961–65	1966–70	1971–75	1976–79	1951–79
United States	4.2	2.3	4.6	3.1	2.3	4.4	3.4
Soviet Union	5.5	5.9	5.0	5.2	3.7	3.0	4.8

Source: Joint Economic Committee, *USSR: Measures of Economic Growth and Development, 1950–80* (Washington, D.C.: U.S. Government Printing Office, 1982), 20.

any estimate) in the period 1980–1982 because U.S. real output stagnated during those years. The CIA estimates are shown in Table 6.4 (as we shall see, the USSR does not calculate GNP officially).

In light of the fact that the Soviet Union continues to invest roughly twice as much of its national output as the U.S., it is important to explore the reasons for this decline in Soviet growth performance. Since growth depends not only on the amount of resources available but also on how productive these resources are, we shall first explore the question of Soviet factor productivity. We shall then turn to a discussion of why Soviet growth rates of combined factor productivity and output have been falling.

Soviet Labor Productivity

A 1960 study by Bergson found that Soviet product per worker was 29 percent of U.S. product per worker in ruble prices but was 58 percent of U.S. product per worker in dollar prices.[28] Appendix 6A will show that both estimates are equally "true," so we can say only that the range was 29 to 58 percent, according to Bergson.

What has happened to Soviet labor productivity since 1960? A study for the Joint Economic Committee of Congress finds that Soviet labor productivity is rising. It concludes that in the Soviet Union: "Nearly twice as much labor would have been required to produce 1972 final demand with 1959 technology as was in fact required in 1972."[29] In relative terms, a study by Wharton Econometric Associates—using a weighted average of ruble and dollar prices—found that the gap in

---

28. Abram Bergson, *The Economics of Soviet Planning* (New Haven: Yale University Press, 1964), 342. This estimate has been reworked several times by Bergson but remains very close to the initial estimate; see Abram Bergson, *Productivity and the Social System* (Cambridge: Harvard University Press, 1978), Ch. 6.

29. D. Gallik, G. Guill, B. Kostinsky, and V. Treml, "The 1972 Input-Output Table and the Changing Structure of the Soviet Economy," in U.S. Congress, Joint Economic Committee, *Soviet Economy in a Time of Change* (Washington, D.C.: U.S. Government Printing Office, 1979), 433.

labor productivity between all Soviet and U.S. workers has declined in this period (in spite of the increasing gap in the agricultural sector). The product per hour of the average Soviet worker was only 30 percent of the U.S. level in 1965, but rose to 41 percent by 1982.[30] Thus, Soviet labor productivity is far behind U.S. productivity, but it is catching up.

Various writers have suggested three reasons for the higher growth of Soviet than U.S. productivity. First, as discussed above, the Soviets have invested more in the training of scientists and engineers. Second, their high rate of investment means that new inventions can be embodied in actual industrial innovations more quickly (but we shall examine the obstacles to this). Third, Soviet population and labor force growth has slowed, so there is a rising amount of capital per worker.

While Soviet labor productivity has grown, its rate of growth has slowed. According to the CIA, it slowed from 3.4 percent per year in 1961–1965 to 1.3 percent during 1976–1980.[31] *Why* it slowed will be discussed below after we have examined the behavior of capital productivity and combined factor productivity.

Capital Productivity

The picture is quite different for productivity of capital. Calculations of output per unit of capital are highly controversial, both because of theoretical problems in measuring capital and because of the practical measurement problem of comparing things in two different price systems. Capital and output must each be calculated in either rubles or in dollars. For what it is worth, Bergson[32] estimated that the Soviet net national product of goods and services *per* unit of reproducible capital in 1960 was 98 percent of the U.S. level calculated in ruble prices or 149 percent in dollar prices. Hence, Soviet output per unit of capital in 1960 was equal to or much higher than U.S. output per unit of capital in most areas of the economy. This result is explainable by the fact that in 1960 in the Soviet Union capital was the relatively scarce factor of production; each unit of capital or each machine was worked relatively by more workers (compared to the factor proportions in the United States). For example, Soviet output of iron per blast furnace was higher than that of the United States partly because they used a much larger number of workers per ton of iron to speed the process. Conversely, their iron output per worker was lower partly because each worker used less capital. For reasons to be explored below, since 1960 Soviet capital productivity has fallen

30. Wharton Associates, "The Soviet Economy under Brezhnev," 1.

31. CIA, *Handbook of Economic Statistics* (Washington, D.C.: U.S. Government Printing Office, 1982), 72.

32. Bergson, *The Economics of Soviet Planning*, 342.

markedly in absolute terms (as its capital stock has risen rapidly).
Today, Soviet capital productivity is below that in the United States.

Combined Factor Productivity

Since the separate measures of labor and capital productivity are
greatly influenced by the relative abundance of the other factor, they
do not serve as reliable indicators of technological development or
overall efficiency in the use of factors. What is needed is a measure of
the combined productivity of both labor and capital. For this purpose
neoclassical economists generally employ the concept of *combined*
or *total factor productivity*. (Many Marxist economists and many post-
Keynesian economists deny the validity and meaningfulness of any
concept of capital productivity or combined labor-capital productivity.)

According to neoclassical economists, the growth rate of total factor productivity (*TFP*) is equal to the growth rate of output minus the
weighted growth rate of the inputs. Algebraically

$$TFP = \dot{Q} - (W_K \dot{K} + W_L \dot{L}),$$

where $\dot{K}$ and $\dot{L}$ are the rate of growth of capital and labor and W_K and
W_L are the weights assigned to capital and labor, respectively.

The weights assigned to each factor correspond to the factor's
share in national income. Assuming the concept is meaningful, there
is still a knotty theoretical and econometric problem. The absence of
capital markets or reported capital shares in the Soviet Union (and
other planned economies) requires that the analyst use synthetic or
estimated factor shares. Some economists have simply assumed
Soviet shares to be equal to U.S. shares, and others have relied on
complicated and controversial production function simulations.

The problem is compounded in the Soviet case because of the
widely divergent growth rates of the capital stock and the labor force,
the former at rates around 7 to 10 percent per annum and the latter at
around 1 to 2 percent per annum over the last two decades. Thus,
when higher income shares or weights are assigned to capital, combined factor inputs appear to be growing more rapidly and total factor
productivity growth rate estimates are lower. Conversely, when
smaller weights are assigned to capital, combined factor inputs are
calculated to be growing more slowly and total factor productivity
growth rates are higher.

In fact, the work of M.I.T. economist Martin Weitzman and others[33]
suggests that the preferred procedure would be to assign capital
higher weights for earlier periods (e.g., the 1950s) and continuously

---

33. For other discussions of Soviet growth, productivity, and efficiency, in
addition to articles already cited, see: M. Weitzman, "Industrial Production,"

Table 6.5
USSR: Average Annual Growth Rates of Total Factor
Productivity, 1960–1980

	1961–65	1966–70	1971–75	1976–80
TFP	1.9%	2.0%	0.6%	0.5%

Source: Authors' calculations based on CIA *Handbook of Statistics* (1982), 72.

diminishing weights thereafter. This is because the so-called "elasticity of substitution" (a measure of the rate at which diminishing returns set in as capital is increased relative to labor) has been repeatedly estimated to be below 1 in the Soviet Union, and usually closer to 0.5. When the elasticity of substitution is below 1 and the capital stock grows more rapidly than the labor input, it means that the capital share falls. Were one to assign falling shares to capital over time, total input growth would be still lower and growth in combined factor productivity still higher.

Although they are complex, it is important to grasp some of these methodological issues before considering actual estimates. In Table 6.5 we present estimates of changes in Soviet total factor productivity since 1960. These estimates are based on (1) CIA estimates for growth rates in Soviet GNP, capital stock, and labor hours, and on (2) the assumption of constant factor shares over the period (as the concept is understood by neoclassical theory). Labor's share is assumed to be 75 percent; capital's share, including land, 25 percent—roughly the same shares as in the United States and Western Europe. Again, were we to have assumed diminishing capital shares, the measure of changes in total factor productivity would have fallen more slowly.

Although the magnitude of these estimates differs somewhat from estimates in other studies,[34] the downward trend is the same. Just as

---

in Bergson and Levine (eds.), *The Soviet Economy: Toward the Year 2000*, (London: George Allen and Unwin, 1983); Martin Weitzman, "Soviet Postwar Growth and Capital-Labor Substitution," *American Economic Review* 60, 4 (Sept. 1970): 676–92; Padma Desai, "The Production Function and Technical Change in Postwar Soviet Industry," *American Economic Review* 66 (June 1976): 372–81; Abram Bergson, "Notes on the Production Function in Soviet Postwar Industrial Growth," *Journal of Comparative Economics* 3 (June 1979): 116–26; Abram Bergson, *Productivity and the Social System: The USSR and the West* (Cambridge: Harvard University Press, 1978); F. Douglas Whitehouse and Ray Converse, "Soviet Industry: Recent Performance and Future Prospects," in U.S. Congress, Joint Economic Committee, *Soviet Economy in a Time of Change* (Washington, D.C.: U.S. Government Printing Office, 1979). 402–22.

34. See, e.g., Bergson, *Productivity and the Social System*; Bergson, "Notes on the Production Function"; and Weitzman, "Industrial Production."

growth rates of industrial and aggregate output in the USSR have fallen over the last two decades, so has the growth rate of total factor productivity fallen. That is, the ability of the Soviet economy to produce more from a given amount of inputs (intensive growth), either from improved technology, organization, or resource allocation, appears to have diminished. Given the projected slow growth (below 1 percent per annum for the 1980s) in the labor force and ongoing natural resource depletion, this trend does not augur well for the Soviet economy—if the CIA estimates and methodological assumptions employed are valid. In the next section, we shall consider various explanations of the decline in Soviet output and productivity growth rates.

The Slowdown in Soviet Growth

Herbert Levine has grouped the possible causes for the growth slowdown into four categories: consequences of a maturing economy; strategic planning decisions; systemic elements; and exogenous factors.[35]

Consequences of a Maturing Economy

As the Soviet economy has grown over time, many of the traditional sources of this growth have been attenuated or exhausted. First, there has been a progressive depletion of their natural resource base, particularly with respect to oil, coal, and iron ore. New resource deposits are difficult to find, involve greater transportation and infrastructural costs, and usually are more expensive to mine. As production costs rise per unit of resource, factor productivity and growth decline. (Of course, this factor may be reduced or even reversed by new technology which uses new resources or which gets more out of old resources. If an economic system encourages enough new technology, there is no natural law that using up of resources must mean a slowing of growth rates.)

Second, with the maturation of the Soviet economy there has been a progressive aging of the capital stock. Again, rather than being a result of some natural law, this condition has been due primarily to the slow rate of retirement of the existing capital stock. In fact, the Soviet capital stock retirement rate was below one-half the U.S. rate

---

35. This section draws heavily from Herbert Levine, "Possible Causes of the Deterioration of Soviet Productivity Growth in the Period 1976–1980," in U.S. Congress, Joint Economic Committee, *Soviet Economy in the 1980s* (Washington, D.C.: U.S. Government Printing Office, 1983).

during the 1960s and 1970s. The rapidly aging capital stock is attributable to incentive problems in industry as well as the cumbersome nature of the Soviet planning hierarchy (discussed in the next several chapters). The consequences of this slow retirement rate are the retention of older, less productive equipment (depressing factor productivities) and the necessity to devote an unusually large share of resources to maintenance and repair. Indeed, a 1981 Soviet study estimated that at times as much as 40 percent of the USSR's machine tool capacity is used for repairing old capital stock rather than for new capital formation.[36]

Third, some analysts have suggested that the opportunities for "catch-up" have decreased as the Soviet economy has modernized. That is, as Soviet technology has become more advanced, the opportunity to copy, borrow, or import foreign technology and machinery has gradually diminished over time.[37]

Strategic Planning Decisions

Two conscious policy decisions made by the Soviet planning authorities also contributed to growth retardation. The first was the decision to allow defense spending to grow at a faster rate than national income. As a consequence, the defense share of GNP grew to nearly 13 percent—at least according to the CIA. (We shall see in Appendix 6B that there is good reason to be skeptical of these CIA estimates.) If we assume that the general direction of the CIA claim is correct, then the military sector in the USSR absorbed an increasing share of the economy's productive resources. In particular, there must have been a growing diversion of resources away from enlarging the capital stock toward military uses as well as a diversion of scarce and skilled manual, technical, and managerial labor toward the defense sphere.

The second decision was to significantly reduce (by one-half) the growth rate of investment during the Tenth Five-Year Plan, 1976–1980. Of course, this was also a decision to increase the relative growth of consumer (and perhaps defense) goods. Although much of the impact of this slower investment growth rate will be felt during the 1980s, it is likely that it also contributed to slower growth during the late seventies. The relative increase in consumer goods resulted from intense political pressures of the Soviet people, pressures that were given more consideration by the leaders in their conflicts for power after Stalin died. Health and education services also rapidly expanded, cutting further into capital investment.

---

36. *Ibid.*, 159.

37. See, e.g., A. Bergson, "Technological Progress," in Bergson and Levine, *The Soviet Economy*, 34–78.

Systemic Elements

There are many sources of waste and inefficiency that plague the Soviet economy, and these will be discussed in detail in the chapters that follow. Unless such inefficiency grew worse over time, however, it is not apparent that the growth rate would be affected. Levine makes two points in this regard. First, as an economy matures, its capital/output ratio increases and it becomes more dependent on technological change as a source of growth. Thus, Levine concludes, the well-known resistance to innovation by Soviet managers had a more deleterious effect on growth in the seventies than in earlier periods.

Second, as an economy grows in size and sophistication, centralized planning becomes more difficult. The growing number of interrelations among sectors makes the problems of central control and coordination more intractable. The Soviets are attempting in many ways to deal with this problem, but they are still experimenting and have not yet found an answer.[38]

Another systemic problem which appears to be getting worse is plan and labor indiscipline. Downward revisions of plan targets during the plan year appear to be an increasingly frequent phenomenon. Additionally, there have been many signs of an increase in lackadaisical work and absenteeism, which some scholars have connected to disillusionment, poor work attitudes among youths, and the growing shortage of labor. The disillusionment thesis is perhaps supported by growing alcoholism, especially among adult male workers.

The growth of the "second economy" (both the legal and illegal activities in the private sphere) accelerated substantially during the 1970s. This development diverted productive efforts away from the public sphere. It also meant that an increasing amount of productive activity was not being counted—just as illegal gambling and drug transactions are not counted in the U.S. GNP. Hence, some of the fall in growth rates may be attributable to a statistical artifact—namely, a smaller share of total production is actually counted.

Another systemic problem is the conflict, contradiction, or tension between the human relationships in the Soviet production process and the potential forces of Soviet production. The human relationships begin with the fundamental fact that a small, self-selected group of *political* leaders (plus a few military leaders) controls the direction of the economy, the use of its products, the activities of its workers in the economy, and even the important technological deci-

---

38. One such attempt is the creation of territorial-industrial complexes; see David Kamerling, "The Role of Territorial Production Complexes and Soviet Economic Policy," in U.S. Congress, Joint Economic Committee, *Soviet Economy in the 1980s* (Washington, D.C.: U.S. Government Printing Office, 1983), 242–66. In July 1983, the Soviets introduced experiments with more decentralization in several sectors.

sions. These human relations of production hold back the progress of the productive forces (1) by stifling scientific thought and research within ideological and censored confines, (2) by arbitrarily directing the planners and managers to make decisions of doubtful use to the economy, and (3) by reducing the interest, participation, and enthusiasm of the average worker. Moreover, with slower growth and, hence, smaller wage increases, a greater motivational burden is placed on intrinsic job characteristics. Since Soviet productivity is now more dependent than ever on science, the lack of complete scientific freedom becomes a more and more limiting factor. The greater complexity of the economy also makes arbitrary decisions by a small, self-selected leadership more and more costly. We return to these problems in later chapters.

Exogenous Factors

These factors are ones that are largely beyond the control of the Soviet economy and are mostly transient in nature. During the 1976–1980 period there were three unusually bad weather years which adversely affected the harvests. Lower agricultural output also meant smaller supplies of raw materials for industry and less food (and/or longer lines) for urban workers. This circumstance, in turn, may have negatively affected work motivation.

Another important feature of the mid and late seventies was the serious international recession in the West which, among other things, lowered Western demand for Soviet exports. This situation left the Soviet Union with less foreign exchange to purchase needed Western materials and equipment.

Finally, the pace of migration from low-productivity rural areas to high-productivity urban areas slowed markedly during the second half of the seventies. The share of the urban population in the total population grew at an average annual rate of 1.33 percent during the 1960s, by 1.29 percent during the first half of the 1970s, and by only .86 percent during 1976–1980.[39]

There are, of course, other factors which may have contributed to the slowdown in Soviet growth, but the most important ones have been discussed. After several pages of analysis about the slowdown in Soviet growth, it is necessary to emphasize that Soviet growth continued to be positive during the late seventies and early eighties, at a time when most of the advanced capitalist countries were stagnating. Despite the manifold problems which afflict the Soviet economy, its system of central planning has proved to be durable and to have several advantages of its own. It is to an in-depth consideration of Soviet central planning that we shall turn in the next chapter.

---

39. See H. Levine, "Possible Causes," 157.

Appendix 6A
Problems with Soviet Statistics

Does the Soviet Union keep two sets of statistical books, a true one for themselves and a false one for foreign propaganda? Most experts answer clearly in the negative, reasoning that accurate figures are so important in a planned economy that the propaganda value of false official figures would be far outweighed by the internal confusion which might result. Of course, there may be and is some cheating and falsification by managers trying to fool superior agencies. There may also be (and probably is) some additional falsification by intermediate agencies trying to mislead the central planners, since promotions as well as the salaries of officials at every level depend on the statistics of their performance.

We should note, however, Alec Nove's famous "law of equal cheating." Suppose that USSR statistics exaggerate in every year from 1928 through 1983. If the percentage of exaggeration remains the same, then the *rate* of growth is unaffected. A fixed rate of cheating could only raise the whole level of apparent production but could not raise the rate of growth. Note also that a law of equal mistakes would say that a constant degree of mistaken estimation would similarly have no effect on the rate of growth.

Although it is generally believed that aggregate Soviet statistics are not intentionally falsified, it is true that the Soviets have simply not released many statistics which would show poor performance. Before Stalin's death, very few Soviet statistics were made publicly available. Since 1957, their availability has greatly increased, and a flood of data has been released, though a few key series are still missing.

There is also the problem of getting correct information from below. For example, U.S. taxpayers tend to underestimate their income to pay lower taxes. Soviet managers tend to overestimate their output to earn bonuses.

Suppose we have Soviet data that are not falsified and are published and available. There may still be very difficult questions of interpretation. In the first place, even a particular physical item of production may be differently defined in the two countries. For example, the Soviets under Stalin measured grain in terms of "biological yield," that is, the amount in the field regardless of how much is lost in gathering, storing, and transport. U.S. grain measures are quite different, taking account of all these losses. The revised Soviet measures are now much closer to the U.S. measures, using the so-called barn yield.

A second area of difference in interpretation arises from the use of different categories and definitions of the aggregates in the national product accounts. For example, there are differences over how to calculate depreciation, though both the United States and the USSR include the result in their concept of gross national product (or its

Soviet equivalent). Most important are the differences over what is to be included in what the Americans call "Gross National Product" and the Soviets call "Combined Social Product." The Soviet's "Product" includes purchases of intermediate goods, for example, the steel that is bought by auto producers. The U.S. "Product," on the other hand, excludes such intermediate purchases as double accounting; that is, American economists consider that the Soviet method counts steel twice, once when it is bought as a raw material and once more as part of the price of the auto or other finished good. There would be no problem if there were only one integrated industrial enterprise or, with respect to the rate of growth, if the degree of vertical integration never changed. In reality, however, increasing specialization and other factors work to change regularly the number of levels of supply and, thereby, alter the accounted value of production. For instance, if a Soviet firm producing primary steel and also fabricating steel split into two firms for the primary production and the fabrication, this arrangement would appear to increase their steel production (because the steel would be counted once by itself and once as part of the fabricated product). Clearly, as a measure of growth (though not for some other purposes), the Soviet measure of economic output is less satisfactory than the Western measure, since it may be affected by changes in the structure of industrial organization. Naturally, this does not say that intermediate goods should not be considered in the planning process.

A contrary bias arises from the fact that the U.S. includes and the USSR excludes from its "Product" what the Soviet Marxists call "nonproductive" labor. This classification comprises mostly services, such as domestic help, advertising, education, health, culture, entertainment, government bureaucracy, and military services. Some Soviet economists wish to reform their accounting to include all services in the GNP. (Incidentally, there *is* some domestic help in the USSR.) Since some of these services (such as education or the military in most periods) are the most rapidly growing sectors in both economies, this exclusion may lower the comparative Soviet growth rate. It should be stressed that by "nonproductive" services, the Soviets do not mean undesirable but merely not engaged directly in the production of material goods. After all, the work of their top leaders is classified as "nonproductive."

In addition to the Combined or Gross Social Product, the Soviets (and their COMECON trading partners) have several other national income accounting categories. The category of Gross Material Product excludes intermediate inputs and, presumably, avoids double counting (the category of Net Material Product or National Income also excludes double counting). Several Soviet National Income categories and their component parts are listed in Figure 6A.1.

Even if we agree on accuracy, availability, and interpretation of statistics, there is still a fourth problem that drastically increases the difficulties of comparing growth rates. This problem is the fact that

---

Figure 6A.1
Categories of Soviet National Income Accounts

Gross Value of Agriculture (incl. Livestock and Forestry)
+ Gross Value of Fishing
+ Gross Value of Industry (incl. Mining and Electrical Energy)
+ Gross Value of Construction

= **Total Material Product**

+ "Productive Services" (Gross Value of Transport,
   Communication, and Trade)

= **Gross or Combined Social Product**

− Intermediate Inputs

= **Gross Material Product**

− Depreciation

= **Net Material Product or National Income**

---

various areas of each economy grow at different rates, and that various inputs are significantly different in their degree of scarcity and in their relative prices in the two economies. For one thing, this means that it may be misleading to compare any particular isolated industry or indicator. For example, the USSR produces more butter than the U.S., but this fact may only reflect different preferences and the availability or lack of different substitutes (such as margarine).

If we wish an overall comparison, it is obviously necessary to aggregate all the different industries into one index of output, like the U.S. Gross National Product or the Soviet National Income. But it is not so simple to add up different products, let alone the services that go into GNP. To construct an index of heterogeneous items all added together leads to the so-called *index number problem.*

Suppose the two economies produce only bread and machinery. If we wish to add up one mix of bread and machinery to compare it with another, this can be done only with a given price for each loaf of bread and each machine. It would be easy if the ratio of prices of bread and machinery were the same in rubles and in dollars, for example, $1 per loaf of bread and $2 per machine in the U.S. and 10 rubles per loaf of bread and 20 rubles per machine in the USSR. In that case the total sales value of bread plus machinery can be expressed either in rubles for both countries or in dollars for both countries, because the ratio of total sales of U.S. to USSR will be the same in either price system.

The problem arises because different items have a different scarcity value (that is, are more expensive to produce or are in greater demand) in the two countries, so there is a different product mix *and a different price structure.* Suppose, for example, that the national product of the USSR is two loaves of bread and four machines, while the national product of the U.S. is four loaves of bread and two machines. Suppose also that in the USSR a loaf of bread costs two rubles and a machine one ruble, while in the United States a loaf of bread costs one dollar and a machine two dollars. Then, if both products are calculated in dollars, we find that the United States produced only eight dollars total and the USSR produced ten dollars. But if both products are calculated in rubles, we find that the U.S. produced ten rubles' worth and the USSR produced only eight rubles' worth.

Which comparison is correct? We can say only that each valuation is "correct" (represents the objective situation) in one country but not the other. So you may take your choice. Notice that the things most valuable in one's own country are always most scarce also, so one's comparison is always more favorable in terms of the other country's price structure. A study by Morris Bornstein found, for example, that the Soviet gross national product in 1955 was only about one-fourth of the U.S. national product when both were calculated in ruble price-weights. When both national products were weighed according to dollar valuations, however, the Soviet national product was about one-half the U.S. national product.[40] Notice that this great difference in estimates arises from only one statistical problem; consider, therefore, the different possible estimates arising from all the varied statistical problems confronting the investigator at once.

We have explored the problem of adding up (or "aggregating") the product mixes of different countries for comparison. An identical problem arises if we wish to observe changes in one country over time, which is another form of the so-called *index number problem*. Thus, the apparent rate of growth of the Soviet economy from 1928 to 1968 is greatly affected by the fact that in 1968 it produced a drastically altered product mix with drastically altered relative prices from those prevailing in 1928. In fact, the Soviet output mix in 1968 is far more different from the Soviet output mix of 1928 than it is from the U.S. output mix of 1968. Yet if all Soviet goods are valued in 1928 prices (or the 1926–27 prices actually used for a long time), the result is very different than if each good in each year is valued at 1968 prices. Again, there is no "correct" way to compare a different mixture of bread and machinery in the different periods.

In practice, it was those products which expanded most rapidly that also experienced the greatest gains in efficiency of production, for example, Soviet steel. Items such as shoes expanded more slowly and gained less cost reduction. Therefore, items like steel have the

---

40. Morris Bornstein, "A Comparison of Soviet and U.S. National Product," in U.S. Congress, Joint Economic Committee, *Comparisons of the U.S. and Soviet Economies*, Part 2 (Washington, D.C.: U.S. Government Printing Office, 1959), 385.

greatest long-run declines in relative prices, and, valued in 1968 prices, steel would contribute much less to overall rapid growth than it would in 1928 prices. On the contrary, the slow expanders and slow efficiency gainers, like shoes, would contribute much more to the overall growth rate if we were using 1968 prices. Since the greatest price reductions happen to be in the most rapidly expanding products, the total difference in growth estimates is considerable. This is also true for the United States. For example, in 1899 prices our production of machinery rose by fifteen times from 1899 to 1939. But valued in 1939 prices, our production of machinery from 1899 to 1939 rose less than two times!

Finally, as a fifth type of problem, this discussion so far has assumed that each product remains physically the same over time and in different countries. Actually, it may be difficult to say whether the quality stays the same, or worsens, or is improving. Furthermore, what is the quality and what should be the price of new products, those that did not even exist in 1926 or 1928? In many areas, such as the chemical industry, new products represent the majority of the industry's output in each decade. This problem is, of course, even more difficult in the Soviet Union where initial prices of new products are rather arbitrarily set by officials, rather than by the market.

Appendix 6B
Soviet vs. U.S. "Defense Spending"

Both the Soviet Union and the United States spend incredible amounts of money for "defense" (they both claim to spend nothing for "offense"). This spending is an enormous burden on the people of both countries.

Exactly how much each spends for "defense" is a mystery and is not easy to estimate. In 1983 the U.S. Department of Defense was authorized to spend $240.5 billion—or a quarter of a trillion dollars. In his budget, President Reagan asked Congress for an increase to $274.1 billion for the Defense Department in 1984. But the Department of Defense budget does *not* include many things that involve military spending. For example, what about military assistance abroad? What about the livelihood, the education, and the care for the injuries and wounds of veterans of the U.S. Armed Forces? What about the enormous amount of interest paid on the debt left by past wars? What about space research for military purposes? What about nuclear research and production for military purposes which falls under the Department of Energy? What about the Coast Guard? All of these items are excluded from the "defense" budget. If they were included, the total would be much higher. In 1981, for instance, it would have been $61.7 billion higher.

Soviet defense spending is at least as difficult to measure. Comparing the U.S. and Soviet "defense" budgets is highly problematic. Consider the two extreme estimates. According to Soviet official figures for 1980, the Soviets spent only 17.1 billion rubles for defense. At the official exchange rate, this was only $27.4 billion—which was only one-fifth of the official U.S. defense spending in 1980 (and is only one-tenth of Reagan's 1984 budget request). At the other extreme, the United States Central Intelligence Agency (CIA) estimates that the Soviets spent about 50 percent *more* than the United States did on defense in 1980. Which estimate is more accurate?

Regarding the CIA estimate, Senator William Proxmire, following Senate hearings in early 1983, commented: "Recent intelligence assessments have created a crisis of confidence concerning what we know and don't know about Soviet military spending and the Soviet economy."[41]

The CIA employs the so-called building block approach, first estimating quantities of everything included in defense—numbers of soldiers, tanks, guns, and so forth. The quantities are taken from (or estimated from) published Soviet materials, satellite reconnaissance photos, and other intelligence sources. But the details are not made available to the public. The CIA only gives value estimates for three aggregate categories: personnel; military equipment; and research, development, and testing. The absence of detail has led many to believe that the CIA makes up the data to suit its propaganda purposes.

For instance, the Stockholm International Peace Research Institute attributes a rapid increase in NATO military spending in recent years to a successful CIA propaganda exercise. The Institute finds that the CIA estimate is "a wholly misleading figure for virtually any purpose." But even if we accept the unreported implicit estimates of quantities of different types of military supplies, there remain serious methodological problems with the CIA estimates.

Most fundamental is our old friend the index number problem. This problem occurs (as shown in Appendix 6A) when nations are at different stages of development, produce different proportions of goods, and have different relative prices. In the Soviet Union, the price of human labor power is relatively cheaper than the price of equipment, compared to U.S. prices. The Soviet Union uses relatively more labor and less equipment. Thus, if the CIA uses U.S. dollar prices as the weights to evaluate Soviet inputs, it is using higher prices for those items used in the USSR in relatively large amounts, while using lower prices for those items of which less is used.

For example, suppose the hypothetical numbers shown in Table 6B.1 are true. If the Soviet military effort is evaluated in rubles, it is 8

---

41. Senator William Proxmire, U.S. Congress, Joint Economic Committee, *Press Release* (April 30, 1983).

Table 6B.1
Hypothetical Figures for Two Military Program Budgets

	USSR		United States	
	Number	Rubles	Number	Dollars
Soldiers	4 million	2,000 each	2 million	15,000 each
Equipment	1,000	20 million each	2,000	10 million each

billion for soldiers and 20 billion for equipment, or 28 billion rubles. At the official 1982 exchange rate of $1.37, the total is $38.4 billion. The U.S. total is $30 billion for soldiers and $20 billion for equipment, or $50 billion total. What does the CIA do to compare the two military programs? It evaluates Soviet men and equipment at U.S. prices! Thus, it multiplies 4 million soldiers by $15,000 and multiplies 1,000 units of equipment by $10 million. This gives $60 billion plus $10 billion, or a Soviet total of $70 billion. Alternatively, using Soviet price weights, the Soviet military budget is 28 billion rubles and the U.S. budget is 44 billion rubles, or the U.S. budget is over one and a half times the Soviet budget. Yet, the statistical bias of the CIA method makes the Soviet military greater than the U.S. military in this case—even though the other methods would be just as "true" or "false."

Another problem is that the CIA basically overlooks the issue of quality. The CIA says that the USSR has 4.3 million uniformed personnel, or twice the U.S. level. The CIA evaluates these Soviet personnel at U.S. rates of pay. Yet the CIA itself discloses the facts that USSR military personnel have: (1) less formal education (in what the CIA claims are inferior schools); (2) lower standards of military training (the U.S. spends twice as much to train each soldier); (3) less exposure to operating power equipment, such as cars, because such equipment is less common in their households; and (4) less military hardware per head. (The Stockholm International Peace Research Institute report states that the number of Soviet soldiers manning a missile is five times the U.S. number.)

With respect to Soviet equipment, former CIA head William Colby admitted during testimony before the Joint Economic Committee of Congress: "There is a systematic upward bias in the valuation of Soviet equipment." How large is the bias? Soviet manufacturing exports receive on the average a 40 percent subsidy to make them competitive on the world market (so Soviet military equipment may be 40 percent overpriced). In 1977, Admiral Turner (then CIA director) suggested that approximately 30 percent of U.S. weapons are beyond Soviet technology. In other words, the CIA believes that the U.S. military gets a bigger bang for the buck.

Once again, in research and development the CIA makes no quality adjustment. Yet the CIA argues in all of its literature that the Soviets are very inefficient in this area. As one example, a CIA report states: "The estimate for Soviet Research, Development, Testing, and Evaluation outlays is the least reliable of our estimates . . . based on highly aggregated and uncertain data, we cannot speak with confidence, nor in detail." Given this uncertainty, one might expect the CIA to be cautious. On the contrary, they go on to assert that the Soviets spend one and a half times as much as the United States on research and development. According to the CIA, it is the fastest growing category of Soviet expenditures—increasing twice as fast as the rest of the military budget.

Regarding the entire military budget, other expert estimates of the comparative Soviet and U.S. military budgets range all over the spectrum, falling everywhere between the official Soviet and official U.S. estimates.

Some have argued the relevant comparison is not Soviet versus U.S. expenditure, but NATO versus Warsaw Pact spending. According to the International Institute of Strategic Services in London, in 1978 total NATO spending (including U.S. spending) was $180 billion, while total Warsaw Pact spending was $160 billion. Again, all such estimates suffer from many deficiencies.

We could go on with the difficulties of comparison at great length, but it may also be said that the whole discussion is silly and on the wrong issues. The main point made by many scientists opposed to further armaments is a simple but powerful one. *Both the Soviet Union and the United States have enough nuclear missiles to destroy the entire world several times over*. Who needs more?

Tentative Conclusions

The whole issue is *not* a trivial matter. According to most of the expert testimony (and the CIA's own testimony on many points), it appears that data is being falsified and distorted by the U.S. government in order to convince U.S. citizens to vote for greater military spending. This is being done by an administration that is attempting to cut peaceful, civilian spending.

We do not presume to answer the political issues for the reader, but it is important to understand the technical issues discussed above as well as the different economic roles played by military spending in the planned Soviet economy and the unplanned U.S. economy. These different roles help to explain some of the differing perceptions and propaganda in the two countries. In the U.S. economy, if the economy is at *full employment*, then it is clear that any dollar shifted from consumption and investment hurts U.S. growth and well-being. If, however, the United States suffers from vast unemployment, then the role of military spending is somewhat different.

Suppose that there are twelve million unemployed (as is true at the time this is being written). If one million are put to work producing napalm bombs, that does not subtract any previously unemployed labor from production of consumer and producer goods. On the contrary, since those one million workers will spend their income on consumption, it will generate more demand for workers in the consumer sector, thus increasing employment on civilian goods as well as military goods. For this reason there is political support in the United States for military spending by workers who get those jobs, by capitalists who will make a profit (usually at a much higher rate than in civilian production), and by politicians who wish to lower unemployment. The only economic argument on the other side is that far more jobs will be generated by many kinds of peaceful spending per dollar than by military spending (because military spending usually uses more capital and less labor). Of course, U.S. military spending contributes indirectly to higher budget deficits and interest rates as well as to possible inflationary pressure and microeconomic inefficiency.

In the Soviet Union, the situation is very different in the purely economic sphere. The USSR normally has full employment and a labor shortage—as do most of the centrally planned economies (for reasons explained in detail in Chapter 8). Therefore, at any given level of production, any increase in production of guns (or other military objects) must come from a decrease in production of bread (or other civilian goods). Thus, most Soviet consumers, workers, and planners see military production as very costly.

Recommended Readings

1. Abram Bergson, *Productivity and the Social System: The USSR and the West* (Cambridge: Harvard University Press, 1978).

2. Though somewhat dated, the best Marxist work on Soviet development remains Maurice Dobb, *Soviet Economic Development since 1917* (London: Routledge and Kegan Paul, 1966 ed.).

3. For comprehensive data and analysis of Soviet agricultural performance, Harry Shaffer, ed., *Soviet Agriculture: An Assessment of Its Contribution to Economic Development* (New York: Praeger, 1977).

4. Alec Nove, *Economic History of the Soviet Union* (London: Penguin, 1968).

5. U.S. Congress, Joint Economic Committee, *Soviet Economy in the 1980s* (Washington, D.C.: U.S. Government Printing Office, 1982), Parts 1 and 2.

6. Franklyn Holzman, *The Soviet Economy: Past, Present and Future* (New York: Foreign Policy Association, 1982).

Recommended Readings for Appendix 6A

1. Gregory Grossman, *Soviet Statistics of Physical Output of Industrial Commodities: Their Compilation and Quality* (Princeton, N.J.: Princeton University Press, 1960).

2. Also see the extensive discussions of methodology in Abram Bergson, *The Real National Income of Soviet Russia since 1928* (Cambridge: Harvard University Press, 1961).

Recommended Readings for Appendix 6B

1. Franklyn Holzman, "Is There a Soviet–U.S. Military Spending Gap?" *Challenge* (Sept./Oct., 1980): 3–9.

2. U.S. Congress, Joint Economic Committee, *Soviet Military–Economic Relations* (Washington, D.C.: U.S. Government Printing Office, 1983).

3. The CIA view is most explicit in National Foreign Assessment Center, *Soviet and U.S. Defense Activities, 1970–1979* (Washington, D.C.: U.S. Government Printing Office, 1980).

7
USSR
THE OPERATION OF
CENTRAL PLANNING

The Soviet Union has at least three different organizational structures at local and regional levels, which converge only at the top national level. It has, like all countries, a *governmental* structure; but it also has an *economic* hierarchy because it is centrally planned; and it has an all-important *political party* structure, representing the one legal party in the society. The organizational structure of these three lines of power is shown in Figure 7.1, and they are described in detail in the following paragraphs.

The Communist party is the most important decision-making body in the Soviet Union structure because it holds ultimate power over both the economy and the government. The Party's highest official is its General Secretary. The General Secretary (Stalin, Khrushchev, Brezhnev, Andropov) controls the Secretariat (comprising ten to fifteen members), which has the power to assign all Communists to any jobs in the country and to transfer them to any other jobs at any time. The General Secretary also presides over the Politburo, a small group of five to twenty members who make all important decisions in the Soviet Union. Nominally, the Politburo is elected by the Central Committee, which has about three to four hundred members. The Central Committee has the power to overrule the Politburo, but the Central Committee meets only a few times a year and, in practice, never overrules the Politburo.

The supreme body, in theory, is the Party Congress, but it meets at most once every two years (and usually less frequently). When it is in session, the Congress can overrule any past acts of the Central Committee or Politburo, and the Congress elects a new Central Committee. The Congress delegates are elected in turn by Party cells all over the country, each containing ten to a hundred members. Thus, in theory the Party structure is democratic, but in practice most elections within it have been controlled from higher levels. In fact, the

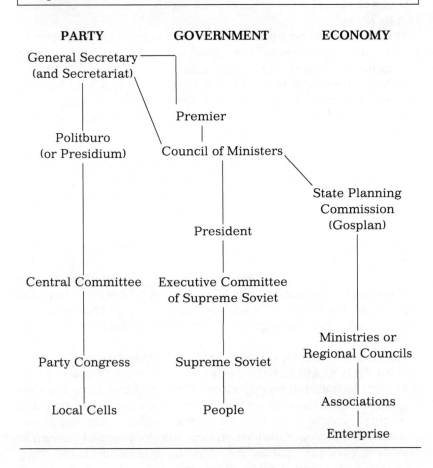

Figure 7.1
Organization of the Soviet Union

General Secretary usually has controlled the "election" of a preselected Politburo, as well as the "election" of the Central Committee, and even the "election" of Congress delegates.

Parallel to the Party apparatus is the governmental structure, which is controlled by the Party. Each locality has a soviet (the Russian word for council), theoretically elected by all the inhabitants. At one time, the local (city and village) soviets elected the regional soviets, or Republic Soviets, which then elected a Supreme Soviet. It should be noted that the Soviet Union is formally a federation of Republics, though in practice it is quite centralized. Since 1936, however, the Supreme Soviet has been chosen by direct election by the universal suffrage of all adult citizens. Candidates run uncontested. The Supreme Soviet is divided into a Soviet of Nationalities (about a thousand members representing different nationalities—from Russian to Uzbek to much smaller groups) and a Soviet of Union (about a thousand members representing equal numbers of population by areas).

The Supreme Soviet meets once or twice a year to pass (or rubber-stamp) laws, to give vent to local grievances, and to elect its Executive Committee composed of two or three hundred members. The Executive Committee meets more often, and it elects a Council of Ministers composed of thirty to one hundred members who act daily on all government matters. The Executive Committee also elects a President of the Soviet Union, who is a figurehead with only ceremonial power. The Council of Ministers is the functioning body, making everyday decisions in all areas from industrial sectors to foreign affairs to health and welfare. The Council of Ministers elects the highest government official, the Premier, or Prime Minister.

Since the Party can issue orders to all Communists, and all top leaders are Communists, the Party can issue orders at every level of government. Thus, the Party has its own men and women in office and can interfere with their actions at any time. Furthermore, lest there be any doubt, the Soviet Constitution allows only one political party in elections, the Communist party. On lower levels, however, the single slate of candidates includes a higher percentage of approved non-Party people, who are sometimes referred to as non-Party Communists.

The General Secretary of the Party not only has extralegal power to control Party elections but also has ultimate power through Party discipline to control the Premier and Council of Ministers. The Premier (also called the Prime Minister, or Chairman of the Council of Ministers), who is also a member of the Politburo, sometimes has considerable power of his own. In turn, the Premier and Council of Ministers exercise control over the top economic bodies. They appoint both the State Planning Commission (Gosplan) and the heads of Ministries and Associations. In the 1980s, however, it appears that Gosplan increasingly receives communications directly from the Central Committee or Politburo of the Party.

The third line of power, the economic structure, draws up the economic Plan, which is a legal document in the Soviet Union, designed by Gosplan and enacted into law by the appropriate government bodies (and usually jointly promulgated by the Party). The Plan is carried into operation at the top level by the Ministries (one minister for each sector of the economy, approximately forty ministries in all). There are usually several, often complex, intermediate bodies below the top level, all of which give orders to the basic economic unit, the enterprise. Since 1973, the number of intermediate planning bodies has been sharply reduced with the spread of Associations (combinations of enterprises). Some have argued that this, in effect, has increased the extent of centralization in the planning system by making it necessary for the Association to go directly to the center for allocations.[1] This contrasts with the stated government position that the Associations will facilitate the decentralization of research, development, and direction.

Forms of Enterprise

The Soviet Union still has a small privately owned sector in industry, and a larger cooperative area, but the vast bulk of industrial production is carried on in government-owned enterprises. The official Soviet data on the percentages of industrial production for some important years by each of these three types of ownership are shown in Table 7.1.

Table 7.1
Soviet Industrial Production by Type of Ownership

	1928	1937	1950	1960	1980
	(in percentages, rounded to nearest percent)				
Public organizations	69	90	92	97	98
Cooperatives	13	10	8	3	2
Private producers	18	0	0	0	0
Total	100	100	100	100	100

Source: Central Statistical Agency of USSR, *Narodnoe Khozaistvo SSSR v 1980 godu* (Moscow, 1982).

On the eve of the planning period in 1928 the private sector of industry was still quite significant and still produced more than the cooperatives. By 1937, however, the private sector was negligible, producing only two-tenths of one percent of industrial production, and it declined still further since then. The cooperative sector was sizable in 1928, but shows a slow and steady decline in percentage of total production ever since.

The largest part of the Soviet national product is produced by public enterprises in industry. The publicly owned industrial enterprise is the creation of the government, and in the past the government has provided its property, assets, and material resources free of charge. The government expects in return that the enterprise will fulfill its plan and return its profits (or a large proportion of them) to the government budget. A director is appointed to be in full charge of operations and is completely responsible for performance of the enterprise, although he or she is checked by various other organizations. He or she has full responsibility to the superior agency for the

---

1. Fyodor Kushnirsky, *Soviet Economic Planning, 1965–1980* (Boulder, Colo.: Westview Press, 1982).

performance of the firm. The primary task of the director is "to fulfill
and if possible overfulfill the output plans" and to utilize the resources placed at his or her disposal with due regard to the national
economy. Successful plan fulfillment results in material bonuses for
the manager and for the workers of the enterprise, as well as the right
to retain a share of profits (the "stimulation fund") to be used for small
investments, collective social consumption, and the formation of the
bonus fund. Although the basic output plan of the enterprise is centrally determined, firms are expected to keep profit and loss accounts
and to be financially independent.

The firm faces a strict set of limitations. Prices of inputs and outputs
are fixed. The supplies of materials are usually subject to control, and
some materials can be obtained only by means of an allocation certifi-
cate. This planning of supplies to each industry or firm is a central
focus of Soviet planning. It is a very complicated and difficult business, and the rigidity of materials allocations results in some major
bottlenecks. It has been one main point of attack in recent Soviet
discussions of reform.

What the firm faces, then, is a set of plans, which are not necessarily
consistent: plans for gross output (recently changed to net output),
profit, cost reduction, wages bill, and materials allocation, among
others. The manager must maneuver within the boundaries of these
material supplies, wage funds, and selling prices in order to achieve
his or her production target and planned profit. Fortunately for the
manager, there are loopholes. Illegal hoarding of materials, the use of
expediters, the firm's use of its own workshops to make supplies not
included in the Plan, and informal contracts between firms all contribute to flexibility.

The Ministry System

From 1932 to 1957 the organization of the planning administration
below the center was by Commissariats or Ministries. Each Ministry
was in charge of a certain sector of industry, and the power of each
was ranked on a priority basis. At first there were just three Ministries: light industry, heavy industry, and the timber industry. These
expanded to thirty or forty ministries, mostly to separate certain
priority industries in the heavy industry sector. Each All-Union Ministry was at that time based in Moscow and had charge of all the
enterprises in its sector all over the nation. It had departmental
divisions for planning, supplies, disposals, deliveries, and other operations. It also had the function of drafting the output and supply
plans for the enterprises to submit to the State Planning Commission.
This State Planning Commission then had the job of coordinating the
plans of the Ministries to arrive at balances between the industries

and a supply and delivery plan for the thousands of centrally allocated goods.

Coordination was extremely difficult partly because each Ministry tended to develop its own self-sufficient empire. A Ministry would often endeavor to create its own input supply system because of the uncertainty of supplies from other Ministries. Thus, a factory producing nails for Ministry A would send its nails to another firm under the same Ministry three thousand miles away, even though a factory under Ministry B was situated right next door and required the nails. Transportation costs could be greatly reduced by using supplies from the other Ministry, but until the 1960s most prices did not include transportation costs. Thus, geographically coordinated planning, or the utilization of local resources on a regional basis, was problematic.

Centrally coordinated planning faces other more fundamental problems. By the crude methods used to date, there are problems in arriving at proper balances between products. There are problems of obtaining sufficient, accurate information and enough time to use it. There is the problem that prices are rather arbitrary and do not always reflect the degree of scarcity, so the result may be inefficient use of resources. There is the problem that overambitious growth plans and weak budget constraints lead to overfull employment and overcommitment of resources or shortages in all areas. All of these and other problems have led each Ministry or enterprise to develop its own auxiliary supply sources, which may be in small, inefficient workshops. There is also the tendency to haul supplies enormous distances. Finally, the enterprises use large numbers of special workers, popularly called *pushers* (corresponding to the so-called expediters in the U.S. economy during the Second World War), who use all sorts of legal and semilegal devices—such as persuasion, bribery, or exchange of one scarce good for another—to obtain necessary supplies.

At any rate, since planning under the Ministry system was very crude, whenever bottlenecks or shortages occurred, deliveries under the formal Plan were superseded by deliveries made according to the importance of the Ministry, that is, its political and economic priority. Both current resources and new capital would then be directed to the Ministry enjoying the higher priority ranking. Each Minister argued for the importance of his industry to the nation's welfare, regardless of what products it produced.

In 1957, under Khrushchev, an attempt was made to solve some of the problems of Ministerial independence by switching to a system of territorial or regional councils. But it was found that this system created worse problems of independence or autarchy by each region. In 1965, after the fall of Khrushchev, the Soviet Union went back to the Ministerial system of industry direction. The switch back to the Ministerial system also enabled Brezhnev to substitute his own men for Khrushchev's planners.

The Organization of the Planning Mechanism

Enterprise managers receive their production directives from a yearly plan. Plans are elaborated in industry for output, investment, inputs, costs, credits, wages, and other indicators. The crucial plan, however, is the plan for materials supply. Once a set of output targets is settled upon, the supply plan must assure the availability and distribution of the material supplies required to fulfill all output targets. This is done by the central allocation of the means of production, including basic raw materials as well as machinery.

The central planning organ of the USSR is the State Planning Commission (Gosplan). It puts into detailed form both the output and the supply plans and bears the responsibility for the consistency and balance of the two. Gosplan, of course, deals with only the most important commodities, those that must be centrally allocated. The scope of its coverage is no small matter, however, involving in recent years some four thousand commodities, up from twenty-seven hundred in the late 1960s.[2] Other commodities are left to the responsibility of the subordinate planning organs.

How is the planning of the main outputs and supplies carried out? Gosplan works very closely with other levels of the hierarchy to formulate a feasible plan. Below Gosplan are the intermediary planning bodies which can be organized along either ministerial (industrial) or regional (territorial) lines. These organs have corresponding subordinate units called chief administrative agencies, or, increasingly since 1973, Associations. These agencies deal directly with the enterprises, which constitute the lowest level. The planning mechanism occurs in six overlapping stages. (The precise number of planning stages is arbitrary, depending on where we make the separations.) The process is discussed below.

First, both Gosplan and the planning departments of the lower units begin to draw up tentative plans for the next year's (the planned year's) production. Gosplan starts first with a statistical analysis of the base year performance in order to uncover failures, bottlenecks, and other causes of supply deficiencies as well as new sources or increases in other material supplies. This process of gathering statistics on past performance from the enterprises requires most of the period from January to June of each year.

In the second stage (June and July) the political leaders set general goals to be specified by the planners. Thus, the Politburo or Council of Ministers decides upon a set of aggregate output targets. These targets reflect political and economic policy decisions regarding the growth rate of certain priority industries and the division of national income between consumption and investment. Using the data col-

---

2. *Ibid.*, 20.

lected on the base year (the previous year), Gosplan then calculates a set of "control figures." The control figures constitute the first estimate of consistent output and supply requirements of each industry, dependent on the overall capacity of the economy.

Meanwhile, the lower organs and enterprises are estimating their input and output requirements based on their performance in the previous year. However, they must await the issuance of the control figures before they can complete even their tentative plans. The control figures serve as guideposts to the industry as to what kind of performance and targets are expected by the central authority (and the industry then devises more detailed targets for the enterprises).

The third stage then follows (from August to October) with a series of bargaining processes between the various levels of the planning hierarchy: the enterprise and its chief administrative agency or Association, the agency and the Ministry, and the Ministry and Gosplan. Each lower level wants as low an output target and as great an amount of supplies as possible, so it can increase the probability of fulfilling its planned target and earn bonuses. The enterprise completes its first draft of supply estimates based on the notion of input norms, or technological coefficients. A technological coefficient describes as a ratio how much of a given input is required to produce one unit of a given output. It is essentially a reflection of the technological development of a given industry. The lower the input norm, the higher the advancement of technology.

The written supply requests are then sent by the enterprise up the hierarchy to its Association (or chief administrative agency). The Association's plan is just a collation of those of the firms it supervises. The Association, however, is well aware of the pressures from above that stress maximum output and economy in supplies. It is also aware of the tendency for the firm to pad its supply requests in order to have a slack or reserve in case of supply failures—or, if possible, in order to use those extra supplies to fulfill the output plan and thus receive a bonus. The Association, however, must also propose a plan for itself that it will have to fulfill; so it will simply add padding at this point. Only much later, after the Plan is made into law, will the Association's or agency's interests diverge somewhat from its enterprises. Then, if the Association or agency can cut down the supplies going to any one of its enterprises, it can save those extra supplies for emergencies that might occur in one of its enterprises elsewhere. After the Plan is approved by higher authorities, the Association or agency may try to reduce the input norm of the enterprise by claiming that the enterprise can produce at a more efficient level, that is, that it can produce the same amount of goods with fewer material inputs.

When the Associations or chief agencies have finished their plan statements, these proposed plans are sent up again to either the Ministry or the regional planning body. Bargaining again occurs, as it is obvious that too low an output plan or too large a request for supplies will be rejected by Gosplan (though again, a Ministry might acquiesce to padded plans until after the Plan has been legally approved). Finally, the aggregated output plans and the supply requirements arrive at Gosplan from the Ministry or Republic.

The fourth stage of Soviet planning (in October and November) is the attempt of Gosplan to balance nearly all of the conflicting estimates of possible outputs and required inputs. It may be recalled here that each enterprise, Association, and Ministry has now submitted its output plan and the amounts of various inputs it will need to achieve the plan. It would be a coincidence, indeed, if there were an exact correspondence between the total proposed output of any product and the total proposed requests for the product by enterprises using it as an input. If the total demand for some input goes beyond its planned output, something must be changed. Theoretically, the whole plan should be recalculated. In practice, an attempt is made to see if more of that one product could somehow be produced with the existing capacity in that industry. Or else an attempt is made to lower the "required" supplies of that product in one (or more) of the following ways: (1) by lowering the "needs" of supplies to other industries by making the other industries be more efficient, that is, by causing them to produce with less of that input per unit of production; or (2) by finding hidden reserves of that input in the industries using it; or (3) by using the centrally kept reserves of some important inputs; or (4) by importing the product. Furthermore, the fact that each lower level has asked for more than the necessary supplies (and keeps emergency inventories) builds a certain amount of flexibility into the planned balance. As a more unwelcome (but often used) alternative, the planners may reduce the output targets of the lowest priority industries, so the scarce inputs can go to the higher priority industries.

If, on the other hand, the planners attempt to increase the output of the scarce input, this circumstance has many repercussions which must be taken into consideration. For example, more steel requires more coal, which in turn requires more steel and more machinery and more labor, and so forth, with such requirements reverberating back and forth in many, many sectors of the economy. As mentioned above, another resort might be an increase of imports, if there is enough foreign exchange to pay for the additional imports. When we examine such balance problems systematically in the next chapter, we shall see that it makes a great difference to the planners whether they must choose an alternative with many repercussions throughout the plan or whether they are able to use means—like imports purchased on credit—that have no effect on other current plans.

Stage five of Soviet planning occurs in about November and December. The complete plan is submitted to the political leaders in the Council of Ministers and the Politburo, who view it from a national perspective. Undoubtedly, some jockeying occurs at this top level as individuals attempt to secure more resources for their own pet projects.

Finally, in stage six (in December and January) the aggregate goals of each industry or region, which have now been adopted at the highest levels, are further specified down to lower levels. Eventually, as a rule after the year begins, the individual enterprises receive their individual plans.

Obviously, there are problems with this system, even assuming fairly perfect theoretical planning techniques. First, if the planners are too optimistic about what can be produced with given inputs, the balances achieved will be quite unreal. Whenever an enterprise is given—by mistake—an increase in output with no additional inputs or with insufficient additional inputs, it has an impossible task to perform. Second, if the annual plan comes to the enterprise any time after the beginning of the year, this lateness will obviously cause a certain amount of misguided work. Third, even the finished plan is much too aggregative (that is, for a group of commodities rather than specific commodities) to specify most of the particular tasks of the enterprise.

An additional problem arises from the fact that plans are frequently changed by amendments after the firm has received the final plan. Changes may come from a superior agency or direct from the Communist party. In many cases the amendments increase the output goals of the firm but do not increase the allocations of inputs from its suppliers. For example, a survey of ninety-five enterprises in the Novosibirsk area revealed that these enterprises together received 1,554 amendments to their annual plan one year without any change in their input allowances.

In the agricultural sector, planning is somewhat different—less precise and less direct. It is less precise because nature is so unpredictable and because so many individual units are involved. It is less direct and more incomplete because most farming units are not government enterprises but are private or cooperative. Private farming now has few restrictions (except by taxation to some degree). Until the 1965 reforms, the cooperative or collective farms were given compulsory minimum delivery quotas to sell to the government but were never assigned fixed total targets. Thus, between the fickleness of nature and the lower degree of central control, it is not surprising that the aggregate agricultural plan is seldom close to the actual agricultural output.

In addition to the plan for current production, there is a plan for investment or expansion of production. Once the State Planning Commission has decided to expand production in a certain industry, a Project Committee is formed of engineers and experts in the area in order to make the technical specifications. They must decide the location and scale of new factories, the exact kind of new machinery, and in general the whole range of technology.

The one-year plans are not the only plans designed by the State Planning Commission (Gosplan). Gosplan also designs highly aggregated five-year plans, which become decrees and are well publicized. Whereas a five-year plan might refer to footwear production, the annual plan will specify shoes, boots, house slippers, and so forth. The five-year plans have been given increasing importance and more detail since the 1979 planning reform. The one-year plans are supposed to conform to the five-year plans. There are also longer-range ten- and fifteen-year plans announced from time to time. Only the one-year plans, however, become law and are given in great detail to the firm to follow as a command.

Also, there are not only physical plans; there are also financial plans in rubles. The financial plans include not only plans for each firm but also national plans for all government revenue and expenditure (these are discussed in the next chapter with respect to the problem of balance and stability). Finally, there are not only domestic plans but a detailed plan for foreign trade (discussed below).

The Price System

We may classify the roles that Soviet prices[3] play into three categories: (1) control and evaluation, (2) allocation, and (3) income distribution. First, to the degree that central planners cannot specify all inputs and outputs in complete detail, the decisions of managers are influenced by the prices set on their inputs and outputs. The manager's performance is evaluated basically in physical terms, but prices are needed to supply a common denominator for the different outputs produced as well as the different inputs utilized. Furthermore, any kind of economic or cost accounting is impossible without prices. Even with distorted prices, cost accounting serves several important functions. One of these functions is to make possible "economizing" of scarce resources by the firm. Another is that it provides a means of checking or evaluating the firm's performance by higher authorities—by stating profits or losses, at least relative to planned profit or losses.

Second, the central planners themselves are influenced by the prices of different substitutes in choosing among technological variants and in allocating investment among different possible investment projects. Prices are used as the common denominator among different products in calculating various aggregate balances,

---

3. The best discussions of Soviet prices are in the many books and articles of Morris Bornstein; see, e.g., "Soviet Price Policy in the 1970s," in U.S. Congress, Joint Economic Committee, *Soviet Economy in a New Perspective* (Washington, D.C.: U.S. Government Printing Office, 1976), 17–66.

such as the balance between the supply and demand for consumer goods. Central planners also use differential wage levels to allocate labor to different areas, industries, and skills. Finally, central planners may use prices to influence farmers, both in the collectives and on the private plots, to allocate their resources to certain agricultural outputs rather than to others.

The third function of prices is to play a role in the distribution of income among workers. The distribution of income is supposed to follow the socialist principle of payment according to work accomplished. This principle implies unequal payments, which provides an incentive for improved and more intensive work or for changing jobs. A person's place in the income distribution is determined, then, by the structure of prices of the goods he or she buys, the money wage, the income tax, and the transfer payments made to him or her by the government.

We may distinguish four important classes of prices that carry out the functions of the price system discussed above. These are (1) retail prices of consumer goods, (2) prices of labor services (wage and salary rates), (3) wholesale prices to industrial enterprises, and (4) prices of agricultural goods. Here, we only wish to introduce and describe the institutional arrangements in each area. The planning problems connected with prices will be discussed more thoroughly in later chapters.

Retail Prices of Consumer Goods

From the viewpoint of the Soviet consumer, the Soviet economy appears to be quite similar to other modern economies. First, the consumer receives a money income. Second, the consumer may spend that income in any proportions he or she likes on whatever goods he or she desires to buy. A wide variety of goods (but quite limited by U.S. standards) is available—though the government does not allow the production or sale of goods like narcotics, sex magazines, or war comic books (so they are not among consumer alternatives).

One obvious difference from the U.S. economy is the much larger proportion of goods available at zero price, for example, public health and all education. A second obvious difference from any private enterprise economy is the lack of any possibility of private investment; the individual may not buy a share in any enterprise. He or she may save money by buying government bonds, by depositing the money at interest in the State Bank, by hoarding cash, or by buying life insurance, but he or she may not invest for profit in a private enterprise. Furthermore, most national Soviet saving is "forced" in the sense that a part of the national income is taken by taxation into the government budget and is used for government investment. Government decisions may result in lower production of consumer goods (in current prices) than total wages and bonuses paid out to producers; this circumstance results in involuntary saving. Thus, unlike a private enterprise economy, the government—not the private investor—makes all investments and decides the ratio between consumption and investment. The only exceptions to this rule are the small replacement investments made by enterprises (which must be sanctioned by the authorities) and the investments by collective farms (which are anticipated by the Plan.)

A very profound difference lies in the fact that Soviet consumers have freedom of choice among goods but no choice among sellers because most goods are sold only by the government monopoly. Consumers do not have "consumer sovereignty" if that is defined as the determination of the output mixture by consumer preferences. If Soviet consumers change their preferences and want other goods not currently being produced, the government monopoly can decide not to change outputs correspondingly. Instead, the government may simply adjust the prices of these goods so that consumer demand is brought back into balance with supply at the new prices—or it may ration the goods or merely allow long lines of consumers. There are "houses of fashion" to show off the latest styles to consumers and to wholesale buyers—and there are surveys of consumer preferences. The Soviet government also influences the quantity demanded by setting high prices on some luxuries, such as cars, while setting low prices on some necessities, such as children's clothing.

Prices of Labor Services (Wage Rates)

Workers for the most part are also free to choose among jobs at prevailing wage rates. They face the same government monopoly, though, in the industrial labor market. They must take some job offered at the going wage level if they wish to work. Now suppose too few workers wish to take a particular job (in a geographical area, an industry, or a skill) compared with the labor needed to fill the output target of that industry. In such a case, the output target is not likely to be changed; more probably, the relative wage for the job is raised.

The relative structure of wages will thus reflect—along with other determining factors—workers' preferences, in the sense that higher wages must be offered to attract workers to more unpleasant, more difficult, or more skilled jobs. The main factors in Soviet wage determination—each of which is given a certain weight in each industry—include: skill required, disutility or unpleasantness of the job, priority of the industry, and locational advantages or disadvantages. The wage rates or bonuses are often used to adjust the supply of workers to the planned demand for labor. The physical plan for output and labor in each area, however, remains as unaffected by changes in rates as it is by changes in retail prices.

Industrial Wholesale Prices

The prices of industrial goods, whether consumer goods passing through wholesalers to retail trade or producer goods for industry itself, are fixed by administrative decree by the State Committee on Prices. They are supposed to include the planned average cost of production plus a margin of profit. These prices are vital guideposts to both planners and managers.

Most Soviet planning is done in physical terms. Yet prices certainly play an important role, or should play such a role if the intention is to plan in an optimal manner. Indeed, the Soviet planners do practice financial planning as well as physical; this is to ensure that money flows will be in balance and consistent with the physical flows. For example, an enterprise is allotted a certain amount of funds to buy supplies, even though it may also have to present a direct allocation order to the supplier. More important, in the aggregate the total amount of monetary capital must be allocated to various new investments, and it would be very difficult to handle these amounts (and other aggregations of things) without using some kind of money prices.

There are also some kinds of physical decision making that cannot be done at all meaningfully without the kind of knowledge reflected in prices and costs. For example, is it cheaper to use coal or oil for railroad engine fuel? To make this evaluation one should know the relative prices (or marginal costs to society) of coal and oil and of the kinds of engines that use them. It should be noted, however, that Soviet prices have been such poor measures of the real costs of most commodities that it is often difficult to allocate resources efficiently. Even Stalin once complained that the price of bread was less than the price of the inputs to produce the bread. If that was so, then Soviet planners could not even balance the inputs of grain with the desired output of bread; and certainly they could not make a rational decision as to the best way of increasing the production of bread.

Soviet industrial price policy, however, is important not only to planners but to managers. Even in a highly centralized economy, many production decisions must be left to each enterprise manager. For example, if an enterprise manager is able to obtain either steel or aluminum for production, and if one of them is cheaper (but perhaps less durable), should the manager substitute the less expensive material throughout? To the extent that the manager is judged by the profits and not by durability, the manager will likely be motivated to employ the cheaper input.

Agricultural Prices

Prices in Soviet agriculture are handled quite differently than in industry. Most similar to the industrial sector are the state farms, which are supposed to be run as factories in the fields. Their prices and outputs are set by the central planners. Even the state farms cannot be so closely planned, however, as is industry. The most important additional problems are: (1) extremely different conditions in different regions, and (2) unpredictably changeable weather conditions.

The collective farms are even less directly controlled. True, they contribute to the government a given quota of output at low, fixed prices. In fact, we have noted that these procurement prices used to be set so low that the procurements constituted a tax on the collectives. Beyond these quotas, however, the collectives are free to sell their output at any price they can get either to the government or to any individual who wishes to buy. During the Stalin era, under the procurement quota system with low prices and high quotas, there was naturally little incentive for producing collective farm goods when farmers reaped such small gains. Khrushchev began to change the situation. He not only continued to lower retail industrial prices but also raised farm procurement prices in 1953, 1958, 1962, and 1963. Khrushchev's successors took the more radical step of lowering or abolishing some procurement quotas.

There is another, higher set of prices for the goods that individuals produce by their own labor on small, private farm plots (which explains their tendency to work harder on these plots than on the collective farms). The vegetables and livestock from these plots are sold in the cities at any price the seller can get. Thus, some part of collective farm produce and all of the surplus private produce of individual farmers are sold at freely fluctuating prices set solely by supply and demand. These markets have usually soaked up, at very high prices, a large proportion of the excess demand for food. When there is so-called repressed inflation (prices set below the equilibrium) in government stores, the rising prices in the collective farm markets are a good indicator of the repressed inflation. It should be noted that the quality of these freely sold goods is generally higher.

The Second Economy

So far, we have discussed only the transactions in the Soviet economy that are exactly within the letter of Soviet law—sometimes called the first, or "red," economy. There is also a large, second economy, or black market, composed of illegal transactions. In fact, there is really a whole spectrum of markets in between, from almost legal, through semi-legal, to illegal.

There are, of course, a huge number of illegal transactions in the United States as well. Organized crime controls large parts of cities (Las Vegas) and industries (the East Coast longshore industry). Orga-

nized crime is even tied into many legitimate businesses and sometimes to agencies of the government.

While the results are somewhat similar in the Soviet Union, the
motivations and structure are quite different. Rather than viewing
themselves as criminals, Soviet citizens are more likely to think of
their activities in the way that a secretary working for the U.S. government, for example, would view his or her use of the office telephone
for private calls, or as a Cabinet member might see the use of his or
her chauffeured car for family transportation.

Since every commercial and industrial enterprise in the Soviet
Union is government owned, there is a huge gray area of semi-legal
transactions. While it is important to recognize that some of these
transactions hurt the Soviet economy by distorting information and
diverting resources to less important uses, it should be noted that
some of these semi-legal transactions help the economy by giving it a
necessary flexibility. The national plan is a very rigid document, with
many mistakes and many omissions. Suppose a truck-building firm
has been allocated all the inputs it needs to build one hundred
thousand trucks, except that it gets no tires for the last twenty
thousand! In this case, by strictly following the law, the firm builds one
hundred thousand excellent trucks, but only eighty thousand with
tires. In Soviet reality, the firm sends out a "pusher" who—by hook or
by crook—gets tires delivered for the remaining twenty thousand
trucks. The pusher and the manager get good bonuses, and the economy gets twenty thousand additional working trucks. It is estimated
that very significant amounts of steel and concrete are obtained by
pushers, who use sweet talk or begging or bribery or unplanned
exchanges. Recognizing that such activities provide needed flexibility, Soviet authorities often look the other way and condone these
unplanned transactions.

A second type of semi-legal or illegal transaction is the construction
of homes by private crews. It is legal to build a house privately (though
not considered as good for the country in the long run as public
construction). But some of these crew members may be doing private
work while they are being paid to work on a public job. And some
large percentage of their materials may have been allocated for use
in public construction.

A third type of illegal transaction encompasses the many employees who lack consumer goods and simply steal from public enterprises. In a fourth type, private production for profit by hired workers
is illegal in the USSR, even if the workers' labor time and materials
are not stolen from state enterprises. Yet some of the goods and
services produced in this illegal manner may be quite necessary, as
they would not otherwise be produced.

Finally, there are many tips, "gifts" to salespeople, and under-the-
counter selling of goods in short supply for higher prices. This, of

course, reduces the supply available to people who are trying to buy goods legitimately.

Some sectors have particularly large amounts of economic crime. Small private subsidiary farm plots are legal, but the farmers illegally use their time when they are being paid to work on the state or collective farm. Some truck drivers have gotten rich by diverting or selling their freight. Most of these economic crimes are discussed by the Soviet press.

Appendix 7A
Soviet Planning for International Trade

All foreign trade in the USSR is conducted by state trading corporations, specializing in export and import trading. Most of these enterprises are under the direction of the Ministry of Foreign Trade. For each product, one trading enterprise is always in a monopoly position, contracting as the exclusive buyer or seller, and acting as intermediary between foreign firms and domestic firms. The Ministry of Foreign Trade keeps fairly tight control over the state trade monopoly by assigning detailed plans for volume, assortment, prices, and transport of trade commodities.

Method of Planning International Trade

The annual plan for international trade is largely based on the requirements of the domestic production Plan. Of course, before annual adjustments are considered, the Soviets begin with a core of more or less regular exports and imports. Thus, they usually export large amounts of armaments, iron ore, coal, and oil, while importing tin, cotton, wheat, and sugar, among others. The annual juggling consists of (1) changes in the amounts of these regularly traded goods, (2) new imports to fill domestic bottlenecks, and (3) new exports from newly discovered unwanted surpluses. Since there is constant pressure to increase imports to ease bottlenecks, there is also constant pressure to find more goods to export and more markets for them. It is important to realize that the Soviets do not look at exports mainly as a way of making profits (which is the view of all private capitalist merchants), but as a way of balancing needed imports.

The sequence of planning the annual adjustments is as follows. First, and most important, the planners scan the domestic Plan to find those areas in which domestic production cannot meet the planned demand, or in which it would be very costly to produce all that is needed. Some of these deficits are chronic, as, for example, those in tin, natural rubber, and tropical fruits. These products and many others are imported at roughly constant levels year after year. Other deficits develop as a result of sudden changes in the Plan through miscalculations in the planning process. On the basis of both the usual needs and the unexpected needs, an import plan is drawn up that will just fill these key domestic deficits.

Next, the planners add up the now-determined imports to see how much total export will be needed to pay for these planned imports. Then they examine the planned domestic production to find which particular goods will be in surplus over domestic needs—or which products can most easily and cheaply be increased in production. Those products are designated for export. It has already been noted that there are many regular exports, such as lumber and petroleum. The Soviets simply plan every year to produce "surpluses" of these commodities for sale abroad. Finally, the export and import plans are supported by detailed plans for geographical distribution and financing.

If at first the import and export plans are out of balance—usually because not enough exports can be found to pay for the imports—the planners attempt to scrape together more "nonessential" goods for export. These exports are usually taken from the low-priority consumer goods industries. In the 1970s and 1980s, the Soviets have benefited from high gold prices and have unloaded large quantities of their gold stocks to meet foreign payments obligations. Extra oil and gas sales were used in this way during 1982 and 1983. The planners are seldom driven to the extreme of cutting down imports which are essential for domestic production, because losing these imports would mean reducing the domestic plan. In theory, it would be possible for the planners to make some adjustments in the domestic plan and then to recalculate the foreign trade plan. In practice, the Soviet planners have so far found such secondary adjustments to be too time-consuming—and too disruptive of domestic planning. So they have usually stopped the process with a foreign trade plan that is heavily influenced by the domestic production plan, but with little or no reciprocal influence.

The Volume of Trade

In general, the foreign trade of the Soviet Union has been smaller, relative to its national income, than the trade of advanced Western economies. For example, in 1981 the Soviet ratio of exports to GNP was only 5.0 percent, whereas the U.S. ratio was 8.1 percent. Furthermore, the trade of the Soviet Union has been less than what it was before the country became a planned economy. It is worth inquiring why this is so.

Immediately after the Revolution, Soviet trade practically ceased for a few years. Then there was a gradual recovery, followed by a rapid increase in the First Five-Year plan. In 1930–1932 exports plus imports rose to about 7 or 8 percent of national income—mostly because imports of machinery were crucial to the industrialization drive. By 1936–1938, however, exports plus imports had fallen to only 1 percent of national income. This decline was due partly to the elimination of the worst bottlenecks for which machine imports were vital and partly to the Great Depression in the capitalist world, which drastically lowered the price offered for Soviet exports.

During World War II, Soviet trade figures began climbing rapidly, since the Soviet government readily accepted economic cooperation and aid from its allies. The higher levels were at first maintained to an extent after the peace settlements. However, as the East and West blocs emerged as separate political-economic spheres of influence and competition, inter-bloc trade stagnated or even declined. Foreign trade thus remained a small percentage of Soviet national income for some years, yet it did rise steadily from the mid 1950s to the 1980s.

Exports rose from 3 percent of Soviet national income in 1955 to 6.5 percent in 1976. This percentage is still somewhat less than in comparable capitalist nations. We can now list the reasons for this lower trade percentage, some of which were already mentioned. First, trade with the Soviet Union was prohibited by the capitalist nations in its earliest years as an attempt to stop its birth. Second, when the USSR did increase its trade in the early 1930s, we have noted that it ran into troubles because of the Great Depression. The Soviets concluded that it is dangerous to be tied into the capitalist trade network because it is subject to very wide fluctuations in volume as well as price.

Third, after the Second World War, during the Cold War of the 1950s, the United States again attempted to prohibit foreign trade with the Soviet Union in a wide range of goods. U.S. allies paid little attention, so Soviet trade grew. This policy was renewed by the Carter administration with a ban on trade in grain and by the Reagan administration with a ban on exports of large pipes for the Soviet pipeline to West Europe. Again, U.S. allies paid little attention, so these embargoes were unsuccessful; but they did have a dampening effect on U.S.–Soviet trade.

Fourth, the complex mechanisms and red tape of Soviet foreign trade may also have some dampening effect. One problem is that Soviet internal enterprises have little incentive for foreign trade because they obtain no extra profit from selling abroad at a high price. If a large profit is made above the domestic price in the transaction, that profit goes to the government treasury rather than to the enterprise. Of course, since foreign trade is strictly controlled by the state, even if enterprises were to have the incentive to export, they might not have the right to do so.

Another problem for Soviet trade is that Soviet currency is exchanged only at a fixed price and is "nonconvertible." This means that Soviet citizens and enterprises may not convert rubles to other currencies without explicit government permission—nor may foreigners with Soviet currency abroad use it to buy Soviet goods without government agreement. Therefore, the Soviet Union must pay for all imports (a) with gold, or (b) in some convertible Western currency, or (c) on credit. This complicates their trading and is one reason they make strict bilateral agreements rather than engage in more flexible trading with all countries.

In spite of the barriers, Soviet trade has not only expanded in total volume, but the share of its trade with the capitalist countries has also expanded. In 1950, only 19 percent of Soviet trade was with capitalist countries, but that figure rose to 40 percent by 1978.[4] Of that 40 percent, almost 30 percent is with the more developed capitalist countries; only a little over 10 percent is with the underdeveloped capitalist countries. The Soviet Union buys many kinds of manufactured goods from the mature capitalist countries and exports many raw materials to them. Yet the USSR exports heavy machinery (and some oil) to the underdeveloped countries, while importing raw materials and agricultural products from them. It is worth emphasizing that the monopoly of foreign trade by the government allows it to import only essential commodities and not spend currency on luxuries. This contrasts with the case in many developing countries where large amounts of scarce Western currency are spent each year to import luxuries for the wealthy.

A vital issue for the Soviet economy is the question of how to coordinate its trade with its planning. We mentioned the theoretical issues earlier, but we must also note the specific problems of its coordination with its communist trading partners, all of whom also have planned economies. Ideally, they should all agree on one international plan for trade that is coordinated with each of their economies. For this purpose they formed the Council for Mutual Economic Assistance (called CMEA or COMECON), consisting of the USSR, Bulgaria, Hungary, East Germany, Cuba, Mongolia, Poland, Rumania, and Czechoslovakia.

COMECON attempts to integrate into a single five-year plan the needs of each trading partner in each industry. It also tries to lay out many joint projects and joint ventures. But these goals are very difficult to achieve because of all the problems of planning already mentioned, as well as some specifically international problems. For example, if all the partners have rather arbitrary price systems, at

---

4. See Paul R. Gregory and Robert C. Stuart, *Soviet Economic Structure and Performance* (New York: Harper and Row, 1981), 267.

what price shall they exchange? Moreover, should the status quo in trade patterns be frozen or should future goods be different? For example, at one point Rumania exported mainly oil and food; the USSR and other COMECON nations thought that was fine, the most efficient use of comparative advantage. But Rumania fought for and obtained the right to expand many branches of its own industry so that it could have a more balanced growth and more independence. When they could stand against Soviet influence, each of the COMECON countries has chosen diversification as a means of gaining greater economic independence.

The existence of planned trade within COMECON helps to remove some of the uncertainty of trade on the international free market. This greater certainty, in turn, facilitates planning the domestic economy. As Soviet trade has been oriented increasingly toward the West, however, and the USSR has come to depend more and more on technological transfers, the Soviet Union has had to accept greater uncertainty in its trade relations (including cyclical changes in prices and amounts demanded by the West). In contrast, its gain from expanding commercial relations with the West has been greater flexibility and a broader access to Western industrial goods and processes.

Recommended Readings

1. The structure of Soviet planning and price setting is discussed in detail in Alec Nove, *The Soviet Economic System* (London: George Allen and Unwin, 2d ed., 1980), Chapters 1, 2, 3, 4, and 7. An excellent, up-to-date introductory primer on the Soviet economy is Franklyn Holzman, *The Soviet Economy: Past, Present and Future* (New York: Foreign Policy Association, 1982).

2. The illegal and semi-legal transactions are discussed in Gregory Grossman, "Notes on the Illegal Private Economy and Corruption," U.S. Congress, Joint Economic Committee, *The Soviet Economy in a Time of Change* (Washington, D.C.: U.S. Government Printing Office, 1979), Vol. 2.

3. Also see Gregory Grossman, "The 'Second Economy' of the USSR," in Morris Bornstein, ed., *The Soviet Economy: Continuity and Change* (Boulder, Colo.: Westview Press, 1981), 71–96.

4. The whole range of legal to semi-legal to illegal transactions (red, brown, and black markets) are discussed in Aron Katzenelenboigen, "Coloured Markets in the Soviet Union," *Soviet Studies,* Vol. 29 (Jan. 1977): 62–85.

5. How the plan is carried out is discussed in Raymond P. Powell, "Plan Execution and the Workability of Soviet Planning," in Bornstein, *The Soviet Economy,* 39–60.

6. A good general introduction to planning is in R. W. Davies, "Economic Planning in the USSR," in Bornstein, *The Soviet Economy*, 7–38.

7. On how the Soviets actually set prices, see Morris Bornstein, "The Administration of the Soviet Price System," *Soviet Studies*, Vol. 30 (Oct. 1978): 466–90.

8. On how Polish prices are actually planned, see Zbigniew Czerwinski, "Prices in a Planned Economy," *Soviet Studies*, Vol. 30 (July 1978): 372–83.

9. Fyodor Kushnirsky, *Soviet Economic Planning, 1965–1980* (Boulder, Colo.: Westview Press, 1982).

10. Janos Kornai, *Economics of Shortage* (Amsterdam: North Holland, 1980).

11. E. H. Carr and R. W. Davies, *Foundations of a Planned Economy* (New York: Macmillan, 1969).

12. M. Cave, *Computers and Economic Planning: The Soviet Experience* (Cambridge: Cambridge University Press, 1980).

13. Michael Ellman, *Planning Problems in the USSR* (Cambridge: Cambridge University Press, 1973).

Recommended Readings for Appendix 7A

1. Alan Brown and Egon Neuberger, *Trade and Planning: Interactions between International Trade and Central Planning* (Berkeley: University of California Press, 1967).

2. Franklyn Holzman, *Foreign Trade under Central Planning* (Cambridge: Harvard University Press, 1974).

3. Franklyn Holzman, *International Trade under Communism* (New York: Basic Books, 1976).

4. Jozef M. van Brabant, *East European Cooperation: The Role of Money and Finance* (New York: Praeger, 1977).

5. "Foreign Economic Relations," Part 8 of U.S. Congress, Joint Economic Committee, *Soviet Economy in the 1980s* (Washington, D.C.: U.S. Government Printing Office, 1983).

8

USSR

PLANNING FOR BALANCE

In this chapter we investigate the following question: How well is the centrally planned Soviet economy able to coordinate the different parts of the economy, such as wages and consumer goods, steel and autos, and so forth?

Aggregate Balance

To obtain an aggregate balance, the resources supplied for investment must just equal the amount required or demanded for investment, and the amount supplied to consumers must just equal the amount they will demand at present incomes and prices. In this section, it is assumed that the politicians have already told the planners what percentage of national output is to be put into investment (as a result of the decisions on growth discussed in Chapter 6). Now the planners must calculate the amounts of consumer goods and the wages and prices that will be consistent with the given investment decision. The analysis presented here examines first the real quantities and problems involved and then some of their reflections in monetary policies.

No General Unemployment

The economy of the United States has been plagued frequently by lack of adequate demand for the products of private enterprise. In the planned economy of the USSR there has *always* been sufficient aggregate demand since planning began in 1928, and there has never been general or aggregate unemployment. The reason is that a lack of aggregate demand can *always* be corrected without great dislocation in a planned economy through the device of additional government investment (or more consumption by payment of higher wages). In reality, the problem has usually been that the Soviet government has demanded much more for investment than could be supplied and has failed to provide enough consumer goods to satisfy household demand.

Since aggregate demand has always more than equaled the amount of resources and manpower available, aggregate unemployment has been nonexistent since 1928. Of course, the Soviet Union does have some "frictional" and "structural" unemployment. Frictional unemployment may be defined as ordinary labor turnover. Structural unemployment occurs when the structure of industry and technology changes, so that workers must change jobs from one place to another, from one industry to another, or from one skill to another. These changes require large amounts of retraining and moving expenses. The number of workers involved and the time necessary for readjustment have recently become great enough in the USSR that numerous observers report significant "unemployment" from this source—but all of the workers are retrained and relocated at government expense. The Soviet Union may also have some seasonal unemployment. This condition occurs because there are times of the year in certain sectors, especially agriculture, when much labor is needed and times when very little labor is needed (but whether utilized or not, the workers are paid their wage). It may not be profitable for a society to transfer these workers to another job for only a few months of the year, although the Chinese use unemployed agricultural workers to build dams and roads as well as to work in small factories.

Although there is no general unemployment in the planned economies (as a result of unlimited government demand), there is alleged to be "underemployment," meaning that workers are not fully utilized. Managers are unsure of the labor supply, so they hoard skilled labor—while hardly using it at times. Furthermore, even when supply and demand would dictate firing workers, the manager often does not do so—either because of an uncertain labor supply, or the rules against firing workers.

Causes of Inflation

As implied above, the main problem of aggregate balance in the Soviet economy (and in all other centrally planned economies) has been due not to lack of demand creating unemployment, but rather to excessive demand causing inflation. The main reason for the inflation of the 1930s and 1940s in the USSR was the excessive increase in government demand for investment goods and military supplies. This situation created an excess demand for all inputs, including labor. The excess demand for labor pushed up wage rates much faster than productivity. Also, the labor force was shifted from consumer goods to military supplies and investment goods. Therefore, workers' demand for consumer goods rose faster than total production and much faster than output of consumer goods.

The excessive wage payments occurred as a result of decisions both at the national level and at the level of each firm. In the initial industrialization and wartime periods, the planners called for much larger increases in investment and military goods than in consumer goods; and the discrepancy was usually even greater in the fulfillment of plans. Related to the high level of investment and military spending was the practice of overfull employment and taut plans; that is, an enterprise was given output targets which, in most cases, were essentially unachievable with the amount of labor and other inputs legally available to them.

In order to meet their production plans, therefore, Soviet managers found themselves competing strenuously for materials and labor. Material goods prices were effectively controlled at the enterprise level, and most deliveries of goods were ordered by direct central priorities and rationing. Workers, however, respond mainly to the incentive of higher wages, so this path was the one followed by managers competing for labor inputs. Managers in the 1930s and 1940s were able to overspend their payrolls with few if any penalties but were under extreme pressure to meet output targets. In that period, they bid notoriously high to obtain the scarce supply of workers, and they even hoarded unneeded workers against future needs.

As a final result of this process, the workers attempted to spend their rapidly increasing wages on the much smaller increase in consumer goods. The consequence was too much money chasing too few goods in the consumer goods market, with resultant steadily rising prices until 1947. From a starting price index of 100 in 1928, Soviet official prices in government stores rose to 700 by 1936, reflecting the all-out industrialization drive, which limited resources for consumer goods in order to shift resources to heavy industry. Then, during the Second World War, the official price index rose again to a level of 3,895 because of the extreme shortage of goods—since much productive capacity was destroyed, while most of that remaining went into war production. In both the 1930s and 1940s, freely moving prices on the collective farm markets, mainly for food, rose even faster—to 3,000 in 1932 and to 13,575 in 1945!

The basic pattern of prewar and wartime inflation was (1) excess demand for labor as a joint result of the high rate of investment and overfull employment planning, and (2) excess demand for consumer goods as a result of wages rising faster than productivity and faster than the output of consumer goods. Since 1947, the problem has been under better control because (1) the state bank allows enterprises to overspend their payrolls only to the extent that they increase output above plan, and (2) the degree of overinvestment, taut plans, and overfull employment appears to have been reduced. Prices have mostly been constant, with some declines and some rises (more rises in recent years). There remains, however, considerable inflationary pressure, which is suppressed by strict government control of official prices.

The Lack of Balance and Its Cure

As a first approximation, ignoring all other changes, it might be said that Soviet consumer goods prices will rise or be inflated if the amount of wages is greater than the value of consumer goods. Neglecting the fact of some voluntary saving, there will be aggregate balance or equilibrium in the consumption sector only if the value of consumer goods just equals the total wages paid. If the value of consumer goods at present prices is less than the total wages, government will have to inflate consumer prices, tolerate long lines of unsatisfied customers, ration, and/or accept the black market. If the value of consumer goods at present prices is greater than the total wages, government will have to deflate consumer prices or there will be goods gathering dust on the shelves.

To add body to this analysis, some more detail must be inserted into the picture. The main point to be considered is that labor may produce not only consumer goods but also investment and military goods (or free welfare goods, which similarly do not soak up wage income). Suppose, with no increased capacity to produce, that some workers are switched from consumer goods to investment goods or military production. In this case, there would be fewer consumer goods but the same amount of wages, thus causing inflationary pressure in the consumer goods market (unless saving or taxation increase).

In the actual Soviet case, productive capacity has been increasing, so proportionate shifts to investment or military goods have meant only a slower growth of consumer goods than wages, rather than an absolute decline. Only in the drastic circumstances of the First Five-Year Plan and the Second World War was higher investment or more military production associated with an actual lowering of consumption. Nevertheless, in most years wages climbed much faster than the slow growth of consumer goods, so inflationary pressures did result.

As a further approximation to Soviet reality, one should note some complicating factors. First, in addition to their basic cost or wholesale prices, all Soviet consumer goods have a large sales or turnover tax placed upon them. Obviously, excess demand might be reduced by raising this turnover tax. Second, wages available for spending may be reduced by personal taxes or license fees, of which the income tax has been the most important to date. Finally, if workers increase their personal savings, by bank deposits or purchase of government bonds, then they obviously have less income left to spend on consumption. If these complicating factors are considered, then the resulting statement is more complex: there will be balance in the consumer goods sector only if the turnover tax plus the cost price of consumer goods times the amount of consumer goods is just equal to the wages paid out in all production, less the amounts of personal saving and personal taxes. Otherwise, there will be imbalance and deflationary or inflationary pressures.

With this analysis, it is possible to examine the cure for a demand and supply imbalance, that is, just what alternatives are open to the planners to correct a financial imbalance. *First*, the amount of labor devoted to consumption versus investment and military goods might be changed. *Second*, technology and the amount of capital might eventually be increased. *Third*, the planners may strive to increase factor productivity.

The *fourth* alternative, as noted all along, is to raise the prices of consumer goods to soak up the wages paid out for additional investment or military spending. How satisfactory a technique is this for meeting the real problems? Actually, price inflation does not directly affect physical planning. However, there are adverse side effects. Inflation does the following: (1) it does actually disrupt the calculations of planning insofar as all prices and accounts are rapidly changing; (2) it changes relative incomes and may reduce the equity of income distribution; and (3) it allegedly may dampen the worker's incentive to work since he or she realizes that extra wages will have less buying power than previously. This latter point, (3), is quite debatable. It is often argued that, with just a little inflation, workers may still be under a money illusion; that is, they may be more conscious of their rising money wages than of rising prices and not be conscious of their declining real wages. It has also been argued that rising prices *force* a worker to work harder in order to maintain income, even though he or she knows that each hour's wages buy less. This is especially the case when the workers concerned are at a very low income level.

A *fifth* alternative reaction to excessive consumer demand at present prices is to leave the disequilibrium as is, doing nothing and allowing so-called repressed inflation. The Soviet Union has often been forced to live with this alternative, but the results are not good. As stocks of goods in stores get very low, people must spend long hours in lines to get anything—and some unlucky consumers will get nothing. This system of distribution is obviously both inefficient and inequitable. Needless to say, the prospect of long hours of waiting in lines and being unable to spend one's money reduces workers' incentives to work and to earn money wages. Repressed inflation or shortages also means that manufacturers can sell almost anything, so there is less incentive to produce attractive, high quality goods. Repressed inflation was particularly serious in the Soviet Union in the years 1929 to 1935 and 1940 to 1947, but it has existed chronically ever since. To sum up, repressed inflation involves: inequity, wasted time standing in lines, lower quality goods, and the spread of black markets. Repressed inflation may also have an adverse impact on incentives to work, since workers accumulate money they cannot spend.

A *sixth* alternative is to leave the imbalance but add rationing to achieve some equity in consumption. Rationing was in force in the Soviet Union when repressed inflation was severe, in the years 1929 to 1935 and 1940 to 1947. In the early 1980s, it has been reintroduced for certain goods in some large cities. Rationing has also had many bad effects, including reduced workers' incentives and reduced satisfaction derived by workers from a given amount of consumer goods. Moreover, if the imbalance is significant and lasts a considerable time, either price controls or rationing—under conditions of excess demand—leads to black markets. Black markets add illegal activity to other woes and undermine the objective of rationing by greatly lessening the equality of distribution. Furthermore, rationing is costly to administer and enforce.

A *seventh* alternative in theory is to lower wage rates in all sectors and, thereby, decrease consumer demand. In practice, this may be politically impossible and is likely to adversely affect incentives to work.

Eighth, taxes may be increased, which is a politically feasible way of reducing wages. Taxation may be in the form of higher personal income taxes, which lower disposable wages after taxes, or in the form of higher sales and turnover taxes, which raise prices after taxes. Either way, taxes lower the volume of goods that workers can actually demand and reduce inflationary pressure. The kind of tax often makes a difference, however. For instance, workers are sometimes more conscious of the loss of real income the taxes represent if higher wages are immediately followed by higher income taxes, which leave take-home pay unchanged, than they are if the higher wages are followed by higher sales taxes and prices.

Finally, *ninth*, the government might offer higher interest rates on bonds or bank deposits in order to encourage voluntary personal saving. From 1927 to 1958, the Soviet government used compulsory bond sales to mop up excess purchasing power. In 1957, all bonds were frozen or declared irredeemable for twenty to twenty-five years. Compulsory bond sales, of course, essentially amount to taxation. Such sales had to be involuntary because voluntary savings in that period were fairly insignificant in the Soviet Union. Involuntary sales were also necessary because a higher interest rate did not elicit a quantitatively important response. For example, interest rates on bonds were 10 to 13 percent in the 1927 to 1931 period, and yet sales had to be forced. The response is limited or "inelastic" partly because previous experience had made doubtful the safety of such money loaned to the Soviet government. Moreover, most Soviet citizens had too low an income to reduce voluntarily their consumption by significant amounts for a higher rate of interest, particularly when there was expectation of inflation (which there was before 1950). As Soviet citizens become more affluent, they are increasing their saving rate. Another reason for higher saving is that, with price controls, many types of goods are unavailable, so consumers are forced to save. In fact, since 1975, according to a U.S. government estimate, Soviet household savings have been increasing by 11 percent a year.[1]

Problems of Coordination

Compared with the latest proposed mathematical models, Soviet planners have used a fairly simple approach called the *method of balances*. For example, according to the form they use, one might state the aggregate balances in the following way.

The personal income of all Soviet citizens might be shown (omitting some details) as a balanced budget of their income and expenditures (see Table 8.1). If there is not enough saving or taxes, then consumer spending may be greater than the available goods, thus leading to inflationary pressure. Also, taxes from workers (and other sources) must be enough to finance government spending.

Table 8.1
Workers' Budget

Sources of Income	Expenditures
Wages	Consumer spending
Transfer payments (pensions, sick pay, student stipends, etc.)	Personal saving
	Taxes
Total income	Total expenditures

The actual revenues and expenditures of the Soviet government for one year (according to official Soviet sources) are shown in Table 8.2. Incidentally, the Soviet government budget amounts to just over 50 percent of Soviet national income, but over half of that is for the government-run economy, which is unlike the case of the U.S. budget.

The same method of establishing a balanced intake and outgo is used for each product or industry. Thus, the balance for the iron industry might be portrayed as in Table 8.3. Of course, it is only the totals that must balance.

The problem of balance may appear in a very dramatic fashion if the planners make mistakes. There have been cases in the Soviet Union

---

1. See Nick Eberstadt, "Overview," U.S. Congress, Joint Economic Committee, *Soviet Economy in the 1980s*, Part 2 (Washington, D.C.: U.S. Government Printing Office, 1983), 199.

Table 8.2
USSR Government Budget, 1978

Revenues	Percentage of total	Spending	Percentage of total
Sales tax (turnover tax)	32	National economy	54
Enterprise profits	30	Social & cultural	34
Social insurance tax	26	Defense	7
Direct taxes on population	8	Administration	1
Other	4	Other	4
Total	100	Total	100

Source: *Narodnoe Khoziastvo SSSR v 1978 g* [The National Economy of the USSR in 1978], published in Moscow (Statistika, 1979), 534.

Table 8.3
Iron Industry

Resources	Needs or uses
1. Imports	1. Exports
2. Reduction in inventory	2. Increase in inventory
3. Production, listed by plants or regions	3. Uses by other industries or regions
Total resources	Total uses

---

where thousands of trucks were finished, but there were not enough tires. Thousands of overcoats have been all ready to be sold in the winter, but the planners forgot to allocate buttons. This is the nitty-gritty issue of getting a proper balance of inputs and outputs for each production process and for the economy as a whole.

An important economic question concerns the units in which commodity balances are stated. For example, the plan for the iron industry may be calculated in tons of iron. The requirements would read x tons of iron needed for exports and inventories, y tons of iron needed for the steel industry in the Urals, z tons of iron needed for the railway industry in the Ukraine, and so forth. The problem with using "tons of iron" is that there are several different types of iron needed by industry. One can add up different types of things only in terms of their values, represented by prices. Therefore, the Soviet planners also present each balance in rubles.

For each type of good, it is only necessary (and sufficient) that the price be constant per unit during the time covered by the plan. It will cause no problem to the balancers that each particular price may be arbitrary in relation to all other prices, because only one price enters into each balance. For this reason, the question of the "value" of a good (discussed in Chapter 9), or the effects of consumer preference, does not affect the balance problem. Hence, although Marxist and non-Marxist writers disagree on how to "value" or price goods, they agree in practice on how to balance industries and sectors.

Because a balance of inputs and outputs can be achieved with any arbitrary prices, Soviet economists have encountered many fewer theoretical difficulties in balancing problems than in optimizing problems.[2] Of course, it is also true that this problem, especially in the macroeconomic area of achieving a *full* employment of workers and resources, is of overwhelming practical importance. Furthermore, this was an area in which Marx did make a contribution.[3] Marx's scheme of balanced economic growth has been translated with some difficulty by several Marxist economists as a simplified type of Keynesian scheme of national income accounting.[4] Marx's scheme has also been translated by the economist Oskar Lange, using a great deal of verbal skill and ingenuity, into a simple input-output model.[5]

Input-Output Method

The Soviet method of balances is a close relative of the Western *input-output method*. The input-output method is simply a mathematical procedure (of simultaneous linear equations) which makes it possible to calculate the required inputs for the whole economy if one knows (1) the desired outputs, and (2) the number of units of each input required to produce one unit of each output at the present technology (usually called the technical coefficient). The input-output method is described in detail in Appendix 8A.

It should be noted that, to their credit, the Soviet economists of the 1920s grappled with most of the problems of balance in a very sophisticated manner. In fact, Wassily Leontief,[6] the Nobel laureate in economics and creator of the input-output method, was an economics student at Leningrad University during the 1920s and undoubtedly benefited from the Soviet experience and debates before he emi-

2. For a sophisticated discussion by a Soviet writer, see A. A. Konus, "Dynamic Intersector Balances in Perspective Planning," *Economics of Planning* 4 (1964): 1–15.

3. See Marx, "The Reproduction and Circulation of the Aggregate Social Capital," *Capital*, Vol. II, Part III.

4. See, e.g., the confused discussion by Shigeto Tsuru, "On Reproduction Schemes," in Appendix A of Paul Sweezy, *Theory of Capitalist Development* (New York: Monthly Review Press, 1958) 365–74.

5. See Oskar Lange, *Introduction to Econometrics* (New York: Pergamon Press, 1959), 218–28.

6. See, e.g., his simplified explanation in W. Leontief, "Input-Output Economics," *Scientific American* (Oct. 1951): 3–9.

grated to the United States. Aside from Leontief, several other Soviet economists constructed models that might have led to a full-blown input-output analysis. Unfortunately, most of these economists were on the most conservative side of the debate on development. When Stalin attacked and even imprisoned some of them in the early 1930s, he condemned *all* of their theories and related theories as "bourgeois" or guilty of "mathematical formalism." The condemnation included early growth models as well as balance models. Given the dogmatic and repressive atmosphere, it was unhealthy to pursue such models any further. Even the Marxist writer Dobb comments that:

> In the second half of the '30's a half-hearted attempt was, indeed, made (prompted, it has been said, by Stalin) to revive a discussion about a synthetic "balance of the National economy." . . . The discussion scarcely got beyond questions of classification (i.e., a listing of the actual relationships of which account must be taken); it was soon to be dismissed by authority as unsatisfactory and was rather abruptly adjourned. After that for two decades silence reigned.[7]

The intensive analysis of input-output relationships was revived only after the anti-Stalinist Twentieth Congress of the Communist Party in 1956. As mentioned above, Soviet economists are now doing a great deal of advanced work in this field. Yet at the present time the planners apparently still use the method of balances in all actual planning. So far, the discussion has produced only a few regional experiments with the input-output method, considerable statistical analysis of the past with this analysis, and much advocacy of its use for future planning.

Problems of the Soviet Balance Method

One of the great difficulties with the Soviet method of balances has been that it does not take into account the secondary effects on other industries of a change in the output of any one industry. For example, an increase in Soviet auto production means an immediate need for more rubber tires, but it also implies that the rubber tire industry will need more rubber as well as more tire-making machinery, and so forth, ad infinitum. By contrast, the input-output method automatically takes into account all secondary and further removed effects (as shown in Appendix 8A).

More specifically, it was observed in an earlier chapter how each Soviet enterprise supplies the State Planning Commission with estimates of its requirements, based on input norms or technical coefficients. A technical coefficient describes in a ratio how much of a

---

7. Maurice Dobb, *Soviet Economic Development since 1917* (New York: Routledge and Kegan Paul, 1966 ed.), 361.

given input, say iron, is required to produce one unit of a given output, say steel. But what happens when all of the enterprise requirements are added together by the Planning Commission, and the Commission finds an imbalance?

For instance, suppose that the planned supply of steel is one million tons short of the total enterprise requirements. If steel production is to be increased, this means additional requirements for iron ore, coal, limestone, and other ingredients. Exactly how much is required of each must be calculated from the respective technical coefficients. For example, if production of one ton of steel requires 1.5 tons of iron ore, then this coefficient, or ratio (1.5/1), means that the production of an additional one million tons of steel requires an additional 1.5 million tons of iron ore. In turn, the additional production of iron ore, coal, limestone, and other inputs into steel must require additional inputs of the commodities used in *their* production. The chain of secondary effects is endless. This endless chain is solved in one calculation by the input-output method, provided all the information is known and various assumptions are made (see Appendix 8A).

If instead of producing additional steel the planners decide to stick with the original plan of steel output, then balance can be achieved only by cutbacks in the output of all commodities dependent upon steel as an input. Thus, depending on their technical coefficients or needs for steel, there would have to be reductions in the planned production of autos, trucks, rails, and so forth. Each of these in turn would mean reductions in other commodities that use them as inputs, another endless chain that could only slowly approach balance as the result of a great number of adjustments.

Thus, by the method of balances, it would be necessary to go through several approximations and changes affecting every balance (because all are interrelated) before getting all the different industries to balance. This process takes so long, even with Soviet shortcuts, omissions, and aggregations, that the balancing process takes not only a great deal of energy but also a lot of time, and it is usually completed late. As a result, the final plan usually arrives at the enterprise *after* the period covered has already begun. Furthermore, this complicated process has been absorbing an increasing percentage of the labor force, which might well be used elsewhere.

Theoretically, the input-output method would remedy the main defect of the balance method, since it does take into account all of the indirect adjustments to any change in one item.[8] It is also more suitable for use with electronic computers. It would not only be faster to

---

8. This is the view of the more liberal Soviet economists; see, e.g., V. S. Nemchinov, "Mathematical Methods in Economics," in V. S. Nemchinov, ed., *The Use of Mathematics in Economics* (London: Oliver and Boyd, 1964, English ed. edited by A. Nove), 24.

calculate one balanced plan by the input-output method, but this method would actually make it easily possible to present several alternative balanced plans, from which the politicians could pick the plan they desire, or even change particular output targets, and yet be certain of all the secondary effects. It can be shown that it is theoretically possible to have an almost infinite number of different balanced plans with given resources, as the desired final bill of goods is varied. (The question, examined in Chapter 9, is: Exactly what is the desired set of final outputs and what is the least costly means of producing it?) It should be noted that the problem of speeding up planning and reaching a final desired approximation to a good balance is now becoming more urgent. This is because (1) Soviet industry comprises a growing number of enterprises, whose relationships are more complex and interrelated, so that secondary effects are harder to calculate intuitively; and (2) the increased complexity makes more difficult the problems of gathering and aggregating the necessary information.

In practice, it is important to mention one Soviet shortcut in the actual use of the method of balances. If more steel is ordered by the politicians, then, as shown above, the planners should theoretically order more iron and coal and other inputs for the steel industry. But this would upset the balances for iron and coal and everything else that goes into steel. To prevent many of these secondary effects from disrupting planning, the planners first try to get each industry to accept a higher target with *no* additional resources. For example, the steel industry may be told that it is wasting too much coal and it should therefore find a more efficient way to use the coal it has. The steel industry might also be told it has excessive reserves or inventories of coal, so it can use some of those to make more steel. In this way, the secondary effects of a change in the amount of one product are kept to a minimum by removing the assumption that a fixed ratio of each resource is necessary for production of each unit of output. Of course, this shortcut can be used only within narrow limits, since it makes the planning more and more taut.

Soviet planners can pressure a firm to produce more without more inputs because they know that most firms keep hefty reserves. The problem is just to give the manager the incentive to use the reserves at the appropriate time. Furthermore, the planners themselves try to keep some reserves in each sector. So if a firm is really missing one key input, they can shift resources to it if it is engaged in a high priority activity.

Another way that flexibility is achieved by firms when under high pressure is the discovery and use of other inputs besides those in the plan. Every firm uses expediters (or "pushers") to go out and find scarce supplies when they are needed by begging, borrowing, or bribing for them. The role of the expediters in supplying more flexibility to the economy is discussed in later chapters.

Another shortcut is the fact that central planning does material balances for only about four thousand commodity groups—not for all twelve million or more individual commodities. This very aggregate planning then leaves the difficult problems of more detailed instructions to the intermediate and lower levels of the economic bureaucracy. Some specific commodities not covered by central ministries or regional balances are planned "according to the level achieved," that is, the previous year's targets are used with or without an added growth factor.

A third shortcut used by the planners is to concentrate attention and priorities on certain important sectors so that they get plenty of resources. For example, whatever the missile industry wants, it gets. Of course, this creates even more problems for other, less prestigious industries, such as shoes or textiles.

Another problem is that Soviet *politicians* have wanted to fix not only the amounts of final goods (such as autos or tanks) but also the amounts of intermediate goods (such as steel or oil). It is easier and more rational for Soviet political leaders to decide only the final bill of goods that is desired and to leave the planning of intermediate goods to the planners.[9]

Limitations of Input-Output Method

Certainly, it appears that the planners could achieve more with the input-output method, which can provide several internally consistent alternative balances for all industry, than with the crude Soviet method of balancing one industry at a time. Yet we must be very clear what the input-output method (as explained in Appendix 8A) can and cannot do. Given the technical coefficients and the list of desired final outputs, planners can calculate the total output (both intermediate and final) required of each industry. If they are also given technical coefficients showing the amount of labor and capital required per unit of output, they can similarly calculate the required amounts of each of these primary inputs.

Yet the limitations of the input-output method are equally clear and should always be kept in mind. First, the input-output method assumes that technical coefficients (that is, the ratio of each input to output in a given process) are fixed for the period of the Plan. Fixed technical coefficients imply that there is only one way to produce each good (in the language of neoclassical economics, in this special

---

9. See the elaboration of such a model in Benjamin Ward, *The Socialist Economy* (New York: Random House, 1967), 44–49.

case, each isoquant happens to consist of a single point rather than a convex line). This assumption is not a realistic one, certainly for any economy with rapid technological improvements, such as the Soviet economy. In fact, the coefficients change over time in particular industries. Moreover, input-output assumes that the coefficients are identical for each firm in an industry, and that they remain constant regardless of the scale of production. In reality the coefficients are different for each firm, change with increases in scale, and vary with changes in technology over time. A really complete model would somehow have to allow for dynamic change of the coefficients within the planning period—though Leontief has defended the input-output method on this point by showing that the U.S. coefficients change slowly enough to have little effect for a number of years. In other words, according to Leontief, it is true that coefficients are always changing, but the change is perhaps slow enough that one may assume them to be constant for a one-year plan.

A second limitation of the input-output method is that it is not as flexible as some practical methods now used in the Soviet setting. If, for example, there is less labor available than the plan of desired final output would require, it would be necessary to set lower final outputs and recalculate the entire plan. In theory, the input-output method could easily be used to calculate a new plan with smaller proportions of all outputs to correspond with the actual available labor supply. Since it automatically takes into consideration the indirect as well as the direct effects of such changes, the input-output method would thus appear to be far more efficient than the method of balances. In practice, however, the Soviet planners do not immediately begin to reduce final outputs if they find a shortage of inputs, whether the shortage is in total labor or in intermediate inputs for some particular industry. Rather, they attempt first to reduce the input-output coefficients, which we have so far taken as fixed or constant.

How do the Soviet planners perform this remarkable feat of reduction of technologically based coefficients, without discovery of any new technology? They do it by pressure on the individual enterprises to increase their efficiency. Thus, for example, the individual enterprise may be induced to introduce new technology which it had previously known but had not used. The enterprise might also have to use new sources of supply which it had previously kept hidden. Soviet enterprises have been notorious for keeping exceptionally high inventories of goods, which they will utilize for just such occasions. The enterprise may also, within the plan or beyond it, hire extra shifts of labor. If the planners are thus able to reduce the direct input-output coefficients by a sufficient amount, they can stop all significant secondary effects. They can then retain the original planned amounts of final output, essentially by squeezing more out of each unit of input. In this way, recalculation of large parts of the Plan can be avoided.

Other practical problems of using input-output methods for a whole economy include the limitations of having to make so many computations, even with computers. The mainframe computers available to Soviet planners in the early 1980s are probably not capable of inverting matrices in excess of 1,000 by 1,000. This would restrict to one thousand the number of material balances processable by input-output analysis, so it would force excessive aggregation of commodities by the planners. With each aggregation, the central planners lose some control. (By *aggregation* we refer to grouping products together, such as considering *farm machinery* as a group instead of separately as threshers, combines, ploughs, tractors, hoes, etc.)

It must also be pointed out that the success of either the input-output or the material balance method depends to a large degree on the central planners' receiving accurate and timely information from below. As we shall see, for a variety of reasons such information is not always forthcoming.

Finally, notice that both the Soviet method of balances and the input-output method provide only balanced or consistent plans among industries. Neither method, however, provides an optimal or most efficient plan in any sense. In other words, neither method helps choose among different technologies, different sets of inputs, or different sets of final outputs, nor do they consider the efficiency with which any firm operates, but rather assume each of these as given. The actual process of decision making regarding the optimal mix of desired final outputs, as well as the optimal choice of technology, will be discussed in Chapter 9. A planned economy may be balanced and still be far from maximum efficiency. Here it need only be added that the input-output problem for the planners remains the same whether planners receive the list of final outputs from the politicians or the individual consumers or some combination of these groups. Nevertheless, although the input-output method does not itself choose an optimal variant, it does allow much more rapid calculation than the method of material balances. Therefore, the planners could prepare several variants of highly aggregated plans and allow the politicians to choose which one they desire.

Appendix 8A
The Input-Output Technique

As an accounting record, the unique feature of an input-output table is that it shows transactions between industries as well as aggregate consumption and other aggregates. Let a very simple form of the Soviet economy be assumed for purely illustrative purposes. All enterprises are owned by the government, and wages are the only form of income. There are no personal savings, no government debts, a balanced budget, no exports nor imports, and no depreciation nor replacement. There are only three industries producing three kinds of products, which are the whole output of the economy. These industries might be called A, B, and C; or, to add a little color to the picture, they might be called the sectors of Agriculture, Manufacturing, and Construction. In reality, there are several other economic sectors, and each of those sectors contains many different industries. Manufacturing alone contains a thousand or so industries, each of which should be analyzed separately, with a separate entry in the table. This simplified input-output table might look something like Table 8A.1.

It is necessary first to explain the individual figures in Table 8A.1 and then to give names to some of the totals. Under the column of *Manufacturing industries*, for example, there is the figure 10 in the row for *Agricultural industries*. This means that 10 billion rubles of the output, or product, of Agriculture became an input into Manufacturing. Notice that the total gross output of Agriculture was 96 billion rubles. Of this gross output 16 billion went as inputs (for intermediate uses) to various industries and so was used up within industry. This 16 billion intermediate use of Agricultural goods includes the 10 billion used in Manufacturing, plus 5 billion used in Construction, *plus* 1 billion used up by Agriculture itself in its own production process.

Subtracting 16 from 96, one finds that the final or net output of Agriculture available for final uses was only 80 billion rubles. Of this 80 billion, 20 went for new investment, 10 for articles of military use, and 5 for public welfare goods, which left only 45 billion rubles of Agricultural product for household or individual consumption. An exactly similar analysis could be made for the rows showing the outputs of the Manufacturing and Construction industries.

If we read down the Input column under Agricultural industries, we find that it used up, out of the intermediate products of industry in this period, 1 billion rubles' worth of its own output, 30 billion of Manufacturing, and 5 billion of Construction. In addition, Agriculture had to pay out 40 billion in wages for labor, 10 billion in profits for the use of capital, and 10 billion as its part of the government military and welfare services. In the centrally planned Soviet economy profit and taxes have been mixed together in the federal budget, so in practice one cannot say that profit goes to pay only for capital and that taxes go only for government services. At any rate, the labor expended in this period, the capital goods used in this period, as well as the government services provided in this period, are the primary inputs needed to keep industry functioning. Welfare, of course, might be considered a part of the payment to all labor. Notice that the input services are valued in the accounts by the payments for them: labor by wages paid, capital by profits paid, and government services by taxes paid.

Discussion has so far centered on the figures in three of the four quadrants into which the input-output table is divided. In Quadrant I

242

Table 8A.1
Soviet Inputs and Outputs (Hypothetical Figures, in Billions of Rubles)

Outputs \\ Inputs	Intermediate outputs			Final outputs				
	Agricultural industries	Manufacturing industries	Construction industries	Investment	Military	Welfare	Individual consumption	Total
	Quadrant I			Quadrant II				
Agricultural industries	1	10	5	20	10	5	45	96
Manufacturing industries	30	30	20	20	5	2	18	125
Construction industries	5	30	1	8	1	8	2	53
	Quadrant III			Quadrant IV				
Wages of labor	40	35	19	5	1	10	14	124
Profits on capital	10	12	2					24
Taxes to government	10	8	6				45	69
Total	96	125	53	53	17	23	124	491

Intermediate outputs: 274
Final outputs: Welfare/Military bracket 274; Individual consumption/Total bracket 93; overall 217
Primary Inputs brackets: 93, 217
Intermediate Inputs bracket: 274

are found the intermediate inputs and intermediate outputs, or the relationships between industries; in Quadrant II, the final or net outputs of material goods from each industry for investment, military, welfare, and individual consumption; in Quadrant III, the primary inputs of labor, capital, and government services.

What do the figures in Quadrant IV represent? They show service inputs (rather than material inputs) into final products. For example, the figures in Quadrant III in the row *Wages of labor* show that labor put 40 billon rubles of work into producing material goods in Agriculture, 35 billion into material goods in Manufacturing, and 19 billion into material goods in Construction. But the figures in Quadrant IV in the row *Wages of labor* show that labor also put 5 billion rubles of work into direct services to investment projects, 1 billion into military service (or soldiering), 10 billion into welfare services (such as nursing or teaching), and 14 billion into services direct to the consumer (for example, by barbers or domestic workers). In addition, note that individual consumers paid out 45 billion (in sales or turnover taxes) for the government services to them.

Next, one may note in Table 8A.1 those items which will always be found in an accounting balance for the last year's record and which the planners must design so as to be in balance for the next year's plan. Obviously, the "value" of what is produced (the intermediate plus the final outputs) by each industry must equal the "value" of what went into each industry (the primary plus the intermediate inputs). This is a necessary accounting and real physical identity, since something cannot come out of nothing, no matter what one's theory of "value" and price is. This necessity of matching the inputs or sources (including initial inventories) with the outputs or uses of each industry's product (including final inventories) is exactly what the Soviets attempt in their physical and ruble balances for each product. In the input-output table for the next year's plan, the total for each industry's input column must equal the total for that industry's output row (for example, Agriculture's total output or input is 96 billion rubles).

If all the industries are summed together, their total inputs (primary plus intermediate) must equal their total outputs (intermediate plus final). In other words, the sum of Quadrants I and II (outputs) must equal the sum of Quadrants I and III (inputs)—identical totals of 274 billion rubles in our example. Of course, the sum of the columns in Quadrant I (intermediate inputs) equals the sum of the rows in Quadrant I (intermediate outputs), since the same numbers are being added together in different directions. By subtraction, the value of Quadrant II, that is, the value of all final material outputs (net of intermediate outputs) must just equal the value of all primary inputs into industry (net of intermediate inputs). Of course, this will not generally be true of any particular industry, because each will have different ratios of its output going to intermediate and final goods.

It was observed that a macrobalance of primary inputs (or incomes) and final outputs (or expenditures) is required, which means that Quadrant III must equal Quadrant II. Therefore, it is no surprise that the value of II plus IV must also equal the value of III plus IV, which is 217 billion rubles in the illustrative example. In other words, the total final output (of material goods plus services) must equal the total primary input (into industry and directly as services). As a sub-balance, notice that if wages just equal consumer goods and services (in the example both are 124 billion rubles), then profits plus taxes must just equal investment plus military plus welfare goods (both sums are 93 billion rubles). Finally, note that the sum of all the rows of all four quadrants equals the sum of all the columns of all four quadrants (each sum is 491 billion rubles).

We shall now turn to a generalized algebraic discussion of the problem. Assume there are n separate industries. The total output of each industry, including intermediate and final outputs, is represented by the letters, $X_1, \ldots, X_n$. The final output of each industry is represented by the letters, $x_1, \ldots, x_n$, and the intermediate output of each industry is represented by the letters, $x_{11}, \ldots, x_{1n}$. The meaning of the subscripts in the intermediate outputs is understood as follows: the first number indicates the industry producing the output, while the second number indicates the industry to which the output is supplied as an input. For example, x_{12} means that this is the amount of output from industry 1 required as an input in industry 2. Thus, the picture of required output from each of the industries is as follows:

$$X_1 = x_{11} + x_{12} + \ldots + x_{1n} + x_1 \tag{1a}$$

$$X_i = x_{i1} + x_{i2} + \ldots + x_{in} + x_i \tag{1i}$$

$$X_n = x_{n1} + x_{n2} + \ldots + x_{nn} + x_n . \tag{1n}$$

Each of these equations may be represented as follows:

$$X_i = \sum_{j=1}^{n} x_{ij} + x_i \quad \text{(where } i = 1, \ldots, n\text{)}. \tag{2}$$

Here i is an individual industry producing output for use as an input into industry j.

At this point, it is necessary to introduce the direct input-output coefficients (sometimes called *technical coefficients*), which represent technical ratios fixed for the duration of the planning period. The direct input-output coefficients are represented by the letters $a_{11}, \ldots, a_{nn}$, where the first number of the subscript represents the industry producing an output, and the second number represents the industry using that output as an input. For example, if there is an intermediate good, x_{12}, it is equal in amount to the coefficient a_{12} times the industry output X_2, where industry 2 demands as an input this part of the output of industry 1; that is, $x_{12} = a_{12}X_2$. To put it another way, the technical coefficient a_{12} represents the ratio of the amount of intermediate goods required by industry 2 from industry 1, or x_{12}, to the total output of industry 2, or X_2; that is,

$$a_{12} = \frac{x_{12}}{X_2}.$$ (2b)

In general, each input-output coefficient represents the ratio between the goods required by the using (or demanding) industry from the producing (or supplying) industry to the total output of the using industry. Thus, where i represents an industry producing an output and j represents an industry using it as an input, the input-output coefficient may be represented as:

$$a_{ij} = \frac{x_{ij}}{X_j},$$ (3a)

or

$$x_{ij} = a_{ij}X_j.$$ (3b)

Utilizing this terminology, plus the assumption that the technical input-output coefficients are fixed and constant during the planning period, it is possible to substitute the coefficients times the total outputs of the using industries for the demand for intermediate goods in every case. In other words, into each of the equations (1a), ..., (1n) may be substituted the amount of coefficient times total output as defined in equation (3b). When this substitution is made, the new picture of required (or demanded) output for all industries is as follows:

$$X_1 = a_{11}X_1 + a_{12}X_2 + \ldots + a_{1n}X_n + x_1$$ (4a)

$$X_i = a_{i1}X_1 + a_{i2}X_2 + \ldots + a_{in}X_n + x_i$$ (4i)

$$X_n = a_{ni}X_1 + a_{n2}X_2 + \ldots + a_{nn}X_n + x_n.$$ (4n)

The input-output method merely requires setting up these equations for every industry and then solving them. If the technical coefficients are known, and the desired final demands are given, it is simple (but very tedious) algebra to solve for each of the total outputs.

In practice, in order to reduce the enormous number of calculations required for a large number of industries, matrix algebra is always utilized. The entire set of technical coefficients may be called the matrix A. The summation of the above equations $(4a), \ldots, (4n)$ may then be written as

$$X = AX + x,\qquad(5)$$

where A is the matrix of technical coefficients, X is the vector of all total outputs, and x is the vector of all final outputs. By rearranging and subtracting, the result is reached that:

$$(I - A)X = x,\qquad(6)$$

where I is the $n \times n$ identity matrix. An identity matrix is simply a matrix whose diagonal entities are all equal to one with all other entities equal to zero. It may be assumed that the matrix A is known and constant; note that the identity matrix I is always known. In this form, therefore, one may assume as given to the planners either the list of desired total outputs (X) or the list of final outputs (x), and the planners will always be able to calculate the other one. For example, suppose the planners are given a list of desired final outputs (x). Since they are assumed to know the technical input-output coefficients $(I - A)$, it follows that total outputs (X) are the only remaining unknowns in the equation, and hence may be calculated.

Note that matrix A, which was called the set of direct input-output coefficients, is derived from the type of data presented in the illustration in Table 8A.1. The calculation of total outputs (X) is performed, then, by dividing both sides of equation (6) by $(I - A)$. This step involves taking the inverse of $(I - A)$. The inverse is represented as $(I - A)^{-1}$. The inverse of a matrix times the matrix equals the identity matrix, I. We then arrive at the desired solution, indicating the total amount of each output to be produced, as shown in equation (7). Soviet planners use their computers to perform matrix inversion calculations:

$$X = (I - A)^{-1}x.\qquad(7)$$

This solution indicates the amount of each output, not only as a result of directly required inputs but also all indirectly required inputs (inputs into inputs).

Recommended Readings

Some excellent sources on problems of planning are:

1. Michael Ellman, *Socialist Planning* (Cambridge: Cambridge University Press, 1979).

2. Alec Nove, *The Soviet Economic System* (London: George Allen & Unwin, 1980), particularly Chapters 2, 3, 4, and 11.

3. Branko Horvat, *The Political Economy of Socialism* (Armonk, N.Y.: M. E. Sharpe, 1982), particularly Chapter 2.

4. A brief and clear introduction to the details of the input-output method is in William M. Miernyk, *The Elements of Input-Output Analysis* (New York: Random House, 1965).

5. A simple Soviet article is L. Berri, F. Klotsvog, and S. Shatalin, "An Experimental Calculation of a Planned Interbranch Balance for 1962," *Problems of Economics* (June 1963): 3–10. Also, A. A. Gatanava, "The Use of the Balance Method in Economic Planning," *Problems of Economics* (June 1963): 11–17.

6. A more advanced work is Janos Kornai, *Growth, Shortage, and Efficiency: A Macrodynamic Model of the Socialist Economy* (Berkeley: University of California Press, 1983).

7. A good comparison of the two planning methods is in Paul G. Hare, "Aggregate Planning by Means of Input-Output and Material Balances Systems," *Journal of Comparative Economics*, Vol. 5 (Sept. 1981): 272–91.

8. On problems of unemployment and inflation, see David H. Howard, "A Note on Hidden Inflation in the Soviet Union," *Soviet Studies*, Vol. 28 (Oct. 1976): 599–608. Also, George Feiwel, "Causes and Consequences of Disguised Industrial Unemployment in a Socialist Economy," *Soviet Studies*, Vol. 26 (July 1974): 344–62.

9

USSR

PLANNING FOR EFFICIENCY

Marx and his earliest followers assumed that it is possible to plan rationally in a socialist society, "socialism" being understood here simply as public ownership of all means of production. They considered it impractical utopianism to describe in detail the problems of the socialist economy.[1] Since planned economies have survived and developed in various countries for a significant length of time, detailed planning can no longer be called a "utopian" project. Soviet Marxists, indeed, take the official position that the possibility of rational, efficient planning has now been proved in practice, so it need not be proved theoretically. Whatever the merits of this squelching answer, the long theoretical debate about the *possibility* of rational planning in socialism teaches many lessons and will serve as a very useful background to our study of optimal planning.

Need for Rational Prices

The most famous denial of the possibility of rational planning came from Ludwig von Mises in the 1920s.[2] Mises argues that the calculation of economic choices requires a knowledge of "rational" prices for both inputs and outputs. For example, if a farmer wishes to know whether to produce oranges or apples, he must know their relative prices at the time in order to maximize his revenues. Or if a planner

---

1. All of the pre-1917 discussions by socialists and antisocialists on this problem are discussed in Carl Landauer, *European Socialism* (Berkeley: University of California Press, 1959), Vol. II, 1602–35.

2. See Ludwig von Mises, "Economic Calculation in the Socialist Commonwealth," in F. A. Hayek, ed., *Collectivist Economic Planning* (London: Routledge and Kegan Paul, Ltd., 1935).

wishes to decide whether railroad locomotives should use coal or oil, he must know the relative prices of coal and oil in order to minimize costs.

In socialism, however, the government owns the coal and oil as well as the locomotives. Therefore, says Mises, since there is no market and no competition among producers, there can be no rational prices. If the coal and oil producers are merely commanded to turn over a certain physical product to the locomotive makers, no one can know which kind of fuel will cost more. In short, there is no free market in socialism, so there are no rational prices and there can be no meaningful calculation or rational planning of the allocation of resources.

Optimal Conditions and Planning

An evaluation of Mises' objection requires a brief explanation of how economists define "rational" prices and "rational" planning. *Rational prices* are defined as those which lead to an "optimal" pattern of outputs and inputs, by the accurate representation of the marginal utility of each output and the marginal cost of each input. As early as 1897 the economist Pareto[3] made explicit the conditions necessary to obtain an optimum welfare situation for all individuals, given the existing technology and the existing distribution of income. He defined what is now called a *Pareto optimum* "as a position from which it is not possible by any reallocation of factors, to make anyone better off without making at least one person worse off."[4]

The Pareto optimum requires at least three conditions. First, there is the condition of consumer satisfaction, the "*Exchange optimum*, which requires that for each individual, the rate of substitution [the ratio of preference of one additional unit of one good to another] be the same for all pairs of goods in the economy."[5] Roughly, this means that each consumer should be equally satisfied with the *last* dollar's worth of each good he or she buys. Second, there is the condition of producer efficiency, the "*Production optimum*, which requires that for each product the rate of substitution between any pair of factors will be the same."[6] Roughly, this means that each producer should get an equal addition to production from the *last* dollar's worth of each input that is bought.

Third, there is a combination of the production and consumption

3. V. Pareto, *Cours d'economie politique* (Lausanne, 1897).

4. E. J. Mishan, "A Survey of Welfare Economics, 1939–1959," in American Economic Association and Royal Economic Society, eds., *Surveys of Economic Theory*, Vol. I (New York: St. Martin's Press, 1966), 163.

5. *Ibid.*

6. *Ibid.*, 164.

conditions in the "*Top Level optimum*. It requires that the subjective rate of substitution, common to all individuals, be equal to the . . . rate of objective substitution for all pairs of goods in the economy."[7] Roughly, this means that the mixture of outputs should be the same as the preference for outputs by all consumers, the mixture of inputs should be the same as the preference for inputs by all producers, and that the addition of one unit of one commodity requires the sacrifice of an equally desirable amount of some other commodity for both consumers and producers. Fortunately, only a very general concept of these conditions—as an allocation of inputs and outputs that cannot be improved—is necessary to the present argument.[8]

It is important to note the limitations of a Pareto optimum welfare situation. First, it *assumes* a given distribution of income; it says nothing about the equity of this distribution of income. Second, it deals only with the most efficient allocation of resources *at a given time* with a given technology, so it says nothing about the dynamics of growth, neither the saving of capital nor the improvement of technology. Third, it assumes that demand equals supply in the aggregate, so it says little that is useful regarding the problems of macroeconomic balance, such as the equilibrium of savings and investment, unemployment, or inflation. So if a private enterprise economy with pure and perfect competition does reach the Pareto optimum, it *may* still have an inequitable income distribution, unemployment, inflation, and no growth.

Within these narrowly defined limits of economic efficiency, as early as 1908, the Italian economist Barone applied a Pareto optimum kind of analysis to a pure centrally planned economy.[9] He points out—or implies, according to later economists—that economic calculation of the Pareto optimum allocation does not require "prices" in an actual market. We need only three kinds of information. First, we must know what resources are available, including people and machines as well as raw materials. Second, we must know the preference scale of "consumers," whether these are individuals or planners or politicians or some weighted sum of these. Third, we must know the "production function" of each output, that is, what combinations of resources are possible to produce each output at the present level of technology.

In a private enterprise economy—as in socialism—the third kind of information (about production possibilities) is furnished by engineers. In the theory of a pure and perfect competitive private enterprise economy, however, market prices *automatically* reflect the first

---

7. *Ibid.*

8. For details on planning and welfare, see Michael Ellman, *Socialist Planning* (Cambridge: Cambridge University Press, 1979).

9. Translated from Italian in E. Barone, "The Ministry of Production in the Collectivist State," in Hayek, *Collectivist Economic Planning*.

and second types of information, that is, the relative scarcity of different resources as well as the relative preference of consumers for different products. *If* a knowledge of the actual information of resource scarcities and consumer preferences can be obtained, however, then socialist planners will be able theoretically to calculate rational "prices" for all resources and for all products. These "prices" would be merely data for planners to use and need not ever be paid to anybody.

If this information were available, the planners of socialist industry could then presumably calculate the optimum allocation of resources for the goal of the maximum welfare of all society (in much the same ways as neoclassical theory claims that private enterprise managers calculate for the maximization of profit).

Since in practice neither a private enterprise system nor a planned socialist economy can achieve the optimum efficiency of a theoretical model, the question is which of these two systems can better approximate allocational efficiency in practice. We shall see that socialist economists reach quite different conclusions from Mises and Hayek.

Information and Computation Problems

In the next stage of debate, Hayek admits that *in theory* the planners might accumulate all the millions of pieces of necessary information and might then solve all of the millions of equations necessary to make an optimal decision.[10] In practice, Hayek argues, no conceivable army of planners could actually gather all of the various kinds of information from every factory and farm, and from every private and public consumer. Furthermore, in practice, even with all of the information, it would take hundreds of years to solve correctly all of the equations for just one year's plan.

Hayek does not directly refer to Soviet experience, but it is clear that he believes that any centrally planned economy must be terribly inefficient. While conceding its theoretical possibility, he argues that any planned economy must base its decisions on only partial bits of information and very rough calculations. The result, he predicts, is far below the optimal allocation of resources compared to that of a competitive private enterprise model.

Nor are these purely academic problems to be dismissed by any socialist. The high rate of Soviet growth proves the possibility of planning; however, it does not tell us how much is lost by the inefficiency of Soviet planning. Even Soviet economists have admitted that with the continued use of present methods and with increasing economic complexity, the Soviet Union would eventually need more

---

10. See Hayek, *Collectivist Economic Planning.*

than its total population just for management of the planning process. Many have argued that this problem could be solved by automated information-collecting and the use of computers. Yet others argue that even these improvements will not suffice to maintain, much less raise, the level of efficiency in Soviet planning.

Central and Decentralized Solutions

The most famous answer to Hayek's criticism of the practicability of socialist planning was given by Lange.[11] He replies that a decentralized or market socialism would have no more trouble than competitive private enterprise in reaching rational prices and optimum allocation of resources. He refers to a system in which the public owns all firms but each firm acts as an independent unit and bases its production decisions on prices which reflect supply and demand conditions in the marketplace. Lange's model is discussed in detail in Chapter 14 on market socialism.

Central planning has been most fully defended by the British Marxist Maurice Dobb.[12] Dobb points to the existence and rapid growth of the planned economy of the USSR as proof of its practicability. He also considers the three problems of socialist planning—growth, balance, and efficiency—and concludes that all three could be better solved under central planning than under capitalism, even though he admits that the planners may have far from rational and accurate price data.

We explore each of these questions in separate chapters, so it suffices here to give a very brief summary of Dobb's stand. First, he argues that growth depends primarily on the ratio of new investment to national product. He maintains that the decision on this ratio does not depend on relative prices because it is not economic but must be primarily political. He believes that the choice will be more conducive to growth when made by a centralized socialist government than by multitudinous private capitalists.

Second, Dobb contends that the problem of a consistent (not necessarily optimal) balance of physical goods and actual money-income flows can be solved with any set of constant but arbitrary prices. Thus, a socialist economy can and does ensure continuous full employment of people and resources, while capitalist economies periodically suffer unemployment.

---

11. Oskar Lange, *On the Economic Theory of Socialism* (Minneapolis: University of Minnesota, 1938).

12. See, e.g., Maurice Dobb, *Economic Theory and Socialism* (New York: International Publishers, 1955), 55–93. But also see the Marxist analysis by Paul M. Sweezy, *Socialism* (New York: McGraw-Hill Book Co., Inc., 1949).

Third, Dobb admits it is true that rational prices are necessary for static Pareto optimal efficiency but argues that this criterion is much less important in economic practice than balance and rapid growth. Anyway, he argues, new computing methods and machines now permit fairly good planners' calculations of the equations for prices and outputs. Moreover, he maintains, capitalist prices are also far from perfectly rational, since there is monopoly on the sellers' side and irrational advertising pressure on the consumers, as well as externalities (discussed in the next section).

A Tentative Summary of Conclusions on Efficiency

How do different economic systems measure up to the criterion of Pareto optimum efficiency? Pure and perfect competition under private enterprise does seem obviously to meet these conditions (with the exceptions and limitations noted below). The rational consumer will buy each good until his ratios of marginal utilities equal the ratios of price, and prices are the same for all consumers. The profit-maximizing producer will buy inputs to the point where the ratios of their marginal products equal their price ratios, and prices are the same for all producers. These facts also mean that for all outputs and inputs the ratios of marginal utilities will equal the ratios of marginal products, which is one way of stating Pareto optimum efficiency.

There are three kinds of exceptions and limitations to how well these rules may work in a competitive private enterprise or capitalist economy. First, the rules do not work under some conditions. For example, there may be "externalities," which are costs or benefits to the public that are not reflected in the firm's costs or prices, such as pollution from automobiles. If there are externalities, then the system does not reach an optimal allocation—and many critics of capitalism believe that externalities are pervasive in any economy. Or, for example, there may be "public goods," that is, goods that can be consumed only collectively, such as public parks, street lights, or military spending. There is no automatic way for the market capitalist system to price or produce these goods. Second, it may be shown that to the degree that competition is imperfect or monopolistic, private enterprise capitalism will not reach the optimum allocation of resources. Third, it has already been noted that this optimum allocation does *not* mean that there is equitable distribution of income, full employment, stable prices, or rapid growth.

What about a competitive or market socialism, in which the government owns all resources but each firm acts independently to maximize its profit by its own price and output decision? Theoretically, if there is pure and perfect competition under market socialism, it turns out that the resulting allocation of resources is exactly as efficient as under pure and perfect competition in private enterprise.

The two may differ only with respect to "equity" or distribution of income and budgets among consumers and among producers (and possibly with respect to growth and aggregate balance). Market socialism will distribute as private income only wages, not profits, nor rent, nor interest. The profit, rent, and interest receipts will be used either to add to wage income or to expand production. Nonetheless, market socialism is also subject to the three types of problem mentioned above: (1) the system is not responsive automatically to externalities or public goods, so it has less than optimal allocation under such conditions; (2) to the degree that competition is imperfect or monopolistic in this system, market socialism will also not achieve an optimum allocation of resources; and (3) it may still be subject to unemployment, inflation, or a low rate of growth. (More will be said on these issues in Chapters 14, 15, and 16.)

Finally, how do the optimum efficiency conditions apply to a centrally planned socialist economy? Recall that the informational ingredients of these conditions are: (1) consumer preferences, (2) availability of resources, and (3) technological possibilities of production. It is not theoretically necessary that these be discovered automatically through the market mechanism. *If* central planners have the complete detailed information on these three items throughout the economy, and *if* they are able to perfectly calculate all of the equations involved, then (as Hayek admits) they can reach the same optimum mix of inputs and outputs as would exist under pure and perfect competition. The same rational prices will also emerge as a byproduct of the planners' calculations, though they are not further needed in a fully planned system.

In reality, just as capitalist systems do not function as pure neoclassical theory claims, central planners will have imperfect information about the millions of preferences, resources, and production processes. They also cannot possibly solve the millions and millions of equations involved for want of time and calculators, even with the use of the most modern electronic machinery. They must, moreover, take more time to make readjustments to new situations than the market does in certain respects. Furthermore, planning in practice costs a considerable amount in terms of the time and effort of people and machines, while the market mechanism is allegedly "free," though there is much duplication of competitive effort in the market. Thus, imperfect planning must involve some considerable departure from optimum efficiency. As with imperfect competition, the difficult question is the quantitative degree of inefficiency under imperfect planning.

One point about propaganda should be kept firmly in mind both here and in the concluding chapter of this book. A debater always considers the theoretical ideal behavior of his or her favorite economic system but stresses the actual imperfect behavior of the opponent's economic system. We should be aware that Mises and Hayek attack the actual or realized operation of an imperfect planned socialist system from the viewpoint of a pure and perfect competitive private enterprise system. Lange stresses the theoretical possibilities of a pure and perfect market socialist system in contrast to the actual operation of imperfect private enterprise economies. Dobb and Sweezy emphasize the theoretical potential of pure and perfect planned economies by contrasting them to the monopolistic and imperfect actual operation of private enterprise economies. *When we examine the pure and perfect form of each of these, we find that in theory they are equally capable of reaching a Pareto optimum condition. The real questions are,* in practice, how close each system approaches static and dynamic efficiency, how their income distribution and aggregate balance compare, and how related political and social behavior compare (all of which are reconsidered in the last chapter of this book).

The "Law of Value" in the Soviet Union

Soviet economists have not discussed efficiency planning in terms of welfare economics until recently, but they have often discussed many of the same issues in the dogmatic form of a debate about the applicability of Marx's *Law of Value* to a socialist economy. The debate over the Law of Value has a long history in the Soviet Union, and it may help to give that setting before we examine the issues as they actually affect present-day planning. The Marxist Law of Value states that the value of any commodity is equal to the amount of average socially necessary labor embodied in it, that is, the amount of labor necessary under present technological conditions. Marx developed his law of value in an effort to understand the workings of capitalist economies.

History of the Debate

During the period of War Communism, from 1917 to 1921, the Soviet Union did not in practice make much use of prices or of money. This lack of prices and money was idealized in theory as a true state of communism. Therefore, during this period it was held very dogmatically that the Law of Value has no application under socialism but is only a description of the situation under competitive capitalism. Then, in the period of the New Economic Policy of the 1920s, trade and exchange became general, and the use of money permeated the economy. In this period there ensued a great deal of debate over the uses of prices in socialism and over the methodology of planning but without much clarification of the use of the Marxist Law of Value. It was in this environment of intense discussion in the mid 1920s that Wassily Leontief studied at Leningrad University and first considered the problems that later led to the input-output method of planning.

Unfortunately, Stalin killed off this promising discussion (and some of the discussants as well) and attacked all model building as "bourgeois, mathematical formalism." As a result, the years of Stalin's dictatorship from 1928 to 1953 were uncreative and terribly dull in economics.[13] The tasks of Soviet economists in these years were characterized by one harsh critic as "perpetual propagation of Marxism, peremptory assessment of the processes of disintegration in capitalism, and exorbitant praise for the success of Soviet industrialization."[14] At any rate, it is a fact that in all those years there were no translations and few discussions of Western economics. It is a more damning fact that in all those years there was published no new textbook of economics and planning; the first weak effort toward a new Soviet textbook was published in 1954. Available statistical data were greatly reduced in the late 1930s, and their publication almost ceased after 1937; Soviet statistical yearbooks began to appear again only in 1957.

During the five-year plans of the 1930s, Stalin stressed that there were no limits to what could be done—there was neither need nor possibility for the operation of an authentic Law of Value but room only for the law of the plan. Soviet economics in this period reverted to a loose Marxist formulation that "value" would disappear in socialism, which was taken to mean that the planners could do anything that Stalin desired. In fact, the official Soviet view urged planners "not to study, but to change economics, to disregard economic laws."[15] Stalinist planning was mostly empirical, using little theory and no attempt to approach optimal efficiency but simply pushing as much investment as possible. Under Stalin, Soviet planners merely used the rule of thumb in basic industry that it is wisest to follow the technology of the more developed United States (with modifications to fit technology to Soviet conditions).

It might also be noted that while Stalin was rejecting any but purely empirical methods of planning, various important theoretical advances were beginning to poke their heads up from the practical operational fields of Soviet engineering and project making. For example, it was in 1939 that the Soviet mathematician Kantorovich was

---

13. For a feeling of the enormous difference that the change in political atmosphere made, read the drivel written on planning in the Soviet textbook *Political Economy* (USSR Academy of Sciences, 1954; English edition published by Lawrence and Wishart, 1957), produced collectively under Stalin's direction. Then compare the brilliant collection of articles issued just five years later in the Khrushchev era by the more progressive Soviet economists, called *The Uses of Mathematics in Economics* (edited by Nemchinov, Moscow, 1959, English edition published by Oliver and Boyd, 1964).

14. Vladimir Treml, "Revival of Soviet Economics and the New Generation of Soviet Economists," *Studies on the Soviet Union* 5, 2 (1965): 4.

15. S. Strumilin, quoted in *ibid.*, 3.

employed by an engineering firm to advise on the optimal use of their machinery. As a result, he published the first paper on what has become the most famous of all planning methods, the method of linear programming. Yet this discovery, too, was buried under the heap of ideological trash produced under the Stalinist dictatorship. It is true that U.S. economists took several years to recognize the importance of linear programming after its first appearance here, but in the Stalinist atmosphere any general utilization of such a radically new economic concept was simply inconceivable. Not only was official dogma promulgated in scholastic detail, but Stalin imprisoned or executed several of the most brilliant and daring economists of the 1930s.

In 1943 came the first official breakthrough and recognition of value problems in the Soviet Union. At that time, in a famous article first appearing in a Soviet journal,[16] there surfaced a vague but definite statement that the Law of Value does apply under socialism. Nothing more concrete, however, evolved in the Soviet discussions until Stalin himself took a hand in the discussion. Stalin in 1952 made his last authoritative pronouncement on the subject, leading to a major debate throughout the socialist countries and the ranks of Western Marxists.[17]

Stalin argues that "wherever commodities and commodity production exist, there the law of value must also exist."[18] By commodity production he means production for sale in the competitive marketplace, just as Marx described competition in the marketplace of capitalism. Stalin saw commodity production in the Soviet Union existing almost exclusively in the collective farm markets, in the exchange of goods between the collective farm and the government-owned factories, and in retail sales. Thus, one sympathetic Western Marxist writes, in agreement with Stalin:

> Under socialism in a country like the U.S.S.R. where a semi-private agricultural sector continues to exist alongside the state sector, commodity production (and therefore the law of value) will also continue to exist, although in a relatively restricted sphere.[19]

The crux of the question, however, is that under pure centrally planned socialism there is no free competitive market exchange of goods between state-owned firms. Therefore, there is no "commodity production" in the sphere of producer goods in the peculiar sense

---

16. "Some Problems in the Teaching of Political Economy," transl. in the *American Economic Review* (Sept. 1944).

17. Joseph Stalin, *Economic Problems in Socialism in the U.S.S.R.* (New York: International Publishers, 1952).

18. *Ibid.*, 18.

19. Ronald Meek, *Studies in the Labour Theory of Value* (New York: International Publishers, 1956), 293.

used by Stalin. Thus, the same writer continues, again in agreement with Stalin:

> So far as manufactured goods are concerned, their situation is somewhat anomalous, since although they are technically "commodities" the concept of a supply price is not really applicable to them, and I can not see that there is much point in attempting to analyse their prices in terms of our conceptual apparatus.[20]

In other words, Stalinist economic theory (really a theology) could admit only that some manufactured goods are "commodities" because they exchange on the market with some agricultural goods, though this is a very small peg upon which to hang a value theory. It was still argued that there is no possibility—or perhaps no need—to plan prices within the manufacturing sector in accordance with value. This very limited recognition of the importance of economic value did very little to improve the quality of the Soviet debate.

It was not until Stalin's death, and especially after the severe and public criticism of Stalin in 1956, that Soviet economists once again felt really free to discuss the importance of money and prices. After 1956, almost all Soviet economists did come to agree that the Law of Value has great importance in socialism; that is, that planning must be based on the objective facts of social needs and costs. And it was only at this time that official Soviet recognition was given to Leontief's input-output discovery and Kantorovich's linear programming discovery—indeed, claiming both as purely Soviet achievements. This claim was made in spite of the fact that the work of both had returned to the Soviet Union only via the extensive research and writings of Western economists.

After it was admitted that the Law of Value does apply to a socialist economy, there arose in the Soviet Union three different views of the value of manufactured means of production.[21] The most restrictive view argues, as Stalin did, that the Law of Value operates only in "market exchange," so values may be calculated only for consumer goods and for the few producer goods exchanged between manufacturing enterprises and collective farms (other producer goods are not traded, bought, and sold but are allocated by the state).[22] The second view maintains that the Law of Value operates under any kind of exchange, so values may be calculated for all exchanges between government enterprises.[23] The third and most radical view argues

---

20. *Ibid.*

21. These three views are discussed in detail in Gregory Grossman, "Gold and the Sword: Money in the Soviet Command Economy," in H. Rosovsky, ed., *Industrialization in Two Systems* (New York: John Wiley, 1966).

22. See, e.g., Ostrovitianov, *Stroitclstvo kommunizma i tovarnodenezhnye otnosheniia* (Moscow: 1962).

23. See, e.g., I. A. Kronod, *Dengi v sotsialisticheskom obshchestve* (Moscow: 1960).

pragmatically that the need for valuation under socialism arises from the necessity in the planning process of measuring the amount of labor expended on each product; so all products must be valued.[24]

These more progressive or radical Soviet writers stress, as seen in detail below, that the current Soviet price structure is highly irrational and misleading. Soviet prices omit rent, interest, and any meaningful category of profits, though they usually include a fixed and arbitrary profit rate. Moreover, most prices remain set for many years, but since supply and demand conditions are constantly changing in any dynamic economy, this implies that prices are far out of line during much of this time. One reflection of this distortion is that many commodities must be subsidized for long periods, while others carry heavy sales or turnover taxes. (Note that some goods are deliberately priced below value for the benefit of society, such as children's clothing, while some goods are deliberately high-priced for social benefit, such as vodka.)

It may be asked why in later years not only the progressives, but even Stalin and his followers, began to talk about the need for rational valuation and calculation in the Soviet economy. The increased need seems to have grown out of the increased complexity of the Soviet economy. For one thing, it has many more enterprise units and more varied products than it did in earlier days—at the present time over two hundred thousand separate enterprises and over twelve million different products. Second, there are many more technological possibilities and variants open to the Soviet planners in each industry. Third, there is a much wider variety of consumer goods to choose among, and the average income now puts the Soviet consumer far above the absolute biological need level. After 1956, the new political atmosphere emphasized prompt satisfaction of the wide variety of consumer needs. Fourth, although there had been plenty of reserve labor in the rural areas in the 1930s, the terrible losses of the Second World War made it urgently necessary to use labor more efficiently. Fifth, the problems of an increased international trade began to call for more rational calculation.

The more progressive Soviet writers emphasize the enormous losses in each of these areas caused by an irrational price structure. The seriousness of the problem not only has been stressed by U.S. critics[25] but was recognized in print by Soviet critics at least as early as 1957.[26] All of the defects in the price system add up to the net result that relative prices do not correctly reflect "value," scarcity, or con-

---

24. See, e.g., I. S. Malyshev, *Obshchestvennyi uchet truda i tsena pri sotsializme* (Moscow: 1960).

25. See, e.g., Jere L. Felker, *Soviet Economic Controversies, the Emerging Marketing Concept and Changes in Planning, 1960–1965* (Cambridge: MIT Press, 1966).

26. See, e.g., I. Malyshev, *Voprosy ekonomiki* (1957), No. 3, p. 32.

sumer demand. Since society is very complex, planners have to make many decisions in ignorance of the information which a rational price system would provide them. One famous progressive Soviet writer says that more efficient planning could increase output by 40 to 50 percent.[27] Although this estimate is very probably an overly enthusiastic one, this is no small matter.

Further reasons for increased Soviet interest in allocational efficiency may be found in the relationship with the Western economies. On the one hand, there is the race to grow more rapidly than the United States, for which maximum achievable efficiency is extremely helpful. On the other hand, there is the fact that great advances in practical methods of planning have been made in the Western countries, and these methods are available for imitation. Of course, the new planning methods have been used in the United States only for planning at the micro or enterprise level, since the United States has no national economic planning. In the USSR, however, the new planning methods not only have been applied at the enterprise level, but also have been applied—or at least the attempt is being made to apply them—at the macroeconomic level of regional economic planning.

Marxist Economic Laws and Planning Models

Is there a conflict between the Marxist economic Law of Value and the modern theories and methods of rational economic planning? Specifically, can the Soviet Union continue to promote Marxist economics while using the latest planning devices? There are three opposing views. First, most Anglo-American experts, such as Robert Campbell, believe that there is indeed a conflict between Marxism and modern planning theory.[28] An extreme view is expressed by Zauberman, who claims

> that the price arrived at in the calculus [of the new Soviet mathematical models] . . . turns out to be in unmistakable conflict with that derived from Marx. Marx's price is a cost price, while the conservative Soviet critics of the . . . mathematical scheme . . . correctly identified . . . [its] value-weights as scarcity prices, typically marginalist in their nature. Many of these critics . . . have rightly pointed to the deep roots of the mathematicians' price in the subjective value concept, and to its incompatibility with Marx's objective value, reducible to "congealed" socially necessary labor.[29]

---

27. See L. V. Kantorovich, *The Best Use of Economic Resources* (Cambridge: Harvard University Press, transl. in 1965).

28. See, e.g., Robert W. Campbell, "Marx, Kantorovich, and Novozhilov," *Slavic Review* 20 (Oct. 1961): 402–18. A discussion of more general conflicts is given by Joseph Berliner, "Marxism and the Soviet Economy," *Problems of Communism*, 13 (Sept.–Oct., 1964): 1–10.

29. Alfred Zauberman, "Revisionism in Soviet Economics," in Leopold Labedz, ed., *Revisionism* (New York: Frederick A. Praeger, 1962), 276.

It follows, according to this argument, that Marxist value economics must be eliminated if the Soviet Union is to plan rationally.

Strangely enough, the major premise of this argument is accepted among the second group, the more dogmatic (orthodox?) Soviet Marxist economists, such as Boiarskii.[30] Boiarskii agrees that there is a conflict between Marxist economics and certain modern theories of planning. Since he believes in the absolute truth of Marxism, however, his conclusion is directly opposite to that reached by Campbell. He concludes that these planning theories must not be followed in the Soviet Union. Particular devices, such as input-output or linear programming, may be used if they are first completely purged of their marginal utility taint.

A third position is that of the less dogmatic (progressive? creative? revisionist?) Marxists in the Soviet Union, such as Novozhilov or Kantorovich.[31] They hold that modern theories of economic planning are quite compatible with Marxism and that the modern instruments of rational planning should be used to the fullest extent. For these views, Novozhilov and others have been labeled as revisionists of Marx both by their own dogmatic Soviet colleagues and by most Anglo-American experts. Nove,[32] a more perceptive critic, writes, however:

> One should not assume, as some Western critics do, that Marxian economics is inherently inconsistent with reality, that the "vulgar Marxist" simplifications of the late-Stalin period are the essence of the theory. Novozhilov, for instance, would certainly argue that his theories are consistent with Marxism; are indeed the correct application of Marxist theory to the circumstances of the Sovet Union.[33]

---

30. See, e.g., A. Y. Boiarskii, "On the Proper Relationship Between Mathematics and Economics in a Socialist Society," transl. in *Problems in Economics* (Jan. 1962): 12–24. Also see the similar views in A. I. Kats, "Concerning a Fallacious Concept of Economic Calculations," transl. in *Problems of Economics* (Nov. 1960): 42–52. A history of the various viewpoints in the Stalin era is available in Gregory Grossman, "Scarce Capital and Soviet Doctrine," *Quarterly Journal of Economics* 67 (Aug. 1963): 311–43.

31. See, e.g., L. V. Kantorovich, "On the Calculation of Production Inputs," transl. in *Problems of Economics* (May 1960): 3–10. Also see Benjamin Ward, "Kantorovich on Economic Calculation," *Journal of Political Economy* 68 (Dec. 1960): 545–56. Further see V. V. Novozhilov, "On Choosing between Investment Projects," transl. in *International Economic Papers*, No. 6 (1956): 67–87. Also see V. V. Novozhilov, "Calculation of Outlays in a Socialist Economy," transl. in *Problems of Economics* (Dec. 1961): 18–28. Finally, his fullest presentation is in V. V. Novozhilov, "Cost-Benefit Comparisons in a Socialist Economy," in V. S. Nemchinov, ed., *The Use of Mathematics in Economics* (London: Oliver and Boyd, Ltd., transl. under the editorship of A. Nove in 1964, Russian ed. 1959).

32. Alec Nove, Introduction to V. S. Nemchinov, ed., *The Use of Mathematics in Economics*, p. x.

33. *Ibid.*

In fact, Novozhilov himself admits that some of his categories of calculation under socialism, such as profits, are semantically similar to those used under capitalism, but he argues strongly that this similarity is due only to the mathematical similarities in all optimization problems.[34] (It must be noted that, for a capitalist economy, if there is pure and perfect competition, as well as constant returns to scale, both Marxist and neoclassical theories agree that value is determined by "cost," though they disagree on the meaning of "cost.")

A great many of the Soviet writers now argue that there is no conflict between Marxism and the modern neoclassical theories of resource allocation.[35] Specifically, the more progressive Soviet writers point out that to advocate a price for capital in a planned economy is quite different from advocating that any profit (or interest) be given as individual income. If the neoclassical theory of allocation happens to meet the problems of socialist firms, there is no reason not to use it.

The progressive Marxists of the West, as in the early writings of Oskar Lange, argue that there is a qualitative difference between the technical problems of planned allocation of resources and the political-ethical problems of class ownership and distribution. They agree that the technical problems of socialist planning may be best discussed in terms of "bourgeois" neoclassical economics. Yet they still believe that the political-ethical questions of income distribution by classes, as well as many macroeconomic problems of capitalism, are to be understood in terms of Marxist political economy.[36]

If the more progressive Soviet attitude were accepted, then there would be no conflict between Marxism and any prospective tool of Soviet economic planning. Since it is far from fully accepted, each action of Soviet planners is still gauged by the politicians in terms of a very dogmatic interpretation of Marxism, as well as their own pragmatic self-interests.

Prices and Efficiency

A careful examination of recent Soviet debates on specific price policy raises two questions: (1) Why are prices essential in Soviet

---

34. *Ibid.*, 189.

35. See, e.g., A. Postyshev, "The Labor Theory of Value and Optimal Planning," transl. in *Problems of Economics* (1967). He identifies the famous "shadow prices" of linear programming with Marx's value in terms of labor.

36. This view of the distinction between Marxist political economy and technical bourgeois economics is presented by the Marxist writers Paul Baran and Paul Sweezy in "Economics of Two Worlds," in *On Political Economy and Econometrics: Essays in Honor of Oskar Lange* (New York: Pergamon Press, 1965), 15–29.

planning for efficiency? and (2) What is the relation of the Soviet theory of value to its practical application in pricing policies?

The Importance of Prices in Soviet Planning

Previous chapters have mentioned some of the uses of prices in the planned Soviet economy. First, wages (with given retail prices) provide much of the stimulus or incentive for workers and managers to do their best work. Moreover, since not every detail is centrally planned, the structure of prices will influence many managerial decisions about inputs as well as output mixtures. This will happen whenever managers' bonuses are based on the value of the total product or on monetary profits.[37]

Second, it was said that many planning decisions about balance involve prices. For example, consumer prices must be set so that demand for goods equals supply at the given prices. Similarly, wages must be set so that the demand equals the supply of workers at the given wages. All of the prices mentioned so far are concerned with the execution of the plan or the influencing of the behavior of workers and managers and consumers in accordance with the plan. But what about prices in the calculation of the plan itself?

Prices enter the problems of balanced growth in a relatively simple way, not involving a theory of value. In theory, balances among industries could be analyzed in wholly physical terms. Physical amounts are used to some degree in Soviet practice in the application of their "method of balances"; physical amounts can also be used in the Leontief input-output method. Where prices are used for purposes of balance, they may be any arbitrary or randomly chosen prices, *provided* that (1) they remain constant during the planning period, and (2) they are consistent among themselves, so that the price of a commodity is not less than the total of the costs of the goods going into it. This is because prices are used in the balancing procedure only for purposes of aggregating different things. This is true, for example, of the sources and the uses side of the balance of a single industry; or, for example, of the total of all wages balanced against the total price of all consumer goods.

The situation is quite different in the other problem of planning, the optimization of resource allocation. Though there are many consistent balances, there is only one *optimal* input and output mix. The choice of that optimal mix depends on what value or price is chosen for each of the inputs and outputs. The optimization problem has two aspects: (1) the choice of a maximum or most preferred output mix,

---

37. An excellent Soviet statement of the importance of rational prices for managers appears in N. Fedorenko, "Price and Optimal Planning," transl. in *Problems of Economics* (1967).

and (2) the choice of a minimum cost or most efficient technology. A solution may be reached *either* by minimizing costs (given a desired set of outputs) or by maximizing the value of output (given available inputs and technology); it is not necessary to do both. In order either to calculate costs properly or to evaluate output properly, however, it is necessary to have prices that rationally reflect social costs and social needs. (A technically detailed discussion of the linear programming method of optimization is in the appendix to this chapter.)

As a concrete example, suppose the Soviet economy produces only two kinds of outputs: apples and oranges. With the given amount of labor and capital inputs available, assume the economy can produce either (1) five apples and ten oranges or (2) ten apples and five oranges. Which output mixture should be produced to maximize output? That obviously depends on the value or price of each output, relative to the price of the other output (for simplicity, we assume each price is constant in its whole range). If the relative prices (values) are two rubles an apple and one ruble an orange, then output is maximized by choosing mixture (2), ten apples and five oranges. But if the prices were one ruble an apple and two rubles an orange, then output would be maximized by choosing mixture (1), five apples and ten oranges.

The case is exactly analogous if planners wish to minimize the cost of production. Suppose the only inputs available are capital and labor. To produce a certain required amount of output (for example, a given number of apples and oranges), there are two technological processes available, involving either (1) the use of five units of labor and ten units of capital or (2) the use of ten units of labor and five units of capital. Each "unit" is a physical measure such as hours of labor expended or numbers of machines used. Which process will minimize the cost of inputs? Again, this depends on the relative prices of the inputs. The planners choose (1) if a unit of labor costs two rubles and a unit of capital one ruble, but choose (2) if a unit of labor costs one ruble and a unit of capital two rubles.

In both cases, it is impossible to optimize, or to make a rational economic choice, without the use of some standard of valuation or price system. In the second example, an engineer could only say that in physical terms either technological process or combination of inputs will produce the same output. But the social welfare cannot be maximized unless the planners know the economic value of the inputs (cost, reflecting the demand for and availability of resources), so they can say which combination produces the output at the least cost to society.

Price Policies

The Soviet views on price policy follow fairly clearly from their different views on value. One view, which has been labeled "voluntarist," is simply to have the planners set prices as they desire. This view derives from the notion that the Law of Value has no application to the socialist economy and that prices need have no effect on planning. Needless to say, this view no longer has any explicit defenders in the Soviet Union.

Nonetheless, the Soviet price structure still bears an unfortunate resemblance to what might be expected of it under such a view. That is to say, in practice Soviet prices do not seem clearly correlated with any particular value theory, though efforts at reform have been made over the last fifteen years. Before the reform, at least, there were many gross and obvious examples of price distortion. Some of these were mentioned earlier. Another, which clearly affects some important decisions, is the fact that consumer goods prices included an enormous turnover tax, while most producer goods were free of any turnover tax. Finding alternative methods of setting taxes, methods that would not distort relative prices, was a major aim of the debate on prices.

Several groups of Soviet economists do agree that the Marxist Law of Value does apply to a socialist economy but offer differing legalistic interpretations of it. All agree that price must equal the total of (1) current labor expenditure, (2) past labor reflected in the cost of materials and capital depreciation, and (3) some profit (called *surplus for society*). Expenditures on current labor, materials, and depreciation are presently included in price. The problem is how to calculate the surplus or profit. The most dogmatic group would calculate the surplus strictly as a given, constant ratio to (1), current labor expenditure. The second would calculate the surplus as a given ratio to (1), current labor expenditure, plus (2), past labor reflected in the cost of materials and capital depreciation. The most progressive group would calculate the profit as a given ratio to the stock of capital, the same formulas on which Marx's "price of production" is based. Finally, the small group advocating price of production shades over into an even smaller group of so-called imputationists. They would set prices, not on the basis of any authoritative theological dogma, but by imputing prices from the objective facts either of social costs or of social needs.

One widely known approach, which falls within the imputationist group, is that of the Soviet economist Novozhilov.[38] In Western economic terms, he calculates the "opportunity costs" of using scarce resources. The reader will recall that opportunity costs are the measure of the sacrifice made in forgoing the best alternative project in

38. See, e.g., V. V. Novozhilov, "Cost-Benefit Comparisons in a Socialist Economy," in Nemchinov, *The Use of Mathematics in Economics*. A similar approach to prices, deriving them strictly according to the needs of optimal planning, is clearly stated by V. S. Dadaian and others in "A Symposium on Problems of Political-Economy," *Problems of Economics* 10 (July 1967): 3–19.

order to use a limited resource in the project under consideration. Novozhilov always calculates these costs in terms of labor so as to maintain Marxist orthodoxy. He calculates not only the usual labor costs but also so-called indirect labor costs. What are these indirect labor costs? If capital and natural resources are used in certain projects in large amounts, then there may not be sufficient capital and natural resources remaining to use them as desired in all other projects. In that case, the other projects will have to switch to the use of more labor and less capital, thus "indirectly" causing an increase of labor costs.

Since these goods are limited or scarce, they must be rationed; that is the function of the calculation of the indirect labor costs. In choosing the alternative with the minimum cost, the planner compares not only current labor costs and the using up of capital and materials but also the indirect labor costs or opportunity costs of directing scarce resources here rather than elsewhere. In this sense the so-called indirect labor costs play a role similar to the rate of profit (and rent) in private enterprise, which rations capital (and natural resources) to different industries so that the marginal return is uniform for all industries in a perfectly competitive environment. If Soviet enterprises borrow all capital from the government, then this calculation acts like a rate of interest, ensuring that (1) investment funds are used where most profitable to the society, and (2) investment goes to just that point where aggregate supply and demand are equal.

Summary of the Planning Debate

What may be learned from this discussion? Mises argued the impossibility of socialist planning because lack of a market would mean lack of knowledge of rational prices. Socialists have answered that optimal planning could be achieved if planners have a knowledge of preferences, resource endowments, and production possibilities. Dobb even argues that planners could do better than the market if society desires not only optimum allocation but also full employment and rapid growth. Hayek objects that in practice the central planners could never get and digest all the necessary information. Lange rejoins that socialism could be decentralized so that a competitive market could provide (directly or indirectly) rational prices for socialist managers.

The Soviet economy is estimated to have some twelve million commodities. Whatever theoretical foundation is used to formulate prices, the task of calculating and recalculating them is formidable. The actual setting of prices in Soviet practice is discussed in Chapter 11.

The Soviet approaches to allocation theory and modern methods of planning have also been examined. The older, more dogmatic Marxist economists believed that Marxist economics is absolutely opposed to modern Western allocation and optimal planning theories. The younger Soviet reformers, however, have reinterpreted Marxism to show that there is no conflict between Marxist economics and optimal planning theories.

Choice of Technology

From where do the technical coefficients (relation of output to input) come, or by whom and how are they derived? In theory, the central planners must determine these coefficients on the basis of their knowledge of all the engineering data on methods of production as well as all of the costs and prices for each output produced by each plant. In practice, many technological decisions are made at a lower echelon than that of the central planners, though this only transfers the problem to local enterprise economists or engineers. Furthermore, as far as the central planners are concerned, most of the means of production now being used were already produced in previous years; so current technological choices may actually be very limited, and the problem arises for the most part only when future investments are planned.

It has been stressed that Soviet planners have usually assumed the final output plan as given by political decision and so have primarily concentrated on the choice of technology. But the choice of technology is mainly the choice among investment projects. New investment, after all, is the area in which most technological choices are made, because established facilities are using certain fixed kinds of capital goods and technological procedures, which may be varied only within narrow limits in current production. Only with new investment—the addition of new capital goods—does the choice between old and new types of technology arise. In the Soviet Union the problem of cost minimization in the choice of new technology has been much debated under the title of the "choice of the best investment project."

One ideological obstacle in the past was the very dogmatic Soviet interpretation of Marx, which held that "capital is not productive," or that "capital produces no value." Somehow, this led Soviets in practice to charge no interest on fixed capital given to enterprises (until the reforms of 1965). It also led them in official planning theory—at least until 1958—to treat capital as a valueless or free good. Assuming capital to be free means that planners would always choose as the least-cost variant that investment project which requires the least labor, *regardless* of how much capital is needed. This thinking would be a mistake anywhere but was an especially unfortunate tendency in the Soviet Union where capital was the relatively scarce factor, while labor was the relatively abundant factor.

For Marxist or any economics and for a socialist or any economy, capital is productive or valuable in one important sense: if capital is added, either output is increased or costs are reduced. This fact is very different from an ethical judgment that the *owners* of capital should or should not be rewarded for its use. When Marx argued that only labor produces "value," although with the help of physical capital goods, he was emphasizing that only workers put human effort into the product. Since, according to Marx, only human effort should be rewarded, the owners of capital should not be rewarded for the use of capital goods. The dogmatic Marxists seem to have confused Marx's ethical conclusion against distributing income to capitalists with the question of whether capital goods could increase labor productivity (which Marx never denied).

In the Soviet debate over the best investment technique for reducing costs, the dogmatists did not want to admit the valuable role of more capital in reducing costs. The practical problem, however, remains: there are an infinite number of possible investment projects in which the added capital could reduce labor and other current operating costs; the planners must choose among these projects because there is only a limited amount of capital at any one time. To repeat endlessly that capital produces no value is no help to the planner.

The general way to make the choice of where to invest more capital is to compare the amount of capital needed with the reduction of cost achieved in each project. Interestingly, without a whisper about theory, Soviet engineers have been doing just that by a crude rule of thumb ever since the 1930s. Their rule is called the Coefficient of Relative Effectiveness (or CRE). The CRE was officially adopted as a useful device for Soviet planning in 1958.[39]

For any new projects, the Soviet CRE directly compares the additional capital needed with the saving in labor and other current costs. Suppose two new projects are proposed, and Project 2 will use more capital investment but will have lower current costs than Project 1. The CRE of Project 2 compared with Project 1 is then defined by the simple formula:

CRE = (Cost in 1 – Cost in 2)/(Capital in 2 – Capital in 1).

As an example of these calculations, suppose that the planners wish to produce 100 million rubles worth of shoes per year and that there are two possible technological ways of doing it. One variant (Project 1) requires an investment of 55 million rubles, and an annual

39. See "Recommendations of the All-Union Scientific-Technical Conference on Problems of Determining the Economic Effectiveness of Capital Investments and New Techniques in the U.S.S.R. National Economy," transl. in *Problems of Economics* 1 (Jan. 1958): 86–90, reprinted in F. D. Holzman, *Readings on the Soviet Economy* (Chicago: Rand McNally, 1962). See a discussion of the earlier Soviet debates on investment criteria in Gregory Grossman, "Scarce Capital and Soviet Doctrine," *Quarterly Journal of Economics* 67 (Aug. 1953): 311–43.

cost of production of another 50 million rubles. The second variant (Project 2) needs an investment of 75 million rubles, but has an annual cost of production of 49 million rubles. Then the Coefficient of Relative Effectiveness of Project 2 as compared with Project 1 can be calculated as:

$$CRE = (50 - 49)/(75 - 55) = .05.$$

In other words, the second variant requires an investment of an additional 20 million rubles for a saving in annual operating costs of only 1 million rubles. The return on the extra investment is 5 percent. This return must be compared with returns for other uses of the 20 million rubles of capital which may have higher or lower CRE's. If the marginal return to existing investments in the economy is 6 percent, then Project 2 would have to be rejected because the additional capital would have inferior returns.

The Soviet CRE is thus a rationing device to distribute the limited supply of capital and is quite similar to some of the rules of thumb used by many U.S. managers and managerial economists (with some differences noted in the next paragraph). One very general textbook rule in the U.S. economy is to continue to invest until additional investment would bring the enterprise's expected profit rate on additional capital (or "internal rate of return") down to the level of the going rate of interest on borrowed capital. In Soviet planning, the project CRE plays the role of the profit rate while the social marginal CRE (or minimum CRE required of new investments) acts as interest rate. In another similar U.S. approach, a minimum CRE of 5 percent might be translated as a twenty-year "payoff period" or "recoupment period," that is, a requirement that any new investment must pay for itself in not more than twenty years.

There are, however, some important differences between the Soviet CRE and the profit or interest rate in the United States. Obviously, no private individual receives the return on capital in the Soviet Union; it is purely a planning device for the optimal distribution of investments. Also, the CRE is a somewhat cruder device than the comparison of internal rate of return with the interest rate. The CRE does not use present discounted values, and it does not take account of the different number of years of savings in costs. The lack of a discounting procedure for income received in the future years means that all future years are implicitly valued equally. Thus, the rate of time preference is zero in the Soviet accounting system. Furthermore, the minimum required CRE is set at different rates in each industry. Because of this, capital is misallocated (by neoclassical criteria) inasmuch as it is used for investment opportunities in some industries where there are low returns instead of in industries where there would be higher returns. Perhaps most important, one must always keep in mind that the distorted price structure makes any such calculations unreliable and potentially misleading.

The CRE approach might also be considered a very, very backward relative of optimal programming. The CRE method requires approximately the same information required for the cost minimization programming problem that was described above. In the Soviet use of the CRE method, the output plan, or rather the plan for the *increase* in capacity to produce, is fixed for each good. The prices of inputs are known, and so are the input-output coefficients for each possible technological method of production. With these facts, the planners can calculate the cheapest ways to achieve the required increases in output capacity. In addition, since capital is limited and to be rationed, the planners have to know in advance the total available investment funds. The Soviet method thus restricts itself to finding the cheapest methods of production within the limits of the available capital. The planners must switch to more labor-using methods to achieve the plan when all the capital would be exhausted too soon by the very cheapest methods. The planners assume that there is always enough labor to achieve the plan. If this assumption should turn out to be wrong, a recalculation of the whole plan would be necessary.

Some U.S. economists argue that it would be much more direct and useful to Soviet planning—at least in theory—if the political leadership no longer established fixed output plans. They could limit themselves to stating their preferences for final public goods and investment goods, while leaving the output mix of consumer goods to consumer preferences. Then the problem could be set up to do what is really desired: to maximize output on the basis of (1) the given demand preferences (of the government and the consumer), (2) the range of technical possibilities, and (3) the limited amounts of each resource. If there were complete information and sufficient calculating ability, the whole problem could theoretically be done as one unified calculation (see Appendix 9A). This course of action is not possible in reality because of (1) the calculation and information problems and (2) the unwillingness of the political leaders to give up detailed control.

By the mid 1960s, it appeared to some that Soviet planning might become thoroughly rational and modernized. Such hopes have not been fulfilled, however, in spite of a vast increase in the use of mathematical economics and an enormous increase in the use of computers. In the case of input-output analysis (discussed in the previous chapter) there has been a great deal of work done in the 1970s and 1980s with many studies of the input-output matrix for various cities and regions and much theoretical discussion of its application to domestic planning.[40] There has, however, been remarkably little application of it in actual planning and almost none at the national level.[41]

---

40. See Albina Tretyakova and Igor Birman, "Input-Output Analysis in the USSR," *Soviet Studies* 28 (Apr. 1976): 157–186.

41. See Vladimir Treml, "A Comment on Birman-Tretyakova," *ibid.*, 187–88.

In the area of efficiency and optimal decision making, there has also been little practical advance. A 1974 Soviet decree directs project makers to consider how to minimize total expenditure, including both current costs and capital costs.[42] There has been a small change in the formulation of the Coefficient of Relative Effectiveness. Rather than comparing just the ratio of costs to capital for two investment projects, it now compares the ratio of profits (defined as revenue minus costs) to capital. In practice, little has changed from the 1958 decree to the present, and there is still no standard CRE for the whole economy.

Decision Making, Democracy, and Efficiency

Once it is accepted in theory that planners should maximize the value of output according to prices determined by the preferences of "society," the practical problem arises as to who represents society. This has led to a sharp debate among East European economists and to a few muted rumblings even among Soviet economists. The issue is very sensitive politically, because all of the choices of both prices and outputs must be consciously planned under Soviet centrally planned socialism. Decisions are not made automatically by the market, because there is no market for producer goods, no market for collective consumption goods (public welfare and military expenditures), and a restricted market for consumer goods.

Individual consumers can choose whether or not to buy available goods, but which ones are to be produced and expanded is a planning decision, which may or may not be made according to consumer preferences. Soviet planners do make extensive use of questionnaires to determine relative consumer preferences. At present, however, Soviet political leaders still set down most of the preferences that planners are ordered to follow. In any modern economy, the political leaders must make decisions in a large sphere of collective spending or so-called collective consumption—road building or defense, for example. These collective or public goods are defined as goods in which all people must share, or in which the benefits cannot be divided; thus, individuals cannot choose to buy these goods or not to buy them. One Communist goal is, in fact, to enlarge the sphere of collective consumption. In the Soviet Union the political leaders must decide between the competing needs for military defense, for medical care, for education, and for all other welfare spending. The Soviet planners attempt to follow the preferences of the political leaders for these collective goods. If Soviet leaders were democratically elected, the choice among public goods could be made in more representative

---

42. Janice Griffin, "The Allocation of Investment in the Soviet Union: Criteria for Efficiency of Investment," *Soviet Studies* 33 (Oct. 1981): 593–609.

fashion. The same argument could be made with regard to the choice between aggregate consumption and investment.

Wlodzimierz Brus, an émigré from Poland who is now an economics professor at Oxford University in England, has been the leading expositor of the theory that lack of democracy is a major barrier to efficiency in centrally planned economies.[43] Brus argues that democracy—or the democratic participation of the people in decision making—is absolutely necessary to efficiency in that type of economy. He claims that the democratic process is, in effect, a factor of production under socialism.

Specifically, Brus contends that lack of democracy causes a blockage of information flows. People are afraid to tell the leaders—or even the planners—about problems, so the problems are not discovered until they become major calamities. Lack of freedom also limits discussion of new technology or alternative ways of doing things. Leaders may become attached to certain technologies for historical reasons, even though such technologies are not economically justified. If there is no discussion and no protest allowed, then the leaders may stick to these uneconomical technologies. Moreover, people who are made indifferent by lack of freedom simply do not inform the central authorities about local conditions. These are the penalties for having little or no public discussion of some of the most vital decisions concerning the national economy, or even the local projects.

Brus claims that lack of information (due to lack of democracy) is the single most important reason for poor planning, misallocation of resources, and arbitrary decision making. Also, the combination of dictatorship and central planning frustrates and prevents local initiative, since decision making is based on commands from above by self-selected leaders. Furthermore, there is an undemocratic and arbitrary selection of intermediate leadership (with no avenues for protest), which results in poor day-to-day management.

Finally, Brus argues that lack of democracy means that because people do not participate in decision making, they feel helpless and alienated from the system. But, as noted above, alienated people are indifferent, so this situation contributes to bad planning, bad intermediate and lower leadership, corruption, bribery, and—equally important—negative attitudes toward work. All in all, to use Marxist terminology, the present Soviet production relations among individuals and classes (which include the political decision-making process under central planning) are a barrier or a fetter holding back the progress of the forces of production.

---

43. Wlodzimierz Brus, "Political System and Economic Efficiency: The East European Context," *Journal of Comparative Economics* 4 (Mar. 1980): 40–55. A more comprehensive work is Wlodzimierz Brus, *Socialist Ownership and Political Systems* (London: Routledge and Kegan Paul, 1975).

Brus cites Poland as the extreme example of lack of democracy leading to an inefficient and almost unworkable economy. Nevertheless, he admits that this hypothesis is hard to prove. It has too many intangibles that are impossible to measure, and there are too many other variables changing at the same time. Still, he does believe that lack of democracy is an important factor in the declining measures of efficiency in most of these countries.

Appendix 9A
Linear Programming in the Soviet Context

Optimal programming may be defined as any technique for reaching an optimal set of inputs and/or outputs in any economic situation. In fact, the techniques of optimal programming are used for even wider applications than economic problems. *Linear programming* is one particular form of optimal programming in which certain artificial restrictions are imposed in order to simplify the problem and the calculations. In linear programming it is assumed that each technological process or activity used in production is linear, that is, a doubling of the inputs will lead to a doubling of the output (and the additivity property obtains). This situation is linear in that such equations will be straight lines on a graph—at least in the case of two inputs and one output.

Linear programming is nevertheless much less restrictive than the input-output method in two important respects. First, input-output allows for only one technological method of production of each output, whereas linear programming allows for several. Second, the input-output method does not put a valuation on the resulting outputs, whereas linear programming does use and require relative prices for each output. Thus, input-output can at the most provide consistent or balanced plans for total outputs and primary inputs with given final outputs (and given methods of technology). Linear programming, however, allows a choice among several techniques of production and also allows planners to choose that mixture of outputs whose total value will be the maximum possible.

The problem of optimization under linear programming may therefore be set up as follows: first, the object is to maximize the value of final output, where value (V) equals prices (p) times final outputs (x); that is,

Maximize $$V = p_1x_1 + p_2x_2 + \ldots + p_nx_n. \tag{1}$$

(The linear programming problem is usually formulated in terms of activity levels or total outputs (X). Total output of each commodity is equal to intermediate plus final output (x). Total outputs, however, can be transformed linearly into final outputs, which we have done in equation (1) for purposes of expositional clarity.)

The maximization procedure is subject to certain constraints, reflecting the objective conditions of production. These constraints are: (1) the fact that there must be sufficient production of each total output to cover its intermediate uses; (2) the fact that there is a limited amount of resources; and (3) the fact that total outputs or activity levels must be non-negative.

The technical coefficients showing the input required for each output are represented as $a_{11}, \ldots, a_{mn}$, where the first number of the subscript to the coefficient shows the commodity which is an input into the output given by the second number of the subscript. Total outputs (intermediate plus final outputs) are represented as $X_1, \ldots, X_n$. Thus, for total outputs the result is the familiar set of inequalities, showing the uses of each total output as an intermediate input into other outputs:

$$a_{11}X_1 + a_{12}X_2 + \ldots + a_{1n}X_n \leq X_1 \qquad (2a)$$
$$a_{21}X_1 + a_{22}X_2 + \ldots + a_{2n}X_n \leq X_2 \qquad (2b)$$

$$a_{n1}X_1 + a_{n2}X_2 + \ldots + a_{nn}X_n \leq X_n \qquad (2n)$$

This set of inequalities differs from the input-output equations only in that in each case the left side of the inequality (the total intermediate uses) may be less than the right side of the inequality (the total output of each commodity) because final demand or final output is omitted from the left side of the inequality. In this way, the model allows for the determination of maximum final outputs as the difference between the total outputs and the intermediate uses—unlike the input-output model where the final outputs or demands were specified exactly.

A second set of constraints represents the limited amounts of primary inputs $(L_1, \ldots, L_m)$. These inputs might be considered as various specialized types of labor as well as various specialized types of capital and raw materials (these latter being regarded, from the Marxist view, as embodied labor). This set of inequalities will show the requirements for primary inputs (the technical coefficients for each primary input multiplied by the respective outputs) added together to give a sum that must be less than or equal to the amount of the primary inputs that is available. In this case, to avoid more confusing subscripts, let the technical coefficients be represented as $b_{11}, \ldots, b_{mn}$, where the first number of the subscript indicates the primary input and the second number indicates the output for which it is used. Thus, the inequalities are:

$$b_{11}X_1 + b_{12}X_2 + \ldots + b_{1n}X_n \leq L_1 \qquad (3a)$$
$$b_{21}X_1 + b_{22}X_2 + \ldots + b_{2n}X_n \leq L_2 \qquad (3b)$$

$$b_{m1}X_1 + b_{m2}X_2 + \ldots + b_{mn}X_n \leq L_m \qquad (3m)$$

The final set of constraints is that total outputs must each be non-negative. These constraints may be stated thus:

$$X_i \geq 0 \ (i = 1, \ldots, m). \tag{4}$$

In this system the technical coefficients for intermediate inputs (the a_{ij}), the technical coefficients for primary inputs (the b_{ij}), the available amounts of primary inputs (the L_i), and the prices of outputs (p_i) are all known and presumed constant. The final outputs (x_i) and total outputs (X_i) are the unknowns, and the function composed of prices times outputs is to be maximized. The actual calculation procedure for the maximization is usually done by converting the inequalities into equalities. Thus, "dummy" variables are inserted into each of the inequalities, using a "slack" variable where the restriction is "less than or equal to." In fact, the dummy variables inserted into equations (2a), ..., (2n) are none other than the final demand $x_1, \ldots, x_n$, which thus enter into this set of equations. In this way, although more variables have been created, it turns out that the constraints have been transformed into an equally large number of equations, each of which represents an equality.

The other problems involved in actually calculating the maximum set of outputs are purely mechanical so they need not be detailed here (for methods of calculation, see selected references at the end of this chapter). Nevertheless, it must be mentioned that very great advances have been made in simplifying the calculating methods. For example, it is known that the optimal solution will be found at a corner point of the feasible set in a graphical sense. The famous *simplex method* of George Dantzig then explains the efficient procedure for checking which corner point is the maximum. These advances make it far more feasible for modern electronic computers to actually do the job of calculation for a very large number of inputs and outputs.

Finally, the typical problem of choice of output mix shown above requires output prices, but it is of interest to note that the solution of this problem can also produce the "prices" of the inputs as a byproduct. These "prices" are not set by the planners for use in any actual transaction, nor are they produced by any actual market exchange; rather, they are purely an intermediate product of the mathematical calculation of maximum outputs. Hence, they are called *shadow prices*.[44] These shadow prices roughly reflect the marginal products of the inputs. Specifically, if a resource constraint is relaxed by one unit, the objective function will increase in value by the shadow price of that resource. Using shadow prices, it would be possible to compute

---

44. On shadow prices, see the simplified explanation in Heinz Kohler, *Welfare and Planning* (New York: John Wiley and Sons, 1966), 121–22; or the mathematical explanation in R. Dorfman, P. Samuelson, and R. Solow, *Linear Programming and Economic Analysis* (New York: McGraw-Hill, 1958), 339–40.

the minimum cost technology. Of course, the central planners would have already decided upon the same technology in determining the way to produce a maximum output, so they would have no reason to repeat the problem.

An Example

The facts represented in Table 9A.1 may be stated algebraically, using symbols defined as follows: M is total output of Manufacturing, A is total output of Agriculture, x_m is final output of M, x_a is final output of A, P_m is price of M, and P_a is price of A.

The problem is to maximize the (transformed) "objective function,"

$$f(x_m, x_a) = P_m x_m + P_a x_a,$$

subject to the following constraints:

$$2A + M \leq 100 \text{ billion hours of labor,} \tag{1}$$
$$2A + 3M \leq 210 \text{ billion units of capital,} \tag{2}$$
$$A \leq 30 \text{ billion tons of natural resources,} \tag{3}$$
$$-0.99A + 0.08M \leq 0, \tag{4}$$
$$0.31A - 0.76M \leq 0. \tag{5}$$

Table 9A.1
Facts for Output Maximization

Outputs / Inputs	Direct inputs per unit of total output		Price of a unit of output (in rubles)	Limits on total number of outputs and inputs
	Agri-culture	Manu-facturing		
Agriculture	0.01	0.08	3.0	greater than zero units
Manufacturing	0.31	0.24	1.5	greater than zero units
Labor (in hours of labor time)	2.00	1.00	not applicable	equal to or less than 100 billion hours
Capital (in numbers of machines)	2.00	3.00	not applicable	equal to or less than 210 billion machines
Natural resources (in tons)	1.00	0	not applicable	equal to or less than 30 billion tons

Inequalities (4) and (5) merely stipulate that intermediate inputs must not exceed total outputs. In order to get the function $P_m x_m + P_a x_a$ into terms of A and M, note that $P_m = 1.5$ rubles, $P_a = 3.0$ rubles, $x_m = 0.76M - 0.31A$, and $x_a = 0.99A - 0.08M$. By substitution the function to be maximized is

$$f(A, M) = 1.5(0.76M - 0.31A) + 3.0(0.99A - 0.08M)$$

or

$$f(A, M) = 0.90M + 2.51A$$

The solution is shown graphically in Figure 9A.1. In this graph, the five constraints are shown by five solid lines, each of which is labeled

---

Figure 9A.1
Optimal Choice of Output Mix by Linear Programming

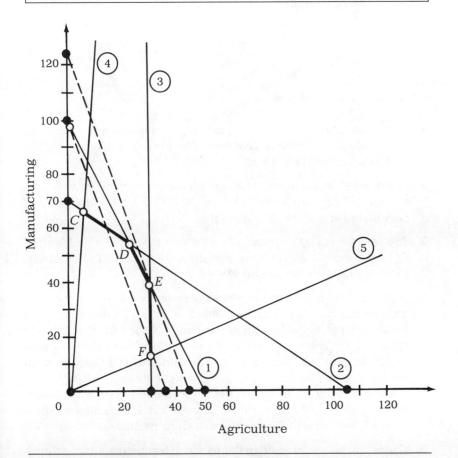

Note: Solid lines are numbered according to equations of constraints in text. C, D, E, and F are extreme points, representing basic feasible solutions. Dotted lines show the slope of the objective function.

with the number of the constraint equation it represents. These five lines set the bounds of feasible production of various combinations of A and M. A heavier line goes through the extreme points C, D, E, and F, each representing a basic optimal solution, one of which must be the maximum value-of-output solution. To find which point is the maximum, the slope of the objective function $0.90M + 2.51A$ is calculated. The two dotted lines indicate the slope of the objective function (which derives from the relative prices and the technical coefficients of x_m and x_a). Then the maximum solution is selected by that dotted line farthest from the origin which still passes through one of the extreme points.

The point so selected is point E. At that point, $A = 30$ billion units and $M = 40$ billion units. Since $x_a = 0.99A - 0.08M$ and $x_m = 0.76M - 0.31A$, the maximum output mix is $x_a = 26.5$ billion units of Agriculture and $x_m = 21.1$ billion units of Manufacturing. It follows also that the maximum value of final output is

$$P_m x_m + P_a x_a = 1.5(21.1) + 3.0(26.5)$$
$$= 111.2 \text{ billion rubles.}$$

Recommended Readings

1. The impossibility of efficient planning in socialism is argued in F. A. Hayek, *Collectivist Economic Planning* (London: Routledge and Kegan Paul, Ltd., 1935).

2. The defense of socialism, especially its decentralized form, is presented in Oskar Lange and F. M. Taylor, *On the Economic Theory of Socialism* (New York: McGraw-Hill, 1964).

3. The case for centrally planned socialism may be found in Maurice Dobb, *Economic Theory and Socialism* (New York: International Publishers, 1955), 33–92 and 239–46.

4. A general review of the Soviet debate on value theory from an anti-Marxist viewpoint may be found in Alfred Zauberman, "The Present State of Soviet 'Planometrics,'" *Soviet Studies* 14 (July 1962): 62–74. The progressive Marxist side of the debate is presented briefly in V. Nemchinov, "Mathematics and Electronics in the Service of Planning," *Problems of Economics* 4, 7 (Nov. 1961): 3–9. A more conservative Soviet view is manifested in P. Matislavskii, "Quantitative Expression of Economic Relationships and Processes," *Problems of Economics* 4, 9 (Jan. 1962): 3–11.

5. Three journals published in English with frequent articles on optimization problems are *Problems of Economics* (translations of Soviet articles), *Economics of Planning* (published in Scandinavia with international contributors), and *Mathematical Studies in*

Economics and Statistics in the U.S.S.R. and Eastern Europe (translations of Soviet and Eastern European articles).

6. The specifics of linear programming are presented in elementary form in W. Allen Spivey, *Linear Programming: An Introduction* (New York: Macmillan Co., 1963). A more advanced neoclassical treatment is: Robert Dorfman, Paul Samuelson, and Robert Solow, *Linear Programming and Economic Analysis* (New York: McGraw-Hill, 1958).

7. Marxist approaches to optimum planning may be seen in K. Porwit, *Central Planning—Evaluation of Variants* (New York: Pergamon Press, transl. from Polish in 1967); and Janos Kornai, *Mathematical Planning of Structural Decisions* (Amsterdam: North Holland Publishing Co., 1967). A review of Kornai's book in the *American Economic Review* of September 1968 says that it "is a landmark in the history of planning and the application of mathematical techniques in socialist countries."

8. A clear discussion of problems and techniques is presented in Michael Ellman, *Socialist Planning* (Cambridge: Cambridge University Press, 1979).

9. For further discussion of the state of Soviet price theory and mathematical planning, see Alec Nove, *The Economics of Feasible Socialism* (London: George Allen and Unwin, 1983).

10
USSR

CLASS STRUCTURE: RULERS, MANAGERS, WORKERS, AND FARMERS

What is the class structure of the Soviet Union? Who constitutes its ruling class? What is the role of managers? How do workers participate in economic decision making and how are wages determined? How does agriculture function, and how do farmers fit into the class structure? These are the questions we shall address in this chapter.

The Soviet Ruling Class

Although they admit that there are different strata among the working class (urban workers, farmers, and intellectuals), Soviet sociologists deny that there is any ruling class in the Soviet Union. Yet Soviet sociologists are quick to speak of an exploitative ruling class in the United States. This stance is parallel to that of the traditional American sociologists, who deny any ruling class in the United States but are quick to find one in the Soviet Union.

There is a vast controversy over the definition of the word "class." For our purposes, a *class* is defined as a group with a common relation to the means of production (factories, equipment, etc.). In the United States, for example, the capitalist class may be defined as those who *own* and *control* the means of production, while the working class may be defined as those who sell their labor power and *work with* the means of production. Soviet classes are not the same as U.S. classes, though they have some things in common. The Soviet working class might be defined the same way as in the United States.

How to define the Soviet ruling class, however, is controversial. The Soviet elite does not *own* the means of production (and the USSR denies that there is any ruling class). In the view of many critics, however, there is a Soviet group that *controls* the means of production. Even though they do not own the means of production, those at the top of the political-economic pyramid control production through the planning process. Through the plan, they determine products, prices, wage levels, new investment projects, and so forth.

There are four main groups in the Soviet ruling class. The first and most important is the top level of the Communist party apparatus, including ten or fifteen people in the highest body, the Politburo, and a few hundred more in the next highest body, the Central Committee. Next, there are the top levels of the government bureaucracy, such as the Council of Ministers, though most of these people also hold top positions in the Party. Third, there are the top officers of the Soviet military establishment. Fourth, there are the top levels of economic management, including the central planners. These four groups are the establishment—or the *Apparat* as they are called in the Soviet Union.

All of these four groups merge and intertwine at the top, and individuals often move from one hierarchy to another at all levels. This merger at the top is one reason we can speak of one ruling class in the Soviet Union; the more important reason, as shown below, is that together they control the use of the economic surplus. Yet the party leaders, whose abilities are political and not technical, are still dominant. In theory, Soviet leaders may lose their class status by being ousted from office (unlike U.S. capitalists, who own their wealth). In practice, however, the top ruling group is not subject to public control, so it is usually a lifetime position and a lifetime class status.

The government bureaucrats, even the very top ones, are still subordinate to the Party, though they have shown somewhat more independence and initiative in recent decades. The power and influence of the economic managers have risen with the increase of technology and industrial complexity, but there has been no technocratic challenge to the clear supremacy of the party apparatus.[1] The military is steadily becoming more professional and independent, for example, pushing for higher levels of military spending. The Party, however, exercises its control of the military through several channels: almost all officers are party members, there is intensive indoctrination at all levels, and there is direct interference from party commissars in individual units.[2]

One way in which the Soviet elite differs from the American elite is in relative size. Whereas the very wealthy and powerful of the American ruling class number up to a million or so (whose main source of

---

1. See Jeremy Azreal, *Managerial Power and Soviet Politics* (Cambridge: Harvard University Press, 1966).

2. See Roman Kolkowicz, *The Soviet Military and the Communist Party* (Princeton: Princeton University Press, 1967).

income is ownership of property), the similar group in the Soviet Union is far smaller in numbers—less than a hundred thousand. "Only the upper strata of the bureaucracy, of the party hierarchy, the managerial groups, and the military personnel, live in conditions comparable to those enjoyed by the rich and the nouveaux riches in the capitalist society."[3] This difference in the size of the two ruling classes results from the fact that all of the middle level of the Soviet elite—such as middle-level managers, local party bosses, majors in the army, and middle-level government bureaucrats—actually live on salaries derived from their own labor. They are paid relatively high amounts compared with ordinary workers, but for lower- and middle-level managers and bureaucrats, these salaries may actually represent—as they are supposed to—differences according to actual ability and quality of the labor that they perform. The top leadership require the lower and middle levels to work hard and earn their money (there are plenty of cases of corruption, but these are punished where discovered).

Only at the top of the Soviet hierarchy are the complete incomes of the leadership a secret, classified for "security" reasons. The official, declared salaries of the top leaders are high by Soviet standards (seven hundred or eight hundred rubles per month), but they could be considered wages for work done. And some Soviet artists and scientists receive higher incomes. In addition, however, the fringe benefits include chauffeured limousines, access to special stores with more and better goods, their own villas in the country, and more. Furthermore, there is allegedly secret, undeclared income going to the very top leaders (Politburo members and Ministers). By its nature, we cannot measure this income. In the case of Czechoslovakia, however, in 1968 a group of reformers came into power and investigated the wealth of President Novotny. During the investigation, he returned thirteen *billion* crowns, which he said were given him by mistake (the investigation was ended by the Soviet occupation of Czechoslovakia). Thus, there is some reason for thinking that at the very top (fifteen to fifty people) true fortunes *may* be involved.

Below that level, the next one hundred thousand Soviet officials live very well—when we include fringe benefits. But their incomes do not compare with the incomes of thousands of American capitalists, who may receive well over a million dollars a year and own private yachts, airplanes, fleets of custom-built cars, several mansions, and so forth (as well as owning millions of dollars in stocks that yield dividends and possible capital gains income whether they work or not).

Thus, it appears that the Soviet ruling class obtains a much smaller percentage of national income than the U.S. ruling class. Yet their

---

3. Isaac Deutscher, *The Unfinished Revolution* (New York: Oxford University Press, 1967), 55.

income is class based, that is, based on control over the means of production and the political and economic process. All Soviet wages and salaries are set by official decree. But who sets the known (and secret) salaries of the top leaders? *Through their control, they set their own salaries and fringe benefits,* which *probably* total far more than the labor they contribute to society (however generously that is measured). Many critics allege, therefore, that some large part of the leaders' income comes from the value created by the working class of the Soviet Union. So, "their incomes are at least partially derived from the 'surplus value' (or profit) produced by the workers."[4] In this view, there is exploitation in the USSR in the sense that some part of ruling class income comes from the value created by Soviet workers, but the amount is probably a much smaller absolute or relative amount than in the United States (for the reasons given earlier).

Yet, unlike the American ruling class, these groups own neither land nor factories, nor can they expand their incomes by investments. The ruling groups have not so far tried to vest their controlling privileges in their children by legal means. The Soviet leaders—and all Soviet professionals—do, however, give their children a head start through an intellectual home atmosphere. According to critics, some Soviet officials also use illegal means to get their children admitted to college or placed in a job. Since all positions are supposedly assigned by merit (and, below the top echelons, most actually seem to be), the role of education is crucial to advancement in the USSR.

The U.S. capitalist class rules through the use of its economic power based on its legal ownership of the means of production (and it hands this ownership on to its children). Because the Soviet ruling class has no legal ownership of the means of production, their need for direct repressive controls is even greater than that of the capitalists. As Isaac Deutscher argues, "The power of property having been destroyed, only the State, that is, the bureaucracy, dominates society; and its domination is based solely on the suppression of the people's liberty to criticize and oppose!"[5] Suppression plus propaganda (and increasing material prosperity) are the means of political domination by the Soviet leadership. The Soviet leaders use their political power to control the means of production.

While the percentage of income exploited is probably much smaller than in the United States, the percentage of all economic decisions (on investment, military spending, and collective welfare) made exclusively by the Soviet ruling class is much greater than the decisions made exclusively by the U.S. ruling class. For example, the Soviet

---

4. Isaac Deutscher, "Roots of Bureaucracy," in Ralph Miliband and J. Saville, eds., *The Socialist Register,* 1969 (New York: Monthly Review Press, 1969), 56.

5. *Ibid.,* 106.

leaders decided long ago to exploit the present generation of workers (by putting huge resources into investment rather than present consumption) for Soviet prestige, military power, and the expected benefit of future generations. Whether this was a good or a bad decision, it was made by the ruling class and was never put to a vote by Soviet citizens.

Mobility

How much mobility is there from the working classes into the elite? Do the children of the Soviet ruling class automatically remain in the ruling class? A very careful study by Alec Nove concludes that the top twenty thousand jobs are not hereditary.[6] Almost no child of the elite holds the same top rank that the parent held. On the other hand, the privileged and the so-called intelligentsia as a whole do tend to keep their children in that same general level. More specifically, there is a very high correlation between the top 10 percent of income receivers in one generation and their children in the next. But there is no correlation between the children of the top twenty thousand leaders and the top twenty thousand leaders of the succeeding generation.

The difference is that getting to the very top in the USSR requires a combination of skill, hard work, a tough personality, and some luck; children are not automatically admitted. Admission to the top 10 percent, on the contrary, depends mainly on education and training. The privileged and the intellectuals are successful in getting a better-than-average education for their children.

One of the more thorough studies of inequality in recent years, by Walter Connor, likewise stresses that economic status in the "socialist" countries cannot be as easily inherited as in capitalism because parents cannot pass on control of accumulated capital. Yet he does show that children of the high income group are helped both by conditioning and by moral support in getting a good education (and perhaps sometimes by pulling some strings). They are also helped by the job connections of their parents. "Children of the visible top political elite, though they do not inherit their father's mantles, often wind up in staff positions, still heavy with privileges."[7]

Connor does emphasize, however, how different are the privileges of such children of the Soviet elite from the privileges inherited by children of the capitalist elite. "Tenure in such positions, however, for them [children of the elite, now in staff positions] and for the less

---

6. Alec Nove, "Is There a Ruling Class in the U.S.S.R.?" *Soviet Studies* 27 (Oct. 1975): 615–38.

7. Walter D. Connor, *Socialism, Politics, and Equality: Hierarchy and Change in Eastern Europe and the USSR* (New York: Columbia University Press, 1979), 258.

elevated but still comfortably privileged, is at the pleasure of those who hold real power; and the strictly private resources that allow the rich in capitalist systems to enjoy privileged lives whoever is in power, to participate in or withdraw from public life at will, are not theirs to command."[8] Thus, most members of the Soviet ruling class have a shaky hold and can fall off the locomotive at any time.

Soviet Income Distribution and Inequality

Income distribution in the USSR is far more equal than in the United States because the Soviet ruling class is so much smaller than the American ruling class and because it exploits a much smaller share of national income from its working class. This fact is clear when we compare the figures on income distribution from both countries (even though both sets of figures contain several kinds of biases and distortions in them). According to Murray Yanowitch, in the Soviet Union in 1960, the top 10 percent of families had a total income which was 4.8 times as much as the income received by the bottom 10 percent of families.[9] In the United States, on the other hand, in 1960, the top 10 percent of families had 30 times the total pretax income of the lowest 10 percent of families. Most of the greater inequality in the United States results from the existence of private profits, rent, and interest income, almost all of which go to the top income group—as well as substantial unemployment, which affects the bottom income group. The Soviets, on the other hand, have only wage and salary income even in the top group.

According to estimates by Soviet scholars, the distribution of income as measured by the decile ratio among all state employees (that is, excluding collective farm workers) grew more equal from the mid fifties through 1968.[10] The Soviet version of the decile ratio takes the income of the bottom percentile of the highest 10 percent (the ninetieth percentile) and divides by the income of the top percentile of the lowest 10 percent (the tenth percentile). By this measurement, the decile ratio fell from 4.4 (those in the ninetieth percentile earned 4.4 times as much as those in the tenth percentile) in 1956 to 2.83 in 1968; it then rose to 3.35 in 1976. However, the rise after 1968, according to Nove, represents an increased number of low income earners counted (as collective farmers have become state farmers) and spe-

---

8. *Ibid.*, 258.

9. See Murray Yanowitch, "The Soviet Income Revolution," reprinted in Morris Bornstein and Dan R. Fusfeld, eds., *The Soviet Economy* (Homewood, Ill.: Richard Irwin, 1966), 237. Also see Murray Yanowitch, *Social and Economic Inequality in the Soviet Union* (White Plains, N.Y.: M. E. Sharpe, 1977), 23–29.

10. Alastair McAuley, "The Distribution of Earnings and Incomes in the Soviet Union," *Soviet Studies* 27 (Apr. 1977): 228.

cial statistical properties of the measure rather than a real increase in inequality.[11] If anything, the evidence presented by Nove suggests an ongoing leveling of incomes during the seventies.

As we have noted, there are many biases in the income data of different countries. For example, the Soviet ruling class probably gets a considerable amount of unreported income, huge fringe benefits in the forms of cars and chauffeurs and country villas, plus access to stores with special availability of high quality and foreign goods. The U.S. ruling class, in turn, gets much income which it is not required to report (such as millions of dollars in interest from tax-free municipal bonds), enormous fringe benefits which are considered as tax-deductible costs of business (such as cars, chauffeurs, meals, and travel), plus supplies taken from businesses and reported as tax-deductible costs. Other income, such as capital gains, is mostly reported but is not included in the U.S. income distribution figures calculated by the Department of Commerce.

The Soviet Union also has a much higher amount of unpriced goods and services that are given free to the general public (such as all health and education), so the Soviet lower income groups have relatively more real income than their money income indicates. This effect is reinforced by the heavy price subsidies conferred upon essential goods, such as rent, utilities, public transportation, bread, milk, children's shoes, and so forth, as well as the high turnover tax (sales tax) levied on luxury items. The Soviet leaders claim that when they reach their goal of full communism, all goods and services will be free to everyone, so there will be perfect income equality.

Stratification of the Soviet Working Class

It is striking that there is not much difference, between the United States and the Soviet Union, in the range of inequality of *just* wage and salary income. However, this comparison is very different from the comparison of overall *income distribution* in the two countries, because the latter includes profit, rent, and interest incomes in the United States. Immediately after the 1917 Revolution, wage and salary incomes in the Soviet Union were, to a very great extent, equalized. In the 1930s, however, Stalin decided that the rapid industrialization drive demanded high wage differentials between workers in order to promote incentives. There was little money income to pay most workers, so the unskilled workers' wages were kept very low. At the same time, those who had the skills to produce more, or to do

---

11. Alec Nove, "Income Distribution in the USSR: A Possible Explanation of Some Recent Data," *Soviet Studies* 34 (Apr. 1982): 286–88. Also, A. McAuley, "Sources of Earnings Inequality: A Comment on Alec Nove's Note on Income Distribution in the USSR," *Soviet Studies* 34 (July 1982): 443–47.

important jobs, were paid very high wages. Therefore, in the 1930s the ratio of most skilled wage rates to unskilled wage rates stood at 3.5 to 1 in the officially prescribed wage scales, and piece-rate bonuses undoubtedly increased this ratio in practice.[12] This was a higher wage differential than prevails currently in the United States. On the other hand, the United States, during our own period of rapid industrialization, had much higher wage differentials than now—it was just about the magnitude of the Soviet Union's in the 1930s.

By the mid 1950s, after the rapid industrialization drive had ended, and after Stalin's death, the leaders came to realize that such wide wage differentials were no longer necessary and might make the mass of unskilled workers angry with the leadership. Therefore, a number of measures were taken to raise the minimum wages of the unskilled, at the same time holding down the wages of the most skilled. As a result, by 1958 the official differential between the wages of the unskilled and the most skilled had fallen to the ratio of 2.8 to 1.[13] Since that time, the range of wages has been somewhat further narrowed, so the degree of wage inequality in the Soviet Union is now somewhat less than in the United States.

A study by Connor found that in 1972, if the average worker's pay was 100, then the pay of intellectual workers (or the intelligentsia) was 120 in Czechoslovakia, 132 in Bulgaria, 134 in the USSR, 142 in Hungary, and 144 in Poland.[15] On the other hand, the pay of routine, nonmanual workers (such as clerical or sales workers) was only 81 in Czechoslovakia, 85 in the USSR, 92 in Hungary, 96 in Bulgaria, and 100 in Poland. Finally, the peasant or farm worker also received below-average pay in most countries: 94 in Hungary, and 98 in Czechoslovakia.

A comprehensive survey of all the research on Soviet inequality by traditional American and West European sociologists concludes: "These studies suggest that the extreme economic inequality of the late Stalinist period has been reduced appreciably in recent years; along with a reduction in interoccupational variation in industrial wages . . . there has been a general leveling and a rise in per capita income."[16] Ideologically, it is worth noting that most Soviet sociologists claim—as do most U.S. sociologists—that some inequality is necessary for incentives to get workers to work efficiently (though they do *not* agree that unemployment is necessary as incentive).

---

12. Yanowitch, "The Soviet Income Revolution," 231.

13. *Ibid.*, 232.

14. Yanowitch, *Social and Economic Inequality in the Soviet Union*, 23–29.

15. Connor, *Socialism, Politics, and Equality*, Ch. 1.

16. Richard Dobson, "Mobility and Stratification in the Soviet Union," in Alex Inkeles, James Coleman, and Neil Smelser, eds., *Annual Review of Sociology* 3 (1977): 302.

Soviet sociologists claim that equality will be possible in the future when work attitudes change.

Soviet sociologists recognize only two classes in the Soviet Union. These are the "nonantagonistic" classes of collective farmers and the working class. The working class includes manual and mental (including professionals), rural and urban, male and female, Russian and non-Russian workers. These two classes have different relationships to the means of production, but they do not exploit each other. What the Soviet sociologists ignore is the ruling class.

The Soviet writers do show the degree of various forms of inequality among strata within the working class as well as some of the difficulties of moving up from lower to higher strata. For example, they show concretely that unskilled workers have less education, lower wages, fewer cultural activities, and less political participation than more skilled workers, who, in turn, have less of all of these characteristics than do the intellectual workers (including engineers) and the supervisors and managers. One study of the machine building industry in Leningrad found that 26 percent of the unskilled workers do not read books at all; perhaps it is more remarkable that 20 percent, according to this study, did read one or more books a week.[17] Another sign of this phenomenon was the finding for three different Soviet cities that participation in "community activities" (political to some extent) was very low among unskilled workers and very high among intellectuals and managerial personnel. Other studies of mobility reveal that families with highly educated parents tend to have the most highly educated children, so that the inequality is reproducing itself in the Soviet as in the American educational system.

In the years of rapid industrialization, there was far more upward mobility in the Soviet Union than in the United States. Sons and daughters of poor peasants could and did emigrate to the cities, to become workers, and often very skilled workers, yet more rarely rising to be technicians and professionals. This vast inflow from the rural areas has been reduced (but is still considerable), so upward mobility is less than it was in the earlier period. Yanowitch, however, indicates that Soviet mobility is still probably greater than in the United States[18]—mainly because the USSR has no private inheritance of income-producing property (except homes, which can be rented). If one can get a higher education in the Soviet Union, the doors are, open to advancement to the highest levels of the society. On the other hand, as noted above, it is clear that the children of educated families

17. A Soviet sociologist in a translated essay in Murray Yanowitch and Wesley Fisher, eds., *Social Stratification and Mobility in the USSR* (White Plains, N.Y.: M. E. Sharpe, 1973), 75.

18. See Yanowitch, *Social and Economic Inequality in the Soviet Union*, 29–30. This study contains several good articles on mobility.

(technicians, professionals, and managers) more often succeed in getting a higher education than the children of ordinary manual workers.

The competition for a higher education is even greater than in the United States. There is less of an economic barrier because every good student gets free tuition plus a very considerable scholarship or stipend (often a significant percentage of the average wage). Nevertheless, the competition for limited places in the universities means that a large proportion of the children of unskilled workers are not likely to get a higher education—mainly because of a less intellectually oriented family environment (though the quality of primary and secondary schools is also lower in some areas). The widespread facilities for training in skills—plus full employment—do mean, however, that most of the children of unskilled workers do rise up the economic ladder to the level of a skilled worker. Upward socioeconomic mobility is thus probably more than in the United States at the present time but is still much less than could be desired.

Soviet Managers

Managers of enterprises are an important group in Soviet society, ranking below the top elite but far above the average worker in status and income. Here, we briefly examine the manager's role before looking at industrial workers and agricultural workers—but we will return to the behavior of managers in Chapter 11, which covers reforms of management.

Soviet managers face somewhat different problems than U.S. managers.[19] Their training and background, therefore, are ordinarily somewhat different from that of their U.S. counterparts. First, a much higher percentage of Soviet managers have college degrees. One reason for this is the traditional prestige accorded all "intellectuals" by European culture. More important is the fact that the Soviet manager, as we shall see, is far more likely to be directly involved with technological problems than is the U.S. manager. From the individual's viewpoint, it is still possible in the United States to achieve a high income position, especially in a family business, without much formal education. In the Soviet Union, on the contrary, a college education is the decisive and almost sole key to high income opportunities, a fact which leads to an even fiercer competition for that education in the USSR than in the United States.

Second, the typical Soviet manager has been educated in engineering and has risen to the top through the production departments of

---

19. See David Granick, *The Red Executive* (New York: Doubleday and Co., 1961).

his or her enterprise. The typical U.S. manager, on the other hand, has majored in business administration and has worked his or her way to the top through personnel work, marketing and distribution, or the financial side of business. The reasons for these differences are not hard to find. In the United States, a major task of enterprise is to increase, by application of marketing techniques, the demand for its product. Even enterprise research in the United States is directed especially toward new products designed to create "needs" and stimulate sales. Thus, a U.S. manager must master marketing techniques: what will sell, how to pick salespeople and advertisers, and how to get financial backing.

The Soviet manager's problem is exactly the opposite. He or she is ordered (at least until recently) to produce as much as possible above the Plan (and even the planned amount is always based on an extremely high estimate of the supply capabilities). And because of taut planning, shortages, and lack of user choice, virtually everything that is produced can be sold. The American businessperson operates in a "buyers' market"; his or her Soviet counterpart, in a "sellers' market." But supplies are restricted and difficult for the Soviet manager to obtain. Since his or her primary concern is to produce the most output from limited supplies, an engineering background is vital.

We may also mention one closely related group of differences in the manager's background and motivation, springing in part from these different needs of the two economies. The highest incomes and prestige in the United States go to the occupations of business, law, or medicine. Engineering is not as high, and until recently science and higher education have been much further down the scale. In the Soviet Union, on the contrary, with the exception of the artists, the highest rewards go to scientists in research institutes or universities. The next highest rewards go to engineers in heavy industry. All other Soviet occupations, including positions in light industry or distribution and in law or medicine, lag far behind in either income or prestige (medicine commands some prestige but little income).

Finally, we may note that Soviet managers tend to be younger than U.S. managers, a characteristic necessarily shared with all very rapidly developing economies. We may also note, on the one hand, that the Soviet pool of managerial talent is restricted (relative to the United States) by the much larger percentage of the population still in the culturally and educationally more backward rural areas. On the other hand, the Soviet pool of managerial talent is enlarged (relative to the United States) because more women are utilized as managers in the USSR than in the United States.

It pays to be a successful Soviet manager. The average manager's salary (including bonuses) is much higher than that of the average worker. In addition, he or she has certain otherwise unobtainable privileges. He or she may be assigned a private chauffeured auto in a society where private autos are still scarce. He or she may also rate a larger apartment or house in a society that is desperately short of housing space, although this reward is not always given. Promotion may open up very inviting political heights.

If the manager fulfills or overfulfills the plan each month, he or she receives an additional large bonus. These bonuses generally run from 25 percent to 50 percent of the manager's salary. One detailed study for 1965 showed managers' bonuses in the high-priority iron and steel industry averaging 51.4 percent of their basic income, although bonuses in the low-priority food industry were only 21 percent.[20] Since 1965 economic reforms have reduced the bonuses for overfulfilling the output target in order to encourage higher target selection and to put more emphasis on quality and on cost reduction, but managers' bonuses remain a large part of their salary.

The unsuccessful manager will lose bonuses and ultimately lose his or her job or be demoted to a less important operation. At an earlier period, a failure was also liable to be interpreted by the government as criminal negligence or even sabotage. Today, the Soviets generally consider the purely social and economic rewards and punishments to be sufficient and do not resort to criminal penalties.

Since the manager is under great pressure to produce, he or she resorts to many evasions. We may note that managerial performance is judged by several criteria, including wage and raw material costs per unit and other indicators of productivity and efficiency. The main success indicator (until the 1965 reforms) was simply the amount of gross output produced. Until 1965, if the planned amount of output was not achieved, the manager received no bonus at all. If, however, the planned target was met exactly, he or she received as much as a full 40 percent bonus, though the average bonus was somewhat less. For each 1 percent overfulfillment of the Plan, managers in high-priority industries received an additional 4 to 6 percent bonus. Since 1965, the extreme emphasis on the fulfillment of the target for amount of gross physical output has been replaced by emphasis on the value of total sales and profitability and more recently on net output, as we shall see in Chapter 11.

The Soviet manager brushes aside bureaucratic regulations and controls when they conflict with the achievement of output goals. To a great extent, the manager evades specific regulations only in order to meet the Plan. This course of action may or may not be to the national benefit. For example, the manager sometimes merely gets around red tape in order to obtain materials that should have been his or hers anyway. On other occasions, however, he or she may obtain materials illegally that could be better used by a higher-priority enterprise. Unfortunately, some of the manager's devices, like lowering quality

---

20. See Joseph Berliner, "Managerial Incentives and Decision-Making," in Bornstein and Fusfeld, *The Soviet Economy*, 116.

in order to produce greater output, yield a bonus for an *apparent* Plan fulfillment which constitutes, in fact, an antisocial act. This type of antisocial behavior is not dissimilar to the well-known evasions of the corporate income tax or antitrust laws by managers of U.S. corporations. The specific practices of some Soviet managers have included: (1) false reports of success, (2) attempts to get easier plans, (3) substitution of poorer quality products, (4) production of only a few styles, (5) a shift of the mix of output to the ones easiest to produce, (6) obtaining of supplies beyond the Plan, (7) hoarding of supplies, (8) use of labor beyond the Plan, (9) use of high-priced materials to produce more "value," (10) intense drives at the end of the month, and (11) resistance to innovations to avoid risk and temporary losses.[21] (These practices are discussed further in Chapter 11.)

The tendencies described do exist, but they should certainly not be taken to mean that Soviet managers are completely inefficient. The Soviet economy *has* produced higher growth than many other economies despite these inefficiencies. This dysfunctional behavior does imply that the growth achieved was at greater cost and sacrifice than necessary, or that growth could have been faster and quality higher with the same amount of effort. The fact, however, that a significant degree of inefficiency does exist in the old system of central planning is the driving force behind the attempts at decentralization reforms.

Many of these evasions of the Plan result in a more flexible functioning of the economy than the official Plan would allow. Planners cannot specify correctly all details because they do not have (1) enough information, (2) enough computer time, or (3) enough planners. Moreover, the planners have conflicting targets and some very distorted prices. Therefore, the managers do somehow carry through the job by various semi-legal means, disregarding impossible tasks and performing others through an informal exchange among enterprises—an exchange not included in the planned allocation of supplies. Still, some managerial infractions, such as using poor quality or improper assortment to achieve most cheaply a large quantity of output, are certainly self-seeking and antisocial in effect. On the whole, however, managers have made the system "work," and work better under imperfect planning than if managers mechanically carried out the plans. (More on this in Chapter 11.)

Soviet Industrial Workers

The Soviet incentive system for labor remains an interesting combination of material rewards (differential wages), nonmaterial rewards (such as social prestige), and penalties. Although basic princi-

---

21. One good article on these problems is Harry G. Shaffer, "Ills and Remedies," *Problems of Communism* (May–June, 1963): 27–32.

ples of the wage system emanate from the highest level of Soviet political leadership, actual specification and control of wage rates are assigned to several planning agencies, the most directly concerned being the Ministry of Finance and the State Committee on Labor and Wages (along with the trade unions, as we shall see).

The wage rates are set in practice to serve two functions. The first is to satisfy the accepted socialist principle of pay according to the quantity and quality of work. The second, a more pragmatic task, is to direct manpower to industries and geographic areas of highest national importance, that is, to distribute labor according to the demand for it. Of course, these two principles need not conflict since a high demand for labor means a high valuation of work done in that area.

The task of planning and controlling wage levels has been a complex one. The government provides for the categorization of all jobs, and about two thousand categories were distinguished in 1965. Furthermore, each job is divided into a variety of grades, with a basic wage rate set for each higher grade.

Labor has been allocated to different jobs in the Soviet Union by a combination of legal force, social pressure, and market influences. We shall see that, although force played a role during much of the Stalinist period, today the predominant role is played by the market. In theory, the Soviets still attack capitalism for buying the worker's time as a "commodity." By contrast, they claim that the Soviet labor supply is "planned" and not affected by market forces. Yet they also speak of the wage differential as a basic tool to achieve the planned allocation—which in effect lets in the labor market by the back door.

In reality, the central planners only plan the *demand* for labor needed for the planned output. This they do by setting the maximum number of workers each enterprise may employ and also the top limit on how much each enterprise may spend for wages. On the *supply* side, however, the planners cannot simply allocate labor as they can allocate supplies of raw materials. The Soviet citizen has the right to choose freely any field and any place in which to obtain training and in which to work. Only by determining how many people can be trained in different fields and occupations do the Soviet planners attempt to control aggregate supply. Aside from wartime, the exceptions to this freedom of movement have been minimal. Even in Stalin's day they consisted mainly of (1) the requirement for students to work during the first three years after college at an assigned job in their specified field, (2) the draft of large numbers of rural youth for industrial training followed by a compulsory assigned job for a few years, (3) penalties to workers for excessive absenteeism or excessive tardiness, and (4) the ordering of Party members to go wherever the Party wants them to go. Of course, this list does not include Stalin's treatment of political prisoners in forced labor camps under terrible conditions.

At present, planners can influence the existing labor supply only by

changes in wage differentials—or in the long run by changes in training and education. The planners can and do influence the potential
labor supply by paying higher subsidies to students in certain fields.
To make matters more difficult for the planners, their market power
is lessened by overfull employment or shortage of labor. Workers can
usually find jobs of some sort where they please, even though planners would like to entice them to higher-priority areas. In fact, there
have always been desperate needs—chronically unfilled—for some
kinds of workers in certain places, even though there were also
unneeded surpluses of other kinds of workers in less important
places. The wage differentials not only attempt to influence the supply of labor by (1) industry or occupation; they also differentiated by (2)
the living conditions of different regions, (3) the necessary training or
skill, and (4) the danger or unpleasantness involved in the job grade.

Education provides the main production line for the training of
workers at all levels of skills, and the Soviets try to plan their educational system so that it will produce the needed workers. Eight years
of elementary school are now required, and the majority of students
now continue with two more years of high school. Each college graduate presumably must spend three years at the first job to which he or
she is assigned. However, there are qualifications to this rule. First, it
is now legal to search out employment mutually agreeable for the
student and an employer before the official decision date. Second, top
students are always offered several possibilities. Third, with the existing labor shortage, if one finds a preferable job while already at
work, it is easy to get the manager of the preferred enterprise to
request a transfer of the assignment. Finally, even under Stalin it was
a seldom-punished crime to quit the assigned job, and it is no longer a
crime at all. The only penalties are possible moral condemnation and
a black mark against the student in his or her workbook by the
enterprise that is deserted.

Aside from the assignment of college graduates, there is remarkably little organized placement of ordinary workers in the Soviet
Union. Since the Soviet Union officially declared unemployment
ended in the early 1930s, labor employment agencies were abolished.
Generally, the individual enterprises advertise by conducting tours
for and having discussions with those leaving school or the army, by
posting notices at factory gates, and by placing ads in newspapers, on
radio, on TV, and on street bulletin boards. Aided by advice from
friends and other workers, people may choose among these jobs
since the jobs are normally more plentiful than applicants.

Once workers are placed, there can still be a serious control problem in the form of tardiness, shirking or slacking off, absenteeism,
and rapid turnover. In the 1930s, the industrial labor force tripled in a
short period and consisted of large numbers of peasants just off the
farms living in miserable housing conditions. Since there was a terrible shortage of labor, managers not only tolerated the casual working

hours and habits but were quick to grab workers from other enterprises with the promise of better conditions. Then in the Second
World War all workers were frozen in their jobs. Many countries
followed this practice in the war period, but after the war Stalin
continued to some extent the freeze on changing jobs (without permission) and retained on the books criminal penalties for excessive
lateness or excessive absences from work.

In practice, these and other Stalinist repressive measures were
allowed to lapse quietly soon after Stalin's death in 1953.[22] Under the
1957 code, if a worker is excessively late or absent, management can
only warn or reprimand the worker, shift him or her to a lower-paid
job for three months, or if the trade union committee approves, dismiss the worker. Since there is still a labor shortage, these noncrim-
inal penalties cannot be very effective. More important today are the
rewards for good behavior that management can give, including
certificates, notices, titles, and medals of honorable or best worker, as
well as valuable gifts, money bonuses, paid vacations at special resorts, and promotions. There are also trade unions which are supposed to protect the individual worker (see Appendix 10A).

Soviet Agricultural Workers

Up to this point, we have discussed the status, conditions of work, and
incentives of Soviet managers as well as Soviet industrial workers.
Now it is time to turn to the third large group in Soviet society (in
addition to the top elite): the Soviet agricultural worker or farmer.
This section examines the status, conditions of work, and incentives
of the Soviet agricultural worker. In addition, within the context of
these agricultural relations of production, we investigate the performance of Soviet agriculture. The three sectors of Soviet agriculture are: (1) private, (2) cooperative or collective, and (3) state or
government; the performance of each of these three sectors is quite
different from the others. According to official Soviet data,[23] as late as
1928 the private sector used 97.2 percent of the sown land, leaving
only 1.2 percent for the collective farms and 1.5 percent for the state
farms. Then came the vast collectivization drive under Stalin's harsh
leadership. By 1937, the private sector was reduced to 5.3 percent, the
state farms had risen to 9.0 percent, and fully 85.7 percent of the sown
land was used by the collective farms.

---

22. See Edward Nash, "Recent Changes in Labor Controls in the Soviet
Union," in U.S. Congress, Joint Economic Committee, *New Directions in the
Soviet Economy* (Washington, D.C.: U.S. Government Printing Office, 1966),
849–71.

23. Summarized in Abram Bergson, *The Economies of Soviet Planning*
(New Haven: Yale University Press, 1964), 18.

The situation remained unchanged for many years. Then after Stalin's death, his heirs decided to switch many areas from collective to state farms. By 1964, the private sector was reduced to 3 percent, the collective farms fell to 52 percent, and the state farms rose to 45 percent of the total sown land. Most of this change occurred in the late 1950s, however, and there has been a fairly slow increase in the percentage of state farms since then. The independent peasant farm has disappeared completely, so the private sector is divided into half-acre farms run as private plots by collective farmers, as well as similar farms run as private plots by workers on state farms, or small plots on the edge of town for urban workers.

A portrait of U.S. and Soviet farms in 1977 finds that the United States had 2.7 *million* farms with an average of 160 hectares per farm and 1.5 workers per farm.[24] The Soviet Union had 27.7 *thousand* collective farms with 6,600 hectares per farm and 539 workers per farm. The Soviet Union also had 20 *thousand* state farms with 17,800 hectares per farm and 588 workers per farm. The reader is reminded that state farms are run like factories, with all profit going to the government. Collective farms are cooperatives in which all profit after taxes goes to the farm workers. Historically, state farms had more conveniences and fringe benefits, but the gap is now almost gone (for example, collective farm workers now have a guaranteed minimum wage).

There is no doubt that agriculture is the weakest part of the Soviet economy and is behind U.S. agriculture. According to the U.S. Commerce Department and Central Intelligence Agency, Soviet farm productivity per labor day was only 14 percent of U.S. labor productivity in 1977.[25] Net farm production in the USSR in 1977 was, according to the Commerce Department and the CIA, only 81 percent of the U.S. level, even though only about 4 percent of the U.S. labor force was in agriculture while about 20 percent of the Soviet labor force was in agriculture (and the Soviet population is larger). Even if we take these U.S. estimates with a grain of salt, they do point to a true difference.

Several reasons for the present low level of Soviet agricultural performance can be identified (some having to do with history and nature and some relating to the system). *First,* czarist Russian agriculture in 1917 was miserable and was way behind U.S. levels. Soviet agriculture then faced a civil war, foreign intervention, revolutionary change in forms, and a fascist occupation of all its best areas in the Second World War. So in 1950, it started way behind U.S. levels (a little

---

24. Douglas Diamond and W. Lee Davis (U.S. Department of Commerce and U.S. CIA), "Comparative Growth in Output and Productivity in U.S. and U.S.S.R. Agriculture," in U.S. Congress, Joint Economic Committee, *The Soviet Economy in a Time of Change* (Washington, D.C.: U.S. Government Printing Office, 1979), 397.

25. *Ibid.,* 21.

over half the U.S. net output level by Commerce–CIA estimates, as we shall see).

Second, the Soviet climate is very badly suited for agriculture. Thirty percent of the land is too cold for any agriculture, another 40 percent is too cold for any but a few hardy crops, and half the land doesn't have enough water—only 10 percent has both enough warmth and enough water for most crops.

Third, Soviet development strategy emphasized industry, not agriculture. The centralized, dictatorial system allowed, but did *not* necessitate, this result. Based on this strategy, in the 1930s and 1940s, resources—including raw materials and the best workers—were removed from agriculture, while almost no capital was invested in it. Lack of inputs helped guarantee lack of output. Since the mid 1950s, as we shall see, the Soviets have put considerable capital (such as tractors and fertilizer) and trained agronomists into agriculture, along with more favorable prices; and the result—not surprisingly— has been improved output performance. Because it had so far to go, however, Soviet agriculture still has far less in the way of tractors, trucks, combines, electric power, and fertilizer per acre than U.S. agriculture.

Fourth, there certainly is a problem of incentives on the farm and a vast migration to the city. Part of the problem is simply that wages are much higher in the city than on the farms. This circumstance exists primarily because prices paid for farm goods by the government throughout the Stalin era were kept artificially low in order to provide another source of industrial capital accumulation. Services are also much worse in the countryside, with little government-built housing, few doctors, little indoor plumbing in many areas, not enough electricity, and terrible roads. Soviet statistics indicate that free (unpriced) goods and services constitute 30 percent of the real wage of the average Soviet worker but only 16 percent of the collective farm real income. The gap between farm and city is lessening, but it still exists (as it exists to some degree in almost all countries today).

Fifth, another problem arises from the fact that an hour spent in a private plot is more profitable for a farmer than an hour spent on a state farm, and far more profitable than an hour spent on a collective farm. It is officially admitted that, "As a rule, income from a day's work on the plot exceeds that from a comparable effort in the socialized sector."[26] Therefore, the private plot exercises a strong pull on the labor supply, and it is difficult to get even the minimum quota of labor on the state and collective farms.

---

26. Communist Party Central Committee Plenum of March 1965, quoted in J. F. Karcz, "Seven Years on the Farm," in U.S. Congress, Joint Economic Committee, *New Directions in Soviet Agriculture* (Washington, D.C.: U.S. Government Printing Office, 1966), 397.

The tiny amount of land in private plots produces a considerable percentage of Soviet food, particularly potatoes, vegetables, eggs, meat, and dairy products (amounting to approximately 25 percent of the total value of agricultural output). This is *not* because the farmer is more productive on his or her private plot. In fact, output per labor hour is highest on state farms, next highest on collective farms, and lowest on private plots.[27] It is simply because farmers put so much of their labor time into these private plots; this extra effort is due to the high prices they obtain in the unregulated market.

Sixth, agriculture is generally less amenable to central planning than is industry. The reason lies in the very large number of different units, the vast distances between planner and farm, the very great differences in conditions in each area, and the important impact of the very changeable weather conditions. As a result of these conditions, and the additional burden of rigidity imposed by the dictatorial thinking and administration, the planners have often made major mistakes in the plans for state farms and in their very considerable influence on the collective farms.

One test of an economic system is its growth and progress. In spite of its many problems of nature and past policies, and in spite of its low beginning point, Soviet agriculture has made significant progress and has been growing faster than U.S. agriculture over a long period of time. To get an appreciation of Soviet progress, it is worth reading a long quote from a source that cannot be accused of pro-Soviet propaganda—two economists from the U.S. Commerce Department and CIA:

> By 1977, Soviet farm output had reached nearly 2½ times the 1950 level. Although progress has been uneven, the average annual rate of growth has been a high respectable 3½ percent per year, nearly double the growth in the United States and more than the 3-percent average for the rest of the world. As a result of this relatively rapid progress, Soviet output by 1977 was more than 80 percent of U.S. farm production, compared with roughly three-fifths in 1950.
>
> Contrary to popular belief, the Soviet regime in this 27-year period has not neglected agriculture. Since 1950, annual inputs to farms have grown by three-fourths and have included costly programs that required heavy support from industry. The difference between the 145-percent growth in Soviet output since 1950 and the 75-percent growth in inputs is the effect of the increased productivity of the resources devoted to agriculture. In the 1970s, the combined productivity of land, labor, capital, and other conventional inputs in Soviet agriculture has averaged more than a third greater than in 1950. This means that a set of resources used in Soviet agriculture in the 1970s would yield more than a third more output than the same resources used in 1950.[28]

27. See Nancy Nimitz, *Farm Employment in the Soviet Union 1928–1963* (Santa Monica: The Rand Corporation, 1965).

28. Diamond and Davis, "Comparative Growth," 20.

To get some more feel for specifics, note that the same Commerce–
CIA study finds, on the input side, that fertilizer use grew twice as fast
in Soviet as in U.S. agriculture in the 1950–1977 period.[29] Land used for
crops fell 4 percent in the United States and rose 23 percent in the
USSR. In 1950–1977, total Soviet investment of fixed capital in agriculture grew 9.7 percent a year, while U.S. investment in agriculture
grew only 2.5 percent a year.

On the output side, the same Commerce–CIA study finds Soviet net
farm output rising from 58 percent of U.S. in 1950 to 81 percent in 1977.
Meat production rose from 47 percent to 83 percent of U.S. production. The main reason for Soviet grain imports has not been to feed
grain to people, since their own production has grown fast enough for
that. The main reason for Soviet grain imports is the rapid increase in
livestock, because it requires between 7.5 and 14 pounds of grain to
obtain 1 pound of meat.[30]

Farm output per hectare rose in the 1950–1977 period by 59 percent
in the United States but by 75 percent in the USSR. Yet, product per
farm worker in the USSR rose about 2 percent a year in 1950 to 1977,
while U.S. agricultural productivity increased 2.5 percent per year.
The Soviet rise in farm labor productivity is reflected in the fact that 76
percent of Soviet population was on the farm in 1914, 42 percent was
still on the farm in 1960, but only about 20 percent by 1980.

Soviet agriculture, however, has benefited from the yearly mobilization of industrial workers, students, soldiers, and others to work
with the harvest. In 1979, these mobilized volunteers amounted to
fifteen million people, more than double the number in 1970.[31] While
boosting agriculture output and productivity, these mobilizations
must cause considerable disruption to production and services elsewhere in the economy.

In the years 1980–1982, the Soviet Union had three consecutive poor
harvests. There are continuing problems with incentives (and it
seems that the Soviets are attempting to solve these problems by
emulating elements of the more flexible and decentralized Hungarian agricultural policy). Nevertheless, a study for the U.S. Congress
released in 1983 finds that "In terms of overall output growth, USSR
agriculture has performed well compared with that in Western
Europe and North America since 1950."[32] The annual growth rate of
Soviet agriculture was 3.0 percent from 1950 through 1980. The prob-

29. Data in this paragraph from *ibid.*, 19–54.

30. See Harry G. Shaffer, ed., *Soviet Agriculture: An Assessment of Its Contribution to Economic Development* (New York: Praeger, 1977), 10–11.

31. See Alec Nove, *The Economics of Feasible Socialism* (London: George
Allen and Unwin, 1983), 88.

32. D. Gale Johnson, "Prospects for Soviet Agriculture in the 1980s," in U.S.
Congress, Joint Economic Committee, *Soviet Economy in the 1980s* (Washington, D.C.: U.S. Government Printing Office, 1983), 8.

lems of Soviet agriculture are reflected, however, in the fact (according to the same study) that the Soviet annual growth rate was 3.9 percent from 1950 through 1971 (when the U.S. rate was only 2 percent), but declined to 1.2 percent from 1970 to 1980.

In summary, Soviet farm output is approaching U.S. levels (by heavy use of additional resources), while Soviet growth rates of farm productivity are of the same magnitudes as U.S. rates. Yet nowhere are the systemic differences between the two economies seen more clearly than in agriculture. In the U.S. market capitalist economy, the biggest farm problem is the lack of demand for farm products. In the Soviet planned economy, the main problem remains how to increase farm production enough to meet demands, especially in poor harvest years. Part of the Soviet solution surely depends on better management and more efficient resource use.

Appendix 10A
Trade Unions

Soviet Trade Unions

Not only is the environment within which unions operate in the USSR determined by the government, but specific functions of trade unions are also affected by decisions of the Communist party. The official view—that the USSR is a workers' government, so workers and their unions can never have interests opposed to the Soviet government (their employer)—creates a conflict within Soviet unions. Should the unions serve the government by striving for increases in production and enforcing labor discipline, or should they serve their members by seeking to increase the workers' share of the current social product and to eliminate inequities that develop in the incentive system?

With wages and fringe benefits being bureaucratically determined, the practice of collective bargaining over wages has not existed. Higher wages would simply mean higher sales. Neither have unions regularly employed the strike mechanism. Instead of local struggles, the general wage policy for the whole country is annually dictated in an agreement between the Central Council of the Trade Unions and the appropriate government Ministries and State Committees. This practice became the rule in the 1930s and has remained ever since. The Soviets claim that a planned economy could never allow separate unions to argue over the total wage bill, because it would then be impossible to make a central plan for output or to determine the level of investment. Local unions do, however, bargain over safety and conditions of labor. Furthermore, some degree of local union service to workers and protection of workers has always existed. Unions do administer a vast social insurance system, provide recreation facilities for their members, and make available grievance machinery in case of managerial abuses. Yet unions have remained primarily instruments of the government, and only secondarily representatives of their members' interests.

In the early period of Bolshevik power, there was much controversy over the place of trade unions in the developing Soviet socialist society. Party policy first expressed by Lenin during 1917, and reiterated at the First Congress of Trade Unions in 1918, held that unions could both remain autonomous and perform vital functions for the government. But alteration of this position was already underway by 1919; a new stance was exhibited at the Second Union Congress of that year. The "government function" of unions was given more emphasis, and Lenin forecast the necessity for unions eventually to "merge with the organs of state power." At the same time Lenin predicted a "withering away" of any government which is elevated and separate from the people, and the emergence of a society where everyone was to learn the business of government. It would be the function of unions to educate the people for this undertaking.

Discussion over the independence of unions continued through 1919 and erupted into heated debate at the tenth Congress of the Communist Party, held in 1920. Opposition to the increasingly centralist tendencies of the new government came from the so-called Workers' Opposition (led by Shliapnikov and Kollontai), which called for a change to an egalitarian regime run directly by workers as represented by their trade unions. At the other extreme were the centralists (led by Trotsky and Bukharin), who urged immediate absorption of the trade unions by the government, since there could be no conflict between a government of workers and the workers themselves. The clash of these political forces and personalities prompted Lenin's famous oration on the "transmission belt" theory of unionism—a "compromise" stand which actually sounded the death knell for the aspirations of the Workers' Opposition. The Party accepted Lenin's proposition: unions were to be conceived of as intermediaries working for the realization of centrally defined goals. After failing to democratize the union role in the economy at the 1920 Congress, the Workers' Opposition began active protest and resistance to the Bolsheviks, culminating in the 1921 Kronshtadt rebellion. The Kronshtadt workers called for workers' control of the enterprises, democratic rights, and soviet power with no Communist party. Their uprising was firmly suppressed, and the active period of the Workers' Opposition came to an end.

Although the concept of unions that were independent of governmental control was officially discarded at the 1920 Congress, it is important and interesting that unions did manage in practice to remain active on behalf of the working masses during the period of the New Economic Policy (1921–1928). Soon after Stalin's consolidation of power in 1928, the last vestige of actual independence was extirpated. In the 1929 purge, Stalin eliminated Tomsky, the head of the whole Soviet trade union apparatus, and all other union leaders who showed resistance to Party enthusiasm for a plan of rapid industrialization, low real wages, and high differentials for skills. The policy of highly differentiated wages was especially emphasized after Stalin's speech of June 1931. Under this strict rule, the trade unions were adjuncts of the government, which arbitrarily assigned and altered union functions.

Among the first tasks of the unions in the 1930s was—and they played a major role in this task—the recruitment and settlement of very large numbers of rural laborers into industrial firms and society. In this regard unions took responsibility for the newcomers' habits, rudimentary skills, housing, and social insurance. They also served in encouraging the new workers to adjust to labor discipline and had a hand in enforcement procedures. They joined with the Supreme Council of National Economy and the Commissariat of Education to form factory schools for technical skills; and they organized general education courses, financed from their own membership dues. Unions were given control of social security benefits and adjudication of benefits. Finally, trade unions were given responsibility for *increasing labor productivity* while sustaining or improving worker morale. Propaganda campaigns for promoting labor competition and "socialist emulation" among workers were the result. The search was for "shock workers" in the early 1930s and "Stakhanovites" after 1935 (when the coal miner, Stakhanov, chalked up some records in production). These record-producing workers were rewarded for exceptional labor by a standard of living that was clearly differentiated from their fellow workers. "Stakhanovism" was finally abandoned because the organization of an enterprise to increase the productivity of a few selected workers proved to be disruptive to the overall productivity of the plant.

During the democratic, anti-Stalinist ferment in the USSR in the late 1950s, official attitudes toward trade unions underwent a basic alteration. More attention was given to worker rights and to working conditions. There were also many reports of increased democracy and "answerability" at the local level, as well as more effective grievance machinery. Soviet journalists and politicians now spoke of unions as service organizations for "improving the condition of work and life of workers."

Specifically, the greatest expansion of the service and protection role of Soviet trade unions was in the liberal 1956–1959 period.[33] In

---

33. See Nash, "Recent Changes in Labor Controls in the Soviet Union," 857–58. For later developments, see A. Goodman and G. Schleifer, "The Soviet Labor Market in the 1980s," in U.S. Congress, Joint Economic Committee,

1956, criminal sanctions against labor indiscipline (absenteeism, slack work, etc.) were removed. In 1957, a new law allowed workers to present more easily their grievances to a labor disputes board, composed half of management and half of union representatives. Grievances were to include questions of job and wage grades, payment for overtime or sick leave, and unfair dismissals or transfers. In 1958 trade unions were given powers (1) to help plan workers' housing and work quotas, (2) to check on management compliance with collective agreements and labor laws, (3) to hold and control general workers' meetings, and (4) to pass on dismissals. In 1959 the trade union constitution was revised so that it not only mentions the primary duty to encourage production, but also emphasizes the duty to protect workers from any management violations of laws or agreements.

Unfortunately, since the early sixties, there have been no concrete signs that further progress has been made, though new legislation during the 1970s did grant workers more *formal* participation in enterprise management.[34] Critics have said that Soviet unions are a success from the government standpoint but a failure from the workers' standpoint.

Polish Trade Unions

In 1944–45 the Soviet army liberated Poland from the German fascist occupation and installed a pro-Soviet government. The Communist party of Poland eventually became the ruler of Poland, with the support of Soviet troops with permanent bases in Poland, and with an implicit agreement between the Polish government and the still-powerful Catholic church. As in the Soviet Union, official trade unions were set up, mostly directed from above and mainly devoted to increasing productivity. As in the USSR, the economy was directed by a central plan.

In June 1956, soon after Khrushchev's attack on Stalinism, the Second Polish Congress of Economists was convened. The conference called for an immediate increase in the living standards in Poland, an improvement in the quality of both producer and consumer goods, and more efficient use of raw materials. In addition, the conference criticized the incentive system, claiming that it rewarded

---

Soviet Economy in the 1980s (Washington, D.C.: U.S. Government Printing Office, 1983), Vol. 2, 323–48; also Blair Ruble, "Soviet Trade Unions and Labor Relations after Solidarity," *ibid.*, 349–66.

34. On worker participation in Soviet management, see Murray Yanowitch, "Hierarchy at the Work Place and Participation in Management," in Yanowitch, *Social and Economic Inequality in the Soviet Union.* Also see Murray Yanowitch, ed., *Soviet Work Attitudes* (White Plains, N.Y.: M. E. Sharpe, 1979); and Blair Ruble, *Soviet Trade Unions* (Cambridge: Cambridge University Press, 1981), 64–118.

waste in materials, transportation, equipment, and labor; the group called for increased initiative on the part of the managers in the enterprise. The major suggestion resulting from this conference was that the economic bureaucracy in Poland be decentralized, thereby enabling the economy to develop along more suitable lines. One economist stated that, "The planners' role should amount to creating such economic conditions that the decisions of the enterprise would go in the direction suggested."[35] Another economist participating in the discussions of the conference noted that, "We became aware of the awful destruction caused by the bureaucratic central system of running the national economy, and to what degree these things had made people lose faith so that even the most trivial matter could not be settled without asking the central authorities."[36]

Ferment and discussion of all aspects of Polish life rose to new heights after this conference in 1956. The public at large had some very sharp words about the weaknesses of the Polish economy. They complained that the economy was not consumer oriented enough and that the quality of household goods had fallen considerably. After the economic conference, even *Trybuna Ludu*—the official newspaper of the Communist party in Poland—ran a series of extremely critical articles on the state of the economy. The Communist party itself called for the liquidation of overly extensive central planning and limitation of central directives, for the institution of incentive schemes designed to eliminate waste, for improvement of the quality of goods produced, for easing of the supply situation, and for planners to base production on more realistic estimates of the capacity of the economy. Public grumblings reached a climax with the Poznań industrial riots, in which workers conducted an illegal, general strike against the government. The old, official unions were abandoned, and the workers replaced them by new, elected unions. The grievances of the workers were numerous. They included, on the economic side, complaints of overindustrialization with lack of concern for consumer desires, increasing prices, low purchasing power, and poor living standards.

In October 1956, a bloodless revolution turned out the Stalinists and put in power the more liberal Communists. Wladyslav Gomulka, who had been jailed for his liberal, pragmatic, and nationalist views prior to the uprising, now became head of the Communist party. The new government felt that they had a popular mandate for change, and high on the agenda was economic reform. In the spring of 1957 the Economic Council's Commission on the Economic Model, under the direction of Oskar Lange, finally drew up a new set of reform theses.

---

35. Quoted in Nicolas Spulber, *The Economics of Communist Eastern Europe* (New York: John Wiley, 1957), 157.

36. *Ibid.*, 201.

Although they allowed some change, the reforms were a compromise and were far more conservative than the nature of the criticisms would suggest.

Nevertheless, decentralization of the economic bureaucracy was begun. The scope of the directives of the central authorities was reduced. The State Planning Commission's function became essentially one of guidance. The Commission was deprived of its quasi-legislative and managerial functions and relieved of its executive functions. Its staff was cut almost in half. Its previous balancing and distributing functions were parceled out among the various ministries, independent enterprises, the City Councils, and the Workers' Councils in the enterprises. The Workers' Councils seemed to foreshadow decentralized, workers' control of the economy, though they were eventually given very limited powers.[37] In addition, because of the poor record of socialized farming, agriculture was decollectivized.

The trend toward decentralization and reform of the Polish economy reached a peak in 1957. There was very considerable free speech, one independent newspaper, and some contested elections between candidates of two factions of the Communist party. Thereafter, the liberalizers came under increasing attack, and the reformers retreated. As a result of economic slowdown, pressure from the USSR, pressures from Party bureaucrats in the economic ministries, inflation, and the failure of farm production to increase markedly, many of the reforms that had been undertaken in the previous two years were attacked as right-wing deviations. Critics accused the decentralizers of loosening the bonds that held the old economic order together. In 1958, the very limited powers of the Workers' Councils were cut back still further—and the Councils were made docile by the addition of official trade union and Party representatives. The official trade unions were restored to power.

Finally, in 1959, the government declared that decentralization had gone too far with the result that a financial breakdown was in the offing, and the coordination of plans was decreasing. Living conditions had improved but at the expense of other "more vital" considerations. Investment in the capital goods sector was lagging dangerously. The government decreed stricter financial control, widening of the role of the State Planning Commission to again include executive functions, and increased investment in the heavy industrial sector.

This episode of uprising (in 1956), reform (1957–58), and retreat (1959–1965) was covered in some detail because it foreshadowed several later cycles in Poland. Every so many years, the Polish people have risen to protest Soviet domination, a dictatorship, and a poorly

---

37. On the rise and decline of Polish Workers' Councils, 1956–58, see Andre Babeau, *Consejos Obreros en Polonia* (Barcelona: Editorial Nova Terra, 1968).

performing economy. There was also pressure from within the Polish Communist party, which was divided into wavering factions. The Catholic church also gave some support to reforms, thereby sustaining the dissidents and legitimizing opposition to government authority.

The next major confrontation with workers began in December of 1970, when the government announced huge price rises in food. Since workers spent about half of their whole budget on food, they immediately became very angry. The anger was increased by the crude way that the government acted, since it announced these price increases all at once instead of slowly over many months. Moreover, it was the worst possible time because it was mid December, a time when Poles traditionally buy large amounts of food for special feasts at Christmas and New Year's. The government's reason—the necessity to sop up "excess" purchasing power—did not impress most Poles. Yet the government position had a basis of truth because many food prices were being highly subsidized, while Polish agriculture was doing very poorly.

Protests began immediately in the Lenin Shipyards in Gdańsk.[38] These workers were soon joined by many other workers in Gdańsk. They marched to the party headquarters to ask questions. The only answers they received were clubs and tear gas. There were many dead and wounded. The workers at each factory elected workers to an interfactory strike committee. The protests and strikes spread to many other towns. The workers in Gdańsk asked for (1) lower prices, (2) recognition of their strike committee as a union, and (3) freeing of those who had been taken prisoner. The government responded by declaring a "state of siege" in the whole country.

Yet the spread of protests throughout the country continued. A week after the prices had been raised, the entire government was ousted. Gomulka, who had been a liberal when he came in, was forced to resign as a reactionary who had been repudiated by the workers. Edward Gierek, considered a liberal, was made Party chief. The new government immediately gave a special allowance to workers with the lowest incomes—but they left the price increases in place.

As a result, Polish workers—in unofficial unions—continued to strike, especially in the important industrial center of Łodz. Gierek was then forced to repeal the price increases. It should be noted that all of this activity came from workers, with very little show of support from intellectuals. Gierek's regime did succeed in raising real wages by 40 percent between 1970 and 1975. This increase did involve, however, substantial imports, using up scarce foreign exchange, and large-scale subsidies for food. The basic problem of Polish agriculture

---

38. Most of the facts in this section are reported in Daniel Singer, *The Road to Gdańsk* (New York: Monthly Review Press, 1981).

is that it combines the worst of two worlds. It has very small and very inefficient peasant farms, but it also has inept government interference in the farm sector.

Slowly, the Gierek regime got into worse and worse economic trouble because of subsidized goods which had to be imported from abroad—as well as all of the other troubles of central planning discussed in the Soviet case. There was good growth but a big foreign debt—the government attempted to buy off consumer protests with a growth strategy, mostly poorly planned, based on foreign capital. The liberal impulses which had originally put Gierek in power also slowly dissipated, and the government became more rigid in its policies.

In June of 1976 the Gierek government repeated almost exactly the same *political* mistake of its predecessor (the *economic* policy may have been correct). The premier announced enormous price increases—for example, the price of meat was to jump by 69 percent overnight. There was an immediate strike in Warsaw at the largest tractor factory. The strike spread to other cities, especially Łodz and Gdańsk. Once again, after a week, the government retreated. It announced that it was not going to raise prices but was merely going to study the issue for several months. Yet, since the liberal period of the Gierek regime was long gone, it used not only concessions to calm people but repression to frighten them. Thousands of workers who had taken part in the strikes were fired. At the same time, there were major protests by intellectuals, who were also punished, but these protests were not coordinated with the workers' strikes.

On July 1, 1980, the government again decided to raise prices, but this time by deceptive means so it would not be noticed very much. A rather low-ranking official quietly announced that some goods would be transferred from regular stores to "commercial stores." The only difference was that commercial stores had long charged much higher prices than other stores and had had more goods available. Polish workers were not fooled and began their most momentous confrontation. There were many strikes, but in order to calm the workers, the authorities gave concessions in almost every case. Nevertheless, more and more strikes occurred all over Poland. As workers won their demands in almost every strike, the lesson soon became clear that strikes and protests could lead to real gains—and that the government was on the defensive.

At this time, a committee of intellectuals, called the Committee for Social Self-Defense, became involved on the workers' side. At first, it merely tried to keep communications and knowledge flowing between the strikers in different towns. Strikes and protests spread so fast that no one could actually keep up with them, but this did mark a new stage in the cooperation of Polish intellectuals and workers, a cooperation that had previously been close to nonexistent.

Then the Gdańsk shipworkers went out on strike and asked for (1) higher wages and (2) reinstatement of a well-liked woman worker who had been fired in the 1970 strike. At this point, Lech Walesa, another previously fired worker at the shipyards, arose at a meeting of thousands of workers and called for a sit-down strike. (The so-called sit-down strike was pioneered in the United States in the 1930s and means that the workers sit down in the factory and take it over until the end of the strike.) After some negotiations, the government conceded (1) reinstatement of all fired workers, (2) guarantees that strikers would not be punished, (3) a monument to the dead of 1970, and (4) a wage increase. The government assumed that these conditions would appease the workers, and the strike committee voted to go back to work. But the workers felt that for the shipyard workers to go back to work by themselves would be a stab in the back for all the other workers who were out on strike. So Lech Walesa changed his mind and supported a solidarity strike with all other striking workers.

At that time, all of the striking factories in Gdańsk formed an interfactory strike committee. The committee asked the government for (1) free and independent trade unions, and (2) the right to strike. This committee's influence extended to all of Gdańsk, while similar strikes spread to many other cities. The strikers put out a newspaper called *Solidarity*.

Finally, in August 1980 the government bowed to the inevitable. The government was shaken up, with six of eighteen members of the Politburo being replaced—though Gierek remained as Party head. The government agreed to negotiate with the Gdańsk strike committee. A committee of intellectuals flew from Warsaw to Gdańsk to help in the negotiations. The workers meanwhile formed a new independent union called Solidarity. The many demands made by Solidarity fell into three separate categories: (1) recognition of free and independent trade unions, (2) greater freedom of speech in Poland, and (3) economic decentralization and workers' control of enterprise decision making. Some extreme factions, never agreed to by all of Solidarity, raised demands for free elections—with Solidarity opposing the Communist party (but these extreme and unofficial demands were vehemently rejected by the government and were later used as one of the excuses for repression of Solidarity). After considerable negotiations and some confrontations between government ministers and thousands of workers, a historic agreement was reached, with twenty-one points in it. The government agreed to recognize independent unions (though they struck out the word *free*) and made many other concessions, both economic (such as greater decentralization and workers' participation) and political (such as reducing censorship). The Solidarity union, in turn, agreed that it was (1) in favor of socialism, (2) in favor of the leading role of the Communist party in the state, and (3) in favor of keeping the present international alliances (with the Soviet Union) with no change.

It appeared that a reasonable compromise had been reached, and many people all over the world were optimistic that Poland had found a new and peaceful road toward a more democratic socialism. Unfortunately, "the two partners [to the agreement] barely concealed their unspoken reservations. The workers assumed that their unexpected victory was only the beginning; having advanced so far, they were ready to pause for a while in order to consolidate, then to venture further on the uncharted road. The rulers, on the contrary, signed hoping that what had to be conceded in the hour of danger would be recovered, or at least neutralized, at leisure."[39]

In fact, the fragile truce survived for a remarkably long time, in the midst of continuing skirmishes between the two forces. At first, it seemed the agreement was being not only carried out but even deepened. Political prisoners were freed. All censorship basically disappeared. The Party leader, Edward Gierek, was removed—and was supposedly replaced with a more liberal leader, Stanislaw Kania (a now familiar story). The union Solidarity spread all over Poland. The government at first wanted unions to be only local, but Solidarity won the right to be a national union. The government at first refused to recognize a farmers' Solidarity union but finally agreed to do so, with some minor cosmetic reservations.

It appeared that free and independent unions could exist in East European planned economies. It appeared that many steps could be taken there toward political democracy (without Soviet intervention). It appeared that all of this could happen relatively peacefully, at least without a civil war. The notion that the Communist governments represented the workers again was severely challenged. It now seemed that a new form of democracy with workers' participation might evolve.

Then, in December of 1981, the tensions became too much. The government thought that it was losing all of its power to the Solidarity union. And some leaders in Solidarity were indeed talking about letting the union run in elections as a political party. The government then declared martial law. Thousands of Solidarity activists were arrested. After many months of indecision, the government outlawed Solidarity itself.

Finally, it is pertinent to observe that the active oppositional role played by Polish trade unions both reflected and reinforced divisions within the Polish Communist party. These divisions, in turn, resulted in stop-and-go attempts at economic reform and frustrated the development of a stable economic environment.[40] It remains to be seen whether a more deliberate and controlled pattern of reform can be implemented by the Jaruzelski government. The conditions of severe

---

39. *Ibid.*, 210.

40. An excellent analysis of this pattern is provided by the Polish economist, Janusz Zielinski, *Economic Reforms in Polish Industry* (London: Oxford University Press, 1973). Also see J. M. Montias, "Poland: Roots of the Economic

macroeconomic imbalance that prevail in Poland in the early 1980s, of course, do not augur well for any economic program, particularly when implemented by an unpopular government.

U.S. Trade Unions

The fact that free trade unions are prevented in the USSR and Poland does not mean that trade unions have every kind of freedom in the United States. There is no space here for a history of U.S. trade unions; their rich history is given in the books cited in Recommended Readings at the end of this chapter. On the basis of that literature, we may note a few major conclusions. First, the historical conflict of U.S. trade unions with employers has been more violent than in Western Europe—but has not been very violent since the 1930s. Since World War II, however, strike incidence has been higher in the U.S. than in Western Europe.

Second, federal, state, and local governments have usually aided employers against unions but have sometimes acted more favorably toward unions under workers' pressure (at the polls and in the streets). In the late eighteenth century, U.S. law held trade unions to be illegal conspiracies; and only people with property could vote in most states. By the 1830s, workers without property could vote, and unions were not illegal *per se*. But *any* picketing to control the supply of labor (preventing strikebreakers from entering) was illegal—and union pickets were attacked by company police, local police, state militia, and even federal troops in some cases. Over the years, hundreds of workers were killed and thousands were jailed. In 1935, with the support of millions of workers' votes, the New Deal passed laws to recognize unions, allow legal picketing, set minimum wages, and set maximum hours. Union membership rose from 10 percent to 35 percent of the labor force in 1945. Then, in the late 1940s and early 1950s, some antilabor laws were passed, and hundreds of union leaders were investigated as alleged Communists by the House Un-American Activities Committee and Senator Joseph McCarthy. Union federations (the AFL and CIO) gave in by purging whole unions with thousands of members. These inauspicious conditions, along with new technology and the growth of U.S. foreign investment, have progressively undermined the strength of organized labor in the United States. By 1984, less than 21 percent of the U.S. labor force was in trade unions.

Crisis," *ACES Bulletin* 24 (Fall 1982): 1–20. Also see D. M. Nuti, "Poland: Economic Collapse and Socialist Renewal," *New Left Review* (Summer 1980), 1–20. Also see Wlodzimierz Brus, "Economics and Politics: The Fatal Link," in A. Brumberg, ed., *Poland: Genesis of a Revolution* (New York: Vintage Books, 1983).

Recommended Readings

1. On managers, the classic study (now out of date, but still the place to begin) is David Granick, *Management of the Industrial Firm in the U.S.S.R.* (New York: Columbia University Press, 1954). For the relationship of managers to planning, to legal markets, and to semi-legal and illegal markets, see the articles by Raymond Powell, Aron Katzenelinboigen and Herbert Levine, and Gregory Grossman in Morris Bornstein, ed., *The Soviet Economy* (Boulder, Colo.: Westview Press, 1981). Also see Joseph Berliner, *The Innovation Decision in Soviet Industry* (Cambridge: MIT Press, 1976).

2. On Soviet labor, the place to begin is a history by Isaac Deutscher, *Soviet Trade Unions* (New York: Oxford University Press, 1950). Then read: Emily Clark Brown, *Soviet Trade Unions and Labor Relations* (Cambridge: Harvard University Press, 1966). Also see Alec Nove, *The Soviet Economic System* (London: George Allen and Unwin, 2d ed., 1980), Ch. 8. Also see Blair Ruble, "Soviet Trade Unions and Labor Relations after Solidarity," in U.S. Congress, Joint Economic Committee, *Soviet Economy in the 1980s* (Washington, D.C.: U.S. Government Printing Office, 1983). Also see David Powell, "Labor Turnover in the Soviet Union," and Gail Lapidus, "The Female Industrial Labor Force," in Bornstein, ed., *The Soviet Economy*. Lapidus' article is the best available brief discussion of women in the Soviet economy, an important subject for which we have no space here. For a historical view, see Gail Lapidus, *Women in Soviet Society* (Berkeley: University of California Press, 1978). See also Jan Adam, "Systems of Wage Regulation in the Soviet Bloc," *Soviet Studies* 28 (Jan. 1976): 91–109.

3. On agriculture, see Douglas Diamond and W. Lee Davis, "Comparative Growth in Output and Productivity in U.S. and U.S.S.R. Agriculture," in U.S. Congress, Joint Economic Committee, *The Soviet Economy in a Time of Change* (Washington, D.C.: U.S. Government Printing Office, 1979), Vol. 2. Also James Millar, "The Prospects for Soviet Agriculture," in Bornstein, ed., *The Soviet Economy*. Also Harry G. Shaffer, *Soviet Agriculture: An Assessment of Its Contribution to Economic Development* (New York: Praeger, 1977). Also D. Gale Johnson, "Agriculture and the Grain Trade," in U.S. Congress, Joint Economic Committee in U.S. Congress, Part 6 of *Soviet Economy in the 1980s* (Washington, D.C.: U.S. Government Printing Office, 1983), and Robert Stuart (ed.), *The Soviet Rural Economy* (Totowa, N.J.: Roman & Allanheld, 1983).

4. On class, mobility, and inequality, some excellent studies are:
    A. Murray Yanowitch, *Social and Economic Inequality in the Soviet Union* (White Plains, New York: M.E. Sharpe, 1977).

B. A good collection of translated Soviet sociologists is Murray Yanowitch, ed., *Social Stratification and Mobility in the USSR* (White Plains, N.Y.: M. E. Sharpe, 1973).

C. Walter D. Connor, *Socialism, Politics and Equality: Hierarchy and Change in Eastern Europe and the USSR* (New York: Columbia University Press, 1979).

D. David S. Lane, *The End of Inequality? Stratification under State Socialism* (Baltimore: Penguin Books, 1971).

E. David S. Lane, *The Socialist Industrial State: Toward a Political Sociology of State Socialism* (London: George Allen and Unwin, 1976).

F. Felicity O'Dell and David S. Lane, *Soviet Industrial Workers: Class, Education and Control* (Oxford: W. Robertson, 1978).

G. Shirley Cereseto, "Socialism, Capitalism, and Inequality," *Insurgent Sociologist* 11 (Spring 1982): 5–29.

H. Hedrick Smith, *The Russians* (New York: Ballantine Books, 1977).

I. Abram Bergson, "Income Inequality Under Soviet Socialism," *Journal of Economic Literature* 22 (Sept. 1984): 1052–1099.

5. A very thorough and sophisticated study of the Marxist theoretical approach to exploitation in socialist economies is in John E. Roemer, *A General Theory of Exploitation and Class* (Cambridge: Harvard University Press, 1982).

6. On the Polish labor movement, see Daniel Singer, *The Road to Gdańsk* (New York: Monthly Review Press, 1981). Also see Jan Adam, "Systems of Wage Regulation in the Soviet Bloc," *Soviet Studies* 28 (Jan. 1976): 91–109.

7. On the U.S. labor movement, see Philip Foner, *History of the Labor Movement in the United States* (New York: International Publishers, 7 volumes, first vol. in 1947). Also see John R. Commons, *History of Labor in the United States* (New York: 1918, 1935, 4 volumes).

11

USSR
REFORM AND REGRESSION, AFTER 1965

In 1965, the Soviet government launched some extensive reforms of their economy. What compelled them to introduce these reforms at this time? For the full answer, we must consider: (1) the ideological roots in Marx, (2) newer socialist economic theories, (3) the Yugoslav experience, and (4) the increasing economic troubles of the Soviet Union (the most important factor).

Political Background of Reform

Marx on Socialism

Karl Marx himself wrote very little about the details of socialism, always insisting that it would be utopian to discuss such details before the advent of an actual socialist economy. His few remarks can be interpreted as support for quite different positions with regard to central planning and decentralization. On the one hand, Marx criticized the unplanned nature of capitalism and showed that its lack of planning is one precondition of its frequent economic crises. On the other hand, Marx spoke of the development of freely associated producers as his goal and denounced all centralized dictatorships—preferring the example of the very decentralized Paris Commune of 1871.

Socialist Economic Theories

By the 1930s, the Soviet experience was long enough that it forced economists to think through some of the problems of socialist planning. The most famous prosocialist book on planning was written by

Oskar Lange.[1] He proposed a more decentralized scheme that would equal in efficiency any capitalist marketplace while retaining all the features that he considered essential to socialism. Lange's views, and those of other prosocialist and antisocialist writers, will be considered in detail in later chapters. Here it is necessary to say only that many Soviet theorists were aware of the various views on socialist planning by the mid 1960s.

Yugoslav Experience

After it broke away from Stalin's control in 1948, Yugoslavia constructed a new socialist system, mostly decentralized and nominally controlled by workers' councils in each firm. The Yugoslav system was denounced in the Soviet Union for many years as a procapitalist and even profascist scheme. Yet serious Soviet scholars began to study it. After Khrushchev restored good relations with Yugoslavia, the study of its system became even more widespread.

Economic Problems Leading to Reform

In spite of much resistance by the Party apparatus and government bureaucrats, the top leadership was in favor of reforms because the economy was not growing as rapidly as it had. No matter whose estimates of Soviet growth we accept, the conclusions are roughly the same. Soviet economic growth performance was outstanding in the 1930s, with very high rates of growth of the gross national product. There was still high growth in the late 1940s and early 1950s. The rate of growth declined in the late 1950s and declined further in the 1960s. The rate of technological improvement was also slowing (for reasons discussed in detail in Chapter 6). For these reasons—plus the debates of Western and Soviet economists, as well as the Yugoslav experience with a decentralized economy—the top leaders were inclined toward reforms.

Why did the economy show a declining rate of growth (though not the absolute declines of national income seen cyclically in capitalist economies)? There is much controversy about this, but many economists would say that the Soviet-type economy is very well suited to the initial leap from underdevelopment to an advanced economy but is much less suited to an advanced economy itself. In the backward Soviet economy of the 1920s, what was most needed was to put to work large numbers of the unemployed, to channel all resources into heavy industry (except those needed for enough consumption to keep people alive), and to put to use the latest technology as seen in Western Europe and the United States. The centrally planned economy can

---

1. Oskar Lange, *On the Economic Theory of Socialism* (New York: McGraw-Hill, 1964, first publ. 1938).

put everyone to work because it need not worry about problems of the lack of effective demand, since the plan can continue regardless of profit levels. The centrally planned system can concentrate all resources because only the government has the legal right to make investments, imports, or exports. The latest technology was borrowed from Western Europe and the United States, with some changes to fit Soviet conditions.

By the end of the 1950s, when the Soviet Union was itself a highly developed and complex economy, the situation had changed. The government could still ensure full employment of resources and labor, but their allocation became much more difficult, as did the adoption of new technology. The modern Soviet economy produces over twelve million separate products. Which ones shall be produced in what proportions? Soviet planners can choose from many different alternative technologies. Which technology shall be chosen? The modern Soviet economy can no longer borrow technology in many fields because it is now on the frontiers in these areas. Therefore, it must create its own technology to continue a rapid growth (rather than falling behind so it can wait for the technology of others to filter through to it). Even where technology is available, it becomes more difficult in some areas to adapt it to Soviet needs, which are now very particular and specialized.

There are problems both at the center and at the enterprise level. The problems of how to construct a plan at the center were discussed in Chapters 7 and 8. Here we need only say, very briefly, that there are two main problems for the central planners. One is that they do not receive enough information, and some of it is inaccurate. In theory, they should know exactly what resources are available and what the preferences are of everyone for every product (or, at least, the sum of preferences for each product). Second, the information that they do get is still too much to be processed through all of the necessary calculations in a reasonable amount of time. It is simply not technically possible to do this in detail for twelve million, or even one hundred thousand, products. More and faster computers can make only a small dent in this problem. Consequently, the central planners must aggregate or group important products together and ignore others. This leaves a significant share of inputs and output unplanned and contributes, along with other factors, to coordination difficulties. Even with the simplifications and aggregations of data, however, output plans often arrive at the enterprise after the beginning of the planning period and frequently are altered during the period.

Problems of the Soviet Enterprise

There were many problems before 1965 in the execution of the Plan by the manager. Most of these problems persist, sometimes in altered form, today. We examine some of them in this section.

(1) False Reports

Obviously, if the production for the month just misses 100 percent of the target by a hairbreadth—and if the manager's bonus depends on meeting the target—then the manager may report achievement of the planned target by inclusion of waste or unfinished goods in order to meet the target on paper. Or, rather than complete falsification, he or she may simply shift the report of some production from a very high month to a low one. Beyond very, very minor juggling of the figures, however, apparently few managers actually do much outright falsification. For one thing, the manager turns in a very large volume of related reports, which are examined for internal consistency by the bank auditors or by a superior agency.

More important, there are many different channels of control over the manager; and these channels are independent enough so that collusion by all of the agents is very difficult. There is first of all the superior agency, which may be an Association or a section of the Ministry. But these superior organs also have a material interest in exaggerating the production reports from "their" enterprises, so other lines of control must also exist.

A second line of control is through the Communist party cell in each enterprise.

A third line of control is through the local trade union. In fact, during the early 1920s when many managers were still hostile to the regime, the local Communist party secretary and the local trade union secretary were often given equal powers in the enterprise with the manager. Today, when most managers are themselves Party members, the manager has sole power and responsibility for the enterprise, but the Party and the unions do have the right to check on the production reports.

A fourth line of control is through the state bank, in which every enterprise must keep its accounts; the bank examines all enterprise transactions to ensure their conformity to the Plan.

A fifth line of control reaches down from the Central Statistical Agency. Closely related are the activities of the Soviet accountant, who is responsible for the accuracy of his or her figures, not only to the manager but also to higher authorities.

It must be noted, however, that most of these people—such as the manager, the Party secretary, the trade union secretary, and the local bank manager—are often very good friends, so they try not to "disturb" each other. The Soviet press often mentions examples of this phenomenon, called "familyness" or, less politely, collusion.

(2) Easier Plans

Suppose the local or superior controllers are alert and that their reports are accurate. The manager still has important devices for improving apparent performance. For one thing, the central planners cannot have perfect knowledge of plant capacities. Therefore, the manager must play a central role in giving information and formulating the Plan. He or she naturally bargains for a lower output target and a higher amount of required supplies. In this way, output targets are more easily fulfilled.

(3) Poorer Quality

If a plan cannot be met in the necessary quantities by producing what is supposed to be produced, it can often be fulfilled by producing a poorer quality of good. In spite of some of the reforms aimed at this problem, many Soviet goods continue to be of poor quality. Since most consumers (either household or industrial) have little choice and only one source of supply, the producer is under no competitive pressure to produce high quality or correctly specified items. Many analysts see this as the Achilles' heel of the Soviet economy.

With the consumer only poorly represented at best, the outcome tends to be what some have called "output fetishism"—that is, a unidimensional focus on quantity. This is often taken to preposterous extremes. For instance, at the end of one quarter the public utility enterprise of Leningrad (*Leninergo*) was admonished for not meeting its output target, expressed in BTUs. The authorities overlooked the seemingly relevant fact that Leningrad had experienced an unusually mild winter.

(4) Fewer Styles

It is much easier to produce a large amount of one homogeneous good than it is to produce small quantities of many different goods. Managers therefore have an incentive to produce as few types, styles, and sizes as they can get away with, rather than a variety, even though consumers would prefer a variety.

(5) Easiest Mixture

In fact, the type or style may be chosen, not on the basis of usefulness to the economy, but because it is the easiest way of achieving the output target. As a result, if the manager is judged by the weight or number of tons produced, then he or she may produce only very heavy goods—for example, very large nails of the heaviest available metal. Thus, a famous Soviet cartoon shows a single enormous nail hanging the full height of a factory, and a happy manager saying, "We met our monthly quota." If the manager is judged by the number of units, then the tendency is to produce millions of very tiny nails. If the performance is judged by volume (in so many cubic feet), then the temptation is to produce very large and light products—for example, bridge girders that are mostly hollow inside, or large nails of the cheapest metals.

One might think it would be easy to correct these tendencies by judging the manager's performance in terms of the value of output, rather than its physical characteristics. Before the reforms, however, many managers were judged by the value of their gross output, but with very little attention paid to costs. The higher the price of the raw materials used, the higher would be the gross value of output. Under those rules, the Soviet manager had an incentive to use the most expensive possible raw materials in his or her enterprise!

(6) Extra Supplies

As we mentioned earlier, it was a well-known fact that the manager kept some employees, called *pushers*, whose only function was to find new sources of supplies outside of the planned sources—using semi-legal or even illegal means. The pushers have expense accounts on which they wine and dine managers of other firms and of various higher organizations who may be able to furnish these supplies by some means.

(7) Hidden Reserves

Wise Soviet managers pile up reserves of any goods they can get their hands on, regardless of whether they happen to need them or not at the moment. When the output target is raised, they can use the extra reserves to meet it. This hoarding freezes large reserves in storage rather than using them in production.

(8) Extra Labor

Managers are given a plan for the amount of labor and the amount of wages that they can spend. Overspending on wages, however, is hardly punished at all, whereas meeting the output target reaps big rewards. Therefore, there is a strong tendency for Soviet managers to use labor extravagantly and to spend more than their allotted wage funds. One reform in banking makes it more difficult to overspend on payroll—unless the enterprise can prove that such overspending would help to overfulfill the plan.

(9) Storming

Bonuses for managers, and for most workers, are usually paid on a monthly basis. The end of each month, therefore, is often a time of feverish activity—called *storming*—in each enterprise. Of course, the result is that people tend to relax again at the beginning of each month. This off-and-on pressure often results in low quality output and poor maintenance of the capital stock (because maintenance workers are shifted to production).

(10) Resistance to Innovations

The Soviet manager frequently does not react with enthusiasm to innovations that may increase productive capacity or may lower costs. Innovations are risky because they may actually lower output for some months while the transition is made to the new process. Soviet managers seldom take the long-run view (1) because their bonuses are (or were) pegged to monthly goals, and (2) because they are often switched to other enterprises on short notice. The idea behind these frequent changes is to prevent corruption and collusion (or "familyness") from developing, but it also means that managers focus their attention on immediate production gains and are not willing to gamble on long-run gains.

Furthermore, the managers knew that if the innovation succeeded in increasing the capacity to produce, then the production targets would also be increased. If a plan was greatly overfulfilled, targets were usually raised by the same amount. So the wise manager preferred to take no risks and to just barely meet or slightly overfulfill the targets.

The resistance to innovations is most damaging in the long run, because the Soviet Union now has very limited supplies of labor (as a result of very slow population growth). Therefore, it must obtain most growth by means of the application of new technology. These, then, were the chief problems that the 1965 reforms were intended to overcome.

The Liberman Debate

These economic problems (in the context of Marxism, recent economic theories, and the Yugoslav experience) led to major debates in the Soviet Union and to eventual reforms. The so-called Great Debate on decentralization in the USSR ostensibly originated with a 1962 article in *Pravda* by Kharkov economist Evsei G. Liberman, proposing to revamp the existing incentive system for Soviet enterprises.[2] The editorial board of *Pravda* footnoted the article with a request for written responses to the proposals; reactions were immediate. The discussion that followed was extended to include nearly every aspect of Soviet economic life, so that the participants could evaluate all of

---

2. Evsei G. Liberman, "Plan, Profit, and Bonuses," *Pravda*, Sept. 9, 1962, transl. in M. E. Sharpe, ed., *The Liberman Discussion* (White Plains, N.Y.: International Arts and Science Press, 1965), 79–87.

the implications as well as the specifics of Liberman's plan. In the press, in technical discussion groups, in the USSR Academy of Sciences, and in the Central Committee of the Communist party, notables and newcomers alike participated in an intensive debate about the present and proposed systems.

Within the atmosphere after 1956 of increased freedom for scientific inquiry, there arose a faction of economists whose approach was quite pragmatic. They analyzed organizational matters and very concrete issues of policy; they sought experiments and solutions to deal with limited problems. The debate was given urgency when the Soviet political leadership became alarmed over the retardation in growth rates apparent in the early 1960s. At the same time, some of the leading economic theorists began to support the proposals for institutional reform. In April 1962, the late academician V. S. Nemchinov gave the pragmatist Liberman a first chance to influence important academic theorists by persuading the Scientific Council of the Academy of Sciences to hear the then obscure Kharkov professor.

The Kharkov incentive system (as Liberman called his plan) openly called for structural changes in the planning process, but only at the level of the firm. All the prices and outputs were to continue to be centrally planned. The relationship of the planning apparatus to the individual enterprise, however, was to be fundamentally changed.

To encourage greater flexibility and initiative, the large number of indicator targets then passed down to the firm was to be streamlined to "key indices" only. Liberman recommended assigning enterprises just those targets which exclusively pertained to their final output mix: quantity and assortment of production, product destinations, and delivery dates. The *input* mix was to be determined by each individual firm; the planners then presumably summed up all of the enterprise needs and provided for them through the centrally planned system of material allocations (though this process would be quite difficult).

How well an enterprise fulfilled society's demand for maximum efficiency was to be assessed solely on the basis of "ultimate efficiency." Profitability—which was defined to be profits expressed as a percentage of total capital—was to serve as this inclusive evaluator and was to be estimated in yearly plans submitted by all firms. Once the stated output goals were attained, the rate of profitability achieved became the sole determinant of the amount of bonus funds awarded to the firm and its employees. Liberman depicted the central planners as "relieved from petty tutelage over enterprises" and from "costly efforts to influence production through administrative measures rather than economic ones."[3] Bonus payments to enter-

---

3. Liberman, in *ibid.*, 79.

prises were to be computed by comparing the profitability rate of a particular firm with a "profitability norm" established for the branch of industry to which the firm belonged. The attempt was to set a "single standard of profitability for enterprises in roughly the same natural and technical conditions."

To motivate directors to attempt as ambitious a plan as their productive potential allowed, Liberman advanced three proposals. First, incentive premiums per ruble of capital invested were to rise as the rate of profit increased. Second, the firm was to benefit more from fulfilling a high profitability plan than from overfulfilling a lower plan. This provision, of course, was designed to discourage enterprises from concealing production capacity. Third, the norms of profitability were to be established "for an extended period of time" (from two to five years or more). This proposal was intended to prevent the harmful practice of raising norms whenever a firm surpassed its planned targets. In this way, the firm directors could count on reaping benefits from successful innovations or particularly effective cost-saving programs. The concern for profitability was also supposed to stimulate the manager to search for cost reductions and to produce the output mix demanded by the firm's consumers.

Both moderate and active supporters of the Liberman system in the Soviet Union agreed that a "rational" price system is a necessary precondition for a profit-based index to serve as an effective evaluator of enterprise efficiency. Although Liberman himself had been somewhat indefinite about the changes in pricing methodology which would be necessary to achieve this "rationality," others (such as V. S. Nemchinov) had taken a strong stand for many years. Since profits derive from selling prices and cost prices, profitability will be a measure of real, and not merely of paper, efficiency only if prices reflect the relative values of all inputs into production.

One group of Soviet writers argued further that the existing material supply system was too complex and inflexible to give enterprises the freedom of input determination envisioned in Liberman's incentive scheme. Therefore, they advocated replacing administrative allocation with a system of "state trade," in which enterprises would negotiate independent agreements with suppliers and customers.[4] Nemchinov boldly argued that all planning of intermediate goods should cease; the State should decide only what final products it needs. The majority of responses to *Pravda*'s 1962 request for discussion, however, were characterized by either total hostility to Liberman's scheme or considerable criticism. Many of these responses came from middle-level bureaucrats, who feared the loss of their power over enterprises.

---

4. See L. Vaag and S. Zakharov, *Voprosy ekonomiki*, No. 4 (1963).

Official Reforms

By 1965, the top Party leadership felt that something had to be done. They instituted organizational reforms, which moved somewhat in the direction of the Liberman proposals. Adopted as law by the Supreme Soviet, the stipulations of the 1965 Reform were conservative and tentative, yet they did begin the process of reform. The section pertaining to the individual enterprise contained four significant new policies.[5] First, and most important, managers' bonuses were to be paid for fulfillment of planned targets for sales, profit or profitability, and physical output. The norms for bonuses were designed to provide relatively higher rewards for fulfillment of higher planned targets than for overfulfillment of lower targets. Moreover, to evaluate the amount of sales, the *gross value of output* indicator was replaced by *output sold.* This change implied the necessity to produce what consumers desire. Numerous target directives were eliminated, including the norms for labor productivity, number of workers and employees, and average wages.

Second, the enterprise was permitted to retain and utilize a proportion of profits (and some portion of depreciation allowances) for bonuses, collective welfare purposes, and decentralized investment. This measure was intended to be a very significant one, giving financial muscle to the decentralization reforms. Third, half of centralized investment was to be financed by repayable and interest-bearing loans from banks, and interest charges were to be levied (in the form of a tax) on all fixed and working capital put at the enterprise's disposal. Fourth, contracts between enterprises were to be more strictly enforced, prohibiting superiors from changing enterprise plans at will during the plan period.

At the same time, the planning hierarchy was reorganized along ministerial (or branch), rather than territorial, lines.[6] A few years later, another reform grouped enterprises together into larger entities, called Associations. These Associations were supposed to take over the planning functions of the intermediate regional planning agencies as well as to conduct research and development on a more decentralized basis (though, in practice, their powers have varied in different regions).

The intended upshot of all of these reforms was that the managers should have fewer constraints, should work toward the very broad target of profits and profitability, and should be able to plan more

---

5. The text of the law was translated in U.S. Congress, Joint Economic Committee, *New Directions in the Soviet Economy* (Washington, D.C.: U.S. Government Printing Office, 1966), Part 4, 1063–66.

6. See David Granick, "The Ministry as the Maximizing Unit in Soviet Industry," *Journal of Comparative Economics* 4 (Sept. 1980): 255–73.

rationally over a longer time period (without interference day-to-day by higher officials). Before evaluating what actually happened under the reforms, however, it is well to note the limitations that remained, even if the reforms had been fully carried out.

Some of the reform measures do approach the spirit, if not the letter, of Liberman's scheme. Attention to what was left out of the Kosygin system, however, gives us a more pessimistic view of the possibility that the reform would implement the kind of changes which Liberman sympathizers were proposing. For example, it was pointed out numerous times that any attempt at a greater reliance on profitability criteria would be useless (or even harmful) without a rational price system. Yet the wholesale price reform was very slow in coming and did not make the more drastic changes requested by Soviet reform theorists. Furthermore, the new committee charged with price policy was told no more than that prices should reflect costs, a remarkably insufficient suggestion considering that economists and planners had been arguing the basic principles for decades.

Moreover, the new economic system continues to maintain the method of direct materials allocation by the central plan. As long as the system of direct materials allocation is continued, the reforms certainly will not result in the Liberman objective of enterprise freedom to vary inputs. Notice that the reformed system also keeps the central limits on total payrolls and allows managers only to choose the labor mix within those limits.

What Happened to the Reforms?

The reforms met bureaucratic obstruction and sabotage from those who might lose power to the enterprise managers. Those against reform included some of the central planning bureaucracy, ministerial staffs, and Party chiefs, so they were able to do a lot of damage. As a result of this situation and other factors, the reforms have not achieved the intended decentralization and improved performance.

It appears most accurate to say that there have been continual reforms ever since 1965, with new changes every few years. Many of the new "reforms" have been back in the direction of greater centralization, but others have tried new directions. In fact, there have been so many reforms and changes one on top of the other that the large number of changes have themselves hindered the systematic operation of management. Let us examine the course of the reforms in each of the four areas discussed above: (1) fewer incentive indicators, with profitability the main one; (2) use of rent and interest on capital loans; (3) decentralized investment; and (4) long-term contracts with no changes.

Fewer Incentive Indicators, Mainly Profitability

The 1965 reforms did away with a large number of indicators. They reduced the indicators to three main ones: profitability rate, total profits, and sales—provided that the main quantitative targets were met, and provided that the enterprise stayed within the wage bill. If the constraints were met, then profits and sales at or above the Plan targets meant large bonuses for the manager and the work force. Unfortunately, as time went on, more performance indicators were added, both diluting and greatly complicating the original idea. Some of these brought back discarded indicators in disguise. For example, the indicator of *gross output* was dropped because it caused so many problems. In 1970, however, a new indicator called *labor productivity* was added, which was gross output divided by employment. Since then, a long list of other indicators has been added. Gross output itself was subsequently reinstated as an indicator but then dropped again in 1979. The new indicator, *net output*, discourages profligate use of materials but encourages excessive use of labor.

Moreover, superior agencies still retain the right to give specific orders to firms. They are not supposed to do so in the spirit of the reforms, but they have done so to an enormous degree. When the enterprise follows such specific orders, it may be in conflict with the best way of fulfilling its performance indicators, such as profitability. So, in effect, it is penalized for following orders.

To make things more complex, there is an additional bonus if the enterprise voluntarily adopts a plan which has higher targets than the one that was proposed by the planners. Such plans are called *counter-plans*. One problem is that if the enterprise fulfilled the higher plan this year, then next year the official plan would probably set even higher targets—the so-called ratchet effect. To get around this, targets are set in the Five-Year Plan for each of the five years (and are not supposed to be changed). This way, the ratchet effect should be of less concern during the early years of a Five-Year Plan period.

Remember, also, that before profitability counts, the enterprise must reach its planned quantitative targets. This requirement brings back all the old problems. For example, many targets are still stated in tons. But that means the heavier, the better. So bridge girders or airplane bodies may be constructed of the heaviest possible materials! Or large size may be used as an easy way of fulfilling the target, as shown in the giant-nail cartoon described earlier in this chapter. Of course, in such an extreme case, the product could not be sold, so the sales indicator would not be met; but the tendency is definitely there. In general, these cases illustrate the conflict between meeting, on the one hand, the detailed norms laid down by superiors and, on the other hand, the needs of customers. Furthermore, no single measuring rod is accurate when there is a mix of products. So when one type of measure leads to distortions, the temptation is to try another; but that only leads to other kinds of distortions.

Finally, the criterion of profitability can have meaning only if prices are consistent, that is, if the sum of the price of inputs applied in the production process is less than the price of the output. As we have seen, the State Commission on Prices generally attempts to set prices on the basis of cost plus a markup (where the markup is a percent of capital stock). With twelve million domestic commodities and constantly changing prices of imports, however, the setting of prices, according to any formula, is a colossal and complex task. For prices to remain consistent, every time an input price changes the output price should also be reset. It is simply impossible for Moscow bureaucrats to avoid frequent oversights and errors in such price setting. Anecdotes telling of irrationalities in the structure of prices, which result in undesirable changes in output mix, are widespread. No matter how well-intentioned and brilliant the bureaucrats, as long as all prices are administered, it appears (to Western neoclassical economists as well as some Soviet economists) that these irrationalities are inevitable.

Use of Rent and Interest on Capital

Since enterprises wasted capital when they were not forced to pay for it, the reforms stated that all new capital would have a charge placed on it which must be paid each year by the firm (in most cases, 6 percent, a relatively low rate of interest). Similarly, an enterprise would have to pay rent for use of rich mineral land. The charges, however, have not been very high. They have therefore not been enough to stop vast wastage of capital, so a great many schemes for changing the charges have been discussed in the Soviet press, though none has yet been adopted. Moreover, as long as the enterprise faces a soft budget constraint (that is, it will be subsidized or bailed out if it experiences losses), it will tend to pay less attention to, or ignore, such capital charges.

Decentralized Investment

The reforms recognized that local enterprises may be the best judges of local needs, so a certain percentage of profits was to be left to the enterprise to make investments in replacement or improved equipment. There was for a time some increase in the flexibility of local enterprises to spend their profits. Thus, the percentage of profits retained by the enterprise rose from 29 percent in 1965 to 40 percent in 1972;[7] these profits would be used for bonuses, collective consump-

---

7. See Alec Nove, *The Soviet Economic System* (London: George Allen & Unwin, 1980, 2d ed.), 94.

tion, and new investment. The planners, however, found that this meant the enterprise could use its funds to buy products when it suited the enterprise. The planners heartily disliked this situation because it could mean sudden drains on resources, unpredictable by the central planners. Thus, the uncertainty of the central plan would be greatly increased, and the control by the planners would be decreased.

In addition, because of the very taut and rigid plans, the desired materials were usually not available in any legal way. Thus, firms frequently resorted to bribes or the black market. This action further reduced the legally available resources and distorted the plan in other areas. Therefore, the decentralized investment allowed by the reforms has now been nullified by a decree which says that the funds may not be spent until the expenditure is included in the central plan. Many U.S. economists had originally seen decentralized investment as the most meaningful and important part of the reform, so its demise signalled the practical end of decentralization to these observers.

Long-term Contracts without Changes

One of the biggest problems of rational management was that plans and orders might be—and were—frequently changed after the Plan had been given out initially. Furthermore, as noted above, a successful firm would be penalized by having its targets increased the next year. To meet these problems, the reforms provided that the Plan would be operational for five years, individual enterprises would draw up five-year contracts within this context, and no changes would be allowed after the contracts were drawn up.

But in spite of considerable efforts by planners, five-year plans continue to be rather general, and only one-year plans are detailed and operational. This situation is so because it is very difficult to draw up a detailed five-year plan, since so many factors are involved and most of them are continually changing and not easy to predict.

There has been an attempt to more rigorously enforce contracts, but it is still very difficult to do. The penalties for suppliers must outweigh the gains from noncompliance, but they seldom do. The supplier is more interested in its own targets than in meeting customers' contracts. Moreover, the rewards for meeting targets go to individuals, whereas the penalty may simply be on the whole firm's books. Therefore, the manager may ignore a contract, with little or no harm resulting to himself or herself, if this action allows the firm to meet its planned goals more easily.

Furthermore, there is still nothing to stop superiors from giving detailed orders at any time to the enterprise. When the manager gets a specific order from a superior agency, the previously announced Plan and the contracts are simply overridden. The manager must follow the new orders of a superior; this course of action creates havoc with long-run planning or contractual obligations.

The supply problem for the enterprise comes about when the central Plan is too taut and overoptimistic, ordering things to be done that are nearly impossible, or requiring an unrealistic amount of supplies. The supply plan may, in fact, bear little resemblance to the output plan—partly because planners still assume that enterprises are hoarding and not reporting supplies. As a result, instead of relying on unenforceable contracts, based on a legal Plan, enterprises rely on other means to get supplies (such as the expediters, or pushers).

Since there is still no assurance of obtaining supplies, and certainly no assurance that next year's plan will not be higher than this one, it pays to have low targets that can easily be met. That way, one is sure to get a bonus and to appear to be a successful manager.

Part of the reforms consisted of an intention to end the central allocation of industrial inputs, so that enterprises could buy them by means of long-run contracts rather than by central allocations. But this intention has not been carried out. The Central Planning Agency still allocates 70 to 80 percent of the value of output. In fact, allocations for 274 particularly important commodities still require approval by the USSR Council of Ministers.[8] Long-term contracts between enterprises have expanded only very slowly. Instead of allowing one enterprise to sell freely to another, the government supply network has been purchasing small industrial items itself and then selling them in its own network of stores. Purchases can then be made by an enterprise, provided it has the proper ration allocation.

Continuing Contradictions

According to one careful study, "A decade of reforming the reforms has not altered the nature of the Soviet economic system in any essential respect. It remains one of rigid, highly centralized planning of production, formal rationing of nearly all producer goods, centrally-fixed prices, and incentives geared to meeting plans."[9] Since the basic problems have not been cured, the performance of the Soviet economic system has not improved. The rate of growth in official Soviet data continues to decline in each five-year period. (For perspective, it should be emphasized that Soviet growth rate has remained positive.) Moreover, the Soviet press still reports large

---

8. Gertrude Schroeder, "The Soviet Economy on a Treadmill of 'Reforms,'" U.S. Congress, Joint Economic Committee, *Soviet Economy in a Time of Change* (Washington, D.C.: U.S. Government Printing Office, 1979), 323.

9. *Ibid.*, 336–37.

numbers of products of poor quality. In 1977 Soviet inspectors reject
ed 10 percent of all garments and one-eighth of all shoes.

There exists a contradiction in the fact that the manager of an
enterprise is supposed to satisfy his or her customers but is also
supposed to satisfy the detailed instructions of superiors. There exists a contradiction between an independent decision by a manager
to switch to other inputs (perhaps cheaper or better) and the fact that
his or her suppliers must stick to a central plan. There exists a contradiction between the fact that there is not enough information (or time
to digest it) for the central planners possibly to know the local situation and the fact that they give orders to local enterprises. Yet, with
central planning and prices that are set somewhat arbitrarily, there is
no way for the local firm to know the needs of society, even if it
ardently wished to meet those needs.

These contradictions are part of the more basic contradiction that
the Soviet Union has social or public ownership but it is not run
democratically. The small group controlling the Soviet Union does
not want to give up any of its major economic functions or its economic power over all production in the Soviet Union. The top leaders
recognize that it might be nice for managers to make a few more
independent decisions within the context of the general goals. But the
middle echelons fear that they would be left with nothing to do, so
they oppose more power for local enterprise decision makers. Both
the middle- and top-level leaders oppose any greater power over the
economy through democratic discussion and election of top leadership. So part of the problem is that they cling to central planning to
protect their own power. Part of the problem is that dictatorship does
not create the necessary climate for rational discussion and open
debate. This circumstance hurts the attempt to discuss new structural reforms. It hurts the attempt to promote scientific progress and
possible innovations in industry. And it makes it difficult to criticize
inefficiency and corruption, except when an individual has already
been destined for being fired by superiors (though the Soviets do
encourage "constructive" criticism on all kinds of detailed issues,
usually within narrowly prescribed limits). Thus, Soviet political-economic relations are in conflict with the further rapid progress
of its forces of production.

Finally, it remains to be said that the failure to decentralize and
make more efficient the operation of Soviet planning does not imply
that all centrally planned economies are unreformable. The extreme
centralization of the USSR economy is a function of Soviet history
(discussed in Chapter 5). The tautness in the planning system, the
unwillingness to allow even small investments on local initiative, the
constant tutelage of bureaucrats reluctant to reduce enterprise indicators, and so forth, can all be traced to the extreme distrust which
has infested the Communist party and the economic hierarchy since

the early days of Stalin's rule.[10] The regime of Communist party leader Yuri Andropov announced in 1983 that it would experiment with decentralized decision making in several industries, but it will be several years before the success or failure of this attempt becomes clear. The demonstrated ability of other centrally planned economies to continue overall planning while effectively decentralizing many detailed decisions, either administratively (e.g., East Germany) or through use of the market mechanism (e.g., Hungary), highlights the special character of economic problems in the Soviet Union. We shall now turn to consider the central planning experience in other socialist economies.

Recommended Readings

1. Marie Lavigne, *The Socialist Economies of the Soviet Union and Europe* (London: Martin Robertson, 1974), has some good material on economic reforms in the USSR and in other East European countries in the period of the 1960s and early 1970s.

2. Waldemar Kuczynski, "Planning and Economic Reforms under Socialism," *Soviet Studies* 31 (Oct. 1979): 505–22.

3. Norman Ireland and Peter Law, "Incentives and Efficiency in the Kosygin Reforms," *Journal of Comparative Economics* 4 (Mar. 1980): 33–39. This article explores the problem of relating bonuses to sales and profit rates. For a review of the literature, see S. Koont and A. Zimbalist, "Incentives and Elicitation Schemes: A Critique and an Extension," in A. Zimbalist, ed., *Comparative Economic Systems: An Assessment of Knowledge, Theory, and Method* (Boston: Klower-Nijhoff, 1983).

4. David Dyker, "Decentralization and the Command Principle—Some Lessons from Soviet Experience," *Journal of Comparative Economics* 5 (June 1981): 121–48.

5. Fyodor Kushnirsky, *Soviet Economic Planning, 1965–1980* (Boulder, Colo.: Westview Press, 1982). This is a first-hand account of an expatriate Soviet planner's experience.

6. For a stimulating and ingenious discussion of the structural constraints on reforming central planning, the advanced student should consult Janos Kornai's *The Economics of Shortage* (Amsterdam: North-Holland, 1980).

---

10. See Seweryn Bialer, *Stalin's Successors* (Cambridge: Cambridge University Press, 1980), Ch. 2.

Four

CENTRAL PLANNING:
THE DEVELOPING COUNTRIES

In Part Three we examined the highly industrialized economy of the USSR. In this part we shall examine the economies of China and Cuba. Both countries have planned economies but are still developing—and both are socialist (under our narrow definition of socialism). One issue in this part, therefore, is the relation between socialist planning and development.

Another issue lies in the fact that both China and Cuba have experimented with different models of socialist economic management. Some of these models involve greater decentralization; others, more democratic input in planning; and still others, less reliance on material incentive and greater stress on equality. What historical factors led to these different models and how did they work out?

China was chosen to be included here because it has the largest population of any country in the world and because it offered a fascinating alternative model of a socialist economy. It is also a good example of a rapidly changing economic model, with frequent, major policy reorientations. Since 1978 more or less, and particularly during 1983 and 1984, the Chinese government has taken significant strides toward a market socialist-type economy. If they can sustain this current policy direction over the years, the Chinese model will command increasing intellectual interest.

Cuba also has many unique and significant features. It is a very small country, whose economy before the revolution was based (and largely remains based) overwhelmingly on sugar. It is also very dependent on foreign trade. Cuba is worth studying in any case because it is our neighbor, just ninety miles from Key West, Florida, and it has figured very prominently in the discussion and formulation of U.S. foreign policy.

12

CHINA
A CHANGING MODEL*

On October 1, 1949, the People's Republic of China was established, and Mao Zedong, Chairman of the Communist party which led the revolutionary movement for the founding of the new state, declared that "the Chinese people have stood up." Indeed, after more than a century of foreign invasion and occupation, civil wars, warlord rule, and recurrent natural disasters intensified by the inability of weak national governments to take protective action, an era of rapid economic growth began. The economic growth was accompanied by dramatic institutional changes and acute struggles for power based on differing notions of what socialism is and how it is to be brought about. An examination of economic development in China, perhaps more than for any other country, highlights these issues.

Background

For more than two thousand years China had been unified under the emperor system until the final imperial dynasty, the Qing dynasty, collapsed in 1911. The Qing had long been weakened, however, and during the preceding century had been helpless to prevent a series of attacks by Great Britain, France, Germany, the United States, Japan, and other foreign powers, attacks that enabled these other countries to establish special privileges and spheres of influence within China. The opening incursion was by the British, who successfully fought the Opium War from 1839 to 1842 to force China to continue importing opium after Chinese officials had sought to halt the rapidly expanding trade. Concerned with its own trade deficits and the consequent outflow of gold and silver, Britain had consciously sought to expand opium exports from India. Since India was then its colony, Britain could readily obtain India's foreign exchange earnings for itself.

---

*This chapter was written initially by Victor Lippit. In order to conform to the style and approach of this book, it was partly rewritten and edited by the authors.

Until late in the nineteenth century, opium remained China's largest import; by that time China had learned to produce its own. The size of China gave it some protection against complete colonization, since the British were concerned about the expense of administering China's vast territory and population. Covering a total of 3.7 million square miles, China is a little larger in size than the United States and second in size only to the Soviet Union. By the middle of the nineteenth century its population had already reached a total of about 450 million (the 1982 census revealed a total of 1 billion, 8 million, excluding Taiwan, Hong Kong, and Macao).

Although the foreign impact on China was harmful in a number of respects, much greater responsibility for China's failure to develop economically must be assigned to its internal social and class structure. Ultimately, it was the replacement of this social and class structure in 1949 which permitted development to proceed.

In the nineteenth century, thirty to forty thousand officials, under the ultimate authority of the emperor in Beijing, ruled China. These officials were chosen from among those who passed a series of written examinations based mainly on the Chinese classics. Since there was no system of public education, typically only the wealthy could afford to hire private tutors for the many years of study that success in the examinations required. Promising boys from poor families, however, were sometimes sponsored by wealthy families—creating some social mobility. Since those who failed could try again, some people spent literally a lifetime preparing for the exams.

Potentially, the rewards were great. Top officials had immense power and income. According to some estimates, up to ninety-five percent of their income came from bribes and gifts, and a few years in office were sufficient to establish their fortunes. When attempts were made in the mid nineteenth century to reform the educational system by stressing science and technology, virtually the entire gentry class—defined as those who had passed at least the lowest level examination or *purchased* an equivalent degree—opposed it. By the nineteenth century, not only the government officials, but the large landowners, merchants, and compradors (Chinese representatives of foreign business firms) enjoyed the privileges associated with membership in the gentry class.

The lowest official was the county magistrate. Since the counties were comparable in size to an American county, containing perhaps 250,000 people or more, the magistrates could not rule alone, even with substantial supporting staffs. They had to rely on the cooperation of the local gentry, a rural stratum of the same class which dominated the life of the villages and small towns. The local gentry constituted the rural elite, and although their incomes were much smaller than those of the big gentry, they were much higher than the incomes of common people. In all, the gentry owned about three-fourths of the farmland which was rented out—that is, they constituted the greater part of the landlord class.

Even today, more than 80 percent of China's population live in the countryside, and an understanding of the rural heritage is essential to an understanding of the modern economy. About two-thirds of China's peasants were poor.[1] Most poor peasants had some land, but it was an insufficient amount to meet their subsistence needs. As a result, they had to hire themselves out as part-time laborers and engage in handicraft production to make ends meet. Even then, they were right on the margin of subsistence; and when adversity struck, as in the form of drought or some other natural disaster, they died by the tens of thousands. According to the missionary Abbe Regis-Evariste Huc, who spent 1839 to 1851 in China and traveled throughout the country:

> Not a year passes in which a terrific number of persons do not perish of famine in some part or other of China; and the multitude of those who live merely from day to day is incalculable. Let a drought, an inundation, or any accident whatever occur to injure the harvest in a single province, and two-thirds of the population are immediately reduced to a state of starvation. You see them forming themselves into numerous bands—perfect armies of beggars—and proceeding together, men, women and children, to seek in the towns and villages for some little nourishment wherewith to sustain, for a brief interval, their miserable existence. Many fall down fainting by the wayside, and die before they reach the place where they had hoped to find help. You see their bodies lying in the fields, and at the roadside, and you pass without taking notice of them—so familiar is the horrid spectacle.[2]

Better off than the poor and landless peasants, the middle peasants constituted some 20 to 30 percent of the rural population. They had about enough land to meet their basic subsistence needs. The rich peasants, about 7 percent of the population, had sufficient land to hire one or more full-time laborers. The landlords, about 3 percent of the population, divided up their land into small plots to rent out, usually for about half the crop or its equivalent; they had nothing to do with the process of production itself. In China as a whole, about 30 percent of the farmland was held by landlords, with the percentage higher in the more productive regions of central and south China.

This picture of rural China did not change significantly right up to the success of the Communist revolution in 1949, despite the major political and military events. The combination of its own internal weaknesses and intensified foreign interventions around the turn of

---

1. In this discussion of peasant income groups, we are following the classification scheme that was adopted by the Chinese Communists at the time of their first land reform.

2. Quoted in Franz Schurmann and Orville Schell, eds., *Imperial China* (New York: Vintage Press, 1967), 30–31.

the century led to the collapse of the Qing dynasty in 1911 and the establishment of the Republic of China in 1912. The new government was too weak to establish control in most of China, however, and the greater part of the country became subject to the rule of warlords or military dictators. In the mid 1920s, the Nationalist party (Guomindang) under Chiang Kai-shek joined forces with the Communist party to organize an army to march north and unify the country. In 1927, halfway through the so-called Northern Expedition, Chiang turned on his allies and had the Communist party members rounded up and killed. Those who escaped were forced to go underground or move to the countryside. In the rural area of south central China, a Communist base area was formed at the end of the decade.

After a number of unsuccessful attempts to attack the base area in the early 1930s, Chiang, with the aid of military advisers dispatched by the Germans, devised a plan to gradually tighten a noose formed by troops encircling the base area. The Communist forces, led by Mao Zedong, suddenly broke out of the entrapment, going to the west of the country and then north in the famous Long March, which took more than a year and covered some six thousand miles. They ended up in 1936 in Yanan, located in a remote part of north central China, which became their new base area until after World War II.

Meanwhile, Chiang was able to unify much of the country under his leadership when he successfully concluded the Northern Expedition in Beijing in 1928. He was not able, however, to generate meaningful economic development or gain popular support. Rural landowners were a major force in the Nationalist party, and although it passed several land reform measures, these measures never had a serious chance to be implemented. Further, as the representative of the propertied classes, the government was unprepared to introduce the taxation measures needed to finance development activities. Although the Nationalist era was a period of modest modernization of institutions, the traditional class structure remained largely intact.

The economic system of the Nationalist era was increasingly capitalist, but the state continued to control many levers of economic activity through its licensing powers, controls over credit allocation, and so forth. The examination system was eliminated, but the power of the bureaucracy remained largely undiminished. Corruption continued to flourish since private businessmen could not hope to operate without paying off state officials. The gentry class as such disappeared with the end of the imperial system, but its power and property remained largely untouched in the Nationalist era.

In 1931, Japan seized northeast China (Manchuria) and established a puppet state called Manchukuo. Northeast China is relatively rich in resources, and Japan proceeded to develop it as a heavy industrial base and as a supplier of coal and other raw materials to Japan; it remains today the major center of heavy industry in China. In 1937, Japan invaded the rest of China, occupying large parts of north and east central China. The Nationalist government fled to Chongqing in far-off southwest China, where it remained throughout World War II. The United States tried to get Chiang to cooperate in the war against Japan, but he preferred to save his troops to use against the Communists by blockading them in their new north central base.

During the two decades of armed struggle, the Communist party realized clearly that its success relied on popular support. Unlike the warlord and other armies, which often abused the local populations and stole their grain and belongings, the Communist army maintained a strict code of conduct toward the civilian population, paid for what it required, produced much of its own food, and helped local peasants with their own farm work. The Communist army became enormously prestigious and remained so after the revolution. The self-reliance the army practiced indeed characterized the entire base area, since the Nationalist blockade cut the Communists off from the rest of the country. Self-reliance and the cooperative spirit that buttressed it subsequently became a source of great pride in China and a hallmark of post-1949 development.

In the areas they controlled, the Communists carried out land reform, not merely by orders from above but by getting the local people, the poor peasants especially, to participate actively. Their reputation for integrity, support for the poor and oppressed—the majority of the population—and their active fight against the Japanese occupation won the Communists great popular support.

When World War II ended, the civil war broke out again. With American money and arms, Chiang Kai-shek's troops were much better supplied, but the Nationalists lacked popular support and his troops had little heart for the fight. Corruption was rife; and since the government had solved its revenue needs simply by printing more money, a classic hyperinflation broke out, currency became practically worthless, and, to a considerable extent, economic exchange reverted to barter. These economic problems brought ruin to much of China's middle class and served to undermine an important source of Nationalist political support. Initially, the Nationalists held the cities, and the Communists held the countryside; but soon it was the Nationalists' turn to be encircled. One after another the cities fell to the Communists, until finally the Nationalist party and its supporters fled to Taiwan province. Taiwan was an ancient Chinese province, which had been under Japanese colonial rule since 1895 but was returned to China following the Japanese defeat in World War II.

Economic Development and the Transformation of the Chinese Economy

The period from 1949 to 1952 was one of land reform and economic recovery which set the conditions for subsequent growth. In the land reform, an estimated 44 percent of China's farmland was redistributed, resulting in greater equality of per capita holdings throughout the countryside. A series of innovative measures was adopted to restore confidence in the paper currency of the new regime. Bank deposits, for example, were made repayable in "real" terms, that is, they were adjusted for inflation. The state took control over wholesale and retail trade and curtailed the activity of speculators. Excess currency was soaked up through semicompulsory bond sales. State expenditures were cut back. With measures like these, inflation was rapidly brought under control. Vigorous efforts were also made to repair the war-damaged infrastructure. By 1952, industrial and agricultural production, which had fallen sharply, were restored to their previous peak levels in most areas.

China's First Five-Year Plan took place between 1953 and 1957. During this time, industrial production rose at great speed and whole new industries were established. Table 12.1 gives an indication of the

Table 12.1
Indicators of Economic Performance during First Five-Year Plan, 1953–1957

	1952	1957
National figures (million yuan):		
Agricultural output value	34,000	42,500
Industrial output value	11,500	25,700
National income	58,900	90,800
Agricultural products (10,000 tons):		
Grain	16,390	19,505
Cotton	130.4	164.0
Edible oil	419.3	419.6
Industrial products:		
Coal (100 million tons)	0.66	1.31
Electricity (100 million kwh)	73	193
Crude oil (10,000 tons)	44	146
Steel (10,000 tons)	135	535
Bicycles (10,000)	8.0	80.6

Sources: Su Wenming, ed., *Economic Readjustment and Reform* (Beijing: Beijing Review, 1982), 208–10; Lin Wei and A. Chao, eds., *China's Economic Reforms* (Philadelphia: University of Pennsylvania Press, 1982), 239.

Note: Similar to other socialist countries, China's national income accounting differs from that used in the West. Agricultural and industrial output figures count the values of raw materials and intermediate goods more than once. National income refers to the net output value of the five sectors engaged in material production or closely related to it: agriculture, industry, construction, transport and communications, and commerce. It omits many kinds of output included in the West under the category of services.

economic performance during the First Five-Year Plan period and highlights the speed of industrial growth.

The Soviet Union made two major economic loans to China in the early to mid 1950s for a total of $430 million. Soviet aid accounted for only 3 percent of China's financing needs in the First Five-Year Plan period, but it was concentrated on the 156 large-scale projects at the core of the plan. Moreover, Soviet technical support was of great importance, especially in the establishment of entirely new industries. Perhaps of greatest importance in terms of Soviet influence, however, was the fact that the Chinese Communist party had no experience managing large-scale industry when it came to power; it was natural for it to look to the Soviet model. It is useful to recall that in economic terms the Soviet model has two basic features: (1) heavily centralized, hierarchical planning and management, and (2) investment priority to heavy industry.

Through the First Five-Year Plan period, China's industrial organization and economic planning indeed closely resembled the Soviet model. Most large-scale enterprises were incorporated in vertical networks with ultimate authority residing in the various industrial ministries in Beijing. Planning was largely a top-down process, with plans formulated at the center. Such plans were unable to permit much flexibility or take account of differing local situations; the problems were quite similar to those which the Soviet Union encountered.

Great Leap Forward (1958–1960)

China responded by carrying out a major decentralization of industry in late 1957–58. Control of most enterprises was transferred from the ministries to provincial and local governments. This reform, it should be emphasized, was an *administrative* decentralization. There was no *market* decentralization in the sense of allowing enterprises decision-making authority to respond to changing input and product prices. Industrial production and pricing remained bureaucratically administered, therefore, but the layers of administration were brought closer to the enterprises.

In 1958, the decentralization effort was extended to the attempted development of very small-scale rural industries, the most famous of which were the so-called backyard steel furnaces. The production of these industries was not meant to divert resources from their large-scale counterparts but was part of China's effort to industrialize by "walking on two legs." This policy was designed to make use simultaneously of modern, technologically advanced, capital-intensive methods on the one hand and traditional, technically simple, labor-intensive methods on the other. The attempt to develop small-scale industries in the countryside in 1958 was part of a massive nationwide movement to increase agricultural and industrial output dramatically in a few short years through the mobilization of the entire population along semimilitary lines to intensify productive activity sharply. The 1958–1960 period became known by the slogan of the time as the period of the Great Leap Forward (GLF).

The GLF was intended to overcome some of the problems that emerged during the First Five-Year Plan. Perhaps most serious of these was the imbalance between industrial and agricultural growth. As Table 12.1 indicates, between 1952 and 1957 industrial output value grew by 123 percent, while that of agriculture grew by 25 percent. As a consequence, the government was unable to meet its food procurement plans for the rapidly growing cities or obtain adequate raw materials for light industry or export, both of which depended heavily on agricultural production. At the same time, net Soviet aid ended in 1955, and from 1956 until 1965, when its debt to the Soviet Union was fully repaid, China's exports to the USSR exceeded its imports from the USSR. China could have restored balance to its economy by cutting back sharply on its industrialization program and devoting the resources released to the agricultural sector. Instead, China attempted to utilize its surplus labor to develop agriculture and rural industries without diverting resources from the industrial sector.

Although the Great Leap Forward constituted a break from the Soviet model of centralized planning and one-man management, it preserved the concentration of investment resources on industrial development. The great bulk of resources used to underwrite the creation of small industry in rural areas came from the rural areas themselves—extensive labor mobilization and use of local raw materials. If anything, real incomes in rural areas were lowered during the Great Leap Forward in order to finance a more rapid industrial development (and because of organizational problems). It was not until the post-1961 period that the Chinese formally repudiated the Soviet policy of according industry priority over agriculture.[3]

As part of the Great Leap Forward, a striking new collective institution, the people's commune, appeared in the countryside; and by September 1958 some 98 percent of rural households were members. The people's communes, which persisted as a major rural institution long after the leap was over, marked the culmination of the process of agricultural collectivization which had begun as soon as the land reform was over. The Chinese leaders believed—with good reason—that small-scale private farming could not bring about the transformation of Chinese agriculture that modernization required, that collective action would be necessary. At the same time, they were well aware of the resistance arising from forced collectivization in the Soviet Union, which held back Soviet agriculture for many years. They resolved to carry out collectivization gradually, on a step-by-

---

3. See the elaboration of this point in Alexander Eckstein, *Communist China's Economic Growth and Foreign Trade* (New York: McGraw-Hill, 1966), 32–34.

step basis, so that people would learn to act together and see the real advantages of mutual prosperity that collectivization was expected to bring. As we shall see, however, the rapid transformation of agricultural organization in the 1950s was anything but gradual in practice.

At first, mutual aid teams, seasonal or permanent, were organized on a wide scale; between 1950 and 1954 the proportion of peasant households which were members rose from 11 to 58 percent. The team members retained their own land and most of their own implements but often chipped in funds to own part of a draft animal or expensive equipment. They would work as a unit, going from one member's land to the next in succession, and usually included about eight households.

In the mid 1950s, elementary agricultural producers' cooperatives (APCs) received increased emphasis. They began to replace the mutual aid teams, and between June and December 1955 the proportion of peasant households which were members jumped from 14 to 59 percent. The elementary APCs usually consisted of natural villages, with considerable variation around the average of about thirty households. Like the mutual aid teams, the elementary APC members retained title to their own plots of land, but, unlike the teams, land use was collectively organized. After the elementary APCs met their various financial obligations—taxes, production expenses, and so forth—what was left over was divided among the members, about half based on the amount of land contributed and half on the amount of labor.

The elementary APCs were considered to be "semisocialist" because part of their members' income continued to be based on the property they had contributed. In 1956, a year after the elementary APCs had been organized on a wide scale, the "fully socialist" advanced APCs replaced them; by December 1956 some 88 percent of China's rural households were advanced APC members. These differed from the elementary APCs in two main respects. First, the return to land was eliminated, making it possible to distribute the net income among the members—after setting some aside for welfare and savings and investment—entirely on the basis of their labor contribution to the collective. Second, the average size of the advanced APCs was about two hundred households, or seven times that of the elementary APCs.

Their larger size enabled the advanced APCs to tackle larger-scale projects in irrigation, terracing of fields, and other forms of rural capital construction. They were not big enough, however, to undertake very large-scale projects, so in the winter of 1957–58, some of the advanced APCs cooperated in carrying out some very large-scale projects. This cooperation paved the way in 1958 to the formation of an unprecedented form of collective institution, the people's communes, which 98 percent of the rural households had joined by the end of September 1958. The people's communes are at once economic, social, and political institutions, organizing the entire life of the countryside into large-scale, relatively self-contained institutions. They carry on everyday agricultural production and farmland capital construction, set up and operate small-scale industries and handicraft workshops, sponsor cultural activities, maintain clinics, hospitals, and public schools through the high school level, and are responsible for the militia and public security. They were formed by merging the local township governments with a group of advanced APCs and, at first, averaged about twenty-five thousand people.

The people's communes were formed at the start of the GLF and were meant to play a key role in the dramatic acceleration of agricultural and industrial growth that was anticipated. While the GLF ended in failure in 1960, the commune system was consolidated and established the economic framework for Chinese agriculture into the 1980s, when a new period of reform began to change its nature and role dramatically. Before its consolidation, however, the commune system had a rocky start. As we have seen, it abruptly blanketed the countryside in a period of just a few months in 1958, without proper planning and without a necessary experimentation period. In fact, a large number of advanced APCs did not even go through a single harvest before being transformed.

The communes have four distinct levels: the household, the production team, the production brigade, and the commune level. (The term "commune" refers both to the institution as a whole and to the highest administrative level. When we use the term "commune" here, we will be using it to mean the whole institution. When we use the term "commune level," we will mean the highest administrative level.) The production team usually corresponds to the former elementary APC or neighborhood and thus averages about 30 households, while the production brigade usually corresponds to the former advanced APC or village and thus averages about 250 households—there is considerable variation about these averages, and some teams and brigades are three or four times this size, or even larger.

One of the major problems encountered when the communes were first formed was a consequence of making the commune level the unit of distribution. Since income was supposed to be based on collective labor input, accurate record-keeping and accounting skills were essential. These, in fact, were lacking, so that no one knew whether or not he or she would be paid for a day's collective labor or how much he or she would receive if paid. The members' income in a true collective is found by subtracting all costs and taxes from gross revenues. After setting aside funds for collective purposes, the remainder is then divided up among the members according to their labor contribution. What the labor contribution will be worth in a true collective is always uncertain because it won't be known until the end of the production period (when the harvest is in), but the manner in which the communes were first set up compounded these uncertainties.

There was no way to know if one's own work contribution would be properly recorded, whether expenses and receipts would be properly recorded, or whether villages several miles distant were inflating their labor claims. Thus, it was unclear whether there would be any financial reward at all for collective labor, and under these circumstances work incentives became quite weak. Moreover, the wide separation between an individual's work effort and net income at the commune level greatly diminished the effect of material incentives. They were weakened still further by the widespread expectation that the communes would usher in a true communist society—one that carried out distribution according to need.[4] They were further weakened by the efforts of rural party cadres, who were responsible for carrying out the rural policies, to speed the transition to communism by providing as many living essentials as possible free of charge. Food, for example, was often provided in this way in communal dining halls. Since food accounted for more than half of most peasant household expenditures, the communes had to withhold a large part of their net incomes to pay for the food rather than distribute the income to their members on the basis of their labor efforts. From the standpoint of individual households, to the extent they received food and other necessities whether or not they worked or however hard they worked, the income incentive to work was reduced.

The national economic policies of the Great Leap Forward further undermined work incentives by the general economic dislocation they caused. The great effort to develop local industries especially tended to tie up the limited rail and other transport facilities, which carried coal and other raw materials while harvested food was left to rot for lack of adequate transport facilities. Most of the frenzied rural industrialization efforts of the GLF were carried out without adequate investigation and led, as a consequence, to massive waste of resources and labor. Thus, the steel manufactured in the backyard furnaces proved to be extremely brittle, snapping too readily in the cold or when subjected to even minor stress.

---

4. One traditional distinction among capitalist, socialist, and communist societies is the distribution system. Under capitalism distribution is according to property ownership and labor, with differences in property ownership accounting for the most significant differences in income. Under socialism distribution is according to labor, while under communism distribution is according to need. These distinctions are useful but insufficient. A more general criterion for distinguishing between capitalism and socialism is according to which class is the principal controller and beneficiary of economic activity. Under capitalism this is the capitalist class, or the owners of private property, whereas under socialism theoretically it is the class composed of workers, peasants, and all who must work for a living.

344 Chinα: A Changing Model

In 1958, most of the year's agricultural work was completed when the communes were formed, with harvesting the only major task remaining; and grain production rose to 200 million tons from 195 million in 1957. In 1959 and 1960, however, output fell precipitously: to an estimated 170 million tons in 1959 and 143.5 million tons in 1960.[5] Chinese government sources officially blamed unprecedented natural disasters for the agricultural collapse in these years. While these disasters were undoubtedly quite severe and contributory, the primary responsibility lay with the adventurism of public policy—hastily putting the GLF policies into effect without thorough testing or consideration of their consequenes. The consequence was a period of severe malnutrition and hardship in the countryside, which—according to unsupported claims of the present government—resulted in "millions" of deaths.

Spurred by the collapse in grain production, the government took steps to change the organization of the newly formed communes. Most important, the unit of account was transferred in the early sixties from the commune level (approximately 3,200 households on average) to the production brigade (approximately 240 households on average) and then to the production team (approximately 30 households on average). That is, the production team became the primary unit for carrying out agricultural production, accounting for profits and losses, and distributing net income among the team members. At the same time, the provision of free food and services was cut back sharply. Rural markets, which had been greatly curtailed, were allowed to revive somewhat. Peasants were allowed private plots of land to produce for the market or their own consumption, and the average size of the communes was reduced; in 1980 there were some fifty-four thousand communes averaging about fifteen thousand members each. Their size depended in large measure on geographical conditions, so that in flat, densely populated regions communes may have had more than fifty thousand members.

The principal economic advantages of the commune system of organization pertain to economies of scale in production and consumption. For instance, it facilitates the effective mobilization and organization of labor during the slack season. To the extent that people could work on rural capital construction projects at this time, investment could increase without any sacrifice of alternative production activities, notably the production of food or other consumer goods. As we have seen, the communes emerged in part from efforts to harness such "surplus" labor, with the main emphasis on water conservancy—such as the construction of dams, irrigation and drainage facilities, and so forth. By the early 1970s, each winter more than

5. U.S. Department of Agriculture, *China: Review of Agriculture in 1981 and Outlook for 1982* (Washington, D.C.: Department of Agriculture, 1982), 36.

one hundred million people participated in rural capital construction work.

The communes have provided the basis for the development of small-scale rural industries at the brigade and commune level. The commune members provide the labor force and often the raw materials and some of the market as well. The industrial enterprises tend to be oriented toward meeting local needs—such as agricultural machinery—or processing locally produced agricultural goods. With initial financial support, mainly from the communes and government loans, the enterprises accounted for about one-third of total commune production value and a substantial share of commune income in the early 1980s.

In 1981, the industrial enterprises at the commune and brigade level employed 19.8 million workers and accounted for 19 percent of China's coal production, 80 percent of its building materials (bricks, tiles, etc.), 40 percent of its garment production, and 70 percent of its medium- and small-sized farm implements.[6] Thus, the commune created a setting in which all-around rural development could take place.

There are also possible economies of scale in agricultural production itself, allowing land and crop rotation or the use of more sophisticated machinery and techniques. Additionally, the commune system allowed for economies of scale in the consumption of certain services, such as health, education, and culture. China's leaders found that the communes facilitated political control in the countryside. The abuse of this control undermined the commune system, however, for it created a tendency toward governing rural areas by means of authoritarian commands rather than persuasion or democracy. This tendency, in turn, contributed to weak work incentives and greater alienation, and, as we shall see, it underlies recent attempts at reform in the commune system.

The Cultural Revolution

The Great Proletarian Cultural Revolution—or Cultural Revolution (CR) for short—is a milestone in China's development. It marks a great conflict between two differing interpretations of the nature of socialist development in China and two opposing strategies for bringing that development about. To a great extent, its genesis lies in the Great Leap Forward and its aftermath.

The GLF marked a radical departure from conventional approaches to economic development. It involved, on the one hand, a great decentralization and reliance on the productive power of the masses, and, on the other hand, a form of centralization in the sense that the masses were consciously directed and mobilized from above

---

6. *Beijing Review*, 25, 48 (Nov. 29, 1982): 3–4.

by the Communist party, which today criticizes its policies of this period as "ultra-left." As we have seen, the collapse of agricultural production began in 1959, the second year of the GLF; a similar collapse of industrial production began in 1960. In each case the decline persisted for two years.

To foster recovery and renewed growth, a relaxation of controls was implemented as part of a general movement back toward a more conventional development strategy. Rural markets revived and private plots were permitted. Professionals, in all spheres, whose advice had been denigrated during the GLF, were once again influential. Under these circumstances, the power of the bureaucracy grew; it appeared that unless some decisive action were taken, an elite would emerge in China, much as it had emerged in the Soviet Union. In Communist countries, those with access to the power of the state potentially have enormous power. Although they are supposed to be exercising that power in the interest of the working people, the question arises, what means can ensure that it will be so exercised?

In China, with a history of bureaucratic power and abuse, Chairman Mao perceived a new elite emerging, an elite of high government officials, educated people and administrators, people with power and income denied to the ordinary man and woman. Most of the Party leadership did not see this as a major problem; and even though Mao was Chairman, being in the minority, he could not implement his ideas through the Party. So he appealed directly to the masses, to young people especially, to revive the revolutionary tradition by challenging directly power holders, including senior Party members. With his enormous personal prestige as the leader of the Chinese revolution, Mao evoked an enthusiastic mass response, and thus the Cultural Revolution was launched. Its active phase lasted from 1966 to 1969, but many of the policies it spawned persisted until Mao's death in 1976; so we may properly refer to the entire 1966–1976 decade as the Cultural Revolution period.

According to Marxian thought, the economic base of society, including its ownership system, can be distinguished from its "superstructure" of ideology and institutions. Although the two interact, it is the economic base which is ultimately decisive. According to the thinking of the CR, however, this would not necessarily be the case. Socialism had indeed replaced a semifeudal, semicapitalist economic system, but most of the values and ideas of the presocialist period persisted in the superstructure. Unless these values and ideas were consciously combatted, unless a cultural revolution took place, the transition to socialism in China would be cut short and a Soviet type of state socialism or bureaucratism would be restored. The advocates of the CR in China contended that the main danger was the "capitalist-roaders" in power, and they sought to remake the culture, institutions, and ideology of the nation. The so-called Gang of Four, headed by Jiang Qing, Mao's wife, were among the leaders of the CR.

Hence, the development strategy espoused by Mao and embodied in the CR was one of *simultaneous* development. The social relations of socialism were to be created simultaneously with the creation of a modern industrial base (or the development of the material forces of production). This approach stands in contrast to the one advocated by Lenin, Stalin, and other Soviet leaders who adhered to a *sequential* development strategy. That is, the material base would have first to be developed and abundance created before socialist consciousness and behavior could emerge. As interpreted by Stalin, this meant the subordination of socialist ideals to rapid industrialization; equality, democracy, and cooperation could be worried about in the distant future.

Perhaps the central slogan of the Cultural Revolution was "serve the people." All those holding positions of social power and responsibility were exhorted to consider their positions as held in trust for the social good rather than as means of pursuing personal benefit. The "May 7th cadre schools" institutionalized this thrust. All people with administrative posts or authoritative social positions were expected to spend six months or so, sometimes longer, at the May 7th cadre schools in the countryside. There they would engage in physical labor, mainly agricultural work, half-time and study and discussion half-time, reading the socialist classics and reflecting on their own social roles—whether they were really doing their utmost to serve the people.

Making a reality of serving the people did not depend on transforming the consciousness of bureaucrats alone. In most work places and institutions "revolutionary committees" would be formed to take control, sometimes incorporating previous leaders but often thrusting them aside. In communes and factories alike, the revolutionary committees assumed control. They were charged with reconsidering the rules and operating characteristics of their institutions from the standpoint of whether they genuinely contributed to the development of a socialist culture.

Consider, for example, the question of working hard for one's own material gain. Bonuses had been widely used in Chinese industry prior to the Cultural Revolution, but in the CR, material incentives were criticized severely for perpetuating the capitalist ethic of pursuing one's own interest rather than that of the group. Thus, bonuses were almost completely eliminated during the CR. In the countryside, too, the method of assigning labor-day credits (on which income distribution was based) to different tasks came under attack. Those people who meticulously cleaned and cared for collective property after using it would earn less, for example, than those who rushed from one task to another without doing so.

In every institution, questions were raised during the CR concerning the suitability of its rules, regulations, and operating practices for a socialist society. At the largest department store in Canton, for example, the staff met frequently to consider this. The members felt that in a number of respects they had not done all they should to "serve the people." In stocking items, too much attention had been paid to profit margins rather than to the importance of the items in people's everyday lives. This practice was remedied. The department store also opened a comprehensive repair service and kept a portion of the store open twenty-four hours to serve workers on night shifts. In addition, it increased surveys to learn the needs of its customers and sent representatives out with samples to take orders from groups which could not readily come to the store.

In education, the CR brought a severe criticism of the existing establishment. College entrance examinations, it was argued, discriminate against peasant children since the schools and home environments in the countryside cannot prepare these children to compete against urban children. The point, of course, was well taken. The CR solution was to drop entrance examinations. Instead, all high school students were to work for at least two years after graduation, and then some of them could hope to be nominated for college by their work places—normally factory or commune. The point of education was not to advance some particular individual's career, it was argued, but to train people imbued with the spirit to serve the community.

The universities were closed for most of the time between 1966 and 1970, and when they were reopened the new admission system was put into effect. At the same time, the curriculum was changed drastically, course examinations were abolished, and great emphasis was put on regular practical work as part of education. Thus, for example, chemistry students were expected to spend ten weeks each year working in a chemical factory as part of their education. The criticism of examinations reflected in large measure a feeling that examinations were suited to the individual-career orientations of capitalist society but not to the collective-cooperative ethos of socialism. It was felt that they inspired students to compete against one another rather than to work together toward common goals, and that they divided students from teachers as well as from one another.

In one sense, then, the CR period was one of high idealism, but it had a much darker aspect as well. We should understand, first of all, that it was a period of intense politicization of all aspects of life. In practically every institution different factions formed and struggled with one another, often violently. Commonly, each faction would claim to represent Mao's "real" thought. People who resisted change or simply held different ideas were commonly called "capitalist-roaders," a term of great opprobrium. They were dealt with harshly, dismissed from their posts, and sent to the countryside for "re-education" through labor. A peasant who wanted to use his private plot to increase his income (the plots had been established for this purpose), a professor who insisted that examinations may serve a proper educational purpose, or a symphony violinist whose crime was playing "bourgeois" music were all vulnerable to attack.

In addition to Western music, most of China's traditional literature and performing arts were banned because they emerged during the "feudal" (presocialist) era and were seen as perpetuating presocialist sensibilities and ideas. Ancient temples and other cultural relics were often attacked and destroyed for the same reason when the CR was in its early, most active phase. The greatest damage, however, was done to individuals. There was no system of individual rights or protection under law—indeed, there was hardly any law as such. Often, the factional conflicts were used to settle old scores or in opportunistic ways to seek personal advancement. The concept of "capitalist-roader"—ostensibly someone whose ideas and practices would lead to the restoration of capitalism—was so vague it could be applied to practically anyone.

Even where the actions taken were sincerely motivated, enormous injustice was often the result. The activities carried out were like those of vigilante groups; people from the top to the bottom of society were affected. Deng Xiaoping, for example, who emerged as the architect of China's reform policies and the most important leader in China after Mao's death (although he declined a title higher than that of Vice Premier), was paraded around Beijing wearing a dunce cap. His crimes included efforts to prevent the ill-treatment of other leaders and playing bridge with people whose relatives had been capitalists. In general, there was no private space for individuals during the CR, and people could be victimized merely for holding "the wrong" ideas. When the CR was over and discredited in China, various official sources estimated that perhaps 10 percent of the Chinese population, that is, one hundred million people, suffered from injustice during the CR. This estimate may be too high, but it is clear that those who suffered number in the millions.

Since "correct" thought or ideology was given such emphasis, it was only natural for China's leaders during the CR to engage in censorship on a massive scale. It was hoped that people would be inspired by the news media and arts to serve the communal welfare unselfishly. Thus, the press would often carry stories about workers at a factory giving up their day off to meet the planned output quota, or about similarly altruistic behavior to serve as an example to others. The reality, however, was more complex.

For every Chinese worker there is a little black book detailing his or her political behavior, kept by the factory director or another official; in the rare case that he or she moves from one enterprise to another, the book goes along. When workers are considered for promotion—or, during the CR, when people were struggled against—their records are consulted. To avoid trouble, it was important not to have black marks against oneself. The first imperative was not to do anything that could single one out in a potentially negative way. Thus, when political meetings were called, as was constantly the case during the CR, everyone would be sure to attend.

Some workers sought to ascertain what the leadership wanted and to behave accordingly. If they saw that factory leaders were under pressure to increase output and wanted them to "volunteer" to work overtime without pay, they would do so. This would put great pressure on the majority, who didn't want to be singled out in a negative way, to do likewise. Thus, what appeared in press reports as selfless collective action typically had a far more complex set of motivations.

In fact, although the ideology of the CR stressed worker control, the economic institutions had not been reformed in a way to permit this. For example, in the great majority of cases, there was no regular method of workers participating in the selection of the revolutionary committees which ran the factories. The factional conflicts that arose in the 1966–1969 period were commonly ended only by the sending in of army officers to establish control and assume authority. Together with party cadres appointed from above, they assumed control of the "revolutionary committees." Despite the title, the old forms of enterprise hierarchy were for the most part replaced by the new ones.

One of the major premises of the CR, albeit an implicit one, was that punishing people in authority—that is, bureaucrats—for holding the wrong ideas could lead to reform of the system. In fact, however, the problem of bringing about a transition to socialist society is far more complicated. In a Soviet-type centrally planned economy, a single political and economic hierarchy tends to emerge. Those who have access to the authority and resources of the state have enormous potential power. Ostensibly, workers, peasants, and all those doing socially useful labor constitute the dominant classes in socialist society; and that power is being exercised in their interest. But institutional reform which invests considerable real power in the direct producers (workers, peasants, etc.) must certainly accompany the moral awakening of bureaucrats if socialism is to be achieved. Public ownership of the means of production may be a necessary condition for socialism; but the full realization of socialist goals can come only when working people take control of their own lives, their own work places, and their own society at every level.

Despite the attacks on bureaucrats, political power in Chinese society became even more centralized and hierarchical during the CR. Ordinary people were afraid to speak out or assume decision-making responsibility, and within enterprises even minor decisions were routinely passed on to the head of the revolutionary committee or the secretary of the factory Party branch. Despite the continuation of formal central administration of the economy, the attack on functional specialists and the bureaucracy made central planning nearly impossible during most of the CR. Central planning, in fact, became weaker and more arbitrary. Five-year plans existed in name only, and data on economic conditions and performance were extremely scarce.

The CR brought to a peak one strand in Chinese socialism: the attempt to create socialist society by reforming people's consciousness through pervasive propaganda appeals on the one hand and the threat of ostracism or harsher sanctions on the other. It was hoped that people would be motivated to work not for material gain or personal advancement but for the welfare of society. Accordingly, after 1957 regular wage increases in industry were discontinued and for two decades real individual wages failed to rise. During the same 1957–1977 period, in agriculture the increase in discretionary income from collective labor was negligible: from 57 to 65 yuan, or slightly more than four U.S. dollars, spread over twenty years. Although incomes rose slightly, the hours of work rose much more; so the earnings per hour worked actually fell—by an amount estimated between 15 and 36 percent.[7]

Changes in consciousness arise through experience, however, not through persuasion; the main lesson the Chinese citizen learned from the CR was that one must be cautious about revealing one's true feelings. Ironically, the wage freeze seemed to make people more concerned with material compensation rather than less. State-owned enterprises have an eight-grade wage system, with workers in the top grade earning about three times the wage in the bottom grade. To a considerable extent, promotion in the system depends on seniority. Since workers in the bottom grades could look forward to wages comparable to those received by workers in the higher grades, to be received when they had attained comparable experience, there was no sense of injustice. When wage increases were stopped, however, this wage increment system was no longer the case. Thus, a worker who began working about 1960 might be frozen at the first-grade wage level while workers who began five years earlier earned much more. In 1970, despite this same worker's ten years of experience, and perhaps comparable or greater productivity, the discrepancy between these wages would persist. Meanwhile, new workers would be earning as much as the worker with ten years of experience, who by this time was apt to have a family to support. (Although both men and women routinely enter the labor force in China today, young workers are often living with their parents and have much lower expenses.) Under these circumstances, substantial inequities arose and people became highly conscious of them.

In education, comparable problems arose which prevented the CR

---

7. Victor D. Lippit, "Socialist Development in China," in Victor D. Lippit and Mark Selden, eds., *The Transition to Socialism in China* (Armonk, N.Y.: M. E. Sharpe, 1982), 116–58.

reforms from having their intended effect. The elimination of examinations and stress on political criteria for entry to and promotion in the educational system simply resulted in a poorly educated generation. Research in pure science was stopped altogether—with consequences still to be felt—as was all graduate education between 1966 and 1978. It was felt incorrectly that professional skills could be developed by merely apprenticing graduates to current practitioners. Student life was completely politicized; and teachers who tried to maintain academic standards were subject to being accused of being capitalist-roaders—that is, counterrevolutionaries—and to being harassed and dismissed from their posts and sent to the countryside for "re-education."

When Mao died in September 1976, the four main leaders of the Cultural Revolution, led by Jiang Qing, Mao's wife, were accused of plotting a coup to seize state power and were arrested. Dubbed the "Gang of Four," they were also accused of many abuses of power during the CR and were brought to trial. Jiang Qing was sentenced to death, but her sentence was later commuted to life imprisonment. At the same time, a thoroughgoing reform movement—reversing the CR—has infused all areas of the Chinese economy and society.

The Post-Mao Reforms

The Cultural Revolution left China with a legacy of problems. For two decades, from 1957 to 1977, real wage payments to individuals failed to rise. During the same period, there was no increase in *per capita* grain production and peasant incomes increased only slightly. Industrial growth continued at a rapid pace—about 10 percent yearly— but only because the share of national income going to investment was raised sharply. This increase in investment limited the production of consumption goods and was reflected in the failure of real incomes to rise significantly. The tendency toward a highly unbalanced economic growth pattern began in the early fifties but was accentuated during the CR.

To justify the inattention to people's material welfare, the Gang of Four placed great emphasis on ideological exhortation and mass campaigns to criticize "counterrevolutionary" thought and thinkers. Socialism was to be brought to China, they claimed, by each individual working for the good of all rather than pursuing personal benefit. This assertion, however, is only partly correct. In a well-working socialist society, the principle of working for the good of others in addition to (not instead of) pursuing one's own interest must have a major place. However, the attempt by the Gang of Four to bring about through rhetoric a complete denial of self, summed up succinctly in the slogan of the period, "fight self," proved to be both misguided and counterproductive.

As the Chinese economy grew after 1958, it increasingly encountered the systemic problems of centrally planned economies. The various enterprises had relatively little room for maneuver or initiative. Higher authorities told the enterprises what to produce, whom to hire, and where to obtain their raw materials, besides approving and funding all capital goods purchases. Further, the state took all the profits and bore all the losses. During the CR, moreover, wage raises and bonuses were, for the most part, eliminated.

In the post-Mao reform period, the legitimacy of improving living standards has been re-established and made a cornerstone of the development strategy. From 1970 to 1978, an average of 36 percent of national income was used for investment; by 1981 this figure had been reduced to 30 percent, and the reform target is 25 percent. For every 1 percentage point decrease in the investment rate, there is a corresponding increase in the share of national income devoted to consumption. Further, within the investment sphere, the share of expenditure devoted to improving people's living standards directly (rather than to expanding production) has risen markedly. Thus, the portion of capital construction funds devoted to worker housing, science, education, culture, and so forth rose from 17.4 percent in 1978 to 33.7 percent in 1980.

Of course, an increase in the present share of consumption does not necessarily mean more consumer goods in the long run. If the decline of investment means less economic growth, then there will be fewer producers' goods and fewer consumer goods in the future. The trade-off is between present consumer goods and future consumer goods. The current Chinese leaders hope that increasing present consumption will strengthen work incentives and enhance growth. If their strategy is correct, the decline in investment will be compensated by improvements in economic efficiency, leading to greater growth in the future.

Instead of basing increased output on channeling almost the entire economic surplus into capital goods and structures, the new strategy seeks to base it on scientific and technological development in conjunction with increased entrepreneurship and initiative at the enterprise level. This, in turn, requires introducing an appropriate system of rewards and inducements to motivate economic behavior. Ideological concerns and unselfish behavior remain extremely important in China, but the one-sided emphasis on ideology of the Cultural Revolution has been replaced by what the Chinese leaders hope to be a more balanced appeal to community interest and self-interest.

Industrial Reform

The basic direction of China's industrial reform is to maintain the overall planning system while increasing the role of the market within it, always leaving the market subordinate. This is done to assure that the basic thrust of economic activity will always be to serve social objectives rather than private profit objectives. Thus, for example, in the early stages of the post-1976 reform when great stress was placed on improving living standards, directives from the state were necessary to reorient economic activity accordingly. Overall capital construction had to be cut down. Capital construction that did take place had to be reoriented toward serving agriculture and light industry rather than serving the further expansion of the capital goods industry. Light industry had to be given priority in obtaining inputs. The market simply could not be relied upon to achieve these objectives.

Under the economic reform, China's industrial enterprises must still meet plan quotas, but beyond these they can produce what they want and sell to the government or on the open market. For such nonquota or overquota items, moreover, they can buy their own raw materials wherever they can get the best prices. These changes have increased flexibility and initiative considerably. Thus, for example, one firm producing precision equipment for the capital goods industry found the sharp reduction in capital expenditures leaving a substantial proportion of its plant capacity unutilized. It developed instead new precision machinery for making watches, machinery very much in demand because of the planned rapid expansion in the consumer goods sector. It advertised its new equipment and received orders from all over the country, enabling it to produce at full capacity.

In another instance, the Seamless Steel Tube Plant of Chengdu, in southwest China, received a government order for eighty thousand tons of steel pipe, leaving thirty thousand tons of capacity unused. On checking with the Ministry of Metallurgical Industry in Beijing, it found that China had plans to import oil pipes of a kind that had not previously been produced domestically. It offered to undertake the production instead and received the order.

Enterprises must have more than the freedom to undertake initiatives like these; they must have the incentive. Under the reform regulations, a large share of profits can be retained by the firms for (1) bonuses, (2) housing and worker welfare, and (3) investment. Further, since promotions within the eight-grade wage system are again possible, good work can be rewarded with promotions as well as bonuses. Typically, the enterprise keeps 5 percent of its planned profit and 20 percent of its above-plan profit, with the rest going to the state. Different practices exist, however, and the system is still in flux with a variety of experiments under way to establish the optimum balance between the interests of the state or whole society and those of the enterprise and its employees.

However, the material incentives (retained profits, bonuses, and higher incomes) are meaningful only if production above plan quotas is a general phenomenon. That is, the desired goods must be available to be purchased. This, in turn, implies the existence of plans that are "slack" (relatively easy to meet) as opposed to "taut" (straining production capacity). In fact, relative to the Soviet Union, China consistently has had slack plans since the mid fifties. This circumstance continues to be true today. Nonetheless, there have been consistent complaints that enterprises cannot obtain the goods they desire to improve enterprise social facilities or to expand production.[8]

Together with the expanded powers handed over to enterprises, efforts are being made to democratize the work place. Elections of section chiefs and workshop heads appear to be increasingly common, and in a few experimental cases even factory directors have been elected by the workers. Previously, the factory branch secretary of the Communist party wielded the real authority, and even routine operating decisions were passed on to him or her. Now, the Party has ordered its branches *not* to interfere in factory management. Additionally, there appears to be an ongoing revival of the congresses of workers and staff, which were eliminated in the CR. The congress, whose members are elected by all the workers and staff members, is responsible, in theory, for the orientation and policy of production and management, factory rules, rewards and punishments, and supervision of the management. The director makes regular reports to the congress, which discusses and must approve them. We do not yet have enough information, however, to determine how much actual worker participation or democratization is being achieved. To be sure, there have even been some indications during 1983 that workplace hierarchy and discipline are receiving renewed emphasis.

Other reforms in the industrial system include giving firms the authority to export directly (rather than through a state export-import company), to obtain loans directly from foreign banks, and to retain a portion of the foreign exchange earnings for their own use. Also, firms which consistently lose money can be closed or merged, and new contractual relationships are being encouraged between enterprises. Thus, for example, a commune factory may receive technical guidance from a state-owned factory and serve as a subcontractor, producing components for the state-owned factory.

The old concept of the "iron rice bowl," or guaranteed jobs, is also being challenged. Layoffs and discharges are now acceptable, although it is questionable how prevalent they will become. It should also be noted that, unlike the USSR and Eastern Europe, there is virtually no job mobility in China, with the exception of a few experiments. Workers are assigned jobs by the state, usually for life. A worker can, of course, apply for a transfer. But transfers are generally

8. Christine Wong, "The Economics of Shortage and the Problem of Post-Mao Reforms in China," paper presented at the Modern China Seminar, East Asian Research Institute, Columbia University, New York, February 10, 1983.

difficult to obtain. With the new system, it will be interesting to see how these characteristics of the labor market might change.

As part of the post-Mao reform movement, young people who had been forced to settle in the countryside were allowed to return to their urban homes, and over ten million did so. At the same time, the high birth rates of the 1960s resulted in a huge influx into the labor market of high school and junior high school graduates. As a result, unemployment has reappeared in urban areas. At the end of 1982, 2.6 percent of the urban labor force was officially unemployed. Eighty percent of this group were recent high school graduates; many were trying to enter college,[9] but most were simply waiting for their first job assignment, which normally took about six months to receive.

Urban cooperatives are also being encouraged, especially as a means of providing employment and increasing urban services. Even individual enterprises are permitted again, although they account for only about 1 percent of total urban employment. The individual enterprises can have no more than a few assistants or apprentices, and they are concentrated in such fields as repair services, snack stands, and other small businesses. Urban cooperatives, by contrast, tend to be much larger and may operate restaurants, engage in handicraft production, and so forth. They are able to provide more employment, as a result of greater labor intensity, for a given level of capital expenditures than state enterprises, have more flexibility, and can provide competitive pressure for state-owned enterprises to improve their services.

In conjunction with the spreading financial responsibility reforms, part of the income of shop employees is now based, in a limited experiment, on their sales performance. Also, the existence of cooperative shops and restaurants puts some pressure on state-owned enterprises to improve their service. The cooperatives, it should be noted, unlike "true" cooperatives, do not pay their members the residual when receipts have been set aside for expenses and taxes. Rather, the members receive wages as one of the prior claims on income. Bonuses and changes in wages, however, tend to be more flexible than those in the state enterprises.

During the CR, such individual enterprises were not possible, and urban collectives were much more limited. The new leadership is considerably more pragmatic, concerned with improving services and employment. It does not fear that the socialist economy will become undermined by permitting more individual and collective enterprise in economically marginal fields, where the development of the forces of production cannot yet justify exclusively state-operated activities. In the five years following Mao's death, the urban employment problem reached a peak. The problem developed be-

---

9. *Wall Street Journal*, Mar. 29, 1983, 33.

cause large numbers of middle school graduates, born before China's family planning policies became strongly effective in the 1970s, entered the labor force at the same time that the young people from the cities who had been forced to settle in the countryside were allowed to return home to the cities and take up jobs there. The flexible attitude toward institutional organization has helped to deal with the problem.

Agricultural Reform

The post-Mao reforms in agriculture have been of two main types. The first, known as the "responsibility system," seeks to tie financial rewards directly to success in raising productivity. The second seeks to promote institutional reform, including change in the structure of the commune, as a means of promoting innovation and raising productivity. Let us look at the responsibility system first, a system which began in 1979 but spread completely throughout Chinese agriculture by the end of 1982.

In the basic form of the responsibility system, a commune production team may assign responsibility for the cultivation of a particular plot of land to a group of households or to a single household. The household signs a contract with the team to deliver a specified quantity of grain. Any excess output—or sometimes a certain proportion of it—goes to the cultivating household. If output is less than the specified quantity (this rarely happens since targets are set low enough to maximize positive incentives), the household may have to make up the shortfall or may be penalized a certain number of workday credits. In communes which are relatively developed, the responsibility system is also used, but only a part of the excess output is retained and the contracts are usually signed with groups rather than individual households. In any event, a great variety of methods are used to reward (or penalize) the commune members. The different practices in use at the Donggucheng Production Brigade of the Taoyuan People's Commune in Hebei Province, north China, are illustrative of the variety.

The Taoyuan commune specializes in fruit production, mainly apples. Specialized teams are selected to be responsible for the apples. Each team must meet a quota of 1.1 million yuan worth of fruit in two years; each member receives in return 350 workday credits per year. If the quota is exceeded, the team members receive 15 percent of the excess output value. If they fall short of the quota, they lose 5 percent of their workday credits. As is the case in China generally, quotas are set low enough so that everyone is expected to meet them; the stress in the responsibility system is on positive incentives rather than negative sanctions.

In the case of grain, the entire output above the quota goes to

Table 12.2
Increase in China's Agricultural Output
during the Early Reform Period, 1978–1981

	1978	1981
Grain (million tons)	304.8	325.0
Soybeans (million tons)	7.6	9.2
Oilseeds (million tons)	5.2	10.2
Cotton (million bales)	10.0	13.6
Tea (thousand tons)	268.0	343.0
Silk cocoons (thousand tons)	228.0	211.0
Pork, beef, and mutton (million tons)	8.6	12.6

Source: U.S. Department of Agriculture, *China: Review of Agriculture in 1981 and Outlook for 1982* (Washington, D.C.: U.S. Department of Agriculture, Aug. 1982).

individuals or individual groups. Those who fail to fulfill plans are responsible for the entire shortfall. In this same brigade, groups sign contracts with the brigade, but the group members divide up responsibility and each one is responsible for his or her own land area. The responsibility system is also used in brigade industries. Between 1978 and 1981, the net income of the average brigade more than doubled.

Much of the gain in income reflects increases during 1979 in government purchase prices for grain (20 percent) and other agricultural products, but much also reflects increased output. Table 12.2 indicates the rise in agricultural output between 1979 and 1981.

The obvious success of the introduction of the responsibility system at the level of the production team led to experimentation with the household responsibility system, that is, the household became the unit of accounting. Although the household is still responsible for delivering a certain amount of output to the production team, under this system individual household income is independent of the performance of the other households in the production team. This modified version of family farming has also proved successful and has been expanded quite rapidly. According to recent evidence,[10] by the autumn of 1982 some 50 percent of production teams in China were using the household responsibility system. The system is more prevalent in less developed regions.

The household responsibility system continued to spread quickly throughout China during 1983. According to some estimates, it had

---

10. See the study by Cathy Hartford, *Once More, With Feeling: The New Stage in Chinese Agricultural Policy*, Harvard Business School, Feb., 1983, 63.

taken hold on over 85 percent of all production teams in China by December 1983.[11]

In addition to the increase in government purchase prices, other shifts in government policy contributed to the rise in agricultural production. Restrictions on private plots—which commune members were supposed to be able to use as they saw fit, but which in fact they often could not—were lifted. Moreover, the maximum amount of commune land that could be used for private plots increased from about 7 percent to 15 percent of their arable land area. (Since private plots tend to be more intensively farmed than communal land, this change will tend to increase output in the short run.) Also, local free markets, previously discouraged and limited, were encouraged and expanded, giving the peasants an outlet to sell their products and further stimulating production. Many peasants have enriched themselves rapidly under these new conditions and have become the subject of friendly derision in newspaper cartoons. Instead of one-sided emphasis on grain production, the government planners now advocate a diversified agricultural production and give the communes much greater leeway in choosing crops most suited to local conditions. Finally, post-1976 government policy has re-emphasized the "agriculture first" approach to economic development—devoting an increasing share of society's investment resources to the agricultural sector.

Paralleling the almost-universal introduction of the responsibility system, the regime has also carried out experiments in institutional reform which may ultimately have an even greater impact. Near Chongqing in Sichuan Province, twenty-six state farms combined operations in 1979 and added processing and sales to their production activities. (The state farms differ from the communes in that their workers are state employees and receive regular salaries, just like state factory workers.) Fifty production teams belonging to local communes also joined; and in 1980 the number expanded to eight hundred and the Changjiang Agriculture, Industry, and Commerce Corporation of Chongqing (CAICC) was formed.

The state farms had individually regularly lost money because of low state purchasing prices, lack of work incentives, and lack of permission to expand into food processing and distribution. From 1966 to 1977 they lost a total of forty-two million yuan. Since 1978, however, when a nominal profit was recorded, their profits began to climb sharply.

The CAICC forms joint enterprises with commune production teams, enterprises in which the teams provide the bulk of the raw

11. Carl Riskin, *Political Economy of Chinese Development since 1949* (Oxford: Oxford University Press, 1985), Ch. 12. Also see William Hinton, "A Trip to Fengyang County: Investigating China's New Family Contract System," *Monthly Review* 35 (Nov. 1983): 1–28.

materials (and receive the bulk of the profits) and the CAICC is responsible for processing and distribution. In 1980, for example, a special citrus company was formed composed of several state farms and three hundred production teams. Each team receives one share in the company for each 10,000 jin (1 jin = 1.1 lbs.) of fruit it guarantees to deliver and makes a capital contribution of two hundred yuan (about one hundred U.S. dollars) per share. Twenty-five hundred shares were purchased, officers were selected from both teams and state farms, and managers were hired.

The company pays regular market prices for the fruit it receives from the teams. It sells some of the fruit to government purchasing agencies, some on the market, and some for export; it retains part of the fruit for processing and then sells it in the same way. Of company revenues, 50 percent was used to pay for the fruit and to pay for labor from the teams used in processing. Thirty percent was used for dividends to the shareholders and 20 percent to set up a citrus research institute with twenty-five experts, a training school for technicians, and a fund for interest-free loans to the teams (they pay back in fruit over three to five years).[12]

This new type of enterprise is representative of a variety of organizational experiments that were initiated during the reform period. By bringing superior administrative and technical resources to the teams in conjunction with the greater material incentives that participation in processing and sales makes possible, the reform promises to stimulate agricultural production and raise agricultural incomes sharply. At the same time, the linking of teams of different communes with noncommune organizations undermines the role of the communes in Chinese agriculture. Indeed, the role of the communes has come increasingly into question for a number of reasons.

As we have noted, over the two decades following 1957, the incomes of commune members failed to rise significantly. It is widely felt among the reformers that a major cause of this failure was excessive integration of the political and economic spheres, with the state limiting and interfering with rural entrepreneurship and incentives in myriad ways, from low purchasing prices to restrictions on land use, restrictions on marketing, and so forth. At the same time, new organizational forms such as the CAICC and the citrus company described require associative links that transcend traditional commune boundaries. In this context, the political and economic spheres are being separated in some regions by separating the township governments from the communes. While the changes are still tentative and experimental, it appears that a multiplicity of institutional forms will come to characterize the Chinese countryside. The most notable

---

12. Sidney Shapiro, *Experiment in Sichuan: A Report on Economic Reform* (Beijing: New World Press, 1981), 23–24.

aspect to date of the current agricultural reform, however, is the thrust toward the household as the unit of account.

Reform Problems

In both the agricultural and industrial spheres, a number of serious problems have arisen as a consequence of the attempt to implement reforms. The most serious of these have to do with the consequences of decentralized decision making, pricing, and material incentives, elements which are at the heart of the reform process.

A market system works, in essence, through price signals. If economic activity is to conform to supply and demand, the prices must reflect relative scarcities. In China, prices have served a host of traditional functions, and they cannot be easily altered to reflect relative scarcities. Prices of certain consumer durables, for example, have deliberately been kept high to assure that state revenue needs will be met. Prices of other goods and services, like grain, house rents, and utilities, have been kept low to assure that people's basic needs will be met. If market allocation based on relative prices were to prevail, production resources would be switched from grain and housing to sewing machines, for example.

An actual problem did, in fact, arise along these lines. Although grain prices were increased during the reform period, prices for other crops were increased by greater amounts. The communes, freed to make their own production decisions, began taking land out of grain to use for other purposes. With the sown area used for grain dropping from 121 million hectares in 1978 to 114 million in 1981, the problem threatened to get out of hand, so minimum grain acreage requirements were again imposed by the central government.

An additional difficulty associated with the decentralization of pricing decisions is the inflationary possibility it opens up. Indeed, China, which for decades had enjoyed essential price stability, began to experience serious inflationary pressures. Prices rose by 6.7 percent in 1980, prompting a state council edict limiting further increases and new restrictions on government spending to balance the budget. The measures to restrain inflation were successful, but they inevitably involved suppressing the working of the market pricing mechanism, negating in part the reform effort. This experience is similar to the experience with pricing reforms in several East European economies.

The new attitude toward material incentives also raises potential problems for the transition to socialism in China. The ideological perspective of the Gang of Four which tended to deny all material aspirations and implied that somehow an aspiration for a tape recorder or wristwatch made one less socialist may have been unreasonable, but the new emphasis on material incentives to motivate work effort clearly has its own hazards. If allowed to develop unchecked, the cooperative ethos that characterized the Chinese revolution may give way to a materialistic culture akin to that found in the West. The establishment of free trade zones in southern China (where concessionary terms are granted to foreign investors) also threatens to "infect" adjacent provinces with unsocialist attitudes.

To be sure, the rapid policy shift from self-sufficient development (during Mao) to development through foreign investment and trade with the capitalist economies (post-Mao) may eventually prove to be politically unpalatable, whatever its economic merit. As the share of trade in National Income has nearly doubled since 1976, foreign loans and investments have multiplied many times over. According to new 1983 regulations, enterprises can now obtain loans directly from the branches of foreign banks operating in China and, as of June 1983, China had received a total of $5.8 billion in foreign investment pledges.

Notwithstanding the new problems and tensions accompanying the reform process, however, the current leadership's pragmatic approach to policy making and management has brought significant economic gains in many areas. The economy has grown rapidly, has achieved a basic balance in its foreign trade, and is approaching a balance in its domestic budget in 1983. Table 12.3 depicts several aspects of this improved performance since 1980.

Conclusion

The historical process involved in the making of China's socialist revolution was entirely distinct from that in the Soviet Union. The

Table 12.3
Macroeconomic Performance of the Chinese Economy since 1980

	1980	1981	1982 (Projected)	1983 (Projected)	1984 (Projected)
Annual growth rate of:					
Total gross output	6.8%	4.6%	8.9%	7.8%	8.2%
Industrial output	8.7%	4.1%	10.5%	8.7%	9.4%
Agricultural output	2.6%	5.6%	5.3%	5.6%	5.2%
Gross Domestic Product per capita	4.6%	3.4%	5.9%	5.4%	5.6%
Balance of trade (millions, U.S. $)	+115	+3,505	+2,000	—	—

Source: Wharton Econometric Forecasting Associates, *Centrally Planned Economies Outlook*, Sept. 1982, 153.

Chinese Communist party, led eventually by Mao, established an active base among China's peasant masses. The leaders of the Chinese Communist party were in the countryside fighting and rebuilding alongside the peasantry for the two decades prior to the revolution of 1949. The revolutionary practice in China built a strong Communist party base in the peasantry, which comprised well over 80 percent of the labor force—in contrast to Lenin's strategy of building the Bolsheviks' base in the diminutive urban proletariat. The revolutionary process in China, unlike that in the USSR, produced a highly mobilized mass of popular support among the peasants, close identification of the peasant base with the Party purporting to represent it, and a popular ideology that included the peasant majority in the Party constituency. These historical conditions, among others, led the Chinese to jettison the Stalinist model of economic development[13] and to experiment with constructing a new model of socialist development.

This experimentation began in earnest in 1957–58 with the Great Leap Forward and continued, first, with the market-oriented recovery policies of 1961–1965, second, with the decade or so of the Cultural Revolution, and, lastly, with the current period of market-oriented reform. A common theme to each of these periods is the tendency to build in greater decentralization in economic management, either through changes in the administrative structure of planning or through use of the market. This impulse toward decentralization and flexibility can be traced back to characteristics of the pre-1949 revolutionary process.

Clearly, one problem for China has been the propensity to swing from one pendular extreme to the other. In the swing to the extreme, the policies of each period yielded decreasing performance and engendered increasing resistance. The Cultural Revolution, for instance, went too far in destroying the planning bureaucracy, undermining the role of specialists, repudiating any form of material incentives, and so on. The attack on bureaucratism of the CR was accompanied by extreme ideological centralism. Conformity to centrally defined norms and work for the commonweal were expected to evolve practically overnight through exhortation. Rather than extending the democratic control that began to emerge in 1965–66, the CR eventually caused the dominating role of the Party to be reestablished. Without genuine popular participation, the goals and processes of the CR came to diverge more and more from an attack on bureaucratism or an elevation of the popular will. For example, the

13. An excellent discussion of the incompatibility of the Stalinist model with Chinese practices and the process of repudiating this model can be found in Franz Schurmann, *Ideology and Organization in Communist China* (Berkeley: University of California Press, 1968), Ch. 4. Also see Stephen Andors, *China's Industrial Revolution* (New York: Pantheon Books, 1977), Chs. 3 and 4.

policy of replacing college entrance examinations with the requirement of working on the commune for two years and being nominated
for college by one's work peers has a certain popular and egalitarian
appearance. Yet the policy was imposed coercively on urban youth
and was not supported with the resources necessary to assist in the
integration of the young people into the countryside.

The period since Mao's death in September 1976 has been characterized by a policy shift back toward the market and material incentives. The idealism of the CR has been replaced by pragmatism.
Although many of the extremes of the CR have been eliminated, the
current reform project has encountered many difficulties. There are
signs of abiding political divisions within the Party, and the extended
use of the market has brought, among other things, greater inequality
with some price instability, a small amount of unemployment, and
new problems of coordination.

Despite strong growth and improved macroeconomic performance, material living standards are still very low. It is too early to
predict whether the incremental gains in the standard of living will be
sufficient to withstand the political and social tensions engendered by
the economic reform. Whether the Chinese can set themselves on a
consistent course toward constructing their own political-economic
model for socialism remains to be seen.

Recommended Readings

1. Alexander Eckstein, *China's Economic Revolution* (Cambridge:
   Cambridge University Press, 1977).

2. U.S. Congress, Joint Economic Committee, *China under the Four
   Modernizations* (Washington: U.S. Government Printing Office,
   1982).

3. Victor Lippit and Mark Selden, eds., *The Transition to Socialism in
   China* (Armonk, N.Y.: M. E. Sharpe, 1982).

4. George Wang, ed., *Economic Reform in the PRC* (Boulder, Colo.:
   Westview, 1982).

5. Carl Riskin, *Political Economy of Chinese Development since 1949*
   (Oxford: Oxford University Press, 1985).

6. Xue Muqiao, ed., *Almanac of China's Economy 1981: With Economic Statistics 1949–1981* (Cambridge, Mass.: Ballinger, 1982).

7. Li Chengrui, "Are the 1967–76 Statistics on China's Economy Reliable?" *Beijing Review* (March 19, 1984): 21–28.

8. Steven Goldstein et al., *The People's Republic of China: A Basic
   Handbook*, 4th Ed. (New York: China Council of the Asia Society,
   1984).

13

CUBA
SOCIALISM NEXT DOOR

Cuba is a small island, 760 miles long and 22 to 124 miles wide, lying only 90 miles south of Key West, Florida. Its population numbers some ten million. The island is poor in mineral and fresh-water resources.

Cuba was the last country in Latin America to gain its independence from Spain. The break occurred in 1898 as a result of what Americans call the Spanish-American war. During this three-year war thousands of Cubans and 266 U.S. soldiers lost their lives. President Teddy Roosevelt appraised the episode as follows: "It wasn't much of a war, but it was the best war we had."[1]

Cuba's independence from Spain subjected Cuba to political and economic domination by the United States. This subordinate relationship was enshrined in the Platt Amendment of 1901, which gave the U.S. the right to intervene in Cuban politics "to preserve Cuban independence," as well as in the treaty leasing Guantanamo Naval Base to the United States.

The overthrow of the Batista government on January 1, 1959, brought Fidel Castro and his 26th of July Movement to power. Castro's efforts to bring Cuba's land and industry under Cuban control and to reduce the island's dependence on the U.S. economy proved to be too great a strain on diplomatic relations. The U.S. cancelled Cuba's sugar quota on July 5, 1960, established an economic blockade on all items but basic food and medicine on October 19, 1960, imposed a total trade blockade on March 23, 1962, and cajoled the rest of Latin America, save Mexico, to go along with the blockade on July 26, 1964. Along with the blockade came repeated acts of sabotage, one major invasion, and ongoing biological warfare, as well as various attempts

---

1. Cited in Ramon Ruiz, *Cuba: The Making of a Revolution* (New York: W. W. Norton & Co., 1968), 21.

to assassinate Fidel Castro.[2] This list does not exhaust the uses to which U.S. tax dollars were put to the intended detriment of Castro. The following is a quote from the U.S. Senate subcommittee report on CIA attempts to assassinate foreign leaders:

> From March through August 1960 . . . the CIA considered plans to under-mine Castro's charismatic appeal by sabotaging his speeches. [One] scheme [was] to spray Castro's broadcasting studio with a chemical which produced effects similar to LSD. . . . During this period, TSD (the Technical Services Division of the CIA) impregnated a box of cigars with a chemical which produced temporary disorientation, hoping to induce Castro to smoke one of the cigars before delivering a speech. The Inspec-tor General also reported a plan to destroy Castro's image as El Barbudo (the bearded one) by dusting his shoes with thallium salts, a strong de-pilatory that would cause his beard to fall out.[3]

The Reagan administration views Cuba as our worst enemy in this hemisphere. More than once, Reagan has declared the Cuban econ-omy to be a dismal failure and has threatened that if the United States does not intervene in Central America then we will face the unthink-able prospect of more Cubas in our hemisphere.

On the one hand, since Cuba has generated such concern and played a central role in the formulation of U.S. foreign policy, it is essential for educated Americans to have a deeper understanding of the realities of the Cuban society and economy. On the other hand, Cuba represents a significantly different brand of socialist economics to merit study in its own right. Whether or not the Cuban model is viable is certainly of profound interest to other Third World countries (for example, Nicaragua, Mozambique, Angola) which are trying to introduce a socialist development strategy.

The fact that Cuba's socialist revolution was home-grown, in con-trast to those in Eastern Europe (save Yugoslavia), meant no external model of economic planning and development was directly imposed. Instead, Cuba learned by trial and error in developing a planning system suitable to its own conditions. Cuba did not have its first five-year plan until the second half of the seventies, and it is fair to say that most of the country's present economic institutions were not in place before then. Thus, the story of Cuba's socialist economy is very much one of ongoing development, probing, experimentation, and continuing evolution. In this chapter we will attempt to outline the structural transformation, the development strategies, and the per-formance of the Cuban economy since the revolution.

---

2. U.S. Senate Report, *Alleged Assassination Plots Involving Foreign Lead-ers* (Washington, D.C.: U.S. Government Printing Office, 1975).

3. *Ibid.,* 72. Another excellent source on the U.S.-C.I.A. continuing efforts to overthrow the Castro government is Warren Hinckle and William W. Turner, *The Fish Is Red: The Story of the Secret Wars Against Castro* (New York: Harper and Row, 1981).

Background

Fulgencio Batista led a U.S.-supported military coup in early 1934 and essentially ruled Cuba as head of state or head of the armed forces until January 1, 1959. In its broad outline Batista's Cuba was characterized by economic stagnation (in 1926 prices, National Income per capita was $201 in 1903–1906 and $200 in 1956–1958), sharp inequality, rampant corruption, and pervasive graft.[4]

United States' direct investment in Cuba exceeded one billion dollars in the late fifties and dominated the modern sector of the economy. U.S. companies owned factories involved in producing nickel, cement, tires, paint, detergent, toiletries, bottles, cans, and paper and in oil refining and auto assembly. These industries employed only 3 percent of the labor force and catered to the demand of the upper 10 or 15 percent of Cuba's income earners. It has been estimated that between 1950 and 1958 80 percent of Cuba's imports went either to service the demand of U.S. corporations or of Cuba's upper class. One interesting statistic is that in 1954 Havana (Cuba's capital city) had the highest per capita consumption of Cadillacs of any city in the world.[5] At the same time, most of the people of Havana were very poor.

Cuba's inability to develop its own entrepreneurial class and domestically owned manufacturing industry is attributable to several factors. Among them, the August 1934 Reciprocal Trade Agreement with the United States provided for preferential tariff treatment by Cubans of four hundred U.S. products. This situation, together with Cuba's geographical proximity to the U.S., left fledgling domestic industry without sufficient protection to establish itself on a competitive basis. Thus, pre-1959 Cuba never benefited from the import substitution industrialization experienced elsewhere in Latin America. The same 1934 agreement limited to 22 percent the share of sugar exports to the United States which could be in the form of refined, as opposed to raw, sugar. This agreement amounted to a statutory limitation on forward linkages, that is, the processing, elaboration, and subsequent marketing of the raw material. The limitation with respect to Cuba's main crop, together with massive profit repatriation by foreign companies to the U.S., contributed to the general retardation of Cuba's industrial growth. Finally, the low level of per

---

4. Between 1950 and 1958 real per capita income continued to fall at an annual rate of 0.3 percent. J. O'Connor, *The Origins of Socialism in Cuba* (Ithaca: Cornell University Press, 1970), 17. Another excellent source for historical economic data on Cuba is Jorge Domínguez, *Cuba: Order and Revolution* (Cambridge: Harvard University Press, 1978). A good English source of post-1959 economic data and its limitations is C. Mesa-Lago, *The Economy of Socialist Cuba* (Albuquerque: University of New Mexico Press, 1981).

5. Ruiz, *Cuba*, 9.

capita income combined with acute inequality severely limited the size of the domestic market.

Inevitably, U.S. economic domination over Cuba went hand in hand with political domination. For instance, former U.S. Ambassador to Cuba during Batista's last year, Earl Smith, explained to a Senate subcommittee in 1960:

> The U.S., until the advent of Castro, was so overwhelmingly influential in Cuba that . . . the American Ambassador was the second most influential person in Cuba, sometimes even more important than the President.[6]

The most blatant symbol of U.S. domination and economic irrationality was Cuba's sugar industry. Between 1951 and 1958 sugar accounted for 82 percent of Cuba's exports, 29 percent of its National Income, and 25 percent of its labor force (two-thirds of sugar workers were wage earners). Seventy-five percent of Cuba's arable land was owned by large sugar companies, most notably United Fruit and King Ranch of Texas. These companies also owned two-thirds of the country's railroad trackage and most of its ports.[7]

The U.S. sugar companies farmed extensively, employing relatively little machinery and fertilizer, sowing only half the land they owned and harvesting only 75 percent of the planted land during the fifties. The average sugar cane laborer worked only 123 days out of the year. Out of eighteen major cane sugar producing countries in the world, Cuba ranked next to the bottom in yield per acre.[8]

Backward linkages (that is, production of inputs used in sugar production) were virtually nonexistent and forward linkages were minimal. For instance, from 1955 to 1958 only 13 percent of Cuba's sugar exports were in refined sugar, and there was no industry for the conversion of milling residue, or bagasse, to fuel, cellulose, or paper. (As of December 1983, the refining process added approximately twelve cents of value added per pound. Since the world price of raw sugar at that time was around eight cents per pound, this means that close to 60 percent of potential value added would be lost for each pound of sugar not refined in Cuba. The production of rum, of course, uses sugar as a base and is an exception.) Loophole-riddled tax legislation also permitted massive profit repatriation to the United States by U.S. sugar companies, further attenuating the sugar sector's possible contribution to general economic development.

---

6. Quoted in R. F. Smith, *What Happened in Cuba?* (New York: Twayne Publishers, 1963), 273.

7. For a more extensive discussion of these conditions see, among others: E. Boorstein, *The Economic Transformation of Cuba* (New York: Monthly Review, 1968), Chap. 1; A. Ritter, *The Economic Development of Revolutionary Cuba* (New York: Praeger, 1974), Chap. 2; and A. MacEwan, *Revolution and Economic Development in Cuba* (London: Macmillan, 1981), Chaps. 1–3.

8. MacEwan, *Revolution*, 17.

Two other aspects of economic dependence on sugar were particularly problematic. First, sugar prices fluctuate wildly in world markets. Since over 75 percent of Cuba's export earnings consistently came from sugar and Cuba relied heavily on imports to keep its industry producing, violent swings in the business cycle were commonplace. In addition to retarding investment and economic growth, this factor undoubtedly contributed to militant working class activity and political instability. Second, the income elasticity of demand (percent increase in quantity demanded divided by percent increase in income) for sugar was low (most estimates place it below 0.5), meaning that it was a poor export commodity to rely on in the long run.

Fidel Castro, son of a well-to-do Oriente sugar planter and himself a lawyer, was a congressional candidate in the 1952 elections. These elections, however, never occurred because of an intervening coup by Batista. Castro appealed to the Supreme Court to declare the coup unconstitutional. When he lost his plea, he turned to armed struggle.

The story of the successful armed struggle against Batista is both involved and interesting but would take us on too long a digression. However, to understand Cuba's post-1959 political economy it is necessary to appreciate some important legacies of the pre-1959 revolutionary experience.

Castro's group, the 26th of July Movement, was nationalist and democratic in its ideology, as distinct from socialist, during 1953–1959. It gained substantial and increasing support from all social classes over this period. Despite logistical support from an urban underground as well as the peasantry of Oriente province, the Rebel Army never involved more than several hundred Cubans in armed resistance. Batista fell not because he was overwhelmed by superior military forces, but because his own military forces crumbled. This collapse, in turn, can be attributed to the growing lack of legitimacy of his government resulting from economic stagnation, acute inequality, and widespread corruption.

Castro, unlike the leaders of the Bolshevik party in Russia, was inside the country, living and struggling from guerrilla encampments among the peasantry of Oriente. His *History Will Absolve Me* speech,[9] delivered at his 1953 trial, about the inequities of the Cuban society, came to be familiar to most Cubans. His willingness to risk his life and fight against terrific odds gained the close attention and respect of the great majority of Cubans. By 1959, his popularity was far-reaching. The Cuban people identified with his leadership—and his years in the Oriente countryside along with the Rebel Army led him to identify and empathize with the plight of the people.

This circumstance conditioned the economic and social policies

9. Fidel Castro, *History Will Absolve Me* (Secaucus, N.J.: Lyle Stuart, 1983).

chosen by the revolutionary leadership after 1959. It ruled out, for instance, harsh, unpopular measures such as a collectivization drive. Yet it is also important to underscore that despite the population's sympathy for Castro and his professed goals, the population had not been extensively mobilized in the fight against Batista. If the population was to be actively incorporated into the new political structure, if it was to participate effectively in the new government, then it needed to be further organized and mobilized. This mobilization of the masses was not accomplished as it was in China and Yugoslavia, and to a lesser extent in Russia, by the revolutionary struggle. This fact helps to explain the deep-seated paternalism of the early years of Castro's government. The absence of mass involvement in decision making was singled out by Castro as the most important determinant of the economic failures of the late sixties.

Early Development Strategy

Castro inherited a stagnant, recession-ridden economy. On average from May 1956 to April 1957, 361,000 out of a labor force of 2.2. million (16.4 percent) were unemployed; an additional 377,000 were underemployed.[10]

The early redistributive and stimulative economic measures of the rebel government were sufficient to put Cuba's idle resources back to work and occasion a significant economic spurt. Prices were frozen, taxes were cut, rents were reduced 30 to 50 percent, luxury imports were choked off, private clubs and beaches were expropriated and opened to the public, 30 percent of industrial profits were to go to the workers, and a first land redistribution was initiated. These policies, among others, bolstered demand and led agricultural output to grow by approximately 4.5 percent per year between 1959 and 1961. Industrial output expanded 29 percent over the first two years.[11] By 1961, however, severe problems began to set in.

One source of these problems was the deteriorating relationship with the United States. It is difficult to identify a single primary catalyst of U.S.–Cuban hostilities, but surely a major provocation occurred in April 1960 when Esso, Texaco, and Shell refused to refine three hundred thousand tons of cheaper Soviet crude oil. When the companies refused, they were expropriated. The U.S. responded by revoking Cuba's sugar quota and, several retaliations later, by imposing an embargo on all trade with Cuba, save food and medicine

---

10. Mesa-Lago, *Economy of Socialist Cuba*, 121. Over this period the unemployment went as high as 20.7 percent during the nonharvest season and as low as 9 percent during the harvest.

11. See Ritter, *Economic Development*, 106–116, for a fuller discussion of economic performance from 1959 to 1961.

exports, in October 1960. The embargo was extended to all goods by presidential order in March 1962 and has been in place ever since. Because virtually all of Cuba's modern plant and equipment came from the U.S. and the blockade made it impossible for Cuba to obtain necessary materials and spare parts, the effect on the Cuban economy was crippling. To compound matters, as relations with the U.S. worsened and strains within Cuba grew, a massive flight of professionals, engineers, and technicians began. Without sufficient skilled personnel, breakdowns in industry were rife and the need for spare parts and repairs became even greater.

Another problem was based in Cuba's efforts to diversify her economy overnight, minimizing dependence on the symbolic sugar albatross. Resources were spread too thin, intersectoral coordination was poor, and bottlenecks became common. Moreover, with lower sugar production (made worse by bad weather in 1962 and 1963) export earnings fell off and a sizable balance of payments deficit first appeared in 1962. These problems were aggravated by opposition-led economic sabotage, lack of political unity in the government, and a corresponding lack of coherence in their approach to economic management.

All these conditions necessitated a new strategy. Briefly, the decision was made in 1964 to promote sugar production and to pursue diversification more gradually. In a sense, the Soviets offered a deal the Cubans couldn't refuse: to buy five million tons of sugar a year for five years at a fixed (above world market) price of 6.11 cents per pound. The Chinese agreed to purchase an additional one million tons at the same price. With guaranteed sales and prices, as well as domestic ownership, the historical economic disadvantages of sugar dependence were for the time being practically eliminated. (Dependence on weather conditions still remained as did the social structure of sugar production until the mechanization of the late seventies.) This new policy might have yielded continuing economic growth had it not been for the introduction of a new, shortsighted approach to economic management.

Planning in the 1960s

Between 1963 and 1965 a debate over incentives and planning took place in Cuba.[12] Two basic positions were propounded. Che Guevara argued for central planning, budgetary accounting, and moral in-

---

12. Two good sources on this debate are: R. Bernardo, *The Theory of Moral Incentives in Cuba* (University, Ala.: University of Alabama Press, 1971); and B. Silverman, ed., *Man and Socialism in Cuba: The Great Debate* (New York: Atheneum, 1973). The latter source contains translations of several original articles from the debate.

centives. Moral incentives, Guevara maintained, were necessary to create a new socialist consciousness, although he recognized that material incentives could not be abandoned all at once. He urged, therefore, that material incentives be collective (that is, they should pertain to a group of workers rather than an individual worker) and be limited in scope. According to Guevara, Cuba's low level of material development meant that an extensive use of material incentives, and the corresponding income differentiation, would re-create the widespread poverty of the Bastista era.

The other side of the debate was represented most forcefully by Carlos Rafael Rodríguez, a prominent member of the Party's Central Committee. He argued for central planning, economic accounting, and material incentives. Under budgetary accounting, enterprises are financed out of the central budget and are not expected to balance their own costs and revenues or to yield a surplus. Rodriguez believed budgetary accounting encouraged inefficiency. Under economic accounting or self-financing, each enterprise would be expected to balance its budget or yield a net income. Material incentives, he claimed, were imperative to motivate Cuban workers who were not ideologically ready (just five years into the revolution) for the Communist principle of distribution: "from each according to their ability, to each according to their need." (This is contrasted with the socialist principle: "from each according to their ability, to each according to their work.") Moral incentives would only be efficacious after the forces of production were more developed.

At the time of the debate, economic management consisted of a rather ad hoc version of central planning, a mixture of budgetary and economic accounting and extensive use of individual material incentives. (Between 1963 and 1966 national wage scales were introduced along with job norms or work quotas. Workers' wages went up 0.5 percent for every 1 percent production increased above their norm.) Guevara's position was the basis for major economic policy changes beginning in 1966. Indeed, new policy with regard to planning and incentives went considerably beyond the proposals of Che Guevara.

In 1966, the powers of JUCEPLAN (the Cuban Central Planning Board) were reduced, and formal one-year planning was abandoned. In its stead was substituted Castro's idea of mini-plans which, in essence, prioritized a few sectors (such as sugar) assuring them of adequate resources. Nonprioritized sectors, however, fared poorly and bottlenecks spread throughout the economy. The combination of bottlenecks and the high investment ratios of the late sixties (gross investment as a share of Gross Material Product reached 27 percent in 1967 and 31 percent in 1968)[13] created serious shortages of consumer goods. Thus, even if the leadership had wanted to, it would

---

13. Ritter, *Economic Development,* 170. The figures reported in Brundenius, *Economic Growth, Basic Needs and Income Distribution in Revolutionary Cuba* (Lund, Sweden: Research Policy Institute, University of Lund, 1981) are somewhat lower.

have been impossible to meaningfully implement a policy of material incentives. That is, workers could hardly be expected to work harder to earn more when there were insufficient price-controlled goods on which to spend their income.

The incentive policies of the late sixties were idealistic in the extreme. The tie between wages and productivity was severed and replaced by a panoply of moral incentives. The economy underwent demonetization as free services were extended to many items. The prices of other basic services and goods were heavily subsidized. The interest rate on credit to enterprises was abolished in 1967 as were income taxes on private farmers. Small private plots on state farms were ended as was overtime pay.

(A second Agrarian Reform Law was passed in 1963. It expropriated all landholdings above 67 hectares. This left two agricultural sectors: state farms, encompassing approximately 70 percent of all farm land, and private farms, accounting for the remaining 30 percent. Since private land can only be passed on to family members working the land, some of the private land has been sold to the state. Today, just over 25 percent of the land is privately owned, and around one-fourth of this is in the form of production cooperatives. In 1982, small private plots on state farms were beginning to reappear.)

Two additional factors contributed to production problems at the time. First, in 1968 it was decided to nationalize all retail and small business, thrusting tens of thousands of workers into the state sector. The organization of the state planning apparatus was already insufficient to plan for and manage large and medium-sized industry. Adding this new sector, very dispersed and numerous by nature, made the tasks of coordination immense. Moreover, the problems of training and disciplining these new workers were monumental.

Second, the government had placed an irrational emphasis on attaining the 10-million-ton sugar harvest in 1970. This resulted in an enormous diversion of resources, including the use of 170,000 industrial workers in the harvest. In the end, the 1970 harvest reached 8.5 million tons, a record, but short of the goal upon which Castro had staked the honor of the revolution.

Production data series for the 1960s are spotty and growth estimates from different sources vary widely.[14] National Income per cap-

---

14. The estimates of growth for this period vary significantly depending on the source (e.g., Cuban government, CIA, *Economist's Intelligence Unit*, or U.N. Commissions). Mesa-Lago, *Economy of Socialist Cuba*, provides a careful discussion of Cuban growth statistics and their difficulties; see especially Chap. 3, Chap. 8, and Appendices 1 and 3. A good discussion of the different estimates on Cuban growth can be found in Claes Brundenius, *Economic Growth, Basic Needs and Income Distribution in Revolutionary Cuba* (Lund, Sweden: Research Policy Institute, University of Lund, 1981). A critical and up-to-date examination of Cuban economic statistics is provided in Wharton

ita appears to have increased slightly from 1962 to 1965 and then fallen slightly from 1966 to 1969. After the initial recuperation to 1962, then, there was a seven-year period of no economic growth.

If overall production per capita stagnated, then consumer good production per capita fell off appreciably. This circumstance, together with the provision of many free services and fixed state prices, led to an excess supply of money in circulation. It was estimated that by 1970 purchasing power exceeded goods supply by 87 percent at existing prices. Before the government could begin to reintroduce material incentives, this surplus of money had to be dried up. Beginning in 1970, several measures were taken to accomplish this end, including large price increases for nonbasic or above-ration goods and a sharp reduction in the investment ratio. More basic, institutional changes were to come.

Economic Change, 1970–1975

In Castro's speech of May 20, 1970, on the failure to achieve the ten-million-ton sugar harvest, he repeatedly emphasized the problem of bureaucratic leadership and poor economic management. In his speech on July 26, 1970, Castro again alluded to the sugar harvest failure and reiterated that "... the leaders of this Revolution have cost the people too much in our process of learning."[15] Castro was quick to add, however, that the problem did not lie with specific individuals; rather, it was a question of the failure of the nation to work as a collectivity:

> We believe this is a problem of the whole people! And we sincerely believe that the only way we can solve the problem we have today is by all working together—all of us—from the men in the highest positions of responsibility in the Party and state right on down to those in the most humble industrial plant and not just those in leadership positions there. . . .
>
> Why should a manager have to be absolutely in charge? Why shouldn't we begin to introduce representatives of the factory's workers into its management? Why not have confidence? Why not put our trust in that tremendous proletarian spirit . . . ?
>
> We don't believe that the problem of managing a plant should fall exclusively to the manager. It would really be worthwhile to begin introducing a number of new ideas. There should be a manager, naturally—for there must always be someone accountable—but we must begin to estab-

---

Econometric Forecasting Associates, *Construction of Cuban Economic Activity and Trade Indexes,* 2 vols. (Washington, D.C.: Wharton Econometric Forecasting Associates, 1983).

15. F. Castro, "Report on the Cuban Economy," in R. Bonachea and Valdes, eds., *Cuba in Revolution* (Garden City: Anchor, 1972), 338.

lish a collective body in the management of each plant. A collective body! It should be headed by one man, but it should also be made up of representatives of the advanced workers' movement, the Young Communist League, the Party and the women's front. . . .[16]

Five days later Labor Minister Risquet made a statement on national television criticizing the lack of democracy in Cuba's factories. He made three recommendations:

(a) the unions should be given an opportunity to perform their role; their first duty should be to see that labor legislation is applied and workers' rights protected; (b) the elections of the directorate of the union should not be restricted; there should not be the slightest fear that conditions would be placed on the election of the representatives; there should be no doubt that the election will be free and open; and (c) an investigation should be undertaken on the potential participation of the workers in factory management.[17]

The first actual step along these lines was to revitalize the trade union movement. On November 9, 1970, secret ballot elections were held to choose new union officials; 26,427 new locals were created and 117,625 officials were elected (87 percent for the first time) for two-year terms. Local union officials represent their work centers on higher union bodies confederated along both geographical and product lines.

In early 1973 preparations were made for the Thirteenth National Trade Union Congress (the Twelfth was in 1966). The "theses" of the Congress were made available at each work center where they were discussed. Delegates were elected to attend the actual Congress in November. Among the major resolutions of the Congress were: (1) the decision to reinvoke the "socialist principle" of remuneration—"from each according to her/his ability, to each according to her/his work"; (2) the decisions to strengthen and extend worker participation in collective management through the union.

Material Incentives

The first resolution entailed linking worker income to productivity. Each job was to be assigned an output quota or norm. If the worker fulfilled the norm exactly, he or she would receive the basic wage set for the job established in the national wage scale. For every percentage point over or under fulfillment the wage would go up or down, respectively, by the same percentage. On the surface, this method resembles the straight-line piece-rate system known in many U.S.

---

16. *Ibid.*, 345–49.

17. Cited in R. Hernández and C. Mesa-Lago, "Labor Organization and Wages," in C. Mesa-Lago, ed., *Revolutionary Change in Cuba* (Pittsburgh: University of Pittsburgh Press, 1971), 245.

manufacturing industries. However, the Cubans claim there is one crucial difference between the two systems in that the Cuban norms are established in consultation with and subject to the approval of the affected workers.

For a variety of reasons these work norms (and their link to income) have been introduced rather slowly. By the last quarter of 1979 only 46.6 percent of the Cuban work force (in the productive sphere) was functioning under this system. One apparent problem is that the norms are generally set unrealistically low. During the last quarter of 1979, 95.5 percent of workers operating with norms either met or exceeded their quotas (see Table 13.1).[18] It is likely that many of the small percentage who fell below the norm did so because of "external" problems (for example, production bottlenecks, supply shortages, machinery breakdowns, etc.).

Table 13.1
Norm Fulfillment (End of 1979)

Percentage of fulfillment	Percentage of normed workers
100–115	40.2
116–135	37.8
greater than 135	17.5

Source: JUCEPLAN, *Segunda Plenaria Nacional de Chequeo de la Implantación del SDPE* (Havana: July 1980), 297.

Strong emphasis was also placed on collectively based material incentives after 1970. Beginning in 1971, work centers were allocated a number of consumer durables and other items for distribution to the center's workers. In some cases, the size of the allocation was tied to factory performance. Since each year's allocation permitted only a small group of workers to benefit, it was necessary to devise a distribution scheme perceived to be equitable. Through collective discussion in a workers' assembly, beneficiaries would be selected according to merit (attendance and work record) and need (size of family, living conditions, etc.).

The same distribution system was used for housing constructed by "microbrigades." Microbrigades are groups of workers (usually fifteen to forty per work center) who leave their usual work place to join a state-supplied construction project for a certain period of time. The remaining members of the work place agree to work harder to maintain production levels. When the housing project is completed, a

---

18. JUCEPLAN, *Segunda Plenaria Nacional de Chequeo de la Implantación del SDPE* (Havana: July 1980), 297.

number of units is assigned to each work center. The microbrigades were begun in mid 1971 and by the mid seventies were building over ten thousand housing units annually. Their role is less prominent today, since these projects have been replaced largely by privately contracted housing construction.

Worker Participation

The resolution to promote greater popular participation has been implemented on a number of fronts. We shall provide a few examples below. First, as suggested in the speeches of Castro and Risquet, one-man management has been replaced by a Management Council, consisting of the enterprise director, top management assistants, and elected representatives from the local Party organization, trade union, and communist youth organization. Generally, this Council meets at least once a week. Second, each production section has a monthly assembly of all workers in the section, where matters of production, material supplies, health and safety, worker education programs, labor discipline, etc. are discussed. Attendance at these after-work-hour meetings is optional and appears to be very high (in the 70-to-95-percent range).[19] Third, each factory workshop elects delegates to attend a quarterly meeting of delegates with the Management Council. In addition, elected trade union committees, labor councils, and other organs are involved in a variety of decisions regarding production, culture, and community at the factory. Popular input into macroeconomic policy and priority setting, however, occurs only indirectly through special commissions of the elected National Assembly of the People's Power, the Cuban Federation of Workers, the Institute of Internal Demand, and various informal vehicles.

There is some evidence of growing worker involvement in enterprise decision making. A 1975 study by M. Perez-Stable found that 85 percent of surveyed workers believed workers must be consulted in enterprise affairs, and 58 percent of this group felt that worker input was already influential and significant.[20] A 1976 survey by Herrera and Rosenkranz of 355 workers revealed that 80 percent of their respondents felt they "always or nearly always" made a personal intervention at production assemblies.[21] Moreover, when asked to mention the most important policy areas discussed and decided upon with the

19. Interviews during visits to Cuba in July–August 1974 and March 1982.
20. Marifeli Pérez-Stable, "Institutionalization and Workers' Response," *Cuban Studies* 6 (1976): 31-54.
21. A. Herrera and H. Rosenkranz, "Political Consciousness in Cuba," in Griffiths and Griffiths, eds., *Cuba: The Second Decade* (London: Britain-Cuba Scientific Liaison Committee, 1979), 48.

direct participation of workers, 95 percent listed production plans. The second highest frequency was education at 57 percent. The entire list is long but the prioritization is striking. According to this survey, then, unlike workers in Yugoslavia or participatory enterprises elsewhere, Cuban workers appear to take a greater interest in production-related matters than in worker benefits.

According to Castro's reports to the First (1975) and Second (1980) Party Congress, the number of workers participating in the discussion of the annual economic plan in their enterprises rose from 1.26 million in 1975 to 1.45 million in 1980 (or by 15 percent). A 1980 Cuban government study reported that the 1979 economic plan was discussed with the workers in 75 percent of all enterprises and the 1980 plan was discussed in 91 percent of all enterprises. Workers' suggestions were used to amend the plan's control figures in 42 percent of the enterprises for the 1979 plan and in 59 percent for the 1980 plan.[22] All of these results suggest a considerably higher level of actual worker participation in Cuban enterprises than in Soviet enterprises despite the existence of formal legislation in the USSR which grants workers significant decision-making power.[23]

Participation in enterprise goal formulation often can lead to identification with or internalization of the goal. This "internal incentive" is alleged to have been a powerful motivating force behind work effort in Cuba since 1970, probably more powerful than the introduction of work norms and individual material incentives.

Although it is impossible to "prove" this assertion, there is some evidence to support it. Labor productivity in Cuba rose rapidly during the first years of the 1970s, including an increase of 21 percent in 1972. These productivity increases preceded (1) the linking of wages to worker output (which only slowly began to occur in 1974) and (2) the elimination of excess liquidity (money) held by Cuban households. Under such circumstances, it is hard to imagine that material incentives were a significant motivating force for Cuban workers at the time.

Income Distribution

A commitment to the collective good or the commonweal, however, also requires an acceptance of the prevailing distributional stan-

---

22. JUCEPLAN, *Segunda Plenaria Nacional*, 27.

23. For additional information on worker participation in Cuba see: M. Harnecker, *Cuba: Dictatorship or Democracy?* (Westport, Conn.: Lawrence Hill & Co., 1979), Chap. 1; and A. Zimbalist, "Worker Participation in Cuba," *Challenge: The Magazine of Economic Affairs* (Nov./Dec. 1975). On actual worker participation in the Soviet Union see: M. Yanowitch, *Social and Economic Inequality in the Soviet Union* (White Plains, N.Y.: M. E. Sharpe, 1977), Chap. 5; and M. Yanowitch, ed., *Soviet Work Attitudes: The Issue of Participation in Management* (White Plains, N.Y.: M. E. Sharpe, 1979).

dards. That is, even if a worker helped to decide upon producing a certain assortment and quantities of goods, if those goods ultimately could be afforded by only an elite group of consumers, it is less likely the worker would perceive his or her enterprise's efforts as contributing to the general welfare of society. The internal or moral component of the incentive would thereby be diminished.

It is relevant, then, to inquire into the Cuban distribution of income. At the beginning of 1982 the minimum wage was 95 pesos per month (at the official tourist rate of exchange a Cuban peso equals approximately $1.20). The highest wage in the national wage scale is 450 pesos per month, although directors of important national institutes seem to earn an additional bonus of 100 pesos. There are also a small number of professionals who still receive their "historical" (pre-1959) wage, which can reach into the 700 to 800 pesos per month range. However, the great majority (probably 70 to 80 percent) of all state workers earn between 120 and 280 pesos per month. The distribution of income of wages and salaries, thus, is very compressed; and, given the absence of property income, the overall distribution of income is extremely egalitarian. An estimate of the Cuban income distribution in 1978 by a Swedish economist is presented in Table 13.2 below. (This discussion excludes private farmers, bonuses, after-hour work, and possible special access to goods for a restricted number of top officials. There is no accurate data currently available on these items, but it appears that the inclusion of these sources would not appreciably change the overall picture of income equality.)

Table 13.2
Cuban Distribution of Income, 1978

Decile	Share of total income
0–10 (bottom 10%)	5.1
11–20	5.9
21–30	6.5
31–40	7.3
41–50	8.0
51–60	8.5
61–70	9.9
71–80	12.8
81–90	14.9
91–100	21.1
Decile ratio = 4.1.	

Source: Claes Brundenius, *Economic Growth, Basic Needs and Income Distribution in Revolutionary Cuba*, Research Policy Institute, no. 32 (Lund, Sweden: University of Lund, 1981), 151.

Note: The author presents two distribution estimates for 1978, the other slightly less egalitarian. We present the above distribution because we believe it is based on more realistic assumptions.

The distribution of consumption is, of course, more equal still, as a result of the free, universal provision of health, educational, and many cultural services and the heavy price subsidies for basic commodities. Conversely, heavy excise taxes are put on nonbasic or luxury goods, reducing the purchasing power of high-income Cubans. Furthermore, practices like rationing, durable good and housing unit allocations to work centers, and equal benefit and access regulations (for example, every worker is entitled to thirty days of paid vacation per year) reinforce the above patterns of equality.

The continuing adherence to generally accepted norms of distributional equity along with growing worker participation and other factors contributed to the favorable economic performance of the early seventies. The average annual growth rate of labor productivity from 1971 to 1975 was an impressive 9 percent, a growth rate that occurred prior to any significant application of individual material incentives at the work place. Gross Social Product, aided by high sugar prices at the end of the period, grew at an average yearly rate of 7.5 percent in constant prices during 1971 to 1975. (The reader will recall that Gross Social Product includes material production as well as the "productive services"—transportation, trade, and communication. It does not include "nonproductive services," like education, health care, culture, etc. Gross Social Product also suffers as a measure because of the double counting of many intermediate inputs.)[24]

Economic Change since 1975

The second half of the seventies witnessed Cuba's first Five-Year Plan as well as the gradual introduction of an economic reform known as the "New System of Economic Management and Planning" (SDPE). Each represents the evolving maturity and institutionalization of Cuba's economic organizations.

The SDPE in many respects is modeled after the 1965 Soviet reforms. It attempts to (1) put enterprises on a self-financing basis, (2) introduce a profitability criterion with its attendant incentives, and (3) generally promote decentralization, organizational coherence, and efficiency. As with the Soviet reform it has met with the obstacles of bureaucratic resistance and an irrational price structure. Yet

24. For sources and growth rates see Table 13.3.

there are indications that these obstacles are being successfully confronted and the Cubans have given the SDPE a good report card.[25]

One interesting organizational change connected with the SDPE has been decentralized control over local enterprises by the elected organs of popular power (municipal or regional governments). Prior to 1976 all enterprises were subordinated to a central state ministry. Currently, some 41 percent of locally oriented enterprises in services, commerce, and industry are responsible to the local organ of popular power. The directors of these local enterprises are named and removed by the organ of popular power, and this body is the link between JUCEPLAN (the Central Planning Board) and the enterprise. The local government is responsible to JUCEPLAN but is given considerable latitude in its choice and prioritization of projects as well as services and goods production.

Furthermore, the allocation of material supplies for many inputs is being decentralized. There are also plans to introduce more flexibility and greater decentralization in other areas of their planning system.[26]

The decentralization efforts of the SDPE have spurred decentralization in other areas. In March 1980, free farmers' markets were introduced where production beyond state procurement contracts can be sold at market prices. At the beginning of 1982 these markets were flourishing. During 1983 it was reported that 58 percent of food distribution was through peasant markets. The state has also sanctioned private services and small-scale goods production. After work hours or during weekend and vacation periods workers can sell their skills (carpentry, plumbing, electrical repairs, etc.) at free market prices. In 1981, thirteen thousand housing units (out of a total thirty-four thousand) were built by private construction cooperatives. Small private plots on state farms were reintroduced in 1982. The new system of free labor contracting permits enterprises to directly hire workers, in contrast to assignment by state agencies. State enterprises can also contract with artisans and the self-employed to provide inputs, using up to 30 percent of their profits.

As shown in Table 13.3, real growth of the Gross Social Product during 1976 to 1980, however, slowed down to a yearly rate of 4.0 percent. The reasons for this slowdown are several, among others: a lower investment ratio during the early and mid seventies with more emphasis on consumer rather than capital goods; the world economic recession, including Eastern Europe and the USSR; the sharp decline in world raw sugar prices from a high of over 60 cents per

25. This, at least, is the conclusion drawn by the compehensive study of the SDPE done by JUCEPLAN in 1980. JUCEPLAN, *Segunda Plenaria Nacional de Chequeo de la Implantación del SDPE* (Havana: 1981). Castro echoes this conclusion in his speech to the Second Party Congress in December 1980.

26. *Ibid.*, 87–91.

Table 13.3

Official Growth Rates of Gross Social Product (GSP), 1962–1983

	Average annual rates at constant prices				
	1962–65	1966–70	1971–75	1976–80	1981–83
GSP	3.7%	0.4%	7.5%	4.0%	7.7%
GSP per capita	1.3%	− 1.3%	5.7%	3.1%	6.8%

Sources: Calculated from C. Mesa-Lago, *The Economy of Socialist Cuba,* p. 34; Banco Nacional de Cuba, *Informe Económico* 1984, p. 17; Comité Estatal de Estadísticas (CEE), *Anuario Estadístico de Cuba,* 1981, p. 67 and 1982, p. 98; CEE, *La Economía Cubana,* 1982, p. 17 and 1983, p. 18.

Note: According to the State Statistical Committee these official rates represent constant price or real rates of growth. Officially recognized inflation (implicit GSP deflator) equalled 0.86% per year between 1976 and 1980, 11.7% in 1981, 1.2% in 1982, and 1.2% again in 1983. There is still some uncertainty about the treatment of price increases, resulting from shifting turnover taxes, in the trade sector reported in these official figures.

pound in 1974, to 20 cents in 1975, and below 10 cents during 1977–1979;[27] agricultural pests such as sugar cane smut, tobacco blue mold, and swine fever, along with severe hurricanes and an oil tanker spill in the prime lobster bed at the end of the five-year period; and growing Cuban foreign aid and military involvement in Africa which incurred economic costs.[28] With the pests overcome and higher world sugar prices during 1980 and 1981, economic growth accelerated again and real Gross Social Product grew by 14.8 percent in 1981. Markedly lower world sugar prices since 1982, however, have contributed to slower economic growth, reportedly 2.7 percent in 1982 and 5.2 percent in 1983 in real terms.

Achievements of the Cuban Revolution

A 1982 study on the Cuban economy, prepared for the Joint Economic Committee of the U.S. Congress, begins with the following acknowledgment:

> The genuine socio-economic and political accomplishments of the Cuban revolution have attracted international attention. These accomplishments include:

---

27. Cuba exported around 70 percent of its sugar over this period to the USSR and received subsidized prices equivalent to 30 to 44 cents per pound. Cuba's terms of trade with non-COMECON countries deteriorated 53 percent between 1975 and 1979.

28. Many of these problems are discussed at length by C. Mesa-Lago in his article, "The Economy: Caution, Frugality and Resilient Ideology," in J. Dominguez, ed., *Cuba: Internal and International Affairs* (Beverly Hills: Sage Publications, 1982).

—A highly egalitarian redistribution of income that has eliminated almost all malnutrition, particularly among children.

—Establishment of a national health care program that is superior in the Third World and rivals that of numerous developed countries.

—Near total elimination of illiteracy and a highly developed multilevel educational system.

—Development of a relatively well-disciplined and motivated population with a strong sense of national identification.[29]

This list could be extended to include: full employment, near eradication of radical discrimination, rapidly improving position of women, rapid growth of and universal access to the arts, and good overall economic growth.[30]

Naturally, a sizable list of shortcomings of the Cuban revolution could also be compiled, including: large-scale economic waste, chronic balance of trade deficits, shortages of consumer goods, consumer inconvenience, and severe restrictions on political opposition. Nonetheless, when Cuba of the eighties is compared with pre-1959 Cuba or with its hemispheric neighbors in Latin America, the contrast in health and education is striking and unambiguously attests to the monumental human achievement of the revolution (see Table 13.4).

Although Cuba still has an underdeveloped economy and development policy has emphasized social consumption (for example, health, education) and meeting basic needs, significant strides have been made in recent years to diversify and increase the availability of commodities for individual consumption. In 1970, 94 percent of a total of 274 generic products sold in Cuba were rationed. In 1980, only 21 percent of generic products were rationed and the number of generic products increased from 274 to 874. In 1980, 51 percent of food products and 17 percent of nonfood products were rationed, compared to 93 percent and 94 percent, respectively, in 1970. Overall, in 1970, 95 percent of consumer spending was on rationed goods while in 1980 this proportion was approximately 30 percent.[31]

Rationing, of course, is simply a means of ensuring that everyone receives a certain amount of a basic good that is in short supply. The price system also "rations" in a sense to those who can afford higher prices. The result of "price system rationing" is greater inequality in consumption, no guaranteed minimal consumption level, and lower administrative costs. The fact that Cuba has sharply reduced the

---

29. *Cuba Faces the Economic Realities of the 1980s*, prepared by Lawrence Theriot, Bureau of East-West Trade, U.S. Dept. of Commerce, 1982, p. 5.

30. This good overall record of economic growth is attributable primarily to strong growth since 1970. The advanced student may wish to consult the critical review of the scholarly literature on Cuban statistics provided by Claes Brundenius and A. Zimbalist in "Recent Studies on Cuban Economic Growth: A Review," *ACES Bulletin* (Spring 1985).

31. M. Bald, "Cuban Consumer at the Crossroads," *Cubatimes* (Summer 1981): 7.

Table 13.4
Health and Social Indicators

	Adult literacy (percentage of population)		No. enrolled in secondary school as percentage of age group		Population per physician	Per capita daily calorie intake	Per capita daily protein intake (grams)	Infant mortality rate[1] (age 0–1)		Child death rate[1] (age 1–4)		Life expectancy
	a	b	a	b	b	b	c	a	b	a	b	b
Cuba	76	97	14	51	626	2,900	75	69	18.5	8	2	73
Colombia	63	—	12	43	1,970	2,364	47	113	—	20	8	63
Brazil	61	76	11	24	1,700	2,562	63	128	92	17	8	63
Venezuela	63	82	21	38	930	2,435	62	72	40	12	5	67
Mexico	65	82	11	39	1,820	2,654	65	78	60	13	5	66
El Salvador	49	62	13	23	3,600	2,051	—	—	60	23	8	63

Note: The letter *a* designates a year between 1958 and 1960; *b*, a year between 1977 and 1981; and *c*, a year between 1973 and 1980. The numbers shown in this table are *averages* and do not denote distributional characteristics.
1. per thousand.

share of rationed goods represents success in increasing the supply and assortment of consumer items as well as less consumer inconvenience.

Finally, many of the newly available goods are consumer durables beginning to be produced in Cuba. By 1982, for every 100 Cuban homes there were 67 televisions, 119 radios, 35 refrigerators, and 34 washing machines.[32]

Soviet Economic Aid

Many critics of the Cuban economy have contended that Cuba's economic achievements are attributable entirely to massive doses of economic aid from the Soviet Union. The CIA, for instance, has estimated that this aid equaled $8 million a day in 1979. (This would amount to 10 to 20 percent of National Income depending on which estimate of National Income is adopted.)[33] Although Soviet aid is very important to the Cuban economy, the magnitude of this claim is misleading and is derived from improper methodology.

The CIA estimates of Soviet aid to Cuba include: the sugar price subsidy, the petroleum price subsidy, the nickel price subsidy, and balance of payments aid. The price subsidies are the difference between the implicit price received from (or paid to) the USSR and the world market price.

In 1979, for instance, the world market price for raw sugar averaged 9.65 cents per pound and the implicit price received from the Soviet Union was an estimated 44 cents per pound—a 34.35 cents per pound subsidy. In 1979, the total sugar price subsidy had a CIA estimated value of $2.3 billion out of $3.1 billion (74.2 percent) of total estimated yearly aid.

The first problem, then, with this estimate of $3.1 billion (or over $8 million a day) is that it was derived for a year when the price subsidy was unrepresentative. In 1980, average world sugar prices rose to 28.7 cents per pound and in 1981 they were 18.4 cents per pound. If we assume the USSR continued to pay Cuba the implicit price of 44 cents per pound in 1980 and 1981, the subsidy per pound in 1980 was less than half of what it was in 1979. Moreover, with higher world market prices the Cubans probably exported considerably less sugar to the USSR, cutting the total sugar subsidy even more.

The use of the world-market price as distinct from the U.S. raw sugar price might also be questioned. Because of import controls, the U.S. price has generally exceeded the world market price. On February 8, 1983, for instance, the U.S. price of raw sugar exceeded the

---

32. CEPAL, "Cuba," Estudio Económico de América Latina, 1982 (New York: United Nations, Nov. 1983), p. 6.

33. Central Intelligence Agency, The Cuban Economy: A Statistical Review (Washington, D.C.: Government Printing Office, March 1981).

world market price by 15.3 cents per pound. If Cuba were not selling its sugar to the USSR and was restored a share of the U.S. market, it would receive the U.S. price for its quota sugar. Naturally, if the CIA used the U.S. price as a basis for comparison, the estimated subsidy would drop significantly.

The Economic Commission for Latin America of the United Nations reported that while terms of trade between Cuba and the USSR were constant from 1975 to 1977, they deteriorated in 1979 as a result of, among other things, a "substantial modification of the contractual base which served to establish the adjustment mechanism, by disconnecting the price paid for sugar from Soviet exports to Cuba." This claim has not been confirmed by other sources, but if it is valid it further undermines the CIA estimates. To be sure, increasing economic difficulties in the USSR and Eastern Europe lend support to the contention that the Soviet Union cannot maintain the favorable price subsidies for trade with Cuba. The stringent measures adopted by the Cuban government since the beginning of 1981 to reduce oil consumption suggest further that the real price of petroleum from the Soviet Union is rising. (The severity, as well as the effectiveness, of these measures is indicated by the fact that twenty-one gallons of petroleum were used per ton of sugar produced during the 1981–82 season compared to seventy gallons per ton used the previous year.)

(If the subsidy mechanism has not been altered, it is probable that Soviet aid increased again, from its reduced 1980–81 level, in 1982 when world raw sugar prices hovered in the six to eight cents per pound range. However, prices began to rise again in mid 1983 and by July 1983 were around eleven cents, implying falling Soviet subsidies once again. Two significant factors behind the weak 1982–83 market are: (1) European government subsidies to domestic beet sugar growers to expand output and exports, ignoring the International Sugar Agreement; and (2) stricter U.S. import quotas to artificially maintain higher prices to benefit U.S. producers, thus making more sugar available on the world market.)

The second problem with the CIA estimate is that it treats implicit prices in primarily barter trade with the USSR as equally valuable to dollar prices in the open market. Eighty percent or more of Soviet payments for Cuban sugar is in the form of goods implicitly priced at COMECON levels. Often these prices are higher than world prices, and almost invariably the quality of these goods is inferior to what could be purchased in the open international market. Cuba has spent countless millions on Soviet products, such as the first vintage of mechanical cane harvesters, which didn't work.

Other disadvantages of trade with the Soviet Union are less apparent to the outside observer. An official of the West Coast Longshoremen's Union, Herb Mills, had the very unusual experience in the fall of 1979 of being allowed onto a Soviet merchant ship in the Odessa harbor bound for Cuba. He observed in near disbelief the loading of tires and rebar steel into two of the ship's three hatches. The job was done so carelessly that Mills estimated the discharge time in the Havana docks would be at least doubled and the danger to the health of the Cuban stevedores multiplied severalfold compared to a properly stowed load. This circumstance obviously imposes hidden costs on the Cuban economy that are not reflected by the officially quoted price subsidies.

The fact, then, that the price subsidy is, in effect, "tied aid" in the form of restricted ruble credits rather than dollars greatly diminishes its true value. Specific information on terms of trade within COMECON is difficult to obtain. Several studies lend support to the conclusion that COMECON prices tend to lie above world market levels.[34] One study by Leon Goure and Julian Weinkle states that "an estimate by the National Bank of Cuba places the total cost of the Soviet goods supplied to Cuba at about 50 percent above what Cuba would have had to pay if it had been able to purchase the same quality and types of goods from non-Communist countries."[35]

The third problem with the CIA estimate is that the calculation does not deduct certain indirect costs that Cuba incurs as a result of its political goals. In addition to committing massive manpower resources to military operations in Africa, Cuba has sent hundreds of doctors to Ethiopia, Angola, and Nicaragua. Altogether there are over 2,500 Cuban public health workers doing service in twenty-seven other countries.[36] Cuba has also sent over two thousand teachers, eight thousand construction workers, and hundreds of technicians to these countries. Further, COMECON has been known to require resource diversion to meet crises within the bloc, exemplified by the case of Poland in the early 1980s. Lastly, some Cuba experts have suggested that Cuba's involvement in Africa is likely to have contributed to the suspension or reduction of economic and technical aid to Cuba after 1976 from Sweden, Holland, Norway, and West Germany. Whether or not one approves of Cuba's international solidarity posture, it entails a significant drain on Cuba's productive resources. This type of commitment is not made by other underdeveloped nations and must be included in the assessment of the ability of the Cuban economy to stand on its own feet.

A fourth problem with the CIA figures is in the category of balance

---

34. See, for instance, the review of this literature in J. Perez-Lopez, "Sugar and Petroleum in Cuban-Soviet Terms of Trade," in C. Blasier and C. Mesa-Lago, eds., *Cuba in the World* (Pittsburgh: University of Pittsburgh Press, 1979). Official pricing formulas in COMECON since 1976, however, are based on world market prices. Whether they are adhered to or not is another question.

35. L. Gouré and J. Weinkle, "Cuba's New Dependency," *Problems of Communism* 21, 2 (Mar./Apr. 1972): 75.

36. Banco Nacional de Cuba, *Highlights of Cuban Economic and Social Development 1976–1980 and Main Targets for 1981–85* (Havana: 1981), 19.

of payments aid from the Soviet Union. The CIA estimates that such aid rose steadily from $150 million in 1975 to $330 million in 1978 and $440 million in 1979. In 1978 (the last year such data is currently available) Cuba ran a balance of trade surplus of $86 million with the USSR and Eastern Europe which, by itself, would imply a flow of funds in the other direction. However, also in 1978, Cuba had a hard currency trade deficit of $273 million. It is probable that most or all of this was covered by Western loans. Even if one made the unrealistic assumption that the USSR lent Cuba hard currency to cover half of this, it would still not explain the CIA estimate of $330 million balance of payments aid. Similar problems exist for the estimates for other years.

Returning to the question of the viability of the Cuban economy in its own right, several additional considerations must be borne in mind. One cost Cuba has paid for its relationship with the Soviet Union is the continuing economic blockade by the United States (and most of Latin America). The blockade still brings a terrific burden upon the Cuban economy. There is still a sizable share of Cuba's productive assets which are of U.S. origin. Without proper parts, machinery which could be cheaply repaired must instead be entirely replaced. The same applies to many consumer goods (Soviet tires don't fit American cars, Soviet light bulbs don't fit American sockets, etc.).

The U.S. has also stepped up the pressure on its trading partners against trading with Cuba and, in many cases, has been effective. The French conglomerate Le Creusot Loire was using Cuban nickel in steel it was shipping to the United States. The steel was banned from entering the United States and Le Creusot Loire canceled its already-underway contract to build two factories in Cuba for converting bagasse to paper. Two Canadian firms negotiating contracts to build a citrus processing factory and a power plant recently backed down under pressure from the U.S. Department of Commerce. During the 1981 dengue fever epidemic, obstructions on a U.S. subsidiary based in Mexico led to pesticides being flown in from Europe at a cost of five thousand dollars per ton, making freight three and a half times more costly than the product.[37] The list of similar incidents is long.

In addition to the explicit and comprehensive blockade by the United States, Cuba must also countenance extensive discriminatory tariffs from the European Common Market. For example, a 47-percent tariff on Cuban cigars takes away Cuba's natural European market edge and gives it to Jamaica, whose cigars enter the Common Market tariff-free. A discriminatory tariff against Cuban rum gives the edge to Bacardi (from Puerto Rico), and so on.

---

37. These examples are based on interviews with Cuban economic planners in March 1982 and reports in the *Economist's Intelligence Unit* quarterly publications on the Cuban economy as well as articles in *Cubatimes*.

Even excluding these manifold disadvantages of being in the Soviet bloc, the base figure of $8 million a day of Soviet economic aid to Cuba is completely unrealistic. It should be pointed out, however, that such aid levels are not unheard of outside the Soviet bloc. Chile, for instance, was running an average $10 million a day balance of payments deficit during 1981 which must have been supported by a corresponding aid program. Yet Chile cannot boast of any of Cuba's economic and social accomplishments.

Prospects

Despite financial and technical reliance on the Soviet Union, Cuba's productive structure is being gradually transformed. Unlike the pre-1959 era when Cuba's economy remained calcified with only a single cash crop in agriculture and some final processing operations in light industry, the last quarter century has brought substantial import substitution as well as industrial and agricultural diversification and export promotion. Capital goods, consumer durables, chemicals, medicines, electronics, computers, and steel are all sectors with negligible or zero output in 1958 that are now substantial and growing rapidly. Others, such as citrus, fish, eggs, nickel, cement, and electricity, have expanded several times over since the revolution. Cuba is now producing a large majority of its new cane harvesters, buses, and refrigerators and other durables.

These developments do not mean that Cuba is on the threshold of nondependence on sugar or of general economic prosperity; rather, there is now a dynamic element in place that is bringing increasing potential for long-run economic strength, diversity, and greater self-sufficiency.

In the short run, the Cuban economy will remain vulnerable to its excessive dependency on sugar exports and the Soviet Union. With extremely depressed sugar prices, lower Soviet aid, and the weak international economy, the prospects for continued economic growth during the remainder of the 1981–1985 Five-Year Plan are uncertain.

Conclusion

As is true for market economies, centrally planned economies are different from one another. Although they experience similar problems and trade-offs, they also make different choices, establish distinct organizational arrangements, and perform quite variably.

It is usually difficult to perceive the breadth of these differences by looking at only the formal structure of planning. It is the case in Cuba, for instance, that a large majority of planning bodies and institutions bear the same names (in translation) and formal relations to one another as in the Soviet Union. In this sense, the 1976 economic reform in Cuba bears a striking resemblance to the 1965 reform in the USSR.

To identify the planning *form*, however, is not the same as identifying the planning *content*. The latter is different in Cuba because the social relations are different. That is, compared with the Soviet Union, there is stricter adherence to professed egalitarian norms and, it appears, considerably greater popular involvement in decision making. This difference is evident as much for production decisions as it is for the position and role of the Cuban consumer.

For instance, the Cuban Institute of Internal Demand is in charge of surveying consumer preferences, goods inventories, and needs. It has a *formal* Soviet counterpart, but the Cuban Institute is more active and powerful in its impact on planning decisions. It also relies for its effectiveness on a network of thousands of volunteers to provide biweekly information on the operation of retail stores, shortages, consumer suggestions, etc. In addition, the Institute publishes its own monthly magazine which reports on new consumer styles, runs campaigns against harmful consumption such as cigarettes and sugar (yes, sugar), and carries eight or ten pages of classified ads. These ads are for a panoply of privately provided services (e.g., repair of appliances, TVs, and cars, massages, carpentry, plumbing, cosmetics, gardening, music lessons, magicians and clowns for children's parties) and production (e.g., privately constructed housing—in 1981, 38 percent of new housing units were built by private contractors). These activities have been sanctioned since the late seventies and represent a level of legal decentralization not present in the USSR or the rest of Eastern Europe, except Hungary and Yugoslavia.

The formal planning system is also more decentralized in Cuba. Forty-one percent of all enterprises are subordinated to local and regional government ("organs of popular power"). Unlike the Soviet Union, local government representatives in Cuba are chosen in open, contested elections; and elected delegates are required to hold regular meetings (at least one every three weeks) with their constituents. Local government bodies elect from among themselves representatives to the provincial and national governments. At these higher government levels, special commissions are formed which study economic problems and discuss with JUCEPLAN and the Council of Ministers the priorities in the One- and Five-Year Plans.

Electoral choice and popular participation does not imply the existence of a political opposition. Cuba is a one-party state and any meaningful opposition is suppressed. Doubtless, the existence of oppositional political parties or greater openness would be exploited by the United States, as it has been in the past, to destabilize the Castro government. The resources of the United States being so immense relative to Cuba's, Castro perhaps has cause for his apprehension and political restrictions. Many scholars believe that the best United States policy to further democratize the Cuban society would be to cease the blockade and other acts of aggression. These facts help us to explain, without approving, the absence of a democratic opposition in Cuba.

Finally, Cuba still has a sizable and flourishing private sector in farming. This sector accounts for over 25 percent of all farmland and has its own political organization, ANAP (National Association of Small Farmers). ANAP has a significant impact on government policy regarding prices, provision of inputs, rural social services, etc. As mentioned earlier, since March 1980 a portion of farm output has been sold at free farmers' markets. These markets exist throughout the island and are becoming an important source of distribution as well as farmer income. (State farms are also allowed to sell surplus produce in these markets.)

The differences in form and content between Cuba's political economy and that of the USSR reflect Cuba's unique social and economic history. As outlined above, an important aspect of this history involves the nature of the revolutionary party, its ideology, its struggle against Batista, and its relationship to the Cuban people.

Cuba has greater latitude for experimentation with its economic institutions than do the countries of Eastern Europe because of its geographic distance from the USSR as well as the circumstances surrounding the Communist takeover in Eastern Europe. This latitude will become even broader if the United States ends its blockade and reduces Cuban dependence on the Soviet Union. (Since early 1982 Cuba has sent numerous signals to the international community that it is eager to improve relations with the United States and to attract foreign capital. For example, Cuba's foreign investment code of February 1982 offers to foreign capital up to 49 percent ownership as well as free pricing, production, and employment policies.[38])

Finally, in this chapter we have emphasized the role of politics and the United States in Cuban economic performance. This has not been done to minimize the internal sources of difficulties and failures of the Cuban revolution but rather to provide a more complete analysis of the situation. In general, developing economies which are (1) small in size and more dependent on trade and (2) geographically close to a superpower—while challenging the economic model adhered to by the superpower—will inevitably be greatly affected by external politics. The case of Chile under Allende and the ongoing experiences of Nicaragua and Cuba make it quite clear that economic policies and performance cannot be adequately comprehended without a consideration of the activities of the United States. The same logic applies, even more so, to the Soviet Union and Eastern Europe.

---

38. According to *The Economist* of April 17, 1982, Castro is also pondering the establishment of an industrial free trade zone.

Recommended Readings

1. Carmelo Mesa-Lago, *The Economy of Socialist Cuba* (Albuquerque: University of New Mexico Press, 1981).

2. Arthur MacEwan, *Revolution and Economic Development in Cuba* (London: Macmillan, 1981).

3. Claes Brundenius, *Revolutionary Cuba: The Challenge of Economic Growth with Equity* (Boulder: Westview Press, 1984).

4. Benjamin Medea, J. Collins, and M. Scott, *No Free Lunch: Food and Revolution in Cuba Today* (San Francisco: Institute for Food and Development Policy, 1984).

Five

MARKET SOCIALISM

This part of the book investigates Hungary and Yugoslavia. These two economies call themselves socialist, but the market plays a larger role here than in other socialist economies. They thus present different issues from those confronted by centrally planned socialism.

In the first chapter, Chapter 14, we present the theoretical model of pure market socialism, as well as the controversies that have raged around it. In the next two chapters, we examine the actual economies of these two countries to see (1) how well they have performed, and (2) how far they deviate from a pure model of market socialism.

(Given the 1984 changes in China's system of economic organization, China too could be included in this group of market-oriented socialist economies. These developments, however, have come after the writing of this book. It remains to be seen whether China can stick to its present course.)

14

THE THEORY OF MARKET SOCIALISM

The reader by this time should be quite familiar with the array of economic problems associated with central planning. As we have seen, these problems have brought forth conscious efforts at economic reform and decentralization as well as spontaneous decentralization through the development of the so-called second economy.[1]

In the Soviet Union and most of Eastern Europe the reforms were cut short and aborted at an early stage. However, in two countries, Hungary and Yugoslavia, the reforms were gradually carried forward and the market gained progressive significance as a coordinating mechanism in the economy. The institutional arrangements in each economy are now sufficiently different from the centrally planned economies to warrant a separate analysis.

The Hungarian experience with a modified market socialism has been successful enough to become a showcase for economic reform among the centrally planned economies. For instance, in the current wave of economic reforms in China (see Chapter 12) policymakers have closely studied the Hungarian model. The present Polish government under Jaruzelski is attempting to follow the Hungarian road to decentralization, although the prevailing state of economic and political disarray bodes poorly for any program.

In the chapters that follow we shall discuss the Yugoslav and Hungarian economies in some detail. Before doing this, however, it is important to look at the theory of and the debate on the economics of market socialism.

---

1. See R. Knaack, "Dynamic Comparative Economics: Lessons from Socialist Planning," in A. Zimbalist, ed., *Comparative Economic Systems: An Assessment of Knowledge, Theory and Method* (Boston: Kluwer-Nijhoff, 1983).

The Economics of Market Socialism

In Chapter 9 we discussed the beginnings of the economic debate on efficiency and socialism. Briefly, just prior to 1900 Pareto demonstrated mathematically that attaining allocational efficiency involved solving the same equations in either a market or a planned economy.[2] That is, *in theory* efficiency was possible in either economic system. Naturally, in a perfectly competitive market economy the solutions flow automatically, under certain assumptions, and in a planned economy they must be calculated and implemented administratively.

Apparently unaware of Pareto's proof, writing in 1920 Ludwig von Mises maintained that economic rationality was impossible under socialism.[3] In the next stage of the debate, Friedrich Hayek conceded that *in theory* the planners might accumulate all the millions of pieces of necessary information and might then solve all the millions of equations to make an optimal decision.[4] *In practice*, Hayek argued, no conceivable force of planners could actually gather all of the various kinds of information from every factory and farm, and from every private and public consumer. Furthermore, *in practice*, even with all of the information, it would take hundreds of years to solve correctly all of the equations for just one year's plan.

The most famous answer to Hayek's criticism of the practicability of socialist planning was given by Oskar Lange.[5] He replied that a decentralized or market socialism would have no more trouble than competitive private enterprise in reaching rational prices and an optimal allocation of resources.

In Lange's system, there is public ownership of the means of production (although he allows for private ownership of small-scale industry, retailing, and farming). The Central Planning Board (CPB) performs several basic economic functions: it appoints directors of enterprises and of whole industries; it sets the rules governing their production decisions; it fixes the prices for all capital goods and nonlabor inputs (consumer goods prices and wages are set freely by the forces of supply and demand in the market); it chooses the rate of capital accumulation (investment) and sets the interest rate in order to equilibrate the available supply of capital with the chosen demand.

The CPB's functions, thus, are extensive but do not include the decision about what to produce, how much to produce, and how to

---

2. V. Pareto, *Cours d'economie politique* (Lausanne, 1897).

3. See Ludwig von Mises, "Economic Calculation in the Socialist Commonwealth," in F. A. Hayek, ed., *Collectivist Economic Planning* (London: Routledge and Kegan Paul, Ltd., 1935).

4. See Hayek, *Collectivist Economic Planning*.

5. Oskar Lange and Fred Taylor, *On the Economic Theory of Socialism* (New York: McGraw-Hill, 1964).

produce (again, with the exception of setting the level of investment). These decisions are made by the managers of enterprises and of industries according to two rules established by the CPB. The first rule is that the enterprise should produce up to the level of output where the marginal costs of production equal the output price set by the CPB. (The industry should produce at the level where the *long run* marginal cost equals the estimated future price.) The second rule is that the enterprise should use the factors of production in such a combination that $MP_i/P_i = MP_j/P_j$ for all factors, where MP is marginal product, P is price, and i and j are different factors of production. In other words, the last dollar spent on each factor should yield the same addition to output. The successful implementation of these two rules will ensure that the optimal level of output is produced and that enterprises are minimizing their production costs (using the optimal combination of inputs).

The CPB is to set prices in such a way as to equilibrate supply and demand. Lange argues that this process is relatively simple and straightforward. If at the prevailing price for, say, an intermediate good there is a shrinking inventory of the good (i.e., demand exceeds supply), then the price of the good should be raised. If inventories are increasing (i.e., supply exceeds demand), then the price should be lowered. The CPB need only look at inventory levels to set prices; no detailed or quantitative knowledge of costs or demand is required. Since prices go up when demand goes up and prices fall when demand falls and since, by rule one, production levels follow prices, Lange's system preserves consumer sovereignty in the neoclassical sense. That is, it does not impose the preferences of a central agency regarding what is to be produced. Finally, if the two rules are followed, together with free markets in labor and consumer goods, the system will generate an efficient allocation of resources.

Lange's model of market socialism, therefore, bears all the positive microeconomic attributes of a perfectly competitive capitalist economy. In addition, Lange argues that his system has several advantages over a competitive capitalist economy. One advantage: since the CPB has a broader vision of the economy than a private entrepreneur when setting prices, it will, if anything, "be able to reach the right equilibrium prices by a much shorter series of successive trials than a competitive market actually does."[6] A second advantage: in setting prices the CPB will be able to explicitly and directly include social costs (not usually paid by private firms) in addition to private costs. Here Lange gives three examples. First, when an employee is discharged by a private firm, certain costs of maintaining that worker are borne by the society and not the firm. In its calculation about firing a worker the private firm in a competitive environment looks at its

---

6. *Ibid.*, 89.

private costs and, hence, does not make a socially optimal decision (see Chapter 3, pages 80 and 81, for an illustration of this point). As a second example, in a private competitive firm there is no a priori cost provision for industrial accidents or diseases although social costs are present. (Of course, government regulations regarding workmen's compensation do often internalize to the firm at least a portion of the social costs.) Again, social and private costs diverge and a socially inefficient allocation of resources results. The last example is the standard case of external economies (e.g., inventions) or diseconomies (e.g., pollution) which are not accounted for by the marketplace.

A third advantage: Lange points out that with public ownership of the means of production there will be no property income. With this source of inequality eliminated, the distribution of income will be considerably more equal under market socialism than under capitalism. This circumstance is desirable since it means that marketplace votes will be more equally distributed, and, from a utilitarian point of view, total consumer utility will be enhanced (a poor person gets more utility out of a dollar than a rich person).

Finally, Lange sees a macroeconomic advantage to his system.

> As a result of the possibility of taking into account all the alternatives a socialist economy would not be subject to the fluctuations of the business cycle. . . . In a socialist economy there can be, of course, grave mistakes and misdirection of investments and production. But such misdirection need not lead to shrinkage of output and unemployment of factors of production spreading over the whole economic system. A private entrepreneur *has* to close his plant when he incurs grave losses. In a socialist economy a mistake is a mistake, too, and has to be corrected. But in making the correction *all* the alternatives gained and sacrificed can be taken into account, and there is no need to correct losses in one part of the economic system by a procedure which creates still further losses by the secondary effect of a cumulative shrinkage of demand and of unemployment of factors of production. Mistakes can be *localized*, a partial overproduction does not need to turn into a general one. Thus the business cycle theorist would lose his subject of study in a socialist economy, but the knowledge accumulated by him would still be useful in finding out ways of preventing mistakes, and methods of correcting those made that would not lead to further losses.[7]

Lange, anticipating his critics, notes two possible disadvantages to his system. First, the rate of capital accumulation is set arbitrarily by the CPB rather than by the forces of supply and demand. Lange, however, sees this as a small problem. Under capitalism, the rate of investment is, he asserts, affected more by the distribution of income ("which is irrational" says Lange) than by the interest rate. In addi-

---

7. *Ibid.*, 105–6.

tion, under capitalism, the public's attempt to save may be frustrated by an inadequate attempt to invest by firms. That is, excess planned saving will result in insufficient aggregate demand so that output, income, and employment will fall.

The second objection to his system, according to Lange, is the possible "bureaucratization of economic life" and he regards this more seriously. However, Lange retorts: "Unfortunately, we do not see how the same, or even greater, danger can be averted under monopolistic capitalism. Officials subject to democratic control seem preferable to private corporation executives who practically are responsible to nobody."[8] Were Lange writing today, he doubtless would point out the marked tendency of advanced capitalist economies toward increasing regulation and attribute this to growing market failures under "monopoly capitalism." Greater government regulation in market economies also contributes to the "bureaucratization of economic life."

Lange did not anticipate all the subsequent criticisms of his model. The two most important orthodox critics of Lange are Friedrich Hayek and Abram Bergson.[9] Grouping their arguments, we present the objections as follows. First, it is contended that price setting by the CPB will be far more problematic than expected by Lange. In a modern, complex economy there will be hundreds of thousands of prices to set and an enormously diverse variety of goods with many styles and prices. How will the CPB obtain accurate and timely inventory information on all those goods? How often will the CPB adjust prices? One response to these very legitimate concerns is to recall that consumer goods prices are not set by the CPB in Lange's economy but are free to fluctuate with supply and demand.

The second objection is how will the CPB know if each enterprise is following the two rules for setting output and minimizing costs? It is maintained that the only way to effectively monitor this compliance would be to probe deeply into each enterprise's operation. Such probing along with the complexity of price setting would engender an awesome central economic bureaucracy which would reproduce many of the costs and irrationalities of central planning.

In evaluating this criticism it is useful to consider two situations. In the first situation, if an industry is competitive and appropriate factor prices are being charged, the monitoring of compliance with rules is straightforward: those firms that do not follow rules will have lower

---

8. *Ibid.*, 109.

9. See F. Hayek, "Socialist Calculation: The Competitive 'Solution'," *Economica* (May 1940): 125–49; and A. Bergson, "Market Socialism Revisited," *Journal of Political Economy* (Oct. 1967): 655–73. A good discussion of the debate can also be found in Benjamin Ward, *The Socialist Economy* (New York: Random House, 1967), Chap. 2.

profits—readily observable by the CPB, to which all profits are transferred.

In the second situation, if the industry is dominated by a few firms with large market shares, then profits may no longer be a reliable index of compliance. This is because it would be in the interest of an oligopolistic or a monopolistic firm maximizing profits to reduce output below the competitive level to the point where marginal cost equaled marginal revenue (assuming the existence of a demand curve for the firm). In so doing, output of the industry would be reduced relative to demand at the existing price, inventories would decrease, and the CPB would be prompted to raise prices. In this second case, however, with only one or a few firms per industry, direct enterprise monitoring by the CPB or its branch representative will present less of a problem because of the reduced number of units to be supervised.

Implicit in this question of rule compliance is the issue of managerial incentives and motivation. (A manager might ignore the rules or a manager might endeavor to follow the rules but fail.) If all profits go to the state and there is no explicit system of managerial bonuses, what will stimulate the managers to (a) want to comply with the rules or maximize profits or (b) engage in a desirable degree of risk-taking and entrepreneurial behavior? Bergson is less worried about the motivation problem for industrial managers than for enterprise managers because "... as he ascends a bureaucratic structure an executive tends to identify more with those at the highest level."[10] (This observation is of particular interest since it is less clear what standard to apply in evaluating the behavior of industrial, as distinct from enterprise, managers.) The prospect of possible promotion may also be a motivating factor for the enterprise manager.

One might also raise the concern about the motivation of average workers to perform at or near their potential. In Lange's system there is no direct bonus for workers, only a general "social dividend" which is shared by the whole society in an unspecified manner. It is a rather remote material incentive for an individual to share the fruits of his or her productive efforts with a whole society. If there is full employment in the economy as Lange expects (and, hence, no "whip of unemployment"), the issue of worker motivation becomes even more pressing. It is noteworthy that Lange includes no provision for worker participation in enterprise decision making or for job redesign. Of course, it is possible that Lange was simply treating the internal workings of a firm as a black box as is conventional in microeconomic literature.

Naturally, it is conceivable that if the society is democratic (as Lange prescribes) and the public feels well represented by the market for consumer goods and by the CPB, there will be a general

---

10. Bergson, "Market Socialism Revisited," 658.

willingness to cooperate. If such social relations do not prevail, however, the likelihood of higher worker absenteeism, shirking, slacking off, and so on, increases.

Alternative Market Socialist Models

The specifications of Lange's models are certainly not the only ones conceivable for a market socialist economy. For instance, one might view the prospect of repeatedly setting and resetting prices for all intermediate goods with sufficient awe to stipulate a model where pricing is decentralized. This provision, in turn, may be modified with another allowing for state regulation of certain key prices.

The work of expatriate Polish economist Wlodzimierz Brus should be pursued by those interested in alternative modelings of the optimal institutions of a market socialist–type economy.[11] One of Brus' most interesting points concerns worker participation in management, an area unexplored by Lange. Brus asserts that such participation is an essential feature of any effective effort at decentralization. It will "release the initiative of those directly engaged in the production process and . . . [create] a feeling of responsibility for the success of the enterprise as a whole which, in turn, cannot be expected unless employees have a real influence in the running of the enterprise."[12] Brus also claims that worker participation will result in lengthening the enterprise's time horizon and, hence, diminish the traditional resistance to technological change which comes from the unidimensional focus by "one-man managers" on meeting the enterprise's quarterly or annual production target. "An enterprise," Brus writes, "must be able to work for its long-term interests and the best way of ensuring this is to develop collective decision-making, collective incentives and collective responsibility."[13]

Apart from the instrumental reasons for introducing worker participation as seen from the perspective of planners and managers, it must be mentioned that industrial democracy has been a central demand of all mass movements for democratic reform in Eastern Europe. Spontaneous worker councils were present and prominent

---

11. W. Brus, *The Market in a Socialist Economy* (London: Routledge and Kegan Paul, 1972); and W. Brus, *The Economics and Politics of Socialism* (London: Routledge and Kegan Paul, 1973).

12. Brus, *Economics and Politics*, 41. Brus refers to a management structure in which workers *participate in* rather than *control* decision making. Hence, the literature on the theory of worker-managed economies with the presumed enterprise objective function of maximizing income per worker (discussed in Chapter 16) would not apply to the case of worker participation advocated by Brus.

13. *Ibid.*

in the Soviet Union in 1917–18, in Czechoslovakia in 1948 and 1968, in Hungary in 1956, and in Poland in 1956 and again in 1981. To be sure, the only East European country which has managed a clear and sustained break from the Soviet model is Yugoslavia, where worker councils and worker self-management are basic pillars of their industrial system.

Finally, it should be observed that market socialism has been criticized from the Left as well. Several authors have suggested that competitive market forces may have an impact on social organization which is antithetical to socialist goals.[14] The economic anthropologist Karl Polanyi, for instance, has argued that the market historically has been very disruptive to social cohesion. The prominent Hungarian economist Janos Kornai has pointed to a possible trade-off between the goal of market-type efficiency, on the one hand, and the goals of equality and solidarity, on the other. More will be said on this later.

Reality is invariably more complex than theory, but theory should help focus our questions on key aspects of reality. Many aspects of Yugoslav and Hungarian economic reality conform to the assumptions in the theoretical discussion on market socialism and many do not. In the next two chapters the reader will have the opportunity to weigh theory against reality by examining the experiences of Hungary and Yugoslavia with their own brands of market-oriented socialism.

Recommended Readings

1. Oskar Lange and Fred Taylor, *On the Economic Theory of Socialism* (New York: McGraw-Hill, 1964).

2. Wlodzimierz Brus, *The Market in a Socialist Economy* (London: Routledge and Kegan Paul, 1972).

3. Deborah Milenkovitch, "Is Market Socialism Efficient?" in A. Zimbalist, ed., *Comparative Economic Systems: An Assessment of Knowledge, Theory and Method* (Boston: Kluwer-Nijhoff, 1983).

4. Janos Kornai, "The Dilemmas of a Socialist Economy," *Cambridge Journal of Economics*, no. 4 (1980).

---

14. See J. Kornai, "The Dilemmas of a Socialist Economy," *Cambridge Journal of Economics*, no. 4 (1980): 147–57. K. Polanyi, *The Great Transformation* (Boston: Beacon Press, 1957); and A. Zimbalist, "On the Role of Management in Socialist Development," *World Development* 9, 9 (1981): 971–77. Also see the interesting debate between Paul Sweezy and Charles Bettelheim in their *On the Transition to Socialism* (New York: Monthly Review, 1971), and the work of W. Brus cited above in footnote 11.

15

HUNGARY

PLAN AND MARKET

Goulash, the Budapest String Quartet, exotic dances—perhaps these come to mind when someone mentions Hungary. A comparative systems economist, however, will more likely associate Hungary with the most substantial and effective economic reform in the Soviet bloc. In 1968, the New Economic Mechanism was introduced and placed the Hungarian economy on the road to what Matyas Timar, President of the National Bank, calls *market-oriented socialism*.

In this chapter we shall concern ourselves with the uniquely reformed Hungarian economy: how it works, how it is different and how it is similar to the traditional centrally planned system, and how well it performs and where it is likely headed. We shall begin with the background to the reform to understand the pressures which gave rise to it and the special sociopolitical and economic context into which the reform was introduced.

Background

Hungary is a small country, roughly the size of Indiana. Its ethnically homogeneous population numbers 10.7 million and is growing slowly. With a few exceptions, its land is poor in natural resources and hydroelectric potential. Eighty percent of its oil is imported. These characteristics, among others, make the Hungarian economy heavily dependent on trade. In the last several years Hungary's exports have amounted to around 50 percent of its National Income.[1]

---

1. In 1980 the value of Hungary's exports amounted to 52.7 percent of its net material product. This proportion was 26.4 percent in 1965, 39.2 percent in 1970, and 44.7 percent in 1975. Rezsö Nyers, "Interrelations between Policy and the Economic Reform in Hungary," *Journal of Comparative Economics* 7, 3 (Sept. 1983): 219.

Table 15.1
Agricultural Labor Force, 1870–1975

Year	Percentage of the gainfully employed working in agriculture
1870	80
1910	64.5
1930	52
1941	49
1960	37.3
1975	20.4

Sources: Ivan Berend and G. Ranki, *Hungary: A Century of Economic Development* (New York: Barnes and Noble, 1974), 74; and Nigel Swain, "The Evolution of Hungary's Agricultural System since 1967," in P. Hare, H. Radice, and N. Swain, eds., *Hungary: A Decade of Economic Reform* (London: George Allen and Unwin, 1981), 227.

The first waves of industrialization followed the creation of the Austro-Hungarian Empire in 1867. Foreign capital accounted for 60 percent of all industrial investment between 1867 and 1873, and for 45 percent between 1873 and 1900.[2] A substantial share of Hungary's industrial capacity was lost in the reduction of Hungarian territory following World War I.

Agriculture was the centerpiece of the Hungarian economy (see Table 15.1). Eighty percent of the gainfully employed worked the land in 1870, and a significant part of industrial activity was in food processing. Indeed, Budapest had the reputation of being the milling center of Europe during the first decades of this century.

The serfs were formally liberated in 1848, but the resulting distribution of land was parsimonious. Sixty percent of former serfs received no land or a plot too small for family subsistence, forcing them to seek supplementary employment. Thus, in 1880 there were some four million rural proletarians (including family members) out of a population of six million. The extremely unequal land tenure encouraged a latifundia system, which flourished economically within the protected market of the Austro-Hungarian monarchy.

The historical legacy of a large rural class of wage laborers in Hungary (as in Cuba), as opposed to smallholders or sharecroppers, probably facilitated the later transition to and improved the performance of collective farming under the Communists. On the one hand, a private landowner or sharecropper is more likely to have a deeper attachment to his or her land and to resist collectivization. On the

2. Gyorgy Enyedi, *Hungary: An Economic Geography* (Boulder, Colo.: Westview Press, 1976), 15.

other hand, rural wage workers tend to focus their aspirations on living standards and conditions of work. State or collective farming may or may not be consistent with the amelioration of these considerations.

From the fourteenth century through today Hungary has been shackled by foreign domination. With the exception of brief periods following the revolution of 1848 and World War I internal politics have been defined or severely constrained by foreign powers. This predicament may help to explain both periodic uprisings expressing fierce nationalism (as in 1956) as well as extended times of resignation and relative political tranquility.

As in the rest of Eastern Europe, with the exceptions of Yugoslavia and Albania, communism was brought to Hungary by Soviet troops rather than an indigenous political movement or liberation army. Prior to the establishment of full (one-party) Communist control in 1949, there were national elections in 1945 and 1947. The Communist party candidates received 17 percent of the vote in the 1945 elections and 22.3 percent in 1947.

The Communists reportedly resorted to intimidation and fraud during the August 1947 elections. The veracity of this claim and the extent of such activity does not concern us directly. The point here is that the Communists were a minority party with clearly less than 25 percent support in the electorate; yet they imposed a one-party dictatorship in 1949. The extent of nonsectarian socialist sympathies in the population was undoubtedly broader, but this is a different matter.

The Hungarian Communist party (and its head, Matyas Rakosi) inherited an economy devastated by World War II. An estimated 40 percent of the national wealth was destroyed and some 90 percent of industrial plants were damaged. After a brief period of political rejuvenation and mass mobilization, including worker-controlled factories and a popular land reform program in 1945, Communist party control was consolidated. Rakosi combined a Stalinist flair for political repression and police terror with the Soviet model for economic development. The former included harsh labor laws, political purges, and the 1949 sentencing of Cardinal Mindszenty to life imprisonment. The latter entailed emphasis on heavy industry and high accumulation rates largely achieved at the expense of the peasantry. Beginning in 1948, Rakosi launched a massive drive to collectivize agriculture along with introducing high taxes, compulsory deliveries to the state, and reprisals against rich farmers.

The death of Stalin in March 1953 strengthened the forces of reform throughout Eastern Europe. Relief came quickly to Hungary. In May 1953 Imre Nagy replaced Rakosi as premier (Rakosi remained Party chief) and launched the so-called New Course: political prisoners were set free; concentration camps were abolished; police terror was curtailed; approximately half of the peasants who had been forced onto collective farms were allowed to leave them; resources were shifted from heavy industry to light industry and agriculture; living standards were improved; etc. With a taste of liberalization the Hungarian people wanted more. A rising tide of dissatisfaction following the removal of Nagy in 1955 gave birth to the mass uprisings beginning October 23, 1956. Nagy was reinstalled as head of government along with a cabinet which included Janos Kadar. This rebel government declared its break with the Warsaw Pact. Worker councils spontaneously emerged in factories throughout Hungary and coordinated their activities at municipal, regional, and national levels. Soviet troops invaded to put down the rebellion. After several weeks of intense fighting the outcome was a new, pro-Soviet (yet anti-Rakosi) government led by Janos Kadar, several thousand dead, and in excess of 150,000 refugees.

Kadar gradually succeeded in fashioning a tight, unified Party structure as well as in placating the masses. This entailed manipulations and purges within the Party and certain concessions to the forces of reform. He achieved a reconciliation with the Church, reduced political repression, brought peace to the countryside, allowed the growth of artisan and small-scale cooperative production and retailing, and pursued an economic strategy stressing reform, material gain, and progressive social legislation—all this while maintaining firm political control in the hands of the Party.

The resulting configuration of forces has produced a remarkably cohesive and stable political and economic environment. This, in turn, has been a central element in the relative success of the economy and the 1968 reform.

Early Economic Reform

The grass-roots workers' councils of 1956 were more tenacious and difficult to eliminate than was the old party leadership. It is not a simple matter to convince workers that they have no part to play in the management of a "workers' state." In the absence of democratic institutions for popular input, there must be other strong reasons to induce workers and peasants to accept the legitimacy of Party rule.

One negative factor behind the acceptance of Kadarist rule was the heavy repression and depletion of rebelling ranks wrought by the Soviet army. But Kadar provided many positive reasons as well. He stuck with the development strategy initiated by Nagy: less accumulation, more consumer goods, and greater stimulus to agriculture.

Among Kadar's first measures was the abolition of compulsory agricultural quotas and the temporary decollectivization of agriculture. When the decision to recollectivize agriculture was taken at the end of 1957, it was done with clear sympathy to the sensibilities of the rural workers: collectivization was spread out over four years; the better-off peasants were voluntarily incorporated; generous provision of state agronomists and other aid to the new farms was made; unencumbered elections for the collective farm leadership were instituted; mandatory planting regulations were lifted; collective farm workers were entitled to their own private plot; restrictions on renting land were eased and the purchase or sale of land up to seven acres was permitted. The first year of collectivization, 1958, produced a bountiful harvest, and Hungarian agriculture has generally flourished ever since (see discussion below).

In addition, there was a clear recognition among the Party leadership and economic planners that the system of centralized, comprehensive physical planning was too wasteful and ineffective. In early 1957 a special committee was established to study alternatives to this system. For the next eight years the government introduced modifications to the planning system piecemeal and gradually, among them: a system of profit sharing; a reduction in the number of compulsory directives; a relaxation of export controls for certain enterprises; and an interest charge on capital assets. These partial measures fared little better than the 1965 reforms in the USSR. Without a new price system, profit incentives and reduced directives created new distortions and irrationalities. By 1965, it was recognized that the piecemeal approach was failing, and in May 1966 a Party directive to introduce comprehensive economic reforms with emphasis on foreign trade was issued.

The New Economic Mechanism

After three years of careful study the New Economic Mechanism (NEM) was inaugurated on January 1, 1968. The basic idea was to "organically combine" planned central control with the self-regulating market mechanism. Before discussing the NEM in some detail, it is necessary to note the special circumstances surrounding its inception. First, the new system was meticulously studied and systematically prepared. This could not have happened without Party unity. Nor could such a far-reaching structural reform have been conceivable in the face of leadership ambivalence or divisiveness.

Second, the long gestation period also provided the opportunity to develop slackness and better balance within the economy. This factor together with the fact that the world economy was booming in 1968 meant that the reform had a smoother, more successful beginning. Third, the 1968 Hungarian reform, unlike the otherwise similar 1968 reform in Czechoslovakia, did not seek to establish worker councils to control enterprise decision making. Worker control at the factory level brings with it the ultimate threat to Party control over the economy and polity. The demand for worker control along with the general political environment in Czechoslovakia in 1968 provides a likely explanation of why the Soviet Union was prompted to invade Czechoslovakia and not Hungary on this occasion.

Under the NEM the state is to guide economic activity through parametric controls (controls over prices, subsidies, taxes, etc.). Physical output targets serve as guidelines but are no longer binding on the enterprise either in the one-year or long-term plans. Profit is to be the primary success criterion as well as the basis for managerial and worker bonuses and for decentralized enterprise investment. In addition, enterprises are allowed to contract and trade freely with one another without bureaucratic approval. That is, the cumbersome and wasteful system of administrative supply allocation was abandoned. Enterprise managers continue to be appointed by the state.

As we saw in discussing the 1965 Soviet reforms, profitability is an unworkable standard unless prices are rational. Prices must correspond to some notion of private or social cost. If this is not the case, then some enterprises may exert themselves fully, make appropriate choices, be efficiently managed, and still not make a profit. Conversely, other laggard and inefficient enterprises may turn large profits simply because their output price has been (centrally) set high relative to their input prices.

The Hungarian reformers were quite cognizant of this issue. They decided to gradually move toward prices set by supply and demand with some state intervention. Initially, there were three categories of prices: free prices (set by supply and demand); bounded prices (with a maximum or maximum and minimum price); and fixed prices (set by central planning authorities). Since a sellers' market (excess demand) still prevailed to some extent in certain sectors in 1968, it was anticipated that many free prices would rise and bounded prices would go to their maxima. Thus, to preserve some price stability as well as to thwart monopoly pricing (see below) and to further social policy (e.g., low prices for basic goods), it was necessary to proceed with great caution.

The consumer price structure and level did not change much. Consumer prices fell 0.3 percent in 1968, then rose by 1.4 percent, 1.3 percent, 2.0 percent, and 2.9 percent in successive years. Industrial wholesale prices followed a similar trend. In addition to the factors mentioned above, this is testimony to the degree of slack that had been built into the Hungarian economy.

The realm of free pricing expanded slowly (see Table 15.2), but extensive government subsidies created wide disparities between producer and consumer prices. These impediments to market pricing, in turn, greatly limited the degree to which the profitability criterion could play its expected role.

We can delineate at least three economic functions for profits in a market context: (1) they are a source of funds for (decentralized) enterprise reinvestment; (2) they signal resource movements among

Table 15.2
Evolution of Free Retail Price Formation, 1969-80

Year	Percentage of retail trade in free prices
1969	25
1974	28
1978	37
1980	50

Sources: Bela Belassa, "Reforming the New Economic Mechanism in Hungary," *Journal of Comparative Economics* 7, 3 (Sept. 1983): 260.

sectors; and (3) they serve to motivate owners, managers, and, with profit sharing, workers to perform effectively. Let us consider each of these functions in turn.

It is commonly held that in a centrally planned economy with binding physical output targets and a soft budget constraint there will be a pressure in both enterprises and ministries toward overinvestment. A soft budget constraint refers to a situation in which an enterprise runs a budget deficit (costs exceed revenues) yet experiences no (or minor) penalty because of overriding state subsidies.[3] By introducing some decentralization in investment decisions along with a profitability criterion (interest charges on capital already existed), it was hoped that the NEM would mitigate overinvestment tendencies as well as rationalize that investment which did occur. However, as Hewett has shown, this did not take place.[4] Actual investment continued to exceed planned investment, the investment ratio continued to rise, and inventory accumulation rose to new highs as a share of National Income.

What accounts for the government's inability to control investment demand? The explanation, in part, is that there was a new source (the enterprise) for investment demand with its own funds. Referring to the years with significantly overfulfilled investment plans (1970-71, 1974-75, 1977-78), Hewett writes:

In each of these cases enterprise investments were responsible for the overfulfillment; state investments were on target in 1970-71 and 1974-75,

3. An excellent discussion of soft budget constraints and their meaning in planned economies is provided in Janos Kornai, *The Economics of Shortage* (Amsterdam: North Holland, 1980).

4. Edward Hewett, "The Hungarian Economy: Lessons of the 1970s and Prospects for the 1980s," in U.S. Congress, Joint Economic Committee (J.E.C.), *East European Assessment*, Part 1 (Washington, D.C.: U.S. Government Printing Office, 1981), 505.

and were slightly below target in 1977–78. Enterprise investments were about thirty percent above planned in 1970–71 and about twenty percent above planned in 1974–75 and 1977–78.[5]

Although the enterprises were no longer bound to a physical output target, the branch ministries in essence still were. They, in turn, could separately reward a cooperative enterprise manager. At the same time, the enterprise manager was insulated from normal risk by government policy to preserve worker job security (and, hence, the enterprises in which they worked).

The government policy to prevent unprofitable enterprises from going under inhibited the second function of profits mentioned above. There was a clear trade-off here between the political goal of full employment with job security (an important gain for workers in an undemocratic "workers' state") and the economic goal of allocational efficiency. This trade-off was somewhat mitigated in Hungary because of high rates of labor turnover, the latter owing to (1) liberal government labor market policy, (2) excess demand for labor, (3) the probable absence of psychologically rewarding work, and (4) the fact that 43 percent of industrial workers are concentrated in Budapest, allowing workers to switch jobs without their having to find new (and scarce) housing.

Fixed producer prices reset in January 1968 were intended to cover costs plus allow for rates of return on capital varying from 1.6 to 9.5 percent.[6] The low profit rate sectors (steel, electricity, mining) were so made deliberately in order to maintain their reliance on state investment. This policy, together with other distortions in the price system, made it difficult for profits to allocate capital more efficiently.

Finally, since profit levels seemed to depend largely on somewhat arbitrary pricing policy (as well as on effective management and effort), the incentive connection of profit was significantly attenuated. Indeed, since profit sharing was in practice and profits in good measure were arbitrary, "unjustified" income differences appeared among workers in different sectors of the economy. Anticipating that this would create political problems, the government acted to curb such inequities by levying extremely high taxes on bonuses out of profits.

> The wages of workers in very profitable firms have only marginally exceeded those in unprofitable operations: above average wage increases are heavily taxed in Hungary while minimum wage increases are guaranteed by the government by means of a wide variety of subsidies for unprofitable enterprises. For example, a Hungarian official recently indi-

5. Ibid.
6. David Granick, *Enterprise Guidance in Eastern Europe*, Part III (Princeton: Princeton University Press, 1975).

cated that enterprises that did not produce any profit in 1978 were still able to increase wages by 8.1% while enterprises that produced profits of more than 20% increased wages by only 9.3%.[7]

Naturally, such policy makes the link of income to effort yet more tenuous.

Two other incentive-related factors tempered the initial zeal for reform. The first is described succinctly by an expert on the Hungarian economy, Richard Portes:

> An egregious mistake in the enterprise incentive system, which had given managers profit-related bonuses ten to twenty times greater than those of manual workers (with the size of total distributions varying inversely with the workers' average wage) created great resentment and was corrected at the end of 1969.[8]

The second is that the partially unleashed market forces created manifold incentives and opportunities to engage in private, often underground and "abusive," economic activity. Together these new sources of income inequality were generating political difficulties. By November 1972, Kadar felt it necessary to act. At the Party plenum he declared that the relative position of industrial workers had dropped, argued that equality had to take precedence over efficiency, and criticized "petty-bourgeois" excesses. This signaled a moratorium on further economic reforms which was to last until 1979–80.

In addition to the internal forces which brought an end to the first phase of reforms, the heightened instability of the international economy reinforced the perceived need for continuing government regulation. For instance, the multiplying price of imported oil along with the recession in the West put terrific strains on Hungary's balance of payments and domestic price structure. In order to cushion the economy from these twin blows the Hungarian government rapidly increased its subsidization of many products and retained its remaining price controls.

Above we have stressed the deficiencies of the first stage of the reform process in Hungary. The fact that the early going encountered some snags, however, is to be expected. By the end of 1972, Hungary had moved further away from the Soviet economic model than any other centrally planned economy, with the exception of Yugoslavia. Many economic benefits accompanied this transition: the growth rate

---

7. J. Kramer and J. Danylyk, "Economic Reform in Eastern Europe: Hungary at the Forefront," in J.E.C., *East European Economic Assessment*, 1981, 563.

8. Richard Portes, "Hungary: Economic Performance, Policy and Prospects," U.S. Congress, Joint Economic Committee (J.E.C.), *East European Economies Post-Helsinki* (Washington, D.C.: U.S. Government Printing Office, 1977), 784.

> **Table 15.3**
> **Annual Growth Rate of National Income**
> **of Hungary, 1961–1975**

1961–65	4.1%
1966–70	6.8%
1971–75	6.3%

Source: P. Hare and J. Wanless, "Polish and Hungarian Economic Reforms—A Comparison," *Soviet Studies* 33, 4 (Oct. 1981), 494.

increased above its previous average (see Table 15.3)[9]; the quality and diversity of goods improved; the sellers' market was weakened; the planning apparatus was sharply reduced in size; bureaucratic delays and inefficiencies diminished significantly as a result of the abolition of administrative supply allocation; consumer and industrial services (e.g., repair work) improved; and so on.

Before we consider the recent wave of "market-oriented" reforms, it is important to fill out some of the institutional context by considering the performance of two vital sectors of the Hungarian economy, agriculture and foreign trade.

Agriculture

Some analysts attribute Hungary's relative economic success as much to agriculture as to policies of the NEM. The favorable reputation of Hungarian agriculture is made clear by the following Eastern bloc joke:

> Stanislaw Kania[10] promises peace in Poland if Brezhnev will grant him three wishes:
> "It was a terrible wheat year, Comrade Brezhnev. I need 100 million tons of wheat."
> "One hundred million tons of wheat, Kania? No problem. You've got it."
> "And potatoes, I need 200 million tons of potatoes."
> "Just 200 million? You'll get them next week. What else?"
> "The last one is easy. I need 5000 oranges."
> "Oranges? Impossible! The Hungarians can't produce them."[11]

---

9. Naturally, other factors could have contributed to this result. If the reader is tempted to make comparisons between Hungary's growth rate and income level and those of other East European economies, it should be borne in mind that Hungary's statistics are generally regarded as being more reliable and accurate.

10. Polish Party leader prior to the imposition of martial law in December 1981.

11. L. Minard, "The Hungarian Exception," *Forbes* (May 11, 1981), 119.

Table 15.4
Agricultural Structure and Productivity

	State farms	Collective farms Com- mon	Family plots	Private farms
(1) Percentage of land area (1975)	10.6	54.5	6.3	5.8
(2) Percentage of total agricultural output (1974)	15.2	48.0	20.3	12.9
(3) (2) ÷ (1)	1.4	0.9	3.2	2.2

Source: Calculated from Z. O'Relley, "Hungarian Agricultural Performance During the NEM," in Joint Economic Committee, *East European Economies Post-Helsinki* (Washington, D.C.: U.S. Government Printing Office, 1977), 375–76.

It might be added that Poland has 26 percent of the total agricultural land in Eastern Europe; Hungary has just above 8 percent.[12] Hungarian agriculture also compares favorably by many standards to Western Europe. For instance, Hungary's grain yield per hectare is above the average for the European Common Market.

In 1975, agriculture employed 20.4 percent of Hungary's labor force; it accounted for 15.9 percent of GNP; and it accounted for 22.6 percent of all exports and 50 percent of nonruble exports (both including food industry). There are three major forms of agricultural production: in 1975, there were 151 state farms; 1,599 collective farms (or agricultural producer cooperatives); 800,000 private household plots; and 120,000 small private gardens, orchards, and vineyards.

In Table 15.4, one can observe from the ratios of output share to land area share that the yield per hectare is considerably higher on the privately farmed plots. These are aggregate ratios. The differential productivity is highest for animal husbandry and is nonexistent for several crops. Although surpassed by small private plots, overall efficiency levels on the communal land of collective farms and state farms are still quite reputable.[13]

---

12. Gregor Lazarcik, "Comparative Growth and Levels of Agricultural Output and Productivity in Eastern Europe, 1965–1976," in J.E.C., *East European Economies Post-Helsinki*, 1977, 305.

13. For more details see: ibid.; N. Swain, "The Evolution of Hungary's Agricultural System since 1967," in P. Hare et al., *Hungary: A Decade of Economic Reform* (London: George Allen and Unwin, 1981), 228; Z. O'Relley, "Hungarian Agricultural Performance during the NEM," in J.E.C., *East European Economies Post-Helsinki*, 1977, 375–76; G. Lazarcik, "Comparative Growth, Struc-

There is no limitation on private livestock holdings: 50 percent of pigs, 75 to 80 percent of poultry, and 26 percent of cattle are privately held. Moreover, the state provides annual subsidies per head of cattle to encourage private ownership and breeding. There is also an active, mutually supportive relationship between the private producers and the state and collective farms. For instance, the socialized farms provide young animals, feed, technical assistance, and marketing and transport services to the private producers who, in turn, raise and fatten the livestock.[14]

Since the predominant mode of agricultural organization is the collective farm, it is appropriate to elaborate on the operation of the collective farms. Collective farms are owned by the farm's members, and the administration is elected by them. Individuals are allowed to privately farm their own household plots. A 1977 regulation enables household plots to double in size (to 1.2 hectares) where adjacent communal land is not in use.

The income position and administrative independence of collective farms have increased since the inauguration of the NEM in 1968. Compulsory targets were reduced to one (sown acreage for bread grains), other business with the state to be left to negotiated contracts with appropriate procurement agencies. With the exception of a few products, farms have been allowed to purchase inputs from and sell outputs to a variety of suppliers and buyers. The residual wage principle gave way to the guaranteed wage plus year-end profit sharing. Collective farm associations were set up at regional and the national levels to lobby for policies benefiting their members.

Two consistent state policies, however, stand out which have bolstered agricultural incomes since the late 1960s. First, state producer prices (fixed wholesale prices for agricultural output) have been regularly adjusted upward to match increases in market prices (see Table 15.5). This has resulted not only in higher agricultural incomes but also in higher output and the absence of a sellers' market in the food sector.

Second, the state has encouraged the growth of ancillary activities

---

ture and Levels of Agricultural Output, Inputs, and Productivity in Eastern Europe," in J.E.C., *East European Economic Assessment*, vol. 2, 1981; E. Csizmada, *Socialist Agriculture in Hungary* (Budapest: Akademiai: Kiado, 1977); I. Benet and J. Gyenis, eds., *Economic Studies on Hungary's Agriculture* (Budapest: Akademiai: Kiado, 1977); and Michael Marrese, "Agricultural Policy and Performance in Hungary," *Journal of Comparative Economics* 7, 3 (Sept. 1983). It is worthwhile to note that differential yield per hectare ratios between private and communal land are much smaller in Hungary than in the Soviet Union.

14. Ann Lane, "U.S.S.R.: Private Agriculture on Center Stage," in U.S. Congress, Joint Economic Committee (J.E.C.), *Soviet Economy in the 1980s*, Part 2 (Washington, D.C.: U.S. Government Printing Office, 1983), 39–40.

Table 15.5 Agricultural Price Indices		
Year	State producer prices	Market producer prices
1958	100	100
1967	130.5	143.8
1974	177.3	169.7

Source: N. Swain, "The Evolution of Hungary's Agricultural System since 1967," in P. Hare et al., *Hungary: A Decade of Economic Reform* (London: George Allen and Unwin, 1981), 228.

(food processing, marketing, services, etc.) on collective farms. Before 1968 some 50 percent of collective farm membership was idle during the winter. Today, such ancillary activities account for 43 percent of the sales receipts on collective farms. By 1972, manual agricultural laborers' average income was above that of skilled manual workers in industry.

In sum, Kadar has succeeded in fashioning a "social compromise" with rural workers based on a flexible and pragmatic approach to policy making. When political forces arose which challenged this compromise and nudged policy temporarily against agricultural interests, such as in 1975, ensuing production problems quickly rectified the errant course. As a result, Hungary has been transformed into the breadbasket of Eastern Europe.

Foreign Trade

In recent years, exports have accounted for approximately 50 percent of Hungary's National Income. Between 55 and 60 percent of its exports go to other COMECON countries, between 30 and 35 percent to the industrialized West, and approximately 7 to 11 percent to the underdeveloped nations. Hungary's broad exposure to the world economy, of course, makes it quite vulnerable to any changes in international markets. Bela Csikos-Nagy, a prominent Hungarian economist and head of the government's Price and Market Board, sees Hungary's domestic and foreign economic decisions as virtually inseparable: "In an economy sensitive to foreign trade almost every investment in production is aimed at the promotion of exports or the substitution of imports."[15]

15. B. Csikos-Nagy, "The Competitiveness of the Hungarian Economy," *New Hungarian Quarterly* 22, 83 (Autumn 1981): 24.

It is, then, not surprising that the energy price explosion and international recession of the 1970s brought serious dislocations and imbalances to the Hungarian economy. At the beginning of the 1970s Hungary's hard currency foreign debt amounted to a few hundred million dollars; by the end of 1975 it stood at $2 billion; by the end of 1979, at $7.6 billion.

There were three major sources of this growing debt. One, as mentioned above, excess investment demand became more prevalent with the partial decentralization of investment decisions of the NEM. Part of this excess demand spills over into increased imports.

Two, Hungary's Gross Domestic Product grew at an average annual rate of 5.3 percent from 1970 to 1979, while the average rate for the industrial West was 3.2 percent over the same period. This meant that Hungary's demand for imports grew more rapidly than the West's.

To aggravate matters, Hungary has a high elasticity of demand for nonruble imports. Econometric work has estimated that, when growth rates of National Income are below 3 percent, for every 1 percent increase in National Income the demand for nonruble imports increases by 1.3 percent. For growth rates in the 3- to 4-percent range, every 1 percent increase in National Income brings an increase of 2 percent in the demand for nonruble imports.

Three, as an importer of 80 percent of its oil, Hungary's terms of trade deteriorated some 20 percent between 1974 and 1980. That is, Hungary paid more to buy the same quantity of imports and/or received less for the same quantity of exports.

The resource price explosion and deteriorating terms trade also generated strong inflationary pressures. Policy makers initially opted to absorb most of this pressure by rapidly increasing subsidies to enterprises and maintaining an overvalued commercial forint. These subsidies increased by 70 percent from 1973 to 1977. To finance the growing subsidies, enterprise taxation increased by 170 percent over the same period. Although these policies held back inflation, they further distorted the price structure and constituted a retreat in terms of the goals of the NEM.

The growing foreign debt and increasing central manipulation of prices along with other economic problems compelled the government to clearly define its course. Signs of a renewed commitment to the principles of the NEM emerged in 1979; unequivocal confirmation of this commitment followed in 1980 and 1981.

Hewett has called the new policy in 1979 the Export-Import Plan.[16] This plan sought to slow investment spending, lower inventory accumulation, improve energy efficiency, and retard overall growth as a means to reduce imports. It also called for a decrease in enterprise and price subsidies. In short, it aimed to restore domestic and inter-

---

16. E. Hewett, "The Hungarian Economy," in J.E.C., *East European Economic Assessment*, 1981.

national macrobalance to the economy. Such a balance is a prerequisite for the circumscribed market mechanism to perform the function envisioned for it in the NEM. The tight fiscal policy continued in 1980 when a non-ruble trade surplus (and, hence, debt reduction) was achieved. The trade balance continued to improve during 1981–83.

NEM: The Second Phase

Prices

Price policy began to change on July 23, 1979, when it was announced (with an uncharacteristically short two-day warning) that prices of foodstuffs would rise 20 percent, electricity 50 percent, and dairy and meat 20 percent. This was a preparatory step for a larger change in 1980 which is described succinctly by Hewett:

> The basic features of the 1980 price system are that most producer prices are to be connected directly to foreign trade prices, and consumer prices are to be connected directly to producer prices (some of that already having been accomplished in the July 1979 changes). A two-level price system will develop in which consumer prices will exceed producer prices, by the amount of a uniform turnover tax. . . . The plan for 1980 was to decrease the proportion of officially-determined prices in consumer goods turnover down to 40 percent from its 1979 level of 55 percent.[17]

The aims of the new policy are to gradually reduce subsidies, bring domestic prices in line with foreign prices, and make Hungary's exports more competitive. According to Balassa, as of December 1981, the new rules for competitive pricing had been applied in approximately two-thirds of Hungarian industry.[18]

The gradual reduction of subsidies and introduction of a uniform turnover tax will bring an end to the common occurrence of retail (consumer) prices being lower than wholesale (producer) prices for all but a few products. Social costs will thus be more fully borne by the consumer, and the major rationale for a dual exchange rate (one for commercial trade, one for tourism and transfers) will be eliminated.

---

17. Ibid., 516.

18. B. Balassa, "Reforming the New Economic Mechanism in Hungary," *Journal of Comparative Economics* 7, 3 (Sept. 1983): 256. Balassa does not clearly distinguish between *free prices* and *simulated market prices*, the latter being administered. The 1980 price reform maintains state-administered prices, which are intended to follow world market prices and, hence, to correspond to Hungary's marginal cost. The fact, however, that prices are administered under complex and discretionary rules does preserve, if not extend, the role of the state bureaucracy in directing the economy. See, for one, Laszlo Csaba, "New Features of the Hungarian Economic Mechanism in the Mid-Eighties," *The New Hungarian Quarterly* 24, 90 (Summer 1983): 44–63.

Hungary moved to a unified exchange rate on October 1, 1981. As Balassa has convincingly demonstrated,[19] this move was made rather abruptly and engendered various difficulties. Yet, it was a first step toward convertibility of the forint and was required of Hungary prior to gaining acceptance into the International Monetary Fund (IMF). Hungary entered the IMF in May of 1982.

Two additional changes should be mentioned. First, the allocation of foreign exchange for travel abroad was significantly increased. The freedom to travel abroad was taken advantage of by 5.2 million Hungarians in 1980. Second, many larger companies were given the right to do their own foreign trading. By the end of 1981, there were 130 such companies. This bureaucratic disentanglement means faster and more appealing business dealings for Hungary's trading partners.

Industrial Structure

Three merger movements, the strongest being in the early 1960s, have produced a high degree of industrial concentration in Hungary. Large enterprises operating in a small market yields considerable market power.

The percentage of Hungarian enterprises employing over one thousand workers rose from 14.7 percent in 1960 to 35.4 percent in 1970, to 44.8 percent in 1979. The number of enterprises fell from 1,368 in 1960 to 812 in 1970, to 702 in 1979. Austria, a smaller country geographically with a smaller population, had 6,830 enterprises in 1979. The fifty largest industrial enterprises in Hungary in 1973 employed 45 percent of industrial labor and produced 58 percent of industrial output. The extent of concentration was even greater than these figures suggest since approximately half of all industrial firms were organized into trusts.[20] Large firms can offer various administrative conveniences to a centrally planned economy. However, firms with appreciable market power represent a challenge to an economic reform which seeks to introduce competitive pricing.

The 1980–81 reforms attempted to deal with this problem. First, in 1980 the three existing industrial ministries were combined into one in an effort to streamline the bureaucracy as well as to restructure the relationship between the state and the production units. This restructuring was intended to reduce administrative interference in enterprise activities and to reinforce enterprise responsiveness to market signals. Second, seventy new firms were created by breaking up horizontal trusts and large firms. Third, the government has promoted the development of small industrial shops which produce

---

19. Ibid.
20. Ibid., 29.

parts, components, and accessories. Lastly, a new regulation which took effect January 1, 1982, provides for the establishment of new and the expansion of existing small and medium-sized producers.

The latter legislation is complicated, but its significance warrants some attention. First, it sanctions artisans to hire up to three workers and to let out piecework. They can also establish partnerships with up to thirty workers. Up to five such partnerships could join a cooperative with 150 total workers. Second, individuals may set up cooperatives with up to one hundred members. Third, state enterprises may enter into a contract with a subunit of the enterprise, the latter to be managed independently.

On the one hand, these new regulations essentially sanction the very large second economy which had grown up since 1968. On the other, they enlarge an already thriving cooperative sector of the economy. Prior to these changes, the state had authorized ninety large industrial cooperatives (excluding food processing cooperatives on the farms), which employed some 250,000 people and produced 6.4 percent of industrial output. One such private cooperative manufactures Rubik's cubes, named after their Hungarian inventor, Erno Rubik, a millionaire. In 1976, twenty-six thousand retail cooperatives accounted for 35.2 percent of retail trade, and, overall, cooperatives accounted for 23 percent of National Income. Thus, the Hungarian economy is distinguishing itself in the Eastern bloc not only in its market orientation but also in its sizable decentralized cooperative sector. Further, the Hungarian government has successfully promoted a number of joint ventures both at home and abroad with foreign companies based in capitalist countries. New 1983 legislation establishes free-trade zones with tariff exemptions to further encourage joint ventures.

Labor

As of January 1, 1981, there were 5,050,000 active wage earners in Hungary, or 47 percent of the population (the corresponding figure in the United States is around 43 percent). This high participation rate is underwritten by extensive social programs, such as generous maternity leave and child care grants as well as a rapidly growing network of day care centers.[21]

There is, by any reckoning, full employment. Until recently, labor market regulations made it very difficult to lay off workers. In 1976, for instance, with total employment over five million, fewer than seven thousand workers were laid off (or just over one-tenth of one

---

21. For more details see: Zsuzsa Ferge, *A Society in the Making: Hungarian Social and Societal Policy, 1945–75* (White Plains, N.Y.: M. E. Sharpe, 1979), 90–128.

percent of the labor force). To be sure, soft enterprise budget constraints greatly diminished any economic pressure to lay off workers.

The 1970s witnessed a shrinking role of the piece-rate system described so graphically by Haraszti[22] and, since 1975, a renewed emphasis on worker participation in enterprise decision making. The piece-rate system was increasingly ineffectual in stimulating greater worker effort and was progressively outdated by new continuous process and microprocessor technology. At the same time, the Hungarian work force with ever higher levels of educational attainment and a strong propensity to switch jobs was ready for more challenging and fulfilling work environments.

The new regulations regarding worker participation seem to have been accompanied by sincere leadership efforts to promote a more democratic work place. Briefly, elected shop stewards have been empowered to make decisions regarding wage policy, use of enterprise profits, and welfare programs as well as to evaluate production plans and management performance. These powers are, of course, often limited by lack of information or by traditional management style; yet genuine attempts to overcome some of these obstacles are being made. The shop stewards' committee is also allowed to call strikes in factories where managers refuse to improve working conditions; and, in 1981, it is reported that twelve managers were forced to resign by the stewards' committee for this reason.[23] Experiments in which workers in state enterprises will elect their own managers, as is done on cooperative farms in Hungary, are expected to begin in 1985. Doubtless the leadership hopes to lower turnover rates and raise productivity, but whatever its motives worker participation appears to have proceeded further in Hungary than elsewhere in the Warsaw Pact nations.

Workers are always more motivated to cooperate in raising productivity when they have job security; otherwise, higher output per worker may result in fewer workers. Job security has been regarded as an irreducible worker right in Hungary. However, job security was redefined at the Twelfth Party Congress in 1980. Workers still have a right to a job but not necessarily the same job throughout their working life. Presumably, this new policy will facilitate greater resource

---

22. Miklos Haraszti, *Worker in a Worker's State* (New York: Universe Books, 1978).

23. There is a growing literature on the operation of the shop steward committees and other worker participation bodies. See, for example: L. Hethy and C. Mako, "Workers' Direct Participation in Decisions in Hungarian Factories," *International Labor Review* 116, 1 (July–Aug. 1977); and L. Hethy, "Trade Unions, Shop Stewards, and Participation in Hungary," *International Labor Review* 120, 4 (July–Aug. 1981). The data on managerial resignations is from Frank Lipsius, "A Choice Not an Echo in Hungary," *The Nation* (June 18, 1983), 761.

mobility in response to the stronger market signals. Unprofitable enterprises, for example, will no longer be the recipients of automatic bail-outs by the government.

The 1980–81 reforms brought an end to the guaranteed 1.5 percent annual wage increase. Tax rates on above-average wage increases in successful enterprises were lowered (albeit still high). This move is made possible by the enhanced rationality of the price structure and is intended to motivate greater work effort.

These changes raise several questions about the long-run compatibility of plan and market forces. Will the strengthening of enterprise budget constraints and the profitability criterion lead to unemployment problems and will these be accepted in the name of allocational efficiency? Will the closer linking of profits to worker and managerial incomes generate politically unacceptable levels of inequality? Will the growth of the cooperative sector attract "too much" skilled labor out of the state sector? Will workers, given the taste of some decision-making power in the enterprise, begin to call for even broader powers? If so, what are Budapest's or Moscow's limits of tolerance?

Evaluation

Economic analysts of the Hungarian experiment with "market-oriented socialism" have drawn varying conclusions. Portes, Balassa, and Murrell,[24] among others, note positive changes toward greater organizational simplicity as well as allocational efficiency. Others, such as Granick and Hewett,[25] have stressed the persistence of certain undesirable characteristics of the centrally planned economy and have drawn less sanguine conclusions. Hungarian economists have registered similarly divergent assessments of the current status and future prospects of their country's reforms.[26]

Even before the 1979–81 round of reforms, however, the visitor to

---

24. Portes, "Hungary," in J.E.C., *East European Economies Post-Helsinki*; 1977; Balassa, "Reforming the New Economic Mechanism"; and Peter Murrell, "An Evaluation of the Success of the Hungarian Economic Reform: An Analysis Using International Trade Data," *Journal of Comparative Economics* 5, 4 (Dec. 1981).

25. Granick, *Enterprise Guidance*; and Hewett, "The Hungarian Economy," in J.E.C., *East European Economic Assessment*, 1981.

26. Some of the more prominent Hungarian economists who have written extensively in English are Janos Kornai, Andrea Deak, Laszlo Drechsler, Gyorgy Varga, Marton Tardos, Michael Simai, Tamas Bauer, and Bela Csikos-Nagy. Those readers interested in pursuing Hungarian economic scholarship should consult the following journals available in English: *Acta Oeconomica*; *Marketing in Hungary, New Hungarian Quarterly*, and *Abstracts of Hungarian Economic Literature*. Also see the *Journal of Comparative Economics*, Vol. 7, No. 3.

Hungary experienced a different economic environment than elsewhere in Eastern Europe: stores plentifully stocked with a wide variety of good quality consumer goods, coincidence of government and free market prices, absence of queues, better services, etc. To dismiss these achievements as straightforward consequences of abundant imports or salutary agricultural performance is too facile. The reforms brought substantial institutional and behavioral change to the Hungarian economy. The new round of reforms, of course, reinforces and extends these transformations.

It is relevant to look at the issue now from a different vantage point. Not: Have the Hungarians departed enough from central planning to gain advantage from use of the market? But rather: Are the Hungarians relying too much on the market to take advantage of the benefits of planning?

To now, we would answer no to this second question. The economy has been steered carefully to achieve a creditable growth record and macrobalance. The direction and amount of investment has been controlled with good success. Kornai describes the situation well:

> Thus, for example, in 1976 almost half of total investment in the economy was allocated by central decisions. The balance, accounting for a little over half the total, is classified as "investment of firms," because it is initiated by the firm and, formally, the investment decision is made by the firm. But only half of the so-called "investment of firms" is financed exclusively from the firm's own savings. Thus only about a quarter of total investment can be considered as fully decentralised. For the other quarter, the firm has to seek government subsidy or long-term credit, which means that the central planning and financial organization, the bank and the firm take part jointly in these investment decisions.[27]

Tighter macro controls have reduced the investment ratio and subdued excess investment spending in recent years. Unemployment has been absent and relative price stability has been attained. The provision of social services is extensive and income distribution is strikingly egalitarian. As seen in Table 15.6, measured by the post-tax decile ratio for the early seventies, the income distribution in Hungary was three times more equal than in the United States and over four times more equal than in France.

The bigger question is: Will the Hungarians be able to balance the conflicting forces of planning and markets in the long run? Is it possible to achieve political and economic equilibrium which reconciles the many tensions and contradictions generated by the Hungarian experiment? The troublesome international economic situation will not make the task any easier. Not only must Hungary continue to trade with recession-ridden Western economies, but it faces in-

---

27. Janos Kornai, "The Dilemmas of a Socialist Economy: The Hungarian Experience," *Cambridge Journal of Economics*, no. 4 (1980): 153.

**Table 15.6
Ratio of Income Share of Top 10 percent of
Income Earners to Bottom 10 percent (after Tax)**

	1962	1967	1972
Hungary	5.8	4.6	5.0
United States	—	—	15.4
France	—	—	21.8[a]

Source: H. Flakierski, "Economic Reform and Income Distribution in Hungary," *Cambridge Journal of Economics* 3 (1979): 23. OECD, *Income Distribution in OECD Countries*, 1976, 19.

a. For the year 1970.

creasingly austere and problematic conditions within COMECON—from extra aid to Poland, to paying the full world price for additional barrels of Soviet crude oil.

Whatever the eventual outcome, however, Hungary's "market-oriented socialism" has charted a new, unique course of economic organization. It will continue to be watched with great interest by economists throughout the world.

Recommended Readings

1. Paul Hare, H. Radice, and N. Swain, eds., *Hungary: A Decade of Economic Reform* (London: George Allen and Unwin, 1981).

2. O. Gado, *The Economic Mechanism in Hungary: How It Works in 1976* (Budapest: Akademiai Kiado, 1976).

3. Edward Hewett, "The Hungarian Economy: Lessons of the 1970s and Prospects for the 1980s," in U.S. Congress, Joint Economic Committee, *East European Economic Assessment*, Part 1 (Washington, D.C.: U.S. Government Printing Office, 1981).

4. Alec Nove, *The Economics of Feasible Socialism* (London: George Allen and Unwin, 1983), 123–33.

5. Janos Kornai, "The Dilemmas of a Socialist Economy: The Hungarian Experience," *Cambridge Journal of Economics*, No. 4 (1980).

6. Wlodzimierz Brus, "The Eastern European Reforms: What Happened to Them?" *Soviet Studies* 31 (Apr. 1979): 257–67.

7. *Journal of Comparative Economics* 7, 3 (Sept. 1983). Special issue: "Hungary: The Third Wave of Reforms."

16

YUGOSLAVIA

SELF-MANAGEMENT AND
THE MARKET

Since its expulsion from the Cominform in June 1948, Yugoslavia has embarked on a unique road of socialist economic development. Collectivized agriculture and one-man management were early eschewed and, more gradually, central planning was also repudiated. What has emerged in their place is a combination of a constrained market mechanism, decentralized indicative planning, and worker self-management.

The nation of Yugoslavia was created in 1918 out of the ruins of World War I and the dissolution of the Austro-Hungarian and Ottoman Empires. The new state brought together six major and eighteen lesser ethnic groupings, three major religions (Catholic, Eastern Orthodox, and Islam), and fourteen commonly spoken languages (three official languages). This heterogeneity has generated intense centrifugal forces which continue to strain Yugoslav political life today.

After an initial unsuccessful experiment with parliamentary democracy following the First World War, Yugoslavia was governed as a monarchy until World War II. In April 1941, the Axis powers invaded Yugoslavia and gained temporary political control through a series of regional puppet governments. At this time, three separate wars were being fought in Yugoslavia: a national liberation struggle against the German and Italian occupiers, one civil war among the Yugoslav nationalities, and a second civil war between the Monarchists and the Partisans. The Partisans were a broadly based national liberation movement led by the illegal Yugoslav Communist party (headed by Josip Broz, or Tito).

The Allied forces at first supported the Monarchists but transferred their allegiance to the Partisans in December 1943. The reason for this shift was explained by Winston Churchill to the House of Commons in May 1944:

The reason why we have ceased to supply Mihailovic (leader of the Chetniks or Monarchists) with arms and support is a simple one. He has not been fighting the enemy (Nazis), and, moreover, some of his subordinates have made accommodations with the enemy, from which have arisen armed conflicts with the forces of Marshal Tito. . . . We have proclaimed ourselves the strong supporters of Marshal Tito because of his heroic and massive struggle against the German armies.[1]

Churchill might only have added that he had become convinced of eventual Partisan victory. The Partisans slowly liberated the country from the Nazis and Monarchists. In liberated areas governance was through elected "people's committees," worker councils were formed in the factories, schools were established, and political education programs were organized. Popular support for the Partisans was widespread as is made apparent in the following somewhat romanticized, but revealing story told by John Darnton:

It was June 19, 1942. Mr. Jankovic, then a 23-year old peasant from the flinty mountains of Montenegro, belonged to the Fourth Montenegrin Brigade of the Partisan forces. They were camped in a forest near the Sutjeska River. Their situation was desperate. They were under fire from the occupying Italians and harassed by the royalist Chetniks and the Croatian Domobrans.

"We were practically surrounded," Mr. Jankovic said. "We were hungry, badly dressed. We were in a pitiful state. We had almost no weapons, little ammunition. Some had five bullets in their guns, some had none. Bread was running out."

"We were told that someone from the Supreme Command would be there, perhaps it would be the Supreme Commander himself, but no one believed it and no one said it would be Tito. Our battalions were lined up."

"All of a sudden this man galloped in from the woods on a white stallion. He had on a fur cap, a jacket, tall riding boots. We knew right away who it was. He looked so fresh, so young, though he was then 50 years old."

"Tito made a passionate speech. He was frank. He admitted the situation was difficult. But he said we would march to northwest Bosnia and join up with the Proletarian Brigades there and establish a new liberated territory. We would steal arms from the enemy. He sounded so optimistic, so confident. We forgot all our troubles and deeply believed everything he said. And you know, that is exactly the way things turned out."

President Tito is a hero to virtually all Yugoslavs, even those who are not Communists.[2]

The final battles against the Germans were fought in the last months of 1944. With only minor, last minute support from the Soviet Red Army, the Partisan forces repelled the Nazi invaders. In March 1945, a new government led by Tito was formed. Yugoslavia was, thus,

---

1. Gordon McDonald et al., *Area Handbook for Yugoslavia* (Washington, D.C.: U.S. Government Printing Office, 1973), 54.
2. *New York Times*, March 1, 1980.

the only self-liberated East European nation (possibly excepting the tiny nation of Albania).

The contrasts between the Soviet and Yugoslav revolutionary struggles are striking. First, the ideology of the Bolsheviks stressed the need to base the revolutionary movement in the urban working class despite the fact that it made up less than 15 percent of the pre-1917 labor force. Tito and the Partisans based their strategy on mobilizing a peasant base since the peasantry comprised over 80 percent of the population. Second, unlike the Bolshevik leaders who were out of Russia for most of the struggle leading to the overthrow of the Czar, Tito was directly involved with the armed struggle and, indeed, was seriously wounded in battle in 1943. Third, the practice of the Partisans in the liberated areas established the basis for more democratic social relations in the new society. Fourth, unlike the Bolsheviks who had little support in the peasantry or middle class and only gained majority support in the urban soviets just weeks before the October Revolution, Tito and the Partisans had extensive contact with and were revered by a broad popular base. (The revolutionary struggle of the Red Army in China shows several similarities with the experience in Yugoslavia.) This revolutionary experience, then, set the foundation for Yugoslavia's independent road to a more popular, decentralized form of socialism.

Tito spoke out against Soviet hegemony within the community of socialist nations, and he resisted the Soviet effort to dominate economic and political life in Yugoslavia. This behavior proved intolerable to Stalin, who arranged for Yugoslavia's expulsion from the Cominform in 1948 and a Soviet-bloc economic blockade of Yugoslavia from 1949 to 1953. Yugoslavia promptly signed aid and trade agreements with Western Europe and the United States.

Yugoslavia suffered heavy losses during the Second World War. These included: the destruction of some 300,000 farms and over one-third of industrial capacity; the death of 1.7 million Yugoslavs and another 3.3 million left homeless. The losses were estimated to total $9 billion and were a heavy burden upon a preponderantly rural, poorly educated (illiteracy was near 40 percent; only 1.3 percent of the population had a secondary education), and industrially backward nation. In 1945, the per capita income in current prices was estimated at under one hundred dollars.[3] The tasks of reconstruction and development inherited by Tito's government were formidable.

Early Economic Policy: The Emergence of the Yugoslav Model

After initially conforming to the centralized Soviet economic model, beginning around 1950 the Yugoslavs began to experiment with the

---

3. Martin Schrenk et al., *Yugoslavia: Self-Management Socialism* (Baltimore: Johns Hopkins University Press, 1979), 14.

construction of a new model for socialist economic management. One early sign of independent economic policy came in agriculture. The Yugoslav campaign for forced collectivization in agriculture was ended in 1951. Compulsory crop deliveries, central government controls over agricultural prices, and rationing were all gradually eliminated. Today, over 80 percent of arable land is privately owned (individual plots cannot exceed ten hectares) and approximately 70 percent of agricultural production is from this sector. The predominance of small plot agriculture has meant that private farmer incomes have been considerably below those of social sector workers, and this has spurred rapid urban migration; whereas in 1960 63 percent of the labor force worked in agriculture, in 1979 only 31 percent did.

A second, more definitive sign of a break from the Soviet model came with the Worker Council Law of 1950. This popular measure bolstered Yugoslav solidarity during the critical stage of breaking with the Soviet Union. The law provided for enterprise policy to be the responsibility of a Worker Council to be elected by all the workers in the enterprise. The Worker Council, in turn, would elect a Management Board responsible, along with the director, for enterprise decision making. The self-management rights of workers were extended in the 1953 Constitution and subsequent legislation. Although Yugoslav enterprise decision making is conducted in a different context than in other market or planned economies, the decision-making prerogatives of the elected Management Board today include the organization of production, the purchase of inputs, shop floor conditions, marketing, financing, wage and salary policy, investment and pricing policies within certain constraints, etc. Yugoslav enterprises are socially (as opposed to state or privately) owned. That is, they are in theory owned by all the people, and the affiliated workers have usufruct rights (rights of production and use) regarding the enterprises' assets (they may not sell them).

This arrangement of worker management and social ownership has persisted to the present day. Yugoslavia is the only economy in either the socialist or capitalist world where democratically elected worker councils are nominally responsible for enterprise direction. In this sense, it appears to conform with the ideals of a socialist economy enunciated by Marx in his writing on the Paris Commune and stands in sharp contrast to socialist management practices elsewhere in Eastern Europe and the Soviet Union. In practice, however, Yugoslav self-management falls well short of these ideals. We shall return to this matter later in the chapter.

Along with the adoption of worker management, Yugoslavia moved after 1950 to decentralize its system of economic planning. The Soviet-style, one-year operational plan with centrally set output targets for sectors and enterprises was repudiated in the early fifties. It was replaced by medium-term plans concerned with basic proportions in the economy (e.g., investment ratio, growth rate), macroeconomic aggregates, and sectoral prioritization. Central control over the majority of investment resources was retained, although appreciable authority was devolved to regional government units. Enterprises were no longer given obligatory output or product mix targets nor did they receive material supply directives. Although there was much back and forth experimentation with this system of planning, there was a general trend from 1950 to 1965 for the central government to become less involved in resource allocation and price control. The sharpest break with government planning, however, was to come with the economic reforms of 1965.

Economic Reforms of 1965

Yugoslavia's thrust toward economic decentralization can be understood partly as the influence of Party theoreticians such as Djilas and Kardelj who in criticizing the bureaucratization of the Soviet-type system suggested the path to a more democratic, decentralized, and efficient socialism. In many respects the drive toward self-management at the enterprise level also recommended the relaxation of central controls of enterprise behavior. However, Yugoslavia's cultural, ethnic, and linguistic cleavages were equally behind these decentralizing tendencies. It was simply not politically feasible to control all economic decision making from Belgrade. To maintain a minimally requisite allegiance from the Republics to the nation it was necessary to offer the Republics considerable autonomy or self-government. Decentralization, then, was required for national cohesion.

The 1965 decision to further engage market forces is understandable in these terms. The economic reforms of that year included the following measures. One, as a result of lower tax rates and a higher depreciation allowance, more income remained within the enterprise for distribution to workers or decentralized investment. The share of investment resources at the disposal of the government (at all levels), for instance, fell from 61.7 percent in 1961 to 17.7 percent in 1967, although the government continued to exercise some power over credit allocation by the revamped, decentralized banking system. Two, remaining government resources and responsibilities were largely transferred from the federal to the republic and communal levels. Three, the dinar (Yugoslav currency) was devalued, a uniform exchange rate was adopted, many quantitative import restrictions were removed, and import duties were significantly lowered. These measures were deemed necessary in order to open the Yugoslav economy to foreign competition in the context of the world market. Four, the scope of government price subsidies was narrowed and enterprises were granted more autonomy in price formation.

A central and natural expectation of the reformers was that the economy would become more efficient and more competitive internationally. The 1965 reforms, however, created more problems than they solved.

On the micro level, intensified competition, largely from foreign sources, increasingly led to the appearance of weak, financially insolvent enterprises. Sociopolitical values and pressures made bankruptcy a difficult, almost unacceptable, outcome. Indeed, between 1964 and 1970 fewer than four hundred workers per year lost jobs as a result of firm failure. Thus, mergers between strong and weak enterprises, buy-outs by large trading enterprises, or bank mergers were not only accepted but, in many cases, encouraged. From 1965 to 1967, 12 percent of all Yugoslav enterprises were involved in a merger. Strong merger activity continued in the seventies. Whereas in 1970 the 130 largest enterprises in manufacturing and mining accounted for 45.1 percent of total sales and 33.7 percent of total employment, by 1977 these shares rose to 70.1 percent and 48.3 percent, respectively. Industrial bigness together with Yugoslavia's relatively small market size (population in 1983 was some twenty-two million) has yielded a highly concentrated, oligopolistic industrial and financial structure.[4] Thus, the expectations of heightened efficiency from the decentralization measures were thwarted by increasing concentration as well as numerous impediments to free capital markets.

The combination of controlled nominal interest rates and accelerating rates of inflation has produced negative real rates of interest. During the 1970s, only 1972 and 1976 witnessed positive, albeit very low, real interest rates. Since real interest rates were negative and did not reflect the demand and supply of capital, they could not perform their role of efficiently rationing capital among investment projects. Instead, the local enterprise-controlled banks have used nonprice criteria to allocate funds within localized or, at best, regionalized markets.

These factors have contributed, among other things, to a less efficient use of capital. Although capital efficiency is difficult to quantify, many economists use the incremental capital-output ratio (ICOR, i.e., the ratio of additional capital to additional output) as a proxy for the same. If the aggregate ICOR is employed, the comparisons can be misleading. Since investment includes expenditures on social overhead capital (e.g., hospitals) as well as infrastructure (e.g.,

---

4. It must be kept in mind that Yugoslav industry was heavily concentrated prior to the 1965 reforms. In 1969, for example, a majority of Yugoslav industries displayed concentration ratios (percent of sales by top four firms) above 70 percent, compared with only 18 percent of U.S. industries in this category in 1963. See Saul Estrin and W. Bartlett, "The Effects of Enterprise Self-Management in Yugoslavia: An Empirical Survey," in D. Jones and J. Svejnar, eds., *Participatory and Self-Managed Firms* (Lexington: Lexington Books, 1982), 87.

roads, bridges) along with productive investment, nations putting a higher share of funds into the former categories will experience less output growth but are not necessarily less efficient in their use of capital. Some analyses finding low levels of capital efficiency in Yugoslavia relative to other middle income countries have made this mistake. When ICORs in only productive activities are compared, however, Yugoslavia seems to use capital slightly less efficiently (slightly higher ICOR) than other middle income countries. But the data in this regard is hardly conclusive. Moreover, it might be a bias toward capital intensity (more capital per worker) in Yugoslavia (also an outcome of worker management, explained below) rather than capital market inefficiencies per se that account for the differential ICORs.[5]

On the macroeconomic front, Yugoslavia has experienced slower growth and greater instability since the 1965 reforms. Whereas Gross Material Product grew at an average annual rate of 8.6 percent between 1956 and 1964, the rate of growth slowed to 6.4 percent between 1965 and 1975 and has continued at the slower pace since. This, of course, is partly attributable to the high energy prices (in 1979 Yugoslavia imported 49.8 percent of its energy) and the stagnant international economy since 1974. But, since the slower growth preceded 1974, it is clearly also a result of domestic factors. Greater enterprise control over the disposal of profits contributed initially to a reduced investment rate after 1965 as workers chose to devote more of enterprise profits to consumption. The ratio of Gross Domestic Investment to GNP fell from 33.7 percent over 1961–65 to 29.7 percent during 1966–70 and 28.4 percent for 1971–75. In addition, the aggravated macroeconomic instability brought government efforts at stabilization which reinforced the slower growth.

The unemployment rate grew from around 5.5 percent in the early sixties to the 7 to 8 percent range by the late sixties and early seventies. Between 1977 and 1980 the unemployment rate averaged 12 percent. The worsening of unemployment during the late seventies is in large measure due to less absorption of Yugoslav migrant workers in West European labor markets after 1974.

The trade-off between unemployment and inflation deteriorated rapidly. Inflation, as measured by industrial producer prices, aver-

---

5. A discussion of Yugoslav capital efficiency as well as total factor productivity is provided in J. H. Moore, *Growth with Self-Management: Yugoslav Industrialization, 1952–1975* (Stanford: Hoover Institution Press, 1980), Ch. 10. Also see Andre Sapir, "Economic Growth and Factor Substitution: What Happened to the Yugoslav Miracle?" *The Economic Journal* 90 (June 1980): 294–313; and Mieko Nishimizu and John Page, "Total Factor Productivity Growth, Technological Progress and Technical Efficiency Change: Dimensions of Productivity Change in Yugoslavia, 1965–78," *The Economic Journal* 92 (Dec. 1982): 920–36.

aged 1.5 percent per year from 1956 to 1964, 10.4 percent per year from 1965 to 1975, and 14.5 percent from 1976 to 1980. During 1981–83 the annual rate was in excess of 35 percent.[6] Contributing to these higher rates of inflation has been the steady devaluation of the dinar, in turn, a product of growing international payments deficits and foreign debt. Yugoslavia's hard currency debt rose from $2 billion in 1970 to over $15 billion by the end of 1979, a real annual growth rate of 10 percent. At the end of 1983, Yugoslavia's foreign debt stood at $21 billion.

Moreover, the decentralization of central government functions and tax revenues occasioned by the 1965 reforms made fiscal policy a feeble and unreliable tool to cope with the instability. All taxes, save the federal sales tax and tariffs, were transferred to the regional level or below. The setting of tax rates was left up to the decentralized government bodies, and, hence, no uniformity of rates existed. Regional and local governments are also legally required to balance their budgets. The lion's share of all government expenditure is non-discretionary, i.e., fixed by legislation or "social compact." This system led to large problems of fiscal coordination and inflexibility. Some economists have even argued that the net effect of this decentralized and poorly coordinated fiscal policy, if anything, has been pro- rather than counter-cyclical—partly because the local governments often spend more at times of rapid growth and less at times of slow growth.

Monetary policy has posed its own set of problems. The money supply grew at an average annual rate of 12 percent during 1966–70, 29 percent during 1970–75, and 22 percent during 1976–80. This rapid expansion of liquid assets has surely contributed to Yugoslavia's increasingly serious inflation; yet there is a poor correlation between price increases and money supply. This reflects, in part, the prevalence of administered prices (in contrast to market prices).

There seems to be a convincing case that monetary policy in Yugoslavia has been derivative rather than independent. It is observed that as a result of sociopolitical forces (see below) when enterprises experience a fall in demand they tend to build inventories rather than lay off workers and lower output. The inventory build-up has been financed out of almost automatic bank loans. If the lower demand level remains for a while, this practice is obviously problematic. In the early seventies it was estimated that one-third of social sector enterprises were in default. Since massive layoffs or bankruptcies are an anathema politically, there has been intense pressure on the banks (largely enterprise-controlled) to expand credit facilities. Accordingly, the money supply more than trebled from 1971 to 1975. Another

6. Unless otherwise indicated, figures are from OECD. *Yugoslavia: Economic Survey*, various years.

factor confounding a steady monetary policy has been the repeated presence of large, unanticipated foreign exchange flows which the central bank has been unable to sterilize.

Income Distribution

The decentralization of the 1965 reforms brought two additional outcomes which many Yugoslavs judged to be undesirable: increased income inequality and increased hierarchy in enterprise management.

The growing emphasis on market forces led to sharper disparities in enterprise performance and income. Stiffer competition also placed a higher premium on certain scarce skills (e.g., managerial, engineering) leading to greater wage differentials. Between 1965 and 1971 the growth rate of income of those in the top 10 percent of income earners was more than double the growth rate of income of those in the bottom 40 percent.[7] Sharon Zukin reports that it is not uncommon to find a ratio of 20 to 1 of top to bottom income within a successful enterprise.[8] This, of course, is considerably below the ratio one might find in a major U.S. firm with a chief executive earning a $1 million salary and a manual laborer with an $8000 wage, or 125 to 1, perquisites and property income aside. Yet it is considerably above the intraenterprise spread of between 3 to 1 and 5 to 1 typically found in the centrally planned countries. If one further considers the absence of sizable property income in Yugoslavia, the resulting degree of overall equality is similar to Sweden's, considerably more egalitarian than the U.S. distribution, and markedly more equal than Venezuela, a capitalist country with roughly the same per capita income as Yugoslavia (see Table 16.1).

Much of Yugoslavia's inequality is accounted for by wide income disparities among the Republics. Social sector enterprises in developed Republics make obligatory loans out of their undistributed profits (amounting on average to 2 percent of value added in each Republic) to investment funds in the less developed regions (amounting on average to 20 percent of productive investment in these regions). However, the problems of regional underdevelopment (lack of infrastructure, human capital deficiencies, high proportion of the labor force in subsistence agriculture, rapid population growth, cultural barriers, etc.) have proved tenacious. The combination of free market forces and only mild government redistribution have led to sharpening regional inequalities since 1965 (see Table 16.2).

---

7. World Bank, *Yugoslavia: Development with Decentralization* (Baltimore: Johns Hopkins University Press, 1975), 105.

8. Sharon Zukin, *Beyond Marx and Tito: Theory and Practice in Yugoslav Socialism* (London: Cambridge University Press, 1975), 37.

Table 16.1
Overall Distribution of Post-Tax Income

	Bottom 20% (%)	Fourth 20% (%)	Middle 20% (%)	Second 20% (%)	Top 20% (%)	Top 10% (%)
Yugoslavia (1978)	6.6	12.1	18.7	23.9	38.7	22.9
Sweden (1972)	6.6	13.1	18.5	24.8	37.0	21.3
United States (1972)[a]	4.5	10.7	17.3	24.7	42.8	26.6
Venezuela (1970)	3.0	7.3	12.9	22.8	54.0	35.7

Source: World Bank, *World Development Report 1981*, 182–83.
a. Without capital gains.

Table 16.2
Regional Inequality in Yugoslavia

	Gross Material Product per capita				Unemployment	
	1954	1964	1970	1975	1971 (%)	1975 (%)
Less developed regions	71	65	61	62		
Bosnia-Herzegovina	82	69	67	69	5.6	11.5
Kosovo	48	37	34	33	18.6	23.5
Macedonia	69	73	64	69	17.3	21.2
Montenegro	53	72	78	70	6.0	14.7
More developed regions	110	118	121	121		
Croatia	119	119	125	124	4.0	5.6
Serbia	84	95	97	92	7.9	12.8
Slovenia	188	187	193	201	2.7	1.5
Vojvodina	88	116	110	121	6.1	10.8
Yugoslavia	100	100	100	100	6.7	10.4

Source: M. Schrenk et al., *Yugoslavia: Self-Management Socialism* (Baltimore: Johns Hopkins University Press, 1979), 248, 287.

In 1975 per capita gross national product in Slovenia, the most developed Republic, was estimated to be $2,979, while in Kosovo, the least developed region, it was $492. Since virtually all social services are regionally financed and administered, the richer areas enjoy better health care, education, transportation, and so on. The disparities are, in fact, wider than the figures in Table 16.2 indicate. For instance, the higher unemployment rates in the less developed regions are accompanied by significantly lower labor force participation rates. These differences are difficult for a self-proclaimed socialist country to accept. Yet stronger redistributive measures would further antagonize regional strains and present a more immediate political problem.

Another undesirable consequence of the 1965 reforms was increasing technocracy and hierarchy in Yugoslav enterprises. This implied decreasing worker participation in management, a hallmark of Yugoslav socialism. Before we discuss this development it is necessary to make a short digression into the economic theory of worker-managed economies.

The Economic Theory of Worker Management

The work of Evsey Domar,[9] Benjamin Ward,[10] Jaroslav Vanek,[11] and others has suggested that worker-run cooperatives or self-managed enterprises might have a different objective than a profit maximizing firm. In particular, they posit that such an enterprise might endeavor to maximize income per worker. If the workers own or have usufruct rights on the enterprise, then they would share among themselves net revenue (total revenue minus total nonlabor costs) at the end of each period. That is, worker income or wage is determined as a residual which is directly affected by changes in the prices of either output or nonlabor inputs.

According to this controversial theory, if the product demand and price go up, workers would be reluctant to increase output by hiring additional workers since this would reduce their own incomes. This result can be demonstrated with a simple numerical example. Assume an enterprise experiencing constant returns to scale has only two inputs, capital (K) and labor (L), and one output (Q) whose price $P_Q = \$1$. Further assume $Q = 100$, $L = 50$, and the marginal product of labor, $MP_L = 1$. As is true for a profit maximizing firm, an income-per-worker maximizing enterprise will hire labor up to the point where the value of the marginal product of labor ($MP_L \times P_Q =$

9. Evsey Domar, "The Soviet Collective Farm as a Producer Cooperative," *American Economic Review* 56, 4 (1966): 734–57.

10. Benjamin Ward, "The Firm in Illyria: Market Syndicalism," *American Economic Review* 48, 4 (1958): 566–89.

11. Jaroslav Vanek, *The General Theory of the Labor-Managed Market Economies* (Ithaca: Cornell University Press, 1970). For an excellent review of this literature, see Deborah Milenkovitch, "Is Market Socialism Efficient?" in A. Zimbalist, ed., *Comparative Economic Systems: An Assessment of Knowledge, Theory and Method* (Boston: Kluwer-Nijhoff, 1983).

VMP_L) equals the going income per worker or wage. Since P_Q = $1 and MP_L = 1, VMP_L = $1. However, if the demand curve shifts upward and P_Q rises to $1.10, then total revenue will equal $110, nonlabor costs remaining at $50, and net revenue will increase to $60. Divided among 50 workers, income per worker will rise to $1.20 (up from $1.00), but with P_Q = $1.10 and MP_L = 1, the VMP_L = $1.10. Thus, temporarily the wage exceeds the VMP_L and this is a signal for the enterprise to cut back employment and output until the VMP_L reaches $1.20 (the worker's income or wage). To recapitulate, the demand for the firm's output has increased, but in response the income-per-worker maximizing firm has decreased production. That is, the firm's (and the industry's) supply curve is negatively sloped.[12]

This short-run, static theoretical result raises questions about the stability and efficiency of a worker-managed economy. Vanek and others have shown that under certain assumptions in the long run a worker-managed economy will attain pareto optimal conditions (as explained in Chapter 9) in equilibrium.

The comparative static nature of the theory, however, offers few, if any, verifiable propositions about the dynamic behavior of the Yugoslav economy. Various assumptions such as competition in the labor and product markets don't match Yugoslav reality. Political constraints on enterprise bankruptcy or layoffs, price or interest rate controls, imperfect markets, factor immobility, and other problems all frustrate the testing of hypotheses from the theory of worker management.

The difficulty of applying the theory to Yugoslav reality can be illustrated with the following example. Other things being equal, the theory would predict that in the short run for an industry with positive economic profits the worker income (wage plus profit share) in a worker-managed enterprise would be higher than in a normal capitalist firm. (In the long run with free entry all firms would receive the same return on their capital.) This higher worker income, in turn, should encourage a more intensive use of the relatively cheaper factor, capital, yielding a higher capital-labor ratio in the worker-managed system. This indeed is found to be the case in Yugoslavia when compared to other countries at a similar level of development. One must be careful, though, not to ascribe this capital intensity to the firm's objective function (maximizing income per worker) or to higher labor costs alone. It should be recalled that Yugoslav capital markets have offered loans at very low or negative real rates of interest. In addition, the Yugoslav system of enterprise taxation,

---

12. The above result can be demonstrated to hold generally with calculus. In the case of a firm with more than one output or more than one variable input, however, the tendency to have a negatively sloped supply curve is weakened.

functioning essentially as a burdensome payroll tax, provides a further bias toward capital intensity.[13] It is not an easy matter to separate out these distinct influences even with the most sophisticated econometric testing.

The same line of reasoning might lead to the expectation that a worker-managed economy would have a slower employment growth over time. Yet the data on employment expansion in Yugoslavia's social sector suggest the opposite, if anything, to be the case. Many analysts have suggested that this anomaly could be explained either by intense political pressure from the Commune (local government) to expand employment or, perhaps, by the possibility of hiring family members or friends. That is, given the opportunity, workers might engage in a modified optimization strategy—maximization of (extended) family income.

The difficulty in testing aside, the economic theory of worker management is useful in helping to identify possible tendencies of the system. It also leads one to ask questions about enterprise saving behavior, worker property rights, time horizons, entrepreneurial activity, new enterprise formation, as well as other issues which can enrich an understanding of the dynamic behavior of the Yugoslav economy.

By itself, however, the microtheory of worker management provides much too narrow a basis to analyze the Yugoslav economy. To be sure, one prominent Yugoslav economist, Branko Horvat,[14] even rejects the central premise of the theory (developed, incidentally, by U.S. economists) in its application to Yugoslavia. He claims that Yugoslav worker-managed enterprises do not treat their wage as a residual and that they do, in fact, profit maximize.

An offshoot of conventional microtheory, the theory of X-Efficiency developed by Harvard economist Harvey Leibenstein offers additional insights into and questions about economic management in Yugoslavia. Leibenstein[15] defines X-Efficiency to be those aspects of

---

13. Tyson and Eichler appraise the Yugoslav enterprise tax: ". . . the taxation system has artificially inflated the costs of labor. Estimates by the ILO indicate that by the 1970s, various taxes and charges levied on labor incomes plus increments to incomes from profit-sharing arrangements amounted to 65 percent of total labor costs. Moreover, these additional labor costs were a higher percent of total labor costs than anywhere else in Europe." Laura Tyson and G. Eichler, "Continuity and Change in the Yugoslav Economy in the 1970s and 1980s," in U.S. Congress, Joint Economic Committee, *East European Economic Assessment*, Part 1 (Washington, D.C.: U.S. Government Printing Office, 1981), 163.

14. Branko Horvat, "On the Theory of the Labor-Managed Firm," in B. Horvat et al., eds., *Self-Governing Socialism* (White Plains, N.Y.: M. E. Sharpe, 1975), 229–40.

15. Harvey Leibenstein, "Allocative Efficiency vs. X-Efficiency," *American Economic Review* 56 (June 1966): 392–415.

the organization of production which are not within the realm of allocational efficiency, such as style of management, worker participation, motivation, organizational structure, and so on. After reviewing the relevant literature, Leibenstein found that in no case had the misallocation of resources brought on a "welfare loss" (reduction in GNP) of more than 0.1 percent. On the contrary, he cited evidence to the effect that X-Efficiency changes accounted for much larger changes in output.

Since Leibenstein's initial essay there has been a considerable body of literature attesting to the potential positive impact that worker participation can have on output. When workers participate in the formulation of enterprise goals and the implementation of policy, they are more likely to identify with or internalize those goals. This factor alone can provide a powerful motivational force, often stronger than material incentives. Insofar as participation produces greater involvement in enterprise affairs, it is likely to lead to not only more work effort but also reduced absenteeism, turnover, and strike activity (or sabotage). If the participation is accompanied by greater job security, then it is also prone to bring forth a stream of worker suggestions and innovations for improving the work process. Without job security (even with open lines of communication between the shop floor and management) worker ideas about increasing quality or productivity might lead to layoffs and, hence, are less apt to be forthcoming.

Since legislation on enterprise management in Yugoslavia provides not only for participation but potentially for control by the workers, it is pertinent to inquire into the impact Yugoslav worker councils have had on economic performance. Unfortunately, the measurement complexities are too intractable to give a firm empirical answer to this question. Although absenteeism, turnover, and strike activity have been relatively low in Yugoslavia, one cannot unequivocally attribute this to worker participation as opposed to high unemployment, social pressure, political repression, cultural influence, or some other factors. The econometric work which has attempted to analyze the sources of Yugoslav economic growth has, on the whole, been consistent with the view that worker participation in management has had a positive impact on production growth.[16] The extent of this impact naturally would be a function of a number of variables such as the level and nature of worker participation as well as worker preferences for growth. Moreover, these relationships are likely to be complex. For instance, effective worker control over enterprise management might result not only in greater worker motivation but also in the decision to distribute a larger share of enterprise profits as worker bonuses as opposed to reinvestment. (This decision

---

16. See, for example, Estrin and Bartlett, "The Effects of Enterprise Self-Management in Yugoslavia."

could be the result of rational calculation as opposed to short worker time horizons. Since workers do not own an enterprise's assets, enlarging those assets will not benefit the worker after he or she retires. Thus, the older the average age of a firm's workers, the lesser will be the tendency for the firm to save and reinvest its profits. This tendency, however, is offset by others such as increasing use of social compacts to ensure a certain level of saving and growing managerial control over enterprise decision making.) These outcomes would have contradictory impacts on growth.

Yugoslav Worker Management in Practice

As already noted, since the early fifties Yugoslav workers have been granted the power to control democratically the affairs of all social sector enterprises. The fact that many of Yugoslavia's industrial workers at that time were transplanted peasants with low levels of educational attainment and little knowledge of manufacturing processes was not conducive to high levels of worker participation. The historical absence of effective democratic governance in Yugoslav territory was not propitious either.

Notwithstanding these and other obstacles, the ideology and practice of worker management were firmly in place by the late fifties. A variety of studies attests to (1) widespread worker desire to influence enterprise decision making, (2) a growing expectation to participate in decision making concerning production as well as personnel, income, and welfare issues, and (3) high attendance at worker assemblies and meetings of other participatory bodies.[17] These trends were all established prior to 1965. The reforms of that year, however, seemed to mark a turning point. In particular, the strong market orientation of the reforms began to generate a new, more hierarchical enterprise power structure. Among other changes, the so-called Amendment XV of 1969 permitted the Management Board (elected by the Workers' Council) to be replaced by a Business Board appointed by the enterprise director.

A careful comparative study by Ichak Adizes of two Yugoslav textile

---

17. Actually, the pre- and post-1965 studies exhibit a high degree of variability in their conclusions regarding the extent, nature, and impact of participation. This variability corresponds to the uneven development and ethnic diversity of Yugoslavia's regions. Three particularly useful studies of worker participation in Yugoslavia are: Gerry Hunnius, "Workers' Self-Management in Yugoslavia," in Hunnius et al., eds., *Workers' Control* (New York: Vintage, 1973); Ichak Adizes, *Industrial Democracy: Yugoslav Style* (New York: The Free Press, 1971); and Ellen Comisso, *Workers' Control under Plan and Market* (New Haven: Yale University Press, 1979).

firms reveals much of the dynamic behind this shift.[18] Following the 1965 reforms one firm made an immediate adaptation to the new market conditions. A new director was hired and the size of the marketing department was expanded from fewer than a dozen people to 39 people within a year. The need to make more rapid responses to the unstable market and the effort to influence actual market conditions meant that decision making was centered more and more in the hands of the enlarged middle management staff. Given the new premium on nonproduction issues, workers had less and less of an impact on decision making, and attendance at worker council meetings naturally fell off.

In the second firm, the management style, at least through 1966, did not change. Worker attendance and participation at council meetings were maintained, and by standard criteria of technical efficiency (productivity of capital and labor) this second firm was more efficient. Nevertheless, the first firm because of its further integration into the market, closer contact with the local bank, and greater willingness to take risks experienced faster growth than the second firm. Adizes adds that on the basis of interviews with managers from several other enterprises there was a general trend toward greater control by professional managers in Yugoslav firms after the 1965 economic reform. This conclusion has been corroborated by several subsequent studies.

Increasingly removed from basic enterprise decision making, worker councils and workers began to relate to the enterprise in more instrumental ways. They progressively took up the concerns of traditional trade unionism (wages, benefits, grievances, etc.) to the relative detriment of participation in central management issues. As the enterprise grew more hierarchical, the conception of the unit as a competitive profit center gained force. It is probable, and there is some empirical evidence to support this, that the objective of profit maximization took increasing precedence over income-per-worker maximization as managers gained more control over the enterprise in its market context.

Materialist motivation and individualism were gaining ideological ascendancy in what was supposed to be an evolving ethos of socialist participation and cooperation. In the words of a leading Yugoslav expert on self-management: "Economization and particularization of interests of the employed are the result of the domination of the competitive system and the result of the domination of the ideology of development and consumption."[19]

---

18. Adizes, *Industrial Democracy*.

19. Josip Obradovic, "Distribution of Participation in the Process of Decision-Making on Problems Related to the Economic Activity of the Company," in E. Pusic and R. Supek, eds., *Participation and Self-Management* (Zagreb: Council of the Federation of Yugoslav Trade Unions, 1972), 185.

The Reforms of the 1970s

It was clear to Yugoslav policy makers that they had gone too far in reaction to Soviet central planning. Their assumption that the market was economically, socially, and politically neutral was seen by the early seventies to be misguided. The 1965 unleashing of competitive market forces was now seen as largely responsible for the growing macroeconomic instability as well as the progressive undermining of the emergent socialist social fabric. Laura Tyson and Gabriel Eichler, two leading U.S. experts on the Yugoslav economy, assess the results of the 1965 reforms in these terms:

> In the opinion of many political and economic leaders, the market system failed to live up to anticipations: growth over the 1965–70 period was disappointing; inefficiencies in the use of capital and labor remained; and foreign trade bottlenecks persisted. In addition, the market seemed to produce certain consequences that had not been bargained for: a deterioration in the trade-off between growth and inflation; an apparent increase in inequality both among regions and among individuals and enterprises within a given region; and the perceived concentration of economic power in the hands of financial institutions, the managerial elite, and wholesale, retail and foreign trade enterprises. These last two tendencies were seen to be at odds with the ideological goals of socialism.[20]

The new 1974 Yugoslav Constitution and the 1976 Social Planning Law endeavor to establish a new basis for self-managing socialism which rectifies some of these problems. Taken together, they contemplate circumscribing the market mechanism with a form of extremely decentralized, medium-term planning along with decentralizing and democratizing the management and market power of economic units. The reforms are very complex and we shall attempt only a brief summary and analysis in what follows.

A basic change is the legislation providing for the formation of "basic organizations of associated labor," or BOALs. According to the law, if the activity of a subunit of an enterprise "can be expressed in terms of value within the work organization or on the market . . . the workers . . . shall have the right and duty to organize . . . [that unit] as a basic organization of associated labor." The purpose of this effort to decompose enterprises into subunits can be seen as threefold: one, to lessen the market power of large Yugoslav enterprises; two, to create smaller units making the material incentives connected to work effort more immediate; and, three, to break up enterprise organizational structures and, thereby, redistribute decision-making power toward the shop floor workers. Although the complete record is not yet in, this reform has encountered a series of problems.

---

20. Tyson and Eichler, "Continuity and Change," 141.

The first problem is that the enabling legislation is sufficiently nebulous to have created confusion regarding the delineation of enterprise subunits or BOALs. To take an extreme example, Professor Stephen Sacks reported on a discussion at a Zagreb conference of business lawyers: "The topic was whether selling alcoholic and nonalcoholic drinks constitute separate activities; if so, it would seem that a bar must have two BOALs, even though the same employees work in both."[21] A less academic example is found in a confectionery factory where "workers who melt cocoa, make a particular style of hard chocolate, and package it are all in one BOAL. Those who work on a different type of candy are in a separate BOAL, although some of the boxes sold by this firm in retail stores contain candy from several different BOALS."[22] Although in theory an enterprise subunit might be easy to define in many cases by observing distinct vertical phases of production or distinct technologies, in practice it is often as difficult as delimiting electoral districts in U.S. politics. The way a subdivision is gerrymandered is the result of the interplay of conflicting political interests attempting to control the new unit.

The problems persist after the identification of the subunits. Since it is now necessary to do separate, detailed accounting for each subunit, a system of accurate intraenterprise transfer prices must be established. This creates additional accounting and administrative costs. In some instances, BOALs from a single enterprise ceased to trade with each other since the established transfer price differed from that for the same input in another enterprise. The purchasing BOAL bought its material at a cheaper price from a BOAL in another enterprise. While this experience might be applauded as a demonstration of competitive pricing at work, it also engenders serious political and social problems for the affected BOALs. Moreover, there is little evidence that competitive pricing has become more generalized since the reforms.

In many cases, the BOALs are simply re-creations of firms which existed previous to the merger activity of the sixties and seventies. Stephen Sacks gathered data for a sample of nineteen large Yugoslav enterprises, varying in size from 1,014 to 32,000 workers. In these enterprises, the number of BOALs per enterprise fluctuated from 4 to 120, and the average BOAL size varied from 71 to 800 workers. If these enterprises are representative, then the new BOALs seem large enough to be divided along previously existing company lines. In such cases, it is likely that the organization of management did not undergo significant change. Indeed, in her interesting case study of a Zagreb machine tool factory, Ellen Comisso found that "most of the

---

21. Stephen Sacks, "Divisionalization in Large Yugoslav Enterprises," *Journal of Comparative Economics* 4 (1980), 12.

22. Ibid.

workers saw the BOALs as a purely cosmetic change and a purely formal reform."[23]

The second major thrust of reform of the 1970s is to create a new system of decentralized medium-term planning. Starting from the BOAL level, economic units are to make five-year legally binding pacts (or "self-management agreements") with each other. These pacts are then made between enterprises, between associations of enterprises in a particular sector, and, finally, between associations and economic chambers (union of all enterprises in a Republic). At the same time, governments at various levels (or sociopolitical communities as they are called in Yugoslavia) are to make agreements (called social compacts) among themselves and between them and production units regarding basic proportions of the economy as well as matters concerning income distribution, wages, investments, subsidies, taxes, bond floats, and so on. "Planning," then, is to be conducted from the bottom up.

The system raises a host of questions. How are coordination and balance among the economic sectors and regions to be achieved? Won't the system require an inordinate amount of meetings and paperwork? How will such decentralized decision making ultimately be different from or able to moderate the operations of the market mechanism?

Unfortunately, no positive answer to these questions has heretofore been forthcoming. With a few exceptions, the economy appears to be functioning about the same as it was prior to the 1974/76 reforms.

In a recent article, Comisso noted three core difficulties with the new planning system.[24] One, given divergent interests, there has been a significant delay in reaching agreement or an inability to agree on compacts. Two, there has been a problem in getting subordinate units of government to go along with compacts concluded by higher units. Three, even where concluded, compacts have frequently been ignored in practice. She concludes her analysis on a pessimistic note:

> What apparently has happened is that while the role of the sociopolitical community in economic development has been enhanced, this has had the consequence of creating tensions between economic organizations expected to conform with social priorities and the political bodies determining them. These tensions, in turn, have jeopardized coordination and agreement among political units themselves, undermined the rationality and feasibility of the decisions and policies which are arrived at, placed serious obstacles in the way of enforcing legislation and agreements and produced economic consequences not desired by either enterprises or political bodies.[25]

---

23. Comisso, *Workers' Control*, 174.

24. E. Comisso, "Yugoslavia in the 1970s: Self-Management and Bargaining," *Journal of Comparative Economics* 4 (1980): 192–208.

25. Ibid., 193. A more optimistic view of the reforms is provided by Martin Schrenk, *Managerial Structures and Practices in Manufacturing Enterprises:*

One area where a government control (social compact) seems to have been effective is with stricter incomes policies in recent years. Since 1979, productivity increases have exceeded real wage gains by appreciable margins.

In other areas of concern, however, efforts to promote uniform policies across regions have been unsuccessful. Despite some government attempts to gain more control over the use of investment funds, the record here leaves much to be desired. The 1976–80 plan, for instance, called for energy's share in total investment to reach 42 percent. In actuality, it reached only 31 percent. With such tenuous control over basic economic levers as investment, it is difficult to conclude that market forces have been circumscribed to the satisfaction of Yugoslav policy makers.

Finally, it has been observed that the current method of enterprise discussions and bargaining within a sector provides more information to and allows for greater coordination among decision-making units. This amounts to a limited and informal system of indicative planning similar to those in Western Europe and Japan. Tyson and Eichler point out one potential advantage of this process:

> In the absence of information about future prices and costs, the market mechanism alone does not guarantee optimal decision-making, because the individual enterprise does not have access to the data required to make the most profitable decision.[26]

A possible disadvantage of this arrangement is that it could undermine any impetus toward breaking up economic concentration and more competitive pricing.

Conclusion

Criticism comes easy. It is less easy, however, to design and effectively implement the first model of decentralized socialist management. After their initial repudiation of the Soviet model, the Yugoslavs have had no other country's experience to learn from. They have traveled an uncharted course.

It is well to recall that Tito's Yugoslavia not only inherited a war-shattered society with a high illiteracy rate, a heavily rural population, and a small industrial base but also was left the legacy of severe, pervasive ethnic cleavages.

A Yugoslav Case Study, World Bank Staff Working Paper No. 455, May 1981. Another pessimistic view which reports signs of a new commitment to the market can be found in Diane Flaherty, "Economic Reform and Foreign Trade in Yugoslavia," *Cambridge Journal of Economics* 6, 2 (June 1982): 105–143. Also see: Laura Tyson, *The Yugoslav Economic System and Its Performance in the 1970s* (Berkeley: Institute of International Studies, 1980).

26. Tyson and Eichler, "Continuity and Change," 145.

Despite the many difficulties and problems discussed above, Yugoslav economic performance has been creditable. The rate of Yugoslav economic growth has generally surpassed that of other middle income countries over the past three decades. Yugoslav per capita income rose from under $100 in 1945 to $2,790 in 1981 (in current dollars). Although Yugoslavia has been confronted with increasing macroeconomic instability (reflected in unemployment and inflation), here again its experience has not generally been inferior to countries at a similar level of development. There is, moreover, more income equality and a wider provision of social services in Yugoslavia than in the capitalist middle income nations.

Although Yugoslavia has so far fallen short of producing a solid model for self-managing socialism, it has pioneered in experimenting with component parts of a more democratic system of socialist economic management at the enterprise level. Furthermore, even though worker participation in enterprise management seems to have deteriorated since the 1965 reforms, the typical Yugoslav enterprise still exhibits a level of worker participation and influence which would be the envy of worker movements in most of the world.

The Yugoslav society has lived through the death of its charismatic national hero, Josip Broz (Tito) in 1980. Whether the new system of a collective presidency (three representatives from each of six Republics and two representatives each from the two autonomous provinces) can stabilize the country in the face of renewed political protest in Kosovo, intensified economic instability, falling real living standards since 1981, a burdensome foreign debt, and poorly defined institutions of management and planning remains to be seen. Regardless of its future course, Yugoslavia's intransigent resistance to Soviet domination and its flexibility and innovativeness in developing a new economic system will remain the subject of study and admiration for some time to come.

Recommended Readings

1. Deborah Milenkovitch, *Plan and Market in Yugoslav Economic Thought* (New Haven: Yale University Press, 1971).

2. Laura Tyson, *The Yugoslav Economy and Its Performance in the 1970s* (Berkeley: Institute of International Studies, 1980).

3. Ellen Comisso, *Workers' Control under Plan and Market* (New Haven: Yale University Press, 1979).

4. Branko Horvat, *The Yugoslav Economic System* (White Plains, N.Y.: M. E. Sharpe, 1976).

5. International Labor Office, *Workers' Management in Yugoslavia: Recent Developments and Trends* (Geneva: ILO, 1982).

6. Martin Schrenk et al., *Yugoslavia: Self-Management Socialism* (Baltimore: Johns Hopkins University Press, 1979).

7. Howard Wachtel, *Workers' Management and Workers' Wages in Yugoslavia* (Ithaca: Cornell University Press, 1974).

8. Saul Estrin, *Self-Management: Economic Theory and Yugoslav Practice* (Cambridge: Cambridge University Press, 1984).

9. Stephen R. Sacks, *Self-Management in Large Corporations: The Yugoslav Case* (London: George Allen and Unwin, 1984).

Six

CONCLUSION

17

COMPARING ECONOMIC SYSTEMS

In this chapter, we attempt to highlight certain recurrent themes and draw some comparisons among the countries studied in this book.

General Remarks

This study has described and analyzed a broad diversity of economic institutions in both capitalist and socialist countries. We have emphasized a political-economic approach, attempting to illustrate the complexity of real world forces which mold economic institutions and systems.

Economies are often systemically classified according to certain basic characteristics: direction by plan or market forces; the nature of property ownership (private, collective, or public); the system of incentives; and the locus and pattern of decision making (for example, the degree of centralization and decentralization). Economies with predominantly public ownership are generally considered to be socialist; conversely, economies with predominantly private ownership are generally considered to be capitalist. It is also the case that economies characterized primarily by private ownership, with some exceptions, make greater use of the market and material incentives, and the government in these economies tends to play a smaller role in coordinating economic activity. Since, in practice, economies possess these traits to varying degrees, it is possible either to construct a taxonomical continuum or, alternatively, to divide the economies into categories: capitalist, market socialist, planned socialist, etc.

In organizing our presentation we have chosen to group economies into categories. The economies within each category tend to display certain similar behavioral patterns or dynamics. It is also true, however, that there are significant differences regarding institutional arrangements and economic performance among economies within each group. We have attempted to highlight both the similarities and the differences.

Among the set of capitalist-type economies, for instance, there are large differences not only in the extent of public ownership or the share of government spending in GNP, but also in the structure of industrial and financial organization, the functioning of labor markets and collective bargaining, government emphasis on supply or demand management, the particular interplay of social, cultural, political, and economic factors, etc. It is tempting to correlate economic performance with specific economic policies or institutions among the capitalist-type economies. Whereas it is clear that certain capitalist economies have performed in a fashion superior to others, it is dubious to attribute this relative success to individual policies or institutions. Economics is not a laboratory science where one can hold other variables constant.

Among the economies usually categorized as "socialist" there are also major differences in institutions and performance. One obvious distinction is the extent to which an economy has been decentralized. There are two roads toward decentralization from central planning: market decentralization and administrative decentralization.

Market Decentralization of "Socialist" Economies

The only successful reforms to date integrating significant market forces into a socialist economy have been in Yugoslavia and Hungary. Other East European nations and the Soviet Union have flirted with such reforms but have failed and, at least for the time being, retreated. (Since the late 1970s, the Chinese have been experimenting with a rather extensive use of market-type institutions.) It seems clear that if a major reform of central planning is to succeed, there must at a minimum be a strong and unified political leadership ready to prepare patiently and to implement the changes.[1] Efficacious market-type reforms require at least two economic preconditions. First, a balanced macroeconomy must be approximated for market forces and prices to be practicable. Second, tautness must be removed from the planning strategy and some slack must be built in to give decentralized resource allocation some meaning. For instance, to allow enterprises to retain a share of their profits is meaningful only if they can actually use their extra income to obtain the desired investment

---

1. See, for one, Zielinski's excellent analysis of the failure of the Polish economic reforms. J. Zielinski, *Economic Reforms in Polish Industry* (London: Oxford University Press, 1973). Also see R. Knaack, "Dynamic Comparative Economics," in A. Zimbalist, ed., *Comparative Economic Systems: An Assessment of Knowledge, Theory and Method* (Boston: Kluwer-Nijhoff, 1983); and W. Brus, *The Economics and Politics of Socialism* (London: Routledge and Kegan Paul, 1973).

goods (or collective consumption goods, such as an enterprise rec-reational vehicle). The establishment of these preconditions may re-quire several years of concerted economic guidance.

Once introduced, the market-oriented reforms will potentially generate serious social tensions and political pressures since certain groups will be threatened or weakened by the initial reform process. The political leadership must be able to withstand these and other pressures. For instance, the inability to sustain the reform process in Poland dating back to the mid fifties and the several abrupt shifts in Polish economic strategy may be traced back to a lack of consensus within the country's political leadership. The unpredictable policy shifts, in turn, contributed to an unstable environment and Poland's poor economic performance. Similarly, Yugoslavia's growing eco-nomic and political problems can be attributed in part to various extreme policy shifts and, more recently, to the leadership confusion following Tito's death.[2]

Administrative Decentralization of "Socialist" Economies

Administrative decentralization as a conscious policy choice has occurred in the Soviet Union during the early 1920s and between 1957 and 1965; in China during several periods after the mid 1950s; in Cuba during the 1970s; and in East Germany, first from 1963 and then from the late 1970s. The essence of administrative decentralization is to move power over resource allocation away from the center and closer to the units of production. That is, central planning functions devolve in part to branch, regional, or local planning agencies. (Since it is impossible in practice for the center to direct the entire economy, administrative decentralization must exist to some extent in all cen-trally planned economies.)

Empowering local agencies or producing units (decentralizing from above) often entails merging enterprises or farms into larger units (centralizing from below). By creating larger production units at the base, these new "associations" of enterprises or "combines" are able to become more self-sufficient (e.g., produce some of their own inputs, perform more repairs, do their own research and develop-ment, have greater financial flexibility, deal directly in foreign trade) and, hence, become less dependent on the center. The center is still responsible for guiding and coordinating the activities of the com-bines, but the center concerns itself more with managing aggregates and less with overseeing supply allocations and the details of enter-prise operations.

The enlarged local units, in turn, gain strength from their size and

---

2. D. Flaherty, "Economic Reform and Foreign Trade in Yugoslavia," *Cambridge Journal of Economics* 6, 2 (June 1982), 105–43.

potentially have a larger impact on the setting of macroeconomic priorities. The formation of, first, associations and, then, larger combines in East Germany bears a close resemblance to this case of administrative decentralization.[3] According to many, East Germany has performed in a superior way to the other centrally planned economies in COMECON; we shall consider part of its record in the appendix to this chapter. Decentralization of the planning mechanism can assume many other, often less structured, forms, such as building slack into the planning system and/or promoting greater worker participation in enterprise, association, or branch decision making. Administrative and market decentralization are not incompatible and, thus, could be implemented jointly.

It should be noted that if decentralization, either administrative or market, proceeds too far, it begins to engender conflicts for a socialist economy. Too much administrative decentralization can result in duplication of efforts, supply bottlenecks, and overall insufficient coordination. Khrushchev's regionalization experiment from 1957 to 1965, which shifted much economic decision making from thirty-odd central ministries to over one hundred regional councils, is an excellent example of this phenomenon. Unconstrained market decentralization may necessitate accepting many of the negative features of capitalist economies as perceived by socialist theory: enterprise bankruptcies, large-scale layoffs and unemployment, greater inequality, price instability, and business cycles. In a sense, then, the task of the socialist planner is to avoid the pitfalls of either excessive centralization or excessive decentralization.

The ability of a centrally planned economy to effectively decentralize along market or administrative dimensions is closely connected to aspects of political and social organization in the country. The system of centralized, hierarchical and taut planning which emerged in the USSR under Stalin reflected the prevailing political and social environment. The Soviet Communist party became severed early on from the "masses" it purported to represent. Isolated from a popular base, there were few checks on the Party's policies or internal functioning. Stalin turned the Party against itself and through his endless purges and persecutions infected the Party and the society with an awesome sense of insecurity and distrust. (The historical context of the Soviet system was discussed in some detail in Chapter 5.)

Unavoidably, this political atmosphere rubbed off on the planning apparatus. Economic control was closely guarded at the center, and subordinate agencies were given unrealistically high targets (taut planning). There was little basis for assuming that branch or enter-

---

3. D. Cornelsen, "The GDR in a Period of Foreign Trade Difficulties," in U.S. Congress, Joint Economic Committee (J.E.C.), *East European Economic Assessment*, Part 1 (Washington, D.C.: U.S. Government Printing Office, 1981).

prise directors or production workers would voluntarily cooperate or exert themselves on behalf of the country's leaders in this atmosphere. A kind of Taylorism was applied not just to factory workers but throughout the economy. Such were the proximate historical roots for the Soviet planning model.[4]

Other socialist nations with different histories, distinct party organizations or ideologies, and greater popular involvement in the party and revolutionary process have found the Soviet model to be ill-suited to their conditions. In the chapter on the Cuban economy, for instance, we saw that despite surface parallels of institutional *form* with Soviet planning the actual *content* of planning is more flexible and decentralized. Notwithstanding Soviet intervention to stop experimentation as in Hungary 1956, Czechoslovakia 1968, or Poland 1956 and 1981, there is an assortment of economic institutions, political structures, and performance results associated with the socialist economies. Moreover, were it not for U.S. intervention in the affairs of other Western hemisphere nations, the range of socialisms would be even broader. U.S. interference in the governments of Castro in Cuba, Manley in Jamaica, or the Sandinistas in Nicaragua has certainly tainted the nature and success of socialist development in these countries. The central U.S. role in, first, subverting the economic policies and, then, assisting in the overthrow of the democratically elected socialist government of Salvador Allende in Chile in 1973 is another case in point.

Finally, it remains to point out that policy movements toward economic reform in the centrally planned economies have often been accompanied by mass movements for democratization. In particular, Poland from 1956 to 1958, Hungary in 1956, Czechoslovakia in 1968, and Poland again in 1981 were all characterized by very spirited movements for workers' control over production units as well as over the general economic plan. Unfortunately, in many cases the economic reform became a substitute for the needed political reform (that is, democratization). Many authors have contended that economic planning would function more smoothly and productively were it to occur in a democratic political and economic environment. While this point seems well taken, it is appropriate here to recall the admonitions of Alec Nove:

A view held by some on the left is that Soviet planning is not planning at all. How can it be "real" planning, when these distortions occur and when the outcome frequently fails to conform with the intentions of the planners themselves? This is more than a matter of terminology, for under-

4. This argument is elaborated in A. Zimbalist, "On the Role of Management in Socialist Development," *World Development* 9, 9 (1981), and in J. Espinosa and A. Zimbalist, *Economic Democracy* (New York: Academic Press, 1981), 24–29.

lying this view is the belief that there could now exist a "real" socialist democratic planning system which would dispense simultaneously with market, bureaucracy and hierarchy, based upon some undefined form of mass democracy. Those who hold this view are usually unaware of the complexities of the modern industrial structure, with its innumerable complementarities and interdependencies. It is not clear where, in this process, is the place for political democracy as an alternative to both market and bureaucracy. Democratic procedures are indeed essential, but these cannot be meaningfully applied to multiple-millions of micro-economic decisions: an elected assembly can vote on broad priorities (e.g., more for primary education, or housing, or developing a region), but hardly on whether three tons of constructional steel should be allocated to this or that building site, or that production of red dyestuffs be increased by 3%.[5]

Evaluating Performance

How do we assess the relative success of socialist and capitalist economies? At the outset it is necessary to acknowledge that such an assessment is fraught with difficulties. The most sound judgment is that there are no easy answers. But the reader who has toiled through to the final chapter deserves some attempt at a carefully qualified answer. We shall therefore proceed cautiously to: first, recall some of the essential methodological caveats inherent to quantitative comparative analysis; second, establish a possible set of criteria for evaluating economic performance; third, offer some general observations on the actual economic performance, as well as the economic trade-offs, in each economic system; and, fourth, in the appendix to this chapter, consider a bit more specifically the cases of East and West Germany.

Methodology

The definitions of statistical categories and the reliability of official estimates differ significantly from one economy to another. Thus, unlike other COMECON countries, Hungary reports only its exports on an f.o.b. (free on board) basis while reporting its imports c.i.f. (cost, insurance, freight). This statistical practice relatively understates Hungary's balance of trade surpluses or overstates trade deficits. To take some other examples: Denmark is the only country where the measurement of unemployment includes part-time workers seeking full-time work as partly unemployed. The reference period for job seeking in the U.S. unemployment surveys is four weeks but it is only

5. A. Nove, "Problems and Prospects of the Soviet Economy," *New Left Review* 119 (Jan./Feb. 1980), 7.

one week in Japan. The age range for inclusion in the unemployment statistics in Sweden is sixteen to seventy-four years, while in Japan it is fifteen years and over with no upper limit, and in the United States it is sixteen years and over with no upper limit.

Another factor confounding statistical comparison is the existence of different systems of national accounts between COMECON and other countries. Apart from Hungary, the Soviet trade bloc does not use the aggregate production categories GNP (Gross National Product) and GDP (Gross Domestic Product). In many economies, but particularly those which are centrally planned, some or most prices are set by the government. Since prices are needed to aggregate output across goods and services, different pricing systems distort the relative valuation of output. Of course, price distortions arising from market imperfections and certain government policies also affect the valuation of output in capitalist economies. These difficulties are compounded by the serious and unavoidable index number problem (discussed in Appendix A to Chapter 6).

Finally, a related issue is the use of exchange rates to convert output of different nations to the same currency base for purposes of comparison. In the planned economies the exchange rate is often multiple and fixed. That is, the conversion rate of the local currency into, say, dollars is different for different types of transactions and the rate does not fluctuate in the market with changing conditions of supply and demand for the currency. Hence, it is ambiguous which rate to use or what it means. In the market economies, exchange rates generally float to varying degrees with the changing supply and demand conditions for given currencies. In some periods exchange rates are highly volatile and it is not apparent whether one should convert at the rate of a given day, week, or month, or, say, a yearly average.

Each of these statistical conundrums has been discussed more fully in earlier chapters. Generally, there is no "best way" to confront these methodological ambiguities, but it is always necessary to be cognizant of the limitations they impose on quantitative comparative analysis.

Additionally, it is important to remember that not all governments are equally reliable in their reporting of economic data. Some governments have smaller statistical agencies or agencies with less qualified personnel or poorer survey techniques or production units with more refined dissimulation skills. Some governments purposefully limit the reporting of data or, on occasion, directly launder or skew the presentation of data. Together, these obstacles to empirical comparison could turn back an army of researchers, but we shall proceed intrepidly forward and assume the reader will read in the appropriate qualifications without being so reminded at every juncture.

Criteria and Performance

Let us assume for the moment that we have all the accurate data we want, for all the countries we desire. How do we go about deciding which economies are performing better or are, overall, more desirable? Do we look at which economy produces the most PACMAN video games or ET T-shirts? Probably not. What about income per capita or GNP growth?

The factors we choose to investigate and the weights we apply to each factor are very much value judgments. Suppose, for instance, we agree that high growth and a relatively equal distribution of income are the only relevant considerations. Country A has a 5 percent yearly growth rate and a decile ratio (top 10 percent of income earners' average income to bottom 10 percent) of 15, while country B has a 3.5 percent growth rate and a decile ratio of 8. The only meaningful way to choose between the relative desirability of the two economies would be to weight the comparative importance of growth and distribution. But if we disagree on the weights to assign to each factor, then the choice becomes personal. Matters are further complicated when we acknowledge that each country has its own values and weights. Do we evaluate a country on its own terms or on ours? What, moreover, does it mean to speak of a country's values and weights? Presumably, these come from a notion of the country's social welfare function, that is, its entire preference map for all goods and services. Is this welfare function chosen by unrepresentative political leaders or is it somehow generated democratically by the country's citizens?

Fortunately, there is a fair degree of consensus among economists about which variables are important in assessing economic perform-ance. Yet, there is no consensus on how to weight the variables, although it is no secret that conventional economics is primarily concerned with efficiency of resource allocation. Let us, then, turn to consider the most commonly employed criteria for evaluating eco-nomic performance, with the understanding that how one views the overall record is very much a function of one's subjective weighting scheme. We shall consider five performance criteria: economic growth, income distribution, economic stability and full employment, efficiency, and economic freedoms and noneconomic factors.

Economic Growth

Here the relevant measure is the average annual rate of growth of GNP per capita. One available estimate (though others differ) sug-gests a slightly higher rate of growth of GNP per capita among the centrally planned socialist[6] countries than the advanced capitalist

---

6. For the remainder of this chapter we shall use the shorthand "planned

countries from 1960 to 1980, the rate among the industrialized socialist countries being around 4.2 percent and among the industrialized
capitalist countries around 3.6 percent.[7] It might also be mentioned
that there is less variability in growth rates over time among the
planned socialist than the capitalist economies. In contrast, the market socialist economy of Yugoslavia has experienced fluctuating
growth cycles typical of market economies. Yugoslavia's annual rate
of growth of GNP per capita was 5.4 percent between 1960 and 1980.

Given the methodological problems mentioned above, it is impossible to say that the higher growth rates of the socialist economies are
statistically significant. It should also be noted that the investment
ratio (gross investment divided by GNP) in the planned socialist countries has been three or four percentage points above that in the
capitalist countries on average over this period. Additionally, the
planned socialist countries on average have lower levels of development and, therefore, are able to borrow technology from the more
advanced economies. Both of these factors should, other things being
equal, lead to higher rates of growth.[8] The available evidence on
growth, then, can be used to support claims of central planning's

---

socialist" to refer to the "centrally planned socialist" economies, unless otherwise specified. Further, we shall stick with convention and consider Hungary's
economic record to belong to the class of centrally planned economies. While
the recent round of post-1978 economic reforms in Hungary may merit clas-
sifying the Hungarian economy as market socialist, for the great bulk of the
years under consideration the economy of Hungary adhered more closely to
the idiom of central planning. Yugoslavia is considered separately, as a market socialist economy.

7. See P. Gregory and R. Stuart, *Comparative Economic Systems* (Boston:
Houghton Mifflin, 1982), 371–75; and World Bank, *World Development Report
1981* (New York: Oxford University Press, 1981), 111.

8. The relationship between the investment ratio and growth can be demonstrated concisely with simple algebra. Let Q be output, dQ the absolute
change in output, $\dot{Q}$ the percent change in output, dK the change in capital
stock which is equal to I or net investment.

$$\dot{Q} = \frac{dQ}{Q}$$

Multiply numerator and denominator by dK:

$$\dot{Q} = \frac{dQ}{Q} \cdot \frac{dK}{dK}$$

Rearrange:

$$\dot{Q} = \frac{dK}{Q} \cdot \frac{dQ}{dK}$$

This reads that the growth rate of output is equal to the investment ratio times
the marginal product of capital. Thus, the higher the investment ratio and the
higher the marginal product of capital, the higher will be the growth rate of
output. The marginal product of capital, of course, will vary directly with
the sophistication of technology and the degree of capacity utilization.
Clearly, possible insufficiency of aggregate demand is assumed away in this
formulation.

superiority or of its inefficiency, depending on the author's perspective. Any such claims should be interpreted cautiously and closely scrutinized.

Efficiency

Efficiency is a very elusive concept. Understood as the relative amount of output produced for a given amount of inputs, efficiency is broader than the allocational approach in microeconomic theory. In practice, it would also include what Harvey Leibenstein has called X-efficiency.[9] X-efficiency is concerned with questions of effective organization, management, motivation, and so on, all of which can vary with any given allocation of resources. A society's welfare function also enters here. If it is decided, for example, that a slower pace of work is more important than extra output, a society may appear in quantitative terms to be less efficient when they are actually maximizing their welfare.

In analyzing planned economies it is useful to think of coordination efficiency or the consistent working out of material balances. Large-scale waste could ensue not only from arbitrary prices but also from bureaucratic mistakes, resource bottlenecks, the absence of complementary goods, etc. In contrast, in analyzing market economies it is relevant to observe the waste which comes from unemployment of labor and other resources, deceitful advertising, imperfect competition, duplication of efforts, and so on.

Quantitative measures of efficiency give insufficient information on other variables as well, such as quality changes which are not reflected in price changes. It is no easy matter to disentangle these issues.

Economists generally use two concepts of efficiency: static and dynamic. Static efficiency refers to the unit of output per unit of input during a specific time period. To measure this in practice would require quantitative evidence on the level of economic development, the quality of labor and other inputs, the quality of output, the total number of hours worked (and perhaps the intensity of work as well), the value of the capital stock, etc. Such evidence is sufficiently intractable that it usually discourages quantitative static efficiency comparisons.[10]

---

9. H. Leibenstein, "Allocative Efficiency vs. X-Efficiency," *American Economic Review* 56 (June 1966).

10. One exception is a controversial study by Abram Bergson where he found static efficiency in the Soviet economy to be far below that in the U.S. economy: A. Bergson, "Comparative Productivity and Efficiency in the U.S.A. and the U.S.S.R.," in A. Eckstein, ed., *Comparison of Economic Systems* (Berkeley: University of California Press, 1971). Students interested in pursuing the difficulties and complexities involved in Bergson's findings should consult the critique by Evsey Domar in the same volume. Also see Bergson's

Dynamic efficiency refers to the growth of output per growth of inputs over time. Since this concept requires data only on rates of change rather than absolute levels, it is easier to measure than static efficiency. This is because equal distortions cancel out when growth rates are considered. One standard measure of dynamic efficiency is the growth rate of "total factor productivity." The growth rate of total factor productivity is defined as the percent change in output minus the percent change of the weighted average of the inputs. Gregory and Stuart make some rough estimates of dynamic efficiency for capitalist and planned socialist countries and conclude that dynamic efficiency was higher in planned socialist countries from 1950 to 1960 and higher in capitalist countries from 1960 to the early 1970s.[11] Their data on capitalist countries, however, goes beyond 1962 only for the U.S. and Japan—with Japan pulling the average up considerably. Over the whole period considered by Gregory and Stuart, the averages for socialist and capitalist economies are very close. This is an area of great controversy, in which other studies have reached very different conclusions.

Although efficiency performance for the market socialist economy of Yugoslavia is equally difficult to quantify, one leading expert, Laura Tyson, has concluded in a recent study that: "The Yugoslavs have made substantial progress in the modernization of their economy, and . . . [their policies] have resulted in overall economic performance that is at least as good as, and in some cases better than, the performance achieved in other middle-income countries with market systems."[12] The reader will recall, however, that, in addition to

---

reworking and extension of his efficiency comparisons in A. Bergson, *Productivity and the Social System: The USSR and the West* (Cambridge: Harvard University Press, 1978).

11. Gregory and Stuart, *Comparative Economic Systems*, 378–80. Also see: A. Bergson, "Notes on the Production Function in Soviet Postwar Industrial Growth," *Journal of Comparative Economics* 3, 2 (June 1979): 116–26; and Bergson, *Productivity and the Social System*. These estimates are sensitive to assumptions regarding, among other things, factor shares, elasticity of substitution, and quality changes in factors as well as to adjustments for hours worked, factor unemployment, and output valuation difficulties. Thus, for example, as a result of an implausible assumption on factor shares, the CIA has estimated unrealistic growth rates for Soviet total factor productivity (cf. CIA, *Handbook of Economic Statistics* (Washington, D.C.: U.S. Government Printing Office, 1982), 72). An excellent discussion of the methodological issues involved in these estimates can be found in M. Weitzman, "Industrial Production," in A. Bergson and H. Levine, eds., *The Soviet Economy: Toward the Year 2000* (London: George Allen and Unwin, 1983).

12. L. Tyson, *The Yugoslav Economic System and Its Performance in the 1970s* (Berkeley: Institute of International Studies, 1980), 106. On dynamic efficiency in Yugoslavia also see J. G. Moore, *Growth with Self-Management: Yugoslav Industrialization, 1952–75* (Stanford: Hoover Institute Press, 1980), Ch. 10; and M. Nishimizu and J. Page, "Total Factor Productivity Growth,

extensively using the market mechanism, the Yugoslav economy is characterized by "worker-managed" firms and, since the mid seventies, a complex system of bottom-up "social planning." These features undoubtedly affect efficiency performance and also counsel against treating Yugoslavia as an archetypical market socialist economy.

It is, then, rather difficult to decide empirically the question of whether capitalist economies on balance exhibit greater efficiency than socialist economies, or vice versa. Given the methodological problems of calculation, plus the very different historical circumstances of the different countries, various experts have reached different conclusions.

Distribution of Income

The planned socialist economies are characterized by a substantially more egalitarian distribution of income than the capitalist economies. Although some investigators[13] have found that earnings (wages and salaries) are more equally distributed in socialist than capitalist countries, the major reasons for greater equality under socialism are: 1) the virtual absence of property income (rent, interest, dividends, and capital gains); and 2) the tendency to maintain full employment with high labor force participation rates. In Table 17.1 we borrow evidence from earlier chapters and present the post-tax decile ratio (share of income going to the top 10 percent of households divided by share going to the bottom 10 percent[14]) for several capitalist and socialist economies. (The decile ratio is one of several possible distribution measures which tend to be highly correlated with one another.)

It is noteworthy that the "capitalist" country of Sweden exhibits a more equal income distribution than the market socialist country of Yugoslavia. The planned socialist countries of the Soviet Union and

---

Technological Progress and Technical Efficiency Change: Dimensions of Productivity Change in Yugoslavia, 1965–78," *The Economic Journal* 92 (Dec. 1982): 920–36. On dynamic efficiency in China see Carl Riskin, *The Political Economy of Chinese Development since 1949* (Oxford: Oxford University Press, 1985), Ch. 11.

13. See, for one, F. Pryor, *Property and Industrial Organization in Communist and Capitalist Nations* (Bloomington: Indiana University Press, 1973), 74–86.

14. It should be recalled that the Soviet decile ratio is defined slightly differently: the ratio of the ninetieth percentile to the tenth percentile. This measure reduces the impact of the extreme top and bottom incomes and, hence, relative to the decile ratio used for the other economies, understates the degree of inequality. The Soviet estimate, moreover, refers only to earnings in the state sector.

Table 17.1
Decile Ratio of After-tax Income, Various Countries

USSR 1976	Hungary 1972	Sweden 1972	Yugoslavia 1978	United States 1972	France 1970
3.4	5.0	7.2	9.2[a]	15.4	21.8

Sources: A. McAuley, "Sources of Earnings Inequality," *Soviet Studies* 34, 3 (1977): 444. M. Sawyer, "Income Distribution in OECD Countries," *OECD Economic Outlook* (Paris: July 1976): 19. H. Flakierski, "Economic Reform and Income Distribution in Hungary," *Cambridge Journal of Economics* 3 (1979): 23. The World Bank, *World Development Report 1982*, 159.

Note: Decile ratio means share of income going to the top 10 percent of households divided by share going to the bottom 10 percent.

a. The decile ratio for Yugoslavia is based on an extrapolation from the lowest quintile to the lowest decile, multiplying the former by .38.

Hungary (it was predominantly a planned economy in 1972) are uniformly more egalitarian than the market economies.

Many socialist economies, most notably the USSR, offer high hidden incomes and privileges to top Party functionaries, consisting of private villas, vacation homes, access to special stores and foreign goods, and so on.[15] Whether or not these unreported sources of inequality exceed the unreported perquisites for corporate executives and high public officials in capitalist countries is open to speculation.

It remains to indicate that actual consumption is yet more equally distributed than income in socialist economies relative to capitalist economies. That is because many basic services (such as health care, child care centers, higher education, food staples, public transportation, etc.), which comprise a larger share of the low-income person's budget than the high-income person's budget, are either free or heavily subsidized by socialist governments.

Economic Stability

We shall treat economic stability as having four components: employment, prices, international payments, and production cycles. Apart from low levels of frictional unemployment or exceptional periods of political turmoil, planned socialist countries have maintained full employment. The market socialist economy of Yugoslavia, however, has experienced substantial unemployment and macro-instability.

---

15. For an interesting discussion of these benefits in the USSR, see Hedrick Smith, *The Russians* (New York: Ballantine Books, 1976), Chap. 1.

The Hungarian economy has maintained full employment even as it approaches a market socialist model. This has been consistently true even during periods of slow growth and despite the generally higher levels of labor force participation, particularly among women, in the socialist economies of Eastern Europe and the Soviet Union.

It is often argued that a cost involved in socialist full employment is that many workers are underemployed (or enterprises are over-staffed). This observation appears to be generally accurate. It should also be recalled, however, that the cost to a private company of laying off a worker is significantly lower than the social cost involved. If based on social rather than private costs, the employment decision in a planned socialist economy may be more allocationally efficient from the society's point of view.

The success of the planned socialist economies in maintaining full employment is all the more impressive in the early 1980s, at a time when many of the developed capitalist economies, as the United States and Great Britain, are experiencing unemployment rates in excess of 10 percent. It is difficult to remain dispassionate in the face of the acute and widespread material, psychological, and social suffering engendered by these depressionlike unemployment figures. It is also well to recall that these unemployment rates are societal averages and particular groups are harder hit than the averages suggest. For instance, in the United States in June 1983, the overall civilian unemployment rate was 10.0 percent, but the rate was 8.3 percent for all whites and 20.0 percent for all blacks.

As a result of broad central control over prices, planned socialist economies tend to have greater price stability. Most planned socialist economies officially report either no or very low levels of inflation each year. Yugoslavia's market socialist economy, however, has experienced significant inflation. As the Hungarian economy has been decentralized, it too has experienced higher, albeit still moderate, inflation.

Although the contention that planned economies have greater price stability is generally accurate, three qualifications should be mentioned. First, when price increases occur in planned economies, it is usually after an extended period of imbalance between supply and demand for the affected commodity. Whereas the price for such a good would be gradually changing in a smoothly functioning market, the set price is changed all at once by decree. Thus, it is not uncommon for the price of a food item to jump, say, 60 percent from one day to the next. So, although there is greater price stability in the planned economies in the aggregate, there can be disruptive, discrete price movements which appear anything but stable to the consumers involved.

Second, price increases are sometimes disguised when authorities treat a slightly improved or otherwise differentiated good as brand new, so that it has no base in the official price index. Hence, there is no registered price increase—simply a new good with a new price.

Third, there is a definite trade-off involved with price controls in planned economies. Lower or no inflation comes at the cost of, among other things, spot shortages, consumer queues, lower quality, black markets, and/or rationing. If quantity demanded exceeds the quantity supplied and the price is frozen, then the consumer often pays by waiting in line or procuring less than the desired quantity of a good at the going price (rather than paying a higher price). The existence of scarcity requires a rationing mechanism—in planned economies it is frequently direct, administrative, physical rationing, while in market economies it is rationing by price movements. Price controls, then, entail greater administrative expense but ensure that ability to pay (income level) will not be a prohibitive factor in a consumer's access to certain commodities.

Nevertheless, having made these qualifications, it should be stressed that planned economies do have a built-in advantage in achieving financial balance and price stability. This advantage derives from the fact that the wage bargain is centrally set at a point where it can be guaranteed more or less that real wage increases do not exceed increases in productivity. Additionally, inflation, to the extent it exists, in the planned socialist economies generally does not have the effect of either lowering investment spending (since inflation causes greater uncertainty or risk) or shifting investment to speculative rather than productive assets.

Another characteristic of economic stability is the degree of balance in a country's international payments. It is well known that since the early seventies attaining international payments equilibrium has been a problem for virtually every nation in the world. The causes for this are complex and go well beyond the parameters of this book. It is relevant, however, to point out that when there is a payments deficit, planned economies are in a better position to manage and rectify it. This is largely because of the greater control over the use of resources in a planned economy. It is also a function of the planned economies' ability to maintain full employment while engineering a growth contraction to alleviate a payments deficit. Tighter political controls in Eastern Europe and the USSR today also facilitate the necessary resource control.

This advantage of the planned economies in achieving payments equilibrium is testified to by the experience of the last several years. The large and growing hard currency debts of most COMECON nations together with the Polish payments crisis created an extremely critical financial situation in Eastern Europe. New loans from the West came to a near halt, and the Western recession constrained the expansion of COMECON hard currency exports. To compound matters, this troublesome environment prompted many Western banks to withdraw their deposits in East European central banks, lowering the latter's foreign currency reserves and provoking a short-term liquidity crisis. In contrast to the foreign payments and debt situations of the industrialized economies of Western Europe and the less developed countries of the Third World, the situation in the COMECON economies appears to have been brought quickly under control. Listen, for instance, to the assessment of the Wharton Econometric Forecasting Associates (and bear in mind that the averages include the unsettling figures from Poland):

> By mid-1982, a remarkable turnaround is evident in Eastern Europe. Already the huge trade and current account deficits are virtually gone and the level of indebtedness has stabilized. Faced with the impossibility of obtaining fresh credits from the West, Eastern bloc planners had little choice but to quickly cut back on imports and boost exports. The six East European member-countries of CMEA reduced their hard-currency imports from $34.3 billion in 1980 to $29.1 billion in 1981 and are likely to import only $28 billion this year. On the other hand, in spite of the strength of the dollar and the global recession, hard-currency exports of these six have remained almost constant since 1980.
>
> In order to achieve this, East European planners were forced to cut domestic growth rates. The magnitude of these adjustments in many cases is unprecedented. Living standards have been lowered, investment rates slashed, crash conservation programs instituted, and overall belt-tightening has taken place throughout the region. The average growth rate of net material product was 4 percent for the region during 1976–80 and by 1981 it was down to 1.2%.[16]

Wharton forecasts positive real economic growth from 1 to 3 percent in 1982 for all of Eastern Europe and the USSR (except Poland) and then slightly higher rates through 1985.[17]

The final aspect of stability is the degree of cyclical fluctuation in production. The market economies have experienced periodic declines in production. It is significant that Wharton's forecast for Eastern Europe does not include a drop in output, only a slower growth rate. In U.S. terms, then, the planned economies will not enter into a recession (which requires falling real output for two consecutive quarters) but will continue to grow at varying positive rates. Although there is no iron law to this effect, the planned economies on the whole have been successful in averting sustained periods of decreasing output. The main reason why output and employment tend to continue rising in planned economies is that saving and investment are controlled by the same agency, the central planning board. When there is excess savings, the board can always invest in new projects.

---

16. Wharton Econometric Forecasting Associates, *Centrally Planned Economies Outlook* (Washington, D.C.: Wharton Econometric Forecasting Associates, Sept. 1982), 2 and 3.

17. Ibid., 11.

(Normally, the problem in planned economies is a lack of sufficient savings for all the planned projects.)

The tendency to continue growth under planning might also result from what Oskar Lange claimed was the ability of the planned economies to prevent snowballing. The government's control over resources enables it to prevent drops in output or demand in one sector from spreading throughout the economy. Of course, this ability to manage the business cycle may also incur costs of longer term inefficiency if it is based on the maintenance of unprofitable or declining economic sectors.

Economic Freedoms

Here we shall consider: (1) the consumer's ability to influence what is produced and to buy what he or she chooses; (2) the worker's ability to influence what is produced and how it is produced; and (3) the worker's ability to choose whatever job he or she wants to choose. All three of these desiderata are immensely complex to interpret as freedoms and we will endeavor only to sketch some pertinent considerations.

Consumer Choice It is well known that in market economies a profit-maximizing firm will produce what is demanded by consumers—hence, consumer sovereignty. Two qualifications should be made here. First, some consumers are more sovereign than others. In the U.S. in 1979, for instance, the top 4 percent of income earners had a mean income of over $70,000 while the bottom 14 percent had mean incomes below $3,000; or, on average, the top 4 percent had twenty-three times more dollar votes per person than the bottom 14 percent.[18] Hardly a democratic outcome! Second, consumers have imperfect and sometimes intentionally distorted information which also impedes their sovereignty.

In today's planned economies consumers can spend their income on whatever goods are available. The availability of goods, however, is determined by the planners. Planners have opted for high investment ratios, and, therefore, a lower share of national output is devoted to consumer good production. Naturally, it is in the planners' interest to produce what consumers want insofar as possible (within the constraints imposed by the budget, demands for the military, public consumption, and new investment). Their ability to do this, however, is affected by, among other things, the amount of information they have on consumers' preferences, how they aggregate those preferences, how much conflict there is between consumer and planner

---

18. U.S. Bureau of the Census, Current Population Reports, P-60, No. 126, *Money Incomes of Households in the United States: 1979* (Washington, D.C.: U.S. Government Printing Office, 1981), 3.

preferences, and how successful they are in inducing the relevant enterprises to produce the appropriate mix and quality of goods. These relationships differ in practice from one planned economy to another. Those planned economies with higher per capita incomes, more channels for consumer input, more fluid social relations within the planning apparatus, and greater decentralization tend to be more successful in meeting consumer demands.

Worker Participation   Economic freedoms on the job are also important since individuals in most societies spend at least one-third of their waking hours at work. How much control do workers have over the conditions of their work in capitalist and socialist countries? Karl Marx argued that worker alienation was inherent to capitalism; yet his vision of work under socialism has hardly been realized. There is, in fact, a great unevenness regarding working conditions and worker participation in economic decision making among capitalist and socialist countries.

Yugoslavia (and, to a lesser extent, Hungary, Romania, and Cuba) has introduced significant reforms over the years which enhance worker influence. Elsewhere in the COMECON bloc workers evidently have little power over production decisions, yet they do appear to have considerable influence over disciplinary and welfare questions and usually enough control to avoid the extreme work intensification found in some factories in the West.

Variability in work-place relations is at least as great among the capitalist as among the socialist economies. In the capitalist world, where there are unions the workers generally have greater rights. In recent years there has been some movement to introduce restricted forms of worker participation in decision making. In the United States there has been a growing interest in shop-floor experiments such as the Japanese quality control circles. It is fair to say, however, that these reforms have not appreciably increased democratic rights for the affected workers. Indeed, in some companies they have been used to weaken unions or keep unions out. Within the "capitalist" world, Sweden has probably gone the furthest in carrying out substantive reform and democratizing the work place.

The wide diversity of experiences with work-place relations and decision-making patterns both within and among countries in either economic system makes simple generalizations very difficult. The student interested in pursuing the subject of industrial democracy should refer back to the chapter discussions and consult the substantial and growing body of literature on the topic.[19]

---

19. For example, see: J. Espinosa and A. Zimbalist, *Economic Democracy* (New York: Academic Press, 1981); M. Yanowitch, ed., *Soviet Work Attitudes: The Issue of Participation in Management* (White Plains, N.Y.: M. E. Sharpe,

Occupational Choice   Workers are generally free in both capitalist and socialist countries to choose their own jobs. There are a few, not very significant, exceptions which have been referred to earlier. Naturally, workers' choices are constrained by the realities of the job market, their own skills, the availability of housing, etc.

Finally, many attributes which are not properly "freedoms" but rather are "rights" should not be overlooked: the workers' right to guaranteed work; the guarantee of a decent minimum wage; the right to stop work if conditions are unsafe or unhealthy; the guarantee of free or affordable health, education, and other services; the right to breathe unpolluted air and drink clean water; the right to nondiscriminatory treatment regardless of race, sex, creed, etc. Some of these attributes bear a straightforward relation to the economic system; for example, in the planned socialist economies workers are guaranteed a job as well as free or nearly free health care and education.

Other attributes have a more complex and controversial relation to the economic system. For instance, most socialist economists argue that externalities are more controllable in a planned economy; hence, they conclude, where production is for the "social good" rather than "profit," there will be, for instance, less environmental contamination. In the extreme form, this argument is extended to claim that nuclear power plants are safe under socialism but dangerous under capitalism. If we were to judge from the experience with commercial nuclear power in the Soviet Union alone, this contention finds little empirical support. Arguing the contrary position, Marshall Goldman and others have held that the obsession with production targets, compounded by inept bureaucracy, have created a more serious environmental problem in the Soviet Union than in the advanced capitalist nations.[20] Similar disagreements prevail over the systemic impact on race and sex discrimination as well as other odiosa.[21]

1979); M. Yanowitch, *Social and Economic Inequality in the Soviet Union* (White Plains, N.Y.: M. E. Sharpe, 1977), Chap. 5; M. Carnoy and D. Shearer, *Economic Democracy* (White Plains, N.Y.: M. E. Sharpe, 1980); J. Triska and C. Gati, eds., *Blue Collar Workers in Eastern Europe* (London: George Allen and Unwin, 1981); and A. Zimbalist, ed., *Case Studies on the Labor Process* (New York: Monthly Review, 1979).

20. Goldman also recognizes the advantage in theory and greater potential for environmental control in a planned economy. M. Goldman, *The Spoils of Progress: Environmental Pollution in the Soviet Union* (Cambridge: MIT Press, 1972).

21. Excellent discussions of this debate on discrimination are provided by R. Buchele, "The Persistence of Racial Inequality," *Challenge* (July/Aug. 1982), and M. Reich, *Racial Inequality* (Princeton: Princeton University Press, 1981).

There is also the question of the relationship between the economic system and the political system. One extreme position argues that political democracy is impossible under socialism because of government ownership and control over the means of production. The other extreme argues that true democracy and capitalism are incompatible since capitalism breeds inequality and, hence, unequal influence and capitalist class domination over the political process.

We have dealt with this relationship between political and economic systems throughout the book. The relationship is, in fact, complex and defies simple correlations. There are varying degrees of openness and democratic influence in today's planned economies, although all socialist countries have formal political dictatorships. The few capitalist countries with stable political democracies are highly developed. The underdeveloped capitalist world is, with a few weak exceptions, also characterized by political dictatorship. Simple empiricism, then, may lead one to correlate political democracy with high levels of economic development or high standards of living. Such a conclusion, although it has some merit, also does injustice to the intricacies of the relationship between economic and political systems.

Inevitably, comparisons between economic systems are muddled because non–system-related differences among countries (e.g., culture, technology, natural resources, etc.) cannot be held constant. Thus, the Soviet Union is not as successful agriculturally as the United States; but is this situation due to socialism per se, or to the nature of socialism in the USSR, or to poorer climatic conditions, an inefficient incentive system, a lower level of economic development, or other factors? The inability to adjust for other factors has prompted many economists to make the "controlled" comparison of East and West Germany. While even here there are many different outside influences, the comparison is worthwhile and interesting. In the appendix to this chapter, a brief comparison of economic performance in East and West Germany is provided.

Final Remarks

There are many interesting and important questions pertaining to the study of comparative economics which we haven't addressed in this book. One such question, for instance, relates to the process of making a transition from one economic system to another, for example, from capitalism to socialism. Such transitions have been undertaken in recent years through peaceful, parliamentary channels in some countries (primarily developed), and through violent, revolutionary channels in other countries (primarily underdeveloped). Each effort at transition has been confronted by political and economic obstacles. We alluded indirectly to such problems in our brief discussion on Mitterrand's political economic strategy in France. Similar issues are present today in Greece, Nicaragua, Mozambique, Angola, and Spain and were present in the 1970s in Portugal, Chile, Peru, and Uruguay to name a few examples.

Some comparative economists have argued that there is a tendency in each economic system (capitalist or socialist) to make a gradual transition toward the other. This proposition is known as convergence. It is observable in the real world that there are no pure market or pure planned economies. Most are mixed to one degree or another. It is, moreover, apparent that pressures develop in planned economies to make more use of the market mechanism and, conversely, pressures develop in market economies to make greater use of planning. However, these pressures seem to advance at some times and retreat at others. Even if they advance more than they retreat, it is unclear how far they can proceed without challenging the basic premises (e.g., private property) of the existing system.

It is also impossible to develop a satisfactory test of the convergence theory. Which variables or institutions do we select as converging? How do we quantify or weight them?

In this study we have tried to develop a more dynamic perspective—approaching a country's economic system as having its own internal logic and made up of political, social, and cultural as well as economic characteristics. Those systems which have tended to be more economically successful (in their own terms) have managed to evolve economic and other institutions which are consistent with one another as well as with economic growth. Although economies can certainly learn from one another's policies, institutions, and experiences, simple transplants are fraught with difficulties.

We hope the reader, rather than forming any final judgment about which economic system is superior, takes away from this study an enhanced ability: to think critically and creatively about economic systems; to apply a richer economic analysis to new situations with a clearer sense of its insights and limitations; to appreciate the distinctiveness as well as commonality of economies with similar economic systems; and, above all, to approach the study of the world's economies, including our own, with a greater curiosity and open-mindedness.

APPENDIX 17A
A Controlled Comparison: East and West Germany

Since the post–World War II bifurcation of Germany, there has been one capitalist and one socialist economy operating on essentially the same historical terrain—with similar language, culture, climate, resource endowment, etc. Many, though certainly not all, of the intervening variables are held constant. The comparison has the further advantage that each economy is an excellent representative of its group. West Germany has outperformed all other developed capitalist economies (except Japan) since World War II, and East Germany is widely regarded to be the most effective centrally planned economy. Let us, then, turn to a brief look at the evidence on comparative economic performance of the two Germanys.[22]

Per Capita Income and Growth

Prior to World War II the two areas which were to become East and West Germany had roughly the same per capita income.[23] However, wartime devastation was proportionately far greater in the territory to become East Germany, where approximately 50 percent of industrial capacity was knocked out, compared to 25 percent of capacity destroyed in the area to become West Germany.[24] Thus, by 1945 per capita capacity in East Germany was only two-thirds that in West Germany. Following the war, with large Marshall Plan assistance, recovery began more quickly in West Germany, and this gap continued to spread for several years. East Germany had also to contend with: (1) a massive exodus of its most highly skilled and youngest citizens to the West which was to continue until August 1961; (2) a burdensome exaction of reparations imposed by the USSR which considerably exceeded the sum set by the Yalta agreement; and (3) the disintegration of the customs union. This latter factor impacted more negatively on East Germany as a result of: prewar trade patterns; the East region's particular trade specialization; and greater overall dependence on trade than in the West region.

During the 1950s, the economy of West Germany grew at a rate close to 7 percent while—in spite of its initial disadvantages—the growth rate for the East German economy was around 6.5 percent.[25] On a GNP per capita basis, between 1960 and 1979 West Germany

---

22. Needless to say, the standard caveats apply. An excellent treatment of the measurement hurdles and ambiguities pertaining to the comparison of the two Germanys is provided by Herbert Wilkins, *The Two German Economies: A Comparison between the National Product of the GDR and the FRG* (Fannborough, Hants: Gower Publishing, 1981).

23. A good summary of the estimates of income per capita in the two Germanys before and after World War II is presented by Peter Sturm, "The System Component in Differences in Per Capita Output between East and West Germany," *Journal of Comparative Economics* 1, 1 (Mar. 1977): 5–24.

24. P. Gregory and H. Leptin, "Similar Societies under Differing Economic Systems: The Case of the Two Germanys," *Soviet Studies* 29, 4 (1977): 521.

25. Ibid., 527.

grew at 3.3 percent per year and East Germany grew at 4.7 percent.[26] In West Germany real GNP grew by 1.8 percent in 1980 and fell by 0.3 percent in 1981; in East Germany real national income grew by 4.2 percent in 1980 and increased by 4.5 percent in 1981.[27] Thus, according to CIA estimates, by 1981 per capita GNP was approximately $9,750 in East Germany and $11,130 in West Germany.[28] That is, East German per capita income had risen to 87.6 percent of West German per capita income. The gap continued to narrow during 1982 and the first half of 1983. The conclusion appears uncontestable that over the entire postwar period East Germany has experienced more rapid growth per head than West Germany, attributable largely to more rapid growth since 1970.

The question then arises whether this faster growth is the result of higher savings and investment in East Germany. The answer appears to be no. In fact, West Germany had considerably higher investment ratios than East Germany throughout the 1950s and into the early 1960s; since then, the investment ratios have been approximately the same at around 25 percent.[29] (By some estimates the East German ratio is higher, and by some it is lower, depending largely on the methodology used.)

Efficiency

The above information on growth rates and investment levels suggests a stronger *dynamic* efficiency in East Germany. The calculations on total factor productivity (as defined above) over the period 1960–1973 made by Gregory and Leptin confirm this: in West Ger-

---

26. World Bank, *World Development Report 1981*, 135.

27. Calculated from the OECD, *Main Economic Indicators*, 1982 various issues; Wharton, *Centrally Planned Economies Outlook*, 87.

28. CIA, *Handbook of Economic Statistics*, 1982, 26–27. Of course all the usual qualifications apply, and the precise figures in the estimate are not reliable. To be sure, various studies offer a range of estimates of relative per capita income. The CIA relative estimate that we give, however, is similar to that made in the very careful study by Herbert Wilkins, *The Two German Economies*, 106. We also remind the reader that relative per capita income does not denote relative living standards for East and West German citizens. Consumers in East Germany, for instance, experience less variety in and lower quality of consumer goods than those in West Germany. Availability, convenience, and the proportion of collective versus private consumption differ as well. East Germany, for example, has relatively more collective consumption goods per person.

29. See T. Alton, "Production and Resource Allocation in Eastern Europe," in J.E.C., *East European Economic Assessment*, Part 2, 365 and 367; Gregory and Leptin, "Similar Societies," 528; and World Bank, *World Development Report 1981*, 143.

many the average annual increase in total factor productivity was 3.0 percent and in East Germany it was 3.4 percent.[30] Although estimates of *static* efficiency are not available, most experts would agree that static efficiency is significantly greater in West Germany.

Stability

In their study Gregory and Leptin write: "It is our conclusion that the GDR (East Germany) has had greater economic stability throughout the post-War period than the FRG (West Germany). . . . By stability, we refer to the stability of economic growth and to the absence of excessive inflation and unemployment."[31]

Income Distribution

In East Germany in 1970, the top 20 percent of income-earning households received 30.7 percent of total household income and the bottom 20 percent received 10.4 percent; the quintile ratio was, thus, 2.95 to 1.[32] In West Germany in 1973, the top 20 percent earned 46.2 percent of total household income and the bottom 20 percent earned 6.5 percent; the quintile ratio was 7.11 to 1, or more than double the inequality by this measure in East Germany.[33]

Other Criteria

We lack systematic data for other variables. Gregory and Leptin state that it is their impression that environmental quality is superior in West Germany. (This might be expected for a country with a higher standard of living.) There is also some evidence that working conditions are better and worker participation is greater in West Germany. A careful 1981 study of the position of women in the two Germanys, however, has concluded that ". . . in all areas of life GDR (East Germany) women have achieved a much higher degree of equality with men than have their counterparts in West Germany. . . ."[34] Finally, although we have been concerned only with economic performance, it is difficult to overlook the more desirable democratic political system in West Germany.

---

30. Gregory and Leptin, "Similar Societies," 526.

31. Ibid., 535.

32. Ibid., 534. Gregory and Leptin present only quintile ratios.

33. M. Sawyer, "Income Distribution in OECD Countries," *OECD Economic Outlook* (Paris: OECD, July 1976), 19.

34. Harry Shaffer, *Women in the Two Germanies* (New York: Pergamon Press, 1981), 164.

Recommended Readings

1. Alexander Eckstein, ed., *Comparison of Economic Systems: Theoretical and Methodological Approaches* (Berkeley: University of California Press, 1971).

2. Andrew Zimbalist, ed., *Comparative Economic Systems: An Assessment of Knowledge, Theory and Method* (Boston: Kluwer-Nijhoff, 1983).

3. There are two professional journals in the field of comparative economics published in the United States. Advanced students wishing to follow current debates in the field should consult the *Journal of Comparative Economics* and the *ACES Bulletin*, both published by the Association for Comparative Economic Studies. There are, as well, various area studies journals, too numerous to mention here.

INDEX

Active industrial policy. *See* Supply management

Aggregate balance (USSR), 226–246
 aggregate demand and, 226–227, 229–232
 alternatives for restoring, 229–232
 causes of inflation, 227–229
 input-output method of, 234–235, 238–246
 limitations of input-output method, 238–240
 Soviet method of, 232–234, 235–238

Aggregation, 240

Agricultural producers' cooperatives (China), 341–342

Agriculture
 Chinese, 341–342, 357–361
 Hungarian, 404, 412–415
 Japanese, 57–58
 Soviet
  collectivization of, 154–156, 166–168
  Five-Year Plan and, 166–168
  government ownership of, 117, 154–156
  New Economic Policy and, 139, 142–145
  since 1950, 182–183
  prices of goods, 217–218
  productivity of, 127–128
  workers in, 295–300
 Yugoslav, 427

Amakudari, 54

Autogestion, 108, 111

Balance of payments, Japanese, 56
Bank of France, 93
Bank of Japan (BOJ), 38, 39
Banks, commercial, 37–38, 39
Basic organizations of associated labor (BOALS) (Yugoslavia), 440–442

Batista, Fulgencio, 367
Bolsheviks, 129–131, 136
Brus, Wlodzimierz, 272–273, 401
Bukharin, N. I., 142, 148, 151, 152, 153, 158

Capital formation, in Sweden, 90–91
Capitalism
 arguments against, 10–11
 arguments for, 9
 defined, 3, 6–7
 democracy and, 17–23
 socialism vs., 7–8
Cartels, Japanese, 58–59
Castro, Fidel, 365–366, 369–370, 374–375
Centrally planned socialism, 11–12
Central planning
 China, 333–364
  cultural revolution, 345–352
  five-year plans, 338–340
  Great Leap Forward, 339–345
 Cuba, 365–391
  early development strategy of, 370–371
  1960s, 371–374
  1970–1975, 374–380
  1975–present, 380–382
 USSR, 204–224, 252–278
  defense of, 252–253
  development of, 147–148
  dictatorship and, 21
  early five-year plans, 165–173
  efficiency and, 253–255
  international trade and, 220–224
  Law of Value and, 255–262
  Ministry system and, 208–209
  New Economic Policy and, 140–141, 147–148

Central Planning (*cont.*)
  operation of, 204–224
  prices and, 248–249, 259–260, 262–266
  price system and, 214–218
  second economy and, 218–220
  under Stalin, 256–258
  university example and, 118–120
Central Planning Board (CPB), 396–400.
  See also Gosplan
Changjiang Agriculture, Industry, and
  Commerce Corporation of Chongqing (CAICC), 359–360
Chiang Kai-shek, 336
China, 333–364
  agricultural producers' cooperatives,
    341–342
  agricultural reform in, 357–361
  background of, 333–337
  Communists in, 337, 363
  cultural revolution of, 345–352, 363
  economic development of, 337–345
  economic system of, 4
  education in, 348, 351–352
  five-year plans in, 338–340
  Great Leap Forward, 339–345
  industrial reforms in, 353–357
  people's communes, 341–345
  post-Mao reforms in, 352–353
  reform problems of, 361–362
  socialism in, 7–8, 11
Class
  defined, 280
  ruling, in USSR, 280–284
Coefficient of Relative Effectiveness (CRE),
  268–271
Collective bargaining, in Sweden, 70, 80.
  See also Unions
Collective farms, 117, 154–156, 166–168. *See
  also* Communes
Combined factor productivity, 188–190
COMECON, 223–224
Commercial banks, Japanese, 37–38, 39
Communes, Chinese, 341–345
Communism
  development in USSR, 129–137
  War, 131–133
Communist Party
  in China, 337, 363
  in France, 94–96
  in Hungary, 405–406
  in USSR, 129–137, 204–205, 281
Company unionism, 48
Consumer choice, as economic freedom,
  465–466
Consumer goods, in USSR, 121–122
Cooperatives. *See also* Collective farms;
  Communes

Chinese, 341–342
Swedish, 69–70
Cordon sanitaire, 146
Corporate structure and finance, in Japan,
  36–41
CRE (Coefficient of Relative Effectiveness),
  268–271
Critical participation (France), 103
Cuba, 365–391
  ANAP, 391
  background of, 367–370
  early development strategy of, 370–371
  economic changes in, 374–382
  economic system of, 4
  five-year plans in, 380
  health indicators in, 384
  income distribution in, 378–380
  JUCEPLAN, 372, 381
  planning in the 1960s, 371–374
  prospects of, 389
  revolution in, 365–366, 369–370, 382–383
  SDPE, 380–381
  social indicators in, 384
  socialism in, 7–8, 11
  Soviet economic aid to, 385–388
  unions in, 375
  U.S. domination of, 367–368
  worker incentives in, 375–377
  worker participation in, 377–378
Cultural Revolution (China), 345–352, 363

Dantzig, George, 275
Debt, in Japan, 38–39
Decentralization
  of socialist economies, 450–454
  in Yugoslavia, 427–428, 431, 451
Defense spending, USSR vs. U.S., 198–201
Demand, aggregate, 226–227, 229–232
Democracy
  capitalism and, 17–23, 63
  defined, 13
  dictatorship vs., 13–14
  economic systems and, 17–23, 26–27
  efficiency and, 271–273
  Swedish, 63, 70–74
  in USSR, 13, 20, 162–165, 271–273
Deng Xiaoping, 349
Developed economies, 14–15
Dictatorship
  vs. democracy, 13–14
  socialism and, 17–23
  in USSR, 135–138, 160–161, 162–165
Dobb, Maurice, 252–253, 255
Dynamic efficiency, 25

Economic dualism, 44

Economic freedoms, 465–468
    consumer choice, 465–466
    occupational choice, 467–468
    worker participation, 466
Economic growth
    economic systems and, 25
    as performance criterion, 456–458
Economic systems
    comparison of, 23–28
    democracy vs. dictatorship in, 17–23, 26–27
    economic growth and, 25
    employment and, 26
    human relations and, 5
    income distribution and, 25–26
    political structure and, 5–6, 16–23
    standard of living and, 23–24
    static efficiency and, 24–25
    technology and, 5
Economy, and government policy, 16
Efficiency
    dynamic, 25
    static, 24–25
EFO model, 77, 79n
Employment
    economic systems and, 26
    in Japan, 44–47
    lifetime, 44–47
    in Sweden, 74–75
Exports
    French, 112–113
    Japanese, 56
    Swedish, 65

Farms, collective, 117, 154–156, 166–168.
    See also Communes
Farm workers, Soviet, 295–300
Five-Year Plans
    in China, 338–340
    in Cuba, 380
    in USSR, 165–171
Fourth Fund (Sweden), 90
France, 93–114
    capitalism in, 8
    Communist Party in, 94–96
    economic history of, 93–106
    economic system of, 3, 93–114
    expansionary policies in, 113
    government's economic role in, 93
    indicative planning in, 96–106
    nationalization in, 107, 109–111
    Socialist Party in, 106–114
    trade by, 112–113
    unions in, 102–103, 105
Freedom. See Democracy
Friedman, Milton, 16–17

Fundamental opposition (France), 102

Gang of Four (China), 346, 352
General Agreement on Tariffs and Trade
    (GATT), 56
General Confederation of Labor (CGT), 94,
    95
General trading companies (GTCs), 37
Geneticists, 148
German-type bank group, 37
Germany, East vs. West, 469–472
Giscard d'Estaing, Valéry, 105
Glazer, Nathan, 42
GOELRO, 147
Gomez, Alain, 109–110
Gosplan (USSR), 118, 147, 208, 210–214
Government
    in France, 93, 106–114
    in Japan, 35, 52–59
    in Sweden, 88–90
    in USSR
        central planning by. See Central plan-
            ning
        Communist Party, 129–137, 204–205,
            281
        Ministry system, 208–209
        ownership of agriculture, 117, 154–156
        ownership of industry, 116–117, 159
        ruling class, 280–284
        structure of, 204–207
Great Leap Forward (China), 339–345
Great Proletarian Cultural Revolution
    (China), 345–352
Guevara, Che, 371–372

Hayek, Frederick, 16–17, 396
Health indicators, in Cuba, 384
Health insurance, 67
Health services, in USSR, 120–121
Housing, in USSR, 121
Human relations, and economic structure,
    5
Hungary, 403–423
    agriculture in, 404, 412–415
    background of, 403–406
    Communists in, 405–406
    early economic reform in, 406–407
    economic system of, 4–5
    foreign trade in, 415–417
    industrial structure in, 418–419
    labor in, 410–411, 419–421
    New Economic Mechanism in, 407–423
    prices in, 408, 410, 415, 417–418
    socialism in, 8, 11
    wages in, 410–411
    worker incentives in, 410–411

Import barriers
  French, 112
  Japanese, 56–58
Income distribution
  in Cuba, 378–380
  equality of, 25–26
  in Japan, 51
  as performance criterion, 460–461
  in USSR, 285–286
  in Yugoslavia, 432–434
Incremental capital-output ratio (ICOR), 429–430
Indicative planning, 32, 55, 96–106. See also Supply management
Industrial groups
  German-type, 37
  large, 37
  zaibatsu-type, 36–37
Industry
  in China, 353–357
  government ownership of, 116–117
  in Hungary, 418–419
  in Japan, 36–41
  in Sweden, 70–74
Inflation
  in USSR, 227–229
  in Yugoslavia, 430–431
Input-output method, of aggregate balance, 234–235, 238–246
Institute for New Generation Computer Technology (Japan), 58–59

Japan, 33–61
  agriculture in, 57–58
  background of, 34–36, 55–56
  balance of payments of, 56
  capitalism in, 8
  company unionism in, 48
  corporate income tax in, 40
  corporate structure and finance in, 36–41
  debt/equity trend in, 38
  economic growth of, 33–34
  economic system of, 3, 33–61
  government's economic role in, 35, 52–59
  import barriers of, 56–58
  labor disputes in, 44
  labor market institutions in, 43–52
  lifetime employment in, 44–47
  population of, 33, 42
  postal savings system in, 39
  savings in, 40–42
  seniority-based wages in, 47–48
  tax exemptions in, 56
  trade by, 56–58
  unemployment in, 43–44
  wages in, 47–48, 50–51
  women in, 43–44, 45
  worker participation in, 48–49
Japanese External Trade Organization (JETRO), 56
Jiang Qing, 346, 352
Johnson, Chalmers, 54
JUCEPLAN (Cuba), 372, 381

Kadar, Janos, 406
Kamenev, L. B., 152
Kharkov incentive system, 320–321
Khrushchev, Nikita, 158, 161, 165, 209
Kooperativa Forbundet (KF), 69
Kornai, Janos, 402

Labor. See also Unions
  in Cuba, 377–378
  in Hungary, 410–411, 419–421
  in Japan, 43–52
  in Sweden, 74–81
  in USSR
    agricultural, 295–300
    as class, 292–295
    education of, 289, 294
    employment of, 226–227
    five-year plans and, 167, 169
    income distribution in, 285–286
    industrial, 292–295
    mobility of, 123, 284–285
    New Economic Policy and, 140
    productivity of, 186–187
    stratification of, 286–289
    unions of, 300–303
    upward mobility of, 288–289
    wages of, 122–123, 216, 228, 286–288, 292–293
  U.S. vs. USSR, 122–123
  in Yugoslavia, 427, 434–439
Lange, Oskar, 396–400
Leibenstein, Harvey, 436–437
Lenin, Nikolai, 136, 163
Leontief, Wassily, 234–235, 239, 255
Less developed economies, 14–15
Liberal Democratic Party (LDP) (Japan), 53, 57–58
Liberman debate, 319–321
Lifetime employment, 44–47
Linear programming, 273–278
LO (Swedish trade union federation), 63–64, 65, 72, 73, 75–76, 91

Malthus, Thomas, 177–178
Managers, Soviet, 289–292

Mao Tse-tung, 164, 333, 346, 352
Market, defined, 3
Market capitalism, 3
Market socialism, 11, 12, 393
   alternative models of, 401–402
   economics of, 396–401
   Hungarian, 407–423
   Yugoslav, 426–444
Marshall Plan, 95
Marx, Karl, 10, 27, 115, 150, 162, 180, 181, 313
Marxism, 115
Marxist Law of Value, 255–262
Mauroy, Pierre, 109, 110
Medical insurance, 67
Medvedev, Roy, 22–23
Meidner, Rudolf, 73, 75–77
Ministry of Finance (MOF) (Japan), 39, 40, 54
Ministry of International Trade and Indus-
   try (MITI) (Japan), 39, 54, 55, 56–57,
   58–59
Ministry system (USSR), 208–209
Mises, Ludwig von, 248–249
Mitterrand government (France), 106–114
Monetary policy
   in Sweden, 86–88
   in Yugoslavia, 431–432
Monnet, Jean, 96
Monnet Plan, 96–98

Nagy, Imre, 405–406
Nationalization, in France, 107, 109–111.
   See also Industry, government ownership of
New Economic Mechanism (Hungary),
   407–423
   agriculture and, 412–415
   evaluation of, 421–423
   first phase of, 407–417
   foreign trade and, 415–417
   industrial structure and, 418–419
   labor and, 419–421
   prices and, 417–418
   second phase of, 417–421
New Economic Policy (NEP) (USSR), 138–
   141, 142–148
   agriculture and, 139, 142–145
   finance and, 140, 146–147
   industry and, 139, 145–146
   labor and, 140
   planning and, 140–141, 147–148
   trade and, 139–140, 146
Nove, Alec, 22

Occupational choice, as economic freedom, 467–468
Optimal programming, 273–278

Pareto optimum, 249–250
Paris Commune, 162
Payroll taxes, in Sweden, 68
Pensions, in Sweden, 68
People's communes in China, 341–345
Performance evaluation, 454–468
   criteria for, 456–468
      distribution of income, 460–461
      economic freedoms, 465–468
      economic growth, 456–458
      economic stability, 461–465
      efficiency, 458–460
   methodology of, 454–455
Planning. See Central planning
Pluralism, 16
Poland, trade unions in, 303–310
Polanyi, Karl, 402
Politburo (USSR), 204–205
Politics, and economic systems, 5–6, 16–23,
   26–27
Preobrazhensky, E. A., 150, 151
Prices
   in Hungary, 408, 410, 415, 417–418
   in Sweden, 87–88
   in USSR
      agricultural, 217–218
      of consumer goods, 215–216, 228, 230
      efficiency and, 262–266
      functions of, 214–215
      of labor services, 126, 227–228, 231
      planning and, 263–264
      policies for, 264–266
      rational, 248–249, 259–260
      retail, 215, 228, 230
      wholesale, 217
Protectionism, 112

Quality control (Q.C.) circles, 48–49

Rákosi, Matyas, 405
Rationalization cartel, 58
Rational prices. See also Prices
   defined, 249
   need for, 248–249, 259–260
Recession cartel, 58
Rehn, Gösta, 75–77
Retirement, in Sweden, 67–68
Riksbank (Sweden), 86
Rodriguez, Carlos Rafael, 372
Rosovsky, Henry, 56
Rubik, Erno, 419
Russia. See Union of Soviet Socialist Re-
   publics
Russian Revolution, 19–20, 129–137
Rykov, A. I., 148, 151, 153

SAF (Swedish employers' federation), 64, 65, 66, 72, 73, 77, 91
Savings, in Japan, 40–42
Schumpeter, Joseph, 13, 18–19
Scissors crisis, 141–142
Seniority-based wages, 47–48
Serfs, 125–128
Simplex method, 275
Social Democratic Party (SAP) (Sweden), 62, 63–64, 65–66, 74
Socialism
    arguments against, 9–10
    arguments for, 11–12
    capitalism vs., 7–8
    centrally planned, 11–12
    defined, 7–8
    dictatorship and, 17–23, 162–165
    market, 11, 12
    in USSR, 7–8, 11, 115–116, 159–160, 162–165
Socialist Party, in France, 106–114
Social services
    in Sweden, 66–69
    in USSR, 120–121
Solidarity union, 308–309
Soviet, 128–129
Soviet Union. See Union of Soviet Socialist Republics
Stalin, Joseph
    collectivization and, 153–156, 166
    economic solution of, 153–156, 159–160
    Party discipline and, 136, 158, 159
    planning and, 256–258
    political positions of, 152, 153
Standard of living, and economic systems, 23–24
State and Revolution (Lenin), 163
State farms, 117. See also Collective farms
State Planning Commission (USSR). See Gosplan
Static efficiency, 24–25
Stolypin Reforms, 126
Supply management, 55, 88–90. See also Indicative planning
Supreme Soviet, 205–206
Sweden, 62–92
    capital formation in, 90–91
    capitalism in, 8
    cooperative sector in, 69–70
    democracy in, 63, 70–74
    economic background of, 63–66
    economic system of, 3, 62–92
    exports of, 65
    fiscal policy in, 81–86
    government's economic role in, 88–90
    industrial democracy in, 70–74
    labor market characteristics and policies in, 74–81
    monetary policy in, 86–88
    price controls in, 87–88
    retirement in, 67–68
    social services and benefits in, 66–69
    supply management in, 88–90
    taxation in, 81, 83–86
    unemployment in, 66, 67, 74–75
    unions in, 64–65, 80
    wages in, 75, 80
    wage solidarity policy of, 75–76
    women in, 74

Tariffs. See also Trade
    French, 112
    Japanese, 57–58
Taxes
    corporate income, 40
    payroll, 68
    in Sweden, 81, 83–86
    in USSR, 231
Technology
    economic structure and, 5
    Soviet choice of, 267–271
Teleologists, 148
Tito (Josip Broz), 424–426, 444
Tomsky, M. P., 153
Total factor productivity, 188–190
Trade
    by France, 112–113
    by Hungary, 415–417
    by Japan, 56–58
    New Economic Policy and, 139–140, 146
    in USSR, 139–140, 146, 220–224
Trading companies, 37
Trotsky, Leon, 142, 148, 149–150, 151, 153, 158

Unconditional participation (France), 102
Underdeveloped economies, 14–15, 20–22
Unemployment
    in China, 356–357, 364
    in France, 98, 106, 111–113
    in Japan, 43–44
    in Sweden, 66, 67, 74–75
    in USSR, 226–227
    in Yugoslavia, 430
Union of Soviet Socialist Republics (USSR), 4, 19–23, 115–329
    aggregate balance, 226–246
        aggregate demand and, 226–227
        alternatives for restoring, 229–232
        causes of inflation, 227–229
        input-output method of, 234–235, 238–246
        Soviet method of, 232–234, 235–238

agriculture
    collectivization of, 154–156, 166
    Five-Year Plan and, 166–168
    government ownership of, 117, 154–156
    New Economic Policy and, 139, 142–145
    since 1950, 182–183
    prices of goods, 217–218
    productivity of, 127–128
    workers in, 295–300
black markets in, 231
Bolsheviks in, 129–131, 136
capital productivity of, 187–188
central planning, 204–224, 252–278
    defense of, 252–253
    development of, 147–148
    dictatorship and, 21, 256–258
    early five-year plans, 165–173
    efficiency and, 253–255
    international trade and, 220–224
    Law of Value and, 255–262
    Ministry system and, 208–209
    operation of, 204–224
    prices and, 248–249, 259–260, 262–266
    price system and, 214–218
    second economy and, 218–220
    under Stalin, 256–258
    university example and, 118–120
choice of technology in, 267–271
classes, 280–300
    agricultural workers, 295–300
    income distribution among, 285–286
    industrial workers, 292–295
    managers, 289–292
    mobility of, 284–285
    rulers, 280–284
    stratification of workers, 286–289
combined factor productivity, 188–190
consumer demand in, 226–227, 229–232
consumption performance of, 182–184
consumption vs. investment in, 180–181
defense spending of, 198–201
democracy in, 13, 20, 162–165, 271–273
dictatorship in, 135–138, 160–161, 162–165
differences from U.S., 116–121
economic growth
    calculation of, 178–180
    decline in, 185–193
    reasons for, 184–185
    vs. U.S. growth, 182–185
economic history
    before 1917, 125–128
    1905–1917, 128–133
    1917–1921, 133–137
    1921–1923, 139–141
    1923–1924, 141–142
    1924–1928, 142–148
    1928–1932, 165–168, 171–173
    1933–1937, 169–170, 171–173

    1938–1941, 171–173
    1941–1945, 174
    1945–1950, 174–176
    1950-present, 176–180
economic problems of, 314–315
economic theories of, 313–314
efficiency in, 271–273
finance in, 140, 146–147, 175
five-year plans
    1928–1932, 165–168
    1933–1937, 169–170
    1938–1941, 170–171
GNP, 184
government
    central planning by, 118–120, 210–214.
        See also Central planning
    Communist Party, 129–137, 204–205,
        281
    Ministry system, 208–209
    ownership of agriculture by, 117, 154–
        156
    ownership of industry by, 116–117, 159
    ruling class, 280–284
    structure of, 204–207
industry
    decentralized investment in, 325–326
    decision making and, 271–273
    1890–1914, 128
    enterprise problems of, 315–319
    five-year plans and, 170
    forms of enterprise in, 207–208
    growth of, 159–161, 182
    New Economic Policy and, 139, 145–146
    1950–present, 176–177
    1945–1950, 174–176
    in 1930s, 171–173
    productivity of, 187–190
    storming in, 318
interest rates in, 231–232
labor
    agricultural, 295–300
    as class, 292–295
    education of, 289, 294
    employment of, 226–227
    five-year plans and, 167, 169
    income distribution in, 285–286
    industrial, 292–295
    mobility of, 123, 284–285
    New Economic Policy and, 140
    productivity of, 186–187
    stratification of, 286–289
    unions of, 300–303
    upward mobility of, 288–289
    wages of, 122–123, 216, 228, 286–288,
        292–293
Law of Value in, 255–262
linear programming applied to, 273–278

USSR (*cont.*)
New Economic Policy in, 138–141, 142–148
political evolution
1905–1917, 128–129
1917–1921, 133–135
1928–1956, 158–161
1956–present, 181–182
population and growth of, 177–178
prices
agricultural, 217–218
of consumer goods, 215–216, 228, 230
efficiency and, 262–266
functions of, 214–215
of labor services, 216, 227–228, 231
planning and, 263–264
policies for, 264–266
rational, 248–249, 259–260
retail, 215, 228, 230
wholesale, 217
private ownership in, 121–122
public health, education, and housing in, 120–121
rationing in, 231
reconstruction following World War II, 174–176
reform, 313–329
economic problems leading to, 314–315
enterprise problems and, 315–319
Liberman debate and, 319–321
official, 322–323
political background of, 313–314
problems of, 323–329
scissors crisis in, 141–142
second economy in, 218–220
similarities to U.S., 121–123
socialism in, 7–8, 11, 115–116, 159–160, 162–165
Stalin's economic solution, 153–156
statistics of, 194–198
strategic planning decisions of, 191
taxes in, 231
trade in, 139–140, 146, 220–224
Unions
company, 48
in Cuba, 375
in France, 102–103, 105
in Japan, 48
in Poland, 303–310
in Sweden, 63–64, 80
in U.S., 310
in USSR, 300
United States
capitalism in, 8
defense spending of, 198–201
democracy in, 13–14
economic system of, 3–4

Soviet differences from, 116–121
Soviet economic growth vs., 182–185
Soviet similarities to, 121–123
trade unions in, 310

Value, Law of, 255–262
Veblen, Thorstein, 10
Vogel, Ezra, 42, 49

Wages
in Hungary, 410–411
in Japan, 47–48, 50–51
seniority-based, 47–48
in Sweden, 75–80
in USSR, 122–123, 216, 228, 286–288, 292–293
Wage solidarity policy, 75–76
War Communism, 131–133
Weber, Max, 23–24
Women
in Japanese labor force, 43–44, 45
in Sweden, 74
Worker Council Law of 1950 (Yugoslavia), 427
Worker incentives, in Hungary, 410–411
Worker mobility, in USSR, 123, 284–285
Worker participation, 48–49
in Cuba, 377–378
as economic freedom, 466
in Japan, 48–49
in Yugoslavia, 427, 434–439

Yugoslavia, 424–444
agriculture in, 427
background of, 424–426
BOALs, 440–442
democracy in, 13
early economic policy of, 426–428
economic decentralization of, 427–428, 431, 451
economic reforms of 1965, 428–432
economic system of, 4–5
economic theory of worker management in, 434–439
income distribution in, 432–434
inflation in, 430–431
monetary policy of, 431–432
reforms of the 1970s, 440–443
socialism in, 8, 11, 20, 21
socialist reform of, 314
unemployment in, 430
Worker Council Law of 1950, 427

Zaibatsu-type bank groups, 36–37
Zinoviev, G. E., 152

B 5
C 6
D 7
E 8
F 9
G 0
H 1
I 2
J 3